HENRY ADAMS

Selected Letters

HENRY ADAMS

Selected Letters

Edited by

ERNEST SAMUELS

The Belknap Press of
Harvard University Press
Cambridge, Massachusetts
London, England
1992

Library of Congress Cataloging-in-Publication Data

Adams, Henry, 1838–1918.
[Correspondence. Selections]
Henry Adams—selected letters / edited by Ernest Samuels.
p.   cm.
Includes index.
ISBN 0-674-38757-0 (alk. paper)
1. Adams, Henry, 1838–1918—Correspondence. 2. Historians—United
States—Correspondence. I. Samuels, Ernest, 1903–   . II. Title.
E175.5.A2A4 1992
973'.07202—dc20

91-19980
CIP

To

Jayne

Preface

THE TWO HUNDRED FORTY letters of Henry Adams gathered together in this volume have been selected from among the nearly three thousand published in the six volumes of the Harvard University Press edition of 1982–1988. In that edition every letter was printed in its entirety and freed from the errors and omissions of previous editors.

The present collection aims to represent all significant aspects of Henry Adams' career. The letters span sixty eventful years, from 1858 to 1918. They begin with the year when the new Republican party nominated his father as an antislavery candidate for Congress and end in the disastrous spring of the last year of World War I.

The letters lift the veil of old-age disenchantment that obscures *The Education of Henry Adams* and exhibit Adams as perhaps the most brilliant letter writer of his time. What is most engaging in the long course of his correspondence is the tireless range of his intellectual curiosity, his passionate effort to understand the politics, the science, and the human society of the world as it changed about him. In his pages we experience as privileged contemporaries the intimate political and social context of his long residence in Washington across the park from the White House. We share his zest for travel in the South Seas, Cuba, Sicily, and much of the rest of the world as he made his way from place to place as a kind of inspector general of civilization. His letters are an unsentimental commentary on the transformation of the United States and the Western world that followed from the influx of new political, industrial, and social forces in the latter half of the nineteenth century.

As the years run on, the style of the letters reflects the increasing pace of change. The factual reports and sober analyses yield to a growing sense of the varied colors of life. The letters grow vivid with metaphor and racy hyperbole. Ironical, perverse, facetious, and contradictory, the later letters are often dazzling feats of intellectual virtuosity in which Adams wore his cloak of historian with a deprecatory air.

In the arresting image of the first page of the *Education,* looking back on his life from the vantage point of old age, Adams reflected that "had he been born in Jerusalem under the shadow of the Temple and circumcised by his uncle the high priest, under the name of Israel Cohen," rather than having been christened, as he had been, by his Unitarian uncle, the minister of the First Church of Boston, "he would scarcely have been more distinctly branded, and not much more heavily handicapped in the races of the coming century." Being the great-grandson of President John Adams and the grandson of President John Quincy Adams should have ensured his success. Instead it became a handicap, and he missed his destiny. His ironical quest for the causes of this failure became in the *Education* a voyage of Odysseus through a sea of errors.

The letters reveal the real nature of that quest and rescue Henry Adams from the self-inflicted stigma of failure. They free him from the artifice that cloaks the "manikin" of that narrative. They make us secret sharers of his thoughts, opinions, interests, and ambitions. They show him concerned with the means and ends of politics, education, economics, and the naked realities of experience.

He wrote his letters not only to inform his correspondents, to share the news of their social world, and to air his views on the passing scene, but also to entertain and beguile them. He sought to give color and savor to gossip and the commonplace. His model was the famous seventeenth-century letter writer Horace Walpole, the son of Prime Minister Robert Walpole, whose letters were filled with witty gossip about the British political and social establishment. Henry's father used to read them aloud to the family, as new editions came out, with keen appreciation of their literary style. In the Adams household, too, letter writing was a serious art. By the time Henry was ten, his father had edited and published four editions of the letters of his grandmother Abigail Adams, the wife of President John Adams.

The example of Horace Walpole's letters was never far from Adams' thoughts. In 1860, when he became private secretary to his congressman father, he announced to his brother Charles, "I propose to write you this winter a series of private letters to show how things loom. Though I have no ambition to become a Horace Walpole, I still would like to think that a century or two hence when everything about us has been forgotten, my letters might still be read and quoted as a memorial of manners and habits at the time of the great secession of 1860." Later, as a journalist in President Grant's Washington, he wrote to an English friend, "What! shall I imitate H[orace] W[alpole] and tell you about his [Grant's] court; a pack of boobies and scoundrels who have all the vices of H.W.'s time, and with none of the wit and refinement." Walpole's chaffing irony and sarcasm, his extravagant allusions and striking figures of speech, his pose of advanced age and world-weariness, all had a lifelong influence on the character of Adams' letters. At seventy he still resorted to Walpole's pages with relish and admiration.

As Adams grew older, the counterpointing of the centuries, the widening disjunctions between the chaotic present and the remembered sureties of the past, steadily heightened his rhetoric. After he abandoned diary-keeping in midlife, he relieved his discontents with increasing freedom in his letters, though aware of the risks he ran. After reading the letters of Robert Louis Stevenson, he commented that letters "perpetuate all one's mistakes, blunders and carelessness. No one can talk or write letters all the time without the effect of egotism and error. They are like a portrait by Sargent; they betray one's besetting vices in youth, and one's worst selfishness in middle-life."

Yet Adams could not stay his pen. He felt compelled to put himself on record whatever the cost, for letters had become the meat and drink of his life. In a moment of revulsion he might exclaim to his chief correspondent and confidante, Elizabeth Cameron, that she should destroy his letters to avoid leaving them about "for female pigs who feed out of the magazine troughs at five dollars a page." Wisely she ignored the rash plea, confident that the historian in him would forget the suicidal impulse. Toward the end of his life he in fact urged her to publish all the letters of their intimate circle as a memorial of a precious time and place.

As a novice writer Henry Adams had hoped for a literary career. The letters in this collection show the successive steps by which he achieved his aim. It is as literature of a high order that his letters can finally be read. From the fertile perceptions that enliven their prose would come the more formal works of the literary imagination.

Contents

Illustrations

John Hay
Photograph by Marian Adams. Courtesy of the
Massachusetts Historical Society

Brooks Adams
Courtesy of the Massachusetts Historical Society

John La Farge
Photograph by Marian Adams. Courtesy of the
Massachusetts Historical Society

Elizabeth Cameron
Courtesy of Arline B. Tehan

Martha Cameron
Private Collection

Elizabeth Cameron, 1899
Drypoint portrait by Paul Helleu. Courtesy of the late Samuel Reber

Henry Adams, 1914
Crayon drawing by John Briggs Potter. Courtesy of the
Massachusetts Historical Society

The Adams Memorial by Augustus Saint-Gaudens
Photograph by Raymond Davis

HENRY ADAMS
Selected Letters

Abbreviations

BA	Brooks Adams (1848–1927)
CFA	Charles Francis Adams (1807–1886)
CFA2	Charles Francis Adams, Jr. (1835–1915)
HA	Henry Adams (1838–1918)
JA	John Adams (1735–1826)
JQA	John Quincy Adams (1767–1848)
MHA	Marian Hooper Adams (1843–1885)

Manuscript Locations

CtY-B	Collection of American Literature, Beinecke Rare Book and Manuscript Library, Yale University
DLC	Library of Congress
I Tatti	Harvard University Center for Italian Renaissance Studies, Florence, Italy
MH	Houghton Library, Harvard University
MH-Ar	Harvard University Archives
MHi	Massachusetts Historical Society
MH-Z	Museum of Comparative Zoology, Harvard University
NN	The New York Public Library, Astor, Lenox and Tilden Foundations
NNC	Rare Book and Manuscript Library, Columbia University
OCIW	Case Western Reserve University Archives
OO	Oberlin College Archives
PHi	Historical Society of Pennsylvania
PPT	Samuel Paley Library, Temple University
RPB	John Hay Library, Brown University
ScU	South Caroliniana Library, University of South Carolina
ViU	Clifton Waller Barrett Library, University of Virginia

I

Apprentice Years
1858–1868

T HE LETTERS in this section span the ten formative years in the life of Henry Adams that transformed him from a provincial Bostonian to a citizen of the world. They begin in the fall of 1858 at a dramatic moment in his life. He is an earnest young man of twenty who has taken lodgings in Berlin at the start of a two-year sojourn on the Continent. In July he had graduated from Harvard College. Honored as Class Day Orator, he had devoted his address on that sweltering midday to the dangers of materialism and the commercial spirit that threatened the age. His stern moral admonitions showed him to be a true descendant of generations of Puritans.

He had come to Berlin with a contingent of classmates who were embarking on the conventional "Grand Tour" of affluent Americans. He was the first of the Adams offspring to venture abroad, having convinced his reluctant father, who feared the corrupting evils of Europe, that his stay abroad would be an opportunity for serious study of civil law in preparation for the practice of law. He had a model in Senator Charles Sumner, a longtime family friend, who had studied civil law and jurisprudence in Europe on his way to eminence as a statesman. Henry also intended to study German and to improve his Latin.

Although the recent decision in the *Dred Scott* case had at last sharply defined the moral issue for the antislavery forces in the North, there was still no reason for anxiety among the young travelers. Controversy would continue but war was unthinkable.

Charles Francis Adams, Henry's father, was elected to Congress that November as a member of the new Republican party, which opposed the extension of slavery to the new states. He would take office in December of the following year, when the Thirty-sixth Congress convened. "The old Free Soilers," Henry exulted to his brother Charles, "are about the winning hosses, I reckon, just now." What was more immediately relevant to his present situation, however, was the rising clash of interests among the European monarchies of Prussia, Austria, France, and Italy. War was in the offing over the control of the Italian kingdoms. But, having the security of American citizenship, Henry could look on the tangle of national rivalries with academic detachment.

When he visited the university halls in Berlin, he was discouraged by the difficult jargon of the professors and decided to enroll in a *Gymnasium* to master German and Latin. The days he spent among the boys there improved his German, Latin, and Greek, but he found the atmosphere stultifying. The Prussian school system seemed vastly inferior to the enlightened one back home. In a first step toward the "literary" career he had envisioned when he contributed his college "Class Life," he set to work on a portrayal of life in a German *Gymnasium*. It proved less manageable than the familiar essays he had contributed to the *Harvard Magazine,* and the fledgling piece remained unpublished until long after his death.

By spring he was "devilish glad" to leave Berlin for a pleasant two months in Dresden. His private study of Georg Puchta's *Cursus der Institutionen* on Justinian and civil law grew desultory, and he yielded to the pleasures of travels with classmates and his sister Louisa and her husband. There was also much time for the opera and the theater and for determined tours of art galleries. But the ground note of his letters to his brother Charles was the vexing question of what satisfying careers might be open to them, whether in the law for Charles or in literature for Henry, in view of their situation as members of a distinguished political family.

In October he returned to Berlin, but the prospect of another cold winter there and law lectures in German that had no more use to an American than "Chinese cannon to a backwoodsman" made him decamp to Dresden, where he felt more at home. He settled in for the winter in the household of a German professor, consorted with visiting Americans, studied engravings, read widely in German, glanced occasionally at Puchta, and shared the social life of his cultivated hosts. Though undersized—"little," Henry James was to call him—young Adams made a dignified appearance on his rounds in Dresden. Carefully groomed and with his hair neatly parted to one side and his cheeks and chin ringed by a narrow new beard, he looked older than his years.

By April 1860 he was off again on his travels. His sightseeing carried him to Vienna and then to Italy. Challenged by the news that his brother Charles had taken on work as a Boston journalist, he began a series of travel letters for the *Boston Daily Courier.* The movement for unification in Italy was now well under way, with Napoleon III taking a decisive role in the struggle of the Italian states against the Austrian occupiers. In the eight letters published in the *Daily Courier* from May to July 1860 Adams largely ignored the military and political fare of the regular correspondents and with a tourist's eye sought local color and human interest. He achieved something of a scoop when the American minister to the Kingdom of the Two Sicilies at Naples deputized him to carry official dispatches to Palermo, where Garibaldi had just vanquished the Bourbon army. There Adams talked with the red-shirted liberator. The surrender of the Bourbon army, which he reported on June 9, 1860, indicated that the "first act of the melodrama" was over. His serious-minded father faulted the letters for not being "essays politico-economical." The self-deprecating Henry agreed that they were "poor" and thanked God that they were finished. Ten days later he reached Paris.

His two-year immersion in European life and culture ended in the autumn of 1860 after two months in Paris, where he studiously polished his French and visited with his sister and fellow Americans. He returned to the family residence in Quincy, Massachusetts, voted for Abraham Lincoln, and lingered on in Boston studying law in the office of Judge Horace Gray. When his father, who had easily won reelection, invited him to come to Washington as his private secretary, he promptly abandoned Blackstone's *Commentaries*.

In Washington, with secession on all lips, Henry's political education began with a rush. He immediately put it to use as the correspondent of the *Boston Daily Advertiser* in energetic support of his father's tactics as head of the congressional Committee of Thirty-Three. Charles Francis Adams aimed to conciliate the opposing factions in the Republican ranks to gain time until the party could take control of the administration upon Lincoln's inauguration. Lincoln, at the urging of Secretary of State William Seward, appointed Henry's father as minister to England, passing over Senator Charles Sumner. Two weeks later Fort Sumter was bombarded and the Civil War began. It was inevitable that Henry should continue to serve as private secretary. The eldest son, John Quincy, would remain in Boston to manage the family's properties, leaving the second son, Charles, free to become an officer in the Union army.

In an attempt to mollify the disappointed Sumner, Henry published a dispatch in the *New York Times* tactfully explaining the appropriateness of certain federal appointments in Massachusetts. He also arranged with the editor to act as the paper's London correspondent. His work would have to be kept secret from his father because the State Department prohibited "all communications with the press." He departed with the family to England early in May 1861.

Henry's education in international diplomacy began immediately, for the queen's "Proclamation of Neutrality" greeted them on their arrival. Thereafter crisis followed crisis in the relations between England and the Union.

Henry conferred daily with his father, and sitting across from him he copied in his neat script the dispatches to be forwarded to Seward. His work required much research in international law and finance. Far wider fields demanded private study as he became aware of the scientific revolution that was sweeping across England and the Continent. Charles Darwin's recently published *Origin of the Species* was shaking the religious establishments and transforming basic principles in geology, physics, chemistry, and the social sciences.

As the American legation became a magnet for people who sympathized with the North, Henry became acquainted with scores of prominent Englishmen—free trade statesmen like John Bright and Richard Cobden, writers like Robert Browning, Edward Bulwer-Lytton, Leslie Stephen, John Stuart Mill, Thomas Huxley, and Louis Blanc. They all contributed to what he called his "English education." It also became clear that he was enjoying the ceremonies and amenities of the upper-class cultural life that centered on Lord Houghton's Fryston Hall. His engagement book showed an increasingly busy social life, and he developed what one friend would describe as an "English cut to his jib."

After six months, fearing that his authorship might be exposed and his father compromised, Henry cut short his contributions to the *New York Times*. On the suggestion of John Gorham Palfrey, a family friend, he turned to research at the British Museum concerning the veracity of Captain John Smith's account of Pocahontas and John Rolfe, figures sacred to Virginians. He also prepared two articles on the instructive parallels to be drawn between England's unfortunate experience with protective tariffs and inconvertible paper currency during the Napoleonic wars and the high tariffs and "greenback" currency adopted to finance the war effort in the North. The article on John Smith and the two learned articles on British finance were published in the *North American Review*. They were followed by an exhaustive review-essay on Sir Charles Lyell's new edition of his *Principles of Geology,* in which Lyell had adopted Darwin's theory of evolution. Adams concluded that Darwin's theory was "in its nature incapable of proof." It was a skepticism that was never to leave him.

The improvement of diplomatic relations with England in the closing months of the Civil War gave Henry's father the hope that he might return to private life in America. His efforts to resign were resisted, however, by Secretary Seward, who needed him for the troublesome postwar negotiations. Charles Francis Adams loyally stayed at his post. He finally won his release toward the close of 1867, his service to end April 1, 1868. Henry now faced the necessity of beginning a new career, a necessity that he had anticipated since the end of the war. As he later wrote John Bright, he had made up his mind "to live in Washington, and, since the field of public position was by our arrangements practically shut to me, to devote myself to a literary career."

Following a round of leave-takings in London, Henry Adams joined the family at the port of Queenstown. They sailed on June 28 and landed in New York on July 7, 1868.

To Charles Francis Adams, Jr.

Berlin.
Wednesday. November. 3. 1858.

My dear Fellow[1]

With that energy of expression and originality of thought for which you are so justly celebrated, you have remarked in your last that the pleasures and pains of life are pretty equally divided. Permit me in the particular instance before us to doubt the fact. In the long run it may be so, but as between you in Boston and me in Europe, I deny it in toto and without hesitation.

I humbly apologize to you for the remarks in my last letter, which were written under the supposition that you had forgotten me. Your letter was satisfaction itself. I already knew the main points, but I can ask nothing more complete than your particulars. As to the nomination I am delighted with the manner of it.[2] The election took place yesterday, and a fortnight from today I shall certainly know all about it, if not from you, at any rate from Gov. Wright at the American Legation.[3]

Here I am, then, in Berlin. It is now night; I am writing in my room, which is about ten or twelve, by eighteen or twenty feet; by the light of a lamp for which I paid yesterday two dollars; independent; unknown and unknowing; hating the language and yet grubbing into it. I have passed the day since one o'clock with Loo, who is now here and remains till Friday, and with whom I go about to Galleries and Museums, and then dine at her hotel.[4] As you say, I am not rich and am trying to institute a rigid economy in all my expenses. There is one advantage in this place; if forced to it, one can live for almost nothing. Today I was extravagant. I ordered a quantity of clothes; an inside suit and an overcoat of expensive stuffs. The over-coat is a peculiar beaver-cloth, a sort of velvety stuff; and its inside is thick fur, like sealskin, I suppose; so thick that I can't have it lined. The suit is very strong, fine cloth, as good, I fancy as the man had. But then I had to pay dear. Altogether it cost me fifty one American dollars. Now in Boston perhaps this is not so much, but here it is a great deal.

Then this frightful German! I have had the most amusing times with my landlady who's a jolly Dutch woman and who has a power of clack that is marvellous. If I have her called in and she once gets agoing I can no more hope to make her understand what I want than if she talked Hebrew. So I have recourse to my Dutch teacher, whom I pay very high even for America, and get him to mediate between us and look over my bills and see that I'm not cheated. He comes every morning at ten and I read and talk with him and he corrects my exercises.

What shall I say of this city? Why, Lord bless my soul, I have got things enough to see and study in this city alone to take me two years even if I knew the language and only came for pleasure. The Museums, picture Galleries, Theatres, Gardens; there are enough to occupy one's time for ever-so-long in mere play. I would like nothing better than to go into the Picture Gallery and make the Art a study, and read up in it all the time for the next six months. Then do the same with the half-million or so, engravings. Lord! *such* engravings!

The truth is, in the soberest earnest, I am quite as pleasantly situated as I ever expected to be. Sometimes of course, I feel a little lonely and shall feel more so, I suppose, when Loo goes away and I have no one to think of as near me. Sometimes too I get angry at the excessive difficulty of this very repulsive language, and wearied to death at the continual and fatiguing learning by rote which is necessary for almost every phrase. But on the whole, life here is exceedingly pleasant; there is no relaxation from continual occupation; no excuse for the blues, which always with me come from ennui. Here one is surrounded by Art, and I defy any one but a fool to feel ennuyéed while he can look at the works of these old masters.

Here you have my life then. It will be for the next two months a continual dig at the language varied occasionally by a moment or so of Art. The evenings at the Theatres, concerts or Balls, perhaps, such as they have here, queer affairs I imagine, and the day in hard study.

(Saturday eve. Nov. 6.)   I resume my letter where it was broken off, and hope to send it tomorrow. I have just left Loo, who is still here but expects to go to Dresden tomorrow night. She is suffering tonight under one of her fearful head-aches, or I should be with her. She has been very kind to me indeed; very kind; we have been together all the time, going from Gallery to Gallery, and I have almost been living at her expense these ten days, for she would not allow me to pay for my own dinners. I sat with her till ten o'clock last night, and have passed all the afternoons with her (that is, from eleven till six) every day. In consequence I have had to sit up till twelve o'clock to write my exercises.

I have received my clothes, and on the whole they are the best I ever wore. The great-coat is a miracle. I look in it like a veteran. German cloth is, if anything even better than English. However, they ought to be good. They cost enough. Apropos to cost, those bills are right. Apply to papa on my account for the money and let him credit it.

My friends here are all right. I received a letter today from Crowninshield in Hannover in answer to one of mine, in which he represents himself as pretty well except for the fleas.[5] I was very bad that way myself on my arrival here and had a very funny scene with my landlady on the subject, which reached so involved a point at last that an interpreter was called in and as he pretended to speak English but didn't, I'm inclined to think the poor woman to this day doesn't understand. However, I instituted vigorous measures and have not been troubled lately. Anderson is settled here.[6] I went to see him once, but he is a long way off, and I've heard nothing from him for some time. Plenty of Americans are here; one in the next house; but I have had nothing to do with them though I met half-a-dozen at the American Legation last Wednesday. They are of all kinds; some, not attractive. As soon as possible I shall make German acquaintances and in a couple of months I hope to be well enough on in the language, to join the University and make acquaintances there among the donkeys who walk round with absurd caps on their heads; rather more offensive than the soldiers.

Apropos to this, you ask me, what my plans are, here and in life. I hardly know how to follow a plan here, for the way is not at all clear. When I left America my intention was, first to accustom myself to the language; then to join the University and systematically attend lectures on the Civil Law, at the same time taking a Latin tutor and translating Latin into German; and to continue this course in Heidelberg or in Paris or in both. The plan was simple enough; useful enough; and comprehensive enough. But now I see difficulties. I must join the University here in the middle of its term; I certainly can not join to any advantage before January. Shall I be likely to learn much Law by breaking in on a course of Lectures in this manner. To be a student of Civil law I must be an absolute master of written and ordinary Latin; though I need not speak it or write it myself. Now, is it well to study law, Latin and German all at once? Can I have time enough to do all this, or ought I to resign the Law and devote myself to Latin? But supposing I were to do this, devote myself to Latin; I may as well give up the University for it would be mere waste time to attend lectures like Corny Felton's at Cambridge,[7] and, as Carlyle says, these Germans are the worst Dryasdusts on the face of the earth.[8]

These objections will, as I advance further and see clearer, either vanish entirely, or gain strength and finally force me into some new course. I hope it will be the former. I already see very clearly that the two years which are allotted to me here, are not nearly enough to do all that I had hoped to do, or a quarter part of it, and I tell you now fairly that if I return to America without doing more than learn German and French, I shall have done well, and these two years will be the best employed of my life. I am satisfied of this, and though I shall not work any the less hard because I believe it, still I shall feel less disappointed when I return without universal knowledge. At present I adhere to my original plan; and this plan as you see, involves the necessity of my omitting Greek entirely. I am sorry enough to do it, but I became convinced that to attempt the study of Greek now and here, would be hopeless unless I gave up Latin. One or the other I must sacrifice. If I were to include this fourth language in my plan, I should never do anything. Two years will not teach one everything. You may think that as a scholar I should have preferred to sacrifice Latin. As a scholar I should, but as a lawyer I must have only one choice. I take it. And this brings me to the other branch of your question.

As for my plan of life, it is simple, and if health and the usual goods of life are continued to me, I see no reason why it should not be carried out in the regular course of events. Two years in Europe; two years studying law in Boston; and then I propose to emigrate and practice at Saint Louis. What I can do there, God knows; but I have a theory that an educated and reasonably able man can make his mark if he chooses, and if I fail to make mine, why, then—I fail and that's all. I should do it anywhere else as well. But if I know myself, I can't fail. I must, if I only behave like a gentleman and a man of sense, take a position to a certain degree creditable and influential, and as yet my ambition cannot see clearly enough to look further.

In a conversation I had with Mr Dana[9] a few days before I left home, I said all this to him, and the latter part of it he treated with a little contempt. He insisted that I was looking towards politics; and perhaps he was right. There are two things that seem to be at the bottom of our constitutions; one is a continual tendency towards politics; the other is family pride; and it is strange how these two feelings run through all of us. For my own ideas of my future, I have not admitted politics into them. It is as a lawyer that I would emigrate and I've seen altogether too much harm done in this way, to allow myself to quit law for politics without irresistible reasons.

So here you have a few of my thoughts about what I am going to do. Here in Europe, away from home, from care and ambition and the fretting of monotony, I must say that I often feel as I often used to feel in College, as if the whole thing didn't pay, and if I were my own master, it would need more inducements than the law could offer, to drag me out of Europe these ten years yet. I always had an inclination for the Epicurean philosophy, and here in Europe I might gratify it until I was gorged. Give me my thousand a year and free leave and a good conscience, and I'd pass as happy a life here as I'm afraid I never shall in St Louis. But now I am hurried; I must work, work, work; my very pleasures are hurried, and after all, I shall get most pleasure and (I believe) advantage, from what never entered into my calculations; Art.

However, there is no use talking. The Magd has just come in to prepare my room for the night, and her "Guten Nacht" tells me that it is nine o'clock; and I want still to write to John.[10] There will be time enough to despond hereafter. Just now I am sure is the pleasantest time I shall ever see, for there is entire independence, no cares, and endless and inexhaustible pleasures. As for my expences I cannot yet calculate them, but when I square my accounts at the end of the month I shall be able to tell with some degree of certainty how I am to come out. Incidentally you might remark in the hearing of the family circle, that an Englishman the other day said in my hearing that Berlin was an expensive place; nothing was cheap in Berlin.

So farewell. I shall not close this letter on the whole till Sunday night, so that I may say if Loo goes.

H.B.A.

(Sunday night)   I have just seen Loo off. She had a bad night, but today recovered and I dined with them as usual. Tonight at seven o'clock they went off for Dresden. They wanted me to go with them and you may imagine I should have liked to have done so. I am now alone here and shall study hard. I shall write to Hollis next week,[11] but probably not home as there will be little to say. Nick came to see me today. He is all right but I shall see very little of him. This letter will reach you about Thanksgiving, when I am to dine at Magdeburg with Crowninshield and the rest. Five of us. Good-bye.

MS:MHi

1. Charles Francis Adams, Jr. (1835–1915), HA's brother, then reading law in Boston.
2. Their father, Charles Francis Adams (1807–1886), won the Republican nomination for Congress when his leading rival withdrew in his favor.
3. Joseph Albert Wright (1810–1867), minister to Prussia.
4. Louisa Catherine Adams (1831–1870), eldest of the six Adams children, and her husband, Charles Kuhn (1821–1899), were traveling abroad.
5. Benjamin William Crowinshield (1837–1892), Harvard classmate.
6. Nicholas Longworth Anderson (1838–1892), Harvard classmate.
7. Cornelius Conway Felton (1807–1862), professor of Greek literature.
8. Thomas Carlyle, *History of Frederick the Great* (1858), bk. 1, chap. 1.
9. Richard Henry Dana (1815–1882), Boston lawyer active in Free Soil politics.
10. John Quincy Adams (1833–1894), eldest of HA's three brothers.
11. Hollis Hunnewell (1836–1884), Harvard classmate.

To *Charles Francis Adams, Jr.*

No. 4.[1]   Berlin. February. 9. 1859.

Dear Charles

I will pay your last letter the compliment to say that it had effect enough over me to make me feel unpleasantly for two days. Not that I found fault with it. I do not do so, and hope that you will continue to write just so. But it bothered me damnably. For what you say as to my remarks on the Boston young ladies, though your criticisms are rather hard on me, I acknowledge that you are wholly in the right. What one writes is considerably influenced by the accidental state of his mind at the instant of writing, and it is not strange if, among so many letters, when I am hurrying to put down the first thing that comes into my head, and fill out a sentence as quickly as possible, it is not strange, I say, if I say many silly things. Your remark about care in writing what the Gov.[2] is to see, surprised me much more than your criticisms, for possessing as I do a mens conscia recti,[3] I would be perfectly willing to have him see all my thought in reference to my country and believe he would approve them all. If he has expressed unfavorable opinions I wonder that his letters say nothing about them. They, on the contrary, have been very kind and mild, and his last, on finances, the contents of which you seemed to know, was even very liberal, so that I have not a single word to say against his mode of treating me. It is true I shall do my best to make no use of this liberality but am none the less obliged to him, on that account. It is a satisfaction to feel that I *can* spend, and have an ample margin.

What you say about next winter's arrangements I have already heard from mamma. She writes that it's not to be mentioned till next summer but seems to consider the division in just the same way as you. I was surprised to hear of the Melodeon purchase. I know nothing of the size or arrangement of the estate but should think it might be a first-rate thing. Of course I have requested the Gov. to take charge of mine.

Money matters are now very easy with me. I have about six hundred dollars on hand, counting the Gov. late remittance as only five hundred; and this here is equal to eight hundred. I owe not a cent except to you and Hill. This latter I should like to see off my hands, and I'd pay him myself devilish quick if he were here, but as I can't do that nor get the money to him, I'm afraid that I shall have to ask you to see to him. For God's sake, though, don't do it if it will inconvenience you. I feel now that I am perfectly well in condition to pay him myself if I could only send the money, but it is so small a sum that it is hardly worth while to send it by the Baring's.[4]

You surprise me by your admiration of Miss Louisa C. I do not take to her, but perhaps it was an old prejudice that I got when I acted with her two years ago. Society however I will leave for a sheet to John which I shall send with this.

In politics you can judge better than I, but I myself believe that Douglass will win.[5] He is playing a devilish hard game; in fact he is repeating in the nation the operation which was so successful in his own state. We shall see.

About myself I have hardly anything to say beyond what I have said in my last letters. I cannot say that my present life is wildly exciting, nor that the capital of Prussia has as yet shown itself to me in any violently attractive light. But at least if I have not had an exciting time, I have at all events not had an unpleasant one, and if the last month has been particularly quiet, there is at least the satisfaction of knowing that it has been a particularly instructive one. My school is perfectly satisfactory, and I am better satisfied of the wisdom of this step than of anything else I have done. I go a good deal to the Opera, which is a great temptation; to the Theatres not so often for the playing is almost poor and the plays, except when Schiller, Goethe, or Shakespeare is produced, not much. I've not been on a real bat for ever-so-long, being in a very quiet and economical set, and though often indulging after the theatre in a steak and glass of beer or bottle of Rhine wine, this never leads to anything worse. As I have to get up six mornings in the week at either seven or eight o'clock, I have also to go to bed early and not drink too much. I'm virtuous as St. Antony and resist temptation with the strength of a martyr. I've not been to a disrespectable ball for a month or nearly a month, but can't say how long this will last. The way the virtue of the purest is corrupted here is wonderful.

You can imagine that my school lessons don't take up much of my time out of school, though the poor little devils of boys have to work all the time.[6] The master inquires if I can recite, and I say yes or no as it happens. My German is slowly advancing under this pressure, but I must say that I never expect to master it as I once expected. It is terribly long and tedious and my advance can be measured not by days but by months. I read very little German, for most of my time for reading is occupied by my Latin. It may seem to you that this sort of life is not exactly what we usually connect with our ideas of life in Europe, but my experience and observation to the slight extent of four months, goes to show that the American idea of life in Europe, as given by such men as Gus Perkins, the Hammonds, &c &c &c is a damned absurd one and just worthy of them. I've not seen Paris yet but it's my impression that to a sensible person who has no particular object in staying there and is not in French society, it's just as slow as any other city, and except in its Galleries and Palaces, no better than New

York. Indeed I've heard sensible fellows who had lived in both places, assert that in its means of enjoyment New York was ahead of any city in Europe that they had seen. I don't undertake to endorse this, but it shows how differently people think on this point, and for my own part I never feel thoroughly jolly anywhere till my whole time is employed.

Lately, it is true I've been rather more out of my room in the evenings than usually, but I hope not to do so much of this after this week. Consult John's sheet for information as to my sights and dissipations.

I will need proceed, my amiable brother, to discuss the last philosophical propositions of yours, and the plan which you propose for my course in life. I confess that it filled me with wonder and general bewilderment. I think in my last I said that you paid me a left-handed compliment, in your idea of my mind. Permit me to retract; humbly apologize. I never made so great a mistake in all my life. I have usually considered myself a conceited fellow. Every one told me so, and I believed 'em. I *had* thought that I set about as high a price on my mental capacities as most other people; perhaps a peg higher. I was mistaken; I've put it's market value up at least twice as high again since your last.

Were you intoxicated when you wrote that I am to "combine in myself the qualities of Seward, Greely, and Everett"?[7] Mein lieber Gott, what do you take me for? Donnerwetter! do you suppose that I'm a statesman like Seward or that my amiable play-philosophy would ever set me up to guiding a nation; do you imagine that I have a tithe of Greely's vigor, originality and enterprise; are you so blinded by the tenderness of your fraternal affection as to imagine that the mantel of Cicero has fallen upon my shoulders, or that I inherit the pride and ample pinion that the Grecian sophist bore? Nimmermehr! What would be the result if I were to return home and gravely and coolly set myself to doing what you propose? Bah! mine brother, you seem to have written under the idea that I am a genius. Give that idea up, once and forever! I never did anything that I should be treated like this. I know what I can do, and I know what a devilish short way my tether goes, and the evening before I received your letter, I had, in my daily lesson in Ovid, read the fable of Phaethon, whose interesting and suggestive story you'll find at the end of the 1st and beginning of the 2d Book of Metamorphoses.

Now a word as to my own condition, and then for our discussion. You know by my last that I have joined a Gymnasium, like our Latin School, only much larger and thorougher. Here I go every day from three to six hours. It is not very good fun; that is of course. But it admirably answers my purposes. Here I pursue my original design of studying Latin and Greek. Here is tremendous practice in hearing and talking and learning German. Here it is very cheap. Here I am free enough and yet must obey the rules where they are not excepted in my favor. I go four mornings in the week at eight o'clock. Three afternoons there is no school and the others are no trouble to me. The boys received me with open arms, and my proceeding caused some noise in Berlin, for every one of the four hundred and odd told it at home, and I became quite famous. One or two of the little fellows I am quite fond of, and you would split if you could see me walking away from school with a small boy under each arm, to whom I have to bend down to talk to. None of them know English, so of course I speak only German, and am familiar enough with it to get along very well. I am stared at as a sort of wild beast by the rest of the school, who only see me when I come and go, for there is no recess, and no outdoor playing, so that I know only the boys in my own room. As yet I only see the boys at school, where they treat me with a certain sort of respect, and yet as one of themselves. They never push me or trouble me in any way, nor play tricks on me. Perhaps they think that I know how to box, and it's as well to let me alone, but anyway they are many of them firstrate fellows, and two especially I cherish with paternal affection. I've not as yet recited in Latin or Greek, but soon shall begin; to translate, that is, into German. I *can* study all the time, or not at all, but I *must* go to school, and that is study enough to satisfy my conscience.

I am also busied during my leisure odd minutes or hours in studying art, and reading and studying theoretically painting. Music occupies me too, during certain hours every week, and more than these certain ones, if there is any that I wish to hear. So you see that I have enough work (or play-work if you prefer to call it so) to occupy me all my time. I seldom do nothing. In my new rooms I seldom see Americans, but know very few Germans indeed. In short I am busy, contented, and only once in a while cross.

Steady application like this implies a harder blow-out than usual when it does come. As for "life" as it is called, it's all humbug. But once in a while one must go on a bat to clear his head, and I can tell you, after a fortnight of school, a fellow feels very willing to kick off the fetters. I very seldom do anything out of the way, and have had only one really hard spree since I came here. This was last Saturday night, at what claimed to be a masked-ball, but if I recollect right, it was to the sober part of the audience, a very dark and dismal failure. I had a pretty high time there, and it took me all the next day to recover. The worst of a bat in Europe is that women are always in it, and a mere drunk is almost unknown. There is an abundance of means of raising the devil, and use one, you must use the other.

So the world wags on here, quietly as possible. The weather is detestable. Formerly it was always bad. For a month we didn't see the sun. Now we have one fine day, and two bad ones. It grows cold and clears, then thaws and clouds up. Still, when one passes nearly all his daytime in school, it doesn't matter much what the weather is.

In money matters I have to be very careful, and this month have rather overstepped my bound as I have bought several expensive books, but I hope to need no more money from home till the first of March, and unless next summer ruins me, I shall get through. It isn't pleasant to have to calculate every cent one spends, but independence is a great thing, and I shall do my best to hold to it. I keep my accounts most rigidly; have no debts except my monthly accounts with my landlady; and always know where I am. As I have always had to be very careful, it is not so hard now. I economize as much as I can, but sometimes can't resist spending too much.

And now as to the last part of your letter, over which I have thought a good deal, and been a little troubled. I acknowledge the force of what you say, and yet I disagree with your conclusions. Let me proceed systematically if possible.

You try to put me on the horns of a dilemma. You attribute to me a certain kind of mind, and argue that if I am to be a lawyer, or in other words, follow my own plan which I have followed for several years, then what I learn in Europe is worse than thrown away. Hence, to be a lawyer I must cease to be what I am. If I acknowledge that my mind is not adapted to my plan, I must give my plan up. If on the other hand I assert that my mind *is* adapted to my plan, I must give Europe up. This I take to be the ground of your letter. I disagree with it, and think that you are mistaken not only in your judgment of my mind, but also in your idea of the necessary result of two years in Europe. But I shall not go into this subject now. Perhaps in another letter I may give you some reasons for believing that what I am learning here in Europe is not in opposition to what I propose to do hereafter. Just now I prefer to attack your position rather than to defend my own. It's easier and there's more fun in it.

I don't deny the truth of what you say, that law is not a pleasant study, and that we are not adapted to make great lawyers. But beyond this I think you lose yourself and run aground. You say that I am not made for a lawyer; but hardly hint at what I am made for. The same things that you say of me, you also apply to yourself. Now let me see if I can carry out your idea to any result that will give a fellow a minute's firm footing.

The law is bad, you say. Wohlan! what then? Why then, you continue, take something that suits you better. And what would be likely to suit me better? What is this kind of mind that you give me? I must say that you pay me a very left-handed kind of compliment in your estimation of me. You seem to think that I'm adapted to nothing but the sugar-plums of intellect and had better not try to digest anything stronger. You would make me a sort of George Curtis or Ik. Marvel, better or worse; a writer of popular sketches in Magazines; a lecturer before Lyceums and College societies; a dabbler in metaphysics, poetry and art; than which I would rather die, for if it has come to that, alas! verily, as you say, mediocrity has fallen on the name of Adams.

But, I suppose, you will deny that your letter leads to this and assert that such men as Mr Everett, Mr Sumner, the Governor, Mr Palfrey and the like, are a wholly different class.[8] I would just suggest that all these began either as lawyers or clergymen; and I merely propose to do the same. But now let's go back to generalities, and see whether something can't be fished up.

In the most general terms then; you would say, I take it, that my mind if not adapted to law, at least *is* adapted to literary pursuits, in the most extensive meaning of the term; and to nothing else. I couldn't be a physician or a merchant, or a shop-keeper or anything of that kind, so well as I could a lawyer. Literary pursuits are very extensive, but I *must* make some money to support me, so we must say, "literary pursuits that produce money." Now literary pursuits that produce money and that I am eligible for, are very few.

To begin with, perhaps, if I were a better man, I might feel inclined to become a clergyman. But as I'm very much a worser man, we'll count that out.

Then you once proposed to me to go into the newspaper line and become an editor. The objections to this are as many and as strong as to law, but if you don't see them, we'll reserve the subject for further discussion.

Of Atlantic Monthly and Putnam and Harper and the men who write for money in them, my opinion is short. Rather than do nothing but that, or make that an object in life, I'd die here in Europe.

No, mein Liebster, this is one of those propositions which would kill any man's chances in America, even though he had all the training of Gorgias (if that was the beggar's name), and all the philosophy of Frank Bacon; (I refer to the Viscount Verulam and not to the young Bostonian of the same name). Yet after all, your idea is not so very distinct from mine, except that it throws out into the strongest relief the object that I proposed to make dependent on circumstances and success in other respects. We are considerably in the same box, brother mine, and what applies to me, applies also, with slight alterations, to yourself. As you say, there are differences between us, and my character isn't your's; in fact, I know many respects in which I wish it were; but still we have grown up in the same school and have, until now, drawn our mental nutriment from the breasts, metaphorically speaking, of the same wet-nurse; indeed we may consider ourselves a case of modern Romulus and Remus, only omitting their murderous propensities. What is still more, we are beautifully adapted to work together; that is, *you* are. I stand in continual need of some one to kick me, and you use cow-hides for that purpose. So much the better. Continue to do so. In other words, I need you. Whether there's any corresponding necessity on your side, is your affair. But it's a case of "versteht sich" that we can work better together than apart. Under these circumstances, let us be very careful how we take a step that will probably knock one of us in the head forever, or so separate us that our objects would become different. I shall hesitate a very long time indeed before I decide to earn my living by writing for magazines and newspapers, for I believe it to be one of the most dangerous beginnings that a man can make. Recollect that threadbare old Arabian Nights magnetic mountain *that drew all the metal out of the ships* and then sunk them.

I say that our ideas are not far different. The real difference is this. Your's begins by assuming as your ground plank and corner stone that I am capable of teaching the people and of becoming a light to the nations. Mine on the contrary begins by leaving that to develop itself in the future or to remain proved on the other side, without suffering a public disgrace from slumping as I infallibly should do under your idea. I said in my last what I wanted of the law; that I considered it the best grounding in the world for anything that we wish or are likely to do; that it is the strongest point to fall back upon and the best position to advance from; at once offensive and defensive; it gives one a position as literary as if he did nothing but write for periodicals and a good deal more respectable; as a profession it offers many inducements; as merely an occupation it offers still more, and there is much more chance both for you and me to work *up* from it, than there is doubt in my mind that I at least should drop like a stuck monkey from the perch on which you want me to place myself. Perhaps it is my wish and hope that we may do something of the sort you propose, but I do not wish for so large a scale of action, because I know my own weakness; I do not wish to go to work in the way you propose, because in the first place I believe it to be a wrong way, tending to fritter away the little power of steady and long-continued exertion I have, and in the second, it seems to me not to offer that firm and lasting ground-work that the law does. I do wish to adhere to my original plan because, though even that is more, I am afraid, than my powers are up to, yet it seems to me as feasible as any that has yet come before me, and if I can do nothing in that, why let me go to the devil at once, for there's no use staying here. Gott bewahr mich from funny Lyceum lectures and rainbow articles in Atlantic Monthlys with a proof of scholarship as exhibited by a line here and there from "the charming old Epicurean Horace" or the "grand thunderbursts of superhuman strength" from God knows what old Greek trotted out for the

occasion. If I was born to be the admiration of girls and Tupperian philosophers, I'll cheat fate and quietly do nothing all my life.[9]

So here I will lay aside this subject and wait for your next. As this letter
has been written partly in school, partly here, and is the work of some six
or eight different sittings, I'll excuse you for finding fault with it, as with
my former one, but you must also excuse the faults. On your theory of my
proper plan of life, however, I ought never to say any foolish things but
my lips should drool wisdom and my paths should be by the side of
Socrates, and Isocrates; (by the way were these two men related and why
have they so similar names). I hope your next will take a more practical
view of life.

Meanwhile this last week I've been exceedingly dissipated; out every
night in one way or another, and able to do very little real work. The last
two days too, the weather has been charming. Yesterday Jim Higginson
and I took Mr Abthorp out on a spree.[10] He has had us there to dine and
gave us some of the best champagne I ever tasted; perhaps the very best;
I've dined twice with him and got talking very fast both times. The ladies
retired to their room and left us to our wine, and as Mr A doesn't stint
the supply and I make it a rule never to refuse a good glass when it's
offered, the inevitable consequence is very clear. A bottle of wine is the
outside of what I can carry, and in both cases I drank devilish close onto
the limit. Yesterday we returned the hospitality by taking Mr A out for a
day of it, to show him the style of our ordinary life. Higginson and I went
for him at two o'clock and carried him off to our dirty little restauration,
and there dined him and gave him a glass of beer. You know the style of
our dinners from my letters, I think. Then we went to a concert till six,
and leaving the concert before it was over, we walked down to a little
theatre called Wallner's, a devil of a way off, and saw a drama called
"Berlin wie es weint und lacht";[11] a thing very popular in Berlin, and has
run 137 nights. It's by far the best drama of the sort that I've seen, too.
Thence we walked back and sat till twelve o'clock in a Wine-cellar, or
Wein-Stube as they call it, which was crowded with exceedingly respectable
old people but which, though very clean, yet hasn't the vestige of a table-
cloth on ary a table, and was hot as hell and filled with clouds of tobacco
smoke. Here we eat and drank and talked and Hig and I smoked, and
passed a very jolly evening, drinking two bottles and a half of Rhine wine,
really better than I've often tasted at home, for which two bottles and a
half we paid something less than an American dollar. This is a dear place
for wines too. On the Rhine, I am told, they cost much less. I very often
come in here after the theatre and drink a bottle, commonly with Higginson,
or if I'm on the heavy cheap, go to a cellar and get a couple of boiled
sausages and a mug of beer. The sausages I tell you are good. My supper

commonly costs quarter of a dollar or less. My dinner the same. As for cigars, I consider myself extravagant when I smoke really good ones which cost me $15.00 the thousand. They're not proud like yours, but curse me if they dont taste as good as any I used to pay at the rate of $50 & 60 for.

So I will now wind up this letter, which though not so long as yours, has yet the excuse that I've more letters to write than you. I will now proceed immediately, as you say, to put on my paint and feathers (devilish dirty paint in the shape of my old dress suit) for a grand ball in the Opera House, at which I suppose all the Court will be, and which I shall try to tell about in my letter to John. I go from a sense of duty though it costs me three thalers and I'd rather stay at home, but one ought to see these things and I presume it will be handsome and stupid as double-distilled damnation. I don't know anyone except Americans there, and if I did, it wouldn't make any difference. Meanwhile, allerhöchstgeborner Herr, accept the assurances of my deep respect. If I knew enough of this cursed language I'd write you a letter in German, but I don't and never shall, curse it.

Give the tokens of my highest consideration to the family at large. My last letter home was Feb 5th to mamma; before that, Jan. 29th to the Congress man. No letters as yet received this week.

Yrs.   H.B.

MS:MHi

1. HA had begun to number the letters, evidently to help the family keep track of their arrival. He quickly abandoned the practice.
2. "Gov.": nickname for their father.
3. *Mens conscia recti:* good conscience.
4. London banking firm of the Baring Brothers.
5. Stephen A. Douglas (1813–1861), reelected to the Senate by the Illinois legislature, and aimed for the presidency.
6. In order to learn German HA had enrolled as a special student in the Friedrichs-Wilhelm-Werdesches Gymnasium.
7. William Henry Seward (1801–1872), leader of the Republican party, secretary of state under Lincoln; Horace Greeley (1811–1872), founder and editor of the *New York Tribune* and a popular sage; Edward Everett (1794–1865), professor at Harvard, congressman, governor, minister to England, president of Harvard, and U.S. senator, known for his eloquence, an uncle by marriage to HA.
8. John Gorham Palfrey (1796–1881), historian, editor of the *North American Review*; "Governor," familiar for CFA; Charles Sumner (1811–1874), U.S. senator from Massachusetts and leading abolitionist.
9. Martin Tupper (1810–1889), philosopher of the commonplace.
10 James Higginson (1836–1911), Harvard '57; Robert Apthorp (1811–1882), prominent Bostonian.
11. Berlin, How It Weeps and Laughs.

To Charles Francis Adams, Jr.

Thun. August. 6. 1859.

Dear Charles

I received your letter of the 2d–9 July the day before yesterday together with a splendid batch of others including one from papa and one from John who seems like the ancient Phoenix to have become young again and this time so devilish thoroughly that I can't begin to keep along with him. When my unhappy conscience will be relieved from this weight of letters Heaven only knows. Some time ago I wrote a line to mamma from Zürich and since then have had every moment taken up, what with mountains and general accelerated motion. Loo however still writes I suppose a la steam engine and she supplies all gaps.

Here I am as you see in Switzerland and have seen this lion or a part of him at last. Very fine he is too but Englishmen have rather injured the primitiveness of the beast.[1] Here in Thun we have been for several days leading a delightfully primitive and lazy life; Kuhn, Theodore Chase, Ben Crowninshield, Loo and I;[2] all economising, and I in particular looking forward to that £100 that should be here in a week, with a firm consciousness that if it doesn't arrive I shall have my movements rather stopped off. Travelling is perfectly frightful. A pound a day is the lowest a man can calculate on. You can see about where I shall be at the 1st of November.

Tomorrow I'm off for Mt Blanc, shall see Fred Hauteville at Vevay,[3] be back here on the 15th and set off immediately with Kuhn, Loo and Theodore over the St Gothard into Italy where we shall visit Turin and Milan and I shall again leave them at Como and come over the Splügen onto the Rhine. This is an innovation on my original plan, but Loo wants me to do it and it will only take about ten days. Then I shall rejoin Ben at Baden and we shall do the Rhine together.

This is the program. Hope they won't find fault with it at home. It will all be done before you receive this letter.

My own conscience smites me at times when I think of what a big plum-cake I've got hold of, and what an indigestion it may give me. I wish to God I was not the first of the family who had done all this for it renders necessary all sorts of carefulness and puts me as it were under obligations and bonds for future conduct. Travel as modestly, yes as meanly as I will, it is wholly impossible to keep independent of the Governor's assistance and that will bring it's discount, I suppose, with it, if not in one way then in another. But what can't be cured must be endured.

Further, as for travelling there's not much to say. The women are all ugly here and I'm not vulnerable that way. Besides I've made an oath that if I can help it I'll not fall in love until it's certain I can't get along any other way. I've come to the conclusion that that's a double edged sort of amusement that cuts a little deep occasionally. Moreover no one has taken the trouble to fall in love with me; another good reason for not indulging in this amusement. Then the travelling is very pleasant and unless it becomes tiresome as it may in time, will satisfy my highest wishes. It may seem absurd to you that a fellow should write as if it were possible that travelling should not amuse him. I notice however that Joe Bradlee returns to Hannover in the middle of this month; *the* travelling season.[4]

Your letter wasn't high-spirited my boy. In fact it was anything but it. Your reply to my remarks about marrying may be satisfactory to you but is not to me. Not by a jug-full. Talk about your father's "alms." Why damn it Sir if you marry, your father's bound to help you and there's no "pensioned beggar" about it. Is Kuhn a pensioned beggar because his father-in-law allows his wife so much a year. Gott bewahr! It strikes me you take too low a tone about this matter. The Governor wants us to marry. Well and good. Like other fathers who can afford it, he is willing to allow us so much. I say, take it and if there's any trouble about it, don't back down as if it was your fault. To my mind there's no dependence about it, unless you choose to live as Ned Everett does.[5]

Now, my boy, I don't undertake to criticise your conduct except so far as I know it. But it does strike me that you're giving yourself up to a morbid feeling that will some day swallow you whole, and you'll be a sort of Gorham Brooks.[6] I don't know anything about your proceedings but I have written what I did write on the theory that you was letting your hobby run away with you, and I tell you fairly that I very much suspect it has cost you already just about ten thousand times what it's worth. If you can consider the subject coolly and impartially I would like to have you reason out from the position of a fair umpire whether it's worth while to allow objections like this to play damnation with the best, most natural and probably the happiest course that your life could take. If you satisfy yourself however that it's all right, then of course I've no more to say except that I hope the end won't be the worse for it.

If however the father proposes to rest his hopes of grandchildren on his third son, meaning me, from present appearances I think it probable he'll have to practice the art of patience to a very considerable extent for I haven't seen yet the woman whom I'd marry and until I do I shall not express any opinion about the result. One thing I do know, however. If I want to marry I shall do it and the father may "taunt" as much as he pleases. If I know myself and him it won't last long. He's not unreasonable if he's once shown the right road to travel and this objection of yours would be my smallest.

So much for this matter. I'm glad to hear you are to be at Washington a part of the session. I believe, you know, in a change of society, or of no society if you please, for so far as I know, you live in a world of waste and one person is no more to you than another. A position that I was in until I went to College and thank the Lord never have been in since and never will be again if I can help it. It's bad for the soul and the body. I'll always have a friend if he's only a nigger-boy.

This letter is short and personal. I can't make it longer for Theodore, Ben and I are going off in a moment to Berne to take a "bain complet" of which you'd better not speak to the moral and the European travellers.[7] Life here is deliciously lazy and jolly; Theodore plays and we listen and joke and indulge in all sorts of nonsense of which I suppose Loo tells you. So ponder over this letter and give credit to the philosopher

Henry.

MS:MHi

1. The English Alpine Club, founded in 1857, had greatly stimulated mountaineering by Englishmen.
2. Theodore Chase (1832–1894), Harvard '53.
3. Frederic Sears Grand d'Hauteville (1838–1918), Harvard '59.
4. Josiah Bradlee (1838–1902), Harvard classmate.
5. Edward Brooks Everett (1830–1861), HA's cousin.
6. Gorham Brooks (1795–1855), HA's uncle.
7. *Bain complet:* expensive room with private bath.

To Abigail Brooks Adams

Dresden. February. 13. 1860.

Dearest Mamma[1]

Your letter of the 24th arrived this morning, and as Mary's letter is intended for you as well as to her so far as news goes,[2] I shall take this for private matters. The news of the engagement startled me some if not more; on the heels of it came a letter from Ben officially announcing it.[3] Ben is considerably astonished but swallows it like a good boy and gives it his entire approval. Under these circumstances I answered the letter in the same spirit, and wish him joy of F.B. The family Mifflin-Warren-Crowninshield has the monopoly of the hog-trade.

I'm glad you're entertaining. I wish you could make your "salons" the first in Washington. You know I'm ambitious; I needn't remind you of it; not on my own account, but as a family joint-stock affair. Now papa has got to make himself indispensable; not only in the wild-beast pen, but out of it too. So far as ability, courage, strength and bottom goes, that is, so far as public business is concerned, we'll all bet heavy on him and give odds; but his weak point is just where you can fill it; he doesn't like the bother and fuss of entertaining and managing people who can't be reasoned with, and he won't take the trouble to acquire strength and influence that won't fall into his mouth. People can be lead by their stomachs as well as by their understandings, and the opening is now a magnificent one. I don't see why you can't make your drawing-rooms as necessary and as famous as you please and hatch all the Presidents for the next twenty years there. Gov. Seward knows well enough how important this is and if he says so much as your letter mentions, and went so far as to bring his daughter-in-law to you without a previous call from you, all I can say is, the Governor knows what he's about and I believe in him more than ever. As for having the "Presidency in view" I hardly think it's desirable with the present occupant's fate before one's eyes;[4] I aspire to the leadership in the lower House and the Departments. Be ambitious, Mrs A. You're young yet! Just begun life! Principle is an excellent thing; very; but it belongs at the bottom and not at the top; it makes the foundation of life but the upper stories are lighter material; one can't eat and drink and live on principles, as you justly say. It's all infernal nonsense, you and papa sacrificing yourselves for the good of your country; I tell you, you're doing nothing of the sort, at least if I can help it; you must take just as many honors as you can get and what's more, you must work to get them and be glad that the paths of duty and of ambition combine for you; for most people they lie in contrary directions.

You just mark what Seward says; he's the man of the age and the nation; he knows more in politics than a heap; he's a far-sighted man and yet he's got eyes for what's near, too. I aspire to know him some day. Pray tell him so if you ever lack matter of conversation. Keep him allied with papa, the nearer the better. If he comes in as President in that case, we shall see fun. Don't scold because I advise so conceitedly. I want you to know the views of a European, and I don't see the use of shutting our own eyes however much we may wish our neighbors to close their's.

More next week.

Yrs Affectly   Henry.

MS:MHi

1. Abigail Brown Brooks Adams (1808–1889).
2. Mary Adams (1846–1928), HA's younger sister.
3. Louisa Crowninshield (b. 1842), Ben's sister, was engaged to Francis Bacon.
4. President James Buchanan (1791–1868) was under hostile congressional investigation for alleged abuse of federal patronage.

To Charles Francis Adams, Jr.

Dresden. March. 26. 1860.

I received your letter of the 5th or thereabouts, this morning, my dear boy, and hurry to answer it, not because it's in need of an answer so much as because I have a good many things to say that won't wait. I hereby acknowledge moreover various papers from you for which I am much in your debt. Of these presently.

You send me a draft-receipt; God knows what for; I never saw one till now, and shall keep it unless the Baring's keep still and don't notify me. Papa's a rum one in money affairs; he writes me at New Years that he makes me a present and mamma too; I buy articles of "luxe" to the amount expecting a remittance of at least £115, as last year; and so count myself nearly $100 out of pocket. I *must* receive another remittance by the 1st June at Florence. Papa will say he's credited me the amount of his present, which is all devilish good but we know, credited or not, it will count in point of fact against me as current expenses.

I have packed and sent off today a box addressed to you. It will go in a sailing vessel to Boston and probably arrrive in the month of June when you will be notified through the Custom-house. The box contains mostly books; some pictures by my hostess here, of which the uppermost one I think is for Mrs Putnam; it can wait till my return; a package addressed to D. Crouse, contains a photograph; forward this at once; a box wrapped in oil-cloth and sealed with my seal, contains somewhere near a hundred dollars worth of engravings; among them your Parce; be careful of these; in an old beer-jug down in one corner you'll find among other things a porcellain medallion, angel's head; I'd be obliged if without ruining me you'ld have it set as a breast-pin and give it to Rebecca as a memento; it's not very costly but pretty. You will I hope be careful with all the things as well as with those which have gone home with Ben Crowninshield's things, and I would be immensely obliged if you'ld put them all together to wait my return. That is, use them as much as you please but don't let them get scattered.

I leave Dresden this day week and notify you of this box so as to have it off my mind. I hope to God it will arrive safe for even the insurance wouldn't represent half it's value to me.

Your letter is healthier than usual. It doesn't smell of Boston Common and State Street and I was devilish glad to get it. I'm glad you had a good time in society. There is no society in Europe as we understand it, so I can't imitate you. Your first letter about the printing-affair I happened to see through Billy Howe;[1] without knowing who wrote it; I executed a pas seule with variations and warhoop accompaniment in my appartment on reading it. Then I sat down and wrote a florid letter to mamma in which I honored your epistle with the epithet "treacherous." A few days afterwards I was rather taken aback by receiving a package of papers with your initials as "Pemberton."[2] The game is a risky one; take care of your incognito or else it may react and people think it was a political trick of the Governor's to help himself. Putting this aside, it was a great success. Indeed I'm inclined to believe that papa's "coup" owed a very considerable part of it's success to that letter, and not a small part to it's low tone. Even the Courier's "Giant among Pigmies" was quite as much a hit at the Advertiser as a bonbon for papa.[3] The Courier fell into that trap beautifully. Anyway I congratulate you on your success which is in it's way quite as decided as papa's. As none of my home letters have mentioned all these letters as your work, I've said nothing about it either, nor to anyone here, and shan't till I hear that you've avowed them.

Seward's speech is a great thing. I think there are as few assailable points in that speech and yet as broad a position, as is possible. Even the New York Herald will blunt it's dirty teeth on that. As a statesmanlike production too I'm proud of it, and we shall do well to take a lessson from it. The Senate in it's best days never heard anything better done.

I took a hint from your last and have been lately writing a series of letters to mamma to do at least all I can to fix her out. She complains in all her letters of the nuisance of going out and that it'll be the death of her, but somehow they're all written in the best of spirits, and for all her protesting that she hates the life, despises the President and is acting a wholly self-sacrificing rôle, I think the attention she gets pleases her as much as it does us, and as I recollect she never could be happy at home without something to worry her, I hope that this present worry is only the old chronic one in a new shape.

You come down in your political philosophy to the principle of education; from different grounds I did the same here some time ago. It's the main idea of all progressists; it's what gives New England it's moral power; Horace Mann lived in this idea, and died in it.[4] Goethe always said that his task was to educate his countrymen; and that all the Constitutions in the world wouldn't help, if the people weren't raised; and he and Schiller did more for it than anyone else. Our people are educated enough intellectually but it's damned superficial and only makes them more willful; our task so far as we attempt a public work, is to blow up sophistry and jam hard down on morality, and there are as many ways of doing this as there are men in the country. This idea was at the bottom of my letter of the 21st Jan. and it's only the manner in which we can invest our strength to the most advantage in prosecuting this idea, that can trouble us. For I for one haven't the courage of Horace Mann. As for the Union, our field of action remains about the same whether it stands or falls.

However because we are virtuous we'll not banish cakes and ale. I've been trying this winter to make my path clear to myself but haven't quite succeeded. I still waver between two and shall leave fate to decide. In the meanwhile I mean to have as good a time as under the circumstances will do, and shan't interfere with others. This apropos to John. Ye Gods, I would like a pretty sister-in-law. I would love her and cherish her and be kind unto her. Damn the odds. Who can tell what the morrow will bring forth? Let us eat, drink and be merry!

Your Washington letters, my boy, have stirred me up. As you know, I propose to leave Dresden on the 1st of April for Italy. It has occurred to me that this trip may perhaps furnish material for a pleasant series of letters, not written to be published but publishable in case they were worth it. This is my programme. You may therefore expect to receive from week to week, letters from me, beginning at Vienna and continuing so long as I don't get tired of it. What the letters will be about depends of course on circumstances. Now, you will understand, I do *not* propose to write with the wish to publish at all hazards; on the contrary I mean to write private letters to you, as an exercise for myself, and it would be of all things my last wish to force myself into newspapers with a failure for my first attempt. On the other hand if you like the letters and think it would be in my interest to print them, I'm all ready. In any case you can do just what you choose with them so long as you stick by your own judgment. But if, under any absurd idea that I wish to print, you dodge the responsibility of a decision, and a possible hurting of my feelings; by showing me up to the public's amusement without any guarantee against my making a slump, you'll make a very great mistake. I could do that without your help. But it needs a critic to decide what's copper and what silver and I suppose you have courage enough not to be afraid to tell me in case my coinage should turn out copper or copper-gilt. So gird on your sword and don't be idiotic enough to bother yourself with family affection or brotherly sympathies.

The life here doesn't change a hair. I feel like a snake thawing out after being frozen in all winter. My family here bores me. Once or twice I've sat up all night playing cards with the Howes. That was my only excitement. I never make calls for they're slow. My books are now all sent off so I've nothing to do but write. The Howes leave this week; the gambling-shop in the Prager Strasse is to be closed, and there will be another winter a closed book. In the whole of it I've not had one good-time. I've digged like a Freshman; hardly once has my pulse beaten faster than usual except at news from home or over plans and thoughts of my own. On the other hand my health has been excellent; my spirits uniform; I've never been unhappy; hardly felt the blues; not been discontented; and usually been more or less amused. So there's pro and contra. The life has been a pleasant life enough and very useful and such as it is, I'm satisfied with it.

Billy and I presented a letter on a Mr de Cramer of the Russ. Leg. which the Mogul (Uncle Sidney) sent me. At my request he included Billy's name. What on earth induces the Mogul to notice me for the first time in his life. Very kind indeed; very; but quite a new trait. He doesn't intend to remember me in his will, does he? No such luck. That's all for his namesakes.

Give my love to all the little goslings, especially Miss Eugenia who by the way is about the only one of all my acquaintances whom I still recollect with amusement. *Do* get Philo engaged before I return. Mrs Frank Bacon in spe[5] is I hope well. Expect another letter within a fortnight.

Yrs ever   H.

MS:MHi

1. William Edward Howe (d. 1875), Harvard '53.
2. CFA2 published two letters in the *Boston Advertiser*.
3. Editorial in *Boston Courier* praising CFA.
4. Horace Mann (1796–1859), Massachusetts school reformer.
5. *In spe*: in hope.

To Charles Francis Adams, Jr.

No. 6.[1]   Rome. May. 29. 1860.

My dear Charles

This is a great age. One may congratulate himself, I suppose, on living in stirring times, indeed, to a certain degree, in heroic times, which will some day be looked on as a golden, or at least a silver age. And here am I directly in the centre of it all, and what good do I get of it? I might as well be in Pekin as here, so far as there is anything to be seen of the course of the time. Rome is externally quiet as death. As I said in my last, mere demonstrations are at an end. There's a deal of seething and boiling in quiet, but to me the eternal city is more than ever only eternal in it's ruins, it's priests and it's beggars. I meet one day a high-churchman, or feudalist or whatever you may choose to name the apologisers of things as they are, and he tells me that Garibaldi is defeated, that the Piedmontese are deserting in swarms and enlisting under Lamoricière, that the Romagna is growing more and more dissatisfied with it's position, and that the democratic party in Piedmont is getting the better of Cavour and trying to bring back the anarchy of '48.[2] The next day I talk with a warm liberal and learn that

Garibaldi has taken Palermo, that Lamoricière has been defeated near the Tuscan frontier by a band from Tuscany, has lost two hundred men, two cannon and half his army deserted, and that nothing can help the country till the Pope, the Cardinals and all are hunted off once and for ever. If I happen to fall on anybody who is a little cooler or more indifferent in the matter, he tells me that no one knows anything in Rome, no one ever was known to do anything in Rome; that the Pope is just as much in the dark as his subjects, and that the Neapolitan Minister here has been posting about to all his associates of the diplomatic body, praying that somebody will tell him something for he for his part knows less about the affairs of his own country than any of the others. This has gone on for a week and even what occurs within fifty miles of the city is a mystery. Today however I saw a couple of riflemen with extensive sword-bayonets before Lamoricière's quarters in the Piazza di Spagna, so I suppose he has cleared off the intruders on that side and has come down here to rest a day or so.

A man more copiously abused than this good General, I've seldom heard of. Of course all the liberals hate him with a really cordial hatred. The French officers sneer at him for his want of success which they take for granted, pity him for the loss of his reputation, and detest him because he is the opponent of their divinity, the Emperor, and the French army. The Cardinals frown at him for cutting into their privileges and kicking their prejudices out of doors. And the officers who have luxuriated in thirty years of faithful service in the Papal army, are utterly disgusted at being ordered up into the country without a week's delay to have their spare shirt washed and leave cards on all their acquaintances. That is the way things are done in Rome. Meanwhile little is heard of the recruits who were promised. The Irish were announced as having arrived. One gentleman declared he had seen them, but his only proof was that early one morning he met a body of ragged-looking fellows marching in file, each with the neck of a bottle sticking out of his coat-pocket, from which he supposed they were Irish. Enthusiasm seized some members of the nobility on one occasion, as you may have heard, and they entered the army as private soldiers. It appears that the other morning they, or two of them, left the city to join their regiments. The departure was described as quite fine, they driving off in a carriage with a number of admirers, of the lower orders, kissing their swords, or trying to. No doubt they would cut their throats too if there were a revolution. The gentlemen in question are young, and one was described as looking decidedly as though he would like to resign his post of honor, while the other kept his spirits up very well.

This you see is all the merest gossip, but it is what we all live on in Rome; that is, those of us who are interested in it. Our news, that is, the really authenticate news, we get from Galignani, and I cannot think that the Papal Government is so illiberal as many persons describe it, when it allows Galignani and the American papers which contain often ludicrously abusive articles about the Pope, to come every day to the public reading-rooms.[3] I think at home I've heard of illiberality worse than that, even in our own enlightened land.

So, as I've said, I feel a sense of personal injury and wrong that everything here should be so quiet. One might just as well live on the Sandwich Islands. Garibaldi and his three thousand might just as well have fought at Thermopylae. Cavour and "il nostro Re" might just as well have ruled a century ago, for all the part that we, who are right in the heart of the country, can take in their troubles or their efforts. There has been only one exception to this rule, I believe. Our well-known gentlemanly Consul here in Rome narrowly escaped being hurt in the affair of last March, when a trooper made a dash at him as he was getting into his carriage. This is a sort of thing quite unpleasant, and our Consul applied for redress for the threatened injury. Cardinal Antonelli, with a quaintness of conceit and a dryness of humor that one would hardly expect from a Cardinal, is said to have replied that it would give him great pleasure to reprimand the trooper in question, if the American Consul would be so kind as to point him out. I really cannot say whether our Consul has taken further steps in the matter or not.

While the world is thus standing at gaze, and watching Sicily, we Romans are making excursions out to Tusculum and Tivoli, or rambling about in the catacombs or lounging and smoking cigarettes in artist's studios. Thanks to the late Spring and cold weather, the Campagna and all the mountain scenery near Rome is looking magnificently. The Villas at Frascati are the very idea of loveliness in nature. I rode out to Frascati the other morning on horseback, passed the day there and at Tusculum and returned in the evening. It is about two hours ride out there, and when that is done, one desecrates the classic ground by riding over it on donkeys. When the party is tolerably large, it's strange how one forgets what one ought to feel. I think we raced our donkeys over the ground that was once a part of Cicero's Villa, and we lay and eat luncheon in the shade, by the side of an acqueduct that was older than Rome. That was one of the sunshiney days of one's life. And then the sun-set as we started back to Rome was one of those sights that make one melancholy to think about.

By the way, in my last letter, speaking of artists here, I mentioned Mr Story's statue of Cleopatra.[4] At that time I did not know that Mr Hawthorne had introduced it into his new novel, and to this moment, in spite of all my efforts, it has been my misfortune not to have been able to get hold of that book.[5] It is not to be found in the bookstores and of course every owner of a copy has pledged it already months deep. When Mr

Hawthorne describes or praises anything, it is time that other people should hold their tongues. Yet he saw it only in plaster and I'm surprised that he admired it so much. Placed side by side at least, there is as much difference between the plaster and the marble as between a chalk sketch and an oil painting.

The truth is, it is a great deal too dangerous to attempt to criticise a work of art, else I would try and give you some of the results of my lounging in the studios of Rome. Of course all artists are unequal and a good many are bad. It is rather peculiar that the bad artists sell as many or more works than the good ones. It is naturally amusing to stand by and listen to the comments of visitors on works that have no prestige and on others that have, fairly or unfairly, got a reputation. To be sure, I wonder in the same way at the man who goes into raptures over the Venus de Medici, so that my taste may be just as questionable as theirs, but it certainly seems to me as if people took pains to seek out the weakest and poorest of all an artist's works, and have it reproduced again and again. Every one seems to have a rage after Venuses, from painted ones to fettered ones, and yet it is tolerably safe to say that a statue of Venus, especially a naked one, in one's parlor, is bad taste, and still more, that, usually, a Venus is the most insipid and meaningless work an artist ever makes. Then there is for instance a work here in Rome called a Boy mending a Pen, that has achieved a considerable success. I've never heard any one say that this statue was good; I have heard many people say that it was very bad. Yet it is a favorite work among buyers and has been reproduced several times. The truth is that popularity is no test. I don't believe for instance that the Cleopatra will ever be popular unless Mr Hawthorne has made it so. So among Mr Rogers' works, the least good seemed the most sought.[6] By the way I am told that Mr Rogers is or will be three thousand dollars out of pocket on account of his bronze doors. Some one was laughing here at a proposal in Congress to appropriate fifty thousand dollars to a statue of Lafayette. People seemed to think that if three thousand of that fifty were passed over to remunerate Mr Rogers, there would still be enough left to make two equestrian statues with.

The studios are a great feature in Rome. It's delightful to take one's luncheon towards two o'clock and then smoke an hour and watch the clay take form or the sketch fill out into color and life, and meanwhile talk nonsense or sense as it happens. The range is enormous. It stretches from art to prize-fighting; and men talk equally well about the Apollo and the Dying Gladiator, or about Heenan and Pryor.[7] Politics as developed in America produce curious effects on Americans who have lived a little while abroad. There is a general sensation or suggestion of bad Bourbon whiskey about American politics that is not pleasant. The Charleston Convention for instance was a crowd to whom I should have thought the red-nosed Mr Stiggins might have remarked "This meeting is drunk; Mr Chairman you are *all* drunk,"[8] with tolerable truth. Just imagine if you can, such a convention meeting in Piedmont or a Pryor and Potter affair coming off in the Turin Parliament. The world would say that Italy had better remain disunited till Italians learned to behave themselves decently. In fact the world would call it barbarism and the world would be about right. Art must exercise a refining influence, and a man who comes here to pass his life, drops Bourbon whiskey and takes to lemonade or Bordeaux at best. Americans who live abroad read the American papers with a sort of groan. To foreigners New York is the Eureka of vice and villainy, and I assure you in all Europe I have never yet seen so much open and unmitigated wickedness as I have seen in one night in that city.

Of course society here is not perfect. The artist world was always famous for jealousies and troubles, and there are plenty of them here. The tone is tolerably low as a whole, in spite of the art which ought to elevate it. But people don't get drunk, for Bourbon whiskey here would be death and if there are jealousies and unfair play, at least it is quiet and not paraded through the streets.

This is my last day here. I leave half Rome unseen, and go away half ruined. You know I suppose, the Roman jewelry and are aware that it's remarkably fine. You know the Roman cameos, that they are very beautiful. You are also aware perhaps that Roman mosaics are pretty, to say the least, and Roman scarfs not unpleasing in their way. Roman photographs are a popular institution, but cost money, and if a traveller is wildly rich he can buy works of art from American artists. For myself, since Castellani showed me his jewelry and named the prices, I've been indifferent to all smaller things.[9] The innocence with which I selected a little thing that I thought I'd like to have, and the utter disgust at hearing the man suggest that the price was "trois cent piastres, Monsieur" cured me of any further desire of possessing any of his objects of art. But if one has three or four gold mines and a rich wife, I should think he might like to have some of Castellani's things.

I feel sad and solemn at leaving Rome as I never have felt about leaving any place before. Partly out of piety towards an old superstition and partly from a belief in it. I have been this evening to the fountain of Trevi and there in the moonlight, in solemn solitude, have drunk of the water and bathed my face in it, for the story goes that he who does that on the last night of his stay, will surely return some day to drink those waters once more. It's hard to think that one will never see the grand old city again. And then the kindness and hospitality that has met me here is something that makes the leave-taking twice as hard.

The Romans seem to think as I do about it and value me on a scale very flattering to my self-esteem, for I had to pay four dollars and a half for my passport. That passport costs a small fortune in one way and another, and the prospect of Civita Vecchia and Naples is anything but bright. One of our gentlemanly Democratic Ministers abroad once crossing a frontier in his normal condition of crazy inebriation, refused to show his passport, and when finally persuaded to do so, flung it with all his force in the officer's face. The principle was correct but the manner faultily suave.

Yrs ever.

MS:MHi

1. Sixth letter in *Boston Daily Courier* July 6.
2. Giuseppe Garibaldi (1807–1882), Italian liberator; Christophe Lamoricière (1806–1876), commander of the papal army; Camillo Cavour (1810–1861), prime minister of Italy 1860–1861.
3. *Galignani's Messenger,* Paris English-language newspaper.
4. William Wetmore Story (1819–1895), expatriate sculptor.
5. *The Marble Faun* (1860).
6. Randolph Rogers (1825–1892), popular American sculptor.
7. John Heenan (1835–1873), American champion prizefighter recently matched with Tom Sayers, British champion; Roger Pryor (1828–1919), Democratic representative from Virginia, challenged John Potter (1817–1899), Republican representative from Wisconsin, to a duel.
8. Charles Dickens, *The Pickwick Papers* (1837), chap. 33.
9. Augusto Castellani (1829–1914) specialized in reproductions of ancient jewelry.

To Charles Francis Adams, Jr.

[Washington] Sunday. Dec. 9. 1860.

Dear Charles

I propose to write you this winter a series of private letters to show how things look. I fairly confess that I want to have a record of this winter on file, and though I have no ambition nor hope to become a Horace Walpole, I still would like to think that a century or two hence when everything else about us is forgotten, my letters might still be read and quoted as a memorial of manners and habits at the time of the great secession of 1860. At the same time you will be glad to hear all the gossip and to me it will supply the place of a Journal.

The first week is now over and I feel more at home though I've not made many acquaintances. It's a great life; just what I wanted; and as I always feel that I am of real use here and can take an active part in it all, it never tires. Politically there is a terrible panic. The weak brethren weep and tear their hair and imagine that life is to become a burden and the Capitol an owl-nest and fox-hole. The Massachusetts men and the Wisconsin men and scatterers in other states are the only ones who are really firm. Seward is great; a perfect giant in all this howling. Our father is firmer than Mt Ararat. I never saw a more precious old flint. As yet there has been no open defection, but the pressure is immense and you need not swear too much if something gives at last.

Of course your first question would be about Seward. He came up here last Tuesday evening and I heard him talk for the first time. Wednesday he came up to dinner and was absolutely grand. No one was there but the family, and he had all the talking to himself. I sat and watched the old fellow with his big nose and his wire hair and grizzly eyebrows and miserable dress, and listened to him rolling out his grand, broad ideas that would inspire a cow with statesmanship if she understood our language. There's no shake in him. He talks square up to the mark and something beyond it.

He invited us down to dine with him on Friday. His wife hasn't come here this winter, so he has persuaded Mr and Mrs Israel Washburne to put up with him till they go off.[1] We six had a dinner, at which the governor caused a superior champagne to be brought out; not his usual tap. Israel was as usual; ugly as the very devil, but good-humored and nervous and kindhearted as ever. The Governor was chipper as a lark and swore by yea and by nay that everything was going on admirably. The state of society here worries mamma very much and she was sorrowing over the bitterness of feeling and change of bearing in her acquaintances but the Governor was implacable. He swore he was glad of it and delighted to see 'em down. He'd been through all that and come out on the other side. They had been all graciousness to him as a Whig while they tabooed Hale and Sumner and Giddings.[2] They had tried to taboo him too, later, but then it was too late, and now he was glad they did feel cut up and meant they should.

He is the very most glorious original. It delights me out of my skin to see the wiry old scare-crow insinuate advice. He talks so slowly and watches one so hard under those grey eye-brows of his. After our dinner we went into the parlor and played whist. Gradually a whole crowd of visitors came in, mostly staunch men such as Potter and Cad. Washburne, Sedgewick and Alley and Eliot &c.[3] Among others who should turn up but the two R.I. senators, Antony and Simmons, both very fishy and weak-kneed.[4] Antony is the man whom mamma gave a tremendous hiding to, last Spring, for a remark he made more than usually treacherous, but he called on us the other evening notwithstanding. The whole company knew all about it however, and Seward knew they did. I was sitting somewhat back, just behind Antony and Seward and watched them both carefully. Antony remarked deprecatingly; Well, things look pretty bad, Governor; don't you think so?—No! growled Seward—I don't see why they look bad—Well! said Antony still more timidly;—these financial troubles coming so with the political ones—Why, answered Seward; You can't run a financial and a political panic together; the first will regulate itself—Poor Antony fairly broke down and acquiesced. The manner in which Seward spoke fairly bluffed him. But Seward was unmerciful. The first thing we knew he dragged mamma out; wanted to put her against some of these Carolinians; she was the person to take care of them; put 'em in a dark room and let 'em fight it out &c, &c; to all which mamma of course answered laughingly while everyone in the room was on the broad grin. I thought he'd never leave off this talk. He wouldn't stop, but rubbed it in and in till Antony looked blue. At the very first pause and change of topic, he got up and took leave. Of course it did not please mamma too well to be used as a sort of a false target in this way but the Governor only smiled grimly and neither apologised nor confessed his intentions.

Dec. 13.   This letter is still waiting to be finished and this week I've been regularly jammed up for time. What with the duties of secretary, of school-master, of reporter for the papers, and of society-man, I have more than I can do well.

Frank Parker arrived here day before yesterday and will be with you nearly or quite as soon as this.[5] To me fell the duty of guiding his steps and I think he imbibed good republican doctrine and lots of it. All day yesterday we were up at the Senate talking in the cloak-room and to-day I left him in the House where he was well looked to. Last evening I took him down to Seward's, and to-day Seward and Mr & Mrs Israel W. came up to dine with us and him. By the way W.H.S. was urgent on me to tell you that he had lately received a letter from his wife in which she said that a letter dated last October I believe, and addressed "Auburn, Mass." had arrived from you after going to its direction. With various complimentary remarks the Gov. said that as he was epistolarily exhausted, he wanted me to acknowledge the receipt of this letter &c &c &c. Mrs S. sent him on the letter I believe, saying that it was too good to be lost.

We had an interesting time to-day. As you of course see, all the mean material we've got is coming out now—Dixon of Con. flattened out, and so has Sherman; so will Antony, Foster, Collamer I believe, and a heap in the lower House.[6] The 33 committee is sitting now every day and all day, and they'll be reporting some damned nonsense or other soon.[7] Today we were all waiting for our good father before dinner, when in he popped in a state of considerable friction and reported that his committee had sprung a resolution on them yielding everything, which had passed in spite of him with only eight negatives; New England, New York and Wisconsin. Seward looked blue and little Washburne was disgusted. However, as it's not to be submitted to the House, but only intended for effect on South Carolina, there's no immediate danger, though it embroils things badly and will inevitably break the Republican line. So we went to dinner and Seward almost killed me by telling some stories and laughing over them. He goes home tomorrow to be gone a week and Mr & Mrs Blatchford who are coming to stay with him will be received by John and entertained by the Washburnes.[8] Why he goes home I don't know. *He* says it's not politics that drives him but W.H.S. is not to be sounded by ordinary lines.

I shall write for the Monday's Advertiser setting some things forth. You may be aware that our good papa bears up the opposition in the 33. I have therefore reserved my fire so far as he is concerned, but now he will have to be sustained. My communications will perhaps be on the crescendo principle and if the battle waxes hot and Charles Hale does not rise to it, you must thumb-screw him a little.[9] Send Dana and Horace Gray round. I shall write to Hildreth too, probably.[10] My theoretical letter of last Monday was good. Damned if it wasn't. I say it because I have my doubts. It takes forty-eight hours for a letter to go and be published so I didn't send one this evening as it would wait till Monday.

We're chipper as can be here and I keep a general look-out over things. Our men are not afraid, but you must prepare for *any* compromise that the South chooses. Our only hope is that they'll kick us out and refuse everything. This is not improbable, but nothing is sure.

I am only making acquaintances so I can't give you much outside news. There is little or no society as yet and will be very little all winter unless the southerners accept the olive-branch. As I am very busy, I don't care much for there is so much life here as to allow one to dispense with balls. Sidney Everett I've seen twice but as yet not to make any treaty with him, so to speak, and I am the less anxious to do so, as he seems wholly taken up with his Carrolls and I see no hurry to get in with them.[11]

The man Bardolph informs me that he himself took the boxes to the steamer or boat or agent, receiving at the same time the bill of lading therefor; the which he is ready to swear to any amount of profanity, as well as the black gentleman who accompanied him. Does that suit you? If not, what would you more?

We are all well and happy. Our mother allows herself to be distressed somewhat by disunion, but in action she is straight and has a reputation such that the fishes are afraid of her. Parker will enlighten you verbatim as to matters here, as he has seen all our side and has gone deep into the state of affairs. I'm afraid however I only speak exact truth when I tell you to prepare yourself for a complete disorganization of our party. If the south show any liberal spirit, the reaction will sweep us out dreadfully and thin our ranks to a skeleton. Luckily we have our President and can hold on till the next flood tide. How many there will be faithful unto the end, I cannot say but I fear me much, not a third of the House. But the Governor will be great; *our* Governor I mean.

Hints of any sort are welcome.

H.B.A.

MS:MHi

1. Israel Washburn, Jr. (1813–1883), Republican representative from Maine, former Whig.
2. John Parker Hale (1806–1873), senator from New Hampshire; Joshua Reed Giddings (1795–1864), representative from Ohio 1832–1842 and 1842–1859.
3. The five Republican representatives were John Fox Potter (1817–1899) of Wisconsin; Cadwallader C. Washburn (1818–1882) of Wisconsin; Charles B. Sedgwick (1815–1883) of New York; John B. Alley (1817–1896) of Massachusetts; Thomas D. Eliot (1808–1870) of Massachusetts.
5. Francis E. Parker (1821–1886), lawyer, partner of Richard Henry Dana, CFA's ally.
6. James Dixon (1814–1873), senator from Connecticut 1857–1869; John Sherman (1823–1900) of Ohio, representative 1855–1861, senator 1861–1877, 1881–1897, secretary of the Treasury 1877–1881; Lafayette S. Foster (1806–1880), senator from Connecticut 1855–1867; Jacob Collamer (1791–1865), senator from Vermont 1855–1865.
7. Committee of Thirty-Three, one congressman from each state; CFA member from Massachusetts.
8. Richard M. Blatchford (1798–1875) of New York.
9. Charles Hale (1831–1882), editor of *Boston Daily Advertiser,* in which HA's letters appeared.
10. Horace Gray (1828–1902), Boston lawyer; Richard Hildreth (1807–1865), journalist and historian.
11. Henry Sidney Everett (1834–1898), first cousin of HA.

To Charles Francis Adams, Jr.

Washington. 31 Jan. '61.

My dear Boy

Papa has just spoken.[1] The House listened with a perfectly intense attention, and you could have heard them breathe, I believe, if you'd tried. They were evidently with him and every word told. The galleries which were pretty full, applauded him several times. His hour out, an extension was granted which is rather rare now, and he finished, applauded at the close. As usual he held them with a regular grip, and when he ended, every one got up and a poor devil who wanted to speak got mad because no one would listen. I didn't see Sumner there, but old Winthrop and Everett were on the floor and seemed rather less well pleased than I should have thought they would have been.[2] After it was over I saw nearly all the delegation come up to congratulate him very heartily, and a perfect host of others.

In my opinion it's a great speech and one that will tell effectively. It's the best stroke the old gentleman ever made yet. It's what the republicans have got to stand on, and you'll see that everyone will ultimately settle on it except the abolitionists and the disunionists.

Papa has been perfectly overwhelmed with congratulations, the delegation being delighted. Winthrop did not speak to him. Everett shook hands and said he agreed with *nearly* everything he said.

I've never seen papa more affected than by the reception he met. Buffinton got it in, inducing Corwin and Sherman to let him have the floor on the Pacific rail-road bill.[3] This is a *very* rare thing.

The Herald man says he's going to telegraph the whole speech on to New York tonight. Fifteen or twenty thousand copies are already ordered for Maryland.

Loo and Mary called him out from the middle of a swarm of people, and hugged and kissed him in the passage before a heap of women who were all trying to congratulate him too.

On the whole, c'est une grande victoire. Voilà tout!

H.B.A.

MS:MHi
1. CFA spoke in support of the compromises offered by the Committee of Thirty-Three.
2. Robert C. Winthrop (1809–1894) of Boston, former congressman.
3. James Buffinton (1817–1875), representative from Massachusetts; Thomas Corwin (1794–1865), representative from Ohio.

To Charles Francis Adams, Jr.

Washington. 8 Feb. 1861.

My dear Charles

On coming back from a little dinner with Kuhn and Loo and Mary at Gov. Seward's, I received your yesterday's letter. You counsel boldness at the very time when a bold step might close my mouth permanently. It was but this morning that C.F.A. cautioned me against writing too freely. The New York Times, which has always shown particular respect towards my letters, gave to one of them the other day an official character, reprinting it as a leader, with comments. This makes it very necessary that I should be exceedingly cautious in what I say, unless I want to be closed up altogether. Besides, in the present state of the delegation, when there are but three or at most four who will follow our lead, I can't be very bold without bringing Pangborn on my back, and getting not only myself (which I would rather like) but Papa into hot water.

As for Sumner, the utmost that can be expected is to keep him silent.[1] To bring him round is impossible. God Almighty couldn't do it. He has not made his appearance here for more than a week, though there is as yet, so far as I know, no further change in the position of matters between him and C.F.A. As usual I suppose he will stand on his damned dignity. Once Gov. Seward and he had a quarrel. The Gov. wanted him to vote for an Atlantic Steamship bill, and after exhausting all other arguments, tried to act on his feelings and urged him to vote for it as a personal favor in order to aid his re-election. Sumner replied that he wasn't sent to the Senate to get Mr Sewards re-election. On which the Governor, losing his philosophical self-command, said, "Sumner, you're a damned fool," and they didn't speak again for six months. I'm of Seward's opinion. Let Sumner get the idea that his dignity is hurt, and he *is* a damned fool. However, you can rely upon it, we shall do all we can to prevent his bolting, and I mean to flatter him all to pieces if I have a chance.

The Convention is in secret session.[2] Like most meetings of this sort, I suppose they will potter ahead until no one feels any more interest in them, and then they may die. I have not yet seen any of our Massachusetts men.

This temporizing policy is hard work. I'm sick of it, but the 4th of March is coming and we shall soon be afloat again. These cursed Virginians are so in-grain conceited that it's a perfect nuisance to have anything to do with them. Let the 4th March pass and unless I'm much mistaken they will be allowed to send their secession ordinance to the people, and have it rejected too. Just now however there is nothing for it but to delay. Our measures will pass the House; and perhaps the Senate; at least I think so, but we shall see. Forty or fifty on our side will oppose them, but not violently.

We expect John and Fanny tomorrow night. When do you propose to come? John and I will have to live out of the house.

The ancient Seward is in high spirits and chuckles himself hoarse with his stories. He says it's all right. We shall keep the border states, and in three months or thereabouts, if we hold off, the Unionists and Disunionists will have their hands on each others throats in the cotton states. The storm is weathered.

Yrs ever   H.B.A.

MS:MHi

1. Sumner had returned to the Senate, where he violently opposed any compromise with the slaveholding states.
2. "Peace convention," called by the commonwealth of Virginia. Twenty-one states were represented.

To Horace Gray, Jr.

Horace Gray Jr Esq.[1]
39 Court Street. Boston. Mass.

London. 17 June 1861.

Learned Doctor

It is pleasing at least, if not always beneficial to have a certain variety in life, and so far I have nothing to complain of against my destiny which has made of me within twelve months now a gentleman traveller in Europe, now a politician and correspondent of newspapers in Washington, now a student of three days under your fostering care, and finally a budding diplomat in this cheerful village. All four occupations have their pleasant sides and at least are capable of furnishing occupation. Whether the variety will be still further continued is somewhat doubtful, but I don't despair.

As for England, I confess to not being very fond of it. The people are too cold and formal. They never laugh and they amuse themselves with such gravity and earnestness of purpose as is appalling to a lazy person of a cheerful disposition. For my own part I believe that the learned Justice Blackstone is their greatest humorist and that his Commentaries are the best commentary on their character and disposition. I dont wonder that such shoals of them wander out to the uttermost parts of the earth after excitement and new sensations, for sensations seem to be prohibited here by act of Parliament to say nothing of Common Law, and society is as dull and stately as wealth and stupidity can make it. They are not many degrees removed from Chinese Mandarins, I imagine, and it seems to be their ambition to make the resemblance close as possible.

We arrived here some six weeks ago, and found things, politically speaking, in a deuce of a mess. It looked at first very doubtful whether we should not be with you again before you quite expected us. The accounts we got were so bad that we hardly knew what to believe, and people evidently knew so little about our affairs that one hardly knew where to begin. The southern Commissioners had been here for some time working like rats and doing their best to sink us, and had made a decided impression which that old imbecile of a Dallas had done nothing to counteract.[2] Two days after our arrival the Queen's Proclamation appeared and of course compelled my father to make an immediate decision as to the course he was to take.

His instructions as you know were clear and unmistakeable and would have justified him and something more in at once refusing to hold any communications with the Government here. We knew too well enough that such a step would be fully upheld at home and if he had wanted to make a noise and make himself conspicuous, it was a first-rate opportunity. No doubt a good many of you at home fully expected it and would have cheered him on. But he decided otherwise and determined not to do anything violent. Cassius Clay and our friend Burlingame devoted themselves to that sort of diplomacy and a pretty mess they made of it, giving us and our party here a heavier load to carry than Cassius's own lazy, fat, conceited old carcass would have been.[3] My father, though a good deal disappointed, went into the fight, bound to try it out, and not be knocked over by such a foul blow as the Proclamation. He had at once an interview with Lord John who was profoundly civil and disavowed all intention of doing us any harm or the southerners any good, and took amiably a pretty smart hint as to the consequences of pursuing his course, concluding the interview by asking my father in to lunch with him and Mrs R. and all the little Russells. This interview over successfully, my father's course was clear. Before long he was deep in society, invited everywhere and making acquaintances with all the Dukes and Marquesses and Earls in the Kingdom. The effect of these changes in our affairs here was soon very evident. The tone of the press began to change and would have done so much more if those devilish fools in Paris had held their blockhead tongues. In parliament our side at once came up, and Lord John and all the Ministry became wonderfully vigorous in extinguishing the unlucky orators who said anything against us. Finally, and what I consider the greatest victory of all, Lord John issued his orders closing the British ports to armed vessels on each side, and the House of Commons came down with a tremendous avalanche on poor Gregory which stopped his mouth permanently.[4] The southern commissioners fled in dismay to Paris and the field was fairly our own.

Now I don't know how you in America will regard all this, but I must say I feel some pride in our having weathered this very critical point without anything breaking. My father has had the option at any time these six weeks of forcing a war. His instructions would have sustained him and so would the country, but I consider our victory as infinitely more complete and satisfactory now than it could have been in any other way, and unless you at home still remain stuffy and pugnacious, I think it is permanent. My father and Lord John are on the best of terms socially and I see no reason why any more difficulties should arise for some time unless they come from your side of the ocean. Everyone here is polite and cordial as they know how, and though I half suspect I see now and then traces of our friend Sumner's hand not wholly favorable to Mr Seward (this is in deep secrecy, and you must never hint it to anyone) still it would be a very captious person who would not be satisfied with our reception everywhere.

My own part in all this has been small enough. Knowing how hard it is for a stranger to get into English society, I have not yet attempted it at all, but have staid at home reading Blackstone and the newspapers, until my mother has made headway enough for me to step in on her train. This I am going to set about at once and expect a labor duller than a treatise on feudal tenures, and which wont pay me half as well when finished. I have a long theory of action to work out. Literary acquaintances to make, legal and social institutions to examine, such as courts and model lodging-houses, the British Museum and the system of taxation, the daily press and the English Church, all which and much more are open to an enquiring even though a somewhat lazy mind. As usual I expect to be sent away from here just when I am getting into a way of obtaining a little practical knowledge and social position; but that is for the future.

I do not know that there is anything here in the way of gossip that would interest you. As yet I am unacquainted with the celebrities so that I have nothing to say about them. We are in the full blast of the London season which is said to be this year dull to what it usually is, in spite of a degree of solemn entertaining that alarms me of simple ideas. The process of working into our places has been nearly completed by my father and mother but not yet begun by me. On Wednesday we are all presented and make our first appearance at the Queen's drawing-room, which is to be in the deepest mourning for the Duchess of Kent.[5] My father and mother meanwhile are out every evening, generally to a dinner and a ball, or two balls, at which they complain grievously, and with reason, for their health suffers and my father looks and feels badly. But the season is nearly over.

This letter is *very* confidential, so don't quote me, for my good name as a diplomat & believe me

Very truly Yrs   H.B. Adams.

MS:MH

1. HA had tried to study law with Horace Gray.
2. George Mifflin Dallas (1792–1864), minister to Great Britain 1856–1861.
3. Cassius Clay (1810–1903), en route as minister to Russia; Anson Burlingame (1820–1870), en route as minister to Austria, was rejected and assigned to China instead.
4. William Henry Gregory (1817–1892), of Coole Park, Galway, whose motion in Parliament to recognize the Confederacy was indefinitely postponed.
5. Victoria Maria Louisa (1786–1861), duchess of Kent, mother of Queen Victoria, had died March 16.

To Henry J. Raymond

(Private & confidential)   London 24 January. 1862.

My dear Sir[1]

Circumstances make it advisable that I should, in the present state of affairs, cease to write or do anything that might be made public or that might by accident bring me into public notice. You will no doubt see how important this is, not only for myself, which I care little for, but for a variety of other reasons.

The position of affairs here is very critical, and yet very misty. Who it is who holds the true key to it, I do not know; but this much is certain. All England believes and asserts openly that France is urging the Ministry to attack our blockade, and all France asseverates no less earnestly that the pressure comes from England and that Napoleon means to remain neutral. There is evidently political trickery somewhere. Now, so far as France is concerned, there are pretty certain reasons for knowing that there is no hostile movement intended. It is equally certain that if such an intention exists in the present English Government, it can only be in a portion of it, and that the first overt act will be the signal for a conflict that will probably destroy the Cabinet and bring a tremendous struggle on the Parliament and people. It looks to me very much as though some contest were now going on here, though so far out of sight that it is only to be guessed at. The case lies thus. Government organs have distinctly made the proposal of intervention, and the Observer and the Morning Post, both Palmerstonian papers, have encouraged it. The Southern agents here have offered, or let themselves appear as offering, terms that amount to nothing less than utter ruin to the South, emancipation among them. This is announced by another well-posted paper, the Scotsman. King Leopold of Belgium is here, and if one is to believe the world, is warmly opposing intervention on any terms. The Times and the Globe, high authorities, have come out on the same side. This all seems to indicate some Ministerial division of opinion, and to those who know Lord Palmerston, it looks much as though he had been advancing the proposal in order to see what reception it would meet.

For the present there seems no doubt that this plot has failed, thanks to the brilliant ability of Mr Seward.[2] But Parliament is going to meet and the Southerners here are working with utter desperation to excite a popular movement. They are at their wit's end and can't stand up much longer. We don't know what success they may have, but everyone knows that agitation almost always gets its end in time, and though the middle classes are neutral in our fight, there is no great feeling in our behalf here that can be organised or made very active. One thing would save us and that is a decisive victory. Without that our fate here seems to me to be a mere question of time.

If we can't get the victory however, or if it's not decisive, we must prepare to stand a hot battle in Parliament, and the main thing for us to do is to strengthen our friends there. Mr Seward's late course has already done this very much. I certainly hope no effort will be spared in America not only to keep down the expressions of ill-will to this country, but to prevent subjects of controversy from rising, and to create points on which our friends here can rest. We have many and very able advocates, and, I believe, a majority of the Ministry. If no new quarrel rises and we suffer no military disasters, or no great ones, I think the Southerners can get little here. They have however the advantage over us in their organisation, and in the steady aid which the Times gives them. The Clubs too are hopelessly anti-American.

The main point of attack now is the Charleston harbor business, but this is to my mind a good sign as it shows how hard they are driven for a point which has any chance of being vulnerable, and as it relieves the efficiency of our blockade from attack and indeed from notice. Still it would be something to take away even this cause of reproach and disavow any intention of permanent destruction.

There is talk of a popular movement against us among the poor of Lancashire and Yorkshire, and it is even said that all the wires are already laid to start it and it only waits for Mason's arrival and sanction. This, however, will be of little account, I think, if the Ministry remain firm.

This is the best summary I can give of our position here. As it is my last, I give it only in the hope that it may be of some little service to you. We are very anxious to hear of a success, but it really must be better followed up than our others if we are to be much strengthened by it here. I hope that what I have written may have been of use, and only regret that I have been unable to speak so openly as I could have wished.

Socially the position of Americans in England is not so pleasant as it might be. There is a cool ignorance and dogmatism about this people that is hard to bear, but I hope to see a spoke put in their wheel some day yet.

Very truly Yrs   H.B.A.

MS:NN

1. Henry J. Raymond (1820–1869), editor of the *New York Times*, with whom HA had secretly arranged to act as London correspondent. HA's last letter appeared Jan. 21.
2. Since Seward had agreed to release the Confederate agents James Murray Mason and John Slidell, who had been taken from the British ship *Trent*, Lord Russell, the British foreign secretary, instructed envoy Lord Lyons on Jan. 10 that Britain regarded the incident as closed.

To John Gorham Palfrey

London 12 February. 1862.

My dear Sir

Your letter of 19 Nov. which you were so kind as to write in answer to my small remarks on the mythical Pocahontas, has remained unacknowledged longer than I wished. But it reached me when we were on the verge of ship-wreck, and I had no heart nor time to think of any female of that age or any other. The storm has passed for a time, however, and I am so foolishly sanguine as to think that it was the crisis in our foreign dangers, and that now, if we must be ship-wrecked, we on this side the water shall have no voice nor hand in the disaster. Our work seems to me to be done, and I feel confident that Europe will now lie still until the home-crisis that seems to be inevitable, shall have come to some positive result. I have made use of the respite to run over again in a very superficial way, the question which we were discussing, and I think I may say, with a certain confidence, that I know considerably less about the matter than I thought I did before.

When I wrote last, I was under serious difficulty from having quite mistaken certain facts; an error which I perhaps shouldn't have made if the way of arriving at these same facts had been easier. I am obliged to Mr Deane for correcting me, and will try not to do so again.[1]

The British Museum, if properly searched, might perhaps give some light on this subject. But I have not yet succeeded in tapping any productive vein. You and Mr Deane are no doubt thoroughly familiar with all the sources of information yet opened. The best that I have arrived at in the way of enlightenment on the history of the romantic young woman, is a portrait purporting to represent her, decidedly hard-featured and wearing a stupendous sugar-loaf hat and garments in the height of the graceful stiffness of James the First's period. No doubt you are well-acquainted with this, as the book is hardly a rare one. In two letters of the day, she is mentioned as "the Virginia woman"; the ungrateful Chamberlain doesn't even give her the title of Princess:[2] But I think he was jealous that the King should have had her "well-placed at the masque." Not a word, however, of her connection with Smith, nor does the State Paper collection seem to mention her further. I can only find Hamer's book in a German translation published in Hanau in 1617.[3] Probably Mr Deane has the original, which is not in the British Museum, or, if it is, I can't find it. He, I notice, speaks of "Pocahuntas" as one "whose renown has spread even to England under the name *Non Parella.*" This is at least more gallant than Chamberlain, but it puzzles me. If the epithet means anything, it must refer either to personal or to mental superiorities. Now, handsome was she not, if I can judge from her picture. Contemporary authority says only that she was not uglier than many English ladies, which, with deference, is barely a compliment to her. Have I not seen their descendents? But if her mental charms were *sans pareil,* what had she done at that time (before her capture by Capt. Argal) to justify the title? Hamer however leaves this all in blank, and her goose of a husband, Rolfe, writes a long letter to justify his marriage, without ever descending to give such a terrestrial reason for it as a regard for his wife, or any merit in her that attracted him, except that she was a Pagan. I confess, this seems to me to show a degree of self-devotion on his part that does not tally with my idea of the character of the Virginia settlers. It belonged rather to the latitude of New England.

Smith's authority being ruled out, I must acknowledge that I have as yet succeeded in unearthing nothing that throws any light on Mrs Rolfe's antecedents. Unless some one else proves luckier than I, we must yield that the chances are in favor of Smith's turning out as powerful a liar as he was seaman. I fully expect that the ghost of John Randolf will haunt you and Mr Deane and me for this impiety,[4] but it wasn't my fault.

I presented Wingfield duly to the British Museum and received a letter of thanks from the Librarian of the Reading Room; and further it was said that the thanks of the Trustees would be offered to Mr Deane on their next meeting. Since then I have not seen nor heard from Mr Watts. I wish to thank Mr Deane also on my side for the trouble he has taken on my account.

We are all flourishing here, and living in firm hope of salvation. About six weeks ago the Boston Courier, by puffing an indifferent poor work of mine that should have remained anonymous, got me into a position that strongly resembled "Damien's bed of steel";[5] for I was roasted with pepper and salt by the English press. Consequently, my small attempts to make progress here, have wholly ceased, and I live the life of a hermit, copying letters. I have, therefore, no news to tell, except that I think it a question whether you would find England as agreeable a residence now, as you once did. My own Anglicism is somewhat wilted.

With best respects to your family I remain

Very respy &c &c	H.B. Adams

Mr Parkes[6] wishes me to acknowledge a letter from you and Mr Dana. He has been quite ill for ten days and is not out of the house. But he has a letter on the stocks for you.

MS:MH

1. Charles Deane (1813–1889), editor of early American documents. Palfrey sent HA's letter to Deane, who, by way of correction, sent his edition of Edward M. Wingfield's *A Discourse*

of Virginia (1608) and urged HA to continue at the British Museum with research concerning Captain John Smith and Pocahontas.

2. John Chamberlain (1553–1627), whose letters date from 1598 to 1625.

3. Ralph Hamor, *True Discourse of the Present Estate of Virginia* (1615).

4. John Randolph (1773–1833), a bitter opponent of JA and JQA, claimed descent from John Rolfe and Pocahontas.

5. Quoted from Oliver Goldsmith's *The Traveller* (1764), alluding to the torture of Robert Damiens, the failed assassin of Louis XV.

6. Joseph Parkes (1796–1865), Birmingham lawyer-politician.

To Charles Francis Adams, Jr.

London 16 May. 1862.

My dear Boy

My last letter to you was dated the 8th. Since then I have received a long one from you dated the 6th April with a postscript of the 11th. I was glad to get it for I had begun to think you had given up the pen for the sword with a vengeance.

Before this reaches you, I suppose you will be in motion, and I hope that the war will be at an end. It would be a mere piece of unjustifiable wantonness for the Southern generals to defend Charleston, if they are defeated in Virginia. So, although I would like to see you covered with glory, I would be extremely well satisfied to hear that you had ended the campaign and ridden into Charleston without firing a shot or drawing a sabre.

Last Sunday afternoon, the day after my letter to you had gone, telling how hard it was to sustain one's own convictions against the scepticism of a nation, I returned from taking a walk on Rotten Row with my very estimable friend Baron Brincken,[1] and on reaching home, I was considerably astounded at perceiving the Chief in an excited manner dance across the entry and ejaculate "We've got New Orleans." Philosopher as I am and constant in a just and tenacious virtue, I confess that even I was considerably interested for the moment. So leaving Sir Charles Lyell regarding my abrupt departure through one eye-glass with some apparent astonishment,[2] I took a cab and drove down to Mr Weed.[3] Meeting him in the street near his hotel, I leaped out of the cab, and each of us simultaneously drew out a telegram, which we exchanged. His was Mr Peabody's private business-telegram;[4] mine was an official one from Seward. We then proceeded together to the telegraph office and sent a despatch to Mr Dayton at Paris;[5] and finally I went round to the Diplomatic Club and had the pleasure of enunciating my sentiments. Here my own agency ended; but Mr Weed drank his cup of victory to the dregs. He spread the news in every direction, and finally sat down to dinner at the Reform Club with two sceptical old English friends of our side, and had the pleasure of hearing the news-boys outside shout "Rumored capture of New Orleans" in an evening Extra, while the news was posted at Brookes's, and the whole town was in immense excitement as though it were an English defeat.

Indeed the effect of the news here has been greater than anything yet. It has acted like a violent blow in the face on a drunken man. The next morning the Times came out and gave fairly in that it had been mistaken; it had believed Southern accounts and was deceived by them. This morning it has an article still more remarkable, and intimates for the first time that it sees little more chance for the South. This is, we think, a preparation for withdrawing their belligerent declaration and acknowledging again the authority of the Federal Government over all the national territory, to be absolute and undisputed. One more victory will bring us up to this, I am confident. That done, I shall consider, not only that the nation has come through a struggle such as no other nation ever heard of, but in a smaller and personal point of view, I shall feel much relieved and pleased at the successful career of the Chief.

You can judge of the probable effect of this last victory at New Orleans, from the fact that friend Russell of the Times[6] (who has not called yet) gravely warned the English nation yesterday, of the magnificent army that had better be carefully watched by the English people, since it hated them like the devil and would want to have something to do. And last night, I met Mr John Bright at an evening reception,[7] who seemed to feel somewhat in the same way. "Now," said he; "if you Americans succeed in getting over this affair, you mustn't go and get stuffy to England. Because if you do, I don't know what's to become of us who've stood up for you here." I didn't say we wouldn't, but I did tell him that *he* needn't be alarmed, for all he would have to do would be to come over to America and we would send him to Congress at once. He laughed and said he thought he had had about enough of that sort of thing in England. By the way, there is a story that he thinks of leaving Parliament.

This last week has been socially a quiet one and I have seen very little of the world, as I have no time to frequent the Club. I don't get ahead very fast in English society, because as yet I can't succeed in finding any one to introduce me among people my own age. It's the same way with all the foreigners here, and a young Englishman, with whom I talked on the subject, comforted me by acknowledging the fact and saying that as a general thing young Englishmen were seldom intimate with any one unless they had known him three or four years. He gave a practical illustration of the principle by never recognizing me since, although we sat next each other three hours at a dinner and talked all the time, besides drinking various bottles of claret. With the foreigners I do much better, but they are generally worse off than I am in society. Except for a sort of conscientious feeling, I should care little for not knowing people at balls, especially as all accounts, especially English, declare young society to be a frantic bore. But to come home without having a Lady Jane, or a Miss Cavendish, to spread about, would make me contemptible in the eyes of Boston; whereas, if I do spread them, I shall be called no end of a damn fool. For mere occupation, I have more than I can manage; for not only do I act the part of confidential secretary, but I have my dry-nurse functions to perform with as great regularity as possible, and then after the day is over and everyone in bed, I generally sit up till two o'clock amusing myself with literary toys; articles which I've had in hand in any quantity ever since I was a boy at Mrs Storey's in Harvard Street, and perpetrated "Holden Chapel."[8]

Of course I'm in love; I make a point of being that; and I know *of* a few eligible girls; but as to knowing them, a bow is the highest distinction I ever hope to receive.

Now as to your letter and its contents on the negro question. I've not published it for two reasons. The first is that the tendency here now is pro-slavery and the sympathy with the South is so great as to seek justification in everything. Your view of the case, however anti-slavery, is not encouraging nor does it tend to strengthen our case. If published, especially if by any accident known to be by you, it might be used to annoy us with effect.

My second reason, though this alone would not have decided me, is that it seems to me you are a little needlessly dark in your anticipations. One thing is certain; labor in America is dear and will remain so; American cotton will always command a premium over any other yet known; and can be most easily produced. Emancipation cannot be instantaneous. We must rather found free colonies in the south such as you are now engaged in building up at Port Royal; the nucleus of which must be military and naval stations garrisoned by *corps d'armée,* and grouped around them must be the *emeriti,* the old soldiers with their grants of land, their families, their schools, churches and Northern energy, forming common cause with the negroes in gradually sapping the strength of the slave-holders, and thus year after year carrying new industry and free institutions until their borders meet from the Atlantic, the Gulf, the Mississippi and the Tennesee in a common centre, and the old crime shall be expiated and the whole social system of the South reconstructed. Such was the system of the old Romans with their conquered countries and it was always successful. It is the only means by which we can insure our hold on the South, and plant colonies that are certain of success. It must be a military system of colonies, governed by the Executive and without any dependence upon or relation to the States in which they happen to be placed. With such a system I would allow fifty years for the South to become ten times as great and powerful and loyal as she ever was, besides being free.

Such are my ideas, and as the negroes would be extremely valuable and even necessary to the development of these colonies, or the Southern resources at all, I trust they will manage to have a career yet.

Ever Yrs   H.B.A.

MS:MHi

1. Baron Egon von der Brinken (1834–1906), attaché of the Prussian legation.
2. Sir Charles Lyell (1797–1875), geologist, friend of the Union.
3. Thurlow Weed (1797–1882), editor of *Albany Evening Journal,* Republican party manager.
4. George Peabody (1795–1869), head of a London banking firm.
5. William L. Dayton (1807–1864), U.S. minister to France.
6. William H. Russell (1821–1907), London *Times* war correspondent.
7. John Bright (1811–1889), M.P., industrialist and reformer.
8. HA's article in *Harvard Magazine* (1885).

To Charles Francis Adams, Jr.

London. 10 October. 1862.

My dear Boy

I have received nothing from you since my last of some weeks back, and with such sharp fighting as is going on, I have a kind of dread of writing.[1] Still, as I suppose it's a pleasure to you to receive letters, I will try and hash up something. Only not about the war. A dozen times within the last two months I have been on the point of leaving this and joining you; and unless something *very* successful happens *very* soon in your profession, you may confidently expect to see me at home and enrolled early next year. Under present prospects here, short-handed as we already are, I must stay till the crash comes.

Our life is placid; our amusements not exciting, and our pleasures few. We drag on from day to day, writing, working and eating. I only wish some of you fellows could come over here and enliven yourselves with it, for it bores me, and yet I don't know what, as a matter of pleasure, I would rather do than stay here; certainly I shouldn't look for much pleasure in seeing people butchered without result, as you are doing. I hardly know how time passes, but it does go on, and as I am never wholly idle, I am well-enough pleased with it. There is almost always some-one passing through here. Some weeks ago it was Jim Higginson who cheered me up under the news of Pope's defeat;[2] Ye Gods! how that cut us up here! You may tell Major Higginson, if you see him, that his brother looked well and was in very good spirits, doing his best to keep up mine.[3] And I almost determined to go home with him, he wanted me to, so much. Then Hull and Lizzy came and just left us yesterday on their return home. Hull was with me a good deal and I was quite jolly under the unaccustomed excitement.[4] We went together to various places of amusement and haunts of vice such as Cremorne, which bored us dreadfully.[5] The poor old fellow's neck is still very bad, and he is not so vivacious as he used to be, but he was still dreadfully droll. I took him to the new Turkish bath here, a gorgeous establishment, fitted up with any quantity of eastern wrinkles, lined and paved with marble, where you lie on divans or carpets or the bare stone, in a dim dim religious light from a big brick dome, with a few holes in it for colored light. I am eastern in my tastes; a perfect satrap; and I affect the religious light, where you lie on marble, which, for marble, is perhaps not so very hard, and smoke your cigar and chibouc too, if you order it, and drink sherbet which is brought to you by grinning and perspiry Ethiop youths, especially imported from the east to minister to our effeminacy. While so reclining and dozing over my cigar in a temperature of 120°, I usually lazily meditate upon you and reflect that this would do you good. Hull and I went together, and Hull began by stubbing his toes with the boot-jack which made him cross, and then flying into a passion with a small boy and cursing him loudly and indiscriminately till I howled over it. Finally we got stripped and he concluded reluctantly to try the public room, into which we were ushered; a sort of dusky Egyptian tomb, with dark figures lying about. When we were fairly reclined, he began to comment on the appearance of the parties present; especially one pot-bellied party, magnificently extended on his back on an elevated platform in the middle of the dome, then undergoing the champooing process, in a state of entire nudity. Hull's public observations kept me in a state of convulsion, and seemed to bewilder the gloomy Englishmen near us, who never smile in London and look with horror on anyone that laughs, damn 'em.

Geo. Howe and his wife are now here. No doubt, mamma will write you all about Alice who looks very ill, I think. George has not changed a single hair. He is as stately and magnificent as in his early days. I drove down to the city with him yesterday at his invitation, and we had a long talk. He and his wife dine with us today without company, as they go nowhere now.

I am buying a horse and we are meditating on a country-house for a few weeks; rather risky experiments with almost a certainty of ship-wreck within three months. However, I am tired of waiting for events; I have wholly drawn out of all society except American; I am occupied to my own satisfaction with other studies; and I am ready to go straight ahead until knocked down. It won't be long. If you really ever come to the conclusion that I had better come home (in case for example of our leaving here for the continent, as is not impossible, or to relieve John of the pressure on him to go to the war, by going in his place), a single word from you will bring me to the Potomac at once.

If you see Ben Crowninshield, tell him I shall answer his letter next week. I am immensely obliged to him for writing.

MS:MHi

1. CFA2's cavalry unit was part of Gen. George B. McClellan's army, which was attempting to drive Gen. Robert E. Lee's forces out of Maryland. It came under heavy artillery fire at the Battle of Antietam.
2. Gen. John Pope (1822–1892), Union general, defeated in the Second Battle of Bull Run (Manassas) in the last days of August 1862.
3. Henry Lee Higginson (1834–1919), whose brother James became a lieutenant in the 1st Massachusetts cavalry.
4. Isaac Hull Adams (1813–1900) and his sister Elizabeth Coombs Adams (1808–1903).
5. Cremorne Gardens, an amusement park in Chelsea.

To *Charles Francis Adams, Jr.*

London. 21 November. 1862.

My dear old boy:

It's some time since I last wrote, but as you never get my letters apparently, perhaps it doesn't much matter. Besides, I had nothing to say, nor have I now. Last week and the week before last we were out of town, and as I always tag after the family, I went with them to the sea-shore, the Chief and I relieving each other. The truth is, I stick my nose to the grindstone so assiduously on purpose. If I were to let up here, and make friends of my own age and enjoy myself, I should destroy my purpose and had better go home. It's only on condition of being bored that I can conscientiously remain. Once too I had visions of an active agency in affairs here. This, even into its remotest branches, I have been forced to foreswear, and now begin by assuring everyone that I am connected in no way with official business, and am merely a visitor temporarily living with my father in England. Under cover of this character I can move much more freely than in any other, and the results of my unfortunate expedition to Lancashire a year ago thoroughly frightened me from every and any act that was likely to expose me even to the risk of a scorching of the same kind.[1] Perhaps the lesson is a good one on the whole. My work is now limited to a careful observation of events here and assistance in the manual labor of the place, and to a study of history and politics which seem to me most necessary to our country for the next century. The future is a blank to me as I suppose it is also to you. I have no plans nor can have any, so long as my course is tied to that of the Chief. Should you at the end of the war, wish to take my place, in case the services of one of us were still required,

I should return to Boston and Horace Gray, and I really do not know whether I should regret the change. The truth is, the experience of four years has done little towards giving me confidence in myself. The more I see, the more I am convinced that a man whose mind is balanced like mine, in such a way that what is evil never seems unmixed with good, and what is good always streaked with evil; an object never seems important enough to call out strong energies till they are exhausted, nor necessary enough not to allow of its failure being possible to retrieve; in short, a mind which is not strongly positive and absolute, cannot be steadily successful in action, which requires quickness and perseverance. I have steadily lost faith in myself ever since I left college, and my aim is now so indefinite that all my time may prove to have been wasted, and then nothing left but a truncated life.

I should care the less for all this if I could see your path any clearer, but while my time *may* prove to have been wasted, I don't see but what yours *must* prove so. At least God forbid that you should remain an officer longer than is necessary. And what then? The West is possible; indeed, I have thought of that myself. But what we want, my dear boy, is a *school*. We want a national set of young men like ourselves or better, to start new influences not only in politics, but in literature, in law, in society, and throughout the whole social organism of the country. A national school of our own generation. And that is what America has no power to create. In England the Universities centralize ability and London gives a field. So in France, Paris encourages and combines these influences. But with us, we should need at least six perfect geniuses placed, or rather, spotted over the country and all working together; whereas our generation as yet has not produced one nor the promise of one. It's all random, insulated work, for special and temporary and personal purposes, and we have no means, power or hope of combined action for any unselfish end.

One man who has real ability may do a great deal, but we ought to have a more concentrated power of influence than any that now exists.

For the present war, I have nothing to say. We received cheerful letters from you and John to-day, and now we have the news of McClellan's removal. As I do not believe in Burnside's genius,[2] I do not feel encouraged by this, especially as it shakes our whole structure to its centre. I have given up the war and only pray for its end. The South has vindicated its position and we cannot help it, so, as we can find no one to lead us and no one to hold us together, I don't see the use of our shedding more blood. Still, my boy, all this makes able men a necessity for the future, and if you're an able man, there's your career. I have projects enough and not unpromising ones for some day, but like most of my combinations, I suppose they'll all end in dust and ashes.

We are very comfortable here in London fog. Some sharp diplomatic practice, but, I hope, not very serious.[3] People don't overwhelm us with attentions, but that is excusable.

Ever Yrs

MS:MHi

1. HA went to Manchester to sound out attitudes toward the Union in that cotton-mill city. His signed report in the *Boston Courier* satirized, in passing, the meager hospitality of his hosts there. The *Times* pilloried him for his gaucherie.
2. Gen. Ambrose Burnside (1824–1881) was placed in command of the Army of the Potomac Nov. 10.
3. Pope's disastrous defeat at Second Bull Run and Lee's progress northward had inspired secret moves in England and France toward mediation based on de facto recognition of the Confederacy.

To *Charles Francis Adams, Jr.*

London. 23 January. 1863.

My dear Charles:

I have but a moment till it grows dark and the bag closes,[1] but I don't think I've much to say, so it don't matter. I've had a hard day's work too, as we generally do on Fridays, and am tired. We are in the dark as to movements at home since the 8th, no steamer being yet in owing I suppose to the awful gales.

We are as usual very quiet, having been dragged the rounds of the Christmas pantomimes and bored to death with them. I wish you or John were here to be funny and amuse people; you know I never could do it, and now I grow stupider and stupider every year as my hair grows thinner. I haven't even the wit left to talk to girls. I wish I were fifty years old at once, and then I should feel at home.

The Emancipation Proclamation has done more for us here than all our former victories and all our diplomacy. It is creating an almost convulsive reaction in our favor all over this country. The London Times is furious and scolds like a drunken drab. Certain it is, however, that public opinion is very deeply stirred here and finds expression in meetings; addresses to Pres. Lincoln; deputations to us; standing committees to agitate the subject and to affect opinion; and all the other symptoms of a great popular movement peculiarly unpleasant to the upper classes here because it rests altogether on the spontaneous action of the laboring classes and has a pestilent squint at sympathy with republicanism. But the Times is on its last legs and has lost its temper. They say it always does lose its temper when it finds such a feeling too strong for it, and its next step will be to come round and try to guide it. We are much encouraged and in high spirits. If only you at home don't have disasters, we will give such a checkmate to the foreign hopes of the rebels as they never yet have had.

We are all well and happy. I am at last on the point of buying a little mare and expect to have to hand her over to Mary, as her own horse is rather too much for her. Also having had my watch, hat and purse stolen at my celebrated Turkish baths, I have succeeded in obtaining a compensation of £15.0.0. with which I propose immediately to invest in a new watch. The exchange would be an inducement to invest at home, where I do not hear that my income has materially increased in spite of the superfluity of money. The mare costs £40.0.0 and will cost me at least £5.0.0 a month in keep.

Lebe wohl. Time is up and the Chief is a cussin and swearin like anythink for my letters.

Ever Yrs.

MS:MHi
1. Diplomatic pouch.

To *Charles Francis Adams, Jr.*

London. 14 May. 1863.

My dear Boy:

The telegraph assures us that Hooker is over the Rappanock and your division regally indistinct "in the enemy's rear."[1] I suppose the campaign is begun, then. Honestly, I'd rather be with you than here, for our state of mind during the next few weeks is not likely to be very easy.

But now that things are begun, I will leave them to your care. Just for your information, I inclose one of Mr Lawley's letters from Richmond to the London Times. It is curious. Mr Lawley's character here is under a cloud, as, strange to say, is not unusual with the employés of that seditious journal. For this and other reasons I don't put implicit trust in him, but one fact is remarkably distinct. His dread of the shedding of blood makes him wonderfully anxious for intervention. A prayer for intervention is all that the northern men read in this epistle, and Mr Lawley's humanity doesn't quite explain his earnestness.[2]

But if our letters from here have any real merit with you, it is because they give you a little change of atmosphere. So I will leave your affairs alone, in spite of your last letter which almost threw your dear mother into permanent dissolution because you said that under the bother of your difficulties you had one day taken to drinking and had struck one of your men. I think it will but slightly need a reminder to bring to your mind the lesson we should have given you, had you been here. "We certainly had thought that an Adams &c &c &c." All I can say is that I hope you stick it out with your regiment, for if you do work through, you will have had a good training not to let your passions trip up your heels. Yet I don't suppose it's an agreeable experience nor a cheerful prospect to look forward to. Don't you recollect that I wrote to you after the first Bull Run, announcing my intention of returning, and suggesting a new regiment then talked of, as my place, and your reply telling me by no means to put myself under that man for a Colonel.

This week has been quite a busy one with us here; socially at least, for politically there is a lull. I won't trouble you with an account of balls, at which I am usually a miserable attendant, looking and feeling like an exhibited horned owl. You already know my opinions about that species of society here, and no doubt you have been the confidant of the feminine portion of our humanity in regard to the silly manner in which I *will* behave. In short, I abhor it! but I go, in silence. Mary, too, drags me to the Park and compels me to ride in Rotten Row, and I submit to that too, though I am not properly mounted for such show work, and it interrupts all my occupations. In fine, I feel more and more every day the want of life in others, and as I never had much of my own, I am slowly but certainly becoming a dead-head.

Once in a while, however, I get a little glimpse into a less offensive existence. If Mary writes to you this week, she will tell you, no doubt about a little dinner she and I were asked to, the other day, by some friends of ours. Our young lady, whom I suspect to be not a little vain, and whose vanity was not a little flattered, was much delighted with the attention she received from Sir Edward Lytton. It was a party of only eleven, and of these, Sir Edward was one, Robert Browning another, and a Mr Ward, a well-known artist and member of the royal Academy, was a third.[3] All were people of a stamp, you know; as different from the sky-blue, skim-milk of the ball-rooms, as good old burgundy is from syrup-lemonade. I had a royal evening; a feast of remarkable choiceness, for the meats were very excellent good, the wines were rare and plentiful, and the company was of earth's choicest.

Sir Edward is one of the ugliest men it has been my good luck to meet. He is tall and slouchy, careless in his habits, deaf as a ci-devant, mild in manner, and quiet and philosophic in talk. Browning is neat, lively, impetuous, full of animation, and very un-English in all his opinions and appearance. Here, in London society, famous as he is, half his entertainers actually take him to be an American. He told us some amusing stories about this, one evening when he dined here.

Just to amuse you, I will try to give you an idea of the conversation after dinner; the first time I have ever heard anything of the sort in England. Sir Edward is a great smoker, and although no crime can be greater in this country, our host produced cigars after the ladies had left, and we filled our claret-glasses, and drew up together.

Sir Edward seemed to be continuing a conversation with Mr Ward his neighbor. He went on, in his thoughtful, deliberative, way, addressing Browning.

"Do you think your success would be very much more valuable to you for knowing that centuries hence, you would still be remembered? Do you look to the future connection by a portion of mankind, of certain ideas with your name, as the great reward of all your labour?"

"Not in the least! I am perfectly indifferent whether my name is remembered or not. The reward would be that the ideas which were mine, should live and benefit the race!"

"I am glad to hear you say so" continued Sir Edward, thoughtfully, "because it has always seemed so to me, and your opinion supports mine. Life, I take to be a period of preparation. I should compare it to a preparatory school. Though it is true that in one respect the comparison is not just, since the time we pass at a preparatory school bears an infinitely greater proportion to a life, than a life does to eternity. Yet I think it may be compared to a boy's school; such a one as I used to go to, as a child, at old Mrs S's at Fulham. Now if one of my old school-mates there were to meet me some day and seem delighted to see me, and asked me whether I recollected going to old mother S's at Fulham, I should say, 'Well! yes! I did have some faint remembrance of it! yes! I could recollect about it.' And then supposing he were to tell me how I was still remembered there! How much they talked of what a fine fellow I'd been at that school."

"How Jones Minimus" broke in Browning; "said you were the most awfully good fellow, he ever saw."

"Precisely," Sir Edward went on beginning to warm to his idea; "Should I be very much delighted to hear that? Would it make me forget what I am doing now? For five minutes perhaps I should feel gratified, and pleased that I was still remembered, but that would be all. I should go back to my work without a second thought about it.

"Well, now Browning, suppose you, some time or other, were to meet Shakespeare, as perhaps some of us may. You would rush to him, and seize his hand, and cry out, "My dear Shakespeare, how delighted I am to see you. You can't imagine how much they think and talk about you on earth!" Do you suppose Shakespeare would be more carried away by such an announcement than I should be at hearing that I was still remembered by the boys at mother S's at Fulham? What possible advantage can it be to him to know that what he did on the earth is still remembered there?"

The same idea is in LXIII of Tennyson's In Memoriam, but not pointed the same way. It was curious to see two men who, of all others, write for fame, or have done so, ridicule the idea of its real value to them. But Browning went on to get into a very unorthodox humor, and developed a theory of spiritual election that would shock the Pope, I fear. According to him, the minds or souls that really did develope themselves and educate themselves in life, could alone expect to enter a future career for which this life was a preparatory course. The rest were rejected, turned back, God knows what becomes of them; these myriads of savages and brutalized and degraded Christians. Only those that could pass the examination, were allowed to commence the new career. This is Calvin's theory, modified; and really it seems not unlikely to me. Thus this earth may serve as a sort of feeder to the next world, as the lower and middle classes here do to the aristocracy, here and there furnishing a member to fill the gaps. The corollaries of this proposition are amusing to work out.

So much for our dinner which has filled my letter and may serve to amuse you on some battle-field or in some temporary resting ground. Browning seemed much pleased to hear of your studies of him on your campaigns. He is at work on something new.

MS:MHi

1. Joseph Hooker (1814–1879), Union general.
2. Francis Lawley (1825–1901), the *Times* correspondent in Richmond. His alleged investing on the basis of insider information was under parliamentary investigation.
3. Robert Browning (1812–1889); Edward Bulwer-Lytton (1803–1873), the popular novelist; and Edward Matthew Ward (1816–1879), whose historical frescoes were in the Houses of Parliament.

To Charles Francis Adams, Jr.

17 July. 1863.

We are in receipt of all your sanguinary letters, as well as of news down to the 4th, telling of Cyclopean battles, like the struggles of Saturn and Terra and Hyperion for their empire, lasting through sunrise after sunrise, in an agony such as heralds the extinction of systems.[1] It's a pity that we're civilized. What a grand thing Homer would have made of it; while in our day, men only conceive of a battle as of two lines of men shooting at each other till one or the other gives way. At this distance, though, even now it's very grand and inspiring. There's a magnificence about the pertinacity of the struggle, lasting so many days, and closing, so far as we know on the eve of our single national anniversary, with the whole nation bending over it, that makes even these English cubs silent. Dreadful I suppose it is, and God knows I feel anxious and miserable enough at times, but I doubt whether any of us will ever be able to live contented again in times of peace and laziness. Our generation has been stirred up from its lowest layers and there is that in its history which will stamp every member of it until we are all in our graves. We cannot be commonplace. The great burden that has fallen on us must inevitably stamp its character on us. I have hopes for us all, as we go on with the work.

And I, though I grumble at my position here and want to go home, feel at times that I don't know what I say, in making my complaints. I want to go into the army! to become a second lieutenant in an infantry regiment somewhere in the deserts of the South! I who for two years have lived a life of intellectual excitement, in the midst of the most concentrated society of the world, and who have become so accustomed to it that I should wither into nothing without it! Why, the thing's absurd! Even to retire to a provincial life in Boston would be an experiment that I dread to look forward to! But for me to go into the army is ridiculous!

The peculiar attraction of our position is one that is too subtle to put one's hand upon, and yet that we shall be sure to miss extremely when we leave it. The atmosphere is exciting. One does every day and without a second thought, what at another time would be the event of a year; perhaps of a life. For instance, the other day we were asked out to a little garden party by the old Duchess of Sutherland at Chiswick, one of the famous nobleman's places of England. Dukes and Duchesses, Lords and Ladies, Howards and Russells, Grosvenors and Gowers, Cavendish's, Stuarts, Douglases, Campbells, Montagus, half the best blood in England was there, and were cutting through country-dances and turning somersets and playing leap-frog in a way that knocked into a heap all my preconceived ideas of their manners. To be sure it was only a family party, with a few friends. You may be certain that I took no share in it. A stranger had better not assume to be one of the Gods.

Or again! I have just returned from breakfasting with Mr Evarts, and we had Cyrus Field, Mr Blatchford and his wife, and Mr Cobden at table.[2] The conversation was not remarkable to me; so little so that I should probably make only a bare note of it. But Cobden gave a vigorous and amusing account of Roebuck, whom he covered with epithets, and whose treatment of himself he described, going over some scenes in Parliament when Sir Robert Peel was alive.[3] He sketched to us Gladstone's "uneasy conscience" which is always doubting and hesitating and trying to construct new theories. Cyrus Field rattled ahead about his telegraph and told again the story of his experiences. Mr Evarts talked about England and the policy of the country, for he goes home today, and indeed left us only to fire a parting shot into Gladstone. We discussed the war news, and Bancroft

Davis came in, arguing that Lee's ammunition must be exhausted.[4] Cobden was very anxious about the battles, and varied his talk, by discussing a movement he proposes to make in Parliament before it rises. He rather regrets that they didn't force Roebuck's motion to a division, and wants to get in a few words before the close.

So we go on, you see, and how much of this sort of thing could one do at Boston! And the camp could only make up for it in times of action. Even the strangely hostile tone of society here has its peculiar advantage. It wakes us up and keeps our minds on a continual strain to meet and check the tendency. To appear confident in times of doubt, steady in times of disaster, cool and quiet at all times, and unshaken under any pressure, requires a continual wakefulness and actually has an effect to make a man that which he represents himself to be. Mr Evarts is grand in these trials, and from him and Mr Seward and the Chief, one learns to value properly the power of momentum.

All this to you seems, I suppose, curious talk, to one who has just got through with the disgusts of one campaign and is recruiting for another, as I suppose you are doing now. We are very anxious about you as you may suppose, but trust that your regiment is too much used up to fight much more without rest. Besides, in the confusion and excitement of the great struggle, we are glad to counteract anxiety by hope. And though our good friends down town do persist in regarding the news as favorable to the South, we on the whole are inclined to hope, and to feel a certain confidence that friend Lee has got his scoring. There is also the usual rumor of the fall of Vicksburg, as the *very* last telegram by the steamer, but we do not put much confidence in stories of that sort. Meade's despatch at eight o'clock on the evening of the 3d is all the news that I put any faith in.[5] And with that I am patient.

As for us, the season is on its very last legs. Everyone is making a bolt for the country. It has been very hot for England, and is as dry as a Virginia road in summer. No rain for a month past. Politically we are trying to get everything in trim in order to have all clear during the next three months when England is without a Government and drifts. There is only one serious danger, and against that we are doing our best to guard. If you could win a few victories, it would be the best guaranty for good behavior, and I am free to say that England has remained quiet as long as we could reasonably expect, knowing her opinions, without solid guaranties of ultimate success on our part.

The week has been so busy, and every evening occupied with society that I have had little time to give to myself. Although not strictly a society man, and free to confess that I don't wish to be fashionable, I go about a good deal and am not so often now as formerly alone in a room. In fact we rather affect to have our own circle of friends, and to be socially as good as English people in society. They themselves seem to have adopted us, and of course it's more convenient to go into society as indigenous than as foreign. Mary has been a success as girls go here. She is being spoiled hopelessly, but I wash my hands of that, as I think she's old enough now to judge for herself and to carry her own washing-basket. I think myself that I see the old Johnson blood cropping out, and faint traces of Mrs John reappearing here and there, that might have been more distinct and may become so yet.[6]

Your shirt goes by this mail. I have got the best I could find for you. Your mamma selected them. This week I send you still another review and next week I shall send you your friend W. H. Russell's Gazette if he has as blackguard a notice of us in it as he usually does.[7]

Ever Yrs

MS:MHi

1. The Battle of Gettysburg took place July 1–3 and ended in the defeat of Lee's army. CFA2's company, held in reserve, did not see action.
2. William Evarts (1818–1901), a leading New York lawyer and prominent Republican; Cyrus Field (1819–1892), then in England to raise new capital for his Atlantic cable company; Richard Cobden (1804–1865), manufacturer, Radical politician, and advocate of free trade.
3. John Arthur Roebuck (1801–1879), M.P. for Sheffield.
4. John Chandler Bancroft Davis (1822–1907), former secretary of U.S. legation and London *Times* correspondent.
5. George Gordon Meade (1815–1872), general in command of the Union army at Gettysburg.
6. Louisa Catherine Johnson Adams (1775–1852), JQA's wife, had been born in London and seemed more French than English.
7. *Army and Navy Gazette*, edited by Russell.

To Charles Francis Adams, Jr.

23 July. 1863.

I positively tremble to think of receiving any more news from America since the batch that we received last Sunday. Why can't we sink the steamers till some more good news comes? It is like an easterly storm after a glorious June day, this returning to the gloomy chronicle of varying successes and disasters, after exulting in the grand excitement of such triumphs as you sent us on the 4th. For once, there was *no* drawback, unless I except anxiety about you. I wanted to hug the army of the Potomac. I wanted to get the whole of the army of Vicksburg drunk at my own expense.[1] I wanted to fight some small man and lick him. Had I had a single friend in London capable of rising to the dignity of the occasion, I don't know what mightn't have happened. But mediocrity prevailed and I passed the day in base repose.

It was on Sunday morning as I came down to breakfast that I saw a telegram from the Department announcing the fall of Vicksburg. Now, to appreciate the value of this, you must know that the one thing upon which the London press and the English people have been so positive as not to tolerate contradiction, was the impossibility of capturing Vicksburg. Nothing could induce them to believe that Grant's army was not in extreme danger of having itself to capitulate. The Times of Saturday, down to the last moment, declared that the siege of Vicksburg grew more and more hopeless every day. Even now, it refuses, after receiving all the details, to admit the fact, and only says that Northern advices report it, but it is not yet confirmed. Nothing could exceed the energy with which everybody in England has reprobated the wicked waste of life that must be caused by the siege of this place during the sickly season, and ridiculed the idea of its capture. And now, the announcement was just as though a bucket of iced-water were thrown into their faces. They couldn't and wouldn't believe it. All their settled opinions were overthrown, and they were left dangling in the air. You never heard such a cackling as was kept up here on Sunday and Monday, and you can't imagine how spiteful and vicious they all were. Sunday evening I was asked round to Monckton Milnes's to meet a few people.[2] Milnes himself is one of the warmest Americans in the world, and received me with a hug before the astonished company, crowing like a fighting cock. But the rest of the company were very cold. W. H. Russell was there, and I had a good deal of talk with him. He at least did not attempt to disguise the gravity of the occasion, nor to turn Lee's defeat into a victory. I went with Mr Milnes to the Cosmopolitan Club afterwards, where the people all looked at me as though I were objectionable. Of course I avoided the subject in conversation, but I saw very clearly how unpleasant the news was which I brought. So it has been everywhere. This is a sort of thing that can be neither denied, palliated, nor evaded; the disasters of the rebels are unredeemed by even any hope of success. Accordingly the emergency has produced here a mere access of spite; preparatory (if we suffer no reverse) to a revolution in tone.

It is now conceded at once that all idea of intervention is at an end. The war is to continue indefinitely, so far as Europe is concerned, and the only remaining chance of collision is in the case of the iron-clads. We are looking after them with considerable energy, and I think we shall settle them.

It is utterly impossible to describe to you the delight that we all felt here and that has not diminished even now. I can imagine the temporary insanity that must have prevailed over the North on the night of the 7th. Here our demonstrations were quiet, but ye Gods! how we felt! Whether to laugh or to cry, one hardly knew. Some men preferred the one, some the other. The Chief was the picture of placid delight. As for me, as my effort has always been here to suppress all expression of feeling, I preserved sobriety in public, but for four days I've been internally singing Hosannahs and running riot in exultation. The future being doubtful, we are all the more determined to drink this one cup of success out. Our friends at home, Dana, John, and so on, are always so devilish afraid that we may see things in too rosy colors. They think it necessary to be correspondingly sombre in their advices. This time, luckily, we had no one to be so cruel as to knock us down from behind, when we were having all we could do to fight our English upas influences in front. We sat on the top of the ladder and didn't care a copper who passed underneath. Your old friend Judge Goodrich was here on Monday, and you never saw a man in such a state.[3] Even for him it was wonderful. He lunched with us and kept us in a perfect riot all the time, telling stories without limit and laughing till he almost screamed.

I am sorry to say however that all this is not likely to make our position here any pleasanter socially. All our experience has shown that as our success was great, so rose equally the spirit of hatred on this side. Never before since the Trent affair has it shown itself so universal and spiteful as now. I am myself more surprised at it than I have any right to be, and philosopher though I aspire to be, I do feel strongly impressed with a desire to see the time come when our success will compel silence and our prosperity will complete the revolution. As for war, it would be folly in us to go to war with this country. We have the means of destroying her without hurting ourselves.

In other respects the week has been a very quiet one. The season is over. The streets are full of Pickford's vans carting furniture from the houses, and Belgravia and May Fair are the scene of dirt and littered straw, as you know them from the accounts of Pendennis. One night we went to the opera, but otherwise we have enjoyed peace, and I have been engaged in looking up routes and sights in the guide book of Scotland. Thither, if nothing prevents and no bad news or rebel's plot interferes, we shall wend our way on the first of August. The rest of the family will probably make a visit or two, and I propose to make use of the opportunity to go on with Brooks and visit the Isle of Skye and the Hebrides, if we can.[4] This is in imitation of Dr Johnson, and I've no doubt, if we had good weather, it would be very jolly. But as for visiting people, the truth is I feel such a dislike for the whole nation, and so keen a sensitiveness to the least suspicion of being thought to pay court to any of them, and so abject a dread of ever giving anyone the chance to put a slight upon me, that I avoid them and neither wish them to be my friends nor wish to be theirs. I haven't the strength of character to retain resentments long, and some day in America

I may astonish myself by defending these people for whom I entertain at present only a profound and lively contempt. But at present I am glad that my acquaintances are so few and I do not intend to increase the number.

You will no doubt be curious to know, if, as I say, I have no acquaintances, how the devil I pass my time. Certainly I do pass it, however, and never have an unoccupied moment. My candles are seldom out before two o'clock in the morning, and my table is piled with half-read books and unfinished writing. For weeks together I only leave the house to mount my horse and after my ride, come back as I went. If it were not for your position and my own uneasy conscience, I should be as happy as a Virginia oyster, and as it is, I believe I never was so well off physically, morally and intellectually as this last year.

I send you another shirt, and a copy of the Index, the southern organ, which I thought you would find more interesting this week than any other newspaper I can send. It seems to me to look to a cessation of *organised* armed resistance and an ultimate resort to the Polish fashion. I think we shall not stand much in their way there, if they like to live in a den of thieves.

Ever

MS:MHi

1. Vicksburg, besieged by land and water, surrendered to Maj. Gen. Ulysses S. Grant (1822–1885) July 4.
2. Richard Monckton Milnes, Lord Houghton (1809–1885), M.P. and literary patron.
3. Aaron Goodrich (1807–1887), secretary of U.S. legation at Brussels. CFA2 met him while campaigning with Seward in Minnesota in 1860.
4. Brooks Adams (1848–1927), HA's younger brother.

To Charles Francis Adams, Jr.

London, 2 October. 1863.

My dear Centaur:

The Scotia's telegram has just arrived, and for an hour or two past, I have been reflecting on the news it brings of what I conceive to be a very severe defeat of Rosecranz.[1] At this distance and with our mere scraps of doubtful intelligence, I am painfully impressed with the conviction that our Government has been again proved incompetent, and has neglected to take those measures of security which it ought to have done, expecting as we all did, just this movement, or the corresponding one on Washington. I imagine that this mischance ensures us another year of war, unless the army of the Potomac shows more energy than usual and more success than ever yet. The truth is, everything in this universe has its regular waves and tides. Electricity, sound, the wind, and I believe every part of organic nature will be brought some day within this law. But my philosophy teaches me, and I firmly believe it, that the laws which govern animated beings will be ultimately found to be at bottom the same with those which rule inanimate nature, and, as I entertain a profound conviction of the littleness of our kind, and of the curious enormity of creation, I am quite ready to receive with pleasure any basis for a systematic conception of it all. Thus (to explain this rather alarming digression) as a sort of experimentalist, I look for regular tides in the affairs of man, and of course, in our own affairs. In every progression, somehow or other, the nations move by the same process which has never been explained but is evident in the ocean and the air. On this theory I should expect at about this time, a turn which would carry us backward. The devil of it is, supposing there comes a time when the rebs suddenly cave in, how am I to explain that!

This little example of my unpractical experimento-philosophico-historico-progressiveness, will be enough. It suffices to say that I am seeking to console my trouble by chewing the dry husks of that philosophy, which, whether it calls itself submission to the will of God, or to the laws of nature, rests in bottom simply and solely upon an acknowledgment of our own impotence and ignorance. In this amusement, I find, if not consolation at least some sort of mental titillation. Besides, I am becoming superstitious. I believe Nick Anderson's killed, though I've not yet seen his ghost. Write me that he's not yet gone under, and I will say defiance to the vague breath of similar chimaeras.

My last week has been wholly occupied in acting as a detective policeman. Our butler has imitated some persons of a better class, and after a long system of undiscovered thefts, at length seceded from the establishment. I have had to seize and arrange his papers, and to investigate his course of villainy. So far we find that he has stolen about £40,0,0.; forged to the extent of £40 more; drunk or disposed of about fifteen dozen of sherry, madeira, port, whiskey, brandy &c &c; besides neglecting his duty, intercepting our correspondence for fear of his affairs being discovered, and destroying our character in the neighborhood. Now here is a case that has completely puzzled all my preconceived ideas. I knew the man to be a coward, and I supposed his cowardice would guarantee us from crime. I knew that he was a liar, and dishonest, but believed that this was the result of education and that his disposition was good. When we discovered his true character, I at once supposed him to be a thorough villain, and took it for granted that he had fled the country. After an absence of three days, he came back, penitent, and wanting to be forgiven and taken back. He confessed the forgeries, and also to the cask of sherry, which he said he "expected" he'd drunk. He lied like a sculpin on every matter where lying was possible, to the last. Yet for months, six months now since the first forgery, he has been struggling to keep his head above water, and while trusted with large sums of money, has generally devoted it to paying bills. The man is a dastardly, rotten-hearted scoundrel, but his character is such a mixture of every meanness and weakness that can make human nature contemptible, all covered with a plausible air of candid, gushing honesty and fidelity, that I would like to have had Balzac or Thackeray analyse and dissect this carrion. The Chief bore it like an angel.

Tomorrow I take the females to Hastings to abide a period.[2] For myself, I am ridiculously attached to London, but still like an occasional sun-beam and sniff of the sea. I come to town occasionally henceforward.

MS:MHi

1. Gen. William Starke Rosecrans (1819–1898), defeated in the Battle of Chickamauga, Sept. 19–20, fell back to Chattanooga.
2. Hastings: a seaside resort on the southeast coast.

To John Gorham Palfrey

London. 15 April. 1864.

My dear Dr Palfrey:

I believe I left your's of the 22d February unanswered, during the busy time of the Captain's presence with us,[1] and since then, as I supposed you would see and talk with him on his return, I thought a letter would be mere superfluity. I gave your message to the good Parkes, who, by the way, has had a very unpleasant time of late with scarlet fever in the house; and now poor Mrs Ellice's death, following that of her father-in-law so soon, troubles him greatly, as the Ellices were his patrons and great admiration.[2] If his letters however are as rambling and futile as his conversation is apt to be, your loss in not receiving any, might be reparable. He is a curiosity; a creature of clubs and aristocratic sunlight; and though no one ever could dislike him perhaps, one can't help laughing occasionally at the pertinacity of his strange delusions about foreign affairs. I gave up long ago trying to argue with him, but even to this day he aggravates my mother's combativeness to a red heat.

Time rattles along so fast that this letter will scarcely reach you before the third anniversary of our departure. We are settled here now nearly as much at home as though we were in Boston, so far as familiarity with our surroundings go, and yet London never seems to me to allow any homelike feelings. I never quit it even for an afternoon at Richmond or a Sunday at

Walton, without feeling a sort of shudder at returning, to be struck as freshly as ever with the solemnity, the gloom, the squalor and the horrible misery and degradation that seem to me to brood over the place. The magnificence I know and can appreciate. It has done its best to make me a socialist and has nearly succeeded. The society I think dull, and the art and literature poor. So that you see I am well suited to return to Boston unspoiled by my travels, a sadder and a wiser man.

Our great event just now is the arrival of Garibaldi, and his reception. Of all curious events, this is the most extraordinary. You know what Garibaldi is; the companion of Mazzini;[3] the representative of the "cosmopolitan revolution"; a regular "child of nature," unintellectual, uncultivated; but enthusiastic and a genius. Every Government in Europe dreads him, or rather his party, and he is the enemy of them all and of none more, whether he will or no, than of England. Suddenly he drops down here, and the people, the real "dangerous classes" go out to meet him with such a reception as never was known before. It was a regular uprising of democracy. But then to our delight, the young Duke and Duchess of Sutherland get hold of him, and at once compromise the whole English aristocracy, and give a hoist to the *rouges* and the democracy throughout Europe, by bringing him to Stafford House and making themselves co-conspirators with every refugee in England, to murder Napoleon, destroy Victor Emmanuel,[4] and proclaim equality and division of property. I don't think I exaggerate the moral effect of this affair on the minds of the democrats. I am a real Garibaldian, and ready to accept, if necessary, his views, at the same time that I think hero-worship, as such, is a precious dangerous thing to meddle with. But here is the whole Clan Sutherland, with the young Duke dancing about at its head, forcing Garibaldi down the throats of English nobility, who daren't openly say no, and who make the worst faces at the process, you can conceive. A few nights since, Stafford House was thrown open for a reception in honor of the General. By the way, what a glorious palace it is. I would like to have such a one at Quincy. We went; the only diplomats there except the Turk. Garibaldi was there; quantum mutatus ab illo Garibaldio that I saw four years ago, surrounded by a yelling mob in Palermo, with a few hundred guerilla troops, and not a nobleman among them! The beautiful young Duchess had him by the arm; she glittering with *the* diamonds; he in a military, loose poncho, or cape. The Duke pirouetted before, behind and on either side. The Duchess Dowager sailed majestically alongside, battling fiercely for the honor of being chief-keeper, but kept silent by her splendid daughter-in-law. In a tangled and promiscuous medley followed the Argylls, Tauntons, Howards, Blantyres, and every Leveson-Gower that draws breath. They paraded through the appartments, as well as Garibaldi could limp along, and we poor lookers-on drew aside and formed a passage for the procession triumphant to pass through. It was superb! And yet almost the last great occasion that Stafford House was open, was to allow this perfect nobility to do honor to Mrs Beecher Stowe, and both then and now the whole thing too strongly resembles a desperate humbug for me to be much impressed by it.[5] Sentimental liberalism is pretty, but it won't hold. Garibaldi is pretty safe to suffer the fate of Mrs Stowe, and American anti-slavery, whenever he stands in need of aristocratic aid. Meanwhile he sits at the feet of the beautiful Duchess (and there he is indeed to be envied) and smokes his cigars in her boudoir, and goes to bed immediately after dinner, and smokes in bed; and has two shirts (the famous red flannel) and a light blue cape lined with red (*rouge,* you see, always), which constitute his entire wardrobe. And in short, I rather doubt whether the good hero yet quite knows where he is, or has any clear idea of how it happens that he who has declared war to the knife against aristocracy and privilege everywhere, has become himself an aristocrat so suddenly. Meanwhile the non-Sutherland aristocracy growl fiercely, but are regularly over-slaughed by the popular wave, and we outsiders think it all as good a practical joke as ever was got up.

When shall we come home? After this season is over, we shall become very restless and if the war is over, as we strongly hope, we must leave here. I wonder whether Sumner wouldn't take the place. I suppose he might get it if he wanted it, on our departure. Then Gov. Andrew could replace him in the Senate, which would be an improvement.[6] I hope to find you and your's, including Frank, well and prosperous at my return; and for my own part am ready to leave the society of Courts to those that are courtiers, and rest awhile at the law-school in Cambridge or elsewhere. My family send their best regards, and I am as ever Yrs

Henry B. Adams.

MS:MH

1. CFA2 had been promoted to captain and was on 70-day leave.
2. Edward Ellice (1781–1863), M.P., deputy governor of Hudson's Bay Company. He and the members of his family had been friends of CFA.
3. Giusepppe Mazzini (1805–1872), republican supporter of Italian unification.
4. Victor Emmanuel II (1820–1878), first king of Italy.
5. Harriet Beecher Stowe (1811–1896), author of *Uncle Tom's Cabin* (1852), had been feted by the duchess of Sutherland after publication of the book.
6. John Albion Andrew (1818–1867), elected governor of Massachusetts in 1860.

To Charles Francis Adams, Jr.

No. 10.   London. 10 June. 1864.

My dear Captain:

As I sat last Sunday at our Club window (by the by, we've built out a bow and made it the best in the street) reading the weekly papers, a brute of a man came running along outside, shouting "Great Federal Defeat, Sir," and brandishing his vile Observers. My face, Sir, was of iron! Quite so! But my stomach collapsed and stopped working. I rose presently with a frown, and lounged with an indifferent air out of the door and round the corner, at which point I pursued with vindictive animosity the wretch, who began now to cry "Great Federal Victory." When caught, he sold me a paper, from which I learned that Lee had retired to the No. Anna. Naturally, the revulsion in my mind was not a little pleasing. At the same time there is no danger of my becoming very sanguine. In fact so far as I can see, our turning Spottsylvania is only a proof that we have failed to defeat Lee there, which I presume was Grant's purpose. Nevertheless, to go forward is an immense gain and as the war seems now destined to assume more than ever its peculiar pulverising character, I can only hope that each step gained is something added to us and lost to them. Only I do trust that Grant will not assault Lee's present position. My plan of campaign is for Grant now to destroy the Virginia Central utterly, as well as Gordonsville, Charlottesville and the road to Lynchburg; then moving down the left bank of the North Anna, cross the Pamaunkey at Hanover Court House or still lower. If Lee now chose to attack, well and good. Grant's aim however, whether before or after a battle, would, I should think, be the James, and he ought to be able to throw the army across the Petersburg and Richmond Railroad if Butler or Smith have a little spirit, before Lee could stop him.[1] At worst however, even if he failed to cut this road, it would be far easier to "fight them rough" from the James than on the North Anna, and whenever we can get the control of the southern approaches of Richmond, we win.

Such are my ideas. I wait therefore with anxiety for the next news. Grant is such an awful fighter that I fear another battle which, so away from our base, must be a more than usually severe one for the wounded and the army.

Your letter of the 19th was highly appreciated. We found also a notice of your squadron as clearing the bridge over the Ny on the 21st from which we infer that head-quarters were hard up for cavalry.

It is almost absurd to talk about London during such amusements at home. Nevertheless the world does move on without even thinking of what happens upon it, and so here we are going along in the old style, so that I become more and more doubtful every day as to what life is made for, and whether this mechanical existence which is led by almost every one I ever heard of, is of so much consequence as our self-conceit affirms. The dullness of mankind in this country is simply appalling. Quite so!

Miss Dayton is staying with us for a few days but our style of existence is not especially changed thereby. This week has in fact been a very quiet one to me; hardly any evening engagements at all and not any agreeable ones at that. I find it a quiet season and I am praying for good news from your army in order to feel free to run out to Mt Felix for a day or two and take a bit of fresh air which we are all beginning to want. Politically I have nothing to tell you from this side, all European affairs being still in a state of simmer. The Conference is still at work, and I lean to the idea that she will hatch something finally, but as yet she only cackles.[2] Some people are not so sanguine. A few feeble barks have been raised against us, but without much effect, so far as I can see, and of course the only probable effect would be to prick up our hostility to these people here. For my own part I've long seen what so many Americans will not see, that our system and the English system are mortal enemies. I mean to write a book about it one day—not for publication however; as I consider stupidity a necessary condition of a good book, and the public read only amusing works. It shall be written for you, my dear boy; for you! to read—if you can!

MS:MHi

1. Gen. Benjamin Butler (1818–1893), later a leading Radical Republican in Congress 1875 and 1877–1879.
2. England tried to mediate the Danish boundary question and end the War of 1864 at a general conference in London. The conference failed, and Prussia imposed the Treaty of Vienna on Denmark (Aug. 1), forcing the cession of Schleswig-Holstein.

To Charles Francis Adams, Jr.

No. 22.   London. 7 October. 1864.

My dear Colonel:

We receive this morning the news of Sheridan's second victory in the valley.[1] The Ealing breakfast-table resounded with shouts of applause over it. To me, although I am still in doubt whether the two divisions of Longstreet's corps were or were not there, it seems to demonstrate that Lee must prepare to quit Richmond. This hurrying small bodies of troops this way and the other, to shut stable doors from which plunder has already been taken, appears to me likely to be now as before, the precursor of a Waterloo. Evidently Lee must send a corps at least towards the valley. If so, he will have to contract his lines at Richmond, will he not? The Richmond papers hint at this, while threatening Grant with new dangers, before they had yet heard of Early's defeat. Am I rash in saying that I think it possible Lee may abandon Petersburg and throw his right well back towards Burkesville, to avoid being caught in a trap by Grant on a line hopelessly long? At any rate I cannot help thinking that Petersburg is to be the reward of Sheridan's victory.

I told you last week that I was going down to Shropshire to visit my friend Gaskell. I only returned last night at eight o'clock, and am off again tomorrow to Derbyshire. My visit to Wenlock was very enjoyable. God only knows how old the Abbot's House is, in which they are as it were picnic-ing before going to their Yorkshire place for the winter. Such a curious edifice I never saw, and the winds of Heaven permeated freely the roof, not to speak of the leaden windows. We three, Mrs Gaskell, Gask and I, dined in a room where the Abbot or the Prior used to feast his guests; a hall on whose timber roof, and great oak rafters, the wood fire threw a red shadow forty feet above our heads.[2] I slept in a room whose walls were all stone, three feet thick, with barred, square Gothic windows and diamond panes; and at my head a small oak door opened upon a winding staircase in the wall, long since closed up at the bottom, and whose purpose is lost. The daws in the early morning, woke me up by their infernal chattering around the ruins, and in the evening we sat in the dusk in the Abbot's own room of state, and there I held forth in grand after-dinner eloquence, all my social, religious and philosophical theories, even in the very holy-of-holies of what was once the heart of a religious community.

Wherever we stepped out of the house, we were at once among the ruins of the Abbey. We dug in the cloisters and we hammered in the cellars. We excavated tiles bearing coats of arms five hundred years old, and we laid bare the passages and floors that had been three centuries under ground. Then we rambled over the Shropshire hills, looking in on farmers in their old kitchens, with flitches of bacon hanging from the roof, and seats in the chimney corners, and clean brick floors, and an ancient blunderbuss by the fire-place. And we drove through the most fascinating parks and long ancient avenues, with the sun shining on the deer and the pheasants, and the "rabbit fondling his own harmless face."[3] And we picnicked at the old Roman city of Uriconium, in the ruins of what was once the baths; and eat partridge and drank Chateau Léoville, where once a great city flourished, of which not one line of record remains, but with which a civilisation perished in this country. Then we dined with a neighboring M.P. whose wife was excentric in her aspirates and asked me if I didn't like that style.

In short my visit to Shropshire was a species of quiet success, so curiously different from the usual stiffness of English society, that I shall always feel a regard for the old barn, though it was as cold a place as one wants to be near. Mr Gaskell was urgent upon me to come up and see them in Yorkshire, and if it is repeated in December, I shall go. Mr Gaskell père, who is a very agreeable man, evidently prefers comfort to antiquity. They are relatives of your friend Lord Houghton, and if anything, a little in his rather sensual and intellectual style.

I have not had time to get you Russell's critique on Sherman, nor have I seen one. Russell's comments on our war have been poor, so far as I have observed, and give me no information. Meanwhile I enclose you a little sketch of Thackeray. You may have seen it, or you may not. I have not read your last letter, so I am not au fait in your affairs, but I understand you are doing well. Pray God we get a few more successes, and our hopes will take a turn homewards.

Ever

MS:MHi

1. Gen. Philip Sheridan (1831–1888) pursued Gen. Jubal Early (1816–1894) and defeated him at Fisher's Hill in the Shenandoah Valley on Sept. 22. The news was received at the Adams residence in Ealing, a London suburb.
2. Mary Gaskell (d. 1869), wife of James Milnes Gaskell (1810–1873), M.P. for Wenlock. "Gask," Charles Milnes Gaskell (1842–1919), son of James. HA met him in London in April 1863. Their lifelong friendship began in Cambridge, where Gaskell and HA's cousin William Everett were about to take their degrees in classics.
3. Tennyson, "Aylmer's Field" (1864).

To *Charles Francis Adams, Jr.*

No. 29.   London. 25 Nov. 1864.

My dear Colonel:

Our last advices announce your arrival at home. I hope you will not return to camp until you have got wholly rid of your dysentery.

The election is over then, and after all that excitement, worry and danger, behold all goes on as before![1] It was one of those cases in which life and death seemed to hang on the issue, and the result is so decisive as to answer all our wishes and hopes. It is a curious commentary upon theoretical reasoning as to forms of Government, that this election which ought by all rights to be a defect in the system, and which is universally considered by the admirers of "strong Governments" to be a proof of the advantage of their own model, should yet turn out in practice a great and positive gain and a fruitful source of national strength. After all, systems of Government are secondary matters, if you've only got your people behind them. I never yet have felt so proud as now of the great qualities of our race, or so confident of the capacity of men to develop their faculties in the mass. I believe that a new era of the movement of the world will date from that day, which will drag nations up still another step, and carry us out of a quantity of old fogs. Europe has a long way to go yet to catch us up.

Anything that produces a great effect in our favor on this side, usually produces a sort of general silence as the first proof of its force. So this election has been met on this side by a species of blindness. People remark the fact with wonder and anger, but they have only just such a vague idea of what are to be its consequences, as shuts their mouths without changing their opinions. Only the most clear-headed see indistinctly what bearing it is likely to have on English politics, and I expect that it will be years yet before its full action gets into play. Meanwhile the Government is now stronger than ever and our only weak point is the financial one. May our name not have to stand guard on that!

You can imagine with what enthusiasm we received the news, and drank to the success of the new Administration. For the time, all interest has centered in the election, and even the incomprehensible state of things in Georgia has been overlooked.[2] How many more campaigns we shall have to make, seems very doubtful, but thus far our rate of progression has been regular, and if continued, ought to bring us to Augusta at the next round. We can afford to be patient however, now, for all we have to fear is pecuniary ruin, and that is tolerably certain.

I don't know that I've anything to tell you that's new or original on this side. Loo Brooks came through this week on her way home after five weeks of most harrassing contact with her mamma-in-law, who appears to have been superbly herself. Poor Loo was happy to escape, and we cheered her and little Fanny amazingly by a few hours at Ealing. I sent by her a cargo of books to the young 'uns, our nephews which ought to keep them in literature till they're old men. By the way, should you go to Washington, try and have a talk with Seward about our affairs. The Chief, by this steamer, sends *privately* a request to be relieved. You can intimate to S. that if compelled to stay, he means at any rate to send his family home and break up the establishment, remaining himself as a temporary occupant till a successor is appointed. He even talks of doing so at once, and sending the women to Italy in January preparatory to their going home in June. Seward must see that a change, if necessary at all, had best be made quickly for the public good. Don't quote me however. On no account let what I say, come back. You will probably get at first hand all the information you want. Best say nothing at all, yet, of the idea of retirement except to S. if you see him. Let me know what he says.

You see we are in a "transition state." But I do not see a chance of release before March,—unless for worse chains.

MS:MHi
1. Lincoln was reelected Nov. 8.
2. Sherman had started from Atlanta Nov. 15 on his march to the sea.

To Charles Francis Adams, Jr.

No. 39.   Sorrento. 2 March. 1865.

My dear Colonel:

    Your's of February 4th reached me at Naples three days ago. As you are now not in active service, and as I am in the middle of a fatiguing, not to say harrassing campaign, my letters necessarily and properly have become fewer. If they average once a month instead of once a week, it is much.

    You have probably heard of our departure from London, our little sojourn at Paris, and then of our slow and stately march across Europe down even to this point. Of the pleasures of the journey I might say a good deal at a pinch. The whole distance from Paris to Leghorn, including especially Avignon, Nice, the Cornice road, Genoa, Spezia and Pisa, was new to me, and very neatly complemented, and dove-tailed itself into my two previous visits to Italy. Our vettura traveling was unexpectedly pleasant. The weather was perfect. We had no mishaps, and in short, I found my duty far easier than I had expected.

    But it is easier to grumble, and still more satisfactory to laugh. Luckily for me, and unluckily for my parent in London, I have a lazy and indolent temper. The duty of acting as a scavenger to society by wrangling about bills, is one which I am weak in performing. Accordingly my soul is disturbed by visions of the unhappy Minister, groaning over my draughts. He has behaved hitherto like an angel. Not a reproach has yet passed his lips. But just four weeks heavy traveling have cost him at the rate of £8.0.0 a day. You can make that calculation if you like, and see what the total amounts to.

    But this is a light evil. The greatest is of a different sort. You know from former letters how I abominate this family work. As for its being a pleasure, I simply laugh at the idea. To be sure, on this journey, I will do my people the justice to say that they have behaved better than I had any idea of. They have not worried my liver and lights out more than once a day. They have not fought more than half the time, nor made my existence intolerable without exceptions. If you could see our sainted mother traveling, you would laugh (unless you swore) even to wildness. Mary rises into humor in describing her, after a lovely day's journey, and an excellent dinner, eaten with excellent appetite, in a most comfortable hotel, sitting before a crackling wood fire, with her feet on the fender, entertaining us thus before going to her warmed and neat bed. "Well, for my part I confesss I do not understand at my time of life the pleasures of traveling. I have seen nothing yet on this journey that any one could call pleasure, and if it weren't for Mary's sake, I never would have left home. Mary's health was our single reason for taking this journey and I do think that Mary is the most perverse and obstinate girl I ever saw in all my life. She will not take care of herself. She will sit with draughts blowing right on her, and there! she's sneezing! yes! she's caught cold! I told her she would in that carriage today. And considering that we have been at all this trouble and expense solely for her sake, she might try to take a little more care of herself, I do think. Henry, I'm homesick! I do wish I were in my own room in Upper Portland Place. It does make me utterly miserable, this never staying two nights in one place; there! it does! and I can't help it. I do want rest so! I get so fatigued with this continual motion. Couldn't we have gone quicker by sea? Why didn't we then? And this is so much more expensive! And you knew I wanted so much to get to Sorrento and it was so necessary for Mary's health! Dear me, what a draught there is! Mary, you are crazy not to wear your jacket! Oh Henry, how you do look with that beard! I really think it is wicked in you to go so, when you know how it pains me and disgusts me to have you seen so! There! now I'm going to bed. Now, do be punctual tomorrow to breakfast. You know you never are, and we start early. Oh dear! there, I am *too* homesick!"

God forgive me for thus ridiculing one of the most devoted of mothers! But I grow old and cynical, and I have learned to be silent, but in return, I must have my laugh. The example I have given is a favorable one. It is far from exaggerated and every word is true. This perpetual feeble worry; this unvarying practice of dwelling on the dark points of a picture, and bearing hardest on me at the most difficult moments, make me contemplate a journey with alarm and complete it with relief. The children are obedient, good-natured and willing, with me. But the battle is perpetual between them and their mother. And if there is one thing that I flinch under, it is the sound of perpetual dispute.

Such are my little amusements, from which I escape as I best can, flying in a cowardly way at the sign of a storm, or maintaining a vigorous silence. In return, consolation and balm sometimes flow into my soul when I climb among the olive-groves, and cool myself in their delicate shade, or ramble through the orange-groves, and smoke my cigar beneath thousands of oranges and lemons which look as poetic as the heart of man could ask. Just now the Tramontana, or north wind, is blowing a tremendous gale across the bay of Naples, and the weather therefore is not altogether agreeable. Your angel mother, who has done nothing but urge me forward all the way, and pray for rest and the repose of Sorrento, is already showing signs of restlessness and an intention to move somewhere else. Meanwhile I have performed my duty. I have brought the party safely here. And I wait new orders from London, whether to return or to stay. You know I am but a subordinate, and obey orders with military precision and silence.

You find fault with my silence about the war, but it seems to me that the silence shows the state of things clearly enough. The rebel cause is in Europe all in the dirt. What may yet happpen, or what has already happened since the 13th Feb. I don't know, but unless we are very unlucky, England has taken her final stand, acknowledges our success, and gives up the case.

I saw Barlow in Paris.[1] Uncle Edward gave him a dinner which perhaps some of your letters have told you about.[2] I know I paid four sixths of the dinner, and our uncle one third, and he ordered it. Barlow was very pleasant and amusing. I hope he did well in London.

What you say about family jars is very true. Kuhn and Loo have already managed to make a pretty wide separation between them and us, which will certainly become a break in time. Loo is near insane, and will kill herself ultimately, I think.

You say nothing about your own plans and I can have nothing to say on that subject myself, as I have no data to go on. You already know my opinion of the necessity of health. As to my plans which you inquire about, I know no more than you. The Minister says I am too useful here to be spared; therefore I am here; not absolutely in Capua, but precious near it. I solace myself in performing this duty of guarding the women and children during the battle, by studying Italian which I shall learn to read at least, and by yielding to the influences of the places we visit. For the time, I am counted out. I was twenty seven the day before we entered Italy. I have been nearly seven years abroad. And I run visibly to seed.

Mary and Brooks and I have this afternoon been rambling up high on the hill-sides. Sorrento was lovelier than you can guess; the air purer and softer than mere intellect can conceive; all the plains below us were dotted and yellow with oranges and lemons; and we sat under the olives with the sunlight filtering down on us; and looked across the Piano del Sorrento, and the bay of Naples, to where Vesuvius was smoking, and beyond Vesuvius the landscape ended in the long line of snow-covered Appenines. It was pretty, oh Fratello mio! quite so! I trust you may come to see it. Come in April or May.

Talk not to me of wars. I have had no letters since one dated the 21st at London. I see no newspapers. We are out of the world, and for all that I know the war in America may be over and peace declared. What I should say would read to you like comments upon Roman history.

We are all pretty well. Mary has got an appetite of the best, and can climb mountains with stout legs. Mamma is given to colds, but otherwise all right.

Ever Yrs.

MS:MHi

1. Maj. Gen. Francis Barlow (1834–1896), in Europe on sick leave.
2. Edward Brooks (1793–1878), eldest brother of HA's mother.

To Charles Francis Adams, Jr.

No. 41.   Rome. 9 April. 1865.

My dear Colonel:

The eccentric course of the world has managed to juggle me back into this city again, five years older than when I was in it last; and with this single exception I rather doubt whether either the city or I have got far ahead of where we then were. It seems as natural as London would; or indeed, as any place except Boston, would seem, and on the whole, I can drag out existence here, if the Minister absolutely will not call me back to more manly duties. As we have not heard from you since your supposed return to camp, and our letters in answer to your engagement must only now be reaching America, I shall write you a long epistle about our proceedings here.[1]

My last was from Sorrento, where we remained nearly through the month. What the weather could do to spoil our residence there, it faithfully did, and if it weren't that Sorrento is one of those few places in this christian world, whose beauty takes hold of the heart of the weary pilgrim, and makes him happy in a peace that passes understanding, I should have learned to dislike it with an energy to which I am not given. Good or bad, however, the time passed over us with no greater excitement than that brought by your letters, and at the beginning of the fifth week we moved round to Amalfi, where the weather was, if possible, still worse, and overflowed rivers barred our road to Paestum.

With our arrival at Naples the skies cleared and the sun brought us summer in a moment. We remained there from the first to the eighth April, just a week, all of which was divided between buying coral and visiting the Museum, with the episode of one day passed at Baja. You, my envied brother, whose acquaintance with women in domestic relations, has yet to begin, and that too, under a form exceptionally agreeable, know little of the meaning of a week's shopping. But when that shopping is for jewelry, and when that jewelry is coral, at Naples, all ordinary shopping becomes an amusement and a jest. Coral is as you are aware, no doubt, a marine product, made for some reason inscrutable to the eyes of purchasers, in different shades of color. These shades vary from absolute white to deep red, but the white is not valuable, neither is the red, nor yet is the light pink esteemed, since it has an imperceptible shadow of yellow. But a certain translucent rose, "rivaling" as Mr Everett says, "the first blush of youthful love", or more precisely I think, "the living carnation" of ditto, is the perfect ideal, the aspiration of young women, and my own nightmare. In search of this, I went through every shop in Naples, and I may say that there is little coral in that city which has not been seen and priced by me. Mary invested a heap of money in it, and kept me for a week in training as a shop-boy. My own purchases were small, but choice, and cost me much anxious reflection and mental toil, but I happily survived it all, and even paid the bills.

The shops however were slightly varied by the Museum, and what time I did not pass in one, I managed to spend in the other, which, if you don't already know it, is one of the most interesting collections in the world. As I recollected it of old, I was not required to *do* it like a tourist, and had a chance to look for what pleased my own taste, and admire that. As the simple savage seems to be about to return to social life, I suppose it won't hurt him to hear that there are some new antiques lately dug out from Pompei, which please me much and which rank high among the gems of art. Two bronzes, both discovered within the last year, both small and both graceful enough to drive our artists frantic, struck me with more satisfaction than I have felt over a work of art for a long time. One of these is a tipsy Silenus, reeling just so much as still to leave his balance straight, and with a drunken flavor oozing out, not only in the face and the limbs, but in the unsteady poise of the figure and the slight forward stagger which seems just enough to show the artist's skill, without becoming coarseness. One hand is raised above his head and on the palm he balances a round vessel, on which a glass vase for wine or flowers once stood. The other hand, stretched down as one does in balancing oneself, held a glass goblet. The bronze is not more than three feet high. For delicacy and freedom of workmanship combined, I have seen few things to beat it.

But though the Bacchus is good, the Narcissus is better. This is a bronze figure about three feet high, clothed carefully in elaborate sandals, and nothing else, except a fillet with light clusters of grapes in his hair, and a goat-skin on, rather than over one shoulder. He stands a little inclined forward, his head bent forward and on one side, one hand resting on his hip, the other with the index finger out, held up as when one listens intently. The face, which is exquisite, has a half smile on it. He is listening—the very poetry of attention. Can you tell me what he is hearing? Is it an echo from some Grecian mountain, or a faintly-heard chorus of nymphs in some legendary forest or stream, or is it the call of the naiad that he is in love with? Am I right in my misty recollection of Narcissus as a youth whom Venus admired in vain, but Luna used to visit on the top of a mountain, and was killed by a wild boar for looking at Diana in a bath? Why the dickins should Narcissus listen, is a question that has bothered me to wildness, and is still unsettled in my mind;[2] but be that as it may, the statue is a touch of perfect grace and delicacy, and so much was I charmed with it that I almost bought a copy, intending it as a wedding present for you and Minnie. But I thought better of it, doubting that the S.S.[3] had not preserved the tastes that would make him happy in the contemplation of bronzes, and doubting still more whether Minnie would be pleased with so classic a gift. I will get her a something pretty here in Rome, and you shall write to me what it is to be. Or rather, you should, if there were time, but I should not get your answer for an age. But now, I think, if my fancy for Narcissus still lasts until my departure from here, I shall buy him for other purposes, since I am not rich enough to sport bronzes of my own. The beautiful face of the divine youth, listening with his raised hand and bent head, to the far-off song of the nymphs, would always remind me of something pleasant, for it all carries with it an odor of summer and song and Greek beauty. But such property does not suit a young man of a wandering turn of mind and debauched habits like myself. I will give him away. I will carry him off to England and leave him there.

Naples was lovely. Not so lovely as it was five years ago next June, when I saw it in its full summer dress, but still there are few places that even make a pretence to beauty beside it. I was sorry to leave it, though I expected to see some of the party catch the fever, and am not even yet at all sure that we have escaped. But we did come on to Rome yesterday, and are already flying about and mixed up in the whole riot of the Holy Week. The Dexters are here and Arthur and his mother are beaming, while Hooker and our Minister's family look after all our sight-seeing.[4] I hope now for a little freedom. Ah, fratello mio; freedom is still sweet, even though I do not deny that a bondage more pleasing than mine, may be still sweeter. The Minister writes as though he expected me to marry at once, but I have tried it at the wrong end, and having once learned what the duties are, without the pleasures, I shall have to wait long before trying either duties or pleasures again, if I've got to take them together.

Still Rome is pleasant even to the head of a family, and the weather has been superb. Your mamma, suddenly become friskey as a young kid, does nothing but run about and see—and see—and see! Mary has required a little nursing. She has had a little bilious trouble, and the deuce take me if

I know how she is ever to get rid of them, nor what new form these attacks may at any moment take. This time however it has not seemed to amount to much more than a trifle.

I have seen little or nothing that is new, unless I except a visit yesterday (13th) with Arthur and his mother to Storey's studio, where we interupted the great sculptor in the act of giving a sitting to no less a person than General McClellan, who is now his guest.[5] And by the way, I will say that a more common, carrotty, vulgar-looking hero than he of Antietam, I have not frequently seen. I exchanged a few words with him and admired his simple want of expression. But it was not of him that I wished to speak, so much as of Storey, who is to my mind, head and shoulders beyond any other sculptor of the day. You know what a success his Cleopatra and Sybil were at London in the Exhibition. Since then he has produced two great works more. One is a Saul; a superb, massive figure, seated, with his right hand and fingers twisted in his beard, like the Moses of Michael Angelo. The face is great. The Spirit of the Lord, as the Bible says, is on it, and though I have only seen it in plaster and in Arthur's photographs, I think it an advance even on the Cleopatra. The other statue is a Medea meditating the death of her children. This is, I firmly believe, the best thing he has yet done. Every line of it is so bold and vigorous that it cuts into one's memory like a knife. It is a standing figure, quite in repose, and draped simply, so as to show the curves of the figure as clearly as possible. The left arm is folded across her, and on the left hand she is resting her right elbow, so that her right hand comes up to her chin. Her head is bent over a little and so rests on the hand. If you understand the attitude, and put anyone into it, you will see in a moment how expressive it is, and how exact it is to suit the instant of determination, or just before the completion of a decisive plan. But the face is something to remember in one's dreams. Such a concentration of idea can't often be worked out of marble. As for describing it—*pas si bête!* Imagine any woman with a face as beautiful and as hard as Greek marble, about to commit a murder under the circumstances mentioned, the idea of elaborating the most ingenious revenge conceivable, predominating in a mind as hard as her face. How Storey can make such statues I cannot understand. He is not a great man. He is vain, flippant, and trifling, and what is worse he has a wife who is a snob! Tudieu, what a snob! And he is under her influence habitually. Until the Cleopatra he had never created anything more than pretty. But the artist actually grows under all this weight of vanity, weakness, folly and flattery, and goes on excelling himself until he promises to reach a height unknown in art for centuries. Understand this who can. To me it is one of the mysteries of human nature.

I have now dosed you sufficiently with art. You may not care for it, but what of that! How can I write of other matters, when I have to get all my accounts of them from so far? All that I can say of ourselves is that your papa is down in the blue dogs at not getting his release; that I am by no means pleased at having to continue as patriarch; that your mamma is delighted with Rome and too much occupied to be thoughtful of other things; that Mary seems well enough, though I have not the least idea whether she is really well or no.

(Saturday. 15th) We have received your letters with Minnie's photograph. There is only one danger now about your position, and that is that the accounts we receive of her from our correspondents, written with more than a lover's enthusiasm, may lead your family to look for more than mortal imperfection can ever supply. The photograph is not calculated to lower these expectations. When you discover any faults in her, let us know. I don't refer to your own epistles, which have been comparatively silent, but to those of aunts, sisters & sich.

(Monday. 17th). We have received the news of the fall of Richmond! What think you, I had best do about it? I waked Arthur up to tell him, and he said he forgave me, but had it been anything else, he wouldn't. General McClellan last night doubted it! Arthur and I exulted over it over Storey's table. Shall I drink up Tiber, eat an obelisk? The Pope illuminated St Peter's last night, of course in honor of the news. The temptation is vehement to do something, but what can I do? With the news, I got your letter of March 26th, which makes me anxious to hear of your safety. If you are all right, I suppose your path is now clear, and you can resign and marry and come out here as soon as you like. Never mind the Minn. Your engagement and this news are the only bits of comfort he has had since we left home, and so you can tell Minnie, if she won't believe what I wrote her myself.

A chaotic letter! But *que veux-tu?*

Ever

MS:MHi

1. CFA2 was engaged to Mary ("Minnie") Hone Ogden (1843–1935).
2 HA mixes all these myths, which appear in Ovid's *Metamorphoses*. The *Drunken Satyr* (Adams' "Bacchus") and the *Narcissus* (now identified as *Dionysus*) are in the National Museum of Naples.
3. S.S.: Second Son (CFA2).
4. Arthur Dexter (1830–1897), a grandson of John Adams' secretary of war, Samuel Dexter, and an intimate friend of CFA2; James C. Hooker (1818–1894), U.S. banker in Rome, unofficial secretary of U.S. legation to the Papal States.
5. Gen. George B. McClellan (1826–1885), first commander of the Army of the Potomac, relieved of the command in early Nov. 1862.

To Charles Francis Adams, Jr.

No. 42.   Florence. 10 May. 1865.

My dear Colonel:

I can't help a feeling of amusement at looking back on my letters and thinking how curiously inapt they have been to the state of things about you. Victories and assassinations, joys, triumphs, sorrows and gloom; all at fever point, with you; while I prate about art and draw out letters from the sunniest and most placid of subjects. I have already buried Mr Lincoln under the ruins of the Capitol, along with Caesar, and this I don't mean merely as a phrase.[1] We must have our wars, it appears, and our crimes, as well as other countries. I think Abraham Lincoln is rather to be envied in his death, as in his life somewhat; and if he wasn't as great as Caesar, he shares the same sort of tomb. History repeats itself, and if we are to imitate the atrocities of Rome, I find a certain amusement in conducting my private funeral service over the victims, on the ground that is most suitable for such associations, of any in the world.

But the King being dead, what then? Are we to cry Live the King again? To me this great change looks like a step downward to our generation. New men have come. Will the old set hold their ground, or is Seward and the long-lived race about him, to make way for a young America which we do not know. You may guess how I have smiled sweetly on the chains that held me here at such a time, and swore polyglott oaths at Italy and everything else that keeps me here. I have looked towards London as earnestly as What's-her-name looked from Blubeard's tower, for the signs of the coming era,[2] but no sign is given. The Minister is waiting also apparently. I have written to him that *of course* now he must remain where he is, but whether he agrees to the of course or not, I can't say. It is clear to me that if Seward lives, he must stay; and if Seward retires, he should leave upon the new Secretary the responsibility of making a change. To throw up his office would be unpatriotic; it would also be a blunder. Do you assent to my doctrine? To be away from my place at such a time is enough to enrage a tadpole. And I can't be back before the end of June.

Are you curious to know about my adventures on the journey from Rome? It was but a repetition of the pleasures I described to you in another letter, with the addition of a violent heat. We drove five days among the Appenines. My hair is thinner in consequence. I have seen some cities that I hadn't seen, and some bad inns that I didn't want to see. One summer evening, returning with Mary and Brooks to our inn after a little excursion to see the falls of Terni, I found Minnie's letters in reply to ours, and smoked a cigar over them on a balcony over a crowd of screaming Italians in the noisy little market-place. Before writing again I wait to hear of your retreat from the army, which I suppose is now on the cards.

The truth is, in regard to traveling, this three months experience has made me old. I grow horribly solemn. I haven't had a good time for an age, nor laughed for a year. They call me Mausoleum, do the children. And well they may, for temper and nerve have been worn to a point that leaves little hope for me except in a tomb. However, I hope to see you before long, and till then—basta! We will have a quiet talk somewhere some day.

What a good time one can have in Italy, though, if one goes the right way about it. This traveling in one's own carriage is luxury itself. One starts in the early morning, and climbs mountains or crosses valleys with historical names and exquisite views; the walls of old Roman or Etruscan cities stare from the tops of hills; great convents rise in the valleys; the vines and flowers of Italy line the road, and if by noon it weren't hotter and dustier than Dante's Purgatorio, one might go on agreeably all day. Towards noon one stops and rests two or three hours, and then jogs on again till he winds up some hill at sunset, on which a very dirty, mediaeval and picturesque town perches itself, and where one looks with a species of distrust of one's own senses, on five centuries ago. But the old peculiarities are fast yielding now, and little remains of them except those which are still protected by the aid of religion, which in this country is the prop and shield of everything degrading, stupid, and bad. Arthur Dexter says that the only good and valuable men in Rome are the atheists. If you are not in a hurry you will miss the old order of things, for in another year railways will run in every direction about Italy, and whatever it may become, the antidiluvian character of the place will be lost. Whether the Papacy will stay or not, who knows? Like many Americans who have lived long in Europe, I have become much more radical in my convictions than is usual in America, where you exist in amusing ignorance of the fact that you are rapidly being caught up with and will soon be left behind by Europe. Of course you may answer this by the usual platitudes about the great republic. It's true enough that you and I never shall see the day when America will stand second, but the fact remains that since 1788 we have with difficulty sustained our position, while Europe has made enormous strides forward. At present there are two great influences holding Europe back. One is the English aristocracy, the other the Roman Church. Both of these will go down as sure as fate. I can't tell you when or how the change will take place, but whether it's ten or whether it's a hundred years, it will come, and when all the world stands on the American principle, where will be our old boasts unless we do something more.

I won't trouble you longer with my ideas on these matters, for they are dull. Perhaps I will write something on the matter some day, and bury it in the depths of the Atlantic—Monthly. At all events I am in theory a violent radical, inclined towards every "ism" in the faint hope of detecting within it some key to the everlasting enigma of progress. How the devil does one add two and two, and what is the answer? Such is philosophy; ditto politics.

At any rate here we are in Florence, which is a live city; an Italian Paris. The place was never a very great favorite of mine, for I never could see why people are so fond of it. We shall stay here till about the 18th; we shall then go to Venice, Milan, and perhaps across Switzerland and down the Rhine, and arrive in Paris on the 20th June. By the 1st July at latest I expect to be at London.

There I shall expect to see you some time towards October, for I do not suppose you will care to punish Minnie by a winter passage for any sins she may have to answer for. Nor will you be wise to trust the equinox. Either the first of September or the first of October is your best time, unless you can make it earlier still.

As to your being married in our absence, I think both your papa and mamma expect it and are waiting to welcome you here. It is so impossible to say in such times what is to happen to us that they have given up every idea of really getting to America. At least they talk so, though what they may do at the last, the Lord knows. You can foresee better from the current of events in America what will be our course, than we can judge it here. Undoubtedly, should Seward go down, there will be a struggle between the factions, more personal than political, for the control of the new Administration. I do not know where to discover in the whole political horizon, a single star whose influence would be favorable to us. Except Seward we have not one friend. Possibly this might be our strength. But on the other hand a vehement push will be made from other directions in favor of the advanced wing of the old Republican party. What their distinctive cry would be, I do not understand, unless it were the reversal of the Shakesperian text "Mercy should temper Justice."[3] But besides the battle between these two, which we won with so much difficulty in 1861, there is the Western element which may cut in between the others, or decide the success of either. For ourselves, we stand merely as cards for other men to play. Of course the Minister does not mix in the fight. But Thurlow Weed has written to London; a very unusual thing, which sets me to thinking, as the movements of that complicated statesman generally do. Does he turn his head that way indeed? If so, he must be hard pressed, for I cannot believe that he has any real taste for our advancement. On the other hand there are but two men with the proper knowledge for the State Department; Sumner and our Minister at London.

Do not imagine that I am anxious for the promotion to Washington. But I do feel that the new emergency opens all the old difficulties, and is of no little importance. Once decided, I shall care little, for then our course will be fixed. In the meanwhile our state of doubt is very embarrassing, and who can say when it will end.

We have received your letters describing your entrance into Richmond. It was just the right ending for your martial life. Now for another kind of experience!

MS:MHi

1. Lincoln died the morning of April 15, the day after he was shot by John Wilkes Booth in Ford's Theatre.
2. In the fairy tale Sister Anne watched for help that would rescue Fatima.
3. Probably a conflation of *The Merchant of Venice,* IV, i, 199f, and Milton, *Paradise Lost,* X, 77.

To Charles Francis Adams, Jr.

London. 21 December. 1866.

My dear Charles:

Two voluminous letters from you have reached me lately; one of 24th Nov., and the other dated the 27th. I will proceed to answer them with that force and skill which is so conspicuous in all my utterances.

Your first letter was very dismal, terminating in thoughts of suicide which were a natural consequence of the frame of mind you were in. As for the suicide, I quite agree with you, having long ago made up my mind that when life becomes a burden to me I shall end it, and I have even decided the process. The only difficulty is that every year I live, I feel on the whole less of this despondency than formerly, and the worst time of all was the earliest; when a boy at school. As a rule I have found this melancholy disposition a consequence of a slightly disordered stomach, or too low system, which was best corrected at this season by a pill and a week or two of cod-liver-oil. This however is only the result of my loose theory of morals, as the Governor rightly calls my ethical opinions. (He gave me a tremendous rasper in connection with this, the other day. Bless his dear old puritanical incorruptible soul! I didn't mind, and he apologised afterwards.) I only suggest the stomach from a materialistic point of view, and having done so, will move up higher.

You may not be aware that Goethe was a great practical genius as well as a great poet. Now this Goethe said one day to his friend Eckerman, who was, as might be said, in your situation: "There must always be a sequence in life."[1] He hit it as true as you live. Life ought to be the demonstration of a mathematical problem; the triangulation of so much time, and your last triangle must, to be correct, have one or more of its sides in common with the preceding one. Now, how stands your case. You can't use your military triangle as the base of your new one. You then go back a step to your legal base. But you can make nothing out of that. What remains but to recommence your operations from a wholly new point, and to slowly and carefully measure your new distances and calculate your new altitudes, calculating to work your old measurements in again so far as possible, as you go along, in order that your old labor may not be wholly thrown away. I don't suppose the process is pleasant, and to be effectual it must and ought to be slow, no doubt. But I dont see that you have any reason to be afraid of the result, except in one alternative. Whatever line you are now drawn into, you must stick to it, for the chances are enormous that a third change would be fatal.

As for me, you mistake the point. I have never varied my course at all. From my birth to this moment it has been straight as an arrow. Such as I am, I am complete. All the accidents of life have fallen in with the bent of my disposition and the previous course of my training. I repeat it, such as I am, the product is unique and positive. I shall get along; and if I am in the end what you in your sublimity call a failure, I shall still have enjoyed what I, in a spirit of more philosophical and milder tendency, consider a rounded and completed existence. Our ideas on this matter are radically at variance, but I think you can understand what I mean if I hammer at you long enough.

For instance, by the time this reaches you I suppose I shall be out in the North American, and perhaps one or two more articles of mine will appear there.[2] But I don't want to repeat my old mishap of five years ago. I don't want to be affiché as the writer of this or that clever or dull or obnoxious or blundering Essay. I would rather my name were wholly unmentioned. Some year or two hence it will all be the same. The estimate the world has of a man, filters ultimately through the masses better in darkness than in the heat of the sun. If five years hence I published a book I would prefer to have the non-reader have a vague idea that I was a clever and rising man, than myself receive a host of newspaper criticisms and society compliments. I don't want to rise by leaps to high position. I don't care for your short cut to eminence. I don't aspire to fill a large or small place in the popular eye as such. I have no fear about what is to happen after my return home. I mean to develope the life I have lived, and to do that I need no external support. I work on the hard pan, if necessary.

So much for our different views of life, which resolve themselves at last merely into a difference of temperament; you, bold, energetic, even arrogant in your demands upon your fellow creatures and on life; I, cautious, timid, and so much inclined to doubt my own mind that I might let the greatest good go by untouched, rather than expose myself to what I should consider an evil. But at any rate, I am patient, and I despise the world and myself so honestly and reflectingly, that whatever fate comes, will probably find me ready to bow to it with a good grace.

This brings me direct to the second point of interest in your letters. I hope that in taking my affairs out of John's hands you did not let him suppose that I wished it. John has taken good care of my affairs during a busy time, and I should be sorry to have him think that I am ungrateful for it. I've no doubt that he is very willing to hand the work over to you, but still I dont want him to suppose that I think your management preferable to his.

I wish that the first work you perform in this connection, would be to send me (unless John has already done it) an exact account of all receipts, disbursements, investments &c. since July, 1865. If not too much trouble I would like for the future a semi-annual account in July and Jan. I shall expect you however, in return, to charge me a per-centage for management as you would anyone else. In that case I can feel at my ease, and find fault with you if I like.

I approve the sale of the factory stock, though I hope you bagged the dividends. Yet I don't understand how the Merrimack can be doing a poor business with a 15 per cent dividend. And if her stock falls much at any time, apart from special reasons of bad-management &c, I wish you would buy in heavily. It has divided 22½ per cent this year, and 23 per cent last year, and John bought at par; the best thing he ever did for me. I go in on factories in the long run.

But I cant see how Michigan Central Bonds at 106 wont shrivel as you say. I should think Chicago City 7.s. at par were cheaper. But I know little of the matter. I wish I were quite as sure of no internal political trouble as you. I wouldn't sell the Phil. Wil. & Baltimore stock though. There's not much and its a great line. The great pressure will, I suppose, fall on the banks and it is well to be clear of them. U.S. Bonds have stood well and are likely to do so. As a rule, I have gone on the principle of scattering my investments, but your movement now is one of concentration and its object is to obtain steady and easily convertible securities. Such are U.S. Bonds, and Massachusetts and Boston Stock. But on the other hand, if Congress expands again, as I fear, I shall be left high and dry for a long time.

The Governor sold your Bonds very well, I believe. He took the '64 bond himself at the home price.

The article you mention in the Edinburgh must have been about two years ago. It was about the Bank rate at 7 per cent, or something of the kind. You can easily find it.

Thanks for your legal notes. I think you are wrong. Gold demonetised is a commodity to be stated not by coin but by weight. So many ounces of gold should be the legal term. Nevertheless your argument will be worth making and I shall be glad to read it.

MS:MHi

1. Johann Peter Eckermann (1792–1854).
2. "North American": the prestigious *North American Review*.

To Charles Francis Adams, Jr.

London. 30 July. 1867.

My dear Charles

I take the first minute of leisure I am likely to have, in order to polish off your article.[1] As we leave England next week, I must either do the work quickly or not at all, and to leave it undone would annoy me, for this kind of criticism very often does more good to the critic than to the critiqué.

Imprimis, I don't hesitate to say that the worm is a good worm. I would publish by all means. Your idea is more than good; it is one of those which seem likely to act as hinges for future statesmanship. Of course it is not original with you, but if you can ride it, practically it is your horse. I say therefore—publish.

But when you ask of me a criticism that shall be only rigid and hostile, I am bound to stop short here with my compliments expressed or implied, and to balance my conclusion—which comes first—by pitching into your whole production with a single purpose of showing that it is too bad for any self-respecting man to own. I know what this means, for I invited Frank Palgrave to treat my Captain John Smith in the same way, and his success was so decided that to this day I can never read that essay without a sense of shame.

My criticism must relate to two separate points, and I have got to begin by drawing the line between the matter and the form of your article—between its argument and its style. As the matter is more important than the form, I will begin with the harder task, after which I promise myself and you much light enjoyment from a right appreciation of your merits as a writer of your native tongue.

I take it that your whole point—that is, in its more limited bearing—rests in the general and notorious fact that the wealth of Boston and its influence are relatively decreasing. The first part of your essay shows or attempts to show why they are decreasing, and the last part is intended to suggest a remedy for the evil. Now let us see how you go to work to prove the causes of your acknowledged fact.

Your argument, if it is an argument, and not an illustration or a contrast, consists of an elaborate comparison between Boston and Chicago. I have no right to parade my personal tastes, or I should express at once my utter fatigue at the strain which Chicago has put upon my intellect. Decidedly Chicago bores me. That western hub is a greater nuisance than ever Boston State House was. Is it absolutely necessary for you to glean the stubble of Parton's harvest?[2] Can't you discover a new case in point? Read the article on the Suez Canal in the Revue des deux Mondes which I am going to send you, and take a hint from Port el Said.

This is only a point of taste, however, and I don't urge it, but I have a much more decisive objection behind and this I do urge. Do your facts justify your argument? Why does Boston not grow like New York and Chicago? You reply: because she does not like New York and Chicago, extend her lines of communication? And why then has she failed to extend her lines of communication? It may do, for your purpose, to throw the blame upon bad legislation, though how bad legislation in Massachusetts could have prevented the Boston, Hartford & Erie from being built in Connecticut, under a Connecticut charter as the road is, I do not comprehend. But though you may make—though you have in fact abundant materials to make a very effective attack upon the legislation, beware of pressing it too far. The truth is, Chicago rose as a colony of New England. She is herself the proof of New England's energy. If you find fault with Boston for backwardness, you must admit that she is weak because she has given her strength to her rival. The question is one of common-sense. If Boston capitalists think that by building railways for Chicago, or sinking copper-mines in Wisconsin, they can double their money, it is unlikely that they will invest it on the Hartford & Erie or any other eastern enterprise which only promises 50 per cent.; and as both are purely and solely questions of investment, the fact is itself the proof; they do not build railways in New England—therefore they must think the other investments better.

I doubt therefore the value of your elaborate argument from the example of Chicago, and I believe that the decline of Boston has been simply due to the fact that other parts of the country were thought to offer, and in fact did offer, quicker and larger returns on expenditure of wealth or of labor than New England could afford to do. So Boston has pitched millions of money into the gutter; she has gambled almost as recklessly—nay, far more recklessly—in gold and copper and petroleum stocks, than ever England did in Grand Trunk, Erie, or Atlantic & Great Western Railway securities. The same feeling has carried her young energy away to New

York, Chicago and San Francisco. The stakes were heavier, the gains larger, and the losses identical, since ruin can only ruin, whether in Boston or the west. To say therefore that this process of depletion was caused by want of enterprise and bad legislation, seems to me to be equivalent to saying that a thing can cause itself, or that what is subsequent in time can be precedent in condition.

If I had my way therefore, I would soften this part of your argument. You don't require it and it gives a tone of injustice and unfaithfulness to your picture. The fact is all you want. New England is depleted. Her wealth and life are drawn irresistibly towards more promising markets. Her capitalists lose millions in wild copper speculations, and refuse money for the Hartford & Erie. They build railways through solitary wildernesses in the west, where wild turkeys and prairie chickens are their only probable passengers, and they despise a line of steamers to Charleston or Europe. Legislation has done its best to create and continue the situation. The representative system in its first stage has broken down, since the legislature has shown itself incompetent to originate a new policy or even to reform its old one. Your statement on this point is full of force and might be developed further with good effect, at the expense of your introduction. I will not try to improve it.

Having thus considered the evil, you now proceed to inquire whether there is any remedy. I agree that you lead up to your point very well, but I think you encourage a little too implicit a confidence in one particular panacea.

The central idea should of course be that as you cannot stop the drain of resources, it is absolutely necessary to husband carefully and to employ economically all the force that is left. In your place I should be strongly tempted here to go more carefully into the whole field of activity; to draw the railways a little back, and to push the adjuncts which you only indicate slightly, a little forward. And finally you can bring out your railway commission as the best available remedy for the most pressing evil, not treating it, however, as a certain success, but as a necessary supplement to the acknowledged deficiencies of our political system. Between ourselves, commissions are a useful, but an unfortunate make-shift. The main-spring of life has got to lie in the people; the capitalists and the thinkers. If capital and thought will run away, commissions will not stop them; and our real hope must be in a reaction from the speculative fever of the last twenty years. All we can do in the interval is to economise our forces, and a railway commission, if it consists of really good men, may do something in that way. What is however of more importance to us is that such commissions open a door to men of our ability. This argument, however, is unfortunately not admissible and must be kept well out of sight.

After this running commentary it is needless for me to say that I think the last seven pages considerably better than the first twelve, and that the whole would be certainly improved by cutting the first twelve down to six, while a considerable addition and developement might be given to the last six, in my opinion, to a corresponding extent. I object to your sketch of Boston thirty years ago. It has a false air of archaeology; one is tempted to ask where are the mediaeval remains. But this is rather a question of style than of substance, and after all, though I got through my Holden Chapel period in College, I have no right to blame others for being deceived by its flimsiness.[3] My main objection is that the argument of your first half is weak and had better be left out. If you confine yourself to drawing a simple contrast between the two cities, which is all you want, half the space is ample. Besides, the lower your key is pitched at the beginning, the more effective will your climax be, and if you are bound to wake Boston, you had best do it in the most dramatic way.

And now I will turn, since your challenge or invitation requires it, to the style of your production, about which I assure you I have much more complaint to make than I had about the substance of it. You are, no doubt, a live American, and like the ancient barbarian kings, you are super grammaticam. Our noble countrymen enjoy as the privilege of their free birth, the right to be proud of ignorance and vulgarity. My criticism therefore will be of no use, but you ask it, and, by the Prophets, you shall have it.

In regard to style in general, I will begin by enouncing an axiom. That is best which is truest. If you wish to write a sentence, how ought you to begin it? I say, like the belier in Hamilton's fairy story: commençons par le commencement.[4] Begin with your subject. You say: No, I prefer to begin by transposing the middle of the sentence, or indeed the end, to its head. I will put my predicate first, or a wholy irrelevant adverb, or needless paraphrase first, in order to give life to my style. And so you mask, or break up and enfeeble the strong lines of honest composition, by an attempt to deceive the eye. If you cannot succeed in lending diversity, elegance or force to your style without sacrificing the solid basis of your sentences, it is better by far that you should abandon the idea of possessing a style at all, and content yourself with writing good grammar.

I maintain the same principle about the whole as about the parts. I execrate—I abhor from my deepest soul every attempt to make a thing what it is not; to write for men as though they were children; to varnish a plain story with a shining and slippery polish; to make use of traps in which the reader's attention may be caught, and the idiot may be waxed into ideas. Let those do such work who like it. No man who knows what a true style is, will condescend to use such upholsterer's art.

Nor have I much more patience with works which offend from excess of knowledge, than with those for which mere ignorance and vulgarity are responsible, or mere harmless affectation. Our oratory is a falsehood which degrades the nation. Our Everetts and our Sumners remind me of the Treasury Building at Washington. A plain flat wall and a set of business offices are by this style disguised like a Greek temple, and our barbarism is made more evident than ever by the shameless audacity of our theft.

Depend upon it, there is but one good style, and that is the simplest and the truest. Such a style may want elegance, but it can't be bad.

Your own writing seems to me to be just this, except in those parts where you attempt more, and there you are dreadfully bad; so bad, that unless I knew how I sin myself, I should be ashamed of you. You wrote better than this at College. Your affectations are intolerable. You flounder like an ill-trained actor in your efforts to amuse and to be vivacious. Nervousness thrusts itself out in your sentences as in your ideas. One seeks in vain for that repose and steadiness of manner, on which alone an easy and elegant style can rest.

But my great objection is to your profuse expenditure of words. This trick, which I am myself painfully conscious of sharing, was, I suspect, an inheritance from Charles Dickens and Frank Palfrey, which principally shows itself in affectations of expression and contortions of thought. This is its worst form. Then comes the habit of saying in two words what can be said in one.

Yet I scarcely know whether on reflection I blame this more than I do the brutal inelegancies and vulgarity of expression which you take no pains to correct or avoid. Why on earth the live American glories in vulgarity, I do not know, but I do know that the Greek, dead or alive, never did so, and that the most active Frenchman takes pride in his language and taste. Let us leave to Parton and the school of which he is far too good a chief, the exclusive possession of these arts by which the people are to be flattered. If you and I have one reason for existence in America, it is that we may do battle with just this national tendency.

I have already mentioned an article in the Revue des deux Mondes, and I come back to it and to that Review generally as my justification in this criticism. You will find in it many styles, but you will seldom find one that is florid employed upon a practical subject, nor one that is imaginative upon a narration of facts. Far seldomer, perhaps never, will you see its severe correctness of language sink into vulgarity. Whenever you and I can write our language as these Frenchmen write theirs, we may hope to accomplish something in our country, for people are vulgar in the mass only because they are ignorant, and they enjoy good-taste the instant they become familiar with it. They will listen to us when we know how to speak.

You will find the first page of your M.S. crammed with as many notes as I could get upon it, and a careful examination of these will illustrate what I have tried in this letter to express more at large. To continue this style of treatment throughout would have been too hard work, and was not neeeded. You can judge for yourself from the specimen. Nevertheless I have dotted a few other notes here and there, while on page 12, I have tried to show you what I meant once by calling your style too fat.

I send you this week a bundle of Parliamentary Papers which Tuke Parker got for me from a Mr Dodson to whom I sent your law article.[5] As Mr Dodson is an M.P. and an authority, you might perhaps write to thank him and so found a correspondence. I do not know how else I could have found the papers. You had better thank Parker too. He may be useful to you.

Brooks arrived last night, well and stout. We leave London on the 10th August.

MS:MHi

1. Manuscript of CFA2, "Boston," part 1, *North American Review* 106 (Jan. 1868), 1–25.
2. James Parton (1822–1891), "Chicago," *Atlantic Monthly* 19 (March 1867), 325–345.
3. "Holden Chapel," *Harvard Magazine* 1 (May 1855), 210–215, the first of HA's eleven published undergraduate writings.
4. Anthony Hamilton (1646–1720), author of "Le Bélier."
5. Henry Tuke Parker (1824–1890), assistant secretary at the U.S. legation; John George Dodson (1825–1897), deputy speaker of the House of Commons.

To Charles Francis Adams, Jr.

Baden. 4 September. 1867.

My dear Charles

I have your letter of the 10th August, all about business and politics. Just now I have dropped these two lines of activity, and am willing to accept on trust all you say. Let us hope that Ludlow will prosper,[1] and the President do right.

I am at it again, as you will have heard, trying hard to drive my team of women. But as Brooks will soon follow this letter to America, I don't think it worth while to write what he will certainly tell you better by word of mouth. So I refer you for family details to him. On the whole I have not had more trouble than I expected.

You will give my love to Minnie. I was relieved to hear that she had got so well through her trial.[2] I read some rubbish you wrote on the subject shortly after her confinement, but as my last letter contained criticism enough for a time, I will refer you to that by way of comment. In a year or two I shall return home and find you training your daughter to theory, I suppose. If I have a chance I'll spoil her as sure as my name is Henry Brooks.

As you know, we passed ten days in Paris while on our way here, and there I saw Hunt's picture of the Minister which he completed while we were there.[3] As you and John no doubt feel an interest in it, I want to say a few words about it.

The picture is not a full-length; it comes only to the knees. The ground on which the figure is painted, is perfectly simple; a warm, foxy color, which age will darken to black. There is no background other than this. The figure itself stands out boldly; the face slightly turned to the left; the black frock coat buttoned up, a scarf covering the shirt, and only the collar showing any bit of white. There is no color anywhere. One hand is thrust into the coat front; the other hangs down with a roll of paper. The expression of the face is marked but not excessively so, and I think you and I have seen him rise to speak in public, when he had almost precisely the same air and manner.

You can understand from the description that Hunt has dealt with his subject in the most honest and straight-forward way. There are no tricks nor devices in the picture. It is in the severest and truest style, so severe that most people will think it commonplace. I imagine that you and everyone else except a few professional men, will look at it with a sense of disappointment, and feel that something is wanting; a bolder or freer touch; a more expressive attitude; more animated features; a less subdued background, or a dash of color in the dress. There is nothing for the eye to fasten upon and to drag away from the whole effect. In your language, as applied to literature, it is dull.

You know by this time my canons of art pretty well, and you know that what pleases the crowd would have a poor chance of pleasing me. Whoever is right, the majority must be wrong. I consider Hunt's picture to be just what a portrait of our papa should be; quiet, sober, refined, dignified; a picture so unassuming that thousands of people will overlook it; but so faithful and honest that *we* shall never look at it without feeling it rise higher in our estimation. I need to see it among other portraits in order to get at its relative merit, but at any rate I don't hesitate to say that I think we have a first-rate likeness of the Governor. I expect it to be in the next Royal Academy Exhibition, and I shall then be able to fix its merits as compared with other paintings. Until then we will let it rest.

Frank Parker has been with us two days and has gone on this morning to Switzerland. We had our usual annual talk, and some pleasant walks in the hills. He was much amused with our life here and scandalised us by suddenly leaving our party to wait for him while he rushed off after Cora

Pearl.[4] The distinguished Cora is only one among many women of the same style here, who this week certainly rule Baden, respectability going hopelessly under. But to see Parker drawn in the train of the most shameless and probably the least pretty of the class, was delicious. I swore we would split on him to Dana. Finally he had the bad grace to come back and abuse poor Cora for the very qualities he and all of us run after her to see.

Mamma is hard at work taking the Griesbach waters here. I do not know yet whether she is better for them, but I certainly do not think she is worse, and she seems contented here. As I am more than ever convinced that it is necessary to do something energetic to prevent the progress of her difficulty, I encourage her staying here. Next week the fashionable season will be over, and I hope we shall have a quiet week more for carrying on the experiment. I doubt whether we start for Switzerland for a fortnight.

If I were here alone with a few thousand pounds to throw away, I should dive into the hell of iniquity we have round us, and try what pleasure there is in a regular blow-out. But alas, I am poor, I am well-known, and I have three shrinking women to protect.[5]

MS:MHi

1. HA's stock in a Ludlow, Mass., factory.
2. Mary Ogden Adams (1867–1933) was born at Quincy, July 27.
3. The Boston artist William Morris Hunt (1824–1879), on an extended visit to Europe, had begun CFA's portrait in London early in the year. It is at Adams House, Harvard University.
4. Cora Pearl (assumed name of the Englishwoman Emma Elizabeth Crouch, 1836?–1886) was a leading courtesan of the Second Empire; mistress of Prince Napoleon 1866–1874.
5. His mother and his sisters, Louisa and Mary.

To Charles Francis Adams, Jr.

London. 22 October. 1867.

My dear Charles

I have received from you at various times letters dated the 10th August, the 24th August, the 6th Sept. and the 5th October. According to your wishes I have sent to you Mr Crawford's Speech on Railway Legislation (N.B. there are no such things as rail-*roads* in this country), and the scientific treatises on railways, the two volumes in one. I have also read your article in the Law Magazine and forwarded it through H. T. Parker to Mr Dodson.

For two or three reasons I preferred to let our argument on the best form of writing drop for a while. In the first place, I was travelling and hated writing at all; after our return I was too busy; but the best reason was that in my own mind I was satisfied that I was right and you were wrong, and that this fact was sure to impress itself little by little on your mind whether you would or no, so as to save me the trouble of wasting Government paper. Now as I take up again your letter of August 24th I feel no doubt that your intelligence must have reached the point where, while still holding fast to all you then said, you will try your hardest to do just the opposite. Your whole argument was too bad for you to defend a month after you had made it. It rested on the supposition that you had not cleverness enough to interest readers unless you made yourself vulgar. You may be right. At any rate you have even here the advantage of me, for whether I am refined or vulgar I begin to despair of ever interesting anyone. But right or wrong you have no business to say it without first trying the better way—and the trial ought to last your life. A life is not such a tremendous time to learn to express your ideas. I don't suppose that Swift when he wrote the Drapier's letters or Cobbett when he edited his Review "fired over the heads of his audience" as you seem to think a man must do who says what he has got to say, and says it in the one-single-sole-unique-possible way.[1] There is but one good way of writing; in the first place, catch your ideas. And now you tell me practically that you've no ideas and have got to take clap-trap. What rubbish! Your ideas are excellent. All that they want is that you should work them up properly. I can tell you I know as well as most men what a labor this is; day after day and week after week I go back to it myself with the feelings, as I should imagine them, of a well-bred dog returning to his vomit. But then I should think myself a mighty ornary cuss if I knocked off this work which is hateful to me as brandy-and-water, calmly remarking, as I sent a crude, half-finished essay to the press: Ah, the public likes it so! The public prefers clap-trap!

You be damned! Yes just that! Give the public a chance. So it is vulgar! So it will drag you down if you let it! But just try once or twice the effect of a clever, pointed article, with all the big words and all the useless words knocked out, written as Heine or Thackeray would write, and then you see which the public will enjoy most. The vulgar experiment may last a day. The other will put you with one jump at the head of American authors. The public is a pretty contemptible thing; that I confess. I've no very high opinion of it myself; but men who propose to influence the public have got to be really great men; otherwise they find themselves talking a deal of stuff in a vulgar jargon, which after all is only an echo of public talk. If I am to drive, I want to sit above my horses. If you are to address an audience you will do well to stand on a platform, morally, intellectually and every other way. So in future stop talking rubbish to me, your dearest brother, and don't deceive yourself with the fancy that your laziness is the same thing with public bad-taste. Just read a page of Macaulay or Balzac or who you please, and then take up a sheet of your or my stuff, and you'll see quickly enough why we still want an audience.

So our friend Stack thought me a humbug![2] His critical acumen is wonderful, and I only wish it had the additional merit of being correct. If I only could manage to endure the drudgery of copying and recopying every word I write, there would be a good chance for me yet to leave half a dozen agreeable volumes in the family library; more than all the rest of the family has ever produced altogether. But unfortunately Stack is in error. I have never copied but one letter since I was a boy, and that one was in answer to Mr Seward's offer of the Assistant Secretary's place here. Stackpole ought to know, and you too ought to know, that when a man has been worried by a subject and thought it over till he does what few people ever will do—that is, knows something about it, his words and sentences flow easily enough, even into "antitheses and rhetorical finish." But I am not going to protect myself under the miserable subterfuge of your combined blunder, bad as it is. I maintain that in calling me a humbug for having (grant I did it) written a familiar letter like an essay, or rather an essay like a familiar letter (take your choice of the charges), you and he said just the thing which is most discreditable to your critical taste. Attack me if you choose for employing art badly, and for not knowing how to write my own wretched style, but don't be so intolerably barbarous as to fancy that art itself is bad. "Copied in cold blood" is your charge, and I wish to God it were true. What of it? If Goethe at eighty could say that he had devoted his whole life to learning to write German, it isn't either you nor friend Stackpole that is big enough to look down upon his labor—no, not by several inches. Clean that idea promptly out of your combined intellects. I am sensitive on points of art. Personally I am willing to acknowledge anything you choose in regard to my own success in employing it, but I consider the meanest bungler who sets to work patiently and with a comprehension of his ignorance on the task of mastering his art, to be worth more than a half dozen clever charlatans who plunge into the most difficult of careers believing that education is a humbug. I have seen Story in Rome work for hours over a lock of hair on a statue, and days on the fold of a bit of cloth. I hope to reach the point when I shall be able by working hours over a sentence, to make it perfect. But whether I do or not is of mighty little consequence. I would rather fail in trying to be a gentleman than succeed in being a turned-up-nose snob. If it weren't for the pleasure of following something above me, I believe I would drop the whole infernal affair.

Bye-Bye Snobs.

MS:MHi

1. Jonathan Swift, *The Drapier's Letters* (1724). William Cobbett published *Cobbett's Political Register* (London, 1802–1835).
2. Joseph Lewis Stackpole (1838–1904), CFA2's classmate at Harvard, was a Boston lawyer.

To Charles Eliot Norton

London. 10 April. 1868.

My dear Sir[1]

You were kind enough in your last letter to express a wish to receive other articles from me. If you are still of that mind, I would like to ask your—and the public's—patience to the extent of some thirty pages in the North American, for a review of Sir Charles Lyell's "Principles of Geology. Tenth Edition."

If you see no objection, I would like further to have my hearing in the October No. I expect myself to return to Boston in July, and will have the M.S. ready by that time, if the confusion I shall live in during the next three months will allow of it.

I ought perhaps to add that I shall try to express more valuable opinions than my own, though I don't wish to be controversial. As it is long since I have had the pleasure of talking with Mr Lowell, and neither your opinions nor his are very well known to me, I would rather run no risk of offering to you anything which might seem not conservative enough for your united tastes.[2] Therefore if you are afraid of Sir Charles and Darwin, and prefer to adhere frankly to Mr Agassiz, you have but to say so, and I am dumb. My own leaning, though not strong, is still towards them, and therefore I should be excluded from even the most modest summing up in the Atlantic, I suppose. It is not likely that I should handle the controversy vigorously— the essay would rather be an historical one—but I should have to touch it.

If you will be kind enough to send me a line, still to the care of this Legation, that I may know what to do, I shall be, as ever,

Very truly Yrs   Henry Brooks Adams.

Charles Eliot Norton Esq.

MS:MHi

1. Charles Eliot Norton (1827–1908), coeditor of the *North American Review* 1864–1868, Dante scholar and man of letters, professor of history of fine art at Harvard 1863–1898.
2. James Russell Lowell (1819–1891), poet, professor of modern languages at Harvard 1856–1876, coeditor with Norton of the *North American Review* at this period.

II

The Conquest of
a Reputation
1868–1885

F REED AT LAST from the "Family go-cart" by his father's resignation as minister to England, Henry Adams went ahead with his plan to establish himself as an independent journalist in Washington, where he had served an exciting apprenticeship eight years earlier. At thirty the pretense of returning to study law in Boston was no longer tenable. His two older brothers, John Quincy and Charles Francis, were already lawyers there, and his younger brother, Brooks, now twenty, would soon help crowd the family roster. As for a possible career in politics, he was later to acknowledge that his father and his elder brothers stood far before him "in the order of promotion."

After his long cosmopolitan existence in London, Boston seemed acutely provincial. Washington was no London or Paris, but the Union victory in the Civil War had made it a world capital, and Adams instinctively gravitated to it. He hoped to make it his home and to earn distinction there. His essay on Captain John Smith, published while he was still in England, may have infuriated Virginians, but their reception of it taught him that breaking shuttered windows to let in light could make a writer's reputation. Everyone knew that postwar Washington needed light. The whole root of its evil, he wrote, "is in *political* corruption." His three articles in the prestigious *North American Review* lent authority to his voice.

Adams allied himself with investigative journalists and political leaders in the movement for reform of the exorbitant tariff, the spoils system, and the debased currency. The Boston economist Edward Atkinson introduced him to E. L. Godkin, editor of the recently founded *Nation,* and Adams became a frequent contributor to that periodical. In Boston his brother Charles began his investigation of the criminal mismanagement of the Erie Railroad, and Henry got Congressman Abram Garfield to supply him with potent evidence. Henry's series of articles on the grave shortcomings of Congress and on the vagaries of government finance made him known in the United States and England as a formidable critic. His most powerful article, "The New York Gold Conspiracy," published in the *Westminster Review* in 1870, exposed the attempt of Jay Gould and James Fisk to corner the American supply of gold bullion.

The reform movement lost headway under President Grant's benign neglect. Since few friends of reform remained in power, Adams was persuaded by his family to accept an appointment as an assistant professor of history at Harvard and as the editor of the *North American Review.* Inspired by the success of the new German scholarship, he pioneered a doctoral program by studying with his graduate students the sources of Anglo-Saxon law. He also kept up a behind-the-scenes relation with such Liberal Republican leaders as Senator Carl Schurz from Missouri and former secretary of the interior Jacob Dolson Cox.

In 1872 Henry Adams married Marian ("Clover") Hooper, the very intellectual daughter of a prominent Boston doctor who had reared his three children since the death of their mother in 1848. As a married man, Adams settled comfortably into his career as an innovative professor of history. His wife became proficient as an amateur photographer. On their wedding journey they spent some months on the Nile, after which he conferred with historians in Europe and England and renewed associations with his wartime friends and acquaintances.

The election of Rutherford Hayes to the presidency in the "stolen election" of 1876 put an end to Adams' political activities. Invited to edit the papers and to write the biography of Albert Gallatin, Jefferson's secretary of the Treasury, he escaped from his professorial chores at Harvard and settled in his beloved Washington as a historian with privileged access to the State Department archives. Thus began his remarkably fruitful middle period in which he and his wife led a charmed social existence. Their salon had at its center the intimate and exclusive "Five of Hearts," whose members included, besides Adams and Clover, John Hay, a journalist and Republican politician; Hay's wife Clara, a Cleveland heiress; and Clarence King, director of the U.S. Geological Survey.

The Gallatin project, which ran to four large volumes, was quickly followed by *Democracy,* a thinly disguised satire of Washington politics under President Grant. The novel, published anonymously, became a sensational success in America and England. During a research year abroad Adams collected diplomatic materials for a project which he had long planned, a multivolume history of the United States during the administrations of Jefferson and Madison. After his return from Europe, he riled Virginians once again with a clinically severe biography of John Randolph, the venomous adversary of John Quincy Adams. Meanwhile, the *History* progressed steadily, and by the beginning of 1885 he was able to circulate among a group of private critics a printed draft of the first half, covering Jefferson's administration. For refreshment he turned to writing another novel, *Esther,* which he published under a pseudonym. It dealt with the impact of the current conflict between religion and science on the life of the heroine, whom Adams modeled on his wife. While busy with that novel he put the seal of permanence on his residence in Washington by joining with John Hay in beginning the construction of adjoining houses facing the White House across Lafayette Square.

This happy and productive period came to an abrupt and tragic end with the suicide of Clover Adams on December 6, 1885. Her photography darkroom supplied the lethal agent, potassium cyanide. The devastated Adams moved in alone to the just-completed house, his life broken in halves.

To Charles Milnes Gaskell

158 G Street. Washington. D.C.
5 Nov. 1868.

My dear Carl

Eccolà! If you can master the idea of streets named after letters of the alphabet, know that the above is my address. Moreover, "D.C." stands for District of Columbia, though you mightn't guess it. The great step is taken, and here I am, settled for years, and perhaps for life. Your last letter was sent on to me a few days ago.

My experiences so far have not been disagreeable, and yet I think and hope they have been the least agreeable part of my experiences past or to come. I left Boston on the 12th of October and stopped several days in New York, intending to come on here and stay at a hotel until I could move into rooms. But one day I met Mr Evarts on the street. You recollect his visit to Cambridge with me in 1863, since which he has become a great man, saving the President in the Impeachment by his skill as Counsel, and in consequence of his services then, appointed a member of the Cabinet as Attorney General not long afterwards. He stopped me to urge that I should stay at his house in Washington until I settled myself. Naturally I assented and we came on together. His family was all away, and he and I kept house for ten days. He took me to call on the President, who was grave, and cordial, and gave me a little lecture on constitutional law. The Secretary of State, as we call the Foreign Secretary, Mr Seward, was also cordial and his major-domo selected rooms for me. With the Secretary of the Treasury, I am on the best of terms and he pats me on the back, not figuratively but in the flesh. Finally the Secretary of War and I are companions.[1] The account so far is a good one, is it not? Unfortunately this whole Cabinet goes out on the 4th of March, and in the next one I shall probably be without a friend. Politics makes a bad trade.

I staid ten days with the Attorney General and then I moved to the house of an aunt I have here, where I still remain while my rooms get into shape. If you come over, I can give you a bed and you can stay as long as you will. You will find all my old books in my cases, my drawings (and memorials of Cannes) on the walls, and my lion and ostrich magnificent and beautiful for ever. My establishment is modest, for my means are exiguous, but it has more civilisation in it than the rest of Washington all together. Come and see.

In fact this is the drollest place in Christian lands. Such a thin veil of varnish over so very rough a material, one can see nowhere else. But for all that, there are strong points about it. From the window of my room I can as I sit see for miles down the Potomac, and I know of no other capital in the world which stands on so wide and splendid a river. But the people and the mode of life are enough to take your hair off. I think I see you trying to live here. You couldn't stand it four-and-twenty hours. Alas! I fear I never shall eat another good dinner.

My geological article was published a month ago, after I left Boston and I have heard nothing of it (the best news I could hear), except that it has paid me £20.[2] I am now beginning Finance again, and you will probably read as much as the title of my next production. In about five years I expect to have conquered a reputation. But what it may be worth when got, is more than I can tell. The sad truth is that I want nothing and life seems to have no purpose.

Our elections as you can see, have passed off as everyone expected and we are approaching a new reign. Personally we have nothing to expect from it. My father is not in sympathy with the party in power, and my brother is a prominent opponent of it. I am too insignificant a cuss to have my opinion asked, but my eyes and ears are wide open, and we mean to be seen and be heard as well as see and hear. I wait now with great interest for your election. Write soon about it. Give my best love to everyone. I shall write again soon.

Ever Yrs   Henry Brooks Adams

MS: MHi

1. Secretary of the Treasury Hugh McCulloch (1808–1895); John Schofield (1831–1906), secretary of war 1868–1869.
2. Review of Sir Charles Lyell's *Principles of Geology, North American Review* 107 (Oct. 1868), 465–501.

To Ralph Palmer

158 G Street. Washington. D.C.
21 November. 1868.

My dear Ralph[1]

In case the above address puzzles you, I will explain that the city of Washington for political reasons was not placed in any State but has an independent territory ten miles square called the District of Columbia (D.C. for short) and that it is barbarous enough to name its streets according to letters of the alphabet. I am on G. When you write, copy this address, and don't imagine you are writing to a states-prison convict.

I received your two letters in close succession, that of the 5th inst. arriving this morning. They relieved me of some anxiety in regard to the fate of the hat, though I had seen Mr Parker on his return, and he told me that he had fulfilled the commission. I have been racking my brain for something to get you to do for me, but as yet without success. Before long, however, I shall have to bother you damnably.

As you can see, I have carried out my projects and am established here with the full determination to make Washington my home. I have enough money to make me independent of the world, even if I can't afford servants or horses or women or vices. My apartment is large enough to supply you with a bed-room and very excellent eating whenever you come to see me. Only don't come between June and October, for then I am at home in (Scotland I was going to say, but meant) New England, where you will be my mother's guest, not mine. I will introduce you into society here, and have the Cabinet Ministers to dine with you, provided they are worth having; for I don't know who will be in the new Cabinet. Socially I don't expect to be a cypher here, I give you my word. So you may count on my performing all I promise. I needn't say that any letter of recommendation you send me shall be properly honored, and if you will keep me informed by post of the exact weight you wish to put on each introduction, I will graduate my attentions accordingly. You need not be afraid of using this offer. If you send me good fellows, you will even do me a favor, for Washington has not much to offer in that way, and I expect to degenerate if I keep the company that I find here.

Your list of engagements shows that somehow or other the aristocracy means in both sexes to copulate according to law, both civil and canonical. This is better than to do it illegally; at least in my opinion; though hitherto I have proceeded on the latter theory. I wish some-one would take the trouble to marry me out-of-hand. I've asked my mother and all my aunts to undertake the negociation, promising to accept anyone they selected. Damn *me* if, one and all, they didn't think I was joking, and nothing would convince them that I was in solemn earnest. That is what society has come to, in this country. All the women acknowledge that no man is fit to choose himself a wife, and yet they all ridicule the idea of doing it for him.

London society has, I suppose, forgotten us, or would have done so, but for Reverdy Johnson and his devilish speeches,[2] so that I have no messages to send, unless some one asks about us. Or perhaps I have, now I think of it. My poor friend Gaskell's mishap has cut me off from the William Herveys, with whom I was very intimate, and I never hear of them.[3] Call there one of these Sundays and write me about them. If you see the eldest one, Mina, tell her that her water-colors of Cannes form a conspicuous ornament to my room here. They are really very pretty now that I have had them framed with about two inches of gold margin. As for Augusta, you can assure her of my highest consideration. But for God's sake, don't allude to my departure last summer, for we were all mixed very deep in Gaskell's affair, and in their minds I am probably always remembered in connection with the sore subject of that engagement. In fact I should be very much embarrassed to pass this next season in London, almost as much so as Gaskell himself, especially with Lady Bristol and Lady Mary about. That was a rough affair, and I was very much involved in it.

Remember me too to Lady Goldsmid if you see her, and Miss Jekyll, and Mrs Russell Sturgis whom you had better call upon and to whom I owe a letter.[4] Write again soon and believe me

ever Yrs   H. B. Adams.

MS: MHi
1. Ralph C. Palmer (1839–1923), a barrister; he became a lifelong friend.
2. Reverdy Johnson (1796–1876), a senator from Maryland just appointed minister to England, toadied to British sympathizers to the Confederacy, recalled in 1869.
3. Lady Mary Hervey had abruptly broken her engagement to Gaskell.
4. Louisa Goldsmid (1819–1908), wife of Sir Francis Goldsmid (1808–1878), baronet, M.P., first Jewish barrister; Clara Jekyll (d. 1922), later Lady Henley; Julia Sturgis, third wife of Russell Sturgis (1805–1887), Massachusetts-born partner of Baring Brothers.

To Edward Atkinson

158 G Street. Washington
1 February. 1869.

My dear Mr Atkinson[1]
I have already a dozen ideas in my head which if elaborated would occupy me years. I shall note the suggestion you make and work it up, if

I get time, but from what I see here I suspect that our people may be properly divided into two classes, one which steals, the other which is stolen from; and we have got to take the matter up with a high hand and drag it into politics if we are to hope for success. If I am right, it follows that our time and labor will be most usefully spent in a regular hand-to-hand fight with corruption here under our eyes. To follow the protectionists over to England is to go off on a false scent. I would rather scarify a few of them personally as they stand. The whole root of the evil is in *political* corruption; theory has really not much to do with it.

You in Massachusetts are not in the Union. Butler is the only man who understands his countrymen and even he does not quite represent the dishonesty of our system. The more I study its working, the more dread I feel at the future. Our coming struggle is going to be harder than the anti-slavery fight, and though we may carry free-trade, I fear we shall be beaten on the wider field.

Are our Boston people mad that they petition against the Alabama Convention?[2] If ever Boston was interested in any matter of Government, she is interested in adopting this Convention. Its rejection means a determination on our part to have, sooner or later, a war with England, and I fear it will be rejected. If our friends are wise they will make all the Eastern Senators support the Treaty, for the West will try to shove us into a struggle in which we alone can be the sufferers.

Very truly Yrs   Henry Brooks Adams.

Edward Atkinson Esq.

MS: MHi

1. Edward Atkinson (1827–1905), Boston cotton manufacturer, economist, and political reformer.
2. The Johnson-Clarendon convention on adjudicating the *Alabama* and similar claims, signed Jan. 14, was now before the Senate.

To John Bright

158 G. Street. Washington. 3 February. 1869.

My dear Mr Bright

Allow me to offer you my congratulations on your coming into office.[1] Whether it is the best step for your own interests, I will not undertake to say, but that it was your duty, I have no doubt. I trust you will remain a long time in power.

I write just now for two reasons. Long before returning to America I had made up my mind to live in Washington, and, since the field of public position was by our arrangements practically shut to me, to devote myself to a literary career. About four months since, I followed out this purpose. I now live in Washington, and I write, not for the newspapers, but for more elaborate periodicals.

Unfortunately for me, I hold opinions upon two points, for which my English education and especially your own influence and that of Mr Cobden are principally responsible. On one side I have a warm feeling of goodwill to England, in spite of all she made me suffer. On the other hand, I am in general principles a firm free-trader. Both these doctrines are much out of favor here just now, and I consider that you are in some sort morally bound to give them all the support you can.

I shall probably soon be obliged to declare as publicly as possible the opinions of our new school here on the questions now before us. On the free-trade issue and our outrageous political corruption, far worse than anything you have to deal with, I know what to say and I shall say it without much caring whose toes I tread upon. But our foreign policy is a more delicate matter. I am told that the Claims Convention has no chance of ratification. Sumner tells me you have written to him anxiously about it.[2] I fear that Sumner will oppose it, and Grant is against it. I cannot conceive what their grounds are, and those I have heard are absolutely trivial. I want you to write me precisely how you feel about it, and I shall make use of your letter in the most effective way I can, without absolute publication. If you could do this so that I could have your opinions within a month, I think I could help the struggle.

Grant is silent and I have no news to write you. We cannot even guess who is to go into the Cabinet, nor what is then to happen. Grant's position is *very* difficult, between the Senate and the people, but he alone can do little. The reform we need must come from the people and the people show no signs of asking it.

In great haste

Very truly Yrs   Henry Brooks Adams.

MS: The British Library, John Bright Papers
1. Bright became president of the Board of Trade.
2. The arbitration treaty for payment of damages by England for losses caused by Confederate raiders was defeated in the Senate on April 13 when Sen. Charles Sumner attacked it as inadequate.

To John Bright

(Confidential)   Washington. 30 May. 1869.

My dear Mr Bright

Your very kind letter of 25th March arrived safely.[1] Since then the situation has been a good deal changed. You probably have more valuable American correspondents than I, but before I leave Washington to pass the summer with my family in the north, I want to answer your letter as carefully as I can. Perhaps you may catch from it some notion of our affairs such as your other correspondents would not think it worth while to give. At any rate I am so anxious about them that I will take the chance of your not reading me.

In the first place, our friend Sumner! I was always aware that you did not understand Sumner, and I suspect that since his speech you understand him still less than before. Do not credit him with too much brain. He passes everywhere either for worse or better than he is, merely because people over-rate his mind.

As he wrote you, the Convention would have been unanimously confirmed a year ago. But Reverdy Johnson's apparent courting of Laird and Roebuck, roused our people to wrath.[2] Seward had lost all control and was utterly unable to guide either the Senate or the new administration. Mr Sumner was now like a school-boy in vacation. The instant Seward's strong hand was removed, and Sumner found that popular feeling ran very strongly against the Treaty, he was inspired by the passion of seizing the direction of our foreign affairs, and I have no question that he had a policy in his mind which he wished to force upon the new Government. In a long article in the North American Review written before Sumner made his speech, I hinted what was the idea in his mind, and it was this. Public feeling, he would say, requires my statement of our wrongs; but it is not yet time to state the remedy; when the time comes I will ride the whirlwind, for which I am not responsible, until a peaceful result will be reached in the cession of territory—say the Hudson's Bay territory.

This was the identical policy you used to charge on Seward and I doubt that Seward did hesitate a moment as to the advantages offered by it, but Seward's mind was large enough to choose the straighter path.

The speech was applauded universally. I was alone in my opposition, for Seward had then gone. Do not believe any disavowal of Senator Grimes or anyone else.[3] I know, for I was here; and both in the press and in society I was alone, and not another voice was raised except by Mr Evarts and

G. T. Curtis.[4] The Senate did approve Sumner; so did the press; so did the people, and it was not till England began to scold, that our people began to hesitate.

But the Administration at once saw that this would never do, and that Sumner and the Senate must not be permitted to seize control of our foreign policy. Mr Fish therefore would have nothing to do with the speech, and Motley's instructions were not based upon it, as Mr Sumner had intended.[5]

Here Sumner's difficulties began. Ordered by the Administration to take his proper place, he did so, and supported the Secretary in an attempt to bring about a renewal of negotiations on a new basis. But here his whole project was knocked in the head by the President who took the bit in his teeth and obstinately declared that he did not want a settlement with England, as he preferred what he calls the "precedent"; that is, to do ourselves at some future time precisely those dishonorable acts of which we have so steadily complained when done by England.

So the matter now stands, so far as I can learn. The President whose mind works in a very narrow compass and in whose character vindictiveness is perhaps more strongly marked than any other trait, is heartily hostile to England, and follows the curious hint given in his curious inaugural. Mr Fish leans to Mr Seward's ideas, but cannot stir at present. Sumner is worried, and uneasy, and I am assured by persons near him, that he would like to retreat from his speech. Until either the President yields, or England gets into trouble, there seems to be no escape from our situation.

There remains the people, and here I confess my doubt. Certainly the eastern States would be unanimously opposed to a mischievous policy the moment they understood its true bearing on their interests. But I am not so certain about the West. I am inclined to think that no one can say with certainty what would be the result of throwing a war-policy into the field of western politics. Individually I know nothing of western sentiment, but I have little doubt that a war-fever once started would sweep all resistance before it, especially in the north-western States, where the temptation of seizing Canada is greatest. I do not want to be an alarmist, but I cannot see any likelihood that either the Republican or the Democratic party would dare to advocate peace if once war were proposed, and whatever individuals may say, these party organisations have little honesty in them and are ruled by ignorant and ambitious men.

How easily the evil might be done, is obvious. If our Government were now to reopen the question, its new demands would necessarily tend to assume before long the character of an ultimatum, and if this were absolutely rejected, it is absurd to suppose that the relations of the two countries could be other than critical. For this reason I am glad that Gen. Grant has refused to reopen the subject diplomatically. To wait is dangerous but it is still more dangerous to act.

I think in a year or two, circumstances will be changed. We have got to meet a period of serious financial pressure which will test our strength severely. We have not yet seen the end of repudiation and the repudiators to a man will advocate a war. We have much to learn about ourselves and the many dangers of the nation. Sooner or later the old parties must break up. I do not know what will then happen, but things look to me very unpleasantly merely as a matter of internal politics and I have already gone so far as to declare my firm belief that without large internal reforms our Government and Union will go to pieces. By that time we shall understand better the bearings of our foreign policy.

Meanwhile England can do much to remove danger, but the essential point is that she should without delay sever her political connection with Canada and all her territory on our continent. That is the key of the difficulty. If after that concession to us, we still make war, we shall hurt ourselves more than you.

This you may think all rubbish and perhaps it is so. At any rate remember me to your family and believe me ever very truly Yrs

Henry Brooks Adams.

Pray do not quote me to anyone, least of all to Americans.

MS: The British Library, John Bright Papers

1. John Bright wrote privately to HA on the basis of his wartime friendship with CFA and the whole family.
2. John Laird (1805–1874), Scottish builder of iron ships for the Confederacy.
3. James Wilson Grimes (1816–1872), Republican senator from Iowa.
4. George Ticknor Curtis (1812–1894), writer on constitutional law.
5. Hamilton Fish (1808–1893), secretary of state; John Lothrop Motley (1814–1877), historian, appointed minister to Great Britain 1869.

To *Charles Milnes Gaskell*

Washington. 23 November. 1869.

Dear Boy:

I sit down to begin you a letter, not because I have received one since my last, but because it is one of the dankest, foggiest, and dismalest of November nights, and, as usual when the sun does not shine, I am as out of sorts as a man may haply be, and yet live through it. Do you remember how, on such evenings we have taken our melancholy tea together in your room in Stratford Place? My heart would rejoice to do it now, but solitude is my lot. This season of the year grinds the very soul out of me. My nerves lose their tone; my teeth ache, and my courage falls to the bottomless bottom of infinitude. Death stalks about me, and the whole of Gray's grisly train,[1] and I am afraid of them, not because life is an object, but because my nerves are upset. I would give up all my pleasures willingly if I could only be a mouse, and sleep three months at a time. Well! one can't have life as one would, but if I ever take too much laudanum, the coroner's jury may bring in a verdict of wilful murder against the month of November. Bah! I never felt it half so keenly when I was in England where there is never any sun.

Now then, where may we sometimes meet and by the fire help waste a sullen day, what time we can from the sad season gaining?[2] And to think that the brute Robert is happy and gay in the sunshine of Rome! I am as lonely as a cat here. Acquaintances without number I have, but no companion. And what avails it to be intimate with all men if one comes home at five o'clock and abhors life! Send a decent Britisher here, do!

Do you know I have taken up the ever youthful Horace Walpole again, and make him my dinner companion. What surprises me most is that he is so extremely like ourselves; not so clever of course, but otherwise he might be a letter-writer of today. I perpetually catch myself thinking of it all as of something I have myself known, until I trip over a sword, or discover there were no railways then, or reflect that Lord Salisbury and not Lord Carteret lives over the way.[3] But all seems astonishingly natural to me; strangely in contrast to what it once seemed. If we didn't know those people—Primoministerio Palmerstonis—then we knew some one for all the world like them. Florence too! Peste! how little the world has changed in a century. Hanbury-Williams and Watkin-Wynn, Hervey; Arlington Street;[4] I know I shall find Lady Sebright further on, and Lady Salisbury will come in for a wipe.

What! shall I imitate H.W. and tell you about this Court; a pack of boobies and scoundrels who have all the vices of H.W's time, with none of its wit or refinement? Or force either, for the matter of that! For where to find a Walpole or a Pitt here, I am at a loss to know.[5] We are all Pelhams,[6] and our President is as narrow, as ignorant, and as prejudiced as ever a George among you. Your friend—que voici—alone, and a few others, have any brain. But what of that! The world goes on, and I send you herewith my last political pamphlet which, I have reason to know, represents the opinions of a minority, and, I think, of a majority of the Cabinet. The violent attack on the Treasury has done me no harm.[7]

I am writing—writing—writing. You must take the New York Nation if you want to read me. I have written that animal Reeve a letter, offering him an article—such an article!—and he does not even answer it.[8] Damme! am I to be treated in this way! I have written to Palgrave to make advances to the Quarterly, and I will make my article *SUPERB* to disgust Reeve.[9] I enclose you a puff—from my own paper. But it is written by a Britisher.[10]

Adieu.

MS: MHi

1. The "grisly troop" in Thomas Gray's "Ode on a Distant Prospect of Eton College" (1747).
2. From Milton's sonnet XX, "Lawrence of virtuous father . . ." (1673).
3. Robert Cecil (1830–1903) became 3rd marquess of Salisbury in 1868; Lord John Carteret (1690–1763), political adversary of Horace Walpole's father.
4. Contemporaries of Horace Walpole. Walpole's London residence was in Arlington Street.
5. Sir Robert Walpole (1676–1745), Horace Walpole's father, prime minister 1715–1717, 1721–1742; William Pitt (1708–1778), sometime Whig prime minister, friend of the American colonies.
6. Corrupt followers of Sir Robert Walpole.
7. *Civil Service Reform*, reprint of HA's article in the *North American Review* 109 (Oct. 1869), 504–533.
8. Henry Reeve (1813–1895), editor of the *Edinburgh Review.*
9. Francis Turner Palgrave (1824–1897), poet and art critic, lifelong friend of HA.
10. The reviewer in the *Nation* 9 (Nov. 11, 1869), 415–416, singled out HA's essay as "by far the most striking and readable."

To Thomas F. Bayard

2017 G Street. Washington.
Tuesday. 8 Feb. 1870.

My dear Mr Bayard[1]

Will you excuse me for doing a little lobbying? As my interference can do no harm, and does not even require a word of reply from you, I venture to ask you a favor.

The Census Bill now before the Senate, is, as you know, a very elaborate piece of work, the result of eight or nine months faithful labor on the part of the very most faithful of our Congressmen.[2] Your Committee, following Conkling, has advised, after a few hour's consideration, the entire abandonment of all that has been done.[3] That Mr Conkling should take such ground, is not encouraging to those of us who wish to improve legislation.

For my own part, I have no argument to make in favor of the Bill. But it is strongly favored by those whose opinion I have most respect for. The favor I have to ask of you is that before committing yourself finally against it, you will have a talk with Wells, or Garfield, or F. A. Walker, or Secretary Cox.[4] If after hearing their side of the question you still decide to follow Conkling, I have nothing to say. As a member of the Committee, your word is of importance, and all our side asks is that the Senate shall act understandingly.

I wish I had known earlier that you were on the Committee. I should have tried to interest you in the success of a measure which all of us reform men think very important.[5]

Very truly Yrs   Henry Brooks Adams.

Senator T.F. Bayard.

MS: DLC, Bayard

1. Thomas F. Bayard (1828–1898), Democratic senator from Delaware 1869–1885.
2. The bill for the ninth census, designed by future president James A. Garfield (1831–1881), then Republican representative from Ohio.
3. Roscoe Conkling (1829–1888), Republican senator from New York 1867–1881 and party boss, opposed reform and reformers.
4. David A. Wells (1828–1898), Massachusetts economist, special commissioner of the revenue 1865–1870; Francis A. Walker (1840–1897), special deputy to Wells; Jacob D. Cox (1828–1900), governor of Ohio 1866–1868, secretary of the interior 1869–1870.
5. Bayard voted with the majority on Feb. 9 to reject the bill.

To Charles Milnes Gaskell

Washington. 7 March. 1870.

My dear Carlo

In a sort of kind of a half way, I thought there might be a letter from you this morning, as my last was dated the 2d February, but if there is one on the way, it is stuck in the snow which was falling all day yesterday. Our winter comes in the spring. As usual, I have nothing to say, except that I am well and have gone through a pleasant season and am now going to church every day, that is to the church door as the young women come from afternoon service. You know me better than to expect more. I have been busy as a Roman flea in May, and have written a piece of intolerably impudent political abuse for the North American for April—but it is finance and you needn't read it—where I am to say that never since the days of Cleon and Aristophanes was a great nation managed by such incompetent men as our leaders in Congress during the rebellion—bien entendu that I am Aristophanes. The editor has not acknowledged it yet, but begged for it piteously.[1] By the way, did you ever receive my pamphlet? I sent you a second copy, but the devil is in the posts. At the same time I write about two articles a month in the Nation, and if I want to be very vituperative, I have a New York daily paper to trust.[2] So I come on and the people here are beginning to acknowledge me as some one to be considered. In my review of the Session, next July, I am going to make an example or two *in terrorem* and go to England to escape retaliation. There! this is all there is about myself, and as for my surroundings I can only say that now Lent has come, society is at an end, and I am left alone, or to the resource of evening visits which may or may not be pleasant. The winter has been very agreeable to me because no other men have been here who could at all interfere with me, and I have had it all to suit myself. As for the other people, many of them are decidedly agreeable and there has actually been no scandal nor quarrelling nor even much ill-nature. For all that amusement, I rely on England. I have read the first day's proceedings in the Mordaunt case, and was delighted with it.[3] As I happen to be in a good humor today, I will say that I am glad to feel satisfied that the girl was really insane. But it's hard on Mordaunt to have—I was going to use a word of Swift's and Defoe's—himself as he has, since he has not proved that he's not cuckolded, and has made himself very ridiculous. And shouts of demoniac laughter must welcome Sir F. Johnstone through this world and the next. What an introduction to society! Who is the man? Do you know him? and whose set is he?

I was wrong about Coore and Jackson. They had not gone when I last wrote. My letter to you was just finished and still on my table, sealed and stamped, when they came in to take leave. So they are now gone for good and all, and I have no more to say about them, except that they were well-behaved and very-very-very English. Lyulph Stanley has not appeared and I hope by this time he is in China or any place he likes that is further away.[4] The members of your Legation tell me that there are some other strolling Britishers in town, but they disturb me not.

You must remember poor Hartman Kuhn in Rome![5] He was a good fellow, though he had too much of the Philadelphian in him, and his wife was a very attractive little woman. I suppose you must have heard of his death at Rome by his horse falling back on him. It was a terrible affair, but I have not heard the details, and am too sorry for him to wish to hear anything so painful. My sister, however, in Florence, has been much distressed about it.

Since my last I have not had a line from any of you. Even Palgrave has not written, and I am waiting to ask him to introduce me—absent—to the editor of the Quarterly, if the Quarterly has an editor. Ecco perché! if that is good Italian. I am about to write an article on a very curious and melodramatic gold speculation that took place in New York last September. It involves a good deal of libelous language which I can't well publish here. I wrote to Reeve offering it to him. He, after three months delay, has just replied that he wants nothing controversial about currency. If this is a pretence, or if he really thinks I am ass enough to open a currency discussion instead of telling a story which has no parallel, I am equally contented to be done with him, but I mean to write the article all the same, and I will offer it to the Quarterly if I can get an introduction to the editor. So I want Palgrave to introduce me. Voilà tout! He need take no further responsibility, and if the Quarterly doesn't want it, I will on coming over find some editor who does. J'y tiens to make Reeve sorry to have lost the best thing his rotten old Review has had a chance to get into its July number. As I have been pulling wires behind the Congressional Committee of Investigation, and have been up to my neck in the whole thing, I know all that is known.[4]

Aweel! aweel!! I have no more to say at this moment, so I will lay this by, and see if anything comes from you tomorrow.

Tuesday.—Nothing at all. So I will close you up and put you into the letter box. I must now go to settle up my income tax,—which amounts to one pound,—to talk with the Special Commissioner of the Revenue about politics, and to lunch with Jephtha's daughter (Chase, C. J.) whose remarks I told her the other day were "twaddle and cant," and I must reconcile.[6]

Ever Yr   H.

MS: MHi
1. Allusion to "The Legal-Tender Act" (with Francis A. Walker), *North American Review* 110 (April 1870), 299–327.
2. The New York *Evening Post*.
3. Sir Charles Mordaunt sued his wife for divorce, a proceeding in which the Prince of Wales's seventeen innocuous letters to her figured among the twenty letters printed by Mordaunt.
4. Edward Lyulph Stanley (1839–1925), later 4th Baron Stanley of Alderley, had been visiting the United States.
5. Hartman Kuhn, brother-in-law of HA.
6. Catherine ("Kate") Chase Sprague (1840–1899) was "Jephtha's daughter" (Judges 11–12) because she was regarded as having sacrificed herself by marrying Sen. William Sprague for his money in an attempt to make her father, Chief Justice Salmon P. Chase, president.

To Charles Milnes Gaskell

Hotel d'Amérique.
Bagni di Lucca. 8 July. 1870.

My dear Carlo
Had I been able to write anything satisfactory I should have written a week ago. As it was, I preferred to wait for your letter which arrived this morning. Many thanks for it. In return I will give you an account of my adventures which have not been gay.

On quitting you I travelled through to Paris where I had four hours for breakfast and bath, and went on to Macon where I was delayed nine hours and went to bed. Crossed the Cenis Wednesday, and reached this place at four o'clock Thursday afternoon, without adventure or incident of any sort.

I found the hotel turned into a sort of camp, and a dozen of my sister's friends regularly keeping guard. Italians, English and Americans, a motley but rather agreeable crew, surrounded her bed-side, and acted in regular relays as nurses, night and day. I found that my sudden summons was owing to the fact that lock-jaw had set in, and for a week my poor sister had been struggling in the very jaws of death, which were by no means locked against her.[1]

It is hardly worth while to describe to you the details of the eight days that have since passed. They have been in many ways the most trying and terrible days I ever had. The struggle has been awful. We have had a series of ups and downs which would test the courage of Hercules. We have swum in cloroform, morphine, opium, and every kind of most violent counter-agent and poison like nicotine and Calabar bean. At times we have abandoned all hope. One night my sister, reduced to the last extremity, gasped farewell to us all, gave all her dying orders, and for two hours we thought every gasp was to be the end. Her breath stopped, her pulse ceased beating, her struggles ended, a dozen people at her bedside went down on their knees, and my brother-in-law and I dropped our hands and drew a long breath of relief to think that the poor child's agony was over even at the cost of suffocation. But after nearly half a minute of absolute silence, the pulse started again, the rattling in the throat recommenced, and presently she waved her arm as though she were ordering death away, and to our utter astonishment commanded us to bring her some nourishment. It has been the same thing ever since. Such a struggle for life is almost worth seeing. She never loses courage nor head. She knows perfectly what is the matter, and her own danger, but in the middle of her most awful convulsions, so long as she can articulate at all, she gives her own orders and comes out with sallies of fun and humorous comments which set us all laughing in spite of our terror at the most awful crises. Of course her talking is only a growl between her teeth and even this often quite inarticulate, but we have learned to understand it pretty well, and habit has made even so horrible a disease as this, so familiar that we stroke and joke it. Indeed the situation, desperate as it is, has its amusing side. Our friends come out in strong colors under such a test as this. They show qualities which go far to redeem human nature. Such kindness I never had seen in mere friends of society, and I can overlook a deal of faults if they are backed up by such courage and patient devotion. As for me, I was at first a wretched coward, but now I am hardened to the impressions and face a convulsion, with death behind it, as coolly as my sister herself.

I can't tell you what will be the end. I haven't a notion how long it will last. I can see no essential difference between the situation now and a week since. As she is still alive and strong after fifteen days of incessant struggle and after swallowing more deadly poison than would have killed all of us about her, who are well, I hope she may pull through. But I ask no questions and make no plans. I am with her about fifteen hours a day, and seldom leave the house at all. I am writing this letter while I attend her, so its style is a trifle eccentric, but you must put up with it for the occasion. Enough for the present. My regards to every one. Give Mrs Sturgis news of me if you can.

Ever Yr   H. B. Adams.

MS: MHi

1. Louisa Adams Kuhn died July 13.

To *Charles Milnes Gaskell*

Washington. 29 Sept. 1870.

My dear Carlo

I wish you had seen me sailing out of the harbor at Queenstown. It blew hard from the south-west, dead ahead, and I, who had been ashore all day, went incontinently to bed, and remained there much the better part of 48 hours, during which the water slopped over us as though we were a tin pan. The voyage on the whole, however, was passable. I made Miss Nilsson's acquaintance, and found a number of friends on board. Mr Mundella, M.P., was also with us.[1] I do not know Mr M., but once happening to go near the spot where he was lecturing an admiring audience, I heard him burst into an eloquent panegyric on John Bright's oratory; "The first orator in the world," said he: "Talk of your Demosthenes and your Euripides, they're nothing to him." I retired in silence. Who knows but that Mr Mundella was right! Euripides might have been surprised at the company he was in, but I was not.

I passed the custom-house safely, unshorn, and reached home without any accident. I found my family as well and as cheerful as I could have expected, only one of my aunts with whom I was very intimate here, had suddenly died in the interval.[2] I found myself growing in consequence. My last article had not only been reprinted entire by several newspapers, but the party press had thought it necessary to answer it, and I cut out some of their notices to send over to you, but forgot to bring them with me.

What is more, I am told that the democratic national committee reprinted it in pamphlet form and mean to circulate two hundred and fifty thousand copies of it. If I get a copy I will send it to you as a curiosity.[3] You see I have a tolerably large audience at least.

But what is much more interesting is that on my return home I found the question of the professorship sprung upon me again in a very troublesome way. Not only the President of the College and the Dean, made a very strong personal appeal to me, but my brothers were earnest about it and my father leaned the same way. I hesitated a week, and then I yielded. Now I am, I believe assistant professor of history at Harvard College with a salary of £400 a year, and two hundred students, the oldest in the college, to whom I am to teach mediaeval history, of which, as you are aware, I am utterly and grossly ignorant. Do you imagine I am appalled at this prospect? Not a bit of it! Impavidum ferient![4] I gave the college fair warning of my ignorance, and the answer was that I knew just as much as anyone else in America knew on the subject, and I could teach better than anyone that could be had. So there I am. My duties begin in a fortnight and I am on here to break up my establishment and transfer my goods to Cambridge where I am fitting up rooms regardless of expense. For I should add that what with one thing and another my income is about doubled, and I have about £1200 a year. With the professorship I take the North American Review and become its avowed editor. So if you care to write thirty pages of abuse of people and houses in England, including Sir Roger, the Sketchbook, and country squires in general, send the manuscript to me and if you are abusive enough you shall have £20.[5]

At the same time Will Everett accepts a tutorship either in Greek or Latin, I forget which. I am glad he has at last gained his chance of success, and if he succeeds he will no doubt be made professor. I have not yet seen him, but am told he is pleased. He has taken a house in Cambridge and will live there.

I think I have now written you news enough and you can reflect upon it at your leisure. My engagement is for five years but I don't expect to remain so long, and my great wish is to get hold of the students' imaginations for my peculiar ideas. The worst of the matter is that I shall be tied tight to the college from the 1st October, to the last of June, which will seriously interfere with my freedom of movement when you come over. This, however, must be managed as we best can. I get three months long vacation in summer, but this is all, except for a fortnight at Christmas. I have nine hours a week in the lecture room, and am absolutely free to teach what I please within the dates 800–1649. I am responsible only to the college Government, and I am brought in to strengthen the reforming party in the

University, so that I am sure of strong backing from above. You can fancy that my influence on the youthful mind is likely to be peculiar to say the least. And yet my predecessor was turned out because he was a Comtist!!![6]

I came on here yesterday, and am very hot, very lonely, and very hard run. I passed an hour today with Secretary Fish, who was very talkative, but there are few of my political friends left in power now, and these few will soon go out. This reconciles me to going away, though I hate Boston and am very fond of Washington. By-the-way, I see John Hervey's name in the papers as having arrived, and Tom Hughes is flying about.[7]

We have an awful drought. At Quincy everything is literally burned and nothing like it ever known. Since coming home I have been roasted.

Ever affecly   H. B. Adams.

MS: MHi

1. Christine Nilsson (1843–1921), Swedish opera singer; Anthony John Mundella (1825–1897), M.P. 1868–1897, industrial reformer.
2. Mary Hellen Adams had died Aug. 31.
3. "The Session," *North American Review* 111 (July 1870), 29–62. In the election year 1872, the article was published as *The Administration—A Radical Indictment!*
4. *Impavidum ferient*: [If the shattered sphere collapse] the ruins will strike him undismayed; Horace, *Odes*, III, 3.
5. Sir Roger de Coverley, the fictitious country squire in Joseph Addison's *Spectator* papers (1711–1712).
6. John Fiske (1842–1901), popularizer of Darwin, Herbert Spencer, and Auguste Comte, gave lectures on "positive philosophy" in 1869–70. When his nomination as instructor in history for the spring of 1870 came before the Board of Overseers, his appointment was almost rejected on the grounds that he was a Positivist. CFA cast the deciding vote in his favor. He was appointed a university lecturer for 1870–71 and an assistant librarian in 1872.
7. John W. Hervey (1841–1902), third son of the late marquess of Bristol; Thomas Hughes (1822–1896), reformer politician.

To Jacob D. Cox

Harvard College. 28 Nov. 1870.

My dear Sir

Your very kind letter of the 25th has just arrived and I hasten to reply to it. If your manuscript is mailed on the 7th Dec., it will be in good time. Let me know if you wish to have the proofs sent to you.

Our New York meeting was very satisfactory. I will try to give you an idea of its results.

There were present, besides the officers of the Free Trade League, my brother Charles and myself; Nordhof of the Evening Post, Godkin of the Nation, Bowles of the Springfield Republican, Horace White of the Chicago Tribune, Grosvenor of the St. Louis Democrat, Mr Bryant, D. A. Wells, Brinkerhoff, and a few outsiders, making twenty or more present.[1] No democrats were asked, and it was understood that the democratic influence was to be held quiet outside.

The first business related to the organisation of the next House. White and Brinkerhoff reported to us that Blaine had sought an interview with them separately and had declared himself satisfied that public opinion and the composition of the House demanded a recognition of our claims.[2] He then pledged himself to give us the Committee of Ways and Means, and any other positions that might be required of him, even beyond our expectations. The question was whether to accept his offer, or to force a contest.

The debate on this point showed that while the League leaned towards a rupture with the Republican party and an alliance with the democrats, all the members of the press favored a different policy. Here at the outset it became evident that neither White nor Grosvenor nor ourselves intended to use the "new party" except as a threat, for the present. It was determined to support Blaine on the avowed ground that he had become one of us, and to throw on the republicans the responsibility of a rupture if they dared try it.

The next debate rose on the question of widening our platform. To my great satisfaction I found that the change in feeling among our friends since last Spring, was very marked. The western men all said that the issue of Civil Service Reform was a stronger one before the people than that of Revenue Reform. It was more easily understood and less easily answered. The League rather resisted its adoption as a part of our system, but it was nevertheless decided that the two measures should be advocated together and that for the present our agitation should be restricted, so far as we acted as a body, to these two issues, although there were others ready to be taken up in case of further success. In this connection I may add that your removal was considered as having more seriously shaken the republican party, than any other event.

Finally, we discussed the propriety of effecting a permanent organisation. We proposed the appointment of a central committee with a view to calling a convention in the summer in case Congress should fail to act. Here a serious difficulty arose in the selection of the Committee. I was soon satisfied that there was great danger of our committing a serious blunder by acting without sufficient preparation, and when it was clear that your name must be put first on the list, without consulting you, I turned round and with Nordhof and my brother, resisted the movement to the utmost. After a long struggle we carried our point and adjourned without naming the committee. As it now stands, we are to wait the doings of Congress, holding our Convention as a threat over the party. Next spring, if a Convention seems desirable, we shall issue a call, signed as generally as possible, and on this it will be necessary for us to have your declared support.

I am sorry to say that the "dodges" as you call them, of the party hacks against you, received so little attention from us that I can scarcely tell what the opinion about them was. The tone of the meeting was one of indifference or contempt for the administration, which was scarcely mentioned at all. We considered it as out of the field—broken down—and our only doubt was whether it was best to break the party down too, or to put it on its good behavior. As for doubt of our own power, I was amused to see how little there was of it. I think your small enemies are best left to chatter.

These were the results of our talk, and the advance since last Spring was very marked. I think you will perhaps strike most effectually by recognising, and, if they meet your approval, by adopting, and leading the movement thus marked out, but this is of course only a suggestion as editor, in case you propose to embrace the general subject in your article. I believe, however, that Blaine's negotiation is for the present confidential.

I saw the Evarts's in New York. I wish you could carry him with you into our movement, but I doubt it. He seems to me to be too careful of his own reputation. Allison was there, also, and in the closest connection with us.[3] Schurz did not venture, but I have an excellent letter from him.

Ever truly Yrs   Henry Adams.

MS: OO

1. Charles Nordhoff (1830–1901), journalist and author, editor of the New York *Evening Post* 1861–1871, Washington correspondent of the New York *Herald* 1874–1890; Samuel Bowles (1826–1878); William Mason Grosvenor (1835–1900), editor of the St. Louis *Democrat,* manager of Schurz's senatorial campaign; William Cullen Bryant (1794–1878) was chief editor of the New York *Evening Post* 1829–1878; Roeliff Brinkerhoff (1828–1911), Cincinnati lawyer active in reform. This was the beginning of the insurgent Liberal Republican movement against President Grant. It brought together free traders, revenue and civil service reformers, and others. Cox broke with Grant and resigned as secretary of the interior.
2. James Gillespie Blaine (1830–1893) of Maine, Republican representative 1863–1876, speaker of the House 1869–1875, senator 1876–1881, and perennial aspirant to the presidency. HA's friends perceived intimations of reform when in fact Blaine characteristically was trying to make a deal.
3. William Boyd Allison (1829–1908) of Iowa, Republican representative 1863–1871, senator 1873–1908. HA and his friends misjudged his apparent sympathy with the Liberal Republican cause.

To Charles Milnes Gaskell

Harvard College. 19 Dec. 1870.

My dear Carlo

It's an age since I wrote, but if you will credit the alarming fact, I am now driven to use the official time of the College to give to you. Here I sit, at the regular meeting of the College Faculty, while some thirty twaddlers are discussing questions of discipline around me, and I have to hear what they say, while I indulge you in all the charms and fascinations of my style. This is what it is to be a Professor, not to say an editor. I have not had a clear hour of time for a month. I have read more heavy German books and passed more time in the printing-office; I have written more letters on business, and read more manuscripts of authors; I have delivered more lectures about matters I knew nothing of, to men who cared nothing about them; and I have had my nose ground down more closely to my double grindstone, than ever a cruel Providence can have considered possible. My happy carelessness of life for the last ten years has departed, and I am a regular old carthorse of the heaviest sort. As for society, I have not seen the hem of a female garment since I came out here. Life has resolved itself into editing and professing. I always swore I never would descend to work, but it is done. Lo! the poor fallen-one!

The curious part of it all is that I don't dislike it so much as I expected. I am so busy that I have not had the time to think whether I enjoyed myself or not, and now the Christmas holidays are nearly here, and I am so nearly half through the year, at least in labor, that it quite bewilders me to think how time goes. I wish you would try a few months of good, hard, work, when you have to count your minutes to keep abreast of the team, and then tell me how you like it. I believe it would do you good. But how these old buffers do bore me! They talk! talk! talk! Ugh!! I wish I could scalp 'em.

Have I sent you my circular? No? I will! It is grand, and involves the deepest interests of literature. I am sending it to all mankind, and of course mankind rushes to see it. Apropos! I have never sent you the reply which Senator Howe of Wisconsin made to my "Session." He blackguards me and all my family to the remotest generation. He calls me a begonia! a plant, I am told. To be abused by a Senator is my highest ambition, and I am now quite happy.[1] My only regret is that I cannot afford to hire a Senator to abuse me permanently. That, however, might pall in time, like plum-pudding or agra-dolce sauce.

At the end of this week, just as soon as I have got my January Review off my shoulders I shall go on to Washington for the holidays. This is the only recess I get for six months, and I want to make the most of it. What do I do after getting there? I go to my dentist's, oh my friend! Yes! I pass a fortnight with my dentist. At any rate he will stop my talking for a time.

Will Everett is here in the room. Shall I ask him whether he has any message to send you? I will——

He says he is going to write to you himself and send you some of his publications.

By the way, I am told that his children's books are not at all bad.[2] Perhaps your mind after Siluria, will be ready to unbend to them. I see poor old Murchison has gone up.[3] He ought to, after such a work. Will is now making a speech. Heaven bless him! Lord, how dull they all are!

What a droll idea it is that you should be running about England, visiting people, and I shut up in this Botany Bay, working like a scavenger. Lord bless me! Do those people really exist, or did I dream it all, after reading Horace Walpole and eating a heavy dinner? I doubt your existence at times, and am not altogether certain about my own. Give my tender love to Gretchen—I mean Lady Margaret. What dress does she wear now? How are the Marguerites?

By the bye! Do you know that I hope to appear soon at the bar of the Old Bailey, or whichever of your Courts has the jurisdiction? James McHenry wants to sue me for a libel.[4] I have written over that this is precisely what would suit me, and that he may try it if he likes. You will, I doubt not, hear of it, if the Westminster Review is brought into Court. Perhaps it would bring me over to England again as I mean to hurt him if he gives me a chance.

I went to New York a month ago to a political meeting, and we laid vast and ambitious projects for the future.

But the Meeting is breaking up, and I must break up too! Thank the Lord! The clack is passed for one week, and a week hence I shall be in Washington.

24 Dec.   I have been too busy to finish the above, and now I start for Washington in an hour, for my holidays. Nothing new from anyone. I am just *done!* Run to death by printers and students. But my work is finished and time is up. I am going to have some fun.

Ever Yrs   Henry Adams.

MS: MHi

1. Timothy O. Howe, *Political History, the Republican Party Defended. A Reviewer Reviewed* (broadside reprinted from *Wisconsin State Journal*, Oct. 7).

2. *Changing Base, or, What Edward Rice Learned at School* (1869); *Double Play, or, How Joe Hardy Chose His Friends* (1870); and others.
3. Sir Roderick Impey Murchison (1792–1871), geologist, *The Silurian System* (1838), active in London society, was struck by paralysis in Nov.
4. James McHenry (1817–1891), British entrepreneur, largest stockholder in the failed Atlantic and Great Western Railway. In "The New York Gold Conspiracy" HA stated that McHenry used his influence on Gould's behalf to plant a deceptive financial article in the *New York Times.*

To Charles Eliot Norton

Harvard College. 13 January. 1871.

My dear Mr Norton

I should have written to you some time ago if I had not been so over-whelmed with work as to reduce me to despair. I now feel a little easier, having got my first number of the North American out and my classes fairly into their work, but even now I am rather ill at ease in the harness and find myself unable to keep up with my correspondents.

Of my success with the Review I am far from sure. As you know I took it as a last resource, since no one else could be found, and at a moment when it was very doubtful whether the publishers would not decide to drop it at once. They determined to try me for one year. If I can make the Review pay for itself, it will go on. If not, it must die. And I do not yet know what the result will be.

I have, however, succeeded in getting hold of Osgood, who has allowed me to change in many ways the business management, and who has really done everything I have asked.[1] If the experiment under these favorable conditions, still fails, I know no resource but to let the Review expire.

I trust that you are not idle in a literary way, merely because you are abroad. I want an article from you on the present condition of Italy. I think it a subject for a philosopher, and I believe you can treat it admirably if you will.[2]

As for the Administration and its appointments or removals from office, I am now happily without even the power of asking a question. I was at Washington last week and found anarchy ruling our nation. I don't know who has power or is responsible, but whoever it is, I cannot find him, and no one confesses to any more knowledge. The official figure-heads at all events are not the ones in power, and it is no use to seek any favor from them. I have not a notion how to help Mr Marsh.[3]

I will try to put more energy into the literary notices. But the truth is, even if I had them all written by a Macaulay or a Sainte Beuve, such is the condition of things that a good page of advertisements would outweigh them all in value to the Review. The first and vital problem is the financial one, and it is now demonstrated that mere literary success will not solve this, though without literary success there is no chance of reaching up to the problem at all. Articles enough, and good enough, I can get, but a page of advertisements would offer me more attractions than the cleverest page of criticism I ever saw.

Allow me to suggest, however, that I believe the Italians print books from time to time, and that an occasional notice of their efforts would not be out of place in the Review.

As for my professorship, the less said of that, the better. A madder choice I can't conceive than that of me to teach medieval history, but they said there was no one better, so I took it as I did the Review, to relieve Gurney's difficulty. It amuses me, certainly, but I doubt whether the professorship was established for just that object. Perhaps in time I may learn something about it, but thus far the only merit of my instruction has been its originality; one hundred youths at any rate have learned facts and theories for which in after life they will hunt the authorities in vain, unless, as I trust, they forget all they have been told. The effect upon our historical criticism, hereafter, will, I imagine, be startling, at least to the mere book-worms of effete Europe.

I suppose you hear regularly from this curious corner of the world, which only the perversity of human nature ever could have conceived to be fit for the existence of animated objects. We are enjoying after our pure-intellectual manner the charms of our season, with the thermometer at zero or at 70 as pleases God. I am in some huge rooms in the old President's-house, and am glad to keep my thermometer up to 40. The University moves on in its established course, and the President is very active. Boston I rarely see, not liking midnight expeditions in mid-winter. I hope you meditate a return shortly. You will find everyone glad to welcome you back.

Pray write from time to time and believe me

Ever truly Yrs   Henry Adams.

MS: MH

1. James Ripley Osgood (1836–1892), partner in Field, Osgood and Company, publishers of the *North American Review.*
2. No such article appeared.
3. George Perkins Marsh (1801–1882) of Vermont, philologist and former U.S. representative, minister to Italy 1861–1882.

To *Charles Milnes Gaskell*

Cambridge. 8 Feb. 1872.

My dear Carl

I had barely put your or rather my last to you in the post, when one arrived from you of the 7th Jan. and now I have your note of the 13th with the Saturday adjoined. Your puff of my poor work is judicious and handsome, better than anything else I have seen on it. As for the Pall Mall, its man has got the wrong book, and reviewed a little publication of my brother's in 1869.[1] I never saw a stupider performance. He has evolved title and author out of his own imagination or memory. However, it probably answers an equally good purpose as an advertisement, and as for the book itself, it is now an old story and must float the best way it can. I have not yet received your notice of Denison, but expect it daily.

From a retired and dignified Professor I have come out again as a social butterfly and waste most of my time at balls where I no longer dance, and in calls where I have no business to be. I still have a contemptible weakness for women's society and blush at the follies I commit. Only last Saturday I made a sensation by giving a luncheon in my rooms here, at which I had the principal beauty of the season and three other buds, with my sister to preside; a party of eleven, and awfully fashionable and larky. They came out in the middle of a fearful snowstorm, and I administered a mellifluous mixture known as champagne cocktails to the young women before sitting down to lunch. There was a matron to do respectability who had known twenty summers and was married a few months since. They made an uproarious noise and have destroyed forever my character for dignity in the College. I assure you, the young women in this land are lively to go, and the curious thing about it is that, so far as I know, these Boston girls are steady as you like. In this Arcadian society sexual passions seem to be abolished. Whether it is so or not, I can't say, but I suspect both men and women are cold, and love only with great refinement. How they ever reconcile themselves to the brutalities of marriage, I don't know.

Your people appear to be making no end of row about the Geneva Arbitration. I can't for the life of me understand what it's about, but I suppose we shall find out. Only I certainly can't compliment Mr Gladstone on his diplomacy. A worse position than he puts himself into if he now breaks up the Commission, I can't conceive, but I suspect that he is driven into some folly or other by one of those utterly imaginary alarms which every now and then run away with us poor idiotic nations. I recommend him to have and to teach a little more quiet to the excitable Bull. The utter astonishment which has seized our people at the goings-on of the London press, is very ludicrous. They don't know what the deuce has got into England and are hesitating whether to laugh or swear.

I suppose my father must be in England at about this time, and not very well pleased at the course things have taken.[2] I confess to being a little nervous myself, for a break-up of the Commission would throw our foreign affairs into the control of a pretty dangerous influence. And I want to go to Europe this year and be a swell.

I am about to dine with the President of the University to meet the Governor of the State![3] Hey! Sounds grand, I guess! And to go to a very select ball afterwards! Quel bonheur d'être professeur!

Ever Yr   H.

MS: MHi

1. Gaskell's review of *Chapters of Erie and Other Essays* appeared in the *Saturday Review* 33 (Jan. 13, 1872), 54–55. The book was a joint publication, containing five essays by HA and three by CFA2. The *Pall Mall Gazette* (Jan. 10, 1872) reviewed Charles's essay "A Chapter of Erie," which had been expanded to a small book.
2. HA's father, who was serving as the U.S. representative to the Geneva Arbitration, returned to the United States when the negotiations were temporarily suspended to allow the public clamor to subside.
3. William Washburn (1820–1887) of Greenfield, Mass., Republican representative 1863–1871, governor 1872–1873, senator 1874–1875.

To Brooks Adams

Cambridge. 3 March. 1872.

My dear Brooks

Your letter of Heaven knows what date, since I have burned it up to prevent accidents, has arrived, and I heartily sympathise with you in your troubles.[1] I only hope you will have a better time of it than I had under the same circumstances. Certainly I was particularly unlucky and you at least have not your family to take care of, as I always had when I got into my worst scrapes. My first experience cost me some two months wretchedness and my later ones as you know were bad enough.

The governor has come home, the Lord be praised, and we are all right again. Mamma is well as ever and everything goes on like clock-work. Whether he will return or not seems very doubtful. I live in the hope that they will all toddle off in May. I have special reasons for hoping so, which I will tell you.

I have had a pretty lively winter of late, going much into society and making myself rather conspicuous in the ultra-fashionable set, especially with the young buds. I rather made an excitement by giving a lunch at my rooms here to Lucy Rathbone and Amy Shaw, at which Mary presided, and of which she will have given you an account. It was very jolly, and your room is still scattered with faded roses left behind by the lovely creatures.

All this however was only a passing amusement on my part, and a dodge. I had more serious business on hand. And now prepare yourself for a shock. I am engaged to be married.

There! what do you say to that? I fancy your horror and incredulity. The fact, however, is indisputable, and you had better here lay down this letter and try to guess the person. Who do you say? Clara Gardner? No! Nanny Wharton? No. It is, however, a Bostonian. You know her, I believe, a little. You are partly responsible, too, for the thing, for I think you were the first person who ever suggested it. I remember well that in our walks last Spring you discussed it. Yes! it is Clover Hooper. So you must stand by me and bear me out.

The truth is, though I didn't think it worth while to confide in mankind, that I have had the design ever since last May and have driven it very steadily. On coming to know Clover Hooper, I found her so far away superior to any woman I had ever met, that I did not think it worth while to resist. I threw myself head over heels into the pursuit, and succeeded in conducting the affair so quietly that this last week we became engaged without a single soul outside her immediate family suspecting it. Nor is it yet out, nor will be, for another week. I'm afraid she has completely got the upper hand of me, for I am a weak-minded cuss with women, and the devil and all his imps couldn't resist the fascination of a clever woman who chooses to be loved.

Such is your brother's fate! Of course the engagement will make a row, and people will discuss it to please themselves. I care little so long as they leave me alone. I know better than anyone the risks I run. But I have weighed them carefully and accept them.

Our plan is to be married and sail for Europe in July. There we propose to stay a year. The winter I want to pass on the Nile. The following Spring I hope to pass in London in society. Then we return to live in Boston.

The parents appear to be pleased and your mamma of course is in a lively condition of excitement. John and Charles are not yet informed. As Clover and I between us are not only tolerably independent of opinion but fairly independent in means, we have no occasion to wait on anyone, and follow our own devices.

Clover is now with the Shaws on Staten Island, but I go on this week to bring her back.[2] The Gurneys smile upon us,[3] and Dr Hooper is resigned.

This, my boy, is all I have to say, and is enough news for one letter. You had better not mention it generally till you hear from us that it is out. I shall expect you to be very kind to Clover, and not rough, for that is not her style. We shall see you in the summer.

Ever Yrs   Henry.

MS: MHi

1. BA, aged 24, had been left in Paris by his father to study French.
2. Francis George Shaw (1809–1882), retired merchant and philanthropist; and Sarah Sturgis Shaw (1815–1902), to whom Marian Hooper was related.
3. Ephraim W. Gurney (1829–1886), professor of history and dean at Harvard, had been editor with James Russell Lowell of the *North American Review*. On HA's marriage he became his brother-in-law, since his wife, Ellen (1838–1887), was MHA's sister.

To Henry Cabot Lodge

Luxor. 2 January, 1873.

My dear Mr Lodge[1]

I received your letter of November 3d just as I was leaving Cairo, and as I have been busily reading myself, I delayed answering till I knew what I had to say. So far as I can see, you are acting on such good advice and working in such good company that I can add very little to your means of getting ahead. Perhaps to a critical eye, the field you have entered may seem rather wide. I doubt whether a man can profitably spread his reading over a very large range unless he has some definite object clearly fixed in his head. My wish is to lead you gradually up to your definite object, but what it must be will depend on the bent of your own tastes. I can only tell you the style of thing that seems to me best.

The first step seems to me to be to familiarise one's mind with thoroughly good work; to master the scientific method, and to adopt the rigid principle of subordinating everything to perfect thoroughness of study. I have therefore advised your learning German, because I think the German method so sound. I am glad you are reading Sohm. But Sohm's work is on too large a scale to imitate. I would like to have you take up some of the smaller works, which have broken the way for him. Read as most kin to your interests, von Maurer's Einleitung; Thudichum's Gau und Markverfassung; Brunner's Entstehung der Schwurgerichte.[2] Study these, not merely for their matter but as literary work. See how the men go at it, and then take an English work, Mayne if you like, or Freeman, and see how they reach their results.[3] I do not mean to set up the Germans as exclusive models at all. But they have the great merit of a very high standard of knowledge. An ignorant, or a superficial work could hardly come from any distinguished German student. I can't say the same for other countries. Great as is Mr Freeman's parade of knowledge, he has never written anything really solid, and Mr—or rather Sir Henry—Mayne's book is precisely such a one as I like to give to students to admire and to criticise. I know of no writer who generalises more brilliantly. But everyone of his generalisations requires a lifetime of work to prove it.

I propose no more to the fellows who are kind enough to think my teaching worth their listening to—those of them I mean who take the thing in the spirit I offer it in—than to teach them how to do their work. The College chose to make me Professor of History—I don't know why, for I knew no more history than my neighbors. And it pitchforked me into mediaeval history, of which I knew nothing. But it makes little difference what one teaches; the great thing is to train scholars for work; and for that purpose there is no better field than mediaeval history to future historians. The mere wish to give a practical turn to my men has almost necessarily led me to give a strong legal bent to the study. Starting from this point, I found that at the outset the Family was the centre of early law. To study the Family therefore in its different relations, was the natural course to follow. From this point we must follow down the different lines of development. The organisation of the Family; the law of inheritance; of testaments; of land tenure; of evidence and legal procedure; the relations of the Family to the community, in its different forms of village, county and state, as well as many other parallel lines of study lay open before me and I have only to indicate them to true students whether of law or of history, and let them go to work and develope them. Of course I don't pretend to have mastered these subjects myself. No one has yet done so. But men like you and Ames can win a reputation by following up any one line of investigation,[4] and the occupation is as good as mathematics for the logical faculty while it leads ultimately to all the nearer subjects of historical study.

Of course our own law and institutions are what we aim at, and we only take German institutions so far as they throw light on English affairs. I think you would do well to keep this in mind and to take some special line of work so soon as you have become tolerably acquainted with the general bearings of things. Of course you will choose whatever you think best suits your tastes. It does not follow that preliminary legal reading is to make you a historian of law, any more than preliminary grammar reading would result in making you a historian of philology. It matters very little what line you take provided you can catch the tail of an idea to develop with solid reasoning and thorough knowledge. America or Europe, our own century or prehistoric time, are all alike to the historian if he can only find out what men are and have been driving at, consciously or unconsciously.

So much is this the case that I myself am now strongly impelled to write an Essay on Egyptian Law; for I have a sort of notion that I could draw out of that queer subject some rather surprising deductions; perhaps I could fix a legal landmark in history; but I have too much on my hands and must let the Cheopses and the Ramses alone.

The Nile is not a bad place for study, and I have run through a library of books here. I want to write to Ames, but until I have got some sort of order into my ideas I shall have nothing to say. But I would be very glad to have a line from him to know how he gets on and whether he has struck any new vein. There are many points I want to discuss with him but they will keep. Meanwhile pray continue to write to me how things are going with you and at Cambridge. Send for a copy of Schmid's Gesetze der Angel-Sachsen; it may be useful to you next year, as I want to go hard at early English law.[5] I have got to learn to read Anglo Saxon, but that is too much to expect from you or anyone not obliged to do it.

Pray give my best regards to your wife. Believe me very truly

Yrs   Henry Adams.

MS: MHi

1. Henry Cabot Lodge (1850–1924), Harvard '71, after a year in Europe was returning to Harvard to study history and law.
2. Rudolph Sohm, *Der Prozess der Lex Salica* (1867); Georg L. von Maurer, *Einleitung zur Geschichte der Mark-, Hof-, Dorf-, und Stadt-Verfassung und der öffentlichen Gewalt* (1854); Friedrich W. Thudichum, *Die Gau- und Markverfassung in Deutschland* (1860); Heinrich Brunner, *Die Entstehung der Schwurgerichte* (1871).
3. Sir Henry James Sumner Maine (1822–1888), professor of jurisprudence at Oxford; *Ancient Law* (1861), *Village Communities* (1871); Edward Augustus Freeman, *History of the Norman Conquest* (1867–1879).
4. James Barr Ames (1846–1910), Harvard '68, LL.B. '72, was teaching HA's classes during his absence.
5. Reinhold Schmid, *Die Gesetze der Angelsachsen* (1832).

To Henry Cabot Lodge

London. 11 June. 1873.

My dear Lodge

Your letter, which I am surprised to find bears the remote date of Feb. 13th, has been an unconscionable time in my pocket, and if an excuse is necessary, I can only put it on the ground of incessant occupation. It reached me somewhere in Italy, and has come with me to London, without ever finding a spare hour of repose. Even here, though we are keeping house and living as regularly as we expect to do in Boston, I find it hard to provide for correspondence.

That you found yourself wallowing in a boundless ocean of history, I can very well imagine. One has a very helpless feeling the first time one plunges into a new existence, no matter what the medium is. Law is as bad as anything else; art should be worse, for art is lower as now practised, than any other profession; and I recollect well that I have found by turn the same sense of helplessness in entering on each new stage of life, both in Europe and at home. Patience is the salvation of men at all such emergencies. I have never found that fail to pull me triumphantly through.

At the same time I do not deny that I thought and still think you were trying to cover too wide a field of mere fact. For the present I was much less inclined to trouble myself about the amount you learned than about the method you were learning. I have, no doubt, more respect for knowledge even where knowledge is useless and worthless, than for mere style, even where style is good; but unless one learns beforehand to be logically accurate and habitually thorough, mere knowledge is worth very little. At best it never can be more than relative ignorance, at least in the study of history. So I wanted you only to read a few specimen books, not large ones either, which would give you an idea of historical method; and I wanted you to learn to use Latin and German with facility; and I suggested Anglo Saxon, which I am studying myself and which is quite amusing. Nor do I see the necessity for your working very laboriously even at this. You will work hard enough one of these days if you ever get interested in the study; if not, what does it matter? The question for you is not by any means whether you can do a great deal; but whether that which you choose to do, be it much or little, shall be done perfectly, so as to give you credit worth your having.

I am inclined to think that you will find you have reached a point a good deal in advance of most historians—so called—, in spite of your discouragement, and that your time has not been ill-spent. At least I hope you could now take up the ordinary historical work of commerce, such as passes for sound even among educated people, and feel at once that it is not what you call history; that it shows neither knowledge nor critical faculty. And I hope too that you are far enough ahead to be able to decipher an Anglo Saxon or a Latin diploma, or to track a given idea through the labyrinths of law and literature. A year is well spent if it only gets your mind into a properly receptive condition,—to use the language of our newspapers.

But I suppose you are pestered by the question which bothers us all when we are at the beginning of a career, especially if, as is usually the case with Americans, we are a little inclined to thinking too much about ourselves. I mean the question of whether a given line of occupation is going to pay; whether you are really ever going to make your scheme work. I am not going to enter into any argument in favor of the course you selected. I don't care to take such a responsibility as that of giving advice to anyone on a matter which involves the occupation of a life-time. If you have seriously become so far discouraged as to think of changing your line of work, and if you have found any other profession or occupation which satisfies you, I have nothing to say against it. But if, in spite of all discouragements you still think a literary life best suited for you, then I hope that we may begin work next term with rather a more definite aim and better defined instruments.

I have this year been engaged in investigating and accumulating notes upon some points of early German law, out of which I expect in time to make a pamphlet or small book. If you like, I will put these notes in your hands next term, and we will proceed to work the subject up together. As I am so much occupied by teaching, I stand much in need of such help. And I think you will find that the work will exercise all your powers and claim no little interest. But it will also require your best knowledge of German, French, Latin and Anglo-Saxon, and I hope you will have more facility than I have, at least in the Latin and Saxon.

If you incline to keep on, then, your path is clear. Don't tell any one the proposal I make, for I am not yet ready to talk about a book. But polish up your languages and on the 1st October, if you are ready to begin, establish yourself in my rooms at Wadsworth.

I shall return to America about August 1st. My wife sends her best regards to yours, as I do mine.

Very truly Yrs   Henry Adams.

H. C. Lodge Esq.

MS: MHi

To Frederick Law Olmsted

91 Marlborough St. 7 April. 1875.

Dear Mr Olmsted[1]

The circulars for the Schurz dinner must be issued this week[2] and as no one else has attended to it, we have undertaken to send it out from here. But there must be found some person or persons in New York who will undertake to act as a committee of correspondence, and of arrangements. The address of such a person ought to be put on our circulars when they are issued. We have written to Godkin, Albert Brown, Whitelaw Reid, and Garrison to urge on them the necessity of immediately appointing a committee and to notify us at once.[3] Could not you act upon it? Or if not, can you not make these gentlemen select a proper person to do so? If you would be the nominal head, some one else might do the work. But at any rate I hope you will hurry their movements and telegraph us some authoritative committee by Saturday.

Yrs truly   Henry Adams.

F. L. Olmsted Esq.

MS: DLC, Olmsted

1. Frederick Law Olmsted (1822–1903), landscape architect, designer of Central Park in New York City and other major urban parks, was active in reform politics.
2. Carl Schurz (1829–1906), Republican senator from Missouri 1869–1875 and strongest leader in the nascent Liberal Republican movement. He did not run for reelection and was departing for Europe. The dinner in his honor on April 27 was an occasion for Evarts, Wells, CFA2, and Schurz himself to restate the Independent program of 1872.
3. Albert Gallatin Browne (1835–1891), formerly a Boston lawyer, was on the editorial staff of the New York *Herald;* Whitelaw Reid (1837–1912), editor-in-chief of the *New York Tribune* 1872–1905; William Lloyd Garrison (1805–1879), former president of the American Anti-Slavery Society.

To Carl Schurz

91 Marlborough St. 12 April. 1875.

My dear Mr Schurz

The danger was over by the time you wrote. Following out the programme, I had entirely withdrawn from all share in the movement, and did not stir till it became clear that something must be done immediately or the whole thing would fall through. Then Sam Bowles, my brother Charles, Cabot Lodge and I, concocted a letter and issued it on Thursday and Friday last (the 8th and 9th) to such gentlemen as were on your lists. Lodge sent it, with the list, to you, and then handed over the whole correspondence to Arthur Sedgwick.[1] He has got a New York committee now raised, and the matter is fairly under way. As you were of opinion that it was best not to give the demonstration the look of an eastern concern, we have not put many New England men on the list. Of course we can have any number, but I presume the really important matter is who will come to the gathering, *prepared to accept ulterior results* and form if necessary an organisation, not who will sign the invitation, for everyone will do this. I don't myself care to see you smothered with a mere crowd that does not mean business.

I suppose it will be well for you to send to the New York committee a reply to the invitation to be ready for publication so soon as a suitable list of names has been made out. The day ought to be published as soon as possible. But as the whole management has now gone to New York, I leave it to New York wisdom to regulate the affair.

I sincerely trust our friends will go to New York with definite notions of a policy to be pursued and practical measures to be carried into execution. You know already that I want organisation and consider the New York meeting only valuable as it leads to and facilitates organisation. Would it not be well to arrange beforehand for a small interior meeting, the day after the dinner, to discuss a policy? The word Convention need not be suggested, but the *thing* Cooperation must be made flesh.

Ever truly Yrs   Henry Adams.

MS: DLC, Schurz
1. Arthur G. Sedgwick (1844–1915), assistant editor of the *Nation*.

To Charles Milnes Gaskell

Beverly Farms, 24 May. 1875.

My dear Carl

Your mysterious and blood-curdling letter of May 3d reminds me of what I have been daily reminding myself, that I have sent you no news for three months. To say that I have nothing to say would be a lie, in intent if not in fact, for one always has enough to say for a letter. To say that I had forgotten to write would be two lies, for I thought of it every day. The only truth that I can think of is that I am no better than a procrastinating cuss and since being married I do less than ever before. Here is another winter gone and I am again nursing nasturtiums and feeding mosquitoes. I am going on to thirty eight years old, the yawning gulf of middle-age. Another, the fifth, year of professordom is expiring this week. I am balder, duller, more pedantic, and more lazy than ever. I have lost my love of travel. My fits of wrath and rebellion against the weaknesses and short-comings of mankind are less violent than they were, though grumbling has become my favorite occupation. I have ceased to grow rapidly either in public esteem or in mental development. One year resembles another and if it weren't for occasional disturbing dreams of decay, disaster or collapse, I should consider myself as having attained as much of Nirwana as a man of my race and temperament can expect to do. And opposite to this mere lump of walking vegetation, three thousand miles away, I dimly descry you prancing about as though ten years were but a day in your sight and youth grew younger by Act of Parliament. Well! let's have your gossip! I am curious to hear it! And it shall be buried in the depths of the American wilderness. By the bye, was it you who wrote the generous notice of me in Routledge's Men of the Time, wherein, with great good-feeling and a most praiseworthy sense of what ought to be the author has calmly credited me with all my brother's writings? Surely some kind friend it must be.[1]

When I last wrote, it was from Washington, I think, where I had just hospitably buried my host and started a new party of dimensions not absolutely gigantic. Since then nothing very startling has occurred. But my new party thrives. It consisted then, I think, of four men. Now it has reached more than that. It would not surprise me if I had as many as forty coadjutors. We felt so happy about our future success that we had a *demonstration* in New York, which, as it was originated, hatched and generally brought into life by me as a result of six months incubation, I may call mine. As it may amuse you to follow my devious and under-ground ways, I send you a report of our proceedings. The secret is told in my brother's speech.[2] But as the devil would have it, no sooner had our speeches been made than the newspapers began to assume that the object of our "new party" was to make my father President next year. And in fact I believe this is to be Schurz's most earnest wish and hope, but emphatically it was no part of my plan, and I am much afraid that we shall all shipwreck on that rock. Nevertheless we shall go ahead and you need not be surprised to hear that we have covered ourselves with eternal ridicule by some new absurd failure, or have subsided into nothing for sheer feebleness, or have actually effected a brilliant *coup,* brought our man in as President, and are the rulers of forty million people. Such is the chaotic condition of our politics that any of these results is possible. Of course it indicates that our whole political fabric is out of joint and running wild, but so it is. My scheme is to organise a party of the centre and to support the party which accepts our influence most completely. But I doubt whether we can absolutely overthrow both parties as many of our ardent friends seem almost inclined to try doing. The worst of it is that in no case can I come in for any part of the plunder in case of success. My father and brothers block my path fatally, for all three stand far before me in the order of promotion. My only consolation is that the chances are two million three hundred and sixty four thousand, seven hundred and eleven to one against our success.

I am glad that you received safely the copy of my grandfather's Memoirs.[3] There will be at least five more volumes I expect, though possibly I may exaggerate. It will ultimately be a very rare work and much sought for. Only 750 copies are printed, as I am told, and the book must unquestionably be forever *the* one great authority for American history during the first half of this century. So I have little doubt that within ten years it will be difficult to find. The publishers seem to be aiming at this intentionally.

With fear and trembling I printed my notice of Palgrave's poems.[4] Heaven knows I dislike nothing more than this kind of task and if it weren't that Palgrave has done so much as many times for me I should have kept very far away from any such extravagance. Still, I am glad it is done, and, indifferent as it is, I hope that Palgrave will not find offence in it. If you will oblige me by expressing to him the strongest and most St James's Parkian contempt for my production, I think you may stir up in him the devil of opposition so far as to make him think it tolerably passable.

I want to write to Robert about his hopes of heirs but dare not yet for fear of a *malheur* in the interval.[5] Give him and all, my best love. Tell Lord Houghton that we are poor but honest and shall be glad to see him here, but he must sleep on husks and eat Indian corn. All well and flourishing. My wife is on tiptoe for your gossip.[6]

Ever truly   Henry Adams

We are just beginning to build our log-hut in the woods. The mosquitoes are so thick that on hot, sunny days they cast an agreeable flickering shade. I have ordered a suit of cinquecento armour to protect me from them.

MS: PPT

1. *Men of the Time: A Dictionary of Contemporaries* (1872), entry under Charles Francis Adams. HA is listed as "a professor in Harvard College" and author of various publications "which have attracted attention for their severity, their ability, and the admirable finish and perfection of their style."
2. CFA2 spoke for those who wanted "a more unselfish standard of public men" and who would, as "independent voters," support either party to attain that end.
3. *Memoirs of John Quincy Adams,* ed. Charles Francis Adams, 12 vols. (1874–1877).
4. "Palgrave's Poems," *North American Review* 120 (April 1875), 438–444. Unsigned.
5. Sir Robert Cunliffe (1839–1905), 5th baronet, of Acton Park, Wrexham, in north Wales, became a lifelong friend of HA.
6. The promised gossip proved to be that Lady Mary Hervey had made overtures in February to renew her engagement to Charles Milnes Gaskell.

To Henry Cabot Lodge

Beverly Farms, Mass. Monday. [21? June 1875]

My dear Lodge

I expected you today and was horrified by your not coming, as it reminded me that I had not answered your notes. I had to go up Friday, and Saturday all day, and in the bother of work, forgot to reply to you. Indeed I expected you anyway, and perhaps I dismissed reply as unnecessary.

Anyway I let it slip my mind, and am specially sorry as I wanted to see you today rather than later as I go to Cambridge tomorrow for the last time, I hope, and could have arranged to meet you there. The fact is, I hardly know what has become of the carpet. It was so full of moths that no one would let it stay in his room, and it was cast into outer darkness. If you receive this note in time and can be at Cambridge tomorrow, you shall take seisin of all there is.

I will resume the "dust and ashes" argument hereafter. I am sorry you think so poorly of Gray, whom I rank very high indeed.[1] But if you insist on having only the naturals classed as poets, why not count in Cowper? I feel a little awkward about literary judgment. Everyone now snubs the last century and I see that Stephen considers Scott to be poor stuff.[2] I confess I do think Pope a poet, and Gray, too, and Cowper, and Goldsmith. But this may be youthful prejudice, or rather prejudice contracted in youth.

I modified your expressions about Chat.[3] not so much because they were too laudatory; that was your affair; but rather because it seemed to me that if his verses were trite, affected, impossible and absurd (I forget your exact words) it was well to modify the praise; and if the praise were correct, the blame ought to be modified; or the balance ought to be more exactly drawn. It was easiest to modify the praise, so I suggested that course.

We are thinking of making our descent on you and your wife one day next week. Will that do?

Forgive my not answering your note. I am much mortified at the bad-manners, but I really assumed that you would come of course and only wanted an answer in case I was not to be at home.

Yrs truly   Henry Adams.

MS: MHi

1. Lodge was serving as HA's assistant editor of the *North American Review*.
2. In *Hours in a Library* (1874) Leslie Stephen (1832–1904) wrote that "the great 'Wizard' has lost some of his magic power" and was guilty of "romantic nonsense."
3. Thomas Chatterton (1752–1770), author of poems which he falsely attributed to Thomas Rowley.

To Sir Robert Cunliffe

Beverly Farms. Mass. 31 August. 1875.

My dear Robert

This morning your letter announcing the coming of the All Hail Here-after,[1] arrived and spread joy at our breakfast table. This year has been a somewhat startling one to me in this respect, for it is but a few weeks since my brother wrote to announce the birth of twin boys.[2] I am however so firm a believer in the necessity of propagating our kind that nothing gives me more pleasure than, like Artemas Ward, to see all my able-bodied friends and relations devoting themselves to this end.[3] I hope you will have a dozen and that they will all be like their father and mother. If you want to give them careers, send them off to the colonies young when they can forget English swelldom. Remember that your rotten old English society can't last another generation, and that new roots are desirable to old trees. A good lawyer, physician, engineer, architect, or editor, can command social position and pecuniary ease in every country except Europe, and upon my soul I consider England an impossible place to live in except for elder sons, or men of extraordinary abilities, or position. You know that though a democrat and a sceptic, I am not fanatically inclined, but I do occasionally thank God that fate did not make me the younger son of an English country gentleman and put me in the army or the church. Of all the forms of English lunacy I ever saw, those two seem to me the most astounding. I would like to send your infant a gift, but as the resources of America are curiously deficient in articles suited to the purpose, I send the advice as above, more valuable than gold or precious gems. Seriously however, I am overjoyed to hear of your triumph and hope one of these days that the young gentleman will do me the honor to visit my lowly mansion and recall to me the manners and features of his papa and mamma. I will try not to instil democratic ideas into his baronetrical mind, and will do my best to make his travels agreeable and instructive. Meanwhile I suppose Lady Cunliffe and you have already settled his entire career in life and that in your minds he is already an elderly gentleman maintaining a dignified position and dispensing a generous hospitality at Acton. I think indeed there can be little doubt that he will be much too grand a personage ever to be quite in sympathy with American friends, and therefore I look in truth to his younger brothers as the real objects of my future care and affection. Please tell your wife that those young cherubs shall be my special favorites. This older representative of a venerable but decaying political system will be above my aid.

And now I must acknowledge your jolly long letter of August 8th which arrived a few days since. Owing to the fact that my eyes suddenly broke down about two months ago, I have neither read nor written anything more than was absolutely necessary since June, and have left my correspondence with Carlo to my wife. He is faithful, however, and I owe to him all the little London news I get, except when Palgrave or you send a despatch. He wrote us of Miss Warren's back-sliding, but gives no hint of any desperate act of his own.[4] But the world now-a-days seems to have got into a sort of back-water; those that are married already, all save one, shall live;[5] the rest shall stay as they are. I never knew a period so absolutely calm, not even a suppressed sore in the political system; no more slavery; no more downtrodden nationalities; no socialists; no anything; which accounts for Carl's getting no wife. I am glad your London house suits you. But what are your plans about Acton? By the bye, I am building a little house here by the sea-side, within an hour of Boston. I told you, I think, that it was in the woods, with a distant sea view, and that my wife and I were the only architects. House and land, of which I have now about twenty acres of rough wood and marsh, will cost us between four and five thousand pounds, and we are now in the act of building and I pass most of my time in superintending the work. Life for the moment hinges on the character of a string-course or the projection of a roof-beam. A vista is the great question on which happiness depends, and the tops of my chimneys are harrassing anxieties. This occupation will, I trust, serve as the amusement of many future summers, for my woods are wild and a century of fussing in them can be passed agreeably. I began my summer furiously in violent desk-work, intent upon my magnum opus, but, for the first time in my life, my eyes put an end to all my ambitious schemes and left me to lounge about my workmen. Heaven only knows when I shall begin study again, but I suppose I shall gradually drift back into the current of work, with the reopening of the University. My sixth year of duty there will soon begin, and I am meditating mischief. University priggishness bores me. I expect there will be a row in the Faculty and that I shall be the victim.

Palgrave's invoice of drawings was a great delight to me. One of the water-colors, a Cousens, is wonderful; the best thing I have; and my little parlor here, only seven feet, six inches, high, is now a gallery of English water-colors; Cousens, Girtin, Cotman, Cox, Varley and Stanfield, besides several more.[6] We bring them with us from town every summer, and they are becoming a sort of serious fact to society which has run almost exclusively here to French art; Troyon, Decamps, Rousseau, Millet and Corot.[7] My drawings are too numerous to carry about, and indeed I must either make a gallery for them very soon, or get a bigger house.

If you know Green or Green's friends, I wish you would have his shoulder jogged in regard to attention to details.[8] His book swarms with inaccuracies which are quite inexcusable. I hinted at this in my notice of it, but did not think myself called upon to notice anything more than such blunders as regarded America. I could have given a long list of others. He seems to have written much without verifying from original sources.

I have been obliged to write a notice of Queen Mary for the October North American.[9] It is rather sharp and I fear Palgrave will not approve.

Life here offers astonishingly little to write about. For months I have seen almost no one. I have not even seen my family but twice since the middle of May. I have not read a book. I do not even keep a dog, though I am looking about for a bull-terrier. Since my eyes gave out I confess to having been bored, a feeling not unnatural to a man who is more utterly devoid of resources outside of books, than any English squire outside of stables. But the work of building ties me down to Beverly, and the beginning of term-time will soon set me to work again. The only disastrous consequence of my stagnation is that when I write letters I find that I really have nothing under the sun to say. Our New England climate and soil do not even breed picturesque situations or incidents. We are but a rather improved low-country Scotland and our lives and deaths are too absolutely unimaginative to adorn a tale. One very worthy neighbor of mine a couple of months ago, being out of spirits because he had too much of all he wanted in the world except content, sat down in his (or his neighbors') avenue, and blew his brains out as calmly and as practically as though he were a Britisher and was bored with life.[10] There was no flourish, no pathos, no moral, and, except for his poor children and his old father and mother, no tragedy about it. We are a practical people. We are sternly conscientious. Our young women are haunted by the idea that they ought to read, to draw, or to labor in some way, not for any such frivolous object as making themselves agreeable to society, nor for simple amusement, but "to improve their minds." They are utterly unconscious of the pathetic impossibility of improving those poor little hard thin, wiry, one-stringed instruments which they call their minds, and which haven't range enough to master one big emotion, much less to express it in words or figures. Our men in the same devoted temper talk "culture" till the word makes me foam at the mouth. They cram themselves with second-hand facts and theories till they bust, and then they lecture at Harvard College and think they are the aristocracy of intellect and are doing true heroic work by exploding themselves all over a younger generation, and forcing up a new set of simple-minded, honest, harmless intellectual prigs as like to themselves as two dried peas in a bladder. It is an atmosphere of "culture," with a really excellent instinct for all the very latest European fashions in "Culture." Matthew Arnold should be their ideal. Ruskin and Herbert Spencer, Morris wall-papers, Corot paintings, Eastlake furniture, are our food and drink. The theories are the very best and latest imported. Our young people have all the most novel intellectual fashions crammed into them with alarming conscientiousness. But I am aghast at the result. Such a swarm of prigs as we are turning out, all formed by prigs and all suffering under a surfeit of useless information, is new to human experience. Are we never to produce one man who will do something himself, is the question I am helplessly asking, and you can imagine that my remarks to my students are gradually growing somewhat sharp-pointed and calculated to get me into trouble some day.

And at last if it doesn't end in a grand howl on my part at the whole University system as practised in England and America, it will be because I know that at heart all America feels just as I do about it and instead of reforming would want to abolish. And it is sometimes hard to see how to reform.

You must keep my memory green in England by telling everyone that I love them and incessantly ask after them. Your wife is however to be an exception. I will send her no such banalities, but only my tenderest sympathies with Sir Robert Junior. I suppose I must give up my hope that you and she would come to America one of these days, unless you do like Lord Houghton and bring the heir[11] to educate. I have not yet seen his Lordship, and expect much gossip from him.

Ever affly Yrs   Henry Adams.

MS: MHi

1. *Macbeth,* I, iii. HA is responding to the birth of Cunliffe's first child, Foster Hugh Egerton Cunliffe (1875–1916), born Aug. 17.
2. Henry Adams II (1875–1951) and John Adams (1875–1964). CFA2's fourth and fifth children were born at Quincy July 17.
3. Artemus Ward of "Baldinsville, Indiany," was the pen name and platform role of Charles Farrar Browne (1834–1867), newspaper humorist.
4. Margaret Warren married Sir Arthur Cowell-Stepney Aug. 24.
5. *Hamlet,* III, i.
6. Artists of the English watercolor school, noted for romantic landscapes and architectural scenes: John Robert Cozens (1752–1799), Thomas Girtin (1775–1802), John Sell Cotman (1782–1842), David Cox (1783–1859), John Varley (1778–1842), and William Clarkson Stanfield (1793–1867).
7. All but Alexandre-Gabriel DeCamps (1803–1860), an Orientalist, were landscapists of the Barbizon school: Constant Troyon (1810–1865), Théodore Rousseau (1812–1867), Jean-François Millet (1815–1875), Jean-Baptiste Camille Corot (1796–1875). Their Boston vogue was begun by William Morris Hunt in the 1860s.
8. HA had reviewed John Richard Green's *A Short History of the English People* in *North American Review* 121 (July 1875), 216–224.
9. "Tennyson's Queen Mary," *North American Review* 121 (Oct. 1875), 422–429. Unsigned.
10. Joseph Peabody Gardner (1827–1875), widower, committed suicide June 12.
11. Robert Milnes (1858–1945), later 2nd Baron Houghton and 1st marquess of Crewe.

To Carl Schurz

Boston. 14 Feb. 1876.

My dear Mr Schurz

Now that we are again thrown back upon the wide question of general policy, I suppose there is no impropriety in my venturing to express an opinion again, in regard to our wisest course. My poor brother Charles to whom I generally leave the duty of declaring our joint opinion, has been very ill and still is too weak and sensitive even to be consulted on the subject. What I have to say, will therefore count for one only.

It is clear that your original scheme must be abandoned. I am not sorry for it. I do not like *coups de main*. I have no taste for political or any other kind of betting, and for us to attempt forcing one of ourselves on a party convention, necessarily entails the jockeying of some-body. It would be the experience of '72 in a new shape, and successful or not it would do no permanent good but rather permanent harm. The caucus system is the rottenest, most odious and most vulnerable part of our body politic. It is the caucus system we want to attack. By making use of it, we lose our own footing.

To attack the caucus system is therefore the end and aim of all my political desires. To that object and to that object only do I care to contribute. Apart from that object, I believe all your political schemes to be mere make-shifts. You wanted to elect my father President. I would prefer to sacrifice him as the candidate of a hopeless minority if I could gain a point in that way against party organisations. Nay, if he were elected, my only ground for giving him support, apart from personal considerations, would be my conviction that he would proceed systematically to purify party machinery by depriving it of the means of corruption.

The present question with me is, then, how to go to work. You have satisfied yourself and me that we are not strong nor united enough to attack in face. The public is not ready to support us. You have therefore, I hope, abandoned that scheme.

The next alternative was to attack in flank. If we could not set up our own man, to support the man who comes nearest to our standard. This is Mr Bristow.[1] He has a strong popular following. He deserves our support. He would make a good President and would probably in time work round to our opinions. We are therefore safe in supporting him.

Unluckily Mr Bristow does not now share in our views. He is a firm believer in party loyalty. He will not accept an independent nomination before the party convention meets. He will refuse to run against the party candidate in any case. He would look with unutterable disgust upon my proposition to force a candidate on a party organisation whose candidacy meant to himself the rebellion against the same party organisation. Our support of Mr Bristow must therefore be avowedly on grounds of policy, not of principle.

Further, nothing is more certain than that Mr Bristow cannot be nominated. We must not let our hands be tied by any delusion as to his strength in the convention.

Here then are the propositions:

1. We must support Mr Bristow.
2. We cannot nominate him as an independent candidate.
3. We cannot let our hands be tied by the support we give him.

The essential point of any policy must be to hold our friends together. Whatever support is given to Mr Bristow or to anyone else, it is all important that we should act ultimately as a unit, and that the certainty of this ultimate action should be the cardinal point of our tactics.

It is now necessary to decide upon these tactics, and after the preceding review of the ground, I will tell you what seems to me the only clear way out of our difficulties.

To effect the essential object of holding our organisation together, it will be necessary to make a demonstration. That demonstration cannot now include a nomination for the Presidency because: 1st. It is our best policy to ally ourselves with Bristow, and his friends. 2d. Mr Bristow will not accept our nomination. 3d. If we nominate him without consulting him, and he is beaten (as is probable) in Convention, he will refuse to run as our candidate, and we shall be left helpless.

The question then rises as to the nature of this demonstration.

My recommendation is that you and half a dozen other gentlemen should write a circular letter addressed to about two hundred of the most weighty and reliable of our friends, inviting them to meet you, say at Cleveland or Pittsburg, one week after the republican Convention meets, there to decide whether we will support the republican candidate or nominate a candidate of our own. I enclose my notion of the draft of the letter.

This letter or address will of course be published. I should suppose it would have all the effects that any demonstration could have, both to unite our friends and to alarm the Convention at Cincinnati. By keeping in your own hands the nominations to our own meeting, you will be able to exclude the most dangerous elements. This is, no doubt, carrying the junto system far. But I have no real fear of juntoes. They are too objectionable in themselves ever to become dangerous like the caucus. And I know no other way of fighting the caucus than with the junto. Together they may not work so badly.

Down to the time of the Convention, let us, within the range of this declaration, work earnestly for Bristow. By establishing close relations with Bristow's friends, we shall probably carry a portion of them with us. If the Convention makes a very bad nomination we may carry nearly all. And Mr Bristow's friends include all the virtue left in the Republican party.

If the Convention nominates Mr Bristow, well and good! Our meeting will merely confirm their action. If not, the serious responsibility will fall upon us of placing a candidate before the people. Our meeting must consist of men who will not shirk that responsibility, and there can be but one ground to rest our action upon; namely, resistance to caucus dictation. We cannot vote the democratic ticket, for that would involve us in the support of a party organisation which it is a hopeless task to reform. But we can found a new party, and are content to bring the democrats into power as the only means of reorganising parties. As I said before, I am willing to sacrifice my father for such an object, if necessary. He used Van Buren for a similar purpose in '48.[2] But I would rather choose some one else if we could find any one. Our action however must depend to some degree on public feeling.

I suppose you are more than any one else alive to the fact that a blunder now would make us helpless for the whole campaign. We must in the nature of things act cautiously for the simple reason that there is no sufficient popular feeling yet to support us in acting boldly. I see no chance of good to result from our making a premature nomination. The public is fairly determined to wait for the action of the parties. But if we can make the public at large feel in advance that they are certain of having an alternative in case the party conventions are unsatisfactory, we shall sap the foundations of party discipline beforehand without exposing ourselves to any possible attack.

I hope these tactics will coincide with your views. Otherwise I shall wait with great anxiety the decision you shall make. But in any case believe me

Very sincerely Yours   Henry Adams.

Hon. Carl Schurz.

[Draft of circular letter.]

—— —— March. 1876.

Sir

The present condition of political affairs is such as to create grave concern in the minds of all reflecting men.

The great party conventions are soon to meet. As yet there is no indication that the choice of these conventions will fall upon persons in whom independent voters can place confidence. All the indications of the time point to the possibility that, in the conflict between personal interests, the interests of the nation may be overlooked, and either a combination of corrupt influences may control the result, or, as has so often happened, the difficulty of harmonising personal claims may lead to the nomination of candidates whom you cannot support with self-respect.

Against such a possibility it is our duty to take every precaution. The Republican Convention will meet on the — of June. We have the honor,

therefore, respectfully to invite your attendance at a conference of gentlemen independent of party ties, to meet at the city of —— on the —— day
of June, to decide whether we can support the nominations made by the
Republican Convention, and if not, to place before the people candidates
of our own selection.

We have the honor &c &c

to —— ——

MS: DLC, Schurz

1. Benjamin H. Bristow (1832–1896), Grant's third secretary of the Treasury 1874–1876,
won the support of reformers by attacking corruption in his department.
2. In 1848 CFA had supported Democrat Martin Van Buren (1782–1862) for another term
as president, with himself as nominee for the vice-presidency, hoping to bring antislavery
Democrats into the new Free Soil party together with his own "Conscience Whigs." The
maneuver succeeded in New England, but the slaveholding Gen. Zachary Taylor (1784–
1850), hero of the war with Mexico, won the election.

To Henry Cabot Lodge

Beverly Farms. 15 May. 1876.

My dear Lodge

I have read your MS. and think it will do you credit. Of course I have
made many alterations, not in the sense, but in the words. I have cut out
all the "we's" I could get at, and tried to make it less objectionably
patronising toward Morse.[1] Probably much further labor may be profitably
expended on it in proof.

You do not of course expect me to acquiesce entirely in your view of
A.H. I can hardly explain the reasons of my own *kind* of aversion to him.
That it is inherited is no explanation, for I inherit feelings of a very different
sort towards Jefferson, Pickering, Jackson, and the legion of other life-long
enemies whom my contentious precursors made. I dislike Hamilton because
I always feel the adventurer in him. The very cause of your admiration is
the cause of my distrust; he was equally ready to support a system he
utterly disbelieved in as one that he liked. From the first to the last words
he wrote, I read always the same Napoleonic kind of adventuredom, nor
do I know any more curious and startling illustration of this than the
conclusion of that strange paper explaining his motives for accepting Burr's
challenge. I *abhor,* says he, the practice of duelling, but "the ability to be
in future useful in those crises of our public affairs which seem likely to
happen, would probably be inseparable from a conformity with prejudice

in this particular."[2] What should you or I say if our great-grandfathers had left us those words as a deathbed legacy? I think we should not have so high a moral standard as I thank those gentlemen for leaving us. And I confess I think those words alone justify all John Adams's distrust of Hamilton. Future political crises all through Hamilton's life were always in his mind about to make him commander-in-chief, and his first and last written words show the same innate theory of life.

But you will not be able to assent to this.

Ever truly Yrs   Henry Adams.

H. C. Lodge Esq.

MS: MHi

1. Lodge's essay reviewed *The Life of Alexander Hamilton* (1876), by his cousin John Torrey Morse, Jr. (1840–1937).
2. From Hamilton's statement on the impending duel. *The Papers of Alexander Hamilton*, ed. Harold C. Syrett, XXVI (1979), 280.

To Moorfield Storey

Beverly Farms. 25 September. 1876.

My dear Storey[1]

I have your's of Saturday and have altered the passage so as to accord with your views.

At the same time I would like to call your attention and that of the Civil Service Reform Club, to a difficulty which they may have to meet.

If we make a law converting the Civil Service tenure into one of life or good behavior, we deprive the President of the power to enforce discipline among his agents. We foment and protect intrigue against him among his own troops and so do what we can to weaken his authority. We increase the power of the "machine" by enabling its creatures to defy their constitutional chief.

John Gray, with whom I have discussed this point, replies that when once the object of such intrigue is taken away by removing the official from personal danger from a change of chiefs, the disposition to intrigue will disappear.[2]

He may be right. The argument rests on so deep a set of human motives that I can't undertake to say it is mistaken. But ought we to face such a risk without actual security? My belief is that American human nature will not be found so pliant, and that the "machine" will find chords to touch. The hope of promotion, the love of politics for their own sake, the sense of personal attachment to individuals, loyalty to party, and many more such influences, will often play a decisive part in such a situation.

There is some reason why I should feel this danger more acutely than most persons, for it is a part of my family history that my grandfather was to no small degree overthrown by it. He honestly acted on the theory of removing no official for political reasons, and it was well known to him and a great complaint against him by his party, that these very officials were intriguing desperately against him and contributed essentially to his defeat.

Let us take care not to make matters worse than they are, by ill-advised reforms.

Ever yrs truly Henry Adams.

Moorfield Storey Esq.

MS: MHi

1. Moorfield Storey (1845–1929), lawyer, coeditor of the *American Law Review.*
2. John Chipman Gray (1839–1915), professor of law at Harvard 1875–1913.

To *Charles Milnes Gaskell*

1501 H Street. Washington. D.C.
25 November, 1877.

My dear Carlo

Your letter of Oct. 21st followed me here and found me at the beginning of a frightful wrestle over a new house and the preparations for an entirely new career. This is my reason for delay in acknowledging it. You may imagine how much pleasure it gave me, and how heartily I congratulate you and your wife on getting happily over this first great condition of marriage.[1] Your life is now much simplified. You have only to do what comes from day to day, and never fear being bored for want of interests.

I am glad to hear that Robert is back at Acton and Frank *not* back at his regiment. Please give them both, my benediction.

As for me and my wife, we have made a great leap in the world; cut loose at once from all that has occupied us since our return from Europe, and caught new ties and occupations here. The fact is, I gravitate to a capital by a primary law of nature. This is the only place in America where society amuses me, or where life offers variety. Here, too, I can fancy that we are of use in the world, for we distinctly occupy niches which ought to be filled. We have taken a large house in which we seem lost. Our water-colors and drawings go with us wherever we go, and here are our great evidence of individuality, and our title to authority. As I am intimate with many of the people in power and out of power, I am readily allowed or aided to do all the historical work I please; and as I am avowedly out of politics, there will, it is to be hoped, be no animosities to meet. Literary and non-partisan people are rare here, and highly appreciated. And yet society in its way is fairly complete, almost as choice, if not as large, as in London or Rome.

One of these days this will be a very great city if nothing happens to it. Even now it is a beautiful one, and its situation is superb. As I belong to the class of people who have great faith in this country and who believe that in another century it will be saying in its turn the last word of civilisation, I enjoy the expectation of the coming day, and try to imagine that I am myself, with my fellow *gelehrte* here, the first faint rays of that great light which is to dazzle and set the world on fire hereafter. Our duties are perhaps only those of twinkling, and many people here, like little Alice, wonder what we're at.[2] But twinkle for twinkle, I prefer our kind to that of the small politician.

After this rather poetical or imaginative description of our surroundings and situation, I have only room to add that we are quite well, very busy, and very happy. One consequence of having no children is that husband and wife become very dependent on each other and live very much together. This is our case, but we both like society and try to conciliate it. My wife sends her warm congratulations to your's and to you. In two years more, if your government will allow it, we hope to see you both—and the babies.

Yrs ever   Henry Adams.

William Story is here now—*not* improved by time.

C. M. Gaskell Esq.

MS: MHi

1. The Gaskells' first child and only son, Evelyn Milnes Gaskell (1877–1931), was born Oct. 19.
2. "Twinkle, twinkle, little bat / How I wonder what you're at!": a parody in *Alice's Adventures in Wonderland* (1865) of the nursery rhyme "The Star."

To Charles Milnes Gaskell

Beverly Farms. 30 May. 1878.

Glad indeed I was, Carlo mio, to see your handwriting on my arrival here two days ago. I had been deferring an epistle until after the scuffle of leaving Washington was over, and your letter came just in time to acknowledge. I had not heard a word about you for months. Robert has long since forgotten me. Palgrave is silent. I was beginning to wonder whether you were still in existence. Even your troubles are better news than I was beginning to fear. Poor Mrs Lindesay![1] When fate takes a prejudice against a woman, it is astonishing with what patient and diabolic cruelty it crushes and mangles her. Men generally resist and die fighting—or swearing, which is moral, and possibly immoral, resistance. But women commonly accept everything and die smiling, and what they call resigned; which means, I believe, that they feel they are powerless. "Is life worth living?" I should say clearly not, under such conditions.[2]

Your brother's troubles too, are hard both on him and his wife, on you and yours, and on your wife's family.[3] He managed to collect a large circle to mourn his misfortunes, and in this there is always a certain wicked satisfaction to the morose disposition of selfish mankind. But I sincerely hope he is all right again.

Of ourselves I can, thank Heaven, give you only pleasant news. We have had a very cheerful winter at Washington. I have worked hard and with good effect. My wife has helped me and has had a house always amusing and interesting. We have had all the society we wished and had found everyone friendly and ready to amuse and be amused. Our little dinners of six and eight were as pleasant as any I ever was at even in London. And Washington has one advantage over other capitals, that a single house counts for more than half a dozen elsewhere; there are so few of them. Among my set of friends this winter has been our old Roman acquaintance Schlözer who is great fun; eccentric as an Englishman and riotous as a wild Highlander.[4] We lament together over our Roman hostess and her *boudins Richelieu*. But you should just try Schlözer's *Gänsebrust* if you want to experience sudden death. Not many of your compatriots have been in Washington, besides Lord Dufferin who was a success and developed uncommon social tact.[5] The young Britishers who are *on the make* as they call their search for rich wives, do not come to Washington. By the bye, one of them, a certain Edward or Teddy Balfour, son of Lady Georgiana Balfour, has just bagged my wife's cousin, a baby with £4000 a year. Do you know anything of him?

After a winter only six weeks long and a spring which began early in February, we were driven from Washington by the heat and came away to brace our constitutions in the east winds and pine woods. Here we propose to abide until November carries us to Washington again. Washington is not very unlike the north of Italy in its climate, malaria included, so that I expect it to become one day or another a favorite winter watering-place.

Do you ever read anything now? If so let me know it, for I am hopelessly out of training. By the way, I saw Will Everett last week, and he asked about you. He is dirtier and more eccentric than ever. The Gurneys return home in September and will, I suppose be in London before then. I am glad you liked Harry James.[6] He has many good points. I never read my friends' books so that I may express no opinions about them. My last volume I have not sent you, as there was nothing of mine in it but the editing. But I have sent you Vol. X of J.Q.A's memoirs. And I enclose you a bill of exchange for £15.19.6 being the proceeds of a paper you had in the North American, invested by me some three years ago, and now turned into cash because I am tired of keeping it.

   With our warmest regards to Lady Catherine,

                              Ever affecly   Henry Adams.

   18 June.   This letter has been kept waiting for the bill of exchange which has only just come. Please observe my financial talents. I invested on your account, four years ago, $50, then equal to about £9.10, and I have by judicious investments made it £16. Don't you wish you had given me £10,000 instead of £10.

   No news. I am living like a hermit in a wood. Work and read ten hours a day, till my mind is scoured like a kitchen copper.

                                           Ever Yrs.

MS: MHi
1. Harriot Hester Lindesay died March 18, 1878.
2. William Hurrell Mallock's essay "Is Life Worth Living" asserted that for atheists and believers alike life has a moral value (*Nineteenth Century* 2 [Sept. 1877], 256).
3. On Dec. 7, 1876, Gaskell married Lady Catherine Henrietta Wallop (1856–1935), daughter of the 5th earl of Portsmouth.
4. Kurt von Schlözer, German minister 1871–1882.
5. Frederick Temple Blackwood (1826–1902), 1st earl of Dufferin, governor-general of Canada 1872–1878, was being succeeded by John D. S. Campbell (1845–1914), marquess of Lorne.
6. Henry James (1843–1916). Gaskell had met James for the first time in 1877.

To Charles Milnes Gaskell

                              Beverly Farms. 21 Aug. 1878.

My dear Carl
   My wife, who takes malicious pleasure in shocking the prejudices of the wise and good, sent you a postal card in reply to your last. Since then we

hear that the Gurney's are to visit you at Wenlock. So we look forward to their return in order to supply ourselves with news. I expect that we shall ourselves be coming out again about a year hence, with a view to passing a winter in Spain and Paris, and a spring in London where we shall probably take a house for the season. I much fear, however, that my diplomacy will get me ashore, for the whole object of my journey is to study the diplomatic correspondence of the three governments, in regard to America, during the time of Napoleon, from 1800 to 1812. Unless I can get this object, I shall throw away my trouble, and so I am straining every nerve to open in advance the doors of three Foreign Offices. I shall come with an official letter of introduction from this Department of State, and shall ask Sir Edward Thornton to give me another.[1] But if you ever see the Salisburys, you might facilitate my movements by sounding for me there. I am afraid that Salisbury has such a suspicious temperament that he will hardly grant such a favor, and I would rather have applied to Derby; but since the great and glorious success which Disraeli has won over Turkey—or was it Russia?—I suppose that Ministry is likely to hold on.[2] Your government is, I believe, very close about its papers and has not thrown them open to anyone later than the close of last century.

If you come across, too, any little box of a house in May Fair which seems suitable for us, please keep your eye on it. I expect to arrive in Liverpool in September or October, and to go on at once to Paris and Madrid, so that I shall hardly get back to London before April. My hope is to pass Christmas in Granada, and making love to Señoritas in Seville and Cadiz. Perhaps we can make a party and bottle a little Andalusian sunshine for our old age. How would your wife like to try the quality of a December moon in the Alhambra? I am now forty and the grave is yawning for me, but I would do my best to smile as I sat on its edge, and to talk as though I were still as young as when you and I first met. Every now and then in my bourgeois ease and uniformity, my soul rebels against it all, and I want to be on my wanderings again, in the Rocky Mountains, on the Nile, the Lord knows where. But I humbly confess that it is vanity and foolishness. I really prefer comfort and repose. I should not now be meditating the passage of that miserable ocean, if it were not for my literary necessities. I am ashamed to seem restless. It is ludicrous to play Ulysses.[3] There is not in this wide continent of respectable mediocrity a greasier citizen, or one more contented in his oily ooze, than myself.

So Lorne is coming over. If he comes to Washington while I am there, I will ask him to dine; but his wife must learn to behave herself like other people. Lord Dufferin has spoiled us in this way. I saw him and his wife again the other day at a little dinner at Mr Winthrop's and found him uncommonly pleasant. Since then my brother Brooks has been salmon-catching in Canada under his auspices. I believe the Canadians adore him, and Lorne will have to improve his manners if he expects to succeed to Dufferin's popularity.

I am now busily engaged in printing again, my normal condition. I have just entered into a contract to bring out four big volumes within twelve months.[4] When I am accouché, I start for Europe; so that I have two years at least laid out before me.

There is no other news on hand. My father and mother seem fairly well. They are now on a visit here, and for the first time for some years I have a chance to see them well; on the whole I hope my life may roll as smoothly as theirs. My sister is calmly established in her own quarters. Altogether, we go on with placidity unequalled, and the only question is, what we live for. Nothing seems to come of it.

I have a letter from Palgrave, and I suppose you, like him, have seen Will Everett. Of Harry James I hear nothing except his Daisy Miller, which I was induced to read and thought really clever. But as England seems to be now marrying in America, I suppose the American girl is likely to be better known there than here. I wish the Prince of Wales were hung, or drowned, or anyway got rid of. He is, to all our pretentious and semi-vulgar people, the successor of Louis Napoleon, and his court has the same influence here that the Tuileries used to have, before the republican broom cleaned out that harpies' den. I shall before long care very little how soon the republican broom sweeps out the Prince and his whole crew, if he is going to make Malborough House a back-avenue for vulgar Americans to reach society.[5] If he had ever been known to be civil to one American who deserved attention, I would forgive him, but as yet nothing could be much worse than his influence on our society.

I am glad you enjoyed your Italian trip, and that your wife had the fun of a run across country. Of your politics I try to keep some little run, and you can imagine that Tancred has considerably amused me.[6] The truth is, your government has cut a very droll figure, but on the whole has got out of the scrape very happily. I am not disposed to quarrel with anyone who preserves the peace. It is the only thing in politics worth preserving. And I never was much of a Gladstonian. He showed us what he was worth during our civil war, and I never got over the impression he then made on me. Are you going to visit Cyprus? I suppose there will be a dozen English Brightons on it before ten years are out. You should buy an Abbey there and get returned to Parliament by it.

Remember us to the Cunliffe's if you ever see them, and to the Doyle's.[7] I shall write again to Palgrave soon. The Gurneys will, I suppose, have made their visit to you before this letter arrives, but as they will then come almost directly to us, we shall have all the benefit of it. Give our kindest regards to Lady Catherine and to the young one.

Ever Yrs   Henry Adams.

Chas. J. Milnes Gaskell Esq.

MS: MHi

1. Sir Edward Thornton (1817–1906), British minister to the U.S.
2. Edward H. Stanley (1826–1893), 15th earl of Derby, foreign minister. The Treaty of San Stefano in March had ended the Russo-Turkish War, which Russia had won. Prime Minister Disraeli was maneuvering to advance British power in the Turkish empire against the advice of Derby, who resigned.
3. Allusion to Tennyson's poem "Ulysses" (1842).
4. HA's edition of the writings of Albert Gallatin and the biography of Gallatin.
5. Marlborough House, the London residence of the Prince of Wales (the future Edward VII), was notorious for attracting American adventurers.
6. The hero of Disraeli's novel *Tancred,* (1847) was a crusading pilgrim to the Holy Land, where he became involved in political intrigue.
7. Sir Francis H. Doyle (1810–1888), poet and man of letters, married to Gaskell's aunt.

To Charles Milnes Gaskell

1501 H Street. Washington.
28 November. 1878.

My dear Carl

Have I had a letter from you since I last wrote? The state of our correspondence has, I regret to say, passed out of my mind. If you owe me a letter, I make you a present of the debt, for I am going to create a new one. Not that I have anything in especial to say, but that time passes and I would not be forgotten.

We broke up our summer establishment a month ago and came here into winter quarters where we find ourselves on the whole more contented than anywhere else in this miserable little planet. I suppose we are of less insignificance here than elsewhere. You see, in London I can't drop in of an evening to the palace to chat with the Queen, nor will Mr Disraeli and Mr Gladstone dine with me whenever I send for them. Here society is primitive as the golden age. We run in at all hours to see everybody. I have a desk in our Foreign Office for my exclusive study, and unlimited access to all papers. We make informal evening calls on the President, the Cabinet and the Diplomates. Ten days ago I went uninvited to Yoshida's, the Japanese Minister's, and played whist with him and his Japanese wife till midnight, after which I beat him at Go-Bang and he showed me how to play Go; after which we closed with oysters and Champagne and *such* a headache the next day.[1] That same day I had called in state on the Chinese Ministers, and was put on a throne and made to drink green tea with the leaves in it. We are bent now on having them to dinner in their national dress, and Secretary Evarts has promised to meet them. Perhaps if I ever go to China, they will return my dinner and impose more green tea-leaves on me.[2] Yoshida, who has since departed for Japan, has already sent me a little blue-and-white Japanese teapot to console me for his absence. You have a dragon of a female at the head of your Legation, who chills my geniality, but I make up for it by a tender attachment for the French Minister's wife.[3]

Such a quaint little society, you never saw or imagined. We do not even talk scandal. There is no scandal to talk about. Everybody is virtuous and the highest dissipation is to play whist at guinea points. I don't even indulge in this. We are all of the Darby and Joan type, and attached to our wives. It is the fashion. We are innocently amused by utterly absurd trifles. We are not ennuyés or blasés. We are good-natured. I assure you, it is like a dream of the golden age. Every morning at nine o'clock my wife and I set out on horse-back and only get back to breakfast at half-past eleven. The riding is excellent hereabouts and the country and weather superb. It holds its own very well against Rome in these respects, and, historical association aside, I am not sure but that I prefer this country for horse-back. It has more variety. For hounds, however, I don't deny that it is badly cut up, but I never have heard of fox-hunting here. We are not so swell.

Meanwhile my ponderous work is more than half done, and there remain only a few more folio volumes to get through the press. After hurling the whole batch at the head of an unconscious public, I shall fly the country next year. As no one will ever read the work, I feel but slight anxiety about its success.

It is a curious fact that while you in England seem to be wallowing about in all sorts of troubles, we in America were never so quiet. As nine tenths of our people, or thereabouts, have passed through bankruptcy in the last five years, we are quite free of debt, and as the operation has been pretty general, every one is about as well off as before. I think on the whole we are faily prosperous. If your people will wait patiently another year or two, we shall be buying your goods as fast as is good for you or for us. But I hope rents will be low when I come over, for I want a nice house on the Park, in May Fair, and I haven't so much money as I used to have, though I think it goes further.

Innocent and peaceful as we are, our Arcadian season has begun, and I must finish my letter in order to dress for dinner. For we have a little dinner tonight, as is not unusual, for we have to entertain all our eminent Boston constituents when they come on. Would you know our company? Behold them! Mr Sidney Bartlett, aged 79, head of the Boston bar, rich, eminent, and considered witty. His son Frank Bartlett, a contemporary of my own. Mr Senator Lucius Quintius Curtius Lamar of Mississipi, the most genial and sympathetic of all Senators and universally respected and admired,— once a Rebel envoy to Russia. Gen. Dick Taylor of Louisiana, brother-in-law of Jefferson Davis, himself one of the best of the rebel Major Generals, a great friend of the Prince of Wales, a first-rate raconteur and whist-player, a son of a former President of the United States.[4] Ecco! Six, you observe. We regret that Lady Catherine and you are not here to make eight. We would teach you to eat terrapin.

Ever affecly   Henry Adams.

C. M. Gaskell Esq.

MS: MHi

1. Yoshida Kiyonari (1845–1891), minister to the U.S. 1874–1881.
2. Ch'ên Lan-Pin, Chinese minister to the U.S. 1878–1881.
3. Lady Thornton; Mme Outrey, wife of Maxime Outrey, French minister 1877–1882.
4. Sidney Bartlett (1799–1889); Francis Bartlett (1836–1913), Boston lawyer; Lucius Quintus Cincinnatus Lamar (1825–1893), Democratic senator from Mississippi 1877–1885; Richard Taylor (1826–1879), son of President Zachary Taylor.

To Sir Robert Cunliffe

17 Half Moon St. 13 July, '79.

My dear Robert

Your last despatch was so long in arriving that I thought you had probably taken offence at my comments on society, and were going to cut my acquaintance. You poor old Britishers are becoming sensitive. I can't make an innocent remark about England that I'm not met with the inquiry how it is in America. I can't persuade people that I am English enough to compare England with herself. But perhaps I am growing old, critical and exacting; ten years ago these things did not strike me as they do now, and especially I was less conscious of the barrenness of politics which now jumps to my eyes. Last week I dined with Forster, and after dinner we sat more than half an hour—six of us besides myself—regaling ourselves with the pettiest chatter of the last debate.[1] It amused me, though there was neither wit, humor, nor taste in it, because it showed me how a political life vulgarises and narrows intelligent people. For my own information I should have preferred to hear the shop-talk of half a dozen stock-jobbers or shop-keepers from the city, who would have talked quite as well, and on matters of more real consequence. I should care less on the subject if I did not see so many acquaintances made victims to this beastly political juggernaut. Here is poor Bryce who should have been now the best historian in England; Albert Rutson, who at least need not have been ridiculous; Broderick, Lord Reay, Cely Trevilian, George Howard, and a dozen others, all the worse for trying to mind other people's business.[2] The ground is literally strewn with such melancholy victims to a diseased appetite. I sincerely hope that you, my dear friend, may escape, and Carlo too; but if you get into Parliament, evidently it will be better for me to avoid England. I certainly will not submit to be bored, and you could no more help boring me than an inmate of any other lunatic asylum could help inflicting his illusions on his visitors.

After this little lecture, I will so far humor your disease as to tell you that so far as I can see, Beaconsfield and the Conservatives have all the cards in their hands, and that the Liberals are quite as incompetent as ever. I have talked much and long with my liberal friends, from John Bright downwards, and they have nothing in them except personal hatred of Dizzy and Salisbury. A liberal leader today, who means to build up a party, must have the nerve to lay his hands on the pillars of the state, and to risk his neck for a distant future. Dilke and Chamberlain know this and are apparently trying to bring themselves up to it, but you know better than I what the length of their tether is.[3] Meanwhile all the Liberals want is to have office again, and all the card they have to play is a bad harvest and commercial depression, for between ourselves the liberal foreign policy is a mere negation, and as bungling in a different way, as Beaconsfield's. Frankly, then, I can't see what good a dissolution is to do to the liberals or to the country, yet this House is so thoroughly used up and disorganised; so completely sterile and unequal to sustained effort, that this cause alone ought to, and I think will, force a dissolution before the end of another session. If I were in Dizzy's place, I would dissolve next month so soon as the Zulus gave in, which will be as soon, I suspect, as the necessary Parliamentary business can be done. *Nous allons voir.* I wish to Heaven you were not going to waste money at such a time on such a trumpery play-thing, or if you must, I wish you had a better cause, wiser leaders, and a clearer sense of what you want. All this, however, is for your private ear. I don't talk this way to other people, and as it's not my business except as my friends react on me, you must take it as quite private and evidence of my attachment.

I need hardly say that my wife and I enjoy ourselves thoroughly. Everyone is civil and yet we are allowed to go our own gait. We have dined out until we are weary. We have seen all we wanted to see, and I have gained my chief object in coming, and have obtained admission to the papers hitherto shut up. Consequently I have declined all invitations into the country; we shall not go to Scotland or to the North, and we shall not be able to see you again, as we had hoped; for I shall probably be kept at work steadily until it is time for me to cross the channel. To make up for our loss, you will have to come up and stay with us next winter when we are housed.

Of society chat I hear very little, not being much in that way. Carlo and Lymington took me down to see Knole last week, and Carl will tell you how much he admires Lord Sackville's hospitality.[4] As usual, the weather is the chief topic of conversation, always followed by that of American cattle, until my wife says that herds of those beasts pursue her in her dreams and she hears nothing but their mournful bellowing.[5] I think Henry James is regarded as one of them, for—again according to my wife's experience—he is always brought forward as a topic of conversation with these. He however is in very good condition, and the most of a society man I know; but then I am afraid my acquaintance is very narrow. For years it has been my highest ambition to know a man who played Polo and shot pigeons, but I shall die without the sight. Carlo has let his social connection escape; he is too much isolated, and I am rejoiced that he has taken a house and gone to social work. You will, I hope, see him in about ten days, on his way north.

I am sorry for your crops, but am really more anxious about the city and the condition of business, which I suspect to be more critical than is openly said. The weak point is the banks, I infer. The country can stand a bad harvest if it must, but a collapse of credit and industry would be most dangerous. I don't know enough about it to have an opinion, but I wish we were a year ahead. I feel sure America will be coming to buy within that time.

I hoped to send you my new book, which is out, I am told, but it has not reached me yet. With our best regards to you, her Ladyship, and Fossie,

Ever very truly   H. Adams.

My wife says that Sutherland's Herbaceous Plants is to be had for seven shillings & six pence. Shall she send it?

MS: MHi

1. William E. Forster (1818–1886), Liberal M.P.
2. James Bryce (1838–1922), professor of civil law, Oxford; Albert O. Rutson (1836–1890), private secretary of Henry A. Bruce, editor; George C. Brodrick (1831–1903), leading political writer on the *Times;* Edwin B. Cely-Trevilian (b. 1833), barrister; George Howard (1843–1911), Liberal M.P.
3. Charles W. Dilke (1843–1911), M.P. 1868–1886, radical leader; Joseph Chamberlain (1836–1914), M.P., aggressive reformer.
4. Newton Wallop (1856–1917), Viscount Lymington, Gaskell's brother-in-law. Knole, in

Kent, a great country house, seat of Mortimer Sackville-West (1820–1888), 1st Baron Sackville.
5. Controversy over importation of American cattle.

To Henry Cabot Lodge

22, Queen Anne's Gate, S.W.
22 February, 1880.

My dear Lodge

Your interesting letter of Jan. 10th reached me on arriving here, after six weeks of dull and dismal hibernation in Paris. At the best of times Paris is to me a fraud and a snare; I dislike it, protest against it, despise its stage, contemn its literature, and have only a temperate respect for its cooking; but in December and January Paris is frankly impossible. It has all the discomforts of London without its mildness; all the harshness of New York without its gaiety. Yet I got my papers, which proved to be most interesting.[1] I did a heap of reading which was indispensable and almost as interesting as the papers. I never have had a better-employed six weeks, and have seldom been gladder to finish them. I rejoiced as much to leave Paris, where I got all I wanted and was perfectly well established, as I regretted to leave dirty, hideous, wretched old Spain, where I was refused everything, and swore at every step. Such is the perversity of human nature. We have now been a month in London, where we took a house next door to Westminster Abbey, Buckingham Palace, and Marlborough House, and about equidistant from all three, which I take to be the ideal situation for an American as it is for a Britisher. It is true that there is about as much chance of my frequenting one as the other of these royal abodes. I am too busy. Just now all my days are passed at the British Museum looking over papers—newspapers, I mean—with nothing in them. Pure loss of time, but inevitable. This will take me a month, working from 11 till 4 every day. Then I must return to the Record Office and complete my work there, which will take another month. By that time I hope to get my papers from France and Spain where Lowell is busying himself for me.[2] I must then go to work with my own pen, an article I have not touched since finishing Gallatin. I want to complete the whole foreign work here, so as to be sure there are no gaps to be filled hereafter. This I hope to accomplish by Aug. 1st. Then I must go to Paris again; make a visit or two in England; sail on or about Sept. 15; reach Boston about Oct. 1st; stay a few days to see my family; rush on to Washington to take a house; pass six weeks between Washington, New York and Boston, trying to furnish the house; and get fairly settled to work again about Dec. 1st.

Such are our plans, which, as you see, are pretty precise. Thus far I have carried out, step by step, the program I made before leaving Washington. If my luck will last to carry me back again, I shall be glad, for, much as I enjoy travelling, and pleasant as London always is, I infinitely prefer home, and I assure you I positively hunger for my Washington life.

So much for myself and our doings. Of you and your's I was glad to get so good an account. Unless you wreck yourself on the rock of the next Presidential election I see no reason why you should not go ahead indefinitely. As for the election, in your place I should have been rather inclined to carry my friends straight to Sherman and to offer him energetic support on the single condition that he would promise not to sell us out to Grant, but to retire, if retire he must, in favor of some other man, or no one. Failing Sherman, I am at a loss to see what can be done, but between ourselves I should think about manœuvring for a renomination of Hayes. What we want is to preserve the present status. Obviously we have not strength to improve it. Therefore—Hayes. But you are on the ground and I am not. Bad as the prospect is from the republican point of view, it seems to me much worse on the democratic side. I can see no candidate worth their putting up, and, as I hear nothing of what is doing, I feel as though anything which would result in an undisputed republican success would be satisfactory to me.

Schurz seems to have got into trouble with his Indian commissioner. This must be a blow to him, but as he has ceased to be anything to us, and so long as he is in the cabinet never can return to his old importance, I don't know that his mischance affects our interests. What interests me far more is to know what our New York independents are doing. They ought to have the names and addresses of ten thousand New York republicans who will vote against Grant at any cost. With such a list behind them, they ought to dictate both the party nominations. Who is leading them? I see they have issued an address.

We are still mourning for Mrs Parkman who has carried with her the largest part of our Beverly society.[3] We could have better spared what is left. I only hope you will invent some one to take her place before we return.

I hear very little from anyone. Brooks occasionally writes me a line. Godkin forced himself up to writing once. But except my mother I have no regular correspondent, and she is not political. I think the world writes fewer letters now than ever, perhaps because there is less to write about. Certainly London has not the material for a letter. It is Sunday afternoon. Harry James is standing on the hearth-rug, with his hands under his coat-tails talking with my wife exactly as though we were in Marlborough Street. I am going out in five minutes to make some calls on perfectly

uninteresting people. Give our best love to your wife, and believe me ever
Yrs

Henry Adams.

H. C. Lodge Esq.

MS: MHi

1. HA was abroad searching archives for his projected history of the United States during the adminstrations of Jefferson and Madison.
2. James Russell Lowell was presently minister resident at the court of Spain.
3. Mary E. D. Parkman (1821–1879), widow of Dr. Samuel Parkman, a relative of the historian Francis Parkman.

To Henry Cabot Lodge

22, Queen Anne's Gate, S.W. 13 May, 1880.

My dear Lodge

Your's of March 21st has been lying a month in my drawer and, grateful as I am for all the news you are the only person to send me, I have so little to say in reply that a letter is hardly writeable. The Boston Sunday Herald and the New York Herald keep me tolerably well posted about home affairs, and Harry Sturgis tells me much more. You will be amused to hear that your friend Portal is soon to be married to a Miss Glyn, a girl rather in the style of Mrs Harry Sturgis at eighteen.[1] I have seen so little of the Portals that I hardly know how the match is liked, but on the face of it I should suppose that it was meant for wear rather than for show. The English are very sensible about these things. Portal is to live in the country and will make an excellent country gentleman, shaming us poor cockneys by his devotion to fox-hounds and cold roast beef.

The American colony is rather large here just now, and decidedly respectable. Besides the Sturgises, Morgans, Walter Burns, Harcourts, Playfairs, Smalleys, and Mistress Alice Mason with her callow brood, there is a swarm of swells whom I don't know and who bask in the smiles of royalty.[2] We are very quiet ourselves, go out little, and as the fashionable people come to town our little tallow-dip disappears in the glare. There is nothing very much worth seeing. No new books have come out to create even a ripple, so far as I know. There is not even a new man of any prominence. Yet society lumbers ahead and one manages to get a good deal of amusement out of it without getting any excitement to speak of. We were more startled by George Eliot's marriage to John Cross than by the elections themselves.[3] As Cross is semi-American by his business connection, she is half-way to emigration. I suppose her American admirers will howl over the fall of their idol, but I can't say I care much for the idol business, and I am clear that if she found her isolation intolerable, she was quite right to marry Cross if she could get him. It is not quite so easy to explain why Cross should have been willing to marry her, for most men of thirty or forty prefer youth, beauty, children and such things, to intellect in gray hairs. Some people say it was a pure marriage of convenience on both sides, but I know that the Cross family have a sort of superstitious adoration of her.

My odds and ends are gradually getting into shape. I have finished with the Record Office, completed my search through the newspapers, collected the greater part of my pamphlets, and sounded all the wells of private collections I could find. In Paris and Madrid copyists are at work for me and ought soon to send their copy. I foresee a good history if I have health and leisure the next five years, and if nothing happens to my collections of material. My belief is that I can make something permanent of it, but, as time passes, I get into a habit of working only for the work's sake and disliking the idea of completing and publishing. One should have some stronger motive than now exists for authorship. I don't think I care much even to be read, and any writer in this frame of mind must be dull reading. On the other hand I enjoy immensely the investigation, and making little memoranda of passages here and there. Aridity grows on me. I always felt myself like Casaubon in Middlemarch,[4] and now I see the tendency steadily creeping over me.

This makes me all the gladder to see you plunged into active life. I envy you your experience at Chicago, though I cannot for my life see how you can manage to worry through it without getting squeezed.[5] I still stick to Sherman. Edmunds is totally unfit to be President[6] and I should prefer Blaine. Massachusetts ought to throw her whole weight energetically for Sherman in convention; it is the only way to be dignified and consistent. If Sherman is withdrawn, then let the State give its vote to the most respectable candidate on the list, but I confess I think it ought in that case, as a mere matter of respect to a most successful administration, throw one complimentary vote for Hayes.

Many thanks for your Pinkney minutes which I shall be glad to have. He and Monroe made an awful blunder in signing that treaty; they were fairly scared to death.[7] Now that I see the English side, they appear utterly ridiculous, and poor dear old Jefferson too, but our beloved Federalists most of all. Ye Gods, what a rum lot they were!

I had nothing to do with your Cobden Club election.[8] Horace White and David Wells are the men there.

Lowell is expected here on the 17th. I fear his wife is still very poorly, but he has not written me the details. He takes a house near Sarah Darwin's in Southampton, and I suppose will come up at intervals.[9] Harry James is expected from Italy at about the same time. He gave us his newspaper criticisms to read, but as I've not read his books I couldn't judge of their justice. These little fits of temper soon blow over, however, and if he is good-natured about it he will get straight again soon.[10]

I am much touched by your loyalty to your venerable Professor, and I feel like two Casaubons, rather than one, at the idea of standing in the attitude of a gray-haired Nestor surrounded by you and Young and poor Laughlin.[11] By the way, did you see how elaborately Stubbs refers to us in his new edition?[12] John Green is one of my intimate friends here, but how he objurgates you fellows for your German style. He says my Essay is bad enough, but you others are clean mad. We chaff each other thereupon.

My wife sends her kindest regards to Mrs Lodge, as do I mine.

Ever Yrs   Henry Adams.

H. C. Lodge Esq.

MS: MHi

1. In 1872 Henry Parkman Sturgis (b. 1847) married Mary Cecilia Brand, daughter of the speaker of the House of Commons. William Wyndham Portal and Florence Elizabeth Glyn were married June 23.
2. Junius Spencer Morgan (1813–1890), founder of the banking firm of J. S. Morgan and Co.; and his wife, Juliet Pierpont Morgan; Walter Hayes Burns (1838–1897), Morgan's son-in-law and successor as head of the firm; Lyon Playfair (1819–1898), later Baron Playfair of St. Andrews, distinguished chemist; and his wife, Edith Russell Playfair of Boston; George Washburn Smalley (1833–1916), European correspondent of the New York *Tribune* 1867–1895; Alice Mason (1838–1913), former wife of Charles Sumner.
3. On May 6 George Eliot married John Walter Cross (1840–1924), of the banking firm Dennistoun, Cross and Co., of New York and London. She was 60 years old.
4. The egregious pedant in George Eliot's 1871 novel.
5. Lodge was a delegate to the Republican national convention in Chicago.
6. George Franklin Edmunds (1828–1919), senator from Vermont 1866–1891, Independent Republican.
7. The treaty signed in 1806 by William Pinkney (1764–1822) and James Monroe, special envoys to England, was so much to Britain's advantage that Jefferson refused to submit it to the Senate for approval.
8. The Cobden Club was a British society of liberals to which Americans were also elected.
9. Sara Sedgwick Darwin (1864–1922), wife of Charles Darwin's son William and sister-in-law of Charles Eliot Norton.
10. Henry James was "attainted of high treason" (Howells' phrase) by American reviewers of his *Hawthorne* (1879) for his insistence on Hawthorne's provincialism.
11. *Essays in Anglo-Saxon Law*, ed. Henry Adams (1876). The book contained an essay by HA and one by each of his three Ph.D. candidates, Lodge, James Laurence Laughlin (1850–1933), and Ernest Young (d. 1888).
12. William Stubbs in *The Constitutional History of England* (1880), I, 86, extensively summarized Lodge's essay.

To George William Curtis

1607 H Street. Washington. 3 Feb. 1881.

My dear Sir[1]

I fear that your aid is now much needed to hold the political machine here in the situation in which you had a chief share in putting it.

Not knowing whether Mr Garfield has consulted you or not, and quite in the dark as to your own views, I want to tell you what is happening here, and you may then judge for yourself whether you should interpose.

The selection of Blaine as Secretary of State was a thunder-clap for our friends here. At first they were quite dumb-foundered. Schurz had set his heart on our having two representatives in the next cabinet, and had hoped to be allowed to name his successor at the Interior. The man he had selected, with the warm support of his friends, was Gen. Francis A Walker, who is, as you know, from Connecticut. The appointment of Blaine however, created a geographical difficulty which seemed insurmountable. Nevertheless Schurz persisted, and has pressed Mr Garfield very strongly and persistently in the matter, while Mr Garfield, professedly inclining towards Schurz's wishes, has not yet ventured either to approve or reject.

Considering Mr Schurz to be our recognised mouth-piece in the cabinet and in the country, I have not hitherto thought the rest of us called upon to meddle; but it was intimated to me last night by John Hay that Schurz ought to be supported and that Walker's appointment should be more widely accepted by our friends if we expected to obtain it.[2]

Next to Schurz, I regard you as the responsible leader of the independent republicans, and I expect to see you on all proper occasions speak for us all. You can best judge whether now you should yourself write to Garfield, or move others to do it, or leave it alone. As I look upon the appointment of Blaine as the most direct and pointed insult Garfield could have offered to the Massachusetts liberals, I certainly can see nothing but the appointment of Walker and McVeagh, among the names proposed,[3] that would relieve us in Massachusetts from the harrow of Blaine's character and patronage, or promise us the smallest hold on Garfield. If we are to stand aloof and criticise, so be it, but Mr Garfield should understand beforehand why we draw away.

I shall do nothing else about it, and have not even consulted my brother

Charles, knowing that he and I rarely disagree in these matters. Publicity of course is to be avoided, but whatever is done should be done
quickly.

                                      I am very truly yours   Henry Adams.
Geo. W. Curtis Esq.

MS: RPB

1. George William Curtis (1824–1892), a leading spokesman for social reform as editor of
   Harper's Weekly 1863–1892, lecturer, and writer; president of the National Civil Service
   Reform League 1881–1892.
2. HA and John Hay (1838–1905) met for the first time when Hay came to Washington in
   1861 as Lincoln's private secretary. They met again briefly in London in 1867. Hay was
   assistant secretary of state 1879–1881.
3. Issac Wayne MacVeagh (1833–1917), lawyer, minister to Turkey 1870–1871, liberal leader
   in Pennsylvania Republican politics.

To Wayne MacVeagh

                                      Beverly Farms. Mass. 18 July. 1881.

My dear Representative
    Your letters encourage me to think that you are still able to be about.
Now that your chief is in a fair way to boss you again, I suppose your
imprisonment will not be so long or so wearing. He is a wonderfully lucky
man, and I don't know but that this bullet is as lucky a hit as any he ever
made.
    Apropos to this subject, inquiry has been made of me in regard to the
course intended to be pursued by him about the "Garfield Fund," whose
projectors wish for subscriptions hereabouts.[1] Of course you can't doubt
my opinion as to the impropriety of such gifts to men in office, but I could
only say that I would try and find out the President's intentions, because,
if he stops it, there is no use in going on. Until it is settled that he consents,
subscriptions will be slow. I need not add that in a political and especially
in a second-term point of view, in the interest of the party, to which you
know by experience my awfully utter devotion, I should regard his accep-
tance of this gift to Mrs Garfield as most unfortunate.
    Why is the District Attorney so eager to prove Guiteau sane?[2] You can't
hang him. Your only chance of shutting him up for life is to prove him *not*
sane. More than this, the assertion that Guiteau is sane is a gross insult to
the whole American people. We are all of us ready to shoot the President
or anyone else if we can find a good reason for it, but we don't go round
banging away with horse-pistols at our neighbors without good cause. To

say that any sane American would do this is a piece, not of insanity, but of idiocy, in the District Attorney. The peculiarity of insanity is the lack of relation between cause and effect. No one has yet succeeded in establishing any *sane* cause for Guiteau's effect. That he is rational proves nothing. We are all more or less rational; it is an almost invariable sign of insanity. I have no doubt the District Attorney is rational, though his course is not.

Will you be so kind as to offer our friendly regards to Mrs McVeagh and inform her that the tables are ordered and will be on their way in about ten days. One plain red at $8. One mahogany and ebonised border, $12. We hope they will give satisfaction and that you will mention us to your friends.

We have been awfully hot here. One day the thermometer rose to 86. If it returns, I shall return with it, to Washington, but just now I am shivering in winter clothes, and we cower over our blazing fires.

Your very obedient and humble constituent

Henry Adams.

Wayne McVeagh Esq.

MS: PHi

1. Shortly after Garfield was shot a fund was established for the relief of his family in the event that he should die.
2. In newspaper interviews in July, District Attorney George B. Corkhill insisted that Charles Guiteau was sane, and despite Guiteau's bizarre behavior at the trial in December, he was found guilty and hanged. At the invitation of Dr. Charles F. Folsom of Boston, a medical witness for the defense, the Adamses went to the trial for an afternoon and met Guiteau in jail.

To E. L. Godkin

Beverly Farms. September 19, 1881.

My dear Godkin[1]

Your's of the 17th has just come. As to the Post Stock, I know nothing about it, more than the man in the moon. I have not a notion whether it is a good or a bad investment or how you have been doing since you took it in hand, or what dividends you mean to make, or whether your combination is working satisfactorily and is likely to last. I take it for granted that there are risks which I know nothing about, and which I don't much care to know unless they are strong enough to break the thing down. This is not my usual way of investing money, for I rather affect business-like principles, but in this case it is with me rather a question of keeping in with my crowd than of investing money, and I want to do precisely whatever suits best the interests of the paper and its managers. Your note is laconic. You do not say how the stock is to be held, or where you would rather see it placed, or whether you have made any allotment of it. I will answer by leaving it to you. Put me down for $20,000 if it suits your interests to do so, (and by *you,* I mean not only you but Schurz and White and the E.P. inclusive). If you find that a smaller allotment is more convenient, make it $15,000; or make it $10,000; or make it $5,000. I will make one, two, three or four shares, as you please; only, for the sake of my credit, please let me know when you will want it, and whether in one payment or in more.

We are going to have a nasty *chopping-sea* in politics for the next three years if Arthur is what we think him.[2] I am a bad sailor, and easily made sea-sick. For God's sake do keep the E.P. steady. I wish I may be drowned if I don't more than half want to stick by the administration through everything, like an old King's friend. We shall go on to Washington early, to try for an office under the new man; an Assistant Secretaryship of Legation somewhere in Germany, I think. Don't let the new Secy. of State [Geo. M. Boutwell of Mass.] know that I hold stock in your concern.[3]

Very truly Yrs   Henry Adams.

E. L. Godkin Esq.

MS: MH

1. Edwin L. Godkin (1831–1902), associate editor of the New York *Evening Post,* of which the new proprietors were Carl Schurz, editor-in-chief; Horace White; and Godkin.
2. President Garfield's death was imminent. He died late that night. Vice-President Chester A. Arthur (1830–1886) was known as a New York machine politician.
3. HA's brackets. George S. Boutwell (1818–1905), representative from Massachusetts 1863–1869, secretary of the Treasury 1869–1873. HA had thought him the weakest of President Grant's cabinet appointments.

To Henry Cabot Lodge

1607 H Street.
Tuesday, 15 Nov. 1881.

My dear Lodge

News travels slow between Lynn and Washington. The Evening Post said you had been beaten, but I have not yet heard particulars, and I write merely to inquire about it.[1]

This is one of the draw-backs to politics as a pursuit. I suppose every man who has looked on at the game has been struck by the remarkable way in which politics deteriorate the moral tone of everyone who mixes in them. The deterioration is far more marked than in any other occupation

I know except the turf, stock-jobbing, and gambling. I imagine the reason in each case to be the same. It is the curse of politics that what one man gains, another man loses. On such conditions you can create not even an average morality. Politicians as a class must be as mean as card-sharpers, turf-men, or Wall Street curb-stone operators. There is no respectable industry in existence which will not average a higher morality.

Whether you have slipped up on this mud-bank, or only have been upset by accident, I do not know, but in any case the moment is one for you to stop and think about it. I have never known a young man go into politics who was not the worse for it. I could give a list as long as the Athenaeum Catalogue,[2] from my two brothers, John and Brooks, down to Willy Astor, Ham. Fish, and Robert Ray Hamilton.[3] They all try to be honest, and then are tripped up by the dishonest; or they try to be dishonest (i.e. practical politicians) and degrade their own natures. In the first case they become disappointed and bitter; in the other they lose self-respect. My conclusion is that no man should be in politics unless he would honestly rather not be there. Public service should be a *corvée;* a disagreeable necessity. The satisfaction should consist in getting out of it.

So much for your mishap, which I hope will still at last strengthen you even politically. I wish I could send you pleasanter news from here, but it is much worse than your affair. Our friend McVeagh, after an heroic and desperate as well as prolonged struggle to drag President Arthur into the assertion of reform principles, has utterly and hopelessly failed. The new administration will be the centre for every element of corruption, south and north. The outlook is very discouraging.

With our best love to your wife

Ever sincerely Yrs   Henry Adams.

MS: MHi

1. Lodge lost a close election to the Massachusetts state senate from the Lynn district.
2. The catalogue of Boston's large subscription library.
3. William Waldorf Astor (1848–1919) of New York, great-grandson of the enormously wealthy John Jacob Astor (1763–1848), lost elections to Congress in 1880 and 1881. He settled in England in 1890. Hamilton Fish, Jr. (1849–1936), private secretary to his father, Grant's secretary of state, was New York assemblyman 1876–1896. Robert Ray Hamilton (1850–1890), great-grandson of Alexander Hamilton, lost the 1881 election to the New York assembly.

To John Hay

1607 H Street. Sunday, 30 April, '82

Sweet heart[1]

Your letter from N.Y. was a good deed in a naughty world.[2] We had hoped for a line without expecting it. On the whole, if you will only behave yourself, live in the open air and seek a tolerable climate, I see no reason why you may not live to pronounce a parting address over the graves of all the other hearts, and my only regret is that I cannot engage you in advance to oust the clergyman at my own funeral. Prayer I won't have, but I want a little speech or two, as: "Fellows, this departed heart first discovered the true meaning of sac and soc; he liked sack and claret; he invented Jefferson, Gallatin and Burr; he laughed at King's puns and Hay's jokes; also at Emily Beale's; and any man who could do all that, deserves all he will get when he gets there."[3]

Your suggestions as to the dear Hamilton shall be followed.[4] To me the man is noxious, not because of the family quarrel, for he was punished sufficiently on that account, but because he combined all the elements of a Scotch prig in a nasty form. For that reason I prefer not to touch him if I can help it, and shall follow your advice by cutting out all I can cut, in regard to him, and emasculating the rest.

First-heart, as you call her, is in bed with a severe cold since Friday, but sends her tender regards to the two of Cleveland. I now keep a hospital. She is in bed in one room, and my brother in the adjoining one. If you were only here in a third, the ward would be full. We couldn't then take King in.

I have a funny dinner today which I wish you could help me with. Hal Richardson the architect, O. C. Marsh, Edmund Hudson of the Boston Herald, old George Bancroft, my brother Brooks.[5] What do you suppose they can talk about?

Ever   Henry Adams.

John Hay Esq.

MS: MHi

1. An allusion to the "Five of Hearts"—John Hay, Clara Hay (1939–1914), HA and MHA, and Clarence King (1842–1901), director of the U.S. Geological Fortieth Parallel Survey. In Nov. 1881 Hay had stationery imprinted for them with a playing-card five of hearts in the upper left corner.
2. *The Merchant of Venice,* V, i. 90.
3. Emily Beale (d. 1912), a vivacious Lafayette Square neighbor, later Mrs. John R. McLean.
4. After reading HA's manuscript on Burr, Hay protested that Hamilton deserved more considerate treatment.
5. Henry H. Richardson (1838–1886), architect, whose style was derivative from the Romanesque; Othniel C. Marsh (1831–1899), Yale paleontologist; George Bancroft (1800–1891), a Washington neighbor whose monumental *History of the United States* had been issued in 1876 in a revised six-volume edition.

To William James

Beverly Farms, Mass. 27 July, 1882.

My dear James[1]

I have read your two papers with that attention which, &c, &c, &c, and am partially prepared to discuss them with you.[2] As I understand your Faith, your x, your reaction of the individual on the cosmos, it is the old question of Free Will over again. You *choose* to assume that the will is free. Good! Reason proves that the Will cannot be free. Equally good! Free or not, the mere fact that a doubt can exist, proves that x must be a very microscopic quantity. If the orthodox are grateful to you for such gifts, the world has indeed changed, and we have much to thank God for, if there is a God, that he should have left us unable to decide whether our thoughts, if we have thoughts, are our own or his'n.

Although your gift to the church seems to me a pretty darned mean one, I admire very much your manner of giving it, which magnifies the crumb into at least forty loaves and fishes. My wife is quite converted by it. She enjoyed the paper extremely. Since she read it she has talked of giving five dollars to Russell Sturgis's church for napkins. As the impression fades, she says less of the napkins.[3]

With hero worship like Carlyle's, I have little patience. In history heroes have neutralysed each other, and the result is no more than would have been reached without them. Indeed in military heroes I suspect that the ultimate result has been retardation. Nevertheless you could doubtless at any time stop the entire progress of human thought by killing a few score of men. So far I am with you.[4] A few hundred men represent the entire intellectual activity of the whole thirteen hundred millions. What then? They drag us up the cork-screw stair of thought, but they can no more get their brains to run out of their especial convolutions than a railway train (with a free will of half an inch on three thousand miles) can run free up Mount Shasta. Not one of them has ever got so far as to tell us a single vital fact worth knowing. We can't prove even that we are.

Meanwhile I enclose your letter to Monod.[5]

Pleasant voyage and happy return. Our love to Harry.

Ever truly   Henry Adams.

MS: MH

1. William James (1842–1910), brother of Henry James, Harvard professor and a leading authority on psychology; *The Principles of Psychology* (1890).

2. "Rationality, Activity, and Faith," *Princeton Review* 2 (July 1882), 58–86; "Great Men, Great Thoughts, and the Environment," *Atlantic Monthly* 46 (Oct. 1880), 441–459.
3. MHA's cousin Russell Sturgis, Jr. (1831–1899), had been zealously raising money for a new YMCA building in Boston to include a chapel.
4. James maintained that great men influence the direction in which society evolves.
5. Presumably a letter of introduction to Gabriel Monod (1844–1912), the French historian. James was going to Europe in September on a leave of absence from his post at Harvard.

To John Hay

Beverly Farms, Mass. Sunday, 8 Oct. 1882.

My dear Hay-oh

Your name naturally prolongs itself into a sigh as I think what fun I should have had if I had been with you in England. Why could not you and King have come over in 1880 when we were living there? Then we would have scaled Heaven and gone down into Hell, but now, look-ye, I am a mud-turtle, and for four months I have burrowed here in the ground without sight of sun or stars. Thank the eternal furies, a fortnight from today we shall be again wallowing in human depravity, at New York, and for the next eight months I think we shall have the better of you. Florence and Nice are frankly *bête* beside Washington.

Long letters from Sir John and Sir Robert, the brace of baronets, sing your praises, and I am really pleased to think that you like them.[1] Robert Cunliffe is one of my few swans; I am very fond of him, and have always found him a gentleman to the core, which is muchissimo dear. The universe hitherto has existed in order to produce a dozen people to amuse the five of hearts. Among us, we know all mankind. We or our friends have canvassed creation, and there are but a dozen or two companions in it;— men and women, I mean, whom you like to have about you, and whose society is an active pleasure. To me, Robert Cunliffe is one of these, not on account of his wit or knowledge, but because he is what a gentleman ought to be.

Next spring, when you return to England, I shall get you to look up at Westminster our friend Ralph Palmer, a dear Dobbin, whom Cunliffe will introduce you to.[2] If you go to Florence, please get yourself introduced to Adela Bossi. Her husband, Count Bossi, is a nice fellow. Adela (I call her so because she was an angel to me once when no one but an angel could have been in such a Hell as I was) is an English-Italian little woman, sympatica and simple. If you meet her or can find her, tell her that I sent you and that I love her just as much as ever. She is not so young now as she was two-and-twenty years ago when I first met her, but she must always be a pleasant acquaintance. All the English, and the old Americans will know all about her.

If you follow your scheme, and write a story "by the author &c," I hope you will take the new *motif* under your eyes.[3] Describe the sufferings of the anonymous author on hearing his book discussed in a foreign country, and how it gradually led him to murder and self-destruction. Although my brain is much disturbed by the whirl of authors known to have written your book, and the vision of you and King and James listening to revelations on the subject is almost too much for me, still I cannot but feel that, had I such a load on my conscience, the listening to British clack would drive me insane. How you have stood it, I tremble to think. Much as I disapprove the *spirit* of your book (resp. Miss Loring's, King's or DeForest's) I can see that in English reflection it must become more terrible to its creator than to anyone else.[4] I can imagine you cowering and crushed under the ignominious popularity you have tumbled into. The situation is tragi-comic in an exceptional degree, and quite new to literature. You can make some atonement for your offence, by explaining the terrors of your atonement. This new crucifixion is unique in history, and should have a great success. After all, to write for people who can't read, as the Frenchman said, may be a severe trial, but the least you can do is to teach them their letters.

I see that the political libel for which you (or De Forest) are popularly supposed to be responsible is to be brought out here in a cheap edition. This, I confess, strikes me as doubtful taste, considering all the circumstances, but perhaps you know best. I am sure you will have been greatly pleased by Folger's nomination in New York, which, to the superficial observer, might seem to lend some color to libels like "Democracy," &c, but which in truth is evidence that we are improving.[5] I am told that the whole Union Club has kicked over the traces and this time there will be fun. You will deplore republican defeat, but you will be glad to see Willy Walter's success and especially his energetic support of the tariff.[6] Like him, I stand up for the tariff as long as that duty on copper is kept up, but if Congress shall be rash enough to touch that key-stone of the system and of our liberties, I go in for free trade pure and simple.[7] On this copper— or iron as the case may be—let Willy Walter, and you and I, take a bold stand.

Gilman of Johns Hopkins gives me a very hopeful account of your new University at Cleveland.[8] I hope to see you Professor of Theology and Ethics, President and Corporation, all at once, some day, and perhaps, when copper is free, you will take me in too, and give me something to do. I don't know any history, but I know a little of everything else worth knowing, and can teach just as well without any knowledge at all.

My John Randolph is just coming into the world.[9] Do you know, a book to me always seems a part of myself, a kind of intellectual brat or segment, and I never bring one into the world without a sense of shame. They are naked, helpless and beggarly, yet the poor wretches must live forever and curse their father for their silent tomb. This particular brat is the first I ever detested. He is the only one I wish never to see again; but I know he will live to dance, in the obituaries, over my cold grave. Don't read him, should you by chance meet him. Kick him gently, and let him go.

Houghton declines to print Aaron because Aaron wasn't a "Statesman." Not bad, that, for a damned bookseller! He should live awhile at Washington and know our *real* statesmen. I am glad to get out of Houghton's hands, for I want to try Harper or Appleton.[10] Which recommendest thou? I incline towards Harper.

Our joint love to Mrs Hay. We are broken-hearted to think of our solitary New York a fortnight hence.

Ever Yrs heartily   Henry Adams.

MS: MHi

1. Sir John F. Clark (1821–1910), 2nd baronet, retired diplomat, owner of estate at Tilly-pronie, Scotland; and Sir Robert A. Cunliffe.
2. William Dobbin, an unselfish and faithful character in Thackeray's *Vanity Fair* (1847–48).
3. HA's anonymous novel *Democracy* (1880), a "political libel" which depicted the corruption of American politics, had been much appreciated in England. Its authorship was a well-kept secret, and Adams and Hay enjoyed bandying each other about it.
4. Various persons, among many others, reputed to be the author of *Democracy*. HA jokingly treats Hay as the author.
5. Charles J. Folger (1818–1884) was nominated for governor despite the opposition of independent-minded Republicans.
6. William Walter Phelps (1839–1894), Republican, U.S. minister to Austria. He was nominated for Congress Sept. 27.
7. HA, like many of his Boston friends, had invested in the Calumet and Hecla copper mines developed by their compatriot, geologist and mining engineer Alexander Agassiz (1835–1910).
8. Daniel Coit Gilman (1831–1908), president of Johns Hopkins University. Amasa Stone (1818–1883), Hay's father-in-law, gave $500,000 to Western Reserve University in 1880. Hay served on the board of trustees 1881–1905.
9. HA's biography *John Randolph* was published in 1882.
10. The Burr manuscript was not published.

To Charles Milnes Gaskell

1607 H Street. Washington. 3 Dec. 1882.

My dear Carlo

Your letter of Oct. 16 has been lying some weeks on my table, and the photographs of your discovered saints[1] have adorned my library. They are interesting, and if you find out when they were done, I would like to know.

Of our news, little can be said. We broke up our villegiatura on the 17th October, and glad we were to get back to life again. The result of four months by the sea-side was only a certain amount of manuscript, and a small volume, of which, after much labor and suffering, I was at last safely accouché at the time of our departure. I did not send it to you because it is so purely American and local in subject, that I knew it would bore you. I have sent no copies to your side of the water.

Before coming away I passed a couple of nights at Quincy with my father and mother. My father declines very slowly; indeed I am not certain that physically he declines at all, and he declares that he is physically stronger than ever. Mentally he is a wreck; that is to say, his memory for recent things is almost wholly gone, and what is worse, he has enough memory left, to remember wrong, and to imagine much that never was. This is always the case, I believe, with this affection of the memory, and luckily it does not make him unhappy. He is quite aware of his failure, and I have noticed for near five years that he was more cautious than ever in talking, but after watching him carefully and talking a great deal with my mother about it, I feel sure that there is no occasion to distress ourselves about him now. He is as contented, and free from pain of any kind, as a man can be. I should not greatly object to going in the same way, if my caste of mind were as composed as his.

My mother grows older, and I fear she is getting a little deaf. On the whole she is not badly off. She is never alone. Her children and grand-children are always about her, and they are as yet all decent people. She is now the head of the family, with the whole care of my father, and an income of some £15,000 a year. On the whole the position is not an unsatisfactory one for old age, and I think she is not more depressed by it than she always was by the various exigencies of life.

A very few years now will bring me and my generation into the fifties and start us down the home quarter. I am working very hard to get everything out of my brain that can be made useful. If my father is a test, I can count on twenty years more brain, if the physical machine holds out.

Do you know that you and I have corresponded for about that time? The other day it occurred to me that Thackeray had written a ballad about an old man alone and merry at forty year, dipping his nose in the Gascon wine, and I laughed as though it were a joke.[2]

I cannot find that boys of twenty have any other poets, novelists histories or loves than those we share with them; for I make it a rule to be friends with all the prettiest girls, and they like me much better than they did five-and-twenty years ago, and talk more confidentially of their doings.

Basta! I grow garrulous and shall soon drivel. How goes it with you? Is Crump yet raising money on post obits? I have but one rule in life. I try to spend every penny of income I have in the world, and if possible a little more, for I care not to pile up wealth for nephews and nieces, especially as I look forward to outliving them all. You will, I hope, do otherwise. Make Crump very rich, so that when England turns communist, he may come over here to spend your money, or what is left of it. Mrs Langtry is carrying ours back to you.[3] I am happy to say that this female has found her level, and my first fears that society would take her up, have proved quite groundless. Luckily Washington is a simple spot, and a small income goes further here than anywhere. I know of no one in decent society who seems to spend more than £5000. Your representative, Mr Sackville West, a very dull little man, with a queer little illegitimate Spanish daughter, quite pretty and baby-like, has, I believe £5000 a year and is thought a great swell.[4] There are plenty of millionaires, but they don't spend money here. Thank a blessed democratic simplicity!

I hear nothing of England but what is in the newspapers—chiefly scandals of that kind for which it seems to me that England has a monopoly, for I never hear of them in other countries. Two or three cases have occurred in our simple-minded society, all of foreigners; one, a Hay, son I suppose of Lord Dupplin, who came to Lenox with letters and a woman who was going to have a baby and answered dinner-invitations as Ruby. I believe they had financial difficulties and disappeared, nor do I know whether they were supposed to be married. Just now we have here a French adventurer in search of a rich wife, Comte de Fitzjames.[5] I wish British sovereigns—de facto or de jure—would keep their mistresses and bastards at home. Then I see that Mandeville has come back again. America is getting to be a nuisance with the European nobility of it.

Luckily some respectable people come over though I rarely see them. Our life and society are so quiet, and come so little in contact with fashion in any form that I can only ask you to tell me what ails the Coutts Lindsays.

Our tender regards to your wife and Crump, and all the larger circle, including especially May Doyle when you see her, and of course F.T.P.[6]

Your nephew seems thus far all right.

Ever Yrs   Henry Adams.

MS: MHi

1. On the 12th-century lavatory panels unearthed in Gaskell's restoration of his residence at Wenlock Abbey.
2. "The Age of Wisdom," in *Ballads* (1855).
3. Lily Langtry (known as the "Jersey Lily") (1852–1929), English actress and famed beauty, made a sensationally successful American tour.
4. Sir Lionel Sackville-West (1827–1908), minister to the U.S. 1881–1888, and his daughter Victoria (1862–1936). Her mother was the Spanish dancer Joseta ("Pepita") Duran de Oliva, who, separated from her husband, lived with Sackville-West until her death in 1871 and bore him five other children.
5. Henri-Marie de Fitz-James (b. 1855), a descendant of James II of England.
6. Mary A. Doyle (d. 1924), related to Gaskell's aunt. F. T. P.: Francis Turner Palgrave.

To John Hay

1607 H Street. 2 Feb. 1884.

Dear Heart

The enclosed, just forwarded to me by Godkin, is a joke, so far better than any I ever thought this world could produce, that I hardly dare send it to you, for fear of its effect.[1] I want to roll on the floor; to howl, kick and sneeze, to weep silent tears of thankfulness to a beneficent providence which has permitted me to see this day; and finally, I want to drown my joy in oceans of Champagne and lemonade. Never, No, never, since Cain wrote his last newspaper letter about Abel, was there anything so droll.

When you have done with it, return it to me. I am going to have it cut in gold letters on the front of our new houses. I would not part with this autograph of my beloved brother for all his cattle-yard stock. Poor though I be, I am richer than common men can dream of, so long as I have the whole Arabian Nights, the Odyssey, and Alice in the Looking Glass, all crowded into one small page of fraternal writing.

Meanwhile, keep perfectly secret about it. To tell anyone would betray us all. Godkin knows my side of the joke, and probably suspects yours. I shall write to him to get the "Note" if possible, and print it with the writer's initials.[2]

Yours arrived yesterday. Richardson will need some little time to work out his plan, as he has got to devise two distinct, harmonious exteriors, and to arrange them for the chance of a seven-story, apartment-building background.[3] I hardly expect anything from him for another week or two; but he has been successful about the Pittsburg competition, and I mean to make the Pittsburgers give us about 20 per cent more house than we should have had.

Oh, but I wish you were here! Can't you and Mrs Hay come on? With jokes like these flying round, life becomes a new, undreamed-of joy.

Ever your poor, coarse and half-educated friend

Henry Adams.

Col. John Hay.

P.S. My coarse and half-educated wife has had a fit over her brother-in-law's Nast-like touch.

MS: MHi

1. The enclosure was a letter from HA's brother Charles to Edwin L. Godkin, associate editor of the New York *Evening Post,* of which the *Nation* was the weekly edition. Charles, ignorant that HA was the author of the novel *Democracy,* suggested that Godkin publish in the *Nation* his discovery that *The Bread-Winners,* a recent anonymous novel having "the same coarse half-educated touch" as *Democracy,* was by the same author; "the Nast-like style of its portrait and painting is unmistakable." Thomas Nast (1840–1902) was famous for his scathing political cartoons in the press. John Hay was the author of *The Bread-Winners.*
2. CFA2's "note," phrased much like his letter but signed "A," appeared in *Nation* 38 (Feb. 21, 1885), 165.
3. HA and John Hay engaged H. H. Richardson to design adjoining houses for them on H Street across from the White House.

To Charles Milnes Gaskell

Beverly Farms, Mass. 21 Sept. 1884.

Dear Carl

Winter is coming again. The grey hairs in my beard are getting the better of the lovely hue which nature first adorned my head with. I grow giddy at times in watching the years fly past, and in wondering at a world so different from that which I first knew. But the amusement is quite as good as ever, and if I could only forget to be serious, or remember to laugh where the jokes come in, I should enjoy myself immoderately.

We are here plunged in politics funnier than words can express. Very great issues are involved. Especially everyone knows that a step towards free trade is inevitable if the democrats come in. For the first time in twentyeight years, a democratic administration is almost inevitable. The public is angry and abusive. Everyone takes part. We are all doing our best, and swearing at each other like demons. But the amusing thing is that no one talks about real interests. By common consent they agree to let these alone. We are afraid to discuss them. Instead of this, the press is engaged in a most amusing dispute whether Mr Cleveland had an illegitimate child, and did or did not live with more than one mistress; whether Mr Blaine got paid in railway bonds for services as Speaker; and whether Mrs Blaine had a baby three months after her marriage. Nothing funnier than some of these subjects has been treated in my time. I have laughed myself red with amusement over the letters, affidavits, leading articles and speeches which are flying through the air. Society is torn to pieces. Parties are wrecked from top to bottom. A great political revolution seems impending. Yet, when I am not angry, I can do nothing but laugh.

I am a free-trade democrat and support Mr Cleveland. I believe he will come in, and in that case my friends will have to reduce our protective duties. The result of this course, if we persevere in it, will be serious to the world; but about ten years more will be needed to effect it.

I am building a house in Washington, which also amuses me, as it will you if I send you a photograph of it. Unfortunately it is now barely above ground and will not be finished for a year.

My history rolls on. I am privately printing my second volume.[1] I hope to finish the whole on or about January 1889. We mean then to go round the world, and I shall want letters to the Governor General of India and the Grand Lama of Thibet. Please take care to be in office. If you see Grant Duff, please thank him for his letter and enclosure to me.

Financially we grub along and talk poor, but as no one here need spend money unless he likes, the loss of thousands of millions has little outward effect. No improvement need be expected until things have got settled to a new economic bottom. Most of us are really better off when the great properties shrink. I am sorry for your Wabash, but conservative people here avoid Mr Jay Gould and expect him to take their money if he can get it.[2] John Hay plays with that edge-tool, but I don't.

The Hays have been passing some weeks near us, and have now gone home to Cleveland where John is presiding over Blaine meetings. We don't talk politics, as we are on opposite sides. Clarence King has returned, but I have not seen him. The Gurneys are here, very much as usual. My own family at Quincy is a wreck. My father is broken to pieces; my mother is barely able to move about. We ought all to get ourselves out of this scrape of life by the time we are seventy, for there is nothing but tribulation afterwards.

My wife is well, and sends her regards to you and yours. We return to Washington in about three weeks to look after our house.

Ever Yrs Henry Adams.

C. M. Gaskell Esq.

MS: MHi

1. The two privately printed draft volumes carried the history of the United States to the end of the second administration of Thomas Jefferson.
2. Jay Gould (1836–1892), railroad financier, whose schemes HA and CFA2 had exposed in their *Chapters of Erie,* had sold most of his stock in the Wabash Railroad to English investors in 1881 at the top of the market.

To Sir John Clark

1607 H Street. Washington. D.C. 13 Dec. 1884.

My dear Sir John

Our two nations have the most unexpected ways of surprising us. They do silly things and then escape the consequences in a manner that baffles belief. We set up an unredeemed scoundrel for President, and were doubly horrified to find that he, chiefly by means of your infamous blackguard Monsignor Capel, had purchased almost all the Irish.[1] Such a combination was enough to scare the equanimity of Caesar Borgia.[2] I never saw decent society before so angry, or so united, but most people thought we should be beaten. As it was, we had barely five hundred votes to spare in a total of ten millions, but we cleaned out the combination. Now I see your old Tories suddenly turning about and passing reform bills which would have made them emigrate in a mass to the Fejee Islands when I had the honor of knowing them five-and-twenty years ago; and I think at that time the Whigs would have joined the circus and emigrated in company. If I live another quarter of a century I expect to see Great Britain admitted into the American Union, and Bradlaugh President of the whole outfit.[3] Every time I make up my mind for a big upset, the world suddenly, instead of going off its head, turns round and laughs. The fact is, we are getting old, and losing our eye-sight. I can only console myself in the terms of King's story about the lamented Laura Fair of Nevada: "Jim, set up the oyster-cans!"[4]

I have not seen King since his return. Hay says he is dead, but I don't believe it. Hay himself is trying to survive the horrors of winter in Cleveland while I build a house for him here. The house-building amuses me, but I think Cleveland does by no means amuse him, and I dread every letter he writes, for fear of bad news.

History grinds itself out like saw-dust. I have privately printed for my own use two heavy volumes containing eight years, 1801–1809; and eight years more remain to be written. Unless I lose my small remnant of brain in burrowing into the mould of forgotten incompetence, I hope to get the task completed in four years more. Then I shall have to quit the country, for the book will make me so many enemies that the interior of China alone will remain for a refuge. I am hesitating between becoming an Arab or a Tartar, but by that time I suppose the Nomads will all vote for President, and nothing but the South Pole will remain for an independent citizen of the world.

Literature is dull here. My friend and cousin Frank Parkman's "Montcalm and Wolfe" is worth your reading.[5] I glanced at Croker, and for the first time thought Macaulay not too severe.[6] Will any future age think the period of the thirties and forties interesting? To me, history and biography end with 1815. After 1830 nothing has flavor, and Sir Robert Peel is the ideal bore.[7] Curious it is, but true, that from the moment men stop cutting each others' throats, they cease to amuse.

Nothing could be pleasanter or less heroic than our lives in this small capital. Just enough society, and just enough variety of interest to make each day different and yet the same. I never feel a wish to wander, and for eight months at a time never even enter a railway train. My wife is worse than I am. Nothing will induce her to contemplate any change except final cremation, which has a certain interest of new experience. We ride when the day is warm; and we sit by our fire and talk with our friends at five o'clock; but we never dream of travel or of office. Satan is powerless over our virtuous lives.

Your country-people turn up quite often;—seldom the swells, who prefer New York; but often very agreeable semi-official gentry like General Strachey, and a young Lubbock with his Herschel wife.[8] Diplomatically your Legation does not shine. In short, to spare your pride as much as possible, I will only say that you are represented by a set of the most copper-fastened, cork-soled, condensing-cylindered idiots and imbeciles I ever met in a diplomatic drawing-room; and I've met more there than anywhere else. An exception seems likely to be deserved in the case of a Mrs Hellyer, wife of the Sec. Leg. She is young, pretty and vivacious. Who is she? Does the aristocracy of England boast of her?

Give our best joint love to Miladi, and assure her of our affection. I know not yet who is to succeed Lowell. If it should be my friend Mr Hewitt, you should know him.[9] You will probably dislike him; most people do; but he is a man worth knowing, and a close intimate of ours. Perhaps his brother-in-law Edward Cooper, may take it; also a good appointment.[10] In any case, the person will be well chosen.

Give our love to our friends, and believe me ever yours

Henry Adams.

Sir John Clark

MS: ViU

1. Blaine, the Republican candidate for the presidency, was said to be supported by Msgr. Thomas Capel (1836–1911), Roman Catholic proselytizer. Blaine, a pet antipathy of HA, lost by a narrow margin.
2. Cesare Borgia (1475–1507), a cardinal noted for his profligacy and murderous intrigues.
3. The Reform Bill of 1884 reduced the financial qualifications for voters. Charles Bradlaugh (1833–1891), atheist and radical politician, had been repeatedly excluded from the House of Commons for refusing to take the oath on the Bible. He was finally admitted in 1886.
4. Laura Fair (1837–1919), keeper of a lodging house in Virginia City, Nevada, shot and killed her lover. She was acquitted in her second trial. King's story turned on her using large oyster cans for target practice when her aim began to fail.
5. Francis Parkman, *Montcalm and Wolfe* (1884).
6. *Memoirs, Diaries, and Correspondence of the Right Hon. John Croker*, ed. L. J. Jennings (1884). Croker, a British statesman and writer, was an opponent of Macaulay.
7. Sir Robert Peel (1788–1850), founder of the conservative wing of the Tory party. Long active in politics, he served twice as prime minister.
8. Sir Richard Strachey (1817–1908), engineer, was in Washington as British representative at the Prime Meridian Conference. Nevile Lubbock (1839–1914) and his second wife, Constance Ann (d. 1939), daughter of the famous scientist Sir John Herschel.
9. Abram S. Hewitt (1822–1903), New York industrialist, Democratic representative in Congress.
10. Edward Cooper (1824–1905), Hewitt's partner in business and in politics.

To Oliver Wendell Holmes

1607 H Street. Washington. 4 Jan. 1885

My dear Dr Holmes

Will you forgive me for writing a few words to say with how much pleasure I have read your volume on Emerson?[1] I fear that Emerson, with all his immortal longings and oneness with nature, could not have returned such a compliment in kind. He had neither the lightness of touch nor the breadth of sympathy that make your work so much superior to anything that we other men, who call ourselves younger, succeed in doing.

As a mere student I could have wished one chapter more, to be reserved for the dissecting-room alone. After studying the scope of any mind, I want as well to study its limitations. The limitations of Napoleon's, or Shake-speare's minds would tell me more than their extensions, so far as relative values are concerned. Emerson's limitations seemed to me very curious and interesting. At one time I had a list of five dicta of his, some of which belonged probably to the narrowed perceptions of his decline. I have forgotten some of them, but they began: No. 1, "There is no music in Shelley." No. 2, "There is no humor in Aristophanes." No. 3, "Photographs give more pleasure than paintings": (i.e. the photograph of a painting gave him more pleasure than the painting itself.). No. 4, "Egypt is uninteresting."

In obtaining extreme sublimation or tenuity of intelligence, I infer that sensuousness must be omitted. If Mr Emerson was in some respects more than human, he paid for it by being in other respects proportionately less.

Will you pardon my asking a favor? When you print another edition, will you not insert more specimens of the poetry? As a rule you cannot underrate the knowledge of your readers. Crass ignorance is the natural condition of the wisest and most learned of men. Even admirers of Emerson may not carry all his poetry in their heads, or have a copy of his works at their elbow. If I were daring enough to hint it, I would even go so far as to say that however much respect the public may feel for Judge Hoar, Mr Freeman Clarke and Mr Alcott, they feel a strong and decided preference for yourself, in the matter of literature; and would be willing to spare no small part of Chapter XV, if by doing so they could correspondingly enlarge Chapter XIV.[2]

This is an Art-criticism which I ought not to venture; but we unillumined, although pleased and proud to admire and study Mr Emerson, must always indulge in a little kick or snort of protest at having Mr Emerson's echoes make themselves heard. Human nature is but a reed shaken by a breeze. The Concord breeze shakes it sometimes like an east wind.

Old Mr Bancroft is quite delighted with your book, and cries for his eighty years again to do it justice. I am, for my own account, sadly struck by the vast superiority you literary gentlemen maintain over us politicians. I cannot but think the poorest volume of the "Men of Letters" better than the best volume of the "Statesmen."

Please give my warmest regards to Mrs Holmes, and believe me very sincerely yours

Henry Adams.

Dr O. W. Holmes.

MS: MH

1. *Ralph Waldo Emerson* (1885), American Men of Letters series.
2. The account of Emerson's funeral in chap. 15 includes eulogies by James Freeman Clarke (1810–1888), Unitarian clergyman and social reformer; Ebenezer Rockwood Hoar (1816–1895); and Bronson Alcott (1799–1888), utopian Transcendentalist and educator. Chap. 14 treats Emerson's poetry.

To Marian Hooper Adams

1607 H Street. Saturday, 28 March [1885]
10 P.M.

Dear Aspasia[1]

Did I promise to write to you tonight? I think I did; and I do obey your command the more obediently in that I foresee myself greatly pressed for time tomorrow. Please imagine me seated by the library fire, writing this on my knee while Boojum snores at my feet.

After the scrawl I sent you last night, I eat my little supper, read a play of Labiche,[2] and went to bed, where I slept harmoniously till eight this morning, and woke with a vile head-ache due to a bottle of pale ale which I had foolishly drunk on the Boston train. At ten o'clock I was starting for Washington from Jersey City, and until the train reached Wilmington I read the last Century and drank green tea. At Wilmington it occurred to me to walk through the cars, and had proceeded through three with no happier result than a nod from Paymaster Bacon, when I was saluted by a Hello, and then and there I saw Clarence King seated next to Bonaparte (whom he did not know) and opposite to his sister who looked very fresh, delicate and pretty.[3] You may imagine that I felt for once in luck. From Wilmington to Washington we talked on time. King was on his way to Mexico tonight; had brought his sister to pass a fortnight with the daughter of some Admiral Simpson in M Street; and refused to stay an hour himself. We talked and talked till we reached Washington, but he would not come up to the house because his train started in half an hour. As he wanted some tea and a tea-ball, I hurried up in the rain and sent him pretty much all that was left of the chest, and my small tea-ball. Then I embraced the dogs who never stopped yelling (poor Possum has been much depressed), and while I was making a cup of tea for myself at half past four, King walked in. His train did not start till ten. We indulged in a cup of tea, and then went out in the rain to look at the houses which he warmly approved. Hay's roof is getting on, but the workmen had gone and we could not see the interiors, so we went to Anderson's[4] and sat half an hour with Madame where Elsie has the German measles. Nothing new could be elicited from Mrs Anderson, so we came back. The only letter I found was one from Hay narrating how he had been in bed, and the children had been there too, and how he wanted to escape from Cleveland and join King, so I was able to do him a good turn by giving the letter to King who promised to telegraph to him. Then we had dinner and pleasant talk till half past nine.

King became a whole-souled convert to the Turner Worcester, and went through all our bric-a-brac, and was as sympathetic and amusing as ever.[5] Little was said of politics, but you will be relieved to hear that he said he could not vote and had not voted for Blaine. He told me much about his European experiences and his purchases of pictures, and half offered to let me have his Turner Whaler and Cotman Castle. He bought of Ruskin the Fluellen of Turner, one of the same Swiss series as our Martigny, and said that Stillman, in the Evening Post, had declared Jim Higginson's Cassiobury to be not a Turner at all. I imagine that Stillman did not know enough to be aware that it was actually an engraved picture, authenticated as few are.[6]

All our best pleasures are brief, and so the Will' o' the Wisp vanished at half past nine, tea, tea-ball and all, on his way to New Orleans, Sombrereto, the city of Mexico and beyond, to be gone, he avers, three weeks, but nearer three months by my tally. He is much better, he says, but I know not. Apparently his trouble is something like Bill Bigelow's.[7]

I find no letters here, but various cards including Frank Parkman's. Not being able to enter the house, I cannot say what work has been done. Hay's roof is beginning to show, but only the rafters. The household seems all right, and the dogs are dirty. Tomorrow I shall go to Maynard and call on John Field.[8] If the weather is decent I shall ride. If I get no telegram by noon I shall send for Lamar. On the whole I shall prepare to start north on Monday and be with you on Tuesday morning. I ought to see Edmondson before going, but I can start tomorrow in case you telegraph before noon.[9]

Of course I have had no time to look about me, or to attend to your commissions. The bills can wait. Margery seems more concerned about your father than about anything in the household, and my only perplexity is to know whether to bring the camera or not. I wish you could telegraph instructions, but I shall have to decide without them.

Perhaps I shall be with you almost as soon as this letter reaches you, so good-night with love to all.[10]

Ever your master   Henry Adams.

MS: MHi

1. Mistress of Pericles, known for wit, learning, and beauty.
2. Eugène Labiche (1815–1888), French dramatist whose comic plays were issued in ten volumes (1878–1879).
3. Albert W. Bacon (1841–1922), naval officer, paymaster on the *Atlanta;* Marian Howland, Clarence King's half-sister.
4. Nicholas Anderson employed H. H. Richardson to build his imposing Washington house for $86,000.

5. HA owned a few Turner watercolors.
6. William James Stillman (1828–1901), painter and critic, disciple of Ruskin.
7. William Sturgis Bigelow (1850–1926), son of Boston surgeon Henry Jacob Bigelow and MHA's aunt Susan Sturgis Bigelow. A favorite cousin of MHA, he was an eccentric dilettante who had gone to Japan in 1882 as a teacher and had become a convert to Buddhism.
8. Edward Maynard (1813–1891), dental surgeon; John W. Field (1815–1887), prominent Philadelphian.
9. Charles Edmondson, a Washington builder, was awarded the contract for the Hay and Adams houses.
10. Marian Adams' father, Dr. Robert W. Hooper, was stricken with heart disease early in March. She helped nurse him for several weeks until his death in mid-April.

To Charles Milnes Gaskell

Sweet Springs. Monroe Co., W. Va.
18 June, 1885

My dear Carlo

You may admire my letter-paper! T'is my all! I have used up my own; and there is no stationer's, of larger resource, within one or two hundred miles of this spot. As you could not, in all human probability, guess within five hundred miles the exact situation of this "Kurbad," I will tell you how and why we came here, and where "here" is.

The city of Washington grows warm and relaxing on the approach of summer. My wife did not care to pass her long summer months at Beverly, which was a gloomy spot to her after her father's death. So we cast about for a refuge. We decided to camp out for six weeks in the Rocky Mountains, but could not go there comfortably, on account of the flies or gnats, before August 1. The month or six weeks intervening had to be filled. We bethought ourselves of the Alleghany Mountains in Virginia. I ran on to Quincy for three days to see my family; returned to Washington on June 10; started by rail the next day, with our two saddle-horses, towards the southwest; and after eleven hours of travels,—perhaps two hundred and fifty miles,—arrived at the White Sulphur Springs some twenty miles north of the place I am now in.

Everything was almost as new and unexpected to me as it might be to you. All my life I had heard of the Sulphur Springs as a great southern watering-place; but very few eastern people ever travel down here, and a country less known to Bostonians could not be found in Europe. Imagine a sloping valley, half a mile or more in width, shut in by moderate mountains densely wooded, and occupied by a huge hotel, and hundreds of cottages dependent on the hotel. Superb oaks are scattered about, and the grounds are practically endless, bounded by wild mountains of indefinite extent. The vegetation is extremely fine and varied. On our first ride, we nearly fell off our horses at seeing hillsides sprinkled with flaming yellow, orange, and red azalea, all mixed together, and masses of white and pink laurel, besides the ordinary common pink azalea, as though such things ought not to be confined to flower-shows. On our second ride we got a long way into the wild mountains by a rough path; and the groves of huge rhododendron were so gloomy and seemed to shake their dark fingers so threateningly over our heads, that we turned about and fled for fear night should catch us, and we should never be seen any more by our dear enemies who would like to have us lost in the woods.

In short, the country was like the most beautiful Appenines; but the hotel, which will hold—cottages and all—two thousand people, and which in these early June days, had about twenty, was so ideally bad that we got on our horses last Monday at eight o'clock, and rode round through the mountains some seventeen miles, which seemed thirty, till we arrived here, at the "Old Sweet"; a broader valley, lower mountains, and even wilder country; where wolves, deer and bear are still tracked on the snow in winter; and where I feel a particular wish to be civil, but not intimate, with rattle-snakes and copperheads. After four hours on horseback with the thermometer Heaven knows where,—down at Washington it was 94° that day,—one feels thirsty; and the sacred spot at this place is a swimming-pool of mineral water, which keeps bubbling like artificial Apollinaris, more or less, with a steady temperature of 76°. Into this I went, head and heels, and came out somewhat intoxicated but happy. The establishment here, which is also in a park and can hold some eight hundred people, was opened that day for the season. We were the only guests and had our choice of everything. We picked out a little wooden cottage, near the bathing-pool; and here we live, quite alone; going for meals to the hotel; swimming, reading, writing, and riding. A vast oak, more than fifteen feet in diameter six feet from the ground, shades our porch. Other magnificent oaks stand round the grounds which look a little like the grounds of an American University. The table is excellent, and only too abundant. The change seems to have set us up already; and my soul yearns day and night for the Apollinaris bath, when the thermometer rises toward 90°.

Here we shall stay till we are tired; then try another spring. I am told there are about sixty; which ought to use up our thirty days. Yet I admit that as long as the cream holds out here in its present abundance, I shall be loath to depart. I am told there are trout in the streams somewhere, and game on the mountains; but I know not. In fact, I am vastly lazy, and, if it were not for the black flies which you call gnats, I should lie all day under my big oak.

Such are our news; while you are, I suppose, fussing with ministries and elections to come. When the summer grows warm, you will follow our example I hope. Scotland is the only enviable possession which England has; for no other spot exists on earth where August and September are tolerable. I have nothing to tell you else. We expect to start about July 25 for the Rocky Mountains; some 2,500 miles journey there, I think; but broken by various cities which contain baths. My camp equipage is ordered; it is to consist of twelve animals, and is a regular eastern caravan;—tents, cook, sheik, and all, except Arabs.

My wife sends her love to you and yours. Tell us about May Doyle's wedding, if she has had one. I am reading Henry Taylor's Memoirs here with some half-surprised amusement at them, and at us who seemed no longer young, but are so.[1]

Ever Yrs   Henry Adams.

MS: MHi

1. Sir Henry Taylor (1800–1886), playwright and poet; *Autobiography* (1885).

To Sir Robert Cunliffe

1607 H Street. Washington. D.C. 29 November, 1885.

My dear Robert

The newspapers today announce that you are a victim to the Tory campaign; and I need not tell you how heartily sorry I am to hear it.[1] The fortune of politics is as queer as the fortune of war. I wish I could say anything that would console you; but at this distance no one can do more than condole.

A very curious law seems to rule elections. I have had occasion to notice here, where no real principle divides us, that some queer mechanical balance holds the two great parties even, so that changes of great numbers of voters leave no trace in the sum-total. I suspect the law will some day be formulated that in democratic societies, parties tend to an equilibrium. In England, five years ago, one saw that the time must come soon when the old Whig liberals must reinforce the conservative party. The Whigs, from Edmund Burke to Carlo Gaskell and even yourself, were always conservatives at heart, and belonged with the supporters of Crown, Peerage and Church. The Tories of today are far more Whig than were the Whigs of five-and-twenty years ago, when I first knew them. Nothing ought to prevent the reorganisation of a conservative party to embrace all the elements of old English society.

As an American I want to see all traces of mediaevalism preserved in Europe;—otherwise Americans will be left without a single place to study history and bric-à-brac; but, American as I am, and devoted—at this distance—to the English Church and Peerage, I admit that neither the Church nor the Peerage strikes me as likely to satisfy any radical, like myself, who happens to live in their shadow. Therefore, if I were one of your party, I should be obliged to follow the potent Chamberlain, and to throw the Whigs over to the conservative side.[2] They must make their option. We radicals mean to reform the whole concern; and if we are to fail, we might as well fail under conservative rule as under any other. Indeed the Tories seem to have got bravely over scruples that still torture Whigs.

You are an early martyr to the new cause, but I suspect you will find so many companions that we shall both of us carry our elections to Heaven's high Parliament before the list is complete. At the same time, I should doubt whether the new Parliament could possibly be long-lived, and you have always your chance of revenge. The Tories are naturally stupid, which is in your favor; but England is terribly conservative at heart, which is not in your favor.

I hope at least you bear defeat with good spirits and temper. The worst effect I have noticed from the pursuit of politics, apart from the fact that it spoils men's morals, is that it depresses their spirits and hurts their tempers.

Perhaps you do not care for sympathy, but the news of your defeat really gave me a little pang, and while the overthrow of the party seems to me a mere step in the necessary path of events, your own disaster has the force of a personal disappointment.

You will now have time to travel again. I hardly want you to come here just now, for my own plans and prospects are a little unsettled and I could not enjoy your visit as I would like; but sooner or later we shall look for you, and perhaps will take a run with you to the Feejees or the Poles.

My wife, who has been, as it were, a good deal off her feed this summer, and shows no such fancy for mending as I could wish, joins me in sending warm love to you and to her serene ladyship, as well as to the young ones. We hear rarely much news of you all; but every now and then comes a ray of light that shows you are all there.

We have no news to send from here. John Hay and I have built a vast pile, glaring into the White House windows, but we are not yet in our new houses, or likely to get there for another month or two. Our affairs, public and private, are otherwise much as of old.

Ever affectionately   Henry Adams.

MS: MHi

1. Cunliffe, a Liberal, was defeated in Denbigh district on Nov. 27. Election results had been cabled.
2. In his 1885 campaign Joseph Chamberlain attacked both Conservatives and Whig Liberals; in 1886 he left the Liberal party as a Liberal Unionist in opposition to Gladstone's Irish Home Rule Bill.

To John Hay

Wednesday, 8 Dec. [1885]

Dear John

Your kind telegram has just arrived.[1] Nothing you can do will affect the fact that I am left alone in the world at a time of life when too young to die and too old to take up existence afresh; but after the first feeling of desperation is over, there will be much that you can do to make my struggle easier. I am going to keep straight on, just as we planned it together, and, unless I break in health, I shall recover strength and courage before long. If you want to help me, hurry on your house, and get into it. With you to fall back upon, I shall have one more support. For the present, Theodore Dwight is coming to live with me.[2]

Give my best love to your wife and the children. Never fear me. I shall come out all right from this—what shall I call it?—Hell!

Ever affecly   Henry Adams.

John Hay Esq.

MS: MHi

1. Marian Adams took her own life on Sunday, Dec. 6, with potassium cyanide, one of the chemicals used in her photographic work. The funeral service was held Dec. 9 at the Adams residence by the Rev. Edward H. Hall of the First Church (Unitarian) of Cambridge. Burial was at Rock Creek Cemetery. In a letter following the telegram, Hay wrote: "Is it any consolation to remember her as she was? that bright, intrepid spirit, that keen, fine intellect, that lofty scorn of all that was mean, that social charm which made your house such a one as Washington never knew before, and made hundreds of people love her as much as they admired her. No, that makes it all so much harder to bear" (Hay to HA, Dec. 9, 1885, Adams Papers, MHS).
2. Theodore F. Dwight (1846–1917), clerk in the library of the State Department, chief of bureau of rolls and library 1882–1888, became HA's secretary and assistant. On March 1, 1886, he wrote a friend: "On [Dec.] 20th I came to live with Mr. A & help him by a sort of devoted doglike companionship to support his bereavement" (George Kennan Papers, DLC).

III

In Search of
Nirvana
1886–1892

O VERWHELMED BY THE SHOCK of Clover's desperate act, Henry Adams sought at first to hide from the world. He had reason to reproach himself for want of vigilance about her photographic hobby and its lethal chemical. When, before his engagement, his mother had urged him to marry Clover Hooper, his brother Charles had blurted out, "Heavens!—no!—they're all crazy as coots. She'll kill herself just like her aunt." Henry had thought the warning farfetched. He was confident that as his wife she would be in no danger. The sensational reports of the tragedy in the newspapers of Washington, New York, and Boston now drove home his humiliating failure. Almost in a penitential mood—for he and Clover had planned such a trip—he escaped the following summer for a two-month tour of Japan with John La Farge.

The journey to Japan began a pattern that would henceforward shape what he was to call his "posthumous" life. He would frequently seek to distract himself by hurrying off on random travel sorties, short or long, alternating with periods of intense concentration on a work in progress. When he returned from Japan he promptly embarked on the first administration of James Madison. The draft volume went to his readers in 1888. Impatient to finish the *History,* he decided to submit the draft of the second administration directly to the publisher, Charles Scribner. In the spring of 1888 he escaped from one of his recurring fits of depression for a month's wandering in Cuba and Florida. There followed several months spent pressing on to the end of his narrative. He was off again in October for a six-week circle tour of the Far West with his English friend Sir Robert Cunliffe. On his return his diary recorded, "I have since worked desperately to prepare my first chapters for the press." There now began the work of simultaneously revising sections of the *History* and proceeding with the arduous tasks of seeing the nine volumes through the press and preparing the formidable index. It was not until July 1890 that he was free to run off again with John La Farge, this time to the South Seas.

Life in his new house at 1603 H Street, after his return from Japan in 1886, fell into a comfortable routine. More and more he resumed an active social existence. At his noon breakfast table pretty nieces and "Queen Regents" gaily matronized. Concerts and theater parties diverted him. By the spring of 1890 he could report that his "little set of Hays, Camerons, Lodges and Roosevelts never were so intimate or friendly as now." Still his thoughts kept turning to the grave in Rock Creek Cemetery, seeking to read its meaning for him. In Japan he had been fascinated by the omnipresent Buddhas and their message that only through suffering could the self be transcended. He engaged the noted sculptor Augustus Saint-Gaudens to create a symbolic figure and set aside the sum of $20,000 for the purpose. As a kind of mortuary accompaniment he began the destruction of all the volumes of his diary, which he had faithfully continued since he was fourteen.

Though he could attempt to close his accounts with the past, the present was soon to become more intractable. He had come to rely more and more for understanding companionship on Elizabeth Cameron, the dazzling young wife of Senator James Donald Cameron. Born in 1857, she was twenty-four years younger than her staid husband and nineteen years younger than Adams. She had become the center of an intimate group of poetizing courtiers headed by Adams. The childless Adams felt keenly drawn to her infant daughter, Martha. As a result his long-standing plan for a year's voyage to the South Seas, China, and Ceylon lost urgency. However, Elizabeth Cameron began to realize that their show of affection for each other was becoming indiscreet. She therefore pressed him to begin his globe-circling travels and herself set out for Europe.

There then began in August 1890 his extraordinary diary letters to her, letters in which he recorded his adventures with La Farge in the exotic worlds of Hawaii, Samoa, Tahiti, Fiji, and Ceylon. His letters—and hers—drew them closer together. Their reunion fourteen months later in Paris and London in the midst of friends and relatives became a succession of frustrating encounters. Though often separated from her impassive husband and greatly flattered by her devoted suitors, Elizabeth Cameron was not one to be swept off her feet by unruly passion. She valued her position in society, and her sense of propriety more than equaled that of Adams. Faced with the impasse, the melancholy Adams resigned himself to play the role of "tame cat" in her life, a role in which the desire for physical possession would give way to the more lasting pleasures of a platonic and idealizing worship.

To Emily Ellsworth Fowler Ford

1603 H Street. 30 March, 1886.

My dear Mrs Ford[1]

Nothing would gratify me more than to be of use in an undertaking like yours; but, in such work, one can rarely be as useful as one would wish, for, in literature, the author must in the end carry his own load, and finds this course easiest. You have much pleasure before you, in preparing the book. If you are like the rest of us, you will find much criticism a greater annoyance than failure itself.

My criticisms are always simple; they are limited to one word:—Omit! Every syllable that can be struck out is pure profit, and every page that can be economised is a five-per-cent dividend. Nature rebels against this rule; the flesh is weak, and shrinks from the scissors; I groan in retrospect over the weak words and useless pages I have written; but the law is sound, and every book written without a superfluous page or word, is a master-piece.

All the same, no one cares to apply so stern a law to another person. One has a right to be severe only with oneself.

I am very truly Yrs   Henry Adams.

Mrs Ford.

MS: NN

1. Emily Ellsworth Fowler Ford (1823–1893). Her uncompleted book was edited by her daughter Emily Ford Skeel and, titled *Notes on the Life of Noah Webster,* was privately printed in 1912.

To John Hay

Nikko. 22 August, 1886.

My son John

I have still to report that purchases for you are going on, but more and more slowly, for I believe we have burst up all the pawnbrokers' shops in Japan. Even the cholera has shaken out little that is worth getting. Bigelow and Fenollosa cling like misers to their miserable hoards.[1] Not a kakimono is to be found, though plenty are brought. Every day new bales of rubbish come up from Tokio or elsewhere; mounds of books; tons of bad bronze; holocausts of lacquer; I buy literally everything that is merely possible; and yet I have got not a hundred dollars' worth of things I want for myself. You shall have some good small bits of lacquer, and any quantity of *duds* to encumber your tables and mantles; but nothing creditable to our joint genius. As for myself, I have only one *Yokomono,*—or kakimono broader than it is long,—and one small bronze, that I care to keep as the fruit of my summer's perspiration.

For Japan is the place to perspire. No one knows an ideal dogday who has not tried Japan in August. From noon to five o'clock I wilt. As for travelling, I would see the rice-fields dry first. I have often wondered what King would have done, had he come with us. I've no doubt he would have seen wonderful sights, but I should have paid his return passage on a corpse. For days together I make no attempt at an effort, while poor La Farge sketches madly and aimlessly.[2]

By the bye, a curious coincidence happened. Bigelow announced one morning that King and Hay were coming from Tokio with loads of curios for us. La Farge and I stared and inquired. Then it appeared that Bigelow and Fenollosa employ two men—Kin, pronounced King,—and Hei,—pronounced Hay,—to hunt curios for them, and had sent them word to bring up whatever they could find. I thought this one of the happiest accidents I ever heard, and I only wish that Messrs King and Hay had brought better things, as their American namesakes expected. They meant well, but they lacked means. Nevertheless they brought a few nice bits, to sustain the credit of their names.

Fairly bored by sweltering in this moistness, I stirred up Mrs Fenollosa to a little expedition last Tuesday. Fenollosa is unwell; La Farge is hard at work; but Mrs Fenollosa, Bigelow, and I, started to visit Yumoto, the Saratoga, or White Sulphur, of Japan. Yumoto lies just fourteen miles above us among the mountains, and with one of my saddle-horses I could easily go there and return on the same day; but such a journey in Japan is serious. Only pedestrians, coolies, or Englishmen, work hard. Mrs Fenollosa summoned five packhorses. All Japanese horses known to me are rats, and resemble their pictures, which I had supposed to be bad drawing; but these packhorses are rats led by a man, or more often by a woman, at a very slow walk. Mrs Fenollosa mounted one; Bigelow another; I ascended a third; a servant and baggage followed on a fourth; the fifth carried beds, blankets, linen, silver, eatables, and drinks. At half past eight the caravan started, and at half past ten it arrived at the foot of Chiu-zen-ji pass, where one climbs a more or less perpendicular mountain side for an hour. I preferred my own legs to the rat's, and walked up. So we arrived at Lake Chiu-zen-ji, a pretty sheet of water about seven miles long, at the foot of the sacred mountain Nan-tai-zan. On the shore of this lake is a temple, where pilgrims begin the ascent of the mountain, sacred to Sho-do Sho-nin, who devoted fifteen years of his valuable existence, in the 8th century, to the astounding feat of climbing it. As it is very accessible, and only 8000 feet above the sea, Sho-do Sho-nin is a very popular and greatly admired saint, and some five thousand pilgrims come every August to follow his sainted steps. Next the temple are some inns, but not a farm or a human dwelling exists on the lake or among the mountains; for if the Japanese like one thing more than another it is filthy rice-fields, and if they care less for one thing than another, it is mountains. All this lovely country, from here to the sea of Japan, is practically a dense wilderness of monkeys, as naked as itself; but the monkeys never seem out of place as a variety, though I have not met them in society, and speak only from association. We stopped at an inn, and while lunch was making ready, Bigelow and I went out in a kind of frigate for a swim in the lake. After lunch, sending our beasts ahead, we sailed to the next starting-point, just the length of a cigar. Another two miles of rise brought us to a moor for all the world like Estes Park and the Rocky Mountains. Crossing this, we climbed another ascent, and came out on an exquisite little green lake with woody mountains reflected on its waters. Nothing could be prettier than the path along this shore, but it was not half so amusing to me as our entrance into the village of Yumoto, with its dozen inns and no villagers; for, by the roadside, at the very entrance, I saw at last the true Japan of my dreams, and broke out into carols of joy. In a wooden hut, open to all the winds, and public as the road, men, women and children, naked as the mother that bore them, were sitting, standing, soaking and drying themselves, as their ancestors had done a thousand years ago.

I had begun to fear that Japan was spoiled by Europe. At Tokio even the coolies wear something resembling a garment, and the sexes are obliged to bathe apart. As I came into the country I noticed first that the children went naked; that the men wore only a breech-clout; and that the women were apt to be stripped to the waist; but I had begun to disbelieve that this disregard of appearances went further. I was wrong. No sooner had we dismounted than we hurried off to visit the baths; and Mrs Fenollosa will bear me witness that for ten minutes we stood at the entrance of the largest bath-house, and looked at a dozen people of all ages, sexes and varieties of ugliness, who paid not the smallest regard to our presence. I should except one pretty girl of sixteen, with quite a round figure and white skin. I did notice that for the most part, while drying herself, she stood with her back to us.

When this exceptionally pleasing virgin walked away, I took no further interest in the proceedings, though I still regard them as primitive. Of the habits and manners of the Japanese in regard to the sexes, I see little, for I cannot conquer a feeling that Japs are monkeys, and the women very badly made monkeys; but from Mrs Fenollosa and other ladies, I hear much on the subject, and what I hear is very far from appetising. In such an atmosphere one talks freely. I was a bit aghast when one young woman called my attention to a temple as a remains of phallic worship; but what can one do? Phallic worship is as universal here as that of trees, stones and the sun. I come across shrines of phallic symbols in my walks, as though I were an ancient Greek. One cannot quite ignore the foundations of society.

23 August.   My poor boy, how very strong you do draw your vintage for my melancholy little Esther.[3] Your letter of July 18 has just reached me, and I hardly knew what I was reading about. Perhaps I made a mistake even to tell King about it; but having told him, I could not leave you out. Now, let it die! To admit the public to it would be almost unendurable to me. I will not pretend that the book is not precious to me, but its value has nothing to do with the public who could never understand that such a book might be written in one's heart's blood. Do not even imagine that I scorn the public, as you say. Twenty years ago, I was hungry for applause. Ten years ago, I would have been glad to please it. Today, and for more than a year past, I have been and am living with not a thought but from minute to minute; and the public is as far away from me as is the celebrated Kung-fu-tse, who once said something on the subject which I forget, but which had probably a meaning to him, as my observation has to me. Yet I do feel pleased that the book has found one friend.

25 August.   I can't say, "let's return to our sheep," for there are no sheep in Japan, and I have eaten nothing but bad beef since landing.[4] As for returning to my remarks on Yumoto as connected with the sexes, I decline to do it. In spite of King, I affirm that sex does not exist in Japan, except as a scientific classification. I would not affirm that there are no exceptions to my law; but the law itself I affirm as the foundation of archaic society. Sex begins with the Aryan race. I have seen a Japanese beauty, which has a husband, *Nabeshame,* if I hear right,—a live Japanese Marquis, late Daimio of Hizo, or some other place; but though he owns potteries, he has, I am sure, no more successful bit of bric-a-brac than his wife is;—but as for being a woman, she is hardly the best Satsuma.

You did not say whether you liked porcelain. I have met only a few little bits, not better than you see in New York everywhere; and not cheap. I have bought one or two on the chance you might fancy variety, but they are not very amusing.

28 August. We go down to Yokohama tomorrow. A week from today we sail for Kobe, Ozaka and Kioto. At Ozaka I shall find your gong. We return to Yokohama, Sept. 23, to sail on the City of Peking for San Francisco on October 2. I should be in Washington, October 25.

Best love to all yours. Mrs Don's letter has rather upset me; but I wrote to her before receiving it.[5]

Ever Yrs   Henry Adams

Yokohama. 31 August. Having today completed purchases of curios to the amount of about $2,500 dollars, I have drawn out your letter of credit. This pleasing news I hasten to communicate, for fear of receiving or inflicting a shock in the future. I can't say when the articles will reach America, as most of them will go by Suez to New York. Some time next spring you will perhaps hear that they have arrived somewhere.

It is hotter than blazes here, but we are supposing ourselves to go to Kobe on Sunday next per Messageries steamer "Volga."

Ever Yrs   H.A.

MS: MHi

1. Ernest Fenollosa (1853–1908), collector of Japanese art, taught Western philosophy and political economy at the Imperial University.
2. John La Farge (1835–1910), painter and muralist, friend of HA since 1872.
3. *Esther,* HA's second novel, published in 1884 under the pseudonym Frances Snow Compton.
4. From a French anecdote in which a digressive lawyer is repeatedly admonished by the judge to return to the subject of the sheep.
5. Elizabeth Sherman Cameron (1857–1944), daughter of Sen. John Sherman of Ohio. In 1878 she married Sen. James Donald Cameron, a widower twenty-four years her senior and a Pennsylvania political boss. Intimates of the Adamses, the Camerons had wished to name their child, born June 25, 1886, after HA's deceased wife, Marian, but, unable to reach HA for his consent, as "Mrs. Don" had informed Clara Hay, they named her Martha after the senator's grandmother.

To Albert Bushnell Hart

1603 H Street. Washington. 3 Dec. 1886.

Dear Sir[1]

I have to thank you for sending me the Outline of your historical course.[2]

I will not attempt to offer any opinion on so considerable an extension of the methods of teaching a subject which hardly admits of being satisfactorily taught. Probably Cambridge has long since forgotten my experiments and—as I judged them—failures, in the field you are toiling over.

Every man must beat out his own path, and I wish the utmost success to yours; but above all I hope that you will discover and fix, what I tried and failed to do—some system of teaching history which should be equally suited to a fixed science and a course of *belles lettres*. Between the two conditions I found compromise impossible, and separate handling impracticable. In other words, I found that a system which taught history as a science, could not be satisfactorily combined with a system which taught history as a branch of *belles lettres* or popular knowledge. For six or seven years I tried experiment on experiment, hoping to satisfy myself by creating a sound historical method for the college, and I spent time, labor and money freely in the effort. I am glad to see you working so vigorously in the same direction; and I wish I could offer you help, but your only valuable help will be in your own energies and your scholars' qualities.

                                        I am yours truly   Henry Adams.
A. B. Hart Esq.

MS: RPB

1. Albert Bushnell Hart (1854–1943), history professor at Harvard 1883–1926.
2. Printed syllabus of Hart's course in American history (*Methods of Teaching History*, 2nd ed., 1885).

To Sir Robert Cunliffe

1603 H Street. 17 January, 1887.

Dear Robert

You are a good boy to write me such long and pleasant stories.

I have nothing to tell you in return. Our public affairs are very dull. My private affairs are still duller. I have not yet recovered interest in the world's doings, but am willing to hope that I shall, although the world seems to understand itself as little as I understand it, and, except for a few discontented people or classes, seems to blunder on with no distinct idea where it wants to come out. Your politics are a specimen. Europe altogether is a specimen still more to the point. As for America, so far as I can see, no one has any ideas at all except to feed, clothe and amuse oneself.

You know that I have for years looked on your political question as simply that of selecting between the democratic and the aristocratic standpoint. Sooner or later all of you will have to range yourselves on one side or the other, and the old Whigs must end by taking the conservative side at last. The present apparent impasse seems to me due only to the inevitable slowness of large bodies of men to shift their ground. You can hardly fail to act with the conservatives if only because you are within sight of your fifties. Men of fifty ought not, and generally are not able, to be revolutionists.

Old Tennyson is an instance. I cannot easily understand how an artist, as he was, can put himself in a frame of mind so artistically bad, as that of his last poem, or can consent to abandon that repose which he knows to be the highest art.[1] Still, he has written an unmelodious shriek which, although it would be undignified even if the universe were shrivelling, contains passages equal in my opinion to his best, as far as energy of expression goes. I suspect some of these verses will live, in spite of the poem.

Sir Francis's book gave me great amusement though it is disfigured by the same fault.[2] Old men should know how to make their exit with grace and good-humor. If the world has treated them well, they owe it as much in return. I am far from denying that mankind is on the high-road to destruction, and I cannot understand how any churchman, with the Thirty-nine Articles in his teeth, can help asserting it; but I do not think that art or manners require us to fling the fact constantly in our neighbors' faces. We don't tell our invalid friends that they are going to die in tortures; we tell them pleasant anecdotes, and fairy-stories about King Arthur and Queen Guinivere. The Carlisles [Carlyles] and Ruskins are bores.

Heaven knows that I say this without meaning anything disrespectful to them. Their motives, apart from the egotism, are all that the Archbishop of Canterbury could wish; but either they are artists or they are not; and, if they claim to be artists, they ought to obey what they know to be fundamental laws of art.

Japan gave me so much to think about that I am eager to start again, not for Japan but for China. As it happens, I have several years of literary work to do before I can wholly close up and dismiss my past life, and set out, after the manner of Ulysses, in search of that new world which is the old.[3] Nothing whatever attaches me any longer to the spots I expected to die in. Neither public nor private relations detain or much concern me. To one who wants nothing, that he can conceive of as a part of his future life, the instinct of wandering is strong, and every day I pass at my desk is passed in the idea that it is so much out of my way. If I can get off, about the year '90, I may, with health and strength, wander ten years before being driven to cover by age; so you need not despair of hearing that I am a Mandarin or an Arab.

Hay and his family, my only stay, go to England in May. You will of course see them. His great work is done, and is now publishing.[4] Very good it is. I am not certain how long they will stay abroad; they say, only till autumn.

King is struggling with destiny in New York. I hope to see him in a few days.[5]

My mother, though old and broken, has got through the shock of my father's death as well as was rationally possible. The death was of course not a surprise, and was quiet and peaceful.

My love to all yours.   Ever truly   Henry Adams.

MS: MHi

1. In "Locksley Hall Sixty Years After" (1886) Tennyson at 77 voiced his loss of faith in the idea of progress.
2. Sir Francis H. Doyle, *Reminiscences and Opinions* (1886).
3. Tennyson, "Ulysses" (1842) and "The Day-Dream. The Departure" (1842).
4. John Hay, HA's next-door neighbor, had begun the serial publication with John Nicolay (1832–1901) of their *Abraham Lincoln: A History* in the *Century* in Nov. 1886.
5. The stockholders at the annual meeting of the Anglo-Mexican Company had forced Clarence King to resign from the management of the Yedras mine.

To Charles Milnes Gaskell

1603 H Street. 8 May, 1887.

My dear Carlo

Your letter of April 9 finds the usual May struggle here; a divided empire between all sorts of seasons, and no kind of objects. Our want of country occupations is a serious thing. With us, one must be either cit or lout; no happy medium exists; one cannot be country squire and city gent at the same time.

My summer is to be passed at Quincy with my mother who is now near eighty, very much broken, and alone, owing to my brother Brooks's taking a vacation in Germany. Four months at Quincy are to me what four months of solitary prison in Ireland might be to you; but it matters very little, and I shall be able to accomplish a deal of heavy work. As I never go into society, or pay visits, I am relieved of the worst burdens of the seasons. The summer will pass, in time; next year I am going to Hawaii for the summer; and two years hence I shall take my first run to Peking; so that the summer question will not bother me again.

Your Irishification is not amusing, and to escape it I have stopped reading English news.[1] Our newspapers are wholly run by Irish for Irish, and the quantity of Irishism is even more obnoxious than the quality. From time to time I see the headlines of some news that makes me wish you had fallen on a pleasanter Parliament; but I console myself by hoping it amuses you. We are doing our best to restore prosperity to your farmers by raising railway rates all over our country; but if your squires can hold on another generation, or perhaps fifty years, I have a strong notion that things will come right for them. Last summer I got a sort of an idea how very small the really cultivable world is, and how fast it is filling. Fifty years more will bring it near the explosive point. I am rather sorry for your children, but I think your grandchildren may find occupation worth having. As for investments, I don't know how the widow and orphan are to live. As trustee, I think it lucky if I can net four per cent for those whom I protect; soon it will be three. To be sure, the nominal capital rolls up; but one gets very little for a million. When I was a boy, and until the last fifteen years, six per cent was the rule. I can take good western mortgages now at that rate, but, for trusts, I fear going so far from home.

Europe will some day become interesting if it does nothing long enough. Heaven only knows how long it is since I have read a new European book, or seen a picture or heard a story from there. By the bye, an intelligent and agreeable fellow has turned up here at your Legation; about the last place one looks for such. His name is Spring Rice,[2] and he has creditable wits. Mad, of course, but not more mad than an Englishman should be. Unluckily he is here only for a short time, and goes back to the Foreign Office in the autumn. He drops in at times on me for meals, and pays in a certain dry humor, not without suggestions of Monckton Milnes's breakfasts five-and-twenty years ago. Other Englishmen twain or more have been here, and, for some unintelligible or unremembered object, have sat at my table; but I forget me as to their names or looks.—Except the Yates Thompsons, who were scourging the land with a wilde, verwegene Jagd.[3] The statistician does not improve with age, and newspapering.

News grow not. Life is dull to scare a Chinese mandarin. I am well, as far as I know; with everything in the world, except what I want; and with nothing to complain of, except the universe. I wish you the exact reverse of my situation; you will find it more amusing if not more to your taste. My love to your wife and children.

Ever Yours   Henry Adams.

Please find out and tell me in your next letter whether old Thomson Hankey and his wife are still living and in their senses. My mother wants to know.[4]

MS: MHi

1. The recently passed Government of Ireland Act had not helped quiet agrarian disorders. A Perpetual Crimes Act had been recently adopted to combat the widespread lawlessness.
2. Cecil Arthur Spring Rice (1859–1918), secretary of the British legation with intervals 1887–1895, ambassador to U.S. 1913–1918.
3. Henry Yates Thompson (1838–1928), owner of the liberal *Pall Mall Gazette*, and his wife,

Elizabeth. "Wilde, verwegende Jagd" (wild, foolhardy hunt) comes from "Lützows wilde Jagd," by Theodor Körner. It was made into a popular patriotic song by Karl Maria von Weber.
4. Thomson Hankey (1805–1893), Liberal M.P. during the time the Adamses were in England, economist and businessman, and onetime governor of the Bank of England.

To Elizabeth Cameron

Vedado. Wed. 7th [March 1888]

My dear Mrs Cameron

I have got your fan. Let me nourish the hope that it will be what you want, for the price it cost was ruinous—not in money, but in morale. As far as money is concerned, the only trouble was to find anything good enough for you to carry; but your responsibility for moral expenditure is beyond calculation. Of course I could not select the proper thing without assuring myself that it was beyond criticism, and the day after our arrival at Havana I found an altogether unexpected chance of educating myself, so that I might defy all the Spanish attachés in Washington to carp at your outfit. A great bull-fight was to take place. Six Andalucian bulls, and three famous Espadas—among them the celebrated Guerrito, of whom you have heard as much as I—were brought over at great expense, for the occasion. Never was such a splendid function in Habaña! I had hitherto refused to see a Corrida de Toros. Even in Spain I carefully kept away from the show, not so much from motives of delicacy for the bull, as from long experience that the consequence of such a spectacle to me would be a more or less violent and sudden attack of sea-sickness; but I was so deeply convinced of the steadiness with which I could face anything in pursuit of your fan, that I only wonder I did not, like the bold but ill-mannered gentleman of the German ballad, accoutre myself as a banderillero, and jump into the arena before the whole circus.[1] I did the next best thing, for I made Dwight go with me. We got the best seats, in the front row, just where the bull enters; but I doubt whether any one of the six bulls was half as much astonished as I was at our meeting. Even after I was fairly seated, I could not shake myself back into a certainty that I was I anyhow, and I began to feel that my mission in life was to be an Andalucian espada with an Astracan cap and a purple jacket. The show was just thrilling, but what turned my poor old addle-brain on end was the dozen or two ladies in more or less soul-moving costumes. One exquisite creature in the costume of an Andalucian bull-fightress,—a feminine adaptation of the matador's dress—reduced me to a pitiable state of imbecile adoration. She was a vision, and I wished I were a picadero or a peccadillo, or anything to her. The thousands of men howled with delight as she entered. Her black Astracan cap and blood-red dress looked, I admit, a little warm for the season; but we hot-blooded Spaniards pay no thought to such trivial details as that. The other ladies wore the white mantilla mostly, which is also fatal to any man with a soul. I was still lost in gazing at these dreams of Roman delight, and watching their fans—the Andalucian vision carried one such as you wanted,—when the barrier opposite was thrown open, and the procession of fighters, headed by the three Espadas, marched across, loaded with costumes of color and gold. If I was enthusiastic before, I was classically sublime at this last vestige of the Roman arena; and the Captain General assumed the proportions of Heliogabalus. I felt that life was still left in the worn-out world. My true archaic blood beat strongly in my heart. I wished for Clarence King to be with me that we might enjoy together the revival of our strong, young lives. Just then the bull rushed in, close by me, and the fight began. He was a handsome animal; but certainly he looked a little out of place; too natural and domestic, and rather Yankee than Roman. From the first I could not impress myself with the idea that he was dangerous. He did not seem to want to hurt anybody. He dashed at the red cloths, but not at the men. Presently they stuck things into him till long patches of blood streamed down his shoulders, and he dashed at a poor, old cab-horse, whose eyes were bandaged, and whose rider held him still, close to the barrier. The bull struck him square on the shoulder, and I saw the horse fall over, feebly kicking, while the bull strolled away. I looked at Dwight. He was blue, purple and streaked. I felt that I looked worse. I turned my glass on the Andalucian beauty. If she felt any pleasure at that moment, she showed none in her face. She looked bored. The fight went on. As I measured it, the time taken to kill that bull was two hours and three quarters. He gored three more horses in the same cool way, without seemingly enjoying it. He fought without enthusiasm, doggedly, as though he were bored, like the Andalucian beauty. Twice he leaped clean over the five-foot barrier, and I could almost touch his back, and might almost have washed my hands in his blood, while he stood at my feet. At last, the Espada came forward, and missed his first *coup*. The next time, I knew by the cries that he succeeded better. I saw the bull trot forward a few steps, the sword sticking up from his shoulder. Then he stopped and began to shake himself. Then a torrent of blood began to pour out of his mouth and nostrils. I judged this to continue fifteen minutes. I watched my Andalucian beauty, who looked straight forward without a sign of interest. The other women mostly looked away; or uneasily about the place. None seemed excited or carried into regions of frenzy. I should say they were all wishing themselves elsewhere. The men howled more or less, but on the whole I was too unwell to watch long; and the moment the bull was dragged out of the arena, I told Dwight that I would keep company with the bull. Dwight acquiesced with some energy. We dropped down a ladder, got our cab, and drove back to town. On arriving we happened to notice the time. The entire fight had not consumed half an hour. I was feeling critically unwell, and if it had not been for a sort of general carnival that afternoon and evening, I should have hardly recovered my balance.

Yet I am not disposed to say that I will never go to another bull-fight. On the contrary I will not only go, but I will carry Martha in my arms, and order for you a whole Andalucian costume, if you will go with me. Nothing would give me more entertainment than to see how you would get through the show; but I admit I should expect to get the fun from you rather than from the bull direct. My offer holds good for a year.

Cuba is fascinating, in the bull-fight way. Habaña is as romantic as anything in Spain, but it is excessively Spanish. Dirt and noise and heat have driven us out three miles to a summer restaurant kept by a Frenchman named Petit, close on the water. Here, looking out over the surf and rocks, and the blue-green-purple sea, I am passing a morning writing to you, with the thermometer at 90° and no appetite for breakfast. I like dirt, and adore heat, and care little for sleep, and prefer the worst possible smells; so I am in Paradise, after a manner; but Dwight is sad and hankers for Washington and Possum. My only trouble is that I can go no further. We cannot get to Jamaica by any means at all that would bring us back in time for Dwight's leave of absence. We cannot even go to St Iago at the other end of the island except once a week, by steamer, and only by starting Sunday which is too late. Tomorrow we shall go to the baths of San Diego to see the western end of the island. Monday we shall go to Matanzas. Wednesday we must start back to Florida, and I suppose we shall be in Washington by Saturday the 18th. I am, of course, eager to return; but probably should come back by way of Panama and New Zealand if my own choice were to guide, so great is my haste.

Habaña seems to devote itself to perpetual masquerade. Last Sunday was nothing but driving, riding, masking and balls. I have passed all my evenings at the opera, selecting the handsomest woman in the boxes for distant adoration. They are fascinating, but I cannot ask them to breakfast, for I foolishly forgot to bring introductions, and my romantic imagination breaks down in the effort to introduce myself. To my surprise I find also the men as handsome as the women. Accustomed to regard men as ugly animals, I never recover from the surprise of having to admit their good looks. I have ransacked the shops, but have found nothing to buy. Cigars and fans are the only exceptions. Not even a Spanish toy for Martha has shown its head. Unless I bring her a cocoa-nut, or a string of bananas, I can do nothing for her esthetic education. I have not even found plants for the greenhouse. Where the whole show is a greenhouse, flowers are scarce and poor. Unless I bring over the whole botanical garden, with its avenues of eighty-foot palms, I must leave empty-handed.

Hasta mas ver! Give my love to Martha.

Ever truly Yrs   Henry Adams.

MS: MHi

1. In Schiller's literary ballad "Der Handschuh" (The Glove) (1798), a lady throws her glove into the lions' cage to test her lover; he retrieves it but then throws it at her face.

To Lucy Baxter

1603 H Street. Sunday, 29 April 1888.

My dear Miss Baxter[1]

Thanks for your letter or letters, for I think I have two to acknowledge. Since the middle of February I have felt waif-like, and have postponed letter-writing as well as everything else. Brooks and Charles kept me informed about my mother's condition, but I wish I had felt easier on account of your own health.

My state, though somewhat like that of the lark at break of day uprising[2] not because he likes to rise but because he can't sleep, is much what it was a year ago, but even more bothered to know what to do. I meant to draw a long breath of relief and cast all my old clothes into the Pacific ocean with a lunatic hope that I might find an excuse for not coming back in the autumn, for I find my mode of existence more intolerable than ever. My mother's wail of despair at Brooks's departure obliged me to give up these hopes in order to comfort her. I turned my thoughts to Quincy, but this summer I need to have Dwight with me, and I could not impose him on my mother. Then I pitched on Beverly. I would rather roast myself over a red-hot gridiron than go back to my house at Beverly, and I doubt whether, when the moment comes, I can make up my mind to do it; yet it has the advantage of comfort and convenience for work, and freedom from daily worries. Probably I should be best off if I went there; but as far as my mother and you are concerned I might as well be in Fiji as I intended. At Beverly I am altogether out of the way; further than John and Charles at the Glades, and able neither to relieve your cares nor my mother's troubles. So I see little good in my going to Beverly, unless it consists in getting a fit of depression that will drive me wholly away next winter. Perhaps I might quarter Dwight somewhere in Quincy, but for this purpose I must be on the spot. Meanwhile summer is coming, and I become more and more perplexed what to decide. Of course I can't talk to my mother about it, as it would only fret her; and I can't do, what I should naturally do, bring Dwight with me, because it would seem to her a burden. Under these circumstances I rather revert to Fiji as the best alternative, and wish that the Lord would kindly show me what to do, as it's not my funeral anyhow, and I never took any such contract.

All this is for your private ear. I don't ask you to do anything because I don't see what you can do; but if you notice indications of insane conduct in me, you may know the reason, and may calm my mother's anxieties by assuring her of my total loss of intellect. The result will be happy, but the process is aberrant.

I warmly hope that your health is improving. From this point of view, and the general question what conduct on my part would most alleviate your burdens, I would like to know what course you would rather have me take.

If profanity, under the most beneficent conditions, tends at times, as philosophy teaches, to smooth our paths through life, I have little doubt that it is acting well on mine at present. Everything is out of joint. I am bothered by a whole bramble-bush of difficulties, and see no resource but to run away, like Marquess, who was always a reflective animal with an eye ahead.[3] The greenhouse bothers me. I must get a new gardner and spoil it at large cost. My little nieces have just left me, and I am not in the least pleased at the state of the eldest's health. My history is slower than ever and more deadly wobbly. The young women have all deserted me, and my house is as dull and gloomy as a comic theatre. Add to these and other comforts of a home, that I am more kinds of a fool than Gladstone, Boulanger[4] and Marcus Tullius Cicero rolled into one; and you will forgive this carol of my lark-notes in the dawn of a sweet day.

Really I am much more interested to know how you are than in my own affairs. Please confide in me with the same cheery optimism which I show in my confidences to you. I can doubtless do much to cheer you up, for I often notice the effect of my society to be decisive on others by calling out all their powers of self-preservation.

If I were you, I would burn this letter, but the recommendation is wholly on your own account. As for me, I could easily write lots as pleasant as this.

Ever Yrs   Henry Adams.

MS: ScU

1. Lucy Baxter (1836–1922), companion to HA's mother, had been a family friend since before the Civil War.
2. Shakespeare, Sonnet 29.
3. Marquess, one of the Adamses' dogs.

4. Gen. Georges Boulanger (1837–1891), leader of a revolutionary movement, was dismissed from the French army in March. He fled the country in 1889 and was convicted of treason in absentia.

To Elizabeth Cameron

Quincy, 29 July, 1888.

My dear Mrs Cameron

The rule that nothing matters much, does not apply to you. According to what I understand to be the teachings of my master, the great Chinese philosopher, Lao-tse, the small is infinitely great and the great infinitely small, and no truth exists of which the opposite is not equally true. I would not have this doctrine vulgarly promulgated, lest, like George de Barnwell's, it might chance to do harm;[1] but in your case I freely admit that I am very sorry you are not coming to Beverly, and still more sorry that you should be sorry. As for the house, you need not waste a thought upon it. I keep it only to lend to friends, and no friend but you has ever wanted it. Of course the house would be better for occupation, and I would gladly hire some friend to pass a month or two in it; but no one wants it, and it is not singular, for the Gurney house is also empty, and, as far as I know, the whole shore is half deserted. Indeed I think you might walk into almost any house there, and have not only house but household as long as you want it, without paying even in thanks, as long as you do not send in your butcher's-bill to the owner.

My philosophy goes no farther than the reflection that I should see no more of you at Beverly than at Harrisburg. My summer is passing, thanks to the dynamic necessities of time, and I suppose some other condition will follow, which I like still less; but, as I have no one within reach whom I care for, and no possibility of seeing such a person, nothing matters much,— not even rheumatism which has caught me directly in the back, and causes me to howl as I ride, for the good of the youth of this neighborhood. My mother is no worse than when I came—perhaps better,—but the best is bad enough. Edward Hooper writes cheerfully from Bethlehem. Clarence King writes despondently from Tuxedo. The Hays are rambling on Colorado mountains. If I had Martha here I could do beautifully. Please send her on.

Ever truly Yrs   Henry Adams.

MS: MHi

1. This sentence is an almost exact quotation from Thackeray's "George de Barnwell" (1847).

To Charles Scribner

Quincy, 1 Aug. 1888.

Dear Sir[1]

Mr Dwight has handed me your letter of July 27, and I will answer it myself to save time.

Your offer is perfectly liberal and satisfactory, but for certain reasons I would rather alter it a little, as I understand it, in your favor.

First, I wish you to understand my position as you would regard it in a business point of view. If I were offering this book for sale, I should, on publishers' estimates, capitalise twelve years of unbroken labor, at (say) $5000 a year, and $20,000 in money spent in travelling, collecting materials, copying, printing, &c; in all $80,000, without charging that additional interest, insurance, or security per-centage which every business-man has to exact. This book, therefore, costs me $80,000; and on business principles I should make a very bad affair if I did not expect to get ten per cent per annum from it for ever. If I bargained according to publishers' rules, I should demand eight thousand dollars a year secured to me; and if I got it, I should still get less than I could probably have acquired in any other successful business.

As I am not a publisher but an author, and the most unpractical kind of an author, a historian, this business view is mere imagination. In truth the historian gives his work to the public and publisher; he means to give it; and he wishes to give it. History has always been, for this reason, the most aristocratic of all literary pursuits, because it obliges the historian to be rich as well as educated. I should be sorry to think that you could give me eight thousand a year for my investment, because I should feel sure that whenever such a rate of profit could be realised on history, history would soon become as popular a pursuit as magazine-writing, and the luxury of its social distinction would vanish.

I propose to give the work outright to the public and the publisher, but I have some objection to admitting the publishers' share in producing it to be greater than my own. This may be a fad, but I have seen the author squeezed between the public and the publisher until he has become absolutely wanting in self-respect, and I hold to preserving the dignity of my profession.

I propose therefore that you shall take all the profits of the book. Having published a number of volumes, and being somewhat familiar with the history-market, I am fairly safe in saying that a twelve-dollar book, in eight volumes, cannot expect a sale of two thousand copies. A sale of fifteen hundred copies will secure the publisher. For still greater security I will add five hundred copies, or a thousand, or ten thousand, if you like; but in making the contract I wish to let it run thus: "After the sale of [say][2] 2000 sets, the author shall receive one half the proceeds, after deducting only the charge for printing, binding, and paper."

I know not what this would come to, but I presume about thirty five cents a volume, and you offer me 22½ cents on all sales over 1500. The difference is not much. In any case the author can hope to receive nothing for two years or more, and in the case of selling three thousand copies, which I regard as an extravagant idea, within three years, the author would be no better off than by accepting your proposal. I intend by my plan to secure you, as far as is in my power, from all loss or risk, and to make over to you whatever profit may be conceived as possible; and all I ask in return is that you shall admit the author to have half the credit, if there is any credit, of the work. For this reason I want expressly to exclude from the cost of the volume the publishers charges of advertising, rent, salaries, putting on the market &c.

With this alteration, I see nothing to interfere with in your plans.[3]

Very truly Yrs   Henry Adams.

MS: ViU

1. Charles Scribner (1854–1930), head of Charles Scribner's Sons. Dwight had initiated negotiations on HA's behalf for publication of HA's *History of the United States During the Administrations of Thomas Jefferson and James Madison;* privately printed draft volumes of the first half had already been circulated to HA's consultants. Only the second administration of James Madison was to be printed from manuscript.
2. HA's brackets.
3. On Aug. 7 Scribner raised his offer from a royalty of 15 percent to one of 20 percent. Sales were to prove disappointing. After ten years the royalties amounted to only $5,000.

To Martha Cameron

Quincy 9 Sept. 1888.

My dear Martha

I love you very much, and think of you a great deal, and want you all the time. I should have run away from here, and looked for you all over the world, long ago, only I've grown too stout for the beautiful clothes I used to wear when I was a young prince in the fairy-stories, and I've lost the feathers out of my hat, and the hat too, and I find that some naughty man has stolen my gold sword and silk-stockings and silver knee-buckles. So I can't come after you, and feel very sad about it. If you would only come and see me, as Princess Beauty came to see Prince Beast, we would go down to the beach, and dig holes in the sand; and would walk in the pastures, and find mushrooms, which are the tables where the very little fairies take dinner; and we would feed Daisy with apples; and go to visit some nice old fairy aunts—very, very old, who would give you beautiful cake;—and Possum and Marquess would be so glad to see you that they would sit up all day on their hind legs, and bring you balls to play with. Then you should help me to write beautiful history in my big library, and build houses with the books, where we would live with the dogs. I am very dull and stupid without you; and have no one but old people to live with.

Please come to Washington as early as you can, if you can't come to me here. Take care of your mamma, for poor mamma does not know very well how to take care of herself, and needs you to look after her, and keep her out of mischief. I know it's a great care to have a mamma to look after, for I have one of my own, and she gives me almost as much trouble as your's gives you; though she is so lame and old that she can't go to parties or walk much, while your mamma can still go about by herself, even if you are not helping her. My mamma has to be wheeled in a chair, and is very cross because she can't walk, or read, or write to her little grandchildren, like you. Give my love to your mamma, and tell her all about me; and that I expect to leave here in about a month for Washington; and that Clarence King has again promised to take me to Mexico in November; and that my history will be finished tomorrow; and that she must take great care of herself, so as to be well and strong when I next see her. I know she must have been in some mischief, because she has not written to me for a month, and I have always noticed that when ladies do not write to me, they are in mischief of some kind. Be sure you write often, so that I may not think you naughty or unwell.

I have sent Mr Dwight up to Lenox to look after you, and he writes me that you have not forgotten me. Be sure to keep on loving

Your affectionate   Dobbitt

MS: MHi

To Charles Milnes Gaskell

Union Club San Francisco
28 October, 1888.

My dear Carlo
Robert's arrival broke the long stilness of the summer, and started me off, on the 13th, to take him wherever he wanted to go. Since then we

have wandered steadily westward, four thousand miles, through all sorts of scenery and people; stopping at Salt Lake; visiting the Shoshone Falls, which tourists have hardly yet discovered in the lava-deserts of Idaho; descending the Columbia River in Oregon; and turning south seven hundred miles down the Pacific coast till we arrived here yesterday morning. I took Robert out to see the sun, setting in a hazy summer light over the Pacific; and I offered to take him on, still westward, as far as the sun went; but he showed at last the effect of age and travel; he refused to go further, and turned his face eastward. Apparently we are at the end.

I think he has enjoyed the trip, though the work is certainly hard, and the fatigue more steadily exhausting than one at first suspects. As for me, I am always contented when in motion, and ask no better than to wander on. Tomorrow we start for the Yosemite; and when we are done with this part of California, we shall go south to the Mexican border, and home to Washington by way of New Orleans. We expect to reach Washington about Nov. 25, and Robert sails December 12 for Liverpool.

Robert is the same pleasant traveling-companion that he was twenty years ago, and takes life as gaily and with as much appreciation as ever. I am heartily glad to have this outing with him, for the chance is small that we should ever renew our youth in any other way. We sometimes speculate whether you would enjoy our adventures, such as they are; and whether you would be intolerably bored by suffocating dust and jouncing carts; vast sand-deserts, and barren sage-brush plains, over which one has to travel, day and night, without much sleep, till one's ideas of the world become altogether upset, and even the solidest Yorkshire valet gets tired of wondering where the country-seats are. Fortunately Robert brought no valet, and we carry our own dust, inch-deep, with a green reflêt, in patience, without being obliged to dust a servant too. I expect to find Robert quite ground away, as by a sand-blast, before I get him across the great southern plains.

For one Sunday we are resting in luxury at San Francisco, with nothing much to do, much bent upon doing it. The baronet is fairly tired, and so am I. The Club is very fine, and the city as bright as sun and movement can make it. Robert has gone to get his hair cut; then we shall breakfast, at noon, and then—I know not what. Some amusement is sure to turn up.

Of course Robert has given me a deal of information about matters in England, and I feel myself almost as well up as I ever was, though this is perhaps no great thing. I am very sorry to hear of Gifford Palgrave's death, which met us on our arrival here.[1] Otherwise we have seemed to strike nothing in the way of news. At this distance I think even Ireland seems a less overpowering element in the cosmos than it seems nearer home; and one finds the Chinaman take the place of the ubiquitous Irishman, politics and all. Both are rather a bore; but the Chinaman bores one in a new way, as Dr Johnson said of the poet Gray.[2]

Robert has returned, and is ordering breakfast. He is wrestling with the California cuisine, and wants me to tell him about all the game-birds he sees, and all the trees. As though I knew! My only labor is to sit on his inquiring mind.

Ever Yrs   Henry Adams.

MS: MHi

1. William Gifford Palgrave (1826–1888), brother of Francis Turner Palgrave.
2. Thomas Gray (1716–1771). "He was dull in a new way, and that made many people think him great"; Samuel Johnson, quoted in James Boswell's *Life* (1791).

To Charles Scribner

1603 H Street. Washington. 26 Nov. 1888.

Dear Sir

On returning to Washington, I find yours of November 13, which I hasten to answer.

John Wilson, at my request, set up a page for me, as I was not satisfied with that he set up first, and which you enclose to me. I enclose the specimen. My only doubt is whether the quotation should be put in smaller type for more contrast. I calculated with Wilson that this page was not only the most elegant, but coincided most closely with my wish to have volumes of five hundred pages each. If you are satisfied, I do not care to alter this specimen unless to reduce the size of type for quotation.

My taste rather inclines towards simplifying the page. I think that the reader who has a table of contents at the beginning, chapter by chapter, and an index for each pair of volumes, besides one for the whole, at the end, would neither need nor look at chapter- or page-headings. If you assent, I propose to drop the arrangement in books, and run the chapters through the volume. Each volume then serves as a Book. Under any circumstances I cannot retain my old arrangement, as the new volume would begin in the middle of a Book; and I can discover no other satisfactory division, suited to the new volume I want. Therefore I propose to number the Chapters consecutively, (except the Introduction, which will make eight chapters) and to make no change in page-headings except for chapters, dates and paging. The result will be such as you see on the specimen, after striking out the Book 1, and enlarging the type of *Chap.* 1.

I want no marginal notes. They were never of use to me in any book, (except Coleridge's Ancient Mariner.)

I infer from your letter that your chief doubt will concern Chapter-headings, and that you regard them as more important than page-headings or marginal notes. I regard them all as quite superfluous. Neither Macaulay nor Mahon used Chapter-headings.[1] The beauty of a page is its absence of all that disturbs the eye. Usage is arbitrary, but one cannot go wrong by being simple. My only doubt is about quotations, for I think the whole page should be in one type; but I must put references in foot-notes, and if one must use small type anyway, one might as well use it in the text. Therefore I yield to this variation from abstract rules, but I see no reason for disturbing the page with unnecessary changes, either before Chapters or elsewhere. I should use the same heading for odd and for even pages, except that the Chapter in one corner would interchange with the date on the other.

Of course you must understand me as expressing only preferences, not fixed prejudices. If you are very decided on any of these points, I do not care to hold out, least of all, about page-headings. I regard them merely as work thrown away. I never regard them in reading, and I do not believe any reader would notice their presence or absence in a history more than in a novel, where uniformity is very common, or in very old books, where it is, I think the rule.

My chief difficulty concerns the maps and plans. These should be nicely engraved to suit the page, as in Napier's Peninsular War.[2] I dislike all the patent processes I have seen. All thicken the lines. Supposing them to be engraved satisfactorily, ought they to be printed on a page, or inserted as in Napier? I care little, but I suppose the insertion to be less troublesome, though more liable to error.

Anyway the engraving must, if possible, precede or at least accompany the printing. The earlier volumes need few plans, but the later or war chapters will require a number. I must furnish them, and must find my engraver. Do you wish to take charge of this matter, or do you prefer that I should find my own man? I know only enough about the subject to dislike every method I ever saw, especially all photographic processes.

I am ready to print as fast as you please, and Wilson can turn out the plates faster than I can correct proof. Whenever you give the order, I will start.

Yrs truly   Henry Adams.

MS: ViU

1. Thomas Babington Macaulay (1800–1859), *History of England* (1849–1861); Philip Henry Stanhope (1805–1875), Earl Stanhope, published his *History of England from the Peace of Utrecht to the Peace of Versailles* (1836–1863) under his previous title of Viscount Mahon.
2. Sir William Napier, *History of the Peninsular War* (1828–1840).

To Lucy Baxter

1603 H Street. Tuesday, 25 March 1890

My dear Miss Baxter

I went down the river for Sunday to inspect a new club I have joined, which stopped my usual Sunday letter-writing. Before I forget it, I wish you would look at the backs of the volumes I sent you, and see if Vol. i matches Vol. ii precisely; and if Vol. iii matches Vol. iv. If not, please send them all back to me, and I will try to get them straight. I find I have mixed the sets, and those that remain are not matches.

Spring comes on apace, and all one's families and friends are coming here at once. The first half of April seems to be the time for everyone to descend on us. The Washingtonians are skurrying about, trying to make up parties for the amusement of visitors, and in consternation because all their friends write to announce immediate arrival. Daisy comes next Saturday to the Lodges.[1] The children come the next week to me. Mrs Cameron's house is packed to the attic. Society consists in hunting for people to amuse guests.

One cannot complain of solitude at this season, for even I, who go nowhere and know nobody, found myself last week unable to escape engagements. They were chiefly concert and theatre parties with my only partners, Mrs Cameron and Mrs Lodge;[2] but the principle is the same.

Your niece's fate seemed to me last summer an impending one; but marriage was so obviously the outcome of her position that you need hardly worry about her chances of happiness. The charm of women is the Hegelian charm of the identity of opposites. You can assume nothing regarding them, without assuming the contrary to be equally true. You all abominate second marriages, yet you all conspire to bring them about. I receive admonitions constantly on the subject, and am aware that my friends take an active interest in selecting a victim to sacrifice to my selfishness. I do not care to interfere with their search. My only precaution is to show a pronounced attachment to married women, so as to preclude any attachment that could cause a rumor of other ties. It would be useless and impossible to argue the matter, or to give reasons for preferring solitude seul to solitude à deux; but the reasons are sufficiently strong, and if I ever should act in a contrary sense, it would be because I should have begun to lose my will, and was in the first stages of imbecility. Just now my only wish is to escape from the dangers that remain in life with the least possible noise and suffering. I have had all I want, and the best. What folly you would think it for a man who had once been a King, to go on trying to be King after he had been deposed and lost his energies and illusions. The best he can do is, like Charles the Fifth, to make clocks.[3]

All the same, no amount of Stoicism can prevent one from hankering, not for the future but for the past; and even Faust, after his famous curse,— "Werd' ich zum Augenblicke sagen"—became so imbecile as to find satisfaction in building a Dutch dyke. I dread the decline of powers, and wish the moment were past when I could still say to the passing moment— Verweile doch, du bist so schön![4] I will try it on Fiji and Gobi.

Ever Ys   Henry Adams

MS: ScU

1. Evelyn ("Daisy") Davis Adams (1853–1926), sister of Anna Cabot Mills Davis Lodge, recently married to BA.
2. Anna Cabot Mills Davis Lodge (1850–1915), wife of Henry Cabot Lodge.
3. As recounted in W. Stirling Maxwell, *The Cloister Life of the Emperor Charles the Fifth* (1852).
4. "Werd ich zum Augenblicke sagen: / Verweile doch! Du bist so schön! / Dann magst du mich in Fesseln schlagen, / Dann will ich gern Zugrunde gehn!" (Should I to the passing moment say Stay! You are so fair! Then you may in fetters bind me, Then will I gladly go to destruction.) Faust to Mephistopheles; Goethe, *Faust,* Part I.

To Theodore F. Dwight

[Late June 1890]

Regular Payments
for H.A.

On the first day of every month
send to William Gray $50.
   "   " Maggy Wade   33.
   "   " John Brent   40.
N.B. Their wages are $35 and $18 respectively, and each receives $15 for board. Brent gets only $5.00 a month for board, and in November will go wholly into Hay's service.
On the 27th day of every month, (after Brooks goes on Sept. 1) send check to W. H. Blanchard, Beverly Farms, for $35.

November 1, send for Washington Tax-bill (perhaps the Collector of Taxes, (Washington, D.C.) will send it to you by mail if you write to him) and pay it by check. Last year it was $827.78
July 1, Water Rents, this year paid $24.00

Every few months, I suppose, a bill will come from C. Powell Noland, Shenandoah, Va. for the horses; $2.50 each per month.

Freeman's bill for taking care of the palms at $10 a month comes in January.

Clubs due January 1:

Knickerbocker	$100.
Metropolitan	50.
Cosmos	35.
Philosophical Society	5.
Quantico	12.
Anthropological	3.
July 1: Quantico	12.

The American Academy of Arts and Sciences sends bills when it pleases. For a year or two dues have not been collected. Pay as applied for.

Twice a year, say Jan. 1 and July 1, send a check for $50 to L. S. Emery, Office of Associated Charities, 707 G. St. Washington, D.C.

At all times bills will drop in for repairs or expenses incurred in the Washington and Beverly houses or grounds.

MS: MHi

To Charles Milnes Gaskell

1603 H Street. 4 July, 1890.

My dear Carlo

As my brother Brooks does not mean to stop in England, and as no one else of my intimacy is going there, I have given the bundle of letters to Spring Rice to send through the Foreign Office to Thornes, where I hope they will arrive within a week after you receive this letter.[1]

I had a letter from Robert yesterday saying that you had been laid up. This seemed to be all the news, and I hope your health is by this time sternly strong.

The summer waxes and still I hang on here, detained by the last sheets of Index, and by hopes of taking John La Farge with me again—this time to the South Seas. Hay also remains here, held by the last sheets of his great work, and we bask in the tropical heat of this empty city, alone in our houses. Hay goes north next week. My own movements are uncertain, but I am liable any day to start for San Francisco and Samoa. I shall need no preparation, for every last order is given; my trunks are ready for packing, and my wardrobe is ready also. I have fitted myself out for two years in the South Seas; but the length of my absence will depend wholly on my feelings. I may return in two months, if I find myself more bored there than here. I may be gone for twenty years if I find myself more bored here than there. I may turn up in England for a change, and you need not be surprised any fine day in April or May to see me walk into your breakfast room. Time is nothing to me, and health is the only unknown element of travel. Barring illness or accident I may go anywhere and do anything. and of nervous strain. The reaction of having nothing to do after steady labor without change for so many years, is severe. Probably it will rapidly disappear with travel. It has hitherto always done so.

Meanwhile I shall amuse myself with the thought of lighting on England by way of Polynesia, and telling you the joys of cannibalism. I expect to reach Samoa at latest by September 1, and for some time afterwards I expect that my safest address will be to the care of the United States Consul at Samoa. From Fiji to Tahiti is my range for next winter.

As far as you are concerned I shall really be nearer there than here, so it is not a matter to regret. My love to all yours.

Ever affely   Henry Adams.

MS: MHi

1. In anticipation of his long absence in the South Seas, HA was returning Gaskell's letters. Thornes, near Wakefield, was one of the Gaskell family residences.

To Elizabeth Cameron

Palace Hotel. 22 Aug. 1890.

I wonder whether I ever told you how delighted I was last year at getting a farewell note from you from shipboard. It seemed to tell me more than a volume on land. My own attempts can have no such success, since you know in advance all that I have to say; but I will send this letter all the same from shipboard. It is now eight o'clock in the morning, and we have a day of preparation before us. Yesterday I accomplished little except to settle on staterooms and get put up at the club.[1] I never feel respectable at San Francisco until I have scrubbed my head with soap and received a card to the club. Yesterday I did both by stages, resulting at last in partial recovery of my color and in a very satisfactory recovery of appetite. Beyond these two qualified successes I accomplished nothing of permanent value to the divine plan, and felt as though I were a tramp begging for a seat on a car-truck rather than like a gentleman with a credit on the Barings and letters of introduction to all the nobility and gentry of Polynesia in my pocket. Well! I hope you are now on the beach with Martha, and I would desperately like to be with you. Now for John Spreckels![2]

Saturday. 6.30 A.M.   At seven o'clock last night I was the tiredest historian in California but I had interviewed all the leading citizens of San Francisco, and had provided for all my expected wants for the winter, including a schooner if I require it. When I am tired I am homesick, and a sudden spasm came over me, just at the foot of the hotel stairs, that I *must* see Martha. I got over it with the help of a bottle of Champagne and a marvelous dinner at the Club, but I am at best homesick enough for Beverly. You have not seen my sonnet on Eagle Head. I will write it out for you on the opposite page. The octave is faulty in too much similarity of rhyme, but I think I like it notwithstanding its defects. By the bye, look into Clough's poems if you can find them, and read a short one beginning *Come back, Come back!*[3] Poor Clough was another wanderer who could not make his world run on four wheels. Here goes, then, for Polynesia! It is seven o'clock, and I must pack and do a thousand things to get on board the "Zealandia" at eleven. I will add a postscript there, and should feel happier if I knew where to address the letter.

Eagle Head

Here was the eagles' nest! The flashing sea,
   Sunny and blue, fades in the distant gray,
   Or flickers green on reefs, or throws white spray
On granite cliffs, as a heart restlessly
Beats against fate, and sobs unceasingly,
   Most beautiful flinging itself away,
   Clasping the rock by which it must not stay,
Sublimest in revolt at destiny.
Here where of old the eagles soared and screamed
   Answering the ocean's restless, longing roar,
While in their nest the hungry eaglets dreamed,
   —Here let us lie and watch the wave-vexed shore,
    Repeating, heart to heart, the eagles' strain,
    The ocean's cry of passion and of pain.

1 P.M.   On board ship. We should have sailed an hour ago, but the mail is late, and we must lie in the baking sun till two o'clock. Our ship is

crowded with English, mostly mild in type, but our staterooms are on deck, in the extreme bow where we should have as much isolation as falls to the lot of cannibals. A small child, rather pretty, howls like Martha in the next stateroom, and serves to remind me of anything you please. San Francisco bay is full of smoke, and the dock is deficient in interest. Awoki, La Farge's Jap., is our only acquaintance, and he seems as little amused as ourselves; but La Farge is always unexpectedly humorous and sustaining. By his aid I keep quite chirpy at times.

2 P.M.   Off, and running out of the bay. The ship is largely filled with cowboys and Indians of the Buffalo Bill persuasion, going somewhere to do something. The usual sprinkling of Jews and Jewesses; the irascible old gentleman, denouncing the company's officials; a few quiet young men, and the conventional British big-nosed female, seem to fill our crew. We are underway, and I am very shortly going to bed, the weather being too fine for confidence in my seamanship. I have done this thing before. So good-bye all! I daren't let myself think. Hasta luego.

MS: MHi

1. The Union Club.
2. John Diedrich Spreckels (1853–1926), president of the Oceanic Steamship Co. (San Francisco and Hawaii). He and his father operated extensive Hawaiian sugar plantations.
3. Arthur Hugh Clough, "Songs in Absence" (1852).

To Elizabeth Cameron

Steamer "W. G. Hall." 13 Sept. 1890.

At sea again, or rather in port, for just now, at seven o'clock in the morning, we are leaving the little village of Kailua, and running along the south coast of the island of Hawaii. We tore ourselves yesterday morning from our comforts at Honolulu, and after a day and night of seasick discomfort on a local steamer, filled with natives, we are now in sight of Mauna Loa, and at evening shall land at Punalu on the extreme southeastern end of the island. As I detest mountains, abominate volcanoes, and execrate the sea, the effort is a tremendous one; but I make it from a sense of duty to the savages who killed Captain Cook just about here a century ago.[1] One good turn deserves another. Perhaps they will kill me. I never saw a place where killing was less like murder. The ocean is calm and blue; the air so warm that I turned out of my sleepless berth at the first light of dawn, and sat in my pyjamas in the cool air with only a sense of refreshment; the huge flat bulk of Mauna Loa stretches down an interminable slope ahead of us, with the strange voluptuous charm peculiar to volcanic slopes, which always seem to invite you to lie down on them and caress them; the shores are rocky and lined with palms; the mountain sides are green, and patched with dark tufts of forest; the place is—an island paradise, made of lava; and the native boats—queer long coffins with an outrigger on one side resting in the water—are now coming out at some new landing-place, bringing mangoes, pine-apples, melons and alligator-pears, all which I am somewhat too nauseated to eat. Our steamer is filled with plaintive-looking native women—the old-gold variety—who vary in expression between the ferocious look of the warriors who worshipped Captain Cook and then killed him, and the melancholy of a generation obliged to be educated by missionaries. They have a charm in this extraordinary scope of expressions which run from tenderness to ferocity in a single play of feature, but I prefer the children, who are plaintive and sea-sick in stacks about the decks, and lie perfectly still, with their pathetic dark eyes expressing all sorts of vague sensations evidently more or less out of gear with the cosmos. The least sympathetic character is the occasional whiteman. Third-rate places seldom attract even third-rate men, but rather ninthrate samples, and these are commonly the white men of tropical islands. I prefer the savages who were—at least the high chiefs—great swells and very much gentlemen, and killed Captain Cook.

Awoki, our Jap, has brought me a pineapple and orange, on which I have breakfasted, with a headache for outlook. We are off again, and on the sunny side of our steamer the heat is too great for comfort. We have to sit on the shady side, and mostly lose the view.

10 o'clock.   We have been ashore to see where Captain Cook was killed, a hot little lava oven where the cliffs rise sharp over deep water,—some old crater-hole—of all sorts of intense blue. Only a hut was there, donkeys and mules, a few natives and a swarm of crabs jumping over the red rocks by the black-blue water. Mauna Loa slopes back for forty miles or so, behind. So now I shall try to take a nap, having done my duty, and will wonder, for amusement, whether you are at Beverly, and how you look there.

Kilauea Volcano House. Monday, Sept. 15. 7 A.M. Our pilgrimage is effected at last. I am looking, from the porch of the inn, down on the black floor of the crater, and its steaming and smoking lake, now chilled over, some two or three miles away, at the crater's further end. More impressive to my fancy is the broad sloping mass of Mauna Loa which rises beyond, ten thousand feet above us, a mass of rugged red lava, scored by deeper red or black streaks down its side, but looking softer than babies' flesh in this lovely morning sunlight, and tinged above its red with the faintest violet vapor. I adore mountains—from below. Like other deities, they should not be trodden upon. As La Farge remarked yesterday when I said that the ocean *looked* quiet enough: "It *is* quiet if you don't fool with it. How would *you* like to be sailed upon?" The natives still come up here and sit on the crater's edge to look down at the residence of their great Goddess, but they never go down into it. They say they're not rich enough. The presents cost too much. Mrs Dominis, the King's sister, and queen-expectant,[2] came up here in the year 1885, and brought a black pig, two roosters, champagne, red handkerchiefs, and a whole basket of presents, which were all thrown on the lava lake. The pig, having his legs tied, squealed half an hour before he was thoroughly roasted, and one of the roosters escaped to an adjoining rock, but was recaught and immersed. Only princesses are rich enough to do the thing suitably, and as Mrs Dominis is a Sunday-school Christian, she knows how to treat true deities. As for me, I prefer the bigger and handsomer Mauna Loa, and I routed La Farge out at six o'clock—or was it five?—to sketch it with its top red with the first rays of sun. Had La Farge not waited to put his trowsers on, he might have caught the rosy-fingered dawn in perfection, but he lost five minutes howling to Awoki for slippers alone. As the clouds cover the mountain by nine o'clock, and rain commonly sets in by noon in floods, one must be economical on dawns. Just now, all is serene and lovely, but one suffers to be beautiful. I am still sea-sick, reeling with nausea, from the horrible two hours of our landing from the steamer in the surf, and La Farge was not much better. I have not been so violently sick and faint for years, as when tossing up and down, six feet at a jump, in the boat by the steamer's side, waiting for fat native women to tumble into it. I wished I was dead and hadn't come, and wondered how I was going through five years misery like that. I am still wondering, for all my suffering is before me, and I think nothing but dreams of Typee sustains us,[3] for La Farge recovers from his sea-sickness slower than I, though he suffers less acutely. The demon of travel sandwiches in a day or two of enjoyment with a day of misery, and lures us on. After the horror of Saturday evening we had a lovely day's drive yesterday up here, over grassy mountain sides, and through lava beds sprinkled with hot-house shrubs and ferns. The air is delicious, and the temperature, when the clouds veil the sun, is perfect either for driving or walking. If we can only escape the steamer on the windward side! but that implies sixty miles of horseback, partly in deluges of rain.

Hilo. Sept. 18.　If you do not know where Hilo is, don't look for it on the map. One's imagination is the best map for travellers. You may remember Hilo best because it is the place where Clarence King's waterfall of old-gold girls was situated.[4] The waterfall is still here, just behind the Severance house where we are staying. Mrs Severance took us down there half an hour ago.[5] She said nothing about the girls, but she did say that the boys used habitually to go over the fall as their after-school amusement; but of late they have given it up, and must be paid for doing it. The last man who jumped off the neighboring high rock required fifteen dollars. Mrs Severance told this sadly, mourning over the decline of the arts and of surf-bathing. A Bostonian named Brigham took a clever photograph of a boy, just half way down, the fall being perhaps twelve or fifteen feet. So passes the glory of Hawaii, and of the old-gold girl,—woe is me!

As La Farge aptly quoted yesterday from some wise traveller's advice to another, à propos of volcanoes: "You will be sorry if you go there, and you will be sorry if you don't go there, so I advise you to go." We went. The evening before last we tramped for two hours across rough blocks and layers of black glass; then tumbled down more broken blocks sixty or eighty feet into another hole; then scrambled half way down another crater—three in succession, one inside the other—and sat down to look at a steaming black floor below us, which ought to have been red-hot and liquid, spouting fountains of fire, but was more like an engine house at night with two or three engines letting off steam and showing head-lights. The scene had a certain vague grandeur as night came on, and the spots of fire glowed below while the new moon looked over the cliff above; but I do not care to go there again, nor did I care even to go down the odd thirty or forty feet to the surface of the famous "lake of liquid fire." It was more effective, I am sure, the less hard one hit one's nose on it. We tramped back in the dark; our lanterns went out, and we were more than three hours to the hotel.

Yesterday morning we had to mount horses at eight o'clock and we rode till half past two,—more than six hours—to get over only fifteen miles of rough lava. Then we struck a road and a wagon, and drove fifteen miles more, to Hilo, in an hour and a half. During the drive we passed through our first tropical forest, and I felt a sensation. You who are comfortably at home cannot conceive the hardship of us poor travellers in trying to imagine we are anywhere else. I pass my time chiefly in trying to explain how Kilauea and Hilo happen to be within driving distance of Beverly. I was bothered to distraction in pitching into the middle of a jungle of tropical trees, creepers, ferns and flowers, when I felt sure that no such thing existed near Salem or Manchester. Perhaps I can show you where it is, but just now I feel constantly puzzled to account for all I see.

Tomorrow we start, through mud and gulches of torrents, on a five day's ride to Kawaihae, eighty miles to the westward, where we take steamer again. If you will believe it, I do this to avoid a day's seasickness.

Steamer "Kinau," Tuesday, 23 Sept. I take it all back. Hawaii is fascinating, and I could dream away months here. Yet dreaming has not been my standard amusement of late. Never have I done such hard and continuous travelling as during the last ten days, since leaving Honolulu. I have told you how we reached Hilo. Friday morning early we left Hilo, according to our plan, with a circus of horses, to ride eighty miles, divided into four days. Rain was falling as we drove out the first eight miles to take horse at the end of the road, but we started off like Pantagruel,[6] and in an hour arrived at a lovely cove or ravine called Onomea where La Farge sketched till noon; one of the sweetest spots on earth where the land and ocean meet like lovers, and the natives still look almost natural. That afternoon we rode eight miles further. The sky cleared; the sun shone; the breeze blew; the road was awful, in deep holes of mud, with rocky cañons to climb down and up at every half mile; but I never enjoyed anything in travel more thoroughly than I did this. Every ravine was more beautiful than the last, and each was a true Paul and Virginia idyll, wildly lovely in ways that made one forget life.[7] The intensely blue ocean foamed into the mouths of still inlets, saturated with the tropical green of ferns and dense woods, and a waterfall always made a back ground, with its sound of running water above the surf. The afternoon repaid all my five thousand miles of weariness, even though we had to pass the night at one of Spreckels' sugar plantations where saturnine Scotchmen and a gentle-spoken Gloucestershire house-keeper entertained us till seven o'clock Saturday morning when we started off again over the same mud-holes and through more cañons, which disturbed La Farge because the horses were not noble animals and warranted little confidence; but to me the enjoyment was perfect. At noon we lunched at another plantation where a rather pretty little German-American woman, of the bride class, entertained us very sweetly, and closed our enjoyment by playing to us Weber's last waltz, while we looked out under vines to the deep blue ocean as one does from the Newport cottages. That was at Laupahoehoe plantation, and that afternoon we passed Laupahoehoe and rode hard till half-past five, when I dismounted before a country-house, and, before I realised it, tumbled up steps into an open hall where three ladies in white dresses were seated. I had to explain that we had invited ourselves to pass the night, and they had to acquiesce. The family was named Horner, and were Americans running several plantations and ranches on the island. We passed the night of Sunday at the plantation of another son, or brother, of the same family, at Kukuihaele, and strolled down to see the Waipio valley, which is one of the Hawaiian sights. Yesterday we rode twelve miles up the hills, stopping to lunch at the house of one Jarrett who manages a great cattle ranch.[8] Jarrett was not there, but two young women were, and though they were in language and manners as much like other young women as might be, they had enough of the old-gold quality and blood to make them very amusing to me. They made me eat raw fish and squid, as well as of course the eternal poi to which I am now accustomed; then after lunch, while La Farge and I smoked or dozed and looked across the grass plains to the wonderful slopes of Mauna Loa and Mauna Kea, the two girls sat on mats under the trees and made garlands of roses and geranium which they fastened round our necks,—or rather round my neck and La Farge's hat. I was tremendously pleased by this, my first *lei*,—I believe they spell the word so, pronouncing it *lay*—and wore it down the long, dusty ride to Kawaihae where we were to meet the steamer, and where we arrived just at dark in an afterglow like Egypt. The girls also drove down, one of them returning to Honolulu by the same steamer. Kawaihae seemed a terrible spot, baked by the southern sun against a mountain of brown lava without a drop of fresh water for miles. When I dismounted and entered the dirty little restaurant, I found our two young ladies eating supper at a dusky table. They had ordered for me a perfectly raw fresh fish, and the old-goldest of the two showed me how to eat it, looking delightfully savage as she held the dripping fish in her hands and tore its flesh with her teeth. Jarrett was there, and took us under his care, so that an evening which threatened to be awful in heat and dirt, turned out delightful. They took us to a native house near by, where a large platform thatched with palm-leaves looked under scrubby trees across the moonlit ocean which just lapped and purred on the beach a few yards away. Then they made the mistress of the house—an old schoolmate, but a native and speaking little English—bring her guitar and sing the Hawaiian songs. They were curiously plaintive, perhaps owing to the way of singing, but only one—Kamehameha's war-dance—was really interesting and sounded as though it were real. A large mat was brought out, and those of us who liked lay down and listened or slept. The moon was half-full, and shone exquisitely and Venus sank with a trail like the sun's.

From this queer little episode, the only touch of half-native life we have felt, we were roused by the appearance of the steamer at ten o'clock, and in due time were taken into the boat and set on board. I dropped my faded and tattered *lay* into the water as we were rowed out, and now while the "Kinau" lies at Mahukana, doing nothing, I write to tell you that our journey has been fascinating, in spite of prosaic sugar-plantations, and that I am yearning to get back to Waimea, where I might stay a month at Samuel Parker's great ranch, and ride his horses about the slopes of Mauna Kea, while indefinite girls of the old-gold variety should hang indefinite garlands round my bronzed neck.[9]

Sept. 24. Honolulu again.   We arrived, seasick as usual, at five o'clock this morning, and returned to our house with a sense of recovering one childhood's home, only worried by the thought of starting again in three days, "sailing, sailing, over the seasick sea." My girl of the Waimea rose-wreath, who came by the steamer with us, was also desperately sea-sick, and I fed her brown eyes with pine-apple, the only refreshment she could take. The distant line of purple ocean still lies to the southward, and the sun still lightens the white surf outside the harbor of Honolulu, as it did when I must have sported here as a child, among the roses and centipedes; but the refuge of our infancy must know us no longer, and I shall be obliged to perpetrate my lurid water-color sketches henceforward somewhere else. Now that I look back on our Hawaian journey of the last ten days, it seems really a considerable experience, and one new to common travellers in gaiters. If you feel enough curiosity to know what others think of the same scenes, read Miss Bird's travels in the Sandwich Islands.[10] I have carefully avoided looking at her remarks, for I know that she always dilates with a correct emotion, and I yearn only for the incorrect ones; but you will surely see Islands of the soundest principles—traveller's principles, I mean,—if you read Miss Bird, who will tell you all that I ought to have seen and felt, and for whom the volcano behaved so well, and performed its correct motions so properly that it becomes a joy to follow her. To us the volcano was positively flat, and I sympathised actively with an Englishman, who, we were told, after a single glance at it, turned away and gazed only at the planets and the Southern Cross. To irritate me still more, we are now assured that the lake of fire by which we sat unmoved, became very active within four-and-twenty hours afterwards. These are our lucks. I never see the world as the world ought to be.

In revenge I have enjoyed much that is not to be set down in literary composition, unless by a writer like Fromentin or a spectacled and animated prism like La Farge.[11] He has taught me to feel the subtleness and endless variety of charm in the color and light of every hour in the tropical island's day and night. I get gently intoxicated on the soft violets and strong blues, the masses of purple and the broad bands of orange and green in the sunsets, as I used to *griser* myself on absynthe on the summer evenings in the Palais Royal before dining at Véfour's, thirty years ago. The outlines of the great mountains, their reddish purple glow, the infinite variety of greens and the perfectly intemperate shifting blues of the ocean, are a new world to me. To be sure, man is pretty vile, but perhaps woman might partly compensate for him, if one only knew where to find her.[12] As she canters about the roads, a-straddle on horseback, with wreaths of faded yellow flowers, and clothed in a blue or red or yellow night-gown, she is rather a riddle than a satisfaction.

I expected a letter by the steamer of the 12th, but nothing comes from the post-office. Only Dwight encloses an exquisite little note, written after you bade me good-bye, which should have reached me before I left Boston, but is even more welcome here. As the mail goes tomorrow I will cut off this piece of island-yarn today, and send it off, hoping to get a real letter on Saturday before I sail. Otherwise I shall be uneasy for fear you or Martha are in trouble.

Ever Yrs   Henry Adams.

MS: MHi

1. Captain James Cook (1728–1779), who discovered the Hawaiian Islands in 1778, was killed in Kealakekua Bay in 1779.
2. Lydia Kamakacha Paki (1838–1917), wife of John Owen Dominis, reigned as Queen Liliuokalani 1891–1893.
3. Herman Melville's idyllic narrative of his stay in the Marquesas, *Typee* (1846), had to sustain HA over some 2,500 miles of open sea before he would reach Samoa, his first destination in Polynesia.
4. Clarence King had visited Hawaii in 1872.
5. The wife of Henry W. Severance of California, U.S. consul general 1889–1893.
6. Pantagruel, son of the giant Gargantua, embarks on a series of adventures with his good companion Panurge; François Rabelais, *Gargantua and Pantagruel* (1552). A handsome new edition in several volumes was in course of publication.
7. Bernardin de Saint-Pierre, *Paul et Virginie* (1787).
8. Paul Jarrett was the manager of the 227,000-acre cattle ranch that John Palmer Parker (1790–1868) of Boston had begun to buy and develop in 1847.
9. "Indefinite girls" refers to the intermarriage between Hawaiians and Caucasians in the dynasty founded by John Palmer Parker. He married the Hawaiian chiefess Kipikane, granddaughter of King Kamehameha I. Samuel K. Parker (b. 1853) was their grandson and one of his main heirs.
10. Isabella Bird Bishop, *The Hawaiian Archipelago: Six Months Among the Palm Groves, Coral Reefs, and Volcanoes of the Sandwich Islands* (1875).
11. Eugène Fromentin (1820–1876), painter, novelist, travel writer, *A Summer in the Sahara* (1857), *A Year in the Sahel* (1859).
12. Reginald Heber, "From Greenland's Icy Mountains" (the "Missionary Hymn," 1819): "What though the spicy breezes / Blow soft o'er Ceylon's isle, / Though every prospect pleases, / And only man is vile."

To John Hay

Vaiale (Apia) 16 Nov. 1890.

My dear John

By this time I had expected to be in Tahiti, but we have found more in Samoa than we expected. Our nasty little pigstye of a steamer sailed for Tahiti a week ago or so, and will not return for a month. Then perhaps we shall sail, and when this reaches you on Christmas Day I hope we shall be established at Papeete. I doubt whether it will have much novelty after

Samoa, but it will give a chance for you to join us. By taking the mail sailing-ship from San Francisco, you can reach Tahiti in about a month; perhaps less, for what I know.

Your letter of October 10 arrived by the last mail. All my letters were very satisfactory, yours highly so, except for Sombrerete, which is sombrereteer than ever.[1] I am brewing a letter to King which I shall write some day, and it will be a volume, for I have seen heaps of things that I can tell him what I don't know about; but the chiefest thing is that a man can still live on these islands of the South Seas for pure fun. The Consuls themselves, the greatest men within a thousand miles, may spend four or five thousand a year. The richest trader can hardly have more. King Malietoa has not a Chilian quarter-dollar to his back. My neighbor and friend Mata-afa, ex-king, goes every morning to work in his *taro*-patch, or to fish on the reef with the villagers. I have had no little difficulty in obtaining a thousand dollars to spend here, and I am regarded as fabulously rich. When I staid in Savaii with Aiga, Malietoa's adopted daughter, my gift at parting was ten dollars; to Lauati, the great orator and chief of Safotulafai, where we staid three days, I gave twenty, which was equivalent to a fine mat, the costliest of possessions; and as a token of regard for Anai, chief of Iva, I am going—God forgive me—to supply his little daughter with a year's schooling at the missionary college at Malua. You see that a dollar still goes a long way in Samoa, and when I tell you that I pay the extravagant rent of ten dollars a month for my native house, and that a horse costs thirty dollars and is not worth riding when he is bought, you can safely assure King that the South Seas can always shelter him though Sombreretes fall. Indeed, for that matter, a great reputation can be made here with mighty small capital. Darwin and Dana and Wallace have only scratched the ocean's surface.[2] The geologist who can explain these islands, and the artist who can express them, will have got a sure hold on the shirt-tail of fame. If I were twenty years younger, and knew anything to start with, I would try it on. King, who is always young and bloomful, can do it at any time.

The curse of money has touched here, but is not yet deep, though mountain forests, covered with dense and almost impenetrable vegetation, are held at ten dollars an acre, and the poor chiefs, whose only possession is a cocoa-nut grove, have mortgaged it to the eyes. By the Berlin treaty, the whites are not permitted to buy more land from natives, but the whites already claim under one title or another, more land than exists in the whole group of islands. If the sugar cultivation is introduced, the people are lost. Nothing can stand against the frantic barbarism of the sugar-planter. As yet, the only plantations are cocoa-nut, and these are not so mischievous, especially as they are badly managed by German companies which spend more money than the copra brings. Yet the social changes are steady, and another generation will leave behind it the finest part of the old Samoan world. The young chiefs are inferior to the old ones. Gunpowder and missionaries have destroyed the life of the nobles. In former times a great chief went into battle with no thought of the common warrior. He passed through a herd of them, and none presumed to attack him. Chiefs fought only with chiefs. The idea of being killed by a common man was sacrilege. The introduction of fire-arms has changed all this, and now, as one of the chiefs said with a voice of horror, any hunchback, behind a tree, can kill the greatest chief in Samoa.

Since I wrote to you last, I have made a journey along the coast as far as Savaii, the westernmost and largest island of the group. We were an imposing party. The Consul General Sewall, whose guests we are, was the head of it, and Sewall is extremely popular among the Malietoa and Mataafa chiefs who consider him to have saved their lives and liberties. Their expressions of gratitude to him and to the United States are unbounded, and they certainly showed that they felt it, for in their strongholds we were received like kings. Our escort was Seumano-tafa, the chief of Apia, Malietoa's right-hand man. You may remember that, in the great hurricane at Apia, Seumano took his boat through the surf, and saved many lives. For this act, our government sent him some costly presents, among others a beautiful boat, perfectly fitted out for oars and sails. On our *malanga,* or boat-excursion, we went with Seu in his boat, and our own boat followed with our baggage and stores. We carried on Seu's boat the Samoan flag; on our own, the American; and our entire party, including servants and crews, was more than twenty men. We were absent some ten days, with fine weather, and visited the most interesting parts of the islands. I felt as though I had got back to Homer's time, and were cruising about the Aegean with Ajax. Of all the classic spots I ever imagined, the little island of Manono was the most ideal. Ithaca was, even in the reign of Ulysses, absolutely modern by the side of it. As the *mise-en-scène* of an opera, it would be perfection. If I could note music, I would compose an opera, on the musical motives of the Samoan dances and boat-songs, gutturals, grunts and all. You may bet your biggest margin it would be a tremendous success, if the police would only keep their hands off. The ballet alone would put New York on its head with excitement. You would rush for the next steamer if you could realise the beauty of some parts of the Siva. There are figures stupid and grotesque as you please; but there are others which would make you gasp with delight, and movements which I do not exaggerate in calling unsurpassable. Then, if I could close the spectacle with the climax of the *pai-pai,* I should just clean out the bottom dollar of W. W. Astor. The *pai-pai* is a figure taboo by the missionaries, as indeed the

Lancers and Virginia Reel are; but it is still danced in the late hours of the night, though we have seen it only once. Two or three women are the dancers, and they should be the best, especially in figure. They dance at first with the same movements, as far as I could see, that they used in many other figures, and as I did not know what they were dancing I paid no special attention. Presently I noticed that the chief dancer's waist-cloth seemed getting loose. This is their only dress, and it is nothing but a strip of cotton or *tapa* about eighteen inches wide, wrapped round the waist, with the end or corner tucked inside to hold it. Of course it constantly works loose, but the natives are so well used to it that they always tighten it, and I never yet have seen either man, woman or child let it fall by accident. In the *pai-pai,* the women let their *lava-lavas,* as they are called, or *siapas,* seem about to fall. The dancer pretends to tighten it, but only opens it so as to show a little more thigh, and fastens it again so low as to show a little more hip. Always turning about and moving with the chorus, she repeats this process again and again, showing more legs and hips every time, until the *siapa* barely hangs on her, and would fall except that she holds it. At last it falls; she turns once or twice more, in full view; then snatches up the *siapa* and runs away.

You must imagine these dances in a native house, lighted by the ruddy flame of a palm-leaf fire in the centre, and filled, except where the dancing is done, by old-gold men and women applauding, laughing, smoking, and smelling of cocoa-nut oil. You are sitting or lying, with your back against an outer-post. Behind you, outside, the moon is lighting a swarm of children, or women, who are also looking eagerly at the dancers. The night air is soft, and the palms rustle above the house. Your legs are cramped by long sitting cross-legged; your back aches; your eyes droop with fatigue; your head aches with the noise; you would give a fortune to be allowed to go to bed, but you can't till the dance is over and the house is cleared. You are half mad with the taste of cocoa-nut oil. You are a little feverish, for this thing has gone on, day and night, for a week, and it is more exhausting than a Pan-American railway jaunt. You are weary of travel and tired of the South Seas. You want to be at home, in your own bed, with clean sheets and a pillow, and quiet. Well! I give you my word, founded on experience, that, with all this, when you see the *pai-pai,* you are glad you came.

Of course the Siva, and especially the figure of the *pai-pai*—beautiful thighs—is made to display the form and not the face. To the Samoan, nine tenths of beauty consists in form; the other tenth in feature, coloring and such details. The Samoan Siva, like the Japanese bath, is evidently connected with natural selection; the young men and young women learn there to know who are the finest marriageable articles. Probably the girl who could make the best show in the *pai-pai* would rise in value to the village by the difference of two or three fine mats and a dozen pigs. In such a case the *pai-pai,* danced by a chief's daughter or *taupo,* does not prove license but virtue. The audience is far less moved by it than a French audience is by a good ballet. Any European suddenly taken to such a show would assume that the girl was licentious, and if he were a Frenchman he would probably ask for her. The chief would be scandalised at European want of decency. He keeps his *taupo* as carefully watched and guarded as though he were a Spaniard. The girl herself knows her own value and is not likely to throw herself away. She has no passions, though she is good-natured enough, and might perhaps elope with a handsome young fellow who made long siege of her. The Frenchman would be politely given some middle-aged woman, more or less repulsive in person, and the mother of several illegitimate children, who would have to be his only consolation for losing the object of his desire. The natives would fully appreciate the joke, and probably nickname the victim by some word preserving its memory.

I have not changed my ideas on the point of morality here. As elsewhere, vice follows vice. We have not sought it, and consequently have not found it. Thus far, no one, either man or woman, has made so much as a suggestion, by word or sign, of any licentious idea. My boatmen probably have license enough, but, as the German Consul warned me, I have none. I might as well be living in a nursery for all the vice that is shown to me, and if I did see it, I should only be amused at its simplicity beside the elaborated viciousness of Paris or even of Naples. I never have lived in so unselfconscious a place. Yesterday La Farge and I snorted with laughter because our boy Charley, a half-caste who acts as our interpreter, informed us that "a girl had just been caught running away with a man." On cross-examination, La Farge drew out the further facts that the pair were literally running, in full sight of half the town, along the main road by the seashore, where they might have dodged into a trackless forest within fifty yards; that the girl was then in a neighboring house getting a scolding from her mother; and that after the scolding she would get a beating. La Farge was so much delighted that he wanted to start off at once to see the girl, with a view, I think, to some possible picture to be called "The Elopement," but he was hard at work painting a sketch of Fang-alo sliding down the waterfall, for Clarence King's satisfaction no doubt, and he could not leave his sketch.

Apropos to cataracts of girls, they are common as any other cataracts here. Any waterfall with a ten-foot pool at its base, and a suitable drop, is sure to be used both by girls and boys, and by men as well. The difficulty is that the coast is mostly flat; the waterfalls are far off, and few of them are suited to the purpose. The only one near Apia is fully five miles away, in the hills, far from any village; and one must make up a party of girls from here, and devote a day to a regular picnic, in order to see the show. For King's sake I did this last week. My friend Fatuleia, Seumano's wife, the chiefess of Apia, took charge of the affair, and summoned half a dozen of the belles of Apia:—Fanua, the *taupo;* Otaota, whose photograph I must have sent you, a pretty girl standing before the grave-monument of a chief; Fang-alo, whose photograph you also have; Nelly, a pretty missionary girl; and two or three others. We rode two hours through the forest, and clambered down a ravine to the spot, a deep valley, with cliffs overgrown with verdure, and topped by high trees far above us. To my surprise I found that the waterfall was little more than a brook, as far as the water had to do with it, though the fall was steep enough; full twenty feet into a deep pool. For this reason the place is called the Sliding Rock, for the water has smoothed the hard stone, and covered it with a slippery grass or fine slimy growth. The girls sit in the running water, and slide or coast down, with a plunge of ten or twelve feet below. They go like a shot, and the sight is very pretty. La Farge and I were immensely amused by it, and so were the girls, who went in as though they were naiads. They wore whatever suited their ideas of propriety, from a waist-cloth to a night-gown dress; but the variety rather added to the effect, and the water took charge of the proprieties.

The most curious part of our experience here is to find that the natives are so totally different from what I imagined, and yet so like what I ought to have expected. They are a finer race than I supposed, and seem uncontaminated by outside influence. They have not suffered from diseases introduced from abroad. They have their own diseases,—elephantiasis is the worst, but skin-troubles and sores are common, and eyes are apt to be affected by blemish,—but they are otherwise strong and would shame any white race I ever saw, for the uniform vigor of their bodies. One never sees a tall man who is thin or feeble. Their standard of beauty varies between six feet, and six-feet-six, in height, but is always broad and muscular in proportion. The women are very nearly as strong as the men. Often in walking behind them I puzzle myself to decide from their backs whether they are men or women, and I am never sure. La Farge detects a certain widening towards the hips which I am too little trained to see; and no wonder, for I have taken enough measurements of typical specimens to be certain that a girl of my height, or say five-feet-six, will have a waist measuring at least thirty-three-and-a-half inches, and hips measuring not more than fortytwo. Her upper-arm will be $14\frac{1}{2}$ inches in circumference; her wrist, eight; the calf of her leg at least sixteen; her ankle near eleven; and yet her foot is but $10\frac{1}{2}$ inches long, and both foot and hands are well shaped. These are masculine proportions, and the men assure me that the women have nearly the strength of men. Child-birth is an easy affair of twentyfour hours. Every motion and gesture is free and masculine. They go into battle with the men, and, as one of the most famous fighting chiefs, Pa-tu, my neighbor, told me of his own daughter who fell in battle by his side, "she was killed fighting like a man."

Now comes the quality which to me is most curious. Here are these superb men and women,—creatures of this soft climate and voluptuous nature, living under a tropical sun, and skies of divine purple and blue,— who ought, on my notions, to be chock-full of languid longings and passionate emotions, but they are pure Greek fauns. Their intellectual existence is made up of concrete facts. As La Farge says, they have no thoughts. They are not in the least voluptuous; they have no longings and very brief passions; they live a matter-of-fact existence that would scare a New England spinster. Even their dances—proper or improper,—always represent facts, and never even attempt to reproduce an emotion. The dancers play at ball, or at bathing, or at cocoa-nut gathering, or hammer, or row, or represent cats, rats, birds or devils, but never an abstraction. They do not know how to be voluptuous. Old Samasoni, the American pilot here for many years, and twice married to high-class native women, tells us that the worst dance he ever saw here was a literal reproduction of the marriage ceremony, and that the man went through the entire form, which is long and highly peculiar, and ended with the consummation,—openly, before the whole village, delighted with the fun,—but that neither actors nor spectators showed a sign of emotion or passion, but went through it as practically as though it had been a cricket-match. Their only idea was that it was funny,—as, in a sense, it certainly was; that is, it was not nice. Sentiment or sentimentality is unknown to them. They are astonishingly kind to their children, and their children are very well-behaved; but there is no sentiment, only good-nature, about it. They are the happiest, easiest, smilingest people I ever saw, and the most delightfully archaic. They fight bravely, but are not morally brave. They have the virtues of healthy children,—and the weaknesses of Agamemnon and Ulysses.

I could babble on indefinitely about them and their ways, but I think you care less about the Archaic than King or I do, and I might only bore you. For myself, I am not bored. I go to bed soon after nine o'clock, and sleep well till half past five. I eat bananas, mangoes, oranges, pineapples and mummy-apples by the peck. I smoke like a lobster. I write, or study water-color drawing all day. The rainy season has begun. Our gay colors and warm lights have washed out into a uniform grey and faint violet. Expeditions are too risky, for one is sure to be drenched, and the rain falls here solid. But we are well, cheerful and dread moving. I ought to take more exercise, but I don't, and time slides as though it were Fang-alo on the Sliding Rock.

Nov. 25. Fine weather again. We are starting on a boat-tour of the island.

Alofa   Atamu

MS: RPB

1. The Sombrerete Mining Co., founded in 1881, which had been one of King's most promising mining schemes, was being liquidated.
2. Alfred Russel Wallace, English naturalist; *Island Life* (1880).

To Elizabeth Cameron

Vaiale, 15 December, 1890.

We find Stevenson still here.[1] He has not gone to Auckland. Apparently we are to see much more of him, for the steamer "Richmond," which is our only conveyance to Tahiti, will not return here for six weeks. La Farge is not yet ready to go; so we have sent for our letters, which cannot arrive till near February, and then only in time for us to acknowledge them before sailing. By that time we shall be well in arrears, for our last letters from home were written early in October. We are to leave Samoa about February 1, and by that time should have three months' arrears of letters to answer on reaching Tahiti.

Having now pretty much exhausted the possibilities of travel in Samoa, I am casting about for amusements during the next six weeks. We are not without distinguished society. Saturday afternoon Mata-afa came over to see us, as he often does; but this time he brought some presents of *tapa* and baskets, explaining that he is now poor and has little to give. The formula is almost a matter of course, but in this case it is probably more than a form, for Mata-afa is an abdicated king, and is struggling with difficulties. I think he would be a marked man anywhere, but he is a long way the most distinguished chief in these islands, and the only one we have met who carries his superiority about him so decidedly as to set him at once apart. He brought me, on Saturday, some old songs I had asked for, and which he had good-naturedly caused to be written out. Two of his oldest followers were with him, and sat at the end of our native house, while Mata-afa himself, in the regulation official white jacket, sat on a chair between us. I had much to ask him about the legendary songs, and he, with a deprecatory smile as though I were a spoiled child, told me at great length the story, or a part of the mass of stories, about Pili, "the Lizard," which seems to be the principal material of Samoan verse. It was not very amusing, and he was aware of it, but I asked him to go on, and he must have toiled an hour, giving sentence after sentence for translation by our boy Charley. I shall not bore you with the doings of Pili, either the father or the son. You can read volumes of such childlike stuff by getting from the Congressional library either Fornandez' great book about Hawaii or Sir George Grey's Maori Legend's about New Zealand, or Turner's volume on Samoa, or half a dozen other books on the South Seas.[2] Polynesians are not imaginative, but eminently practical, with childish ideas as to what is humorous or imposing. My object is only to find out what they have done; so I listened with gravity to Mata-afa, who labored on, until at length Stevenson dropped in, and we turned to discussing the latest appearance of a certain interesting spirit or female enchantress who recently killed a young chief, in whose father's house we stayed at Vao-vai. I thought then that we were rather an interesting company, as the world goes. Mata-afa may fairly rank as one of the heroic figures of our time. Stevenson is a person sufficiently known to fame; and La Farge will probably not be less well known a hundred years hence than now. The group struck me as rather a peculiar one, considering that we were a good many thousand miles from places where people usually hunt lions, and I felt encouraged to think that even here I was not in an atmosphere of hopeless mental stagnation. Stevenson stayed to dine with us, and was quite on his manners, but as usual had to borrow Sewall's clothes. La Farge and I promised to come up to his place the next morning (Sunday), and to send our breakfast before us. I cannot conceive why they should ever be without food in the house, but apparently their normal condition is foodless, and they not only consented but advised my making sure of my own breakfast.[3] Stevenson himself seems to eat little or nothing, and lives on cheap French *vin ordinaire* when he can get it. I do not know how this régime affects his complaint, for I do not know what his complaint is. I supposed it to be *phthisis,* or tubercular consumption; but am assured here that his lungs are not affected. The German physician here says that the complaint is asthma; but I am too weak in knowledge to explain how asthma should get relief from a saturated climate like this, where constant exposure leads also to severe colds, not easily thrown off. Asthma or whatever you please, he and his wife, according to their own account, rarely have enough to eat in the house, so I sent off a native, at seven o'clock in the morning, with a basket of food, while I started on foot at half past ten, and La Farge followed at eleven on horseback. This was my first experiment at walking hereabouts. The climate is not stimulating to legs. Since we arrived, the season has changed; the blessed trade-wind has died out, and the apparent heat is much greater. I walked very slowly, under an umbrella, but was soon in a state of saturation, and, as the path is not interesting, I found pedestrianism a bore, but arrived just at noon, letting La Farge precede me a few minutes. We found Stevenson and his wife just as they had appeared at our first

call, except that Mrs Stevenson did not now think herself obliged to put
on slippers, and her night-gown costume had apparently not been washed
since our visit. Stevenson himself wore still a brown knit woollen sock on
one foot, and a greyish purple sock on the other, much wanting in heels,
so that I speculated half my time whether it was the same old socks, or the
corresponding alternates, and concluded that he must have worn them ever
since we first saw him. They were evidently his slippers for home wear. He
wore also, doubtless out of deference to us, a pair of trousers, and a thin
flannel shirt; but, by way of protest, he rolled up the sleeves above his
shoulders, displaying a pair of the thinnest white arms I ever beheld, which
he brandished in the air habitually as though he wanted to throw them
away. To La Farge and me, this attitude expressed incredible strength, and
heroic defiance of destiny, for his house swarmed with mosquitoes which
drove us wild, though only our heads and hands were exposed. Of course
it was none of our business, and both Stevenson and his wife were very
friendly, and gave us a good breakfast,—or got it themselves,—and kept
up a rapid talk for four hours, at the end of which I was very tired, but
Stevenson seemed only refreshed. Both La Farge and I came round to a
sort of liking for Mrs Stevenson, who is more human than her husband.
Stevenson is an *aïtu*,—uncanny. His fragility passes description, but his
endurance passes his fragility. I cannot conceive how such a bundle of
bones, unable to work on his writing without often taking to his bed as
his working-place, should have gone through the months of exposure,
confinement and bad nourishment which he has enjoyed. Their travels have
broken his wife up; she is a victim to rheumatism which is becoming
paralysis, and, I suspect, to dyspepsia; she says that their voyages have
caused it; but Stevenson gloats over discomforts and thinks that every
traveller should sail for months in small cutters rancid with cocoanut oil
and mouldy with constant rain, and should live on coral atolls with nothing
but cocoanuts and poisonous fish to eat. Their mode of existence here is
far less human than that of the natives, and compared with their shanty a
native house is a palace; but this squalor must be somehow due to his
education. All through him, the education shows. His early associates were
all second-rate; he never seems by any chance to have come in contact with
first-rate people, either men, women or artists. He does not know the
difference between people, and mixes them up in a fashion as grotesque as
if they were characters in his new Arabian Nights. Of course he must have
found me out at once, for my Bostonianism, and finikin clinging to what I
think the best, must rub him raw all over, all the more because I try not
to express it; but I suspect he does not know quite enough even to hate
me for it; and I am sure that he would never have the fineness to penetrate
La Farge, though, compared with La Farge, I am a sort of Stevenson for

coarseness. He is extremely civil, and gives me things of his own to read, which have not been published, and he would not trust to strangers;[4] he gives us letters to Tahiti, and shows a strong wish for our society; but I dare not see him often for fear of his hating me as a Philistine and a disgrace to humanity, because I care not a copper for what interests him. On the other hand he is perfectly safe with La Farge, and La Farge is still safer with him. After all the extreme intimacy of my long acquaintance with La Farge, I am always more and more astonished at the accuracy of his judgment. I knew how fine it was, and how keen, but the infernal triumph of the man is his correctness. I have never managed to catch him in an error. His judgment of men and women is as unfailing as his judgment of a picture, and he understands a Polynesian quite as well as he does a New Yorker. He sees all round a character like Stevenson's, and comments on it as if it were a painting, while Stevenson could never get within reach of him if they were alone on an atoll. The two characters in contact are rather amusing as contrasts; the oriental delicacy of La Farge seems to be doubled by the Scotch eccentricities and barbarisms of Stevenson who is as one-sided as a crab, and flies off at angles, no matter what rocks stand in his way.

December 18. The "Richmond" sailed for Tahiti yesterday and I was sorry not to sail in her. La Farge wishes to remain here, and I care so little whether I go or stay, that I assent to any decided wish of his; but we have now been here nearly three months, and I am beginning to find time drag. The wet and hot season has come, and the trade-wind has ceased blowing. Sir John Thurston writes to me not to visit Fiji till the dry weather returns.[5] On becoming acquainted with the South Seas, I find that the island-groups of interest are very few. I could not stand the flat, coral islands more than a day or two, and the high islands, with scenery and Polynesian natives, are limited to this group, the Marquesas and Tahiti. Our long stay here, among the least changed natives, has made us comparatively indifferent to the natives of Tahiti, who may be superior in every way, but are very few in number, and have abandoned native customs and costumes. I think a month at Tahiti would probably more than satisfy me, and if I give another month to a cruise among the Marquesas, nothing will remain in Polynesia to amuse me. Then I shall turn to New Zealand and Fiji, which are not likely to occupy me long, especially if La Farge leaves for home. Should he leave me, I should certainly become very restless. I shall then hurry to eat my *durian* in the Malay archipelago, and turn off to Ceylon and India. Naturally, China would be the next stage, but I do not look forward so far, though, if health and endurance last, I ought to pass next winter at Pekin. I do not venture to think of what I might do if I knew what is going on at home. At Tahiti I shall be quite as near home as here, and can change my movements to suit. Meanwhile we are to pass six weeks more in Samoa, where we are comfortable enough, and have plenty of acquaintances, but, as far as I am concerned, nothing to do. The Polynesians are a singularly superficial people, and, except to sketch, have nothing but their mysterious origin to occupy one's mind. I try to study their old customs and laws, but the *patria potestas* and the system of female descent are dry food. I find that the only result of trying to sketch is disgust at the results, and constant bucking against my own limitations, not merely in technique, though the inability to draw is bad enough, but still more in artistic sense both of color and mass. Even La Farge's work does not satisfy me any more than it does him, though he has all that I lack. My only consolation is that I should be far more at a loss for occupation at home.

Two more personages of interest to us have come to dinner. One is named Atwater; he was formerly our consul at Tahiti; a Yankee who married into the chief native family, and, through his wife, got large interests in cocoa-nut plantations and pearl islands.[6] He suffers from asthma and cannot live in Tahiti now, but is on his way there, to attend to some business. For taking the fun out of anything, a Yankee matches a Scotchman, and Mr Atwater has perhaps been long enough in the south seas to reach the universal lava-foundation of commonplace. Even the natives are not exempt, and I found, on our last tour round the island, that the happy and indolent islander is extremely bored by his ideal existence. I was slow to believe it, but the *taupo* were frank on the subject, and the young men were devoured by the wish for something new. I believe that ennui is the chief cause of their wars; but at a large village called Saangápu, in the district of Safata, I met an example of restlessness that beat even my own or Atwater's. In the dusk of evening, as I returned to our hut after a stroll along the beach, I was surprised to find a native talking English with La Farge. He turned out to be our host, Angápu, the chief of the village, and a nephew of our chief, Seumano-tafa, our companion and escort. Angápu is a dignified, middle-aged man, and speaks English with the same high-bred beauty of tone and accent that struck us so much in old John Adams at Apia. He has been a great traveller as a common Kanaka-seaman, and has been to San Francisco, New Orleans, New York, Liverpool, Glasgow, Hamburg, as well as to Australia, China, Japan, and all over the Pacific. I asked him whether he was satisfied to stay at home now, and he replied that he would like to go off again; but Seumano, who, as head of the family, can control his movements, would not consent. Angápu was bored by the smallness of Samoan interests and the restrictions of society, yet he is a considerable chief, belonging to a powerful family; his position is one of power and his duties and responsibilities must be constant enough to give him steady occupation. His village was one of the largest and richest we saw. With all this, he was unhappy because he could not go off as a common sailor before the mast, to knock about the ocean in cold climates which were his horror. In his presence I felt myself an ideal representative of stay-at-home, immoveable fixity and repose. Atwater is another example of restlessness. Evidently Tahiti bores him, and he finds San Francisco a relief. He calls himself a bad sailor, yet he wanders from San Francisco to Sydney, and back again, as though the ocean were a French play. He told us much about his pearl-fishing, which seems to have amused him most, but he says that in New York or Paris he can buy pearls cheaper than he can fish them, and in infinitely larger quantities and of better quality. He says that he can buy pearls at San Francisco and sell them at a profit in Tahiti, and that the pearl industry is but an adjunct to that of mother-of-pearl; a sort of accidental margin for the business.

Atwater was very friendly and promised to prepare the way for us at Tahiti, especially with his brother-in-law, Tati Salmon, the head of the greatest native family on the island, to whom Stevenson had already given us a letter. Tati Salmon is half London Jew; half hereditary high chief of the Tevas or Tefas; and looks down on the Pomares with lofty contempt, as parvenus.[7] We shall probably put ourselves at once under his protection, and fly from Papeete where Pomare and Frenchmen have sway.

Our other distinguished visitor is named Shirley Baker, and dined with us last evening.[8] In these parts of the world, three persons seem to be preeminent among the English. One is old Sir George Grey of New Zealand, about whom you can read much in Mr Froude's dull book called Oceanica.[9] I shall probably never meet Sir George Grey, for I have no letters to Auckland. The second is Sir John Thurston at Fiji, whose guest I expect to be. The third is Shirley Baker, who ruled despotically the Tonga group of islands, called Friendly on the maps, several hundred miles south of Samoa. Thurston at Fiji did not approve of Baker's doings at Tonga, and at last, just before we left home, took the strong step of sending a war-vessel to deport Baker, and practically to annex Tonga to his own government. I have taken care not to know anything about the subject, that I might have no prejudices about the men, but the affair has made a great noise in these hollow oceans. Baker was naturally angry, and I imagine that he wants revenge and reinstatement. He has lately come here from Auckland, perhaps with the idea of going to Washington and seeking aid from you and sister Anne. Last evening he dined with us, a London-aldermanic looking person, doubtful on his aspirates, but singularly quiet, restrained and intelligent. His talk was very interesting to us, for he is a converted missionary who has been thirty years at Tonga, and knows more than anyone else of Tongan history and affairs. You are happily ignorant that Tonga was the missionary stronghold where they played pranks such as uncontrolled priesthoods commonly indulge in. Tonga too is or was a stronghold of the Polynesian race, and a central point of its distribution. Probably New Zealand got its Maoris from Tonga, for the Tongans were great navigators, while the Samoans never ventured far to sea, or attempted foreign conquests. Baker had a great deal to say on these subjects, and said it well; but I suspect he is writing a book, for he seemed cautious about telling all he thought; and on the Polynesian battle-ground where everyone has an exclusive and extravagant theory to argue,—the source of the Polynesian race,—he would go no further than suggest that the race and the pig came together, and must be traced back to Asia together. This strikes me as inadequate treatment, but perhaps I do not sufficiently respect the pig; and I have an opposite hobby, that the race came necessarily with the trade-winds,—not against them,—which Baker rejects, riding too confidently on his pigs against the wind. I refer the dispute to you for arbitration, as Baker would certainly reject your only rival, Sir John Thurston.

December 24. (23). Another storm yesterday. The wind and rain were strident, and, with the surf, made us feel at sea again. In this open-air existence, where we never close doors, but take our meals on the verandah, and sit till bed-time, reading, talking and smoking as though it were La Fayette Square in July, we are amusingly badgered about by a storm, and have to hunt for a spot where the wind will let a lamp burn, and the rain will not splash directly on one's head. The interior of the Consulate is untenable, for the wind blows through the open eaves and extinguishes the lamps. Another annoyance is the result of wind. Swarms of very minute winged insects gather round our lamp, blown to leeward, and end by driving us to bed. Last night, in spite of difficulties, I hung on to my book— Stanley's big Africa—till half past nine o'clock, and then had to give it up.[10] Thousands of the little flies were lying on the table, burned, or on the lamp, caught in the kerosene oil that adheres to its inequalities of surface. This morning Awoki reports that the ants have carried away all the flies. Of course we mildew apace, but not so much as I should have expected, considering how little dry weather we get. My ideas of the south seas have changed not a little under the influence of closer acquaintance, but we are now, I suppose, in the rainy season, and can expect worse and worse until April. Our life is perfectly uniform. We sleep a great deal. I go to bed at ten o'clock and get up at about seven, which for me is immense; and La Farge sleeps still more. The first act of the day is to take a shower-bath, and dress. Then I take my breakfast, usually alone;—two mangoes, an orange, two boiled eggs, and coffee. Then I come to my native house, and write or try to paint. Natives come with mats or *tapa* or other things to sell; or visitors drop in, usually chiefs, to chat with us. The chiefs are always welcome to me, but I make them useful by cross-questioning them on every subject I can think of. Especially old To-fai, who is a very high chief, has to earn his entertainment. I have pumped him about history and institutions until he gets too deep even for his own dignity. My last effort was to drag out the whole of his family-organisation, and the nature of his authority as its head. You are properly indifferent to Roman law, and know little in theory of the *patria potestas,* but To-fai tells me that he has nearly two hundred persons under his authority as head of the family, and none of them can do any important act without his assent, under penalty of being beaten more or less severely, or expelled from the family with the consequent loss of protection and rights. The chief has another authority over his village or district, but this seems to be political or military, and interests me less. Every chief has an official name which carries with it the authority. For instance, To-fai is really a title, like an English peerage, but not strictly hereditary, for the persons who elect him may prefer a younger son or a nephew, to a less competent eldest son. Then the elder brothers as well as the uncles and older relations are equally subject to the authority of the younger man. Does this bore you too much? Even to me it is not passionately exciting, but it is more than I have got out of books. The chiefs interest me much more than the common-people do, for they are true aristocrats and have the virtues of their class, while the common people would sink to the level of the Hawaiians if the chiefs were to become extinct. Sometimes I am confounded by an exhibition of feeling which upsets my theories. Certainly the Polynesian is as superficial as you like, but every now and then, here as elsewhere, one is a good deal startled to find that there is no dependence on apparent superficiality. One of our village-chiefs is Pa-tu, an older half-brother of To-fai. Pa-tu, as I have somewhere told you, was the great warrior of the late wars. La Farge says he suggests your uncle Tecumph in look and manner, and it is true.[11] In the war, some two years ago, Pa-tu's daughter was killed in battle, fighting by her father's side, and Pa-tu felt her death deeply. La Farge was struck by the character of her face, as he saw it in a photograph at the photographer's; and with the idea of using the type, had an enlargement made. He thought that he would take two impressions, one for himself, one for Pa-tu, as a present; so the other day, when Pa-tu happened to come in, La Farge gave him the enlargement. Apparently Pa-tu had no idea what to expect, and was quite unprepared, so that I, who was sitting above him, in a chair, while he sat on the mat, watched curiously to see what effect the picture would have on him. He took it as though he supposed it to be what he was familiar with; then he looked at it some time without a word, but I could see his face growing more and more fixed as though he were trying to control himself; then he slowly bent his head down nearly to his knees, still holding the photograph as a sort of veil before him. Naturally La Farge and I were almost as much disturbed as he was, and felt very uncomfortable, but he quite finished us at last by sitting up again, his eyes streaming with tears, and saying, quite simply, a few words which were interpreted to us to mean: "Thank God, I have this day once more seen my daughter as she lived." There was no pretence at thanks or forms. The old man was thinking only of his daughter.

Fanua's wedding invitations are out, for the 31st. She marries an English trader named Gurr, and this time the marriage is English, not Samoan. I like Fanua, who resembles Aenga a little, in being shy and sensitive, though not handsome either in face or figure. As the adopted daughter of Seumano and Fatuleia, and the *taupo* of Apia, we must give her a wedding-present, and go to the feast. Meanwhile another German war-vessel has arrived. The "Sperber" has long been here, and Captain Foss who commands her, has been a very agreeable acquaintance. We must now pay a visit to the Admiral on the "Leipzig." Our own tub, the "Iroquois" is at Pango-pango, and is to come over for the arrival of our Swedish Chief-justice who is to arrive by the next mail-steamer. Then we shall have awful festivities, which I would gladly escape.

December 30. The obstinately wicked get their reward. Here is an outcast who fled from his own country to escape the interminable bore of its nickel-plated politics and politicians; yet when he seeks refuge in an inaccessible island of the South Seas, ten thousand miles from an Irishman, he finds politics running round like roosters without heads. Politics are commonly more or less *bouffe,* but here the whole thing is pure Offenbach. The bloody villain is Stuebel, the German Consul. If Stuebel says it rains, he means mischief. If he says it doesn't rain, he lies. If he says nothing, he is deep in conspiracy. War is to break out in Savaii at once; Manono is coming to seize Malietoa; Stuebel has written to Tamasese to be ready,[12] the "Sperber" is going to Tutuila; the "Leipzig" is going to fetch the new Chief Justice; Malietoa is to be deposed, and the Germans are to seize the island. Stuebel is at the bottom of it all. Every day these stories come to us. Old Samasoni waddles up, almost insane with native rumors, and predicts civil war within twentyfour hours. Mata-afa always has some absurd native story which he tells us with his grave, quiet smile, as though he were sorry to amuse us with his people's folly. You can imagine me in this poultry-yard. After several times expressing myself in my usual offensive and dogmatic manner on the character of this small beer, I have sunk into silence more or less sullen, and let the talk go on as it will. As far as I can see, it is all the play of these brown-skinned children, who are bored for want of excitement, and are quite capable of getting up a fight about nothing, but meanwhile we are standing along the shore, glasses in hand, watching for the smoke of the "Iroquois" which is supposed to be bringing our Swedish Chief Justice from Tutuila. The Chief Justice is to settle everything, it appears; but what is to happen if the unfortunate man should prove to be a tool of the wicked Stuebel? I give it up, and the mail goes out immediately, so I hand over the problem to your superior wisdom. Anyone who can understand Pennsylvania politics, can grapple with Samoa.

Luckily the weather is again fine, and of late I have been able to go out towards sunset in my native canoe and paddle far and wide along the shore and over the reef. Of course it is ideally pretty. The water is shallow, and one sees the fish and coral almost as clearly as the clouds and mountains. The sunsets are miraculous. They are too evanescent and soft to allow one even to think of catching their tones in paint, and although La Farge has attempted it, his success is not so brilliant as to encourage me to a trial. I can only let my canoe turn round and round, while I wonder which part of the scene is most indescribable. Out on the reef, one is alone and at peace with the fishes, even the sharks, and this evening hour, before dinner, is the pleasantest of the day.

Lieutenant Parker and his wife return home by this steamer and will be in Washington soon after this letter. If you are properly devoted to the White House, you will see little Mrs Parker, who has been very sweet and fragile, and has added greatly to the humanity of our consular household. I have never mentioned your name to her, so that you can ask what questions you like with tolerable certainty that she will not conceal our faults or follies.

9.30 P.M.   The mail is just in, with your letter of Nov. 17–Dec. 2d; and to my horror I learn that the return mail goes off tomorrow morning at seven. I have no time to look at anything, or to learn all that has happened, for your's is my only letter except a note of Dec. 2 from Miss Leiter telling me that Marquis is dead.[13] You are an angel to write double. Your Cleveland letter has not reached me. Did you not send it to Tahiti? I shall write to Miss Leiter by the next mail, four weeks hence. Do not forget to go out to Rock Creek Cemetery, and tell me whether my work is done, for no one seems to think me important enough to write business letters to. I send another despatch through the State Department, with an account of my Upolo circuit, but I dread your finding all this a bore, and at times I feel as though it would be much wiser for me not to try your patience so far. Forgive me, as Tennyson somewhere remarks, where I fail in tact, and in your wisdom, make me wise.[14] The truth is that I find pleasure in talking to you, and I go on doing it, even when I think you asleep. It is not the first time.

Your news is startling enough, but I am heartily glad that my brother is out of the Union Pacific, and in the rest there is nothing to disturb me.[15] Give my love to Martha; try to make her remember me. I was out in my canoe till seven o'clock watching the arrival of the new Chief Justice, who will, I suppose be largely the subject of my next letter. He was not brought from Tutuila by the "Iroquois," but was dumped off the port by the "Alameda," which has deranged all our plans, and obliges me to stop now, and bid you good-night.

Good-night.

Nonsense! I have just found your Cleveland letter in this mail. The big photograph caused it to be set aside as a parcel. A million thanks! You are my only friend, literally as well as in sentiment, for no one else has hit me. Luckily the delay of a month has done no harm, for nothing requires an answer. Your winter will be half over when you receive this, and by that time you will have your new set of adorers. Tell me about them. I want to know that they are better than the old lot. Your remarks on my travels, or rather, on my choosing to travel, are beautiful. I am glad to keep them by me, and to feel that you have such correct views of my love of freedom and Polynesia. Once more, good-night! You have given me no end of pleasure. Two letters when I dared not hope for a line.

MS: MHi

1. Robert Louis Stevenson (1850–1894) settled in Samoa in 1889. His wife was an American, Frances Van de Grift (1840–1917), who had been divorced from Samuel Osbourne in 1880.
2. Abraham Fornander (1812–1887), *Account of the Polynesian Race and the Ancient History of the Hawaiian People* (1878–1885); Sir George Grey (1812–1898), *Polynesian Mythology and Ancient Traditional History of the New Zealand Race* (1855); Rev. George Turner (1817?–1891), *Samoa, A Hundred Years Ago and Long Before* (1884).
3. "We have had enlightened society: Lafarge the painter, and your friend Henry Adams: a great privilege—would it might endure. I would go oftener to see them, but the place is awkward to reach on horseback. I had to swim my horse the last time I went to dinner; and as I have not yet returned the clothes I had to borrow, I dare not return in the same plight . . . They, I believe, would come oftener to see me but for the horrid doubt that weighs upon our commissariat department; we have *often* almost nothing to eat; a guest would simply break the bank; my wife and I have dined on one avocado pear" (Stevenson to Henry James, Dec. 29, 1890; *The Letters of Robert Louis Stevenson*, ed. Sidney Colvin [1911], III, 269).
4. Probably portions of his book *A Footnote to History: Eight Years of Trouble in Samoa* (1892).
5. Sir John Bates Thurston (1836–1897), British governor of the Western Pacific 1887–1897.
6. Dorence Atwater (1845–1910) of Connecticut, U.S. consul at Tahiti 1871–1897, married Moetia Salmon (1848–1935).

7. Tati Salmon (1850–1918), younger brother of Moetia Salmon Atwater; King Pomare V (1837–1891).
8. Originally sent to Tonga by the Australian Wesleyan Mission, Shirley Waldemar Baker (1836–1903) became officially premier of Tonga in 1880. His only book was *An English and Tongan Vocabulary* (1897).
9. Sir George Grey was colonial governor of New Zealand 1845–1853, 1861–1867, member of the house of representatives at Auckland 1874–1894; James Anthony Froude, *Oceana, or England and her Colonies* (1886).
10. Henry Morton Stanley (1840–1904), *In Darkest Africa* (1890).
11. William Tecumseh Sherman (1820–1891).
12. Oskar Steubel (1846–1921), German consul at Samoa. Tamasese had been the puppet ruler supported by the Germans in the recent civil war.
13. Mary Victoria Leiter (1870–1906), American heiress, later Lady Curzon; Marquis, HA's dog.
14. Tennyson's prayer in the prologue to *In Memoriam* refers to failures in "truth," not "tact."
15. As Union Pacific president CFA2 was unable to obtain a loan sufficiently large to maintain solvency, and he was obliged to surrender management of the company on Nov. 26, 1890, to Jay Gould.

To Elizabeth Cameron

Papeete, Feb. 23, 1891.

At last we are about to leave Papeete where we shall have staid near three weeks instead of one, as I had expected. The only result of staying the extra time is to make us more glad to go. Papeete is one of those ideal spots which have no fault except that of being insupportable. Stevenson warned us of its character, yet I am not sure but that, at some future day, when the halo of its distance again surrounds it, we may look back on our stay here with wonder that it bored us. The sun and moon leave nothing to desire. The mountains and the sea are fit for all the Gods of a Deological Cyclopaedia. The town is different from anything I ever saw in the long catalogue of towns I have met, and has an expression of lost beatitude quite symbolic of Paradise, apart from its inhabitants. As for the inhabitants, I cannot imagine why I should be worried by them, but I am; and yet they are more amusing than we had a right to expect. My chief trouble is the pervasive half-castitude that permeates everything; a sickly whitey-brown, or dirty-white complexion that suggests weakness, disease, and a combination of the least respectable qualities, both white and red. To be cooped up among two or three thousand such people, in a dirty shanty, with similar so-called cottages within ten feet on either side, makes one forget how exquisitely the morning sun filters through our vines and lights up our breakfast-table, and how blue the sea is, before our gate, to say nothing of the tones of the mountains of Moorea in the distance. Yet even when I forget the half-breeds and the cottages, and go swimming, so to speak, in the blue and purple light, I never lose consciousness of a sort of restless melancholy that will not explain why it should want to haunt a spot that by rights ought to be as gay as a comic opera. If Samoa were not a proof to the contrary, I should think that the fault was mine, but Samoa was never melancholy, though it was sometimes tiresome. Taïti, or at least Papeete is distinctly sad. Towards evening, when the thermometer begins to climb down from 88°, and the heat becomes less oppressive, La Farge and I commonly drive or walk out of town. Sometimes he catches an outline or a figure for a sketch, while I stroll along the shore or round the hills, poking the ground with my umbrella in the vain chance of finding a stone implement, or any sort of object, geological or unexpected, to diversify the charms of undiluted nature. My favorite stroll is back to the saluting battery, which stands on a shoulder of the central mountains, several hundred feet above the town. After Taïtian fashion, the battery is there, with the paraphernalia of a fort, but without other sign of life. I can lie down on the decaying parapet, and watch the sunset without society; and what strikes me more and more, with every visit, is the invariable tone of pathos in the scenery. Upon my word, even the French tricolor looks softly purplish and shockingly out of place. Lovely as it is, it gets on my nerves at last—this eternal charm of middle-aged melancholy. If I could only paint it, or express it in poetry or prose, or do anything with it, or even shake it out of its exasperating repose, the feeling would be a pleasant one, and I should fall in love with the very wrinkles of my venerable and spiritual Taitian grandmother; but when one has nothing else to look at, one rebels at being forever smiled upon by a grandmother whose complexion is absolutely divine, and whose attitude indicates the highest breeding, while she suggests no end of charm of conversation, yet refuses to do anything but smile in a sort of sad way that may mean much or mean nothing. Either she or I come near to being a fool.

One other result our stay at Papeete has had, for it has brought us into rather friendly relations with the Salmonidae, of whom I told you in my last letter. We have dined with the Darsies, who, by the bye, are to sail for San Francisco by the "City of Papeete" which departs on March 15, carrying also our Consul Doty, and this despatch. Taati Salmon, the head, or representative chief of the Tevas, has come here, and proves to be a very pleasant acquaintance. La Farge says he suggests Richardson, our old friend the architect; and he has the effect of bigness and good-nature that was poor Rich's charm. The whole family have the same effect. Not only Tati, but Mrs Darsie, Mrs Atwater, and Marao the ex-Queen, look as large and genial as whales. Tomorrow we start off at seven o'clock in the morning, and drive to Papara, about three hours, to stay with Tati, and pay our respects to his mother, the Chiefess of the Tevas, who, though only sixty-something years old, is regarded as the only person left on the island who belongs to the old times and retains the old royal tradition. We shall stay awhile at Papara and then go on to Tautira, as I warned you in my last letter. Our household goes to Tautira in advance, and carries our cooking-stove, our china and glass, and all our outfit for a month or so. We are to live on oysters, shrimps and bananas, to be served with French sauces and such other additions as M. Peraudot will kindly devise. M. Peraudot has already caused me one sharp attack of dyspepsia, and with such resources he can hardly fail of great success in causing more. At Tautira we shall be formally out of the world. Not even in our journeys round Samoa have we ever been so very far from your blessedness as there; but even Tautira is an industrial and social centre compared with the Marquesas, our coming destiny. Nukaheva is so remote that we seriously doubt our getting there. Nothing short of a fortnight on a schooner, beating against the trade-winds, will carry us to the Typee valley. We doubt whether we can do it, for these voyages seriously impair our health, and we do not want to be nervous dyspeptics for the short rest of life. Even you would give me up if dyspepsia supervened.

Pápara, 26 February.   We escaped from Papeete two days ago. At eight o'clock in the morning La Farge and I, leaving Awoki and Peraudot to take charge of our household movement, mounted into a wagon, and were driven off for fresh wanderings. Unlike Samoa, Taïti has a road. The French built it, and it is not bad, at least on this side of the island. If you can stand another dose of geology, you will understand better why the road is good; why the drive was pretty, and why Mr Darwin and Mr Dana are the eyes and lungs and liver of science and geology, for they have made an immortal name by discovering that all this part of the Pacific has sunk, is sinking, and is morally bound to sink, in order to explain how the coral polyp can, at the rate of an inch a year, more or less, keep the eighty coral atolls of the neighboring Paumotu archipelago just flush with the surface of the ocean. This is clear as the sun, isn't it? You see the whole mystery as plain as you see me, sitting here on Tati Salmon's broad porch, at seven o'clock, in the morning, with the velvet-green mountains, streaked by long white threads of waterfalls, looking down on me as though they wanted to know when they are to sink and disappear under water, to leave only a coral atoll above them, as I can certify that they are morally obliged to do, in order to be scientific. Bear me out now, and never let on that I question the truth of the universe. If Darwin and Dana choose to sing this song of McGinty, and insist that Taïti must have sunk to the bottom of the sea,[1] I, who swear by them, have no scruple in adopting and believing their faith;—

only the road from Papeete here runs the whole distance along the foot of an old line of sea-cliffs, carved and modelled in charming variety by water-action, and evidently extremely ancient. At the foot of these old sea-cliffs is a strip of flat ground, evidently the old coral reef, sometimes a few yards wide, sometimes half a mile or more, and elevated barely ten feet above the sea-level. Out at sea, sometimes near, but never very far away, is the more modern barrier reef with its surf as usual. So, here as in Samoa, instead of subsiding, the wretched island has certainly—at least on this side—risen ten feet in its last geological movement, after having remained stationary for many ages; and neither above nor below, in the water or out of it, can I see the faintest trace of a sign that anything ever was different; which is the reason why the road is level and good; the scenery charming, and Darwin always right.

At eleven o'clock we arrived at Papara, and were set down at Tati's door. Door is not the right word, for one is not very conscious of doors here-abouts; but Tati's house is an old French affair, and though not very different from a Mexican adobe house, is planned with some regard to exits and entrances. From the first moment, I felt contented—and I assure you, the sensation was both pleasant and unaccustomed, for some months have passed since I have felt disposed to say to the passing moment,— Stay![2] The house stands flat on the sea-shore, and as I shook hands with Tati, and his old mother, and his sister, I caught glimpses of an intense blue sea, through the open doors and windows behind; a sea that came close up to the grass, and had three lines of surf rolling in, through an opening in the reef, and rolling close up till they sent small waves into the entrance of the little river that flows close by the house. We sat down to breakfast on the inner verandah, that looks up to the hills, and we had at last the delight of feeling the cool mountain air again, coming down just to oblige us. Tati is charming as a host, and his resemblance to Richardson is more and more striking. He is intelligent, well-informed, full of interest especially in all matters that concern his tribe and island, and a grand seigneur such as can seldom be seen in these days; for the eight Teva districts of the island have no will but his, and his influence is greater than that of the French government, the Pomares and the church together. Tati is a young man still, thirty-eight years old, and his wife is not here. I never like to ask about wives, in the South Seas, so I have not yet disturbed this part of the family. The present lady of the house, ad interim, is Tati's sister, a young lady lately returned from Hamburg, with health affected by a German climate, and with no small amount both of intelligence and beauty of the Miriam type, which, you remember, I like more than you do.[3] In her, Miriam is stronger than the old mother, who is pure native, and delightful; almost as untouched by Europe as my Samoan matrons were.

Old Mrs Salmon will not sit at table with us; she sits on the floor, like a lady, and takes her food when she wants it. When she is inclined to talk, she tells us about pagan Taïti; old songs, superstitions and customs. We know almost all of it, for we have been over the ground in Samoa, and we recognise here the wreck of what was alive there; but here the women wear clothes and no longer dance or swim on the reef. Long ago, each district had its professional beauties who were carried about on *malangas* and matched with the professional beauties of other districts. The great swells made songs for themselves, to be sung when they went out to show their figures by riding their planks on the surf. No more beauties exist. Neither Tati nor any other chief can show me a handsome woman of pure blood. Instead of fifty or sixty thousand natives, five or six thousand are scattered in straggling houses round the island, without social life except in the church. Tati summoned his people to give us a *himene*, all that is left of the old song and dance. The very name—hymn—shows why this fragment has survived. The singing was almost identical with the Samoan, but more finished and elaborate. Some of the songs were old, and some were Teva warsongs; but the life was gone.

Early yesterday morning, our consul Doty, the British Consul Hawes, and two of the Brander boys, dropped on us, having walked by night most of the way from Papeete, twentyfour miles. All went away in the evening, and Tati also, except Winfred Brander who stayed to go with us tomorrow to Tautira, and introduce us to our new hosts, Ori and Arie. These last three days have been charming. Taïti begins to be worth while.

Tautira, March 1.   The old chiefess kept us till twelve o'clock of Thursday night telling the legend of a young chief of marvelous power, whose process of selecting a wife involved such difficulties of translation as kept Miss Pree and Master Winny much wider awake than I was. We all lay on mats on the verandah, in the moonlight, while the surf roared softly near by. Only La Farge and I had remained. Tati had gone to Papeete; a place he hates, and calls a nasty hole. Winny Brander stayed to take us to Tautira. We were quite happy so. The old chiefess was fascinating; and her daughter whose nickname is Pree, short for Beretania,—Britain,—has great charm, both of face and manner. I think you would enjoy the manner if not the face, but you will never see her. She is about twentyfour, I believe. At Hamburg, while studying music, she broke down; her lungs were affected, and the doctors ordered her home. She came,—by way of Cape Horn, Valparaiso and Easter Island,—but she saved only her life, not her lungs. She coughs incessantly, and is bored besides. One may survive either of these afflictions, but not both. I tried to photograph the old lady, but I had not the heart to risk spoiling Pree's Syrian beauty by distorting it in my camera.

Friday morning we bade goodbye to Papara. For once I was heartily sorry to leave a place, and would gladly have lingered; but no solid excuse seemed to offer itself, and as both our hostesses were soon to go to Papeete to bid Mrs Darsie goodbye, we felt a little in the way. So off we went, taking Winny Brander with us, and sending our luggage on, in another wagon. The drive this day was enchanting. Certainly Taiti is lovely beyond common words. I seemed almost to feel again the freshness of my first travels, when the sun had not grown so stupid and prosaic as it is now. Of course Taiti is not so grand in scale, or so varied in landscape as Hawaii, but it is exquisitely graceful in outline, and radiant in light and color. I have seen more brilliant blues and greens in Samoa, but never so enchanting a variety of light and shade, or of vegetation. We drove always on the level strip at the foot of old sea-bluffs, but, as we advanced, the vegetation became richer; the orange trees and bread-fruit gave a deeper green to the roadside; the ferns grew thick on the dripping banks, and the sea actually glowed blue through a lace-work of the long pandanus and cocoanut leaves. I wondered what sort of landscape you were looking at, in your February, and whether you would really enjoy being with us for this one day which has to stand as the traveller's only compensation for months of ennui and discomfort. We stopped for two hours at a very dirty Chinaman's eating-place to lunch. This was on the isthmus of Taravao, as you can see on the map I enclosed in my last letter. There the road crosses from the west to the east side of the island; and from there we entered the peninsula of Taiárapu. Plunging through mountain streams which were luckily low, we rattled along till about five o'clock when we performed what resembled a double-somerset into the river at Tautira. The view here is what you can see in the photograph I mean to enclose; but we struggled through the stream and beyond the valley, half a mile further, till we came to our house in the village of Tautira, looking out over the reef, for all the world exactly like our quarters at Apia. Awoki and Peraudot had everything ready for us. Our host, Ori, Stevenson's friend and brother, beamed on us. We called at once on Arié, the chief, a conventional official, with a round face, who speaks French, and has been to Paris. You can judge of our remoteness by two details. Here we are at the end of the inhabited island; the road stops, and there are no villages beyond. Here, too, we can find no interpreter. Except Arié and the French priest; a Scotchman, deaf as a block, and bearing, if you please, the name of Donald Cameron, boat-maker; and a waif long ago wafted from England, named Parker, who lives on the road to Taravao, no one here speaks or understands a foreign language. Winny Brander stayed a day to start us, but could find no interpreter for us. I sent at once for Donald Cameron, who was an old man at whom I howled wildly orders to make tables and stands. With Ori we try to hold converse by dictionary. Stevenson stayed here two months in the same situation, but we do not willingly put up with deprivations that Stevenson thrives on. In other ways we are better off. The house is comparatively large and has a good big room in the centre, for living in. We can get neither milk nor meat, but Peraudot manages to feed us in one way or another. My only grievance is that they wont let me swim in the sea, for fear of some poisonous fish or coral, I know not what; while the river is full half a mile away. Then, too, as in Apia, one's walking ground is confined by streams that cross the road at short intervals and have no bridges. Still I think I can manage to hold on for some weeks, or even a month, if La Farge wants to paint; and as the natives all wear clothes of some kind, the temptation to paint is less than in Samoa. I will try to paint too, for I find that the occupation absorbs me, miserable as the result must always be. Indeed, if I painted as well or as ill as the best painter alive, I should feel no better satisfied with the result than with my school-boy daubs. Perhaps I should feel less so, for the sense of disappointment would be added to that of incapacity.

Anyway here we are! Taiti offers no more, unless I take to the mountains; and even these would not take time enough to occupy one very long. Perhaps canoeing will prove a resource, though the reef here is not so good for canoeing as at Samoa. You have nearly finished your winter. Congress will rise in three days. I shall have the occupation of wondering where you are, and what you are doing. I suppose no woman can have the heart to object to being made love to, if the offender remains ten thousand miles away. Even Miss Grundy can say very little that is ill-natured on such a theme.[4] I take for granted that the most exacting husband would take it as a good marital joke; and so I will let myself have full swing in that amusement if in no other.

Tautira, March 4.   Your letter of Jan. 10–24 arrived here yesterday afternoon, with others. Long as it is, I think I know it by heart already, or at least can repeat everything in it. The general formula that you are an angel has become so monotonous that I hate to bore you with it. Love is more trite, if possible, than angels. I know no new combination of love and angel to offer you, and am reduced to sheer bêtise, which, at a seven thousand mile dilution, is exasperatingly stupid; but you can at least to some degree imagine what sort of emotion I might be likely to feel at having you take me by the hand and carry me on with your daily life till I feel as though I had been with you all the month. This sort of flattery is even more seductive than what you say of myself, for although I suck in, with the delight of a famished castaway, the flattery which you and Hay are alone in feeding me with, I know myself and my work too well to be changed in my estimate of either; but the other sort of flattery raises my love both for myself and for you. To be sure I want to talk over everything with you, and object strenuously to having to listen without comment or reply. When you say that you wish I would come back, I want to break in with observations on that subject which would soon tire you out. Yet what is the use? How can I come back? Matthew Arnold asked what it boots now that Byron bore, with scorn that half concealed his smart, from Europe to the Aetolian shore, the pageant of a bleeding heart.[5] I am not Byron, and bear no pageant, nor, for that matter, a bleeding heart,—any more than he did,—but I wish you would tell me how I can come home and be contented there.

You will say that I am not contented here. True! but I am not in mischief; I am doing no harm to anyone; I am able to bore myself in many innocent ways; and in some slight degree I am even able to be of use to others. Do you really think I should improve matters by going home? Certainly I often wish I were there, and with quite as much energy as is good for me. I have repeatedly offered La Farge to take the next steamer to Auckland, and go straight to Paris to pass the summer. I am ready to go anywhere or do anything, except go to sea in a copra schooner, or pass a month in Berlin. If you think I ought to come home,—I am willing to accept you as judge,— I will agree to come. Can I say more than that?

This is by way of being disputatious, and because Tautira offers little or nothing to write about. We are comfortable enough, but the thermometer is at 88° every day, and although the wind tempers the heat, we do not feel much like making physical exertion. Stevenson to the contrary notwith-standing, the people are not specially interesting. I have, since arriving here, passed my time in writing letters so as to have them ready in case, as is possible, we should suddenly be offered passage to the Marquesas in a French war-vessel which is soon to take the Governor on his tour of inspection. We cannot afford to throw away such an opportunity, and we might have only a day or two of notice. So I have not resumed my efforts at painting, though your pleasure in my poor little attempt is a strong motive for doing so. I wish I could give you even a faint idea of the beauty of the coloring in these skies and seas. Every evening La Farge and I stroll to about the point from which the enclosed photograph is taken, and there we wait for the after-glow, which lasts about half an hour, and gives a succession of lights that defy imitation or description. La Farge is trying to suggest them in water-color, and some day you may see what he makes of it; but glass is the only possible medium for such tones, and even glass could not render all. Should you go to New York, you might stop at his studio, and ask to see the sketches he has sent home. They would certainly amuse you, after reading my letters about the same things. Only I fear you would be ashamed of me for venturing to touch a brush when he was near. He has a wonderful faculty for getting light into his color. I study in vain to find out how he does it, though I see all his processes. I mix my colors by dozens, and lay one deep wash over another; but the result is always feeble and timid. He splashes in deep purples on deep greens till the paper is soaked with a shapeless daub, yet the next day, with a few touches it comes out a brilliant mass of color and light. Of course it is not an exact rendering of the actual things he paints, though often it is near enough to surprise me by its faithfulness; but whether exact or not, it always suggests the emotion of the moment.

Our days are quiet beyond anything you ever knew. As the chief Ariié told us at our arrival, nothing ever happens here. The people have but one social amusement. Nearly every evening they sing in a sort of concert which they call a *himene,* and which is in fact a curious survival of the old dance-music such as we knew so well at Samoa, but appropriated as hymn-music for church-purposes. It is pretty and well-done; better than the Samoan, and more developed; but it is monotonous and to me it wants the accompaniment of the dance-movements for which it was made. The dance degenerated here so low that it had to be abolished. La Farge hopes to find means of seeing it, but I cannot believe that the women I see here could possibly dance well, or that the men are well enough trained to make an effective show. The people have lost the habit, as they have lost that of kava-drinking, human sacrifices, and other harmless and simple pagan practices. People who wear clothes can't dance. So they sit on the ground and sing.

You think that the "Earl and Doctor" give a low impression of morality in these parts. The immorality is mostly a foreign importation. Polynesians belonged to a stage of society earlier than modern morals, and when sex was a simpler affair than now. Apparently La Farge and I are hopelessly respectable, for in these immoral communities we have been so absolutely neglected that we might as well have been in our nurseries. No Fayaway has come near us.[6] No Princess has made love to us. Except old Mrs Salmon, the chiefess, no woman has shown a disposition to encourage our attentions. Naturally I am much disgusted, for I expected to be quite besieged by splendid young female savages. They are a fraud.

March 8. The Governor has sent word that perhaps he will take us to the Marquesas in the ship-of-war "Champlain," probably next month. In that case I may miss writing by the next mail. Please address yours to care of our Consul at Samoa, as of old. More and more, Samoa tends to become the distributing centre for the South Pacific. Our island mail goes on the 12th, so I must close up, and send this letter to Papeete, with a bundle of others. By the way, is sister Anne offended? She has never acknowledged my letter, written ages ago. Don't put her up to answering it, for I don't care to split my letters, and give you only half; but if Cabot has forbidden her to communicate with me, I shall feel very pleased and proud.

You will find another water-color enclosed; surely not to show you that I "can do anything I choose"; for the drawing shows plainly, to anyone who ever tried to draw, that I "chose" to do something very much better than I succeeded in doing. It is childish enough, but perhaps for once its childishness is almost what is least *manqué*. It is meant to show the morning light, and is taken from our breakfast-table at Papeete. I should not send it as a drawing; I am not bête to that point; but I tried to make it a literal reproduction of light and color, and it is really so near that my eye calls it correct;—though my eye is not La Farge's. It is meant to show you our Taïti weather; since our arrival, it has been the same, varying only in intensity. Yesterday the thermometer touched 90°. We are so remote from Europeans here, and the mosquitoes are so merciful, that I have reduced my costume to the native scale,—shirt and table-handkerchief. At Apia I wore this undress only in my canoe. Here I can wear it all day, and its only objection is that Stevenson did the same. Apparently we are destined to play seconds to Stevenson. For myself I don't care, and am willing to play second to anyone who goes first,—Stevenson or Goward or even James G. Blaine or Benjamin Harrison,—but it is hard on the immortal Scotchman.[7] If you have read his ballad of Rahero just out, you will see it is dedicated to Ori, and the dedication is rather the prettiest part of it. Ori exchanged names "in the island mode" with Stevenson, giving him the name Teriitera, and Stevenson takes it *au serieux,* as the ballads show. Much was said on the subject, and Stevenson's native name here is always Teriitera. I dreaded a repetition of this baptism, and tried to show total indifference to the native custom; but last evening when we were taking our absynthe before dinner, Ori informed me that I was to take his name, Ori, and then and there, I became—and had to become,—Ori, and he Atamu. La Farge also had to go through the same process. Although Ori is, I think, only a nickname, and probably not an island title like Teriitera, it happens to be the name used by Stevenson in dedicating his poem. I presume that Stevenson—or Tereetera—and I, are brothers of the Teva clan, and that his poem bears my name. The situation is just a half-tone too yellow-green. I fear that Stevenson will fail to enjoy the jest, and I am myself not altogether clear about it, for without the express approval of Tati and his mother, I do not care for such adoption. Ori seems intimate with Marau,—Marao,—the divorced Queen, and I wonder a little whether she put him up to it. I have seen Marau less than any of her sisters,—Mrs Darsie, Mrs Atwater and Pree,—though she is really the most interesting; for it was Marao who made, in her divorce suit, an answer that I consider sublime. The King in giving evidence, said that the last child was not his. "None were his!," broke out Marao. For an exchange of insults, I know nothing finer. As for the justice of either charge, that is an insular detail hardly worth attention; but public opinion rather tends to the idea that the oldest daughter of Marao may have been a Pomare, as the King thought; which makes Marao's insult the more murderous. I liked Marau, or what I saw and heard of her; for she seemed a little more Polynesian and possible-savage, than the rest; she had a certain external indifference that might be assumed or occasional. She is, too, with Mrs Atwater, engaged in a fearful family feud with their sister, Mrs Darsie. The depths of this, where I have caught glimpses into it, seem to me grandly black, like old Taïtian mysteries. There is my Polynesian romance all made; and it is not Pierre Loti, *par exemple!*[8] One could make pure Balzac of it, with red-hot Chili pepper added; but the story is too well-known, and the family too respectable to maltreat in such a way; and Pomare is almost too vile for art. Marau writes often to Ori, and perhaps Ori may have consulted her about naming us. If possible, I hope to escape talk about it, for Stevenson's sake. Meanwhile I am quite contented here at Tautira. The retreat is a hermitage, pure and simple; we see no one, and the days are too hot to do anything but write or paint. I try to do both, and find occupation in it. The weather is divine beyond imagination; the scenery, a sort of Paradise for lost souls, the beauty of archangels fallen. Every evening at five I paddle out over the reef and care not if my rippling skiff move swift or slow from cliff to cliff; with dreamful eyes I watch the—flies, according to rhyme,[9] but really the fish, and the strange, positively wierd forms of coral, with patches of color, and sudden sinking, from coral rocks that scrape my canoe, down to dark green depths to a bottom which the sun barely reaches, two or three hundred feet below. I ought to write a canoe-song to native music, but all the native music has the lilt of a quick march—like Kamehameha's march at Hawaii,—and is not fitted for the purple peace of the coral polyp. Even for you, I cannot make the verse or the motive suit the music. The coral will not dance. So I can only watch the sea beneath, and the less rich sky above; and on calm evenings paddle out, from behind the protection of the reef, upon the great bay, where the ocean swell swings me up and down its long sweep of bottomless and endless waves. When the afterglow dies out, at half past six, I come ashore, for my absynthe and my baptism. As for La Farge, he paints,—but oh! how he does paint!

"Farewell! thou art too dear, &c."[10] H.

MS: MHi

1. In the popular song "Down Went McGinty," the hero's imprudence ends with him at "the bottom of the sea."
2. Goethe, *Faust;* see HA to Lucy Baxter, March 25, 1890, note 4.
3. Loïs ("Pree") Salmon (1863–1894), Jewish in appearance, like Miriam in Hawthorne's *The Marble Faun* (1860).
4. Facetious reference to Mrs. Grundy, symbol of conventional propriety, from the character in Thomas Morton's play *Speed the Plough* (1798).
5. "What helps it now, that Byron bore, / With haughty scorn which mock'd the smart, / Through Europe to the Aetolian shore / The pageant of his bleeding heart?"; "Stanzas from the Grande Chartreuse" (1855).
6. Fayaway, a lovely girl in Herman Melville's *Typee* (1846).
7. Gustavus Goward (d. 1908), commissioner sent to Samoa to put into effect the Treaty of 1878 giving the U.S. the right to establish a naval station at Pago Pago; Benjamin Harrison (1833–1901), U.S. president 1889–1893.
8. Pierre Loti, *Le Mariage de Loti* (1860).
9. "I heed not, if / My rippling skiff / Float swift or slow from cliff to cliff;— / With dreamful eyes / My spirit lies / Under the walls of Paradise"; T. B. Read, "Drifting."
10. "Farewell! thou art too dear for my possessing"; Shakespeare, Sonnet 87.

To Martha Cameron

Government House, Fiji. [16? June 1891]

My dear Martha[1]

Your beautiful letter came to me at last, after traveling ever so many weeks over the ocean. I have lots of things to tell you. Do you remember that I asked you to come with me to see the people that eat little girls, and you said that you would not go to be eaten. I have just reached that country, and am living among the people. Ask your mamma to show you some day where it is. Tell her to show you a globe of the world. Then, if you are in England, on top, look directly down under your feet, and if you can only see through the ground far enough, you will see this island where I am. It is exactly under you, but we have to walk on our heads here, when you are on top. You wouldn't mind walking on your head, but it is sometimes rather hard for old people to get used to it, and it often makes me sick, especially at sea. Now that I have got here they tell me that the people dont eat little girls any more. Isn't it too bad. I have come all this long way to have girls to eat, because I like tender little girls, and now I cant have any, and must come home again without knowing how nice they are. You might have come with me after all, if you had known that. You would have seen the fishes flying like birds all over the sea, and you would have had lots of new fruits to eat, and you would have seen the bread growing on trees, and the loveliest blue and green and yellow and red fishes playing at the bottom of the water; and the water is so warm that you could play all day in it, and sail beautiful little boats that the little boys make, and go faster than any boats you ever saw. The children here go out on the water in big wooden bowls which they paddle with their hands, and when they upset, they laugh at each other. One day, I upset my canoe and tipped Mr La Farge with me into the water, and the little girls laughed at us, and ran in, and set the canoe up again, and pulled us along in it till we got home. I think you would have great fun here. The people are almost black, and wear very little clothes, but their hair is thick, and they comb it out straight so that their heads look as big as drums, and as though they were too heavy to carry. The hair is red at the ends, and dark underneath, and makes the men look as though they would eat us, but they are very nice men and kind to little children, and never cross.

Some day I will tell you all about them when I come home again. Remember to love me, and be very good to me when I come back; and come to play with me. I love you, and am always your only devoted

Dobbitt.

MS: MHi
1. This letter is inscribed in block capitals for the 5-year-old Martha.

To Charles Milnes Gaskell

Steamer "Jumna." 17 August, 1891.

Dear Carlo

Your letter, dated I don't know when, for it is locked up in some trunk in the hold, reached me on my arrival at Sydney about three weeks ago. I have wandered now over a vast amount of oceans, and the worst part of oceans is that one might as well be in one as another, for all looks much alike, and has the uniformity of the seasickness which is for me its single invariable pleasure. Up and down the Pacific for many grey weeks, my friend La Farge and I have paraded our ennui, freshening, at intervals of rest, on the little green islands that dot that sea of misery, like very small stars in a very big sky. We passed most of your winter in Samoa; the spring in Tahiti, and part of the summer in Fiji, where we were guests of Sir John Thurston at the Government House, and tramped with him through the remotest recesses of his small empire, guests of ancient cannibals now ornaments of human nature. I will say no more of my travels, because I am now on my way to England where I expect to arrive within a month after this letter reaches you. Where I now am, I do not know; but, somewhere within the vagueness of the Malay Archipelago, I am lounging along towards Batavia where we are due a week hence. These seas are all vast. Two thousand miles is the regular measure of distance between points of departure and arrival—except when it's four thousand. We left Tahiti, June 5, and went two thousand miles to Fiji. We left Fiji, July 23, and sailed two thousand miles to Sydney. We left Sydney, August 6, and came two thousand miles along the eastern coast of Australia to Thursday Island in Torres Straits. We left Torres Straits and Thursday Island thirtysix hours ago, and have two thousand miles to do to Batavia. Then Singapore; then Ceylon; and then I dare not ask how many thousand miles to Brindisi or Naples or Marseilles.

With all this, we are well, in good spirits, pleased with our adventures, and not in the least anxious to return to the world. As La Farge cannot help himself, and as I need some patching, we shall turn our steps to Paris and London, but my future movements are vague, and will depend on my own waywardness. Enough of that! If you are in England in October, or say about Nov. 1, drop a line to me—Baring Brothers, Bishopsgate Street, or Hottinguer &Cie, Paris, to let me know your whereabouts, and I will come to you. Please remember that I never go into society; that I never dine out, except in the most domestic familiarity; that I am nowadays horribly bored by "people"; that I never try to amuse, and am easily satisfied by being amused; and that as far as I know, all the society of Europe contains no one whom I particularly care to know. Let this discharge your mind of all responsibility about me, and all care for my entertainment. I will go anywhere you say in order to be with you and your wife, but unless you can recall those whom we used to love to meet— your father and mother, your aunt Charlotte, your uncle Sir Francis, Lord Houghton and the associations of five-and-twenty years ago, you can do mighty little to make England gay to me.

Talking of Houghton and his world, I have just read the "Life." I am rather disposed to be harder on it than you are. The man who writes it is a feeble twaddler, but that I could to a degree overlook.[1] He has not a qualification for his task; he has not a particle of wit, yet undertakes to write of men who were wits by profession; he has not a spark of humor, yet mangles one of the most genial humorists of the century; and his acquaintance with his victim was too late to help him except to mislead.

All this is bad enough, but I object still more to the slovenly way the work is done. Can no one any longer do literary work thoroughly? England seems to me to be the worst sinner now going in the literary way. I see nothing but *décadence*. No doubt I am wrong; somewhere something competent must exist, but the trashy way in which people for the most part seem pleased to work, grates on my literary nerves which were never very steady. If Houghton had read his own Life, he would have needed all his own good-nature to bear it without murdering his biographer. In fact, unless one or two biographers are assassinated, no considerable man can hope for peace in Heaven—or, for that matter, in Hell. Self-defence is a natural right, and what should be done with a wretch who kills your soul forever, and piles feather-bolsters on it till eternity becomes immortal struggling for breath and air. I hate to growl, but Lord Houghton was one of the best subjects for biography that our time has produced, and to throw it away like this is to throw away the lighter and gayer part of our age. Almost any one of the innumerable visitors at Fryston would have given a better idea of it than this book does. Indeed except Carlyle's visit, no idea at all is conveyed. You yourself could tell more than the two volumes contain. Even I, who was never but once at Fryston, and that in my youngest days, could give a better account of it from memory at thirty years distance, though my memory is as bad as the Life is. I do not complain because I miss the presence of the persons I knew best, and who, in my associations, were and are inseparable from Lord Houghton. Most of them are dead, and very likely left little trace of their talk or their intimacy. What annoys me is the want of art; the lack of a sharp outline, of moving figures and defined character; the washed-out feeling as though the author sponged every one's face; the slovenly way in which good material is handled; above all, the constant attitude of defence, almost apology, and the complaints of non-appreciation which are worse than stupid. If Houghton never understood himself, this is no excuse for his biographer's not understanding him. The greatest men generally pride themselves on qualities which the world denies them; but their biographers do not accent the weakness. Houghton as a statesman was a failure; as a poet, he was not in the first rank; as a social centre for the intelligent world he was an unrivaled and unapproachable success; but the biographer proves only the two introductory axioms.

The moral seems to be that every man should write his own life, to prevent some other fellow from taking it. The moral is almost worse than the vicious alternative, and, after all, the sacrifice would not ensure safety. I know no other escape except to be so obscure as not to need gibbeting at all; but who is safe even then? Poor Lawrence Oliphant was not a conspicuous man; only his insanities were such as to claim passing notice; yet his unlucky life must be ripped up in two volumes to amuse the subscribers to circulating libraries.[2] Had he told the story himself, it might have been good as literature, and instructive as a warning against high living and pure thinking; as it stands, I shrink from reading it. I thought W. E. Forster's Life shockingly poor, and dipped into Earl Russell's with the same result. On the other hand, your uncle Sir Francis, who took the biographic bull by the horns, gave us all something really himself.[3]

The world wants so much to be amused, or thinks it does, that, if every known figure in the Men and Women of the Time is to be made to dance and grimace and grin and blubber to entertain it, at least the utmost possible entertainment ought to be got out of the unlucky actor.[4] I hate botched work. Our American way of doing things is more conscientious, but not much more entertaining. Did you look into the Life of Motley? Did ever "brilliant" historian write such letters?[5] I remember his telling me once that an English dinner was the perfection of human society. He seems to have carried out his theory to the point of thinking that lists of English dinner-parties were the perfect letter-writer's companion. He failed only in omitting the *menus,* which often must have been more interesting than the company.

All this is selfish, because I am mortified at seeing what a mean figure my time will present hereafter. We have Horace Walpole, Doctor Johnson, Fanny Burney, all master-pieces for the last century. Nothing could be said against the way Walter Scott has been put before us. Byron was well-done.[6] Yet I know not one good picture of the society of the middle of our century. Perhaps George Trevelyan's Macaulay is the best.[7] No very representative characters except Gladstone and Tennyson remain to do. Gladstone is sure to be treated politically, and I fear Tennyson's life has been too secluded to be representative. Strange, too, how dull everyone became from the moment her present majesty mounted the throne. Even Greville from that instant seems to yawn like a Queensland crocodile.[8] One is almost grateful to the Prince of Wales and his baccarat. One hour of the Prince Regent is worth a cycle of Prince Albert. In history, nothing amuses but the vicious.

You owe this literary essay to the enforced leisure of the Malay Archipelago. I am weary of reading; I have done little for a year except watch the wine-dark sea; the people on board this ship are quite impossible; I have thought out all my thoughts long ago; so you fall a victim to my need for taking life of some sort. Wreak it on the grouse who are innocent like yourself! Surely Tennyson indulged his Lotos-eaters in a dark-blue sky, vaulted o'er a dark-blue sea! What authority had he for it? If Homer or the Greeks ever said it, I should like to see the passage. I have seen more blue sky vaulted over dark-blue sea than was ever seen by any lotos-eater, Greek or Egyptian; but the peculiarity is that no matter how dark-blue the sea is, the sky is in my experience always light-blue. The sea seems to water it, and wash out the color. This explains its effect on me. I am washed-out, like the sky. I've not an energy left; all has yielded to sea-sickness and Polynesia. I know not why I am so simple an idiot as to pass my life on water when I detest it beyond expression; but really the world contains so very little travelable land, that, after all, I have not given the ocean anything near its proportion of my time.

Should you see the amiable and perfectly virtuous baronet, you had better tell him that I am coming; but I do not know of anyone else whom I care to notify. I should merely be put to the odious necessity of refusing invitations, if anyone cared enough to invite me, or to the mortification of receiving no invitations to refuse. You know of old the precise frame of mind. With me, the refusal is no longer an affectation of indifference or industry. I have been so long a recluse, that a party of mixed acquaintances would be a trial that I am a little afraid to attempt. Total strangers I mind less, for I can turn my back and go home if I like. I can't talk. Nothing is more fatiguing. I never drink champagne except when I feel like it. Finally, although quite willing to admit with Motley that an English dinner-party is the perfection of human society, I have for so long a time been accustomed to prefer the imperfection of my own dinner-table that I have debased my taste and must be left to wallow in my trough.

At the same time, certain persons must be still living whom I should go to see. In a general way I assume that everyone is dead, for I never open a newspaper or a book without noticing the ascension of some former acquaintance, or at least some one more or less known to me. I imagine that not a house in London is now open,—to me—into which I ever entered in former days. Still, here and there, probably, old acquaintances or friends are stranded whom I should express interest in, to the extent of a call. Try and think them over. Annotate them. Make memoranda of their diseases, the dates of their first husband's deaths, and their children's convictions for sodomy or card-cheating. Get a list ready for me in case I should stay more than a week in England. Luckily I come when London is empty, and society is as dull as the weather, and probably I shall be gone long before any old friend can recover from the effects of her or his last fit of gout or lethargy, enough to hear or think of me.

Positively the tropics are not bad. I have not had half bad fun; but damnably and middle-agedly respectable and correct.

Ever Yrs   Henry Adams.

MS: MHi

1. Sir T. Wemyss Reid, *The Life, Letters, and Friendships of Richard Monckton Milnes* (1890).
2. Margaret Oliphant, *Memoir of the Life of Laurence Oliphant and of Alice Oliphant, His Wife* (1891).
3. Sir T. Wemyss Reid, *Life of the Right Hon. W. E. Forster* (1888). Sir Spencer Walpole, *The Life of Lord John Russell* (1889). Sir Francis Doyle, *Reminiscences and Opinions of Sir Francis Doyle, 1813–1885* (1886).

4. *Men and Women of the Time, A Dictionary of Contemporaries,* 13th edition (1891).
5. *The Correspondence of John Lothrop Motley,* ed. G. W. Curtis (1889).
6. Frances Burney, Madame D'Arblay (1752–1840), *Diary and Letters* (1842–1846) and *Early Diary* (1889). John Gibson Lockhart, *Memoirs of the Life of Sir Walter Scott* (1837–1838). Thomas Moore, *Letters and Journals of Lord Byron: With Notices of His Life* (1830).
7. Sir George Otto Trevelyan, *The Life and Letters of Lord Macaulay* (1876).
8. Charles C. Fulke Greville (1794–1865), acute political observer as clerk of the privy council 1821–1859, was the most important English diarist of his generation.

To Elizabeth Cameron

Tuesday, September 8, 1891.

I hope to bring you this letter just a month from today at Paris, but to provide against accident I will go on with the story so that, in case I am delayed, I can let you know all about it by just putting the sheets into an envelope.

We landed at Colombo at eight o'clock Sunday evening, in a temper and with feelings of the most depraved sort. Although we were the only passengers to Colombo, the Messageries officers, stewards and all, totally neglected us, gave us no notice when, where or how to land, and after causing us to lose two hours of light, deliberately let us go off at last as we could, at our own expense, in a native boat, handling our own luggage, without apology, although our situation was again and again, with the utmost civility, made known to them, with the request, not for aid, but only for information. I do not think we do this sort of thing in America, but it has happened twice to us since leaving Brisbane, and is, I think, the rule in the east. Steamers do not land passengers, but forget them. Had I been in my usual form, I should not have cared, but I had a cracking headache and a cold, and could not eat all day, and was exhausted by the moist heat, and generally felt more like a dead beetle than ever before since I bade you good-bye. When we got to a hotel, I crept to bed, and tried to find a spot on my pillow where my head would lie without cracking open, and so dozed till morning with the prospect of the long-expected fever at last. In the morning the headache departed, but I was left very weak, and terribly oppressed by the damp heat of Colombo,—a rice-field heat—which has made me think that if Bishop Heber had known more of the matter he would have made an improvement in his poetry, and would have altered it to: "What though the ricey breezes, blow damp oer Ceylon's isle!"[1] Spice, I know not, but Colombo is in a big rice-swamp, and I felt as though I were in a Turkish bath, and could not get out. All this was owing, I am sure, to something eaten on the "Melbourne,"—I suspect the Camambert cheese—and to being obliged to pass the nights on deck with little sleep and no comfort. Steamers in the tropics are made just like steamers in Greenland. I have not yet seen one—except the American line to Australia—constructed with any reference to the passengers' comfort, or any means of making them comfortable; and if I could hang a few constructors, I would certainly do it in memory of the suffering I have seen them cause to women and children; but the stupidity of the European man is quite radiant, and no one proclaims it louder than the officers who are condemned to command European ships. Between French cheese and French cabins, my life was not worth taking; but my life is a trifle; and I wanted to take some Frenchman's when I saw what happened to others. A delicate little English girl, about Martha's age, was on board; colorless and thin, like all these tropic birds, but talking broken Malay, and rather interesting. On our last night on board, the heat in the cabin was great; the child was taken very sick, and while her mother was examining her, at the table in the saloon, by the light, the little creature feel flat on her face in a dead faint. She was not seasick, but exhausted; and the mother was not allowed to change cabins, or to have air, or to give the child any relief, though the ship was empty, until in a state of ferocity, she went to the Captain. She was howling furious about it, and I gave her what sympathy my sufferings tended to rouse.

Of course our first act, Monday morning, was to seek the Consulate, which I found at eleven o'clock in charge of a small native girl who was then sweeping it, but who seemed to divine my character, for she pointed to a pigeon-hole where I found letters; two from you, one written on the "Teutonic," mailed at Queenstown, and forwarded from Samoa; the other, your dear brief note of August 10, written after receiving my Sydney telegram. You are a wonderful shot with letters, but you never hit a mark closer than this. The letter was just what I wanted to set me up. Perhaps one or two are still missing, but I shall get them, and nothing important can have escaped. Had not your note been very encouraging, I think I should have broken down and gone to bed; for I was grievously disappointed about steamers. I felt too used-up to start again before Saturday the 12th, and wanted a good boat to sail between the 12th and 15th; but the devil forbade any boat at all between the 10th and 17th; and then gave only the P. & O. "Paramatta"; an old ship, of comparatively small tonnage, and of a line I wished to avoid. Instead of reaching Brindisi October 1, we shall be lucky to arrive October 5, and, if not quarantined, reach Paris October 8. Yet, I shall be well-pleased, even with this success.

Colombo seemed to furnish nothing for us, beyond your letter, and I was quite feverish to escape; so we hurried off our small jobs, and took the railway-train at two o'clock for Kandy. A meaner man than I, when I dropped on my seat in that train, I care not to meet; but I could not even lie down without fearing to faint, the oppressiveness of the want of air, and the heavy heat, though only 81° or 82°, were so deadly to me. Two or three times in the day, I had been scared by vertigo, and obliged to steady myself. A weary wight I was when the train began to move, and an impatient one for the next two hours while we jumbled over a rice-swamp where humped cattle lay with their noses just above water, and naked natives paddled in the freshet of the young monsoon; but the green was intense, and the country, even there, was interesting. By the time we had reached the hills, at four o'clock, I had revived; and the next two hours, to Kandy, when the rail rises 1700 feet through superb scenery, made me well. Ceylon is certainly the most interesting and beautiful island we have seen, taking its many-sided interests into account. In one way, Hawaii is grander; in another, Tahiti is more lovely; but Hawaii is a volcano and Tahiti a dream; while Ceylon is what I supposed Java to be, and it was not:—a combination of rich nature and varied human interest, a true piece of voluptuous creativeness. We have seen nothing to approach the brilliancy of the greens and the luxury of the vegetation; but we have been even more struck by the great beauty of the few girls we have caught a glimpse of; especially their eyes, which have a large, dark, far-off, beseeching look, that seems to tell of a coming soul—not Polynesian.

September 10. Kandy is pretty—very; and the surrounding country is prettier still, full of hills and valleys, flowers, elephants, palms and snakes. Monkeys are here also, but I have seen none wild. Another Paradise opens its arms to another son of Adam, but the devil of restlessness, who led my ancestor to the loss of his estate, leads me. I cannot stay three days contented. Socially Kandy seems as impossible as are all these colonial drearinesses, and intellectually man is indubitably vile, as the bishop justly says. In all Ceylon I cannot buy or beg a book on the Ceylon art, literature, religion or history. Of all that has been published on India, not even a stray volume of Max Müller have I seen here, except in the little library of the Sacred Tooth, the Buddhist Temple where the true faith is now alone taught by aid of our master's Tooth, or Tusk—for it is said to be ivory.[2] Of course we visited the famous temple at once, for here is now the last remaining watchfire of our church, except for Boston where Bill Bigelow and Fenollosa fan faint embers. The Temple—Dalada Maligawa, Palace of the Tooth,— was a sad disappointment after the Japanese Temples. The art is poor, rather mean, and quite modern, and even the golden shrine of the Tooth had little to recommend it except one or two cat's-eyes. Occasionally a refined piece of stone carving,—a door-way or threshold,—built into a coarse plaster wall, shows where some older temple has been used for modern ornament, and gives an idea that Ceylon had refinement in the thirteenth century. Hence our tears, or rather our restlessness; for photographs tell us of immense ruined cities in the jungle, a day or two distant; cities as old or older than our aera, where Buddhism flourished like the wicked, more than two thousand years ago. To get there, we must travel day and night in ox-carts; but what of that? We swallow the oxen more willingly than the fevers, snakes, leeches and ticks, with which the deserted cities are said to be now inhabited. So we start tomorrow for Anuradhapura, and, if possible, for Polonnaruwa, and shall return only just in time to take our steamer, the seventeenth. I hope my telegram of the 8th arrived promptly, and was intelligible. "Start seventeenth. Brindisi fifth." After all, I am not at all certain of starting the 17th, for I will not go on the Paramatta without ample comforts and space; I would rather wait a few days more; but my message was as exact as I could make it at a dollar a word, and a ten dollar address. I had half a mind to send you this sheet by the steamer which goes today, but I shall follow so soon that the information would be useless; and I can telegraph both from Suez and from Brindisi in advance of any letter. Almost I hope for another line from you by the mail due here today; but probably you could not calculate so nicely. Only I hope that at breakfast this morning, six hours from now, you will receive my big Sydney letter, and will see that I have behaved like a very nice little boy, and deserve a good mark. Indeed, if it were not for this unreasonable delay here, I would have reached Europe by October 1st as I told you from Tahiti I would try to do. So now for the ox-cart, and the dreadful voyage to Suez; and then—I shall have much to say.

Anuradhapura, Sunday, 13 Sept.   The ox-cart was funny, but not bad, if one must pass nights in these hot regions. We have come about eighty miles from Kandy, and have passed portions of two days inspecting this very sacred city, which is very much out of the world, in a burned jungle, with perfect roads, an excellent government-inn, or Rest-house, and a poor native village, much fever-stricken, infested by jackals, with no whites except government officials in the whole district. I wanted to see the island, and this is it, I suppose, or at least the dry part of it, and sufficiently undisturbed by Europeans, of whom only a few travellers ever come here. I have looked through the inn-book, and found not a name known to me, during a record of eight or ten years; but, for that matter, since leaving San Francisco I have come across no one I ever knew before, so I could not count on finding them here. Yet Ceylon is a place where vast numbers of travellers come—or at least pass—and these ruined cities are the chief interest of the island; so they are visited by about one Englishman a month, thank Buddha, and praise to Siva and Vishnu, not even the photograph-fiend is here. As for the ruins, they are here, beyond question, and we have duly inspected them. Do you want my impressions? I don't believe you do, but it is noon; the day is scorching; we have just breakfasted; I am lying on my bed, trying to keep cool, out of the glare; and why should I not talk to you, even if you go to sleep as I should do in your place. Please imagine a great plain, covered with woods. Dumped on this dry plain are half a dozen huge domes of solid brick, overgrown with grass and shrubs; artificial mounds that have lost their architectural decorations and their plaster covering, but still rise one or two hundred feet above the trees, and have a certain grandeur. Each of these dagobas represents an old temple which had buildings about it, stone bathing-tanks, and stone statues of Buddha, chapels and paved platforms decorated with carved or brick elephants-heads, humped oxen, lions and horses. When Buddha flourished here, two thousand years ago, vast numbers of pilgrims came to worship the relics supposed to be hidden under the dagobas, but still more to pray at the sacred bo-tree, which is the original shoot brought here more than two thousand years ago from the original bo-tree under which Buddha attained Nirwana.—This, then, was Anurajpura; the bo-tree; six dagobas with relics; and one or two temples more or less Brahmanic, that is, rather for Siva or Vishnu than for Buddha, though Buddhism ran here a good deal into Brahmanism. As long as Buddhism flourished, Anurajpura flourished, and the kings went on, building tanks, both for bathing and for irrigation, some of the irrigation tanks being immense lakes, with many miles of embankment. When Buddhism declined, the place went gradually to pieces, and nothing but what was almost indestructible remains. Of course we cared little for the historical or industrial part of the affair, but came here to see the art, which is older than anything in India, and belongs to the earliest and probably purest Buddhist times; for Anuradhapura was the centre of Buddhism even then. I expected—never mind what—all sorts of things—which I have not found. To my surprise and disappointment, all the art seems to me pretty poor and cheap. Compared with Egypt or even with Japan, Ceylon is second-rate. The huge brick-dagobas were laid out on a large scale, with a sense of proportion that must have been artistic, but the want of knowledge or use of the arch makes the result uninteresting. The details are not rich; the stone carving is not fine; the statues are not numerous or very imposing even in size; and all the stone-work, even to the bathing-tanks, is so poorly and cheaply done, without mortar, rivetting or backing, that it can't hold itself up. I have hunted for something to admire, but except the bigness, I am left cold. Not a piece of work, big or small, have I seen that has a heart to it. The place was a big bazaar of religion, made for show and profit. Any country-shrine has more feeling in it than this whole city seems to have shown. I am rather glad the jackals and monkeys own it, for they at least are not religious formalists, and they give a moral and emotion to the empty doorways and broken thresholds. Of course we went at once to the sacred bo-tree, which is now only a sickly shoot or two from the original trunk, and under it I sat for half an hour, hoping to attain Nirwana. La Farge says I am always trying to attain Nirwana, and never get near it. I don't know. Sometimes I think that intellectually I am pretty close to it, if isolation from the world's intellect is Nirwana; but one or two personal interests or affections still bar the last leap to total absorption and silence; even under Buddha's most sacred tree, I thought less of him than of you; which was not the Nirwana that Buddha attained. Probably I am not the first to go through that experience on that spot; though I imagine this to be the first time that the intrusive Siva has been incarnated in you. I left the bo-tree without attaining Bhuddaship. Towards evening we got an ox-cart; a real cart with two wheels, and two slow, meditative, humped oxen, who are also sacred cattle, and who have the most Bhuddistic expression in their humps and horns that ever was reached by God's creatures. The cart was hooped over with thatch, and we put two chairs inside, and were slowly driven by a naked Tamil, as though we were priests or even Hindu deities, through the woods, every now and then clambering out to inspect some stone tank or temple among the trees, and in secret deadly terror of ticks, leeches and cobras, not to speak of centipedes and scorpions. Dusk came on just as a family of monkeys scampered up the trees and jumped across above our heads. I felt no sense of desolation or even of remoteness; sensations have palled on me; but the scene was certainly new, and in a way beautiful, for the evening light was lovely, and the ruined dagobas assumed a color that art never gave them. This evening we resume our travelling ox-cart, with the dainty little trotting oxen, more like deer than cattle; and travelling all night, we reach Dambulla in the morning where we have to look at some rock-temples. I have no longer any hope of finding real art in Ceylon; even the oldest looks to me mechanical, as though it were imported, and paid by the superficial area; but we want to be sure we have seen all the styles, and the rock-temple is a style. I would rather travel by night than by day, even when packed tight in a cart, with my boots sticking out behind. The moon is sweet, and the air exquisite, jackals and all.

September 15.   Before leaving Anuradhapura, we had a dance, after the traditional style of Ceylon. Four men, ornamented with brass arm-plates, silver bangles, and other decorations belonging to their profession, and making music for themselves by thrumming small hand-drums, danced for us, before the Rest-house. They danced well, their training was good, and the dance itself was in a style quite new to us, with a good deal of violent physical exertion at times; but it did not interest me much, and I could see no trace of meaning in it; not even the overlaid, solemn elaboration of

Chinese or Japanese movements, which no one can any longer explain. We paid what seems here, among these terribly poor people, rather a high price for the show,—fifteen rupees, or a little more than a sovereign; but we always encourage native industries. At about eight o'clock in the evening, our mail-cart came for us, and we started on the return-journey. I think the night-travel amused me more than the ruins did. The night-air is pleasantly cool, and the moon was bright. We lay on our backs on a mattrass, with just room—and barely—for us two. Our little white oxen, with their mystical straight horns, and their religious sacred humps, tripped along, sometimes trotting and sometimes running, their bells tinkling in the quaintest way; and the two-wheeled cart, which luckily had springs, tipped about, as though it enjoyed the fun. I slept a good deal, smoked a little, and watched the moonlight on the road and the jungle. We did twentyeight miles in seven hours, reaching a Rest-house at three o'clock in the morning, where we had to change into a less comfortable horse-coach. We knocked up the keeper of the Rest-house, and while he boiled water and made tea, we sat in the dark on the porch, listening to the creak of ox-mills, and to the wierd cries of the jackals, which seemed to fill the woods, and which are the uncanniest night-sound I ever heard. We were on the road again long before dawn, but at six o'clock we reached Dambulla, and climbed up to the Rock-temple, about a mile away. When we got there, the priest and the keys were away, and we had to send back for them, while we sat on the rocks and looked over miles and miles of forest-jungle, to distant mountains. The cave-temples were an exasperating disappointment, mean outside, and stupid within. Not stupid, La Farge insisted, but priestlike; long rows of dirty cotton curtains ran round each temple, carefully hiding the statues in order, no doubt, to extort money for showing them. The statues or figures have no merit as art, but are only conventional Indian Buddhas, sitting or reclining, and coarsely colored; their only value is as decoration, and of course their effect was not only lost but caricatured by concealing them. I think La Farge was angrier than I; but anyway I should not have cared much for the temples which are mere rough holes, without architecture or form. We hurried back to the Rest-house, and kept H.M.'s mail waiting for us till we had breakfasted; then at eight o'clock were on our way again, and at two in the afternoon were in Kandy, which seems deliciously cool and moist after the dry, hot, weary parchment of the plains. We like Kandy as much as though we were children, and it were assorted. The walks and drives are charming, and the peace is almost as ideal as that of Papeete.

Colombo, 18 September. The Parramatta went off last night, but we did not go in her. When I try to explain even to myself how it happened that this steamer, which we had taken every possible trouble to catch and with which we had apparently nothing to do, except to go aboard, should have managed to lose us, I am really puzzled. Everyone in the east would say simply that I should not have tried to go by the P. & O. which is the most unpopular corporation in the celestial system. Not a good word have I ever heard man speak for it, and my own experience fully bears out the prejudice. Yet the P. & O. people must have a certain genius, if they could get rid of passengers so firmly bound as we were. No victim ever entered their slaughtering-pen more resigned than we were when we went to the office yesterday. All we asked was to know whether our cabins were comfortable and where they were to be. The agent could tell us nothing except that the ship was empty; eightyfive vacancies to some sixty berths occupied; but he had no idea what special cabins were vacant; he made a rule not to keep plans of the ships in the office, and therefore could not show me where the cabins were, or what were their numbers or their sizes; his office would close at five o'clock, and the ship would sail in the night. Not disgusted by this cavalier treatment, as soon as the ship arrived, at half past three o'clock in the afternoon La Farge and I pulled out to her, a mile down the bay, and went aboard. A less inviting steamer I have read of, but seldom seen. An atmosphere of Scotch-English-Colonial middle-class grime pervaded the ship and all its arrangements. Dirt, clumsiness and stupidity were its only recommendations. All the same, we got the steward, looked at the rooms said to be vacant, selected two, and hurried back to the town. La Farge, as usual, was very busy buying photographs, for which my hatred has now become a real photo-phobia, and left me to secure the passages. I reached the office just at five. The agent was closing his desk. I gave him the numbers of the rooms chosen. He explained that both were otherwise engaged, but I could have two neighboring ones. He had no ship's plan to show where these were. I suggested that I could not make a decision without consulting La Farge which would take ten or fifteen minutes. He turned his back and went on locking his drawers. I turned my back, and walked gently down stairs. Such is the tale. I admit only to have been, after the first shock of surprise, excessively glad to escape from the P. & O. and its ships. This morning we mean to secure cabins on the Messageries Steamer Djemneh which sails next, three days after the Parramatta, and which will land us at Marseilles October 10, as I shall telegraph you from Aden or Suez. So we have three days more at Colombo, with nothing to do. I have already looked at all the cat's-eyes, and find none worth having at less cost than a thousand dollars, which would, I think, buy as good or better in London. No pearls; moonstones by the bushel, but little different from *nacre;* and only what are called star-stones, or star-sapphires, rather amusing. I like all the stones that appeal to the imagination, like opals and cat's-eyes; and the Asteria, or star-stones, have to me the additional charm of not being in the fashion. Yet I enjoy looking at most gems, and really delight in buying them, except that the pleasure is too costly for my means. You must take me, in Paris and London, to see gems. I must go with you to Phillips's in Cockspur Street. Here I have seen nothing fit for you.

September 27. Two thousand more miles run off—twelve thousand since Tahiti. I feel as though the journey were done, for we have seen the last of the Indian Ocean, and tonight we reach Aden. The voyage has been very quiet and pleasant, all but yesterday when the motion made me so seedy that, as they will not serve anything to eat on deck, I declined to eat at all. At sea, when sick, I can go three days without eating, but yesterday improved and I got dinner. The nights are hot—about 80°—and I passed them mostly on deck. The steamer is the Messageries Djemnah, an old boat, like the Melbourne but smaller. The passengers are few and usual. Some Dutch swine whom I am condemned to sit next; some Portuguese pecora; some French, as unsocial as myself; some English, rather better than common; and some hybrids. Their chief merit is that they are few and quiet. I read much; sleep much; and enjoy the fine weather and the tropic sea,—although for that matter one sea is like another to me except in its good or bad temper. Our last days at Ceylon were rather thrown away. We went out for a night to a hotel on the sea at Mt Lavinia; pretty and slow. We got a juggler who did tricks. I was very warm. Voilà tout!

29 September. I went ashore yesterday at Aden, and sent you my telegram, which will, I hope, prevent your writing to Brindisi, and will bring me a note to Marseilles. La Farge and I telegraphed recklessly—ten pounds worth—all round the universe, to divert our minds from the heat. Aden should mean oven. Only the camels seemed baked enough to suit it. The sun hits one like a base-ball. On board, my thermometer stood at 92° all day; on shore I know not what. My cabin was above 90° all night; but I was not in it—not much. I lay on a chair on deck where it was about 86°, with air; and very pleasant. I like the Red Sea today, though it is 91° without rest, and thirteen hundred miles long. The water is smooth, like a canal, which is just my style of ocean wave, and it is not red but blue, with porpoises, and now and then a bit of bare, baked rock, but generally no land in sight. Before dawn this morning the sailors fairly hunted me down below with their deck-washing, so I took a shower-bath in the dark, and, to my alarm, little fire-flies seemed to play all over me; but it was only phosphorous and didn't bite. We are all languid with the heat; but the sun is going to set soon, very soft and saffrony, as though it were gentle and childlike—fraud as it is,—and we shall have dinner with champagne and ice and punkahs, and my Dutch hog on one side, and a poor Frenchman on the other, whose child died this morning, I think; for I passed the cabin at the time and caught a glimpse of that white horror which becomes so terribly familiar as life goes on; but on board ship no one is supposed to die. Nothing is said, and I do not venture even to ask. The family came on board only yesterday at Aden, and are not known to us.

Saturday, Oct. 3.   We entered the Suez Canal at ten o'clock last night, and this morning at seven were stopped by a steamer aground ahead of us. The delay will cost us a day, I fear, and I shall see you so much later; but the weather is beautiful, the temperature charming, (80° in my cabin at two P.M. and 70° last night), and we are patient, though very dull. If we get through by this evening, we shall still be in Alexandria tomorrow morning. This is our only excitement, and I note it only to bar reflections on my slowness.

Thursday, October 8.   We should have reached Marseilles today, but our detention in the Suez Canal lasted twenty hours; we passed the greater part of Sunday at Port Said; reached Alexandria Monday morning at six; sailed again at half past eight, and for the last three days have run steadily ahead, with beautiful weather and a calm sea, until now we are well through another brace of thousand miles from Aden, and have but some nine hundred more to Paris. Last evening, after dark, we came through the straits of Messina which were like a French boulevard between the rows of gas-lights on either side. Tonight we pass between Corsica and Sardinia. Tomorrow afternoon at about five o'clock we should reach Marseilles. The voyage has been charming, though as quiet as a Pacific island. We have found no exciting society and nothing to tell about. I have read a volume a day, and thought abominably about the future, which will not arrange itself or let me alone. For the first time I am beginning to feel that the long journey, which seemed interminable, is really ended, and that all the old perplexities, with plenty of new ones, are going to revive. The pleasure of seeing you once more overbalances everything else; but in the depths of my cowardice I feel more than ever the conviction that you cannot care to see one who is so intolerably dead as I am, and that the more you see of such a being, the more sorry you will be that you ever tried to bring him back to life; but, as for this, you are the best judge, and, anyway, you can always send me back to the east again by a word. Yet how can I manage not to bore you? If I only knew that, I should feel quite master of the world; but a whole year of vegetation in lonely corners of the ocean, where no social effort was required, and where I have not met one person whom I ever saw before, is shocking bad training for Paris and London. Poor La Farge has been my only victim, and on his sufferings I could look with a calm countenance, or even with a certain amount of sardonic amusement; but I could not bear yours. Men are certainly the most successful invention the devil ever made, and when they arrive at a certain age, and have to be constantly amused, they are even harder to manage than when they are young, mischievous and tormenting.

Marseilles. 9th.   On shore at last, and answered your letter by telegraph at once. Perhaps I shall see you before you receive this closing despatch.

MS: MHi

1. For Bishop Heber's poem, see HA to EC, Sept. 13, 1890, note 12.
2. Friedrich Max Müller, *The Rig-Veda,* 6 vols. (1849–1874).

To Elizabeth Cameron

Wenlock Abbey, Nov. 5, 1891.

A long, lowering, melancholy November day, the clouds hanging low on Wenlock Edge, and stretching off to the westward where you are streaming along the Irish coast and out to sea; for I am writing in the hour before dinner, and you must be just losing sight of land. I have shivered over the fire, chatting feebly, and this afternoon have ridden for two hours over the sodden fields, in the heavy air, talking with Gaskell in our middle-aged way about old people, mostly dead; but always mentally wandering from the talk and the dim landscape to you and your ship. As fate sometimes does temper its sternness with pity, the day, sad as it was, has been calm, as though the storm and strain were over. I was glad for your sake, and a little on my own account, for, as usual, I have passed a bad *quart d'heure* since bidding you good-bye in your Hansom cab across the darkness of Half Moon street. I ought to spare you the doubtful joy of sharing my pleasures in this form; but you, being a woman and quick to see everything that men hide, probably know my thoughts better than I do myself, and would trust me the less if I concealed them. You saw and said that my Paris experiment was not so successful as you had meant it to be. Perhaps I should have done better not to have tried it, for the result of my six months desperate chase to obey your bidding has not been wholly happy. You do not read Mrs Browning. No one does now. As a collegian I used to read Aurora Leigh and Lady Geraldine's Courtship and the Swan's Nest on the River, and two lines have stuck:

"Know you what it is when Anguish, with apocalyptic *Never,*
To a Pythian height dilates you, and Despair sublimes to Power?"[1]

The verse is charmingly preposterous and feminine, for a woman never recognises an impossibility; but an elderly man, when hit over the head by an apocalyptic *Never,* does not sublime to Power, but curls up like Abner Dean of Angels, and for a time does not even squirm;[2] then he tumbles about for a while, seeing the Apocalypse all round him; then he bolts and runs like a mad dog, anywhere,—to Samoa, to Tahiti, to Fiji; then he dashes straight round the world, hoping to get to Paris ahead of the Apocalypse; but hardly has he walked down the Rue Bassano when he sees the apocalyptic *Never* written up like a hotel sign on No. 12; and when he, at last leaves London, and his cab crosses the end of Cork St, his last glimpse of No. 5A shows the Apocalyptic *Never* over the front door. More than once today I have reflected seriously whether I ought not at once to turn round and go back to Ceylon. As I am much the older and presumably the one of us two who is responsible for whatever mischief can happen, I feel as though I had led you into the mistake of bringing me here, and am about to lead you into the worse mistake of bringing me home. Not that I take a French view of the matter, or imagine you to be in the least peril of falling into the conventional dilemmas of the French heroines; but because, no matter how much I may efface myself or how little I may ask, I must always make more demand on you than you can gratify, and you must always have the consciousness that, whatever I may profess, I want more than I can have. Sooner or later the end of such a situation is estrangement, with more or less disappointment and bitterness. I am not old enough to be a tame cat; you are too old to accept me in any other character. You were right last year in sending me away, and if I had the strength of mind of an average monkey, and valued your regard at anything near its true price, I should guard myself well from running so fatal a risk as that of losing it by returning to take a position which cannot fail to tire out your patience and end in your sending me off again, either in kindness or in irritation; but I cannot sublime to power, and as I have learned to follow fate with docility surprising to myself, I shall come back gaily, with a heart as sick as ever a man had who knew that he should lose the only object he loved because he loved too much. I am quite prepared to have you laugh at all this, and think it one of my morbid ideas. So it is; all my ideas are morbid, and that is going to be your worst trouble, as I have always told you. Yet I would give you gladly as many opal and diamond necklaces as Mr Cameron would let you wear if I could only for once look clear down to the bottom of your mind and understand the whole of it. I lie for hours wondering whether you, out on the dark ocean, in surroundings which are certainly less cheerful than mine, sometimes think of me, and divine or suspect that you have undertaken a task too hard for you; whether you feel that the last month has proved to be—not wholly a success, and that the fault is mine for wanting more than I had a right to expect; whether you are almost on the verge of regretting a little that you tried the experiment; whether you are puzzled to know how an indefinite future of such months is to be managed; whether you are fretting, as I am, over what you can and what you cannot do; whether you are not already a little impatient with me for not being satisfied, and for not accepting in secret, as I do accept in pretence, whatever is given me, as more than enough for any deserts or claims of mine; and whether in your most serious thoughts, you have an idea what to do with me when I am again on your hands. I would not distress you with these questions while you were fretted, worried and excited by your last days here; but now that you are tossing on the ocean, you have time to see the apocalyptic Never which has become yours as well as mine. I have dragged you face to face with it, and cannot now help your seeing it. French novels are not the only possible dramas. One may be innocent as the angels, yet as unhappy as the wicked; and I, who would lie down and die rather than give you a day's pain, am going to pain you the more, the more I love.

Nov. 6. Another dark, still day. We had a meet of the hounds this morning, and I rode to it with the Gaskells, and capered over the muddy fields on a pulling poney till my back is sore as never before, and some muscle is so gone wrong that I almost howl every time I rise from my chair. The hunt left us, and we rode home and killed a fox in the Abbey grounds as though the fox had meant to pay me a personal attention. This afternoon I wandered alone across Wenlock Edge and through miles of soaked meadow. The air is still calm, and I thought always of you, but you are near a thousand miles away already, and this weather is no longer yours. Curiously enough, I feel rather peaceful and contented in this dank, dark, dripping, dreary atmosphere, where the hills melt or freeze into dim outlines of mist and cloud. For the moment the world seems stationary, and I can stop too. Nothing has changed here since I first came in the year '64. For once I find perfect stability and repose; even Gaskell seems hardly altered. My long, tearing, wild jaunt of the last five months, ends here in a sense of ended worlds and burnt-out coal-and-iron-universes. Tomorrow I am going over to Birmingham to pass Sunday with the Chamberlains. I have offered myself to Mrs Dugdale—don't be alarmed![3] only for a call. I go to Tillypronie next week. Am I not social and human? I try to be civil, because you tell me I'm rude, and I want to please you. In secret I dread returning to the solitude of hotels and the weariness of self—self—self, and the temptation to commit any folly that would give amusement or change.

Highbury. Sunday, November 8. Here I am with the Chamberlains in their big house with a suburb of greenhouses and forests of orchids. They— Chamberlains and orchids—are charming hosts, and Madame, younger than ever, and like the younger sister of her step-daughters, quite shines with new light as a *grande dame*.[4] Only a few young people are here, and all seems serene and happy. The girls are decidedly agreeable, and my host is admirable in the domestic relation. I feel quite like your brute when I see how gentle and deferential he is. How I wish you would make me a social gem; but you neglect your duties. We have strolled about the place, and the sun actually shone. My virtue shines too, for I suddenly burn with interest for English politics, and talked till near two o'clock last night with my Right Honorable friend on the prospects of the coming general election. With his usual frankness he announced his expectation of the defeat of his party.[5] What ought I to have said? In truth I cared much more to know how your voyage was getting on and whether you were as cold as I am; but the weather is still so very fine and calm that I hope for the best. How I wish you were here with us, and how I should have enjoyed a peaceful Sunday with you among the orchids, admiring *Odontoglossum grande,* if that is its name! I should have had nothing to say to you; I never have anything; but you could have gone to sleep among the palms and ferns, and I could have read to Martha.

Monday. Nov. 9. Wenlock again this evening. Mrs Dugdale telegraphed that she was at Ascot or London or some such neighborhood, so I was spared that effort. This morning I made a special inspection of the Chamberlains' heating and lighting apparatus. Joseph has five big boilers and a gas boiler; a big and little dynamo, and so on. I would like to resemble him in this as in other matters; apparently he takes no thought of money, but he takes less thought of his house, which he leaves to wife and son; and he declared that no one had ever asked to see his boilers before. Then Mistress Mary drove me to the town to show me, also at my request, her portrait now on exhibition there. I thought it much better than I expected. Millais, whatever his weaknesses, is neither a fool nor a lunatic.[6] On the whole Mistress Mary is lucky, and I would give much to see an equally pleasant portrait of you and Martha. How good it might be! Then she took me to church to see Burne Jones's glass, which is—not so bad as I expected.[7] Then we went to the Art Museum to see an exhibition of Pre-raphaelitic pictures—Burne Jones, Holman Hunt, Rosetti, &c,—and these, on the whole were fully as bad as I expected.[8] Then we parted and I came back to Wenlock. I am waiting only to hear of your safe arrival, to mail this letter, probably just as I start for Scotland on Thursday or Friday. Last night the wind blew violently, but you were two thousand miles away, and that gust, at least, could not harm you. I wish you were here with us. You would have to sleep all day, or ride in fields soaked with mud. I am still stiff as a martyr on a gridiron.

Tuesday, 10th. All day out doors, walking or riding, either along muddy roads or through fields and lanes like sloughs. I rather like it still. I feel as though I had reached harbor, and the dull, wet skies and brown foliage leaves me more cheerful than I was in the most perfect tropics. Yet I was tired this evening, and after dressing for dinner I was waiting before the fire in the Abbott's room for Gaskell and Lady Catherine to come down, when a footman brought me a bundle of shirts forwarded by my order from the Hotel Bristol, and in the bundle was a lot of letters, among them your sweet note from Queenstown. Did I not just feel like a horrid brute? No! the fruit and butter came not from me; I hesitated and said to myself that you didn't want them. No! I did not even send a farewell telegram to Queenstown! I hesitated and said to myself that you didn't want it. No! I was glad not to have gone with you to Crewe! I hesitated, and said to myself that you did not want me, and I had suffered already enough in parting. Always when I reach the desperate stage you say or write something that makes me feel unreasonable and brutal, and ashamed of everything but loving you. Why send you what I have written in this letter? I know it cannot give you pleasure, and is likely to give you pain. Yet it is all true, and the pain is actually mine, not yours; your position is right enough, and easily held; mine is all wrong and impossible; you are Beauty; I am the Beast, and until I turn into somebody else I cannot with propriety lead a life fit for you to associate with. I must be a nuisance to you and myself—like Hamlet or Prince Bulbo.[9] But I am really annoyed that you thought my good-bye abrupt, and had no idea it was to come then. I thought I had told you in the afternoon that my good-bye was intended to be our last words in your rooms, for, later, I should have no chance for more than a mere word of farewell. After all, it was only of a piece with my whole visit,—fragmentary, interrupted and unsatisfactory. The fault is mine; you are as gentle, obliging and thoughtful as ever, and nothing remains for me but to be sorry after all is over. Yet I wish—I wish—I wish, I could see clear through your mind. You have a nature like an opal, with the softest, loveliest, purest lights, which one worships and which baffles one's worship.

Thursday, 12 November. The Times today announces the arrival of your Teutonic at New York yesterday morning; less than six days therefore from Queenstown. I feel greatly relieved, for I can at least hope that the voyage was good. The relief was the greater because a change of weather set in here on Sunday which has culminated in a violent storm, and had your ship been delayed, I should have feared that you might have passed through this gale, and suffered. I suppose La Farge sailed from Queenstown today into the teeth of the gale; at any rate I did for him what I was too low-spirited to do for you,—I both telegraphed and wrote farewell. We had been so long together, and had intended to meet again in London, but missed it! We have never had a quarrel, or even a disagreement, which surely proves that he must have a wonderfully sweet disposition. Apart from this, he is the only man of genius I now know living, and though he had seven devils, I would be his friend for that. If I could only give him a big window to do, like Chartres or Amiens![10] So I am now all alone for the first time; you gone; he gone; and myself the gonest of the lot. I still linger at Wenlock, partly because the Clarke's have set Saturday for Tillie-pronie, partly because I feel at home here, as though I were in hiding. Lady Catherine is very nice indeed; she has grown simpler and more natural than in the old sun-flower days, and is very gentle and sympathetic; but I think my true source of repose here is not so much in her or in her husband as in the place itself. An atmosphere of seclusion and peace certainly lingers in these stones, and I have thought much of the life I should certainly have led here had I come with the same experiences five hundred years ago, to the same retreat. Progress has much to answer for in depriving weary and broken men and women of their natural end and happiness; but even now I can fancy myself contented in the cloister, and happy in the daily round of duties, if only I still knew a God to pray to, or better yet, a Goddess; for as I grow older I see that all the human interest and power that religion ever had, was in the mother and child, and I would have nothing to do with a church that did not offer both. There you are again! you see how the thought always turns back to you. Goodbye now! I shall post this letter tomorrow on my way north. My next will follow in about a fortnight. To the last moment I doubt the wisdom of sending this letter; but: Kismet! Let fate have its way.

MS: MHi

1. HA quotes from "Lady Geraldine's Courtship" (1844); he mistitles "The Romance of the Swan's Nest" (1844). *Aurora Leigh* (1857).
2. Abner Dean's fate in the Bret Harte poem "The Society upon the Stanislaus" (1871): "He smiled a kind of sickly smile, and curled up on the floor / And the subsequent proceedings interested him no more."
3. Alice Trevelyan Dugdale, sister of George Otto Trevelyan.
4. Joseph Chamberlain, twice widowed when he married Mary Endicott, had six children by his previous marriages. His eldest daughter was the same age as his young wife.
5. The Liberal Unionists.
6. Sir John Everett Millais (1829–1896) was much in demand as a portrait painter.
7. Sir Edward Burne-Jones (1833–1898), eminent painter of romantic themes and designer of stained glass.
8. Chamberlain as mayor of Birmingham 1873–1875 virtually rebuilt the city center and began the expansion of the museum, which had in 1885 moved into new quarters.
9. A lovesick character in Thackeray's *The Rose and the Ring* (1855).
10. La Farge had written from Brittany about his study of medieval cathedral windows and his wish that he could do the stained glass for a large building.

HENRY ADAMS IN BERLIN, 1859

ABIGAIL BROOKS ADAMS

CHARLES FRANCIS ADAMS

CHARLES FRANCIS
ADAMS, JR.

CHARLES MILNES GASKELL

MARIAN HOOPER, 1869

HENRY ADAMS, 1875

HENRY ADAMS AT 1607 H STREET

THE ADAMS HOUSE AT 1603 H STREET

CLARENCE KING, EARLY 1880S

JOHN HAY IN HENRY ADAMS' STUDY, 1883

BROOKS ADAMS

JOHN LA FARGE IN HENRY ADAMS' STUDY

ELIZABETH
CAMERON

MARTHA CAMERON

ELIZABETH CAMERON, 1899

HENRY ADAMS, 1914

THE ADAMS MEMORIAL BY AUGUSTUS SAINT-GAUDENS

To John Hay

Paris, 21 December, 1891.

Mon Cher

I expect a letter from you soon. That is the reason why I select this vast canvas of paper. I wish to do honor to the letter which ought to be entering my republic. Also I have nothing to do this evening. I have been here a week, which has just served to exhaust all the theatres, and the night is so cold that I shiver at the idea of beginning on the Cafés Chantants. For the first time in my life I am in Paris without society of any kind, as solitary as the sun or the moon. I converse with no one but my dentist and my bookseller, and when I am not squirming in the dentist's chair, I am burrowing in the archives of the Ministère des Affaires Etrangères, discovering blunders that adorn my history. Would that you were here! You would be bored to extinction, which would make you excellent company for me.

Naturally, with such inducements, I have taken arduously to improving my mind, and to picking up the lost pieces of broken crockery scattered over twenty neglected years of French manufacture. As yet, the painting and the sculpture have made me only sea-sick; with all the good-will in the world I have not been able to face the terrors of French art, but I will still try, mon ami,—I will try. In the theatre I have done better. To be sure, the theatre is weaker than I ever knew it before, and I am, I find, a severer critic than one should be; but I have got pleasure out of Réjane, and I find Jane Hading fairly satisfactory.[1] The Palais Royal and the Variétes are very amusing—almost as much so as they used to be. Generally the acting averages well, but I am pained to see that no distinctly first-rate actor or actress is on the stage, and as yet nothing approaching a first-rate new play has met my anxious eyes. At the Français—a theatre which irritates my sensitive nerves—I have seen the old Monde où l'on S'ennuie, and was considerably overcome at finding that, with all its wit, it impressed me as being saved from failure only by the visible efforts of the actors; its intrigue is excessively commonplace, and it hangs together very loosely.[2] At the Vaudeville I have seen the reprise of Nos Intimes, and felt to the full extent the admitted weakness of its last Act. At the Variétés, the Cigale and Nitouche were delightful, but there too the last Acts were not good enough for the first. All these plays are reprises, and some of them from a long way back. The new plays are faulty the other way; they are better constructed; the climax is well worked up, and the last Act is the strongest;

but, oh, my blessed virgin, what situations! Nothing so revolting and horrible ought to be allowed to be seen. I have not been to the Théatre Libre, where I observe by the Figaro that a rape and abortion are to be given on the stage at an approaching performance, but I would as lieve see either or both as see some of the situations I have seen. At the same time I am not so much impressed by indecency as I expected; in fact it seems to me no worse than in old times.

Curiously enough the thing that pleases me most in Paris is the newspapers. Think of that! I can read them. They are uncommonly well written, especially the feuilletons which seem to me better than ever. Jules Lemaitre is delightful. Anatole France is always good. Sarcey you know of old.[3] I kept his yesterday's comments on Ibsen, thinking that I would send them to you, as they seemed to express our views with excellent fooling; but I don't know;—shall I, or shall I not? These things hardly keep their aroma through a sea-voyage. I know of nothing else to send, unless it is Jules Lemaitre's last volume of causeries. Books by the score are poured out, but Maupassant and Loti are the fashions of the day, and you know them both. I am keeping the Goncourt's journal for my next long voyage.[4]

The Opéra here strikes me as poor both at the Grand and the Comique. I have endured Ambroise Thomas until flesh, to ignore blood entirely, rebelled. Lohengrin is better, but that damned swan bores one at last; and why should we not at least have Wagner in some less familiar form! Melba I heard only in Hamlet which is an intolerably commonplace opera.[5] On the other hand Paris is immensely strong in concerts, and on Sunday one can choose between three big orchestras of the first class, all playing Beethoven, Wagner and Berlioz, and all crowded with audiences so respectable that Boston is fin de siècle compared with them.

As for the restaurants—well! I am shaving fiftyfour and things don't taste as they used to do. Perhaps the Café Anglais is as good as ever; but I should say that the cuisine had fallen off. Not but what it is good; only it wants go. I have made superhuman efforts to try all the restaurants far up the boulevards, where foreigners are unknown, and I much prefer them; but the cuisine is the same old story, or even more so. I prefer Delmonico.

December 25.   Forgive me! it was not a rape; it was a "prise de possession." I enclose an account of it in this morning's paper.

I can tell you nothing of the world of society. I have seen absolutely no one. The last time I went to the Legation, I was told that the minister was about to depart for Spain. I did not see him because he was not at the office. I did see Gussy Jay; also I called on his wife.[6] This represents my whole acquaintance. If anyone else is here whom I ought to call upon, I do not know it. I trust that whenever you come here to educate Helen and

Alice, you will find society such as the world elsewhere cannot offer. For my own part, Apia and Papeete were socially gay compared with Paris.

I have an idea for the amusement of our future lives. Let us get possession of an evening newspaper, and write alternate feuilletons once a week. I think I could do it for a time with some enjoyment, if I were exempted from writing under my own name. If we were indecent enough, we could always make a success, and French literature would supply us with indecencies to perpetuity. Reflect on this! I am sure it has possibilities.

No letter from you. Gredin, va![7] While you are butterflying in the salons of Washington, I am grubbing in the desolation of Paris, and you do not give me a thought. If you have nothing to say, why not say it? À revoir! My love to all yours.

Ever   Henry Adams.

MS: RPB

1. Gabrielle Réjane (1857–1920), an outstanding French actress, played in Henri Meilhac's and Ludovic Halévy's *La Cigale*. Jane Hading (1859–1934) appeared in Victorien Sardou's *Nos Intimes*.
2. *Le Monde où l'on s'ennuie* (1881), by Edouard Pailleron.
3. Lemaître, drama critic for the *Journal des Débats;* Anatole France (1844–1924), fortnightly columnist and literary editor of *Le Temps;* Francisque Sarcey (1827–1899), drama critic for *Le Temps*.
4. The *Journal* of the brothers Edmond and Jules de Goncourt (1822–1896; 1830–1870) was being selectively published in nine volumes, 1887–1896.
5. Charles-Ambroise Thomas, composer of *Mignon* (1866), a staple of the Opéra-Comique repertory, and of *Hamlet* (1868). *Lohengrin* (1850), by Richard Wagner, was first performed in Paris Sept. 16, 1891. Nellie Melba was the stage name of Helen Porter Mitchell Armstrong (1859–1931), Australian soprano.
6. Augustus Jay (1850–1919), second secretary of U.S. legation.
7. *Gredin:* villain.

To John Hay

Paris, 9 Jan. 1892

My dear John

On this last night of my imprisonment "dans cet immense égout qu'on appelle Paris," my suppressed rage feels the necessity of explosion.[1] I will come home, and immediately, if you will join me in writing, under any assumed name or character you please, a volume or two of Travels which will permit me to express my opinion of life in general, and especially of the French, their literature and their art. I wont do it alone. Such a book, to be amusing needs variety of treatment and experience. The world is too big for one—or even for two. If King could be induced to join, so much the better; but I would do it with you alone, and put into it all the vinegar, pepper and vitriol necessary to make it a success of scandal if nothing else. I am fairly tired—bored beyond endurance—by the world we live in, and its ideals, and am ready to say so, not violently, but kindly, as one rubs salt into the back of a flogged sailor, as though one loved him.

I have said and stick to it, that I will never again appear as an author, but I don't mind writing anonymously as one does in the newspapers, and Travels that say anything are nowadays read. Of course I should not touch the South Seas; I could not without betraying myself. We could start with San Francisco and go through America to England and France, which is a big mouthful enough.

If you want me to come home, try this experiment, which is only our old scheme revived and enlarged.

Without some such occupation I can't hold out long anywhere; and the occupation must be joint, in order to keep me going. My notion of Travels is a sort of ragbag of everything; scenery, psychology, history, literature, poetry, art; anything in short, that is worth throwing in; and I want to grill a few literary and political gentlemen to serve with champagne.

London. Monday, 11th.   The comforts of European travel in winter fill me with admiration for America. Yesterday I came over from Paris. Being still off my correct form, with a cough and general poorness of condition, I felt the effort more than usual. Actually thirty years ago I did the same thing without a sign of change. The Calais steamer is now somewhat larger than then; otherwise, not a shadow of improvement or alteration. Wedged into the old compartment with the old crowd, shivering over cold foot-warmers of the last century, I got to Calais, with nothing to eat, and went on the steamer in an icy fog that froze my back-bone. I shook with cold. Seizing a stateroom and shutting myself up, I wrapped every coat and rug I had, or could find, round me, and lay down under a heap, and rang for hot tea. Slowly I recovered warmth enough not to shiver, but was too cold to sleep. Yet surely a steamer might be warmed. At Dover again the old English compartment with its foot-warmer, freezing; and at Charing Cross half an hour of custom-house in a chill like salted ice. Everything on this main mail route was identical with what it was when I first knew it, except that the terminus was then at London Bridge. I can understand that their art should be bad and their literature rotten and their tastes mean, but why the deuce they should inflict on themselves cold and hunger and discomfort, hang me if I can understand. Actually, in Europe I see no progress—none! They have the electric light, voilà tout!

This is the end! If nothing more has been done in these last thirty years, that have produced our Atlantic steamers and our railway system in America, nothing more need be expected from Europe. The people are stupid. They grow stupider and coarser as their aristocracies disappear. They have no longer even the refinement of manners and tastes of their old society.

Then, I have arrived. The end is here, and I have seen all there will be to show. One can't mistake a drift of thirty years. I am furious and astonished, like a bull that has butted a brick wall, and reflects.

13th London is lovely; just a rich brown tone, and nothing else. Occasionally a red ball glows in the southern sky, and once or twice has cast a shadow. I thrive in it, and have already recovered my appetite and wax fat. As for people, I know little indeed. I sat with Harry James an hour or two yesterday afternoon, and found him in double trouble between the death of his friend Balestier and the steady decline of his sister.[2] Everyone is still out of town. Everyone has influenza, or has had it, or expects to have it. As yet I've not discovered a single English acquaintance, and shall have to begin laboriously knocking at doors from street to street to ask where everyone is. Did I tell you that my last act in Paris was to breakfast with Whitelaw Reid. I liked his wife; she seemed very simple and sympathetic.[3] Whitelaw drank white wine, and in consequence talked like three Frenchmen. He was extremely civil and cordial, had much to say about you, and generally seemed to me greatly improved, with the air of one who has arrived, and need bother no more to be long-haired.

Lincoln is in bed with influenza, and when I went to the office yesterday, White had gone off to nurse him. The Whites are still in the country.[4]

Larz Anderson and I are in the same house, in Clarges Street, and breakfast together, and go about dining at the various clubs and haunts of fashion.[5] I have learned to drink Champagne and read Truth. No, that's a lie! I can't read Truth yet, but try and hope. Meanwhile I read Mr Blowitz and the Times, and feel a deep interest in Maupassant, whose mental condition in his healthiest state worried me greatly because he seemed totally unconscious whether he wrote excessively funny or excessively stupid things.[6]

A revoir bientôt! I want to visit Truxton at Teheran but can find no companion.[7]

Ever Yrs   Henry Adams.

MS: RPB

1. Alfred de Musset, "Lettre à M. de Lamartine" (1836).
2. Charles Wolcott Balestier (1861–1891), American novelist and publisher, died Dec. 6. Alice James (1847–1892) died in London March 6.
3. Reid was minister to France 1889–1892, ambassador to Great Britain 1905–1912; Elisabeth Mills Reid (1858–1931), New York social leader and philanthropist.

4. Robert Todd Lincoln (1843–1926), U.S. minister to England; Henry White (1850–1927), first secretary of U.S. legation in London 1886–1893, 1897–1905. The Whites had a country house in Berkshire.

5. Larz Anderson (1866–1937), second secretary of London legation 1891–1894, son of Nicholas Longworth Anderson.

6. Henri de Blowitz (1825–1903), Paris correspondent of the *Times* 1870–1902; Guy de Maupassant (1850–1893), French novelist, attempted suicide.

7. Truxton Beale (1856–1936), minister to Persia 1891–1892, brother of HA's Washington neighbor Emily Beale.

IV

A Faustian Traveler
1892–1899

AﬁﬀFTER PARTING from Mrs. Cameron at the end of October 1891, Adams stayed on abroad for three months to attend to troublesome dentistry and the removal of an unsightly wen from his shoulder. He also made a precautionary search of diplomatic archives in Paris with a view to corrections in the *History*. He returned to Washington to find himself at loose ends; no long-term historical project awaited his diligent pen like the one which had preoccupied him for ten years. True, he had brought back from Tahiti some materials for a history of the island dynasties to honor his hosts, but it would have to await their further search for legends.

While his house was readied for him, he joined John Hay for a ten-day visit with the Camerons at their vacation house at St. Helena Island, South Carolina. In Washington his active social existence resumed, and once again nieces, in fact and in wish, made themselves at home and his dinners attracted political figures, diplomats, and scientists. But time hung heavily on his hands, and he dreamed restlessly of more travel, seeing himself, like Goethe's Faust, unable to find pleasure anywhere in repose. So began a new avocation, shepherding his wife's nieces on visits to Scotland and Paris, or dashing off with a companion in search of a fresh horizon. He journeyed to Cuba in February 1893 with William Phillips, a Washington lawyer, and celebrated its exotic culture in colorful diary letters to Elizabeth Cameron. Twice he journeyed to the Chicago World's Fair, where he was dazzled by the architecture of the White City and awed by the mysterious power of the dynamos.

In between the two visits in 1893 he vacationed in the Alps with Senator Cameron and Elizabeth. The great financial panic of that year suddenly intruded on the holiday to give a new and absorbing direction to his thought as he hurried home at the anxious summons of his brother Brooks. There thus began their prolonged collaboration to understand the global inter-relations of politics and economics which had led to the crisis. As the free coinage of silver had precipitated the panic by a rush on gold, the international bankers had driven out silver from an important place in the world money system by forcing the adoption of the single gold standard. To the Adams brothers that strategy seemed an act of tyranny against the debtor classes.

Now a confirmed and passionate tourist, Adams was off again in February 1894 with Clarence King for two months in the back country of Cuba, where he became, like King, a partisan of the revolutionaries. At the end of July he set off on a two-month camping trip to Yellowstone Park and the Tetons with Hay and his son Del. He went on alone to Banff and Vancouver, enjoying "the queer Nirvana" of "never thinking about any consecutive subject." Before the year was out he was wandering in Mexico and the West Indies with twenty-one-year-old Chandler Hale, the son of Senator Eugene Hale. He did not get back to Lafayette Square until April. The chief pleasure of travel, Adams chose to say, was in the movement itself. He was to seek that ambiguous pleasure almost to the end of his life.

In 1896 Henry and his brother Brooks supported William Jennings Bryan's candidacy for the presidential nomination, responding like many others to Bryan's electrifying challenge "You shall not crucify mankind on a cross of gold." The failure of his crusade showed them that the evils of the "gold-bug" culture of finance capitalism would have to be fought in a larger arena. Henry thus helped his brother revise his *Law of Civilization and Decay*, a vehement attack on mercantile values; and he himself began a systematic and destructive analysis of world trade and international finance. Worthington Chauncey Ford, chief of the Bureau of Statistics at the Treasury, kept him supplied with information concerning the movement of international trade.

By way of defense against the "gold-bug" enemy, Henry's thoughts also turned, as Brooks's had done earlier, to a study of what they saw as the more virile and wholesome values of the period before the capitalist revolution, the period of the late Middle Ages. When Henry toured the cathedrals of Normandy with the Lodges in 1895 he felt a moment of revelation before the wonders of Chartres and the majesty of Mont Saint Michel. The age that built these marvels struck him as the true home of his spirit. He began to take pleasure in translating the Old French *chansons* and felt kinship with Richard Coeur de Lion.

The turbulent politics of his own time engrossed him as the international rivalries and tensions of the nineties, exacerbated by the financial panic, seemed to him to presage increasing disorder and chaos. He saw socialism casting its shadow over France while a militant Germany seemed bent on finding a larger place in the sun. Spain was bogged down in Cuba, unable to subdue rebellion despite the fiercest repression. When Adams went there with Clarence King, he too took up the cause, writing to Hay, "Come and revolute Cuba." Soon his house in Washington became a haven for Cuban leaders, and he helped prepare Senator Cameron's resolution of American support as he had earlier coached the senator in the silver fight.

When France was riven by the bitter factional struggles over the Dreyfus case, Adams closed ranks with the conservative members of his Paris circle who regarded the defense of Dreyfus as part of a Jewish conspiracy to discredit the army and the Catholic church. His anti-Semitism became so extravagant that his friend Hay remarked that when Adams "saw Vesuvius reddening the midnight air he searched the horizon to find a Jew stoking the fire."

Adams' distaste and fear of public notice and his protective habit of self-depreciation kept him in flight from his duties as president of the American Historical Association, an honor to which he had been elected in his absence. To escape making his address at the Washington meeting in 1894, he pleaded absence in Mexico and sent "The Tendency of History" to be read at the annual meeting. In it he warned that historians must now create a science of history which would fix with certainty "the path which human society has got to follow." He also warned of a desperate impasse, for such a science would be opposed by every powerful vested interest of Church, State, and Labor.

As he became more and more involved behind the scenes in politics, his "breakfasts" attracted an array of foreign diplomats. The most significant political experience came with the appointment of John Hay as ambassador to England in February 1897. When he joined his friend in London, Adams took on the role of devil's advocate and, amidst hyperbolic and ironic chaff, provided Hay with wide-ranging global analyses. While he was touring Egypt with the Hays, news came of the sinking of the *Maine* on February 15, 1898. War broke out within a month. Sure of American superiority, Adams continued his travels alone into the eastern Mediterranean and on up to Vienna, filling his letters with vivid political and social perspectives against a background of global speculation.

The destruction of the Spanish fleets marked for Adams a decisive turning point in history because it presaged a major shift in the international balance of power. Back in England by June 1898, he proposed a generous peace plan to Hay; Hay responded that his own plan was "almost" like Adams'. At palatial Surrenden Dering, which Hay and Cameron had rented, Adams made himself at home and dispensed his learned and resourceful commentary on world affairs. Appointed secretary of state, Hay had to return to the United States. Adams soon followed, only to discover that, though Hay had thought to use his services in a diplomatic post, presidential prerogatives tied his hands. But if an active role in government was denied him, Adams' position as a privileged observer close to the center of power inspired a brilliant running commentary in his letters, whether written from Washington or from amidst his foreign travels.

The decade of the nineties ended with Adams off once again with congenial friends on a cultural reconnaissance of Sicily and Italy, avid for art and the picturesque. At the end of 1899 he settled once more in Paris and began serious study of the Middle Ages in France, "growing frightfully learned on French art of the Crusades." He was launched on the far-ranging study that would go into the making of *Mont Saint Michel and Chartres.*

To Elizabeth Cameron

Washington. Sunday, 5/6, '92.

You bring me blue, as Suzanne says.[1] How can you take an hour out of your few squeezed minutes, to write to me, when you might wait till you get to Beverly; and when you know that I am so well trained and whipped that I shall not complain if you wait forever? I think I will go back to the South Seas, for as a matter of fact I see more of you when I am there than when I am here, and get more satisfaction from your letters than from your dagoes and Dunns. My only satisfaction is that this time I am the one who takes life easiest. For once, I aint sayin' nothin'. Washington without you is commonplace enough, but so am I, and the two commonplaces get on like army mules together, even without you to drive them. While you were eating your 16th century dinner under the shadow of Diana,[2] I was modestly dining at home, or rather I was dining with the Roosevelts, Hays, and Ward Thoron, in their and your house, and going to hear the Gondoliers afterwards.[3] Was that Wednesday? What in the world did I do Thursday? I can remember only dimly—ah! Clarence King was here on his way to Florida where he is to pass a month in phosphate pits, with a certainty of getting a fever, a probability of getting a twelve foot rattlesnake into each of his boots, and a remote possibility of making a hundred thousand dollars. Of course we were together most of the day. Then Truxton and Arnold Hague dined with me, and discussed central Asia, and Becker, who had just blinded one eye with a ginger-ale cork, and is waiting to know whether the sight is lost or not.[4] Friday, after a hot day, I rode a new horse out to the Rock Creek Church to inspect my planting; then across through the wood to Saul's,[5] and having done with Saul I rode across through his fields to come out through the bars opposite the Argyle on the 14th St road near the Brightwood race-track, when my horse shied at a nigger, caught his hind-foot in a deep, muddy rut, and in half a second rolled over, catching my right leg under him. As we were going a slow walk through thick grass, no bones were broken, both of us were up in an instant, and I did not lose the bridle, but my ankle was bruised, and painful, and I had a pretty tough time getting home. Yesterday the ankle was inflamed and much too stiff for walking on. So I had to hop about on my left leg, or shove a chair before me. Yarrow has put me under a douche of Pond's Extract and hot water.⁶ Apparently the ankle is bruised only, but I am condemned to one-legged confinement for some days; possibly to a splint; certainly to a crutch; and of course I shall not think of traveling till my ankle is quite strong again. You may imagine me hobbling about my house for the next ten days at least, and you can also imagine with what regret I shall lose Constance's wedding.⁷ If any sceptic makes disrespectful remarks, you may assure him that my latest letter to you is written with a certain degree of bashful reticence because my right leg is on a chair, swathed in flannels and Ham-amelis. He may reply that it did not prevent my dining at the Country Club last night with the Hays, Herberts and Roosevelts, which is true, but I hopped there mostly on one leg, and could not possibly stay away seeing that your beloved Herberts were of the party.⁸ I am still waiting to catch the holy flame of affection for Mrs Herbert which your orders and example oblige me to burn. As yet she has said nothing to me that warranted mad devotion, and has only looked like pretty much all the other New York women I know. The type is to me one of the least attractive of all feminine types, but select specimens may be better than the average, and as I am obliged to accept your decision on such matters, I did the best I could last night to win her affections from Mungo. As it was your affair, not really mine, I hope that I hopped into her love. Of course the great excitement was Blaine's resignation. My ever-respected Great-grandfather, John Adams, some ninetyodd years ago, addressed to a distinguished predecessor of Mr Blaine, to wit: Timothy Pickering, a letter beginning: "As I perceive a necessity of introducing a change in the administration of the office of State";⁹ Blaine has judiciously reversed the proceeding; his letter runs: "As I perceive a necessity of introducing a change in the administration of the office of President." Both sides are greatly upset; Blaine's friends have lost their breath, and feel that at last the party has got to pay a pretty considerable bit of piping; Harrison's friends are outspoken in bitterness, and plainly say that Blaine always was a liar and traitor. Roosevelt dances from one to the other, and comes in gaily with the latest remarks of both sides. As for me, I adore H and toss my cap for Blaine without prejudice for Harrison, with a sad and increasing conviction that my own man, Gorman is to occupy the White House, and that H is lost.[10] Yet I had hoped some day to know one White House occupant;—but then even H would cheat me out of it by marrying a drunkard from a sense of duty before March 4.

Love to Mrs Gulliver.[11] Mind the burning of insect-powder if the mosquitoes get into the house.

MS: MHi

1. Suzanne Bancroft (Mrs. Charles) Carroll, granddaughter of historian George Bancroft, brought up in France.
2. Mrs. Cameron had dined in Sanford White's tower apartment in the Madison Square Garden building, which was crowned with Saint-Gaudens' statue of Diana.
3. Theodore Roosevelt (1858–1919), U.S. Civil Service Commission 1889–1895; Edith Kermit Roosevelt (1861–1948); Ward Thoron (1867–1938), young Washington lawyer. *The Gondoliers* (1889), by W. S. Gilbert and Sir Arthur Sullivan.
4. Arnold Hague (1840–1917) and George F. Becker (1847–1919), geologists with the U.S. Geological Survey.
5. John Saul (1819–1897), chairman of Washington Park Commission.
6. Harry C. Yarrow (1840–1929), a member of the medical faculty of George Washington University.
7. Constance Lodge (b. c. 1873), daughter of Henry Cabot Lodge and Anna Cabot Mills Lodge, married Augustus Peabody Gardner June 14, 1892.
8. Michael ("Mungo") Herbert (1857–1903), secretary of British legation; Lelia W. Herbert (d. 1923), a Tennessean, married Herbert in 1888.
9. Timothy Pickering (1745–1829), a political enemy of President John Adams. Blaine resigned suddenly as secretary of state to become a candidate for the presidency.
10. Senator Arthur P. Gorman (1839–1906), Maryland politician, a Democratic compromise candidate. "H" is Harriet Blaine.
11. Martha Cameron's nicknames for HA and herself were Mr. and Mrs. Gulliver.

To Charles W. Eliot

Private.

1603 H Street. Washington
12 June, 1892.

My dear Mr Eliot[1]

Your private note of the 9th has given me much tribulation. You know that for ten years past I have not appeared in the world, even so much as in a drawing-room; and the idea of facing a crowd of friends and acquaintances in order to receive a distinction troubles me more than you, who are used to such things, will readily believe.

Yet such an invitation from the College is in my eyes so nearly a command that I should face the ordeal without hesitation if I were not distressed by another and more practical difficulty. The College is singularly sparing, not to say jealous in its distinctions. Anyone on whom it confers its honors stands before the public much in the attitude of a successful candidate to the French Academy; he tacitly assumes to be the first in his profession. I cannot accept such a situation. The public would infallibly consider the degree to be given, whatever might be the expressed motive, for work done in American History; and the public, I think justly, would regard it as favoritism. I cannot stand alone before a great crowd of people, in such a position. The mere attitude would, in my conscience, be impertinent. No work of mine warrants it in itself; and still less when compared with other contemporary work. Indeed, in my opinion, the College should long ago have conferred degrees on the authors of what I consider far the first work on American history in popular and political importance that has appeared in my time; I mean the Life of Lincoln. If I am in error, you can correct me, but as far as my literary knowledge goes, no great man of any time in any country has ever had from his contemporaries a biography that will compare with this whether in scope, taste or literary execution. Nothing that I have ever done, or ever shall do, will hold its own beside portions of the Lincoln, as for example the account of Gettysburg. The admirable character of the work, which raises it above all books of the kind; the subject, peculiarly interesting to Harvard College; the opportunity to testify respect for the fame and character of Lincoln; the chance for once to escape from the circle of University limitations, and to take a lead in guiding popular impressions; all these motives struck me as overwhelming in dictating recognition of the history. I could not without positive shame put myself in a position where I should seem to countenance the idea that any work of mine compared in importance either of purpose, of moral value, or of public interest to the singularly noble and American character of this monument to the greatest man of our time.

With Hay and Nicolay beside me I could stand up before public criticism, but alone I cannot. Please reflect on this, and give me advice. This letter is not meant for communication to the Board.

Ever truly Yrs   Henry Adams.

MS: MH-Ar

1. Charles W. Eliot (1834–1926), president of Harvard University 1869–1909. The university had invited HA to accept an honorary degree. His personal presence would be required.

To Charles F. Thwing

Fayerweather St., Cambridge.
1 July, 1892

My dear Scholar[1]

Many thanks for your very kind letter. Among the things one has attempted to do in life, that upon which I think we shall look back in a future existence with the most surprise and amusement will be the attempt to teach. To my fancy, as one looks back on life, it has only two responsibilities, which include all others: one is the bringing new life into existence; the other, educating it after it is brought in. All betrayals of trust result from these original sins. As you know, I accepted the responsibility of education, and the result of seven years experience was to satisfy me that all forms of education were necessarily wrong, and that my utmost hope must be that on the whole I had done no more harm than might probably have been done by the person who would have taught if I had not. Any evidence to that effect, like your letter, is *pro tanto,* a relief to my mind, especially since you were one of my most willing victims, and might fairly bear me a grudge, if anyone did.

The Degree is another matter. For that, I am in no way responsible, and can accept it without rousing internal questions of my own ignorance or errors. For that, I feel no self-reproach, and no thought but gratitude for your good opinion.

Ever truly Yours   Henry Adams.

Rev. Charles F. Thwing D.D.

MS: OCIW

1. Charles F. Thwing (1853–1937), president of Western Reserve University, had once been a student under HA at Harvard. Hay, a trustee and benefactor, had proposed HA for an honorary degree of doctor of laws. HA's attendance was not required.

To Samuel P. Langley

1603 H Street. 3 May, 1893.

My dear Mr Langley[1]

Many thanks for remembering the demon.[2] He is not much of a demon, after all, and leaves me about as much in the dark as before he sorted.

The trouble is in my brain, which does not sort. I cannot drive the kinetic theory into it. "The molecules of all bodies," says Maxwell, "are in a state of continual agitation. The hotter a body is, the more violently are its molecules agitated."[3] Conversely, the colder a body is, the less violently are its molecules agitated, until, in a body actually deprived of heat, the molecules cannot agitate at all, which contradicts the first of Maxwell's assertions.

Evidently I am wrong there. Yet if I am a sorting demon, and take a molecule deprived of heat, I cannot sort, under Maxwell's law, without putting more and more heat into it.

Clearly Maxwell must mean that every molecule must have a definite minimum of heat inherent in it as matter. That is, the molecule is the heat plus other forms of energy, of matter.

Yet I am obviously wrong there too, for I understand that the kinetic theory contemplates the total dissipation of energy in any body as a necessary consequence of waste.

Or is only the surface energy dissipated, and does the internal energy remain? Does the kinetic theory assume that the energy due to the translation of the molecule as a whole can be totally dissipated without dissipating the internal energy of the molecule?

This would merely bring the difficulty down one stage, and renew it on subdividing the molecule into its atoms. A molecule would be a sort of closed vessel or box, with the same problem inside it; but the idea itself seems repugnant to the laws of the kinetic theory, as it seems to require that the superficial surface of every molecule should be a non-conductor of any form of energy.

A molecule of hydrogen gas is now bouncing about in the nebula of Orion. As I understand, it is not the molecule of a "body"; it is free. "The hotter a body is, the more violently are its molecules agitated," but in the nebula molecule there is no question of a "body," and the surrounding temperature of space is presumed to have been −450° from eternity. How then does the molecule bounce?

Granting that it bounces, surely it must (on Maxwell's doctrine of the relation of bounce to heat) bounce with very little violence in a temperature of −450°.

Granting that it bounces with such energy as to radiate heat and light on coming in contact with another molecule, or even to radiate without impact, how is the energy thus wasted to be made good?

Supposing it to be lost, what is the status of the molecule. Obviously in a series of years, say twenty million, at the observed rate of dissipation of energy, many molecules must be dead. Maxwell gives me no definition of a dead molecule. I do not remember that Thompson deals with the subject;[4] yet a dead molecule must be something very different from a living molecule.

I am quite aware that in reality the dead molecule is really myself, and that is the reason why I am so stupid, and cannot bounce "violently" enough to understand the kinetic theory; but that was my starting-point.

Yrs truly   Henry Adams.

MS: RPB

1. Samuel Pierpont Langley (1834–1906), astronomer, secretary of the Smithsonian Institution 1887–1906.
2. HA is referring to the "sorting demon," a figure of speech used by physicist James Clerk Maxwell (1831–1879) to describe the random behavior of heat molecules irreversibly passing from a hotter body to a cooler one.
3. *Theory of Heat*, 3rd ed. (1872), p. 286.
4. William Thomson, Lord Kelvin (1824–1907), "The Sorting Demon of Maxwell," in *Popular Lectures and Addresses*, I (1889), 137–141.

To Franklin MacVeagh

1603 H Street. 26 May, 1893

My dear Mr. McVeagh[1]

During my flying visit to Chicago last week I took the single hour unoccupied by sight-seeing to call on you and Mrs. MacVeagh.[2] She was kind enough to hunt us up, and leave a note which we answered by telegraph. Having now partially recovered from the journey, I write to thank Mrs. MacVeagh for her kindness, and to explain that Senators are inexorable, and that our party was highly senatorial.[3]

Although this is the only proper cause of my writing, I have more to say than you would care to read on the Exhibition itself. You have known from the first all that was to be said. On me it dawned suddenly, and my two days were hardly enough to take it in. Indeed the mental excitement and disturbance have upset my usual balance so much that I am not yet quite willing to trust myself to talk or write on the subject. A man who has passed his life, and has come well to the limit of activity of his generation, always thinking and despairing of seeing his age rise to the creation of new art, or the appreciation of the old, cannot all of a sudden see his idea take shape in a form far more magnificent than he had ever dreamed it, without being for the moment stunned by the shock. Though I have lived among the men who are doing this work, and though I thought I knew their powers as well as their limits, I never supposed they could have risen to a level so high as this.[4] They have exceeded their own powers with humbleness of heart and contriteness of spirit. I feel grateful to them for letting me run along by their side, and babble in infantile wonder.

If I was upset by the shock of seeing what my friends and contemporaries could do in art, you may imagine my incredulous bewilderment at seeing the attitude of Chicago. As I returned from the first visit to the Fair, every building in Chicago seemed to me to be twice the height it was before.[5] I was crushed flat. The very winds became sarcastic and sardonic. I supposed I knew that Chicago could do business and make money, but I was not prepared to have her turn on me on my own ground, and tell me that she would now give me a little lesson of modesty, and would teach me something that was not business but beauty. Even you, who are of it, must admit that no matter-of-fact human being could have imagined that Chicago would suddenly, without apparent cause or consequence, lavish millions on millions of money, and infinite effort, in order to produce something that the Greeks might have delighted to see, and Venice would have envied, but which certainly is not business.[6] That Chicago, of all places, should turn on us, with this sort of defiant contempt, and fling its millions into our faces, in order to demonstrate to us that we understand neither business nor art, was not to be expected; but I admit that the demonstration is complete.

In short, as you may infer from my remarks, I returned from Chicago a wiser and a gladder man. Although I sail for Europe June 3, I hope to return to pass October in Chicago. More than ever I feel that I ought to have taken that house. Perhaps I can still get one for October. I would crawl back on my venerable legs rather than not see again the only work my age has produced really worthy of it.

Ever yrs   Henry Adams.

Source: typescript, MHi

1. Franklin MacVeagh (1842–1934), Wayne MacVeagh's younger brother, head of a leading Chicago wholesale grocery firm.
2. Emily Eames MacVeagh, sister of Sen. James Donald Cameron.
3. HA went to the World's Columbian Exposition as a guest of Senator and Mrs. Cameron in a private railroad car that arrived in Chicago on Saturday, May 20.
4. Richard Morris Hunt, Charles F. McKim, Stanford White, and Louis Sullivan were the principal architects. Frederick Law Olmsted landscaped the fairgrounds. The sculptors Augustus Saint-Gaudens, Daniel Chester French, and Frederick MacMonnies and the muralists Francis D. Millet and Kenyon Cox were the foremost artists. The Chicago architect Daniel H. Burnham organized and supervised the design, construction, and decoration of the exposition. Charles B. Atwood, New York architect, was designer-in-chief.
5. Over the past ten years, Chicago architects had pioneered in skeletal steel construction and had built, in the concentrated downtown area, some twenty of the first modern skyscrapers.
6. Burnham achieved the Parian glow of the "White City," as the exposition was called, by sheathing the buildings in plaster of paris and by the use of electric lighting on a large scale. Olmsted created a Venetian effect with lagoons, fountains, and bridges.

To John Hay

Quincy, 12 Aug. '93

Dear and Envied Mortal

You are mighty lucky to be out of this howling madhouse. I got here last Monday after a wet and dismal, but calm and foggy voyage; and I found Boston standing on its head, wild with terror, incapable of going to bed and brushing its weary old tusks in the morning; all this only because no one could get any money to meet his notes. As I had no notes to meet, and on inquiry found I had plenty of money for a year ahead, I was not inclined to join the dance, and retired here to wait until it is over, as it must soon be; for our stocks are all low, and another month will exhaust them.

We are sound, and in another six months we will be on our legs again. I am now watching with immense curiosity to see whether it will be the same with England. The more I think about it, the more I suspect that England is in truth insolvent, and is going into bankruptcy this time forever. This is pretty startling, and would sound more absurd to most Americans than to many an Englishman. We shall soon see. England has tried her best to save herself by squeezing us, and forcing up the price of gold on all her debtors. The squeeze has beggared us for the moment, but we have now got the squeeze on her. We shall see how she stands it. My belief is that the old bully will go on her knees.[1]

True, I am pretty mad about it. In fact, I am furious, and in no frame of mind to be judicial or historical. I am intensely curious, too, for I think we may be on the verge of a general collapse of the social fabric in Europe. I doubt whether Europe can stand what we are enduring, and if she has it at all, she will have to stand a strain much more severe. We have never seen such a prolonged or so intense a pressure since our society existed. It will be nip and tuck with us to keep order if it lasts over the year. What strains our social arrangements to the dangerous point, ought to break Europe all up. You will have the fun of seeing it; but don't get caught! Rome and Paris and London may yet be uncomfortable places before another year is out.

Am I scared? Well, I just am; about the scaredest man you know. I was scared last November; I was scareder last May; and I have gone on getting more and more scared ever since. For America I am now a bull; I would back the rise freely, if I were in that line; but I am in a blue funk for Europe, and fully expect a grand collapse there, financial, social, political and moral.

Other news I have none. The dogdays rage, and I stay as quiet as possible in the house all day. Quincy is just the most solitudinous spot on earth, and I feel not the faintest wish to see anyone in it or out of it. My sister Ann is not at Washington with her Pinkie,[2] but Nahant, where gentlemen daily commit suicide off her rocks by walking into the water with their clothes and hats on.[3] My sister-in-law, with whom I pass half my time,— and who is unwell just now, rather to our uneasiness as we don't know what ails her—keeps me informed.

Love to all yours.   Ever   H.A.

MS: RPB

1. HA had been summoned home from Europe by his brother Brooks to help the family deal with the effects of the worldwide financial panic on their investments. By Aug. 12 the outflow of gold from the U.S. had been checked, and British and European investments in the U.S. had reversed the international exchanges.
2. Mrs. Lodge's nickname for Henry Cabot Lodge.
3. The *Boston Daily Advertiser* had reported that a prominent shoe manufacturer had committed suicide in this way on the Lodges' property at Nahant.

To Wayne MacVeagh

Old House. Quincy.
31 August, 1893.

Dear MacVeagh

My brother Brooks tells me that, when Quincy leaves the State Department, as he has announced his intention of doing,[1] he (Brooks) intends to suggest his own name to the President for the appointment of Assistant Secretary of State, with such support as he may be able to obtain from the Democratic leaders of Massachusetts. His chief difficulty seems to be want of acquaintance and relations with Secretary Gresham;[2] and knowing that you are personally acquainted with the Secretary, he has asked me to consult you, and if possible obtain your support.

You know how little I mix in such matters, and for more than one reason I doubt whether any interference or appearance of mine would help a candidate for that position. I am acquainted neither with the President nor with Secretary Gresham. I am far from eager to place any member of my family in office in Washington. But if Brooks wishes for the opportunity of serving, I am free to say that he is better equipped for the office than any other person I can suggest; that his abilities are, I believe, sufficiently well known to need no guaranty of mine; and that, whether socially or officially, he would probably be a distinctly useful, and perhaps even a very valuable, assistant to the Secretary.

I do not know whether any such considerations, or any considerations at all, will warrant you in offering your assistance, or in acting as an ally in the matter, but if you are on such terms with Secretary Gresham that you can write him a note in support of Brooks's appointment, I am inclined to think that your aid might be of great service to the candidate. At all events Brooks thinks so, and I should think so, in the same position.

Next to success in the attempt, Brooks's chief anxiety is to escape newspaper notice. In that, I warmly agree with him, and therefore beg you will consider the matter as confidential between the Secretary and the sufferers. One is badly enough off when one is a candidate for anything, without newspapers to make it worse.

Give my love to Mrs MacVeagh and your daughter. The times are rough enough to bring us together before long.

Ever Yrs   Henry Adams

Hon. Wayne MacVeagh.

MS: PHi

1. Josiah Quincy (1859–1919), prominent Democrat, mayor of Boston 1895–1899.
2. Walter Quintin Gresham (1832–1895) of Indiana, secretary of state 1893–1895. Both Gresham and MacVeagh had left the Republican party in 1892 to support Cleveland.

To John Hay

1603 H Street. 18 Oct. 1893.

Dearly beloved

Your letter from Paris, October 5, reached me yesterday on my return from Chicago where I have just passed a fortnight. For a poor old ghost like me, just barely hovering on this earth for which my ethereal nature unfits me, the Midway Plaisance was a sweet repose. I revelled in all its fakes and frauds, all its wickedness that seemed not to be understood by our innocent natives, and all its genuineness which was understood still less. I labored solemnly through all the great buildings and looked like an owl at the dynamos and steam-engines. All the time I kept up a devil of a thinking. You know the tenor of my thought, so I will spare you; but if we ever write those Travels of ours, I've a volume or two to put in for the Fair. I want to talk among other matters about the architecture, and discuss the question of the true relation between Burnham, Attwood, McKim, White, Millett, &c, and the world. Do you remember Sargent's portrait of Mrs Hamersly in London this summer?[1] Was it a defiance or an insult to our society, or a rendering in good faith of our civilisation, or a conscious snub to French and English art, or an unconscious revelation of the artist's despair of reconciliation with the female of the gold-bug?[2] I say the female, because the male has been the butt of the artist for centuries. Well! the Chicago architecture is precisely an architectural Mrs Hamersly. I like to look at it as an appeal to the human animal, the superstitious and ignorant savage within us, that has instincts and no reason, against the world as money has made it. I have seen a faint gleam of intelligence lighten the faces even of the ignorant rich, and almost penetrate the eyes of a mugwump and Harvard College graduate, as he brooded, in his usual stolidity of self-satisfaction, on his own merits, before the Court of Honor.[3] Never tell me to despair of our gold-bugs after this; we can always drown them. Burnham, Stanford White, Millett, and the rest, are a little more violent than I. They rather want to torture the very Chicago gold-bugs who have given them the money, beginning with Higginbotham.[4] As for me, I was always humane. I would only drown them without torture, or electrocute them with their own dynamos, painlessly. The mugwump, I admit, is a difficulty; death cannot end his self-esteem; but even Gilder ought to be treated without vindictive feelings.[5] Besides, he has been already flayed alive by the Sun and Tribune, and really means well, and is a cherub.

I came back at midnight, Monday evening, to plunge into a bath of boiling politics. You never lost so much as in missing this silver fight. During the fortnight of my absence, matters have grown irretrievably worse. Cleveland has driven on the passions of the Senate until we are in a really dangerous temper. I fully expect that some one will be killed, unless the situation is immediately relieved. My dear democracy is all in pieces; not a rag of decency is left. Every debate is a four-sided fight; the republican attacks the democrat; the eastern democrat flies at the throat of the western democrat; all three then attack Cleveland. Yesterday John Sherman just danced on Morgan and Hill, while Morgan and Hill were rolling round, gouging each other; and all of them were wild to burn Cleveland alive.[6] The poor mugwumps are the unhappiest of all. They have, with their accustomed simplicity of soul, chosen poor Van Alen as their peculiar grievance, and we are told that Schurz has forced Harper's Weekly to declare war on Cleveland for this awful iniquity—after swallowing Garland and Joe Quincy and Maxwell, and the Lord only knows what iniquities of patronage to buy Voorhees and his brother senators.[7] Wall Street and its various ramifications are howling for a *coup d'état* in the Senate. Cleveland is trying to effect one. The silver-men challenge it. Oh, cock-a-doodle-doo! if I were not a pessimist and a fatalist, a populist, a communist, a socialist, and the friend of a humorist, where would I be at?

As I can see nothing but universal bankruptcy before the world, whatever way it turns, and whatever standard it prefers in which to reckon the balance-sheet of its insolvency, I take little stock either in gold, silver or paper, except that I want all I can get of them all; and most cool men, like those who run the Sun, the Tribune, and such conservative sheets, seem to hold the same view; but with Cleveland for President, and Populism as my only refuge after he has kicked me out of the Democratic party, my toes are getting cold with a very familiar sensation of being shut out-doors in the blizzard.

Socially, too, I am likely to be left alone. You are gone. During my absence at Chicago, Mrs Sherman died, and Mrs Cameron returned only yesterday from the funeral at Cleveland.[8] I have not yet had time to talk with her, but I've no doubt she will go to St Helena for the winter. Arnold Hague has convulsed society by announcing his marriage on the 14th November next to Mrs Walter Howe, or something of that kind; a widow of New York, known to Teddy and the wives of various people; said to be well off in gold and interest-bearing bonds; and a drowned husband at Newport two years ago.[9] So Arnold is lost. Ward Thoron is dropped the next day; so my sole young lover disappears from my stage. Even Rebecca Rae has migrated with all her live-stock, to Annapolis to teach school at the Academy.[10] Except Loonatic Phillips and Loonatic Teddy and Senator Loonatic Cabot, I have no one left;[11] and these three Loons do not make a winter.

Of King I hear nothing. His bank busted with the rest, and I fear he has gone under. Frank Emmons, too, is busted.[12] The Fortieth Parallel always had the devil's bad luck, and yet Arnold Hague marries. The ruin has, I fear, not yet fairly begun, and will not be fully known till the Chicago Fair is closed, and business becomes settled on the bottom-mud.

I have looked into your house to see your windows, which are exquisite.[13] Perhaps after all, I will accept your offer, and move into your house, just to live with the windows. Better than widows, anyhow.

If not that, you may see me any day. If you will go with me to the Taj, telegraph, and I will start within four-and-twenty hours.

Love to all yours   Ever   H. Taura

MS: RPB

1. Portrait of Mary Grant (Mrs. Hugh) Hammersley, by John Singer Sargent (1856–1925).
2. HA applied the epithet "gold-bug" to members of the financial and commercial community who insisted that gold be the sole basis of international and domestic exchange.
3. The architectural center of the fair.
4. Harlow N. Higinbotham (1838–1919), president of the World's Columbian Exposition Association and partner in Marshall Field & Co., Chicago's leading department store.
5. Richard Watson Gilder (1844–1909), editor of the *Century*.
6. Sen. John T. Morgan (1824–1907) of Alabama supported the free coinage of silver against Sen. David B. Hill (1843–1910) of New York in the bitter Oct. debate.
7. James J. Van Alen (1846–1923), heavy contributor to Cleveland's campaign, resigned his appointment as ambassador to Italy when he was accused of bargaining for the office. Carl

Schurz was now the editorial writer for *Harper's Weekly*. Augustus H. Garland (1832–1899) of Arkansas, former attorney general; Robert A. Maxwell (1838–1912) of New York, fourth assistant postmaster general. Daniel W. Voorhees (1827–1897), Democratic senator from Indiana, though known as a strong silver man, cast the deciding vote in committee for repeal of the Silver Purchase Act.

8. Eliza Williams Sherman, Elizabeth Cameron's mother, had died Oct. 1.
9. Mary Robins Howe (d. 1922) was the widow of Walter Howe, who drowned at Newport in Aug. 1890.
10. Rebecca Dodge Rae, wife of Lt. Charles Rae, U.S.N. (1847–1908).
11. William H. Phillips (1853–1897), international lawyer, a Washington companion of HA.
12. Samuel Franklin Emmons (1841–1911), former Quincy neighbor, geologist with the Fortieth Parallel Survey.
13. Two stained-glass windows made by John La Farge for Hay's dining room.

To John Hay

Dos Bocas. Santiago de Cuba
27 February, 1894.

Querido[1]

Doubtless letters from you are wandering somewhere over the infinitudes, and will strike me when the sure revolutions of the world permit it; but since I wrote you from Tampa, on the 3d, I have seen no portion of human vanities like letter-posts, and, except for news of you, I can dispense with them still for a term or terms. King and I carried out our project of going to Havana. We had a lovely trip across, and found Havana as noisy, dirty, and fascinating as ever, although King, as usual, goes on protesting that the ideal negro-woman is mas allá, lejos,[2]—not at Havana, which is a wretched worn-out wreck of anæmic horror, but at Santiago de Cuba, where the charming little plaza is the evening resort of five hundred exquisite females, lovely as mulatto lilies and graceful as the palm-tree whose height—of a hundred feet—they rival. Of course I said, as I always say, that there happiness lay, and we would go. In truth we had to go somewhere, and unless we went to Mexico, no other resort than the east end of Cuba seemed open to the prows of swift ships. Havana knows no neighbors except Florida and Vera Cruz. So in the depths of night, on the 11th, we took a dim train, and started for the Southern Cross, which was the only guide in sight. In two brief hours we crossed Cuba to Batabano, and took the coasting steamer Josefita, on which we passed four days, chiefly among mangrove islands, but occasionally at sea in the trade-wind which is my nightmare from oceans of unforgotten seasickness. Our company on board was Cuban of the commonest, in which I become wildly patriotic, but it was glorified by the presence of a really great, though physically small, hero, el famoso espada, Minuto. To my surprise, King did not embrace him—or anyone else. Yet Minuto, when not drunk, or seasick, was an amusing little cuss; talked brightly, sang pleasantly, and had a very intelligent face. My dexterity with the idioma of Andalucia was not as remarkable as his with the bulls of the same, so I had to hold aloof and study the phrase-book. Our voyage brought us ashore at various places, Cienfuegos, Trinidad, Manzanillo, etcetera, until we left our mangrove sea, and plunged into the howling gale that prances off Cabo Cruz, and accompanied us all night until we found repose in the harbor of Santiago de Cuba before dawn Thursday morning.

This happy home, so long desired, was my yearned-for heaven, with five hundred mulatto houris on its plaza in mantillas. As soon as I could get on my clothes in the dark, I hurried ashore, and King threw me into a carriage. We ascended darkly some streets to the plaza. At five o'clock in the morning I did not expect to see many beautiful women, but we did count on rooms in the hotel. Nada! For an hour we drove from one door to another, until we had hammered loudly on most of the doors of the small city, begging for rooms which were denied us, until at last we bowed our heads and entered the inn of the Telegraph, where I would have had you see us. We discussed at some length which of us was Don Quijote and which was Sancho. The inn needed no discussion. For dirt, noise and smell, it out-spaniarded Castile and Leon.

I was rather disturbed at the situation, for Cuba had done King no visible good. Getting little sleep, no food to speak of, and infernal noise day and night, sometimes does temporarily incommode Bloomingdale patients. Otherwise he was all right, or as bright and straight as ever he was, which, as I told him, meant nothing, since he ought to have been sent to Bloomingdale in early youth, and kept there, along with my other friends and myself. Staying in Santiago was impossible. My only chance was to hire a house in the suburbs. We hunted up Ramsden the British Consul, an old friend of King's, one of the British firm of Brooks &Co.[3] Ramsden was civil and asked us to breakfast for the next morning. We took meals at the Restaurant Venus, on the Plaza, and sat there, on the Plaza, with lizards up our legs and down our necks, while the band played, and the five hundred beautiful women did not come. Not a one! King was broke up. He had lived only on this dream of unfair women,[4] and he could not believe it was thin air. Not a one! Not a mantilla! Not a laugh or a glance to gladden our united hundred and eight years. It was a case of befo' the woh. I need not add that, as usual, it was a case of mas allá, and muchissimo lejosisimos. Our next jump into the infinite must be a thousand miles of trade-wind to Martinique or Domenica where all the women were notoriously even handsomer than at Santiago.

Ramsden saved us. We laid our desperate situation before him and his wife at breakfast the next morning. We must get a house in the country! Within a few hours, we had our choice. We chose the country-house of his partner, Ernest Brooks, an elderly Englishman with a Jamaica-Cuban-Mobilian wife. We moved up here on Monday, the 19th. For a pantomimic transformation scene, my travels have rarely matched it. Dos Bocas is absolutely delightful. It is a narrow mountain valley, with no water-view, but the air, the temperature, the mountains, the walks, the repose, the palms and the views, are enough to make life what it ought to be. True, we have not found a satisfactory type of female perfection. The ideal nigger-woman is mas allá. She is now geographically vague. We have not settled on her next residence. We are to take a short trip next month through Hayti, Porto Rico, St Kitts, Nevis, Domenica, Martinique, and South America, returning through Mexico, certain to find her there anyhow, because King knows her well in Central America and Mexico. Meanwhile, having heard this vision for the last twenty years, I cultivate my garden, and try to sketch our orange-trees, pomegranates and palms. I would read Candide, but the Brooks children seem to have been allowed to read no satire except your detestable and ribald novel Democracy which glared at me from the shelf at my first entrance. King seems now quite well; sleeps, tramps for hours, and is almost contented sometimes to be quiet.

Love to all Yrs.   Ever   H.

MS: RPB

1. *Querido:* beloved.
2. *Más allá, lejos:* further, much further away.
3. Frederick Ramsden (1839–1898), British consul for the province of Santiago da Cuba.
4. An allusion to Tennyson's "A Dream of Fair Women" (1832).

To Charles Milnes Gaskell

1603 H Street. 28 April, 1894.

My dear Carlo

I found your letter of April 11 waiting me here last Monday, when I arrived at my house after four months absence in the south. The spirit of unrest which drives me from one form of seasickness to another has hunted me this season through Cuba and the Bahamas, regions mostly new to me, and with much that has amused me immensely. One effect of years I can now take as constant. I love the tropics, and feel really at ease nowhere else. A good, rotten tropical Spanish island, like Cuba, with no roads and no drainage, but plenty of bananas and brigands, never bores me. Your

Consul at Santiago, a very good fellow named Ramsden—of the Yorkshire Ramsdens, I think—borrowed a country-house for us at Santiago, and made our winter possible. King and I geologised and lived on cocidas and frijoles without destroying our digestions, and I pretty much made up my mind to buy a coffee plantation somewhere in the Antilles, and to abandon all further pretence of civilisation. Every time I come back to what we are pleased to call civilised life, it bores me more, and seems to me more hopelessly idiotic; and, as I do not care to imitate Carlyle and Ruskin and Emerson and all the rest of our protesting philosophers by trying to make a living by abusing the society of my time, nothing remains but to quit it, and seek another. I am satisfied that Pearson is right, and that the dark races are gaining on us, so that we may depend on their steadily shutting down on us, as they have already done in Haiti, and are doing throughout the West Indies and our southern States.[1] In another fifty years, at the same rate of movement, the white races will have to reconquer the tropics by war and nomadic invasion, or be shut up, north of the fortieth parallel. I know that with our fatuous self-esteem, our newspapers admire themselves too much to admit their own possible inferiority to niggers without newspapers; but as I rather prefer niggers to whites, and much prefer oriental art to European, I incline to make the most of the tropics while the white is still tolerated there.

My return here is not of a sort to discourage these notions. If ever one saw an enormous exhibition of imbecility, we give it here. We dont know what is the matter with us, yet we all admit that we have had a terrific shock of some sort. We see no reason at all for assuming that the causes, whatever they are, which have brought about the prostration, have ceased, or will cease, to act. On the contrary, as far as we can see, if anything is radically wrong, it must grow worse, for it must be in our system itself, and at the bottom of all modern society. If we are diseased, so is all the world. Everyone is discussing, disputing, doubting, economising, going into bankruptcy, waiting for the storm to pass, but no sign of agreement is visible as to what has upset us, or whether we can cure the disease. That the trouble is quite different from any previous experience, pretty much everyone seems to admit; but nobody diagnoses it. Probably, in a year or two, we shall pick ourselves up again, and go ahead, but we shall know no better what hit us. To judge from what I can gather from the Economist and other European sources of financial wisdom, Europe is rather more in the dark than we are. Europe and Asia are used to accepting disease and death as inevitable, but to us the idea is a new one. We want to know what is wrong with the world that it should suddenly go to smash without visible cause or possible advantage. Here, in this young, rich continent, capable of supporting three times its population with ease, we have had a million men out of employment for nearly a year, and the situation growing worse rather than better. Society here, as well as in Europe, is shaking, yet we have no bombs, no violence, and no wars to fear. I prefer my Cuba, which is frankly subsiding into savagery. At least the problems there are simple.

Thus far I have not suffered. As well as I know, I have not lost a dollar either in capital or income. Of course this cannot last. Probably within another year, I shall feel the shrinkage. At present I feel it only through others, and chiefly in the form of physical collapse. All my brothers have gone, or are on their way, to Europe for rest. They need it. Men of sixty wear out fast under steady anxiety. Edward Hooper has also gone over, probably for the same reason, although he says nothing of his health.[2] My friend La Farge is with him, also for health, although collapse in his case is not due to finance, I suppose. Clarence King woke up one day to find himself in Bloomingdale Asylum. He stayed there some weeks, till the congestion of his fifth or fifteenth or fiftieth vertebra subsided, and then went with me to Cuba. He is still with me, never better, but dreading return to New York and care. These private instances of the collapse would not bother me so much except that I feel the same unhealthy exciteability and worry in society, high and low, rich and poor, industrial, financial and political. Moreton Frewen is rushing about, quite out of character, with feverish activity to cure creation.[3] Spring Rice is furious with Frewen. Sir Julian Pauncefote has taken to gout and worry.[4] Young Ford, our old friend Clare Ford's son, has exasperated one set of women by going off to Cuba with a certain Lady de Clifford.[5] Don't quote me! Your embassy looks dark at the mention of their names, and mysteriously solemn. I presume they talk tariff, but when I heard the lady talk last, her care seemed to be tarpons,—which are fish. They make me tired, all the same. My favorite girls, too, have all got married—which is a bore.

Never mind! We have had our little day.

Love to you all.   Henry Adams.

I agree with you about Lowell's letters. They are deadly.[6] But what letters are not, now? Do tell me of a new book.

MS: MHi

1. Charles Henry Pearson, *National Life and Character: A Forecast* (1893).
2. Edward William Hooper (d. 1901), HA's brother-in-law, treasurer of Harvard 1876–1898.
3. Moreton Frewen (1853–1924), British entrepreneur, bimetalist, silver and tariff lobbyist in Washington.
4. Sir Julian Pauncefote (1828–1902), British ambassador to the U.S.
5. John Ford (d. 1917), attaché at the British embassy in Washington 1893, was the son of Sir Francis Clare Ford (1830–1899), ambassador to Italy 1893–1898. Lady de Clifford

was Hilda Balfour Russell (1861–1895), widow of Edward Southwell Russell, 24th Baron de Clifford, who had died at Monte Carlo on April 6.
6. *Letters of James Russell Lowell*, ed. Charles Eliot Norton (1894).

To Elizabeth Cameron

1603 H Street. 13 July, 1894.

A week hence I hope to be at St Paul, and in a fortnight deep in the Yellowstone country. So do not look for letters. If I had anything to write about, perhaps it would be worth while, but although Washington and New York are now very pleasant cities, as the people are all away, they afford less to tell. We are hot again and burned dry. I have dined once or twice at the Chevy Chase Inn for a change. Once the Endicotts took me there.[1] Mostly I stay in my house and read Cicero and other gold-bug literature of Rome, not in the original, I am sorry to say, but in Mr Bohn's veracious translations.[2] Generally I dine at the Club, and see queer, stray, people, like myself. Two days ago, it was Joe Quincy. Cabot and Theodore are at home. Springy is still with Theodore. Sir Julian remains, but the Pattens go away next week, as I hear from Lotty who was here last evening.[3] I hope your husband is also away. The last week has been more than usually awkward for politicians. Cleveland has won another colossal victory for his friends the gold-bugs; a greater than his silver triumph, for he has settled the working-man forever. Now that the gold-bug has drunk blood, and has seen that the government can safely use the army to shoot socialists, the wage-question is as good as settled. Of course we silver men will be shot next, but for the moment, the working-men are worse off than we.[4] Of course, too, the Senate has unanimously approved of Cleveland. I hope your husband was not there, for, to my mind, the men who endorsed Cleveland made the gravest kind of a blunder. The proof is that the House did not dare do it. Bellamy Storer introduced the Resolution, but so many members of both parties came to him to beg him to desist, that he had to do so.[5] This I learn from Rockhill and Phillips.[6] Of course every gold-bug in the country, and all the newspapers are radiant and violent in support of Cleveland. Indeed I am very much inclined to think that his second great victory settles everything. The gold-bug has got us cold. For my part, I do not object. I never think it good sense to try to reverse the processes of nature, and my idea of politics is to hasten rather than retard results. Silver is really in the interests of money, and would prolong indefinitely the money-lender's reign, whereas gold is fatal to it. Were you, in your former lives, ever acquainted with one Midas, a Greek banker, who has typified the gold-bug for three thousand years? If not, look him up in your Ovid, in the 11th Book of Metamorphoses, lines 90 to 190. "Ille male usurus"— that outrageous usurer—turned everything to gold, and had asses ears; two infallible signs of a banker. Bacchus kindly gave him free silver, and saved his life and ears. I am no Bacchus, and, if possible, would prefer to take his life and cut off his ears.

Your husband had better keep dead quiet now, till things take another turn. He is really helpless, and at most can only keep his head above water till time shall show whether we are to have a chance once more. Debs has smashed everything for the present. The working-man is so brilliant a political failure—so suicidal a political ally, that until he is dead and buried, the gold-bug must rule us. George M. Pullman and Andrew Carnegie and Grover Cleveland are our Crassus and Pompey and Caesar,—our proud American triumvirate, the types of our national mind and ideals.[7] We are under a sort of terror before them. The Senate bows down, and even I, who want not so much as a protective duty on my books, think life easier if I hold my tongue and let Midas's ears alone.

Luckily Carlisle and Ruskin and Thackeray and Mat. Arnold, as well as various other gentlefolk, have said all that the occasion requires, and my brother Brooks is always on hand. My riding is better by your leave. We start Wednesday;—John Hay and Del; Iddings, Phillips and I.[8] Let's hope we shall give pleasure to some of us.

MS: MHi

1. William Crowninshield Endicott, Jr. (1860–1936), Boston lawyer, son of the secretary of war; and his wife, Marie Thoron Endicott.
2. Henry Bohn (1796–1884), founder of Bohn's Classical Library.
3. Charlotte ("Lotty") Wise Hopkins (1851–1935), HA's cousin, a civic leader in Washington; the Patten sisters (Edythe, Mary, Josephine, and Helen) were active in Washington society.
4. The strike of the Pullman Car Workers in Chicago, led by Eugene V. Debs (1855–1926), was supported by the American Railway Union, of which Debs was president. It led to much rioting and paralyzed rail traffic. The strike was broken on July 10 by the intervention of federal troops. Debs was jailed. Converted to socialism, Debs thereafter ran five times as the Socialist candidate for president.
5. Bellamy Storer (1847–1922), Republican representative from Ohio. Cleveland secured the repeal of the Silver Purchase Act, thus ensuring the primacy of the gold standard in the currency system.
6. William Woodville Rockhill (1854–1914), policy adviser to the State Department, famed Tibetan explorer, minister to Greece 1897–1899.
7. George M. Pullman (1831–1897), president of the Pullman Car Co.; Andrew Carnegie (1835–1919), Scottish-born industrialist, a leader in the steel industry.
8. Adelbert Hay (1876–1901), son of John Hay; Joseph P. Iddings (1857–1920), recently with the U.S. Geological Survey. The party planned a camping trip to the Snake River and the Teton mountains.

To Sir Robert Cunliffe

Cuautla. Mexico. 8 Jan. 1895.

Beloved Barnet

Why you should suddenly occur to my mind just now, I do not know; but my conscience, which has been dull enough of late, wakes me up this morning with an order to write to tell you something—I don't know what.—Pax! I trust all still goes well in your pilgrimage. As I have been wandering, since Dec. 1, where letters could not follow me, and where telegraphs were little useful, I know not what news may wait my reappearance in the world. All news, at our time of life, is bad news. So I thought three months ago, when, on coming out of the Rocky Mountains, my only letter told me that my eldest brother was dead. So I think now, when I try to imagine whether any possible news that may await me, can be good news. My best prayer for you and yours is that you have no news to send.

Certainly I have none to send you. What does Petrarch say in that forgotten, but very much fin-de-siècle sonnet beginning "Dell'empia Babilonia," and continuing "aqui me sto solo"? (unless my Spanish has mixed itself with what little Italian I once thought I knew.)[1] At any rate, here I am passably solitary. For a month I have been drifting about Mexico, until mules and mountains so wearied me that I have stopped at this small town to rest, and to cure an obstinate cold. I do not know that you feel even a gleam of curiosity to know where the town is, and I am not, myself, quite sure of its latitude and longitude, but, as I came here, it stood about a hundred miles, more or less, to the south of the city of Mexico. I came here because it was the way to Acapulco where I was trying to get, and where I found I could not get, at least in time for the steamer; so after riding a hundred and fifty miles on mule-back, in a sugar-loaf hat, leather jacket and trousers, and spurs that weigh many kilos, I dropped back here, under the slopes of Popocatapetl, and lie all day on my bed, looking at the red Poinsettias and oleanders and hybiscus flowering in the garden, and the eternally blue sky over the snow of Popocatapetl, and wondering whether the dust and the dirt and the heat of midday, and the cold of midnight and the bad food and the general beastliness will let me stay quiet another day. Do you know that I have travelled to every place on earth which travellers have described as most fascinating, in the hope of finding one where I should want to stay or return, and have found that Faust had a sure horse on the devil in his promise about the passing hour: "Bleibe doch, du bist so schön!"[2] Three days in any place on earth is all it will bear. The pleasure is in the movement, as Faust knew when he let the devil in to the preposterous contract. Mexico is exceptionally amusing, not in the romantic way I expected, but in a prosaic, grimy, Indian, scarlet-vermilion way of its own, impossible to describe, and disappointing to realize. It is another money-making machine, like the United States or England or Italy, but uses peculiar and rather successful processes of its own, remnants of the Roman Empire, which still survives here in full flower. As far as I could judge, living as I have done, in their mud huts, and eating their tortillas and chile by their side, among the pigs and hens and dogs that fill the interstices of their cabins, I saw nothing whatever that I should not have seen in a like journey in the Spain of Hadrian. Every detail of the pottery, the huts, the mule-trains with their loads, the food, the clothes, and the roads where no wheel had ever passed, might have been Roman, and the people have the peculiar look, though all really Indians, that the Roman empire left forever on its slave-provinces. Thanks to its silver coinage, Mexico is now flourishing, chiefly at the cost of the United States and England. Agriculture, manufactures and mines are all splendidly suc-cessful, and the poorest labor is well employed. I see the country at its best, and admit that it is right, and we are the failures. Mexico can lose nothing, for it is at the bottom in respect to its wants. She is bound to clean us out.

Artistically the old Mexico, both ecclesiastical and secular, was charming, and has astonished me much.

I have done with it now, and in a week expect to be in Havana, hoping to reach the Windward Islands through Porto Rico, having failed to get round through Panama. Towards April I should drift northward again, and hope then to find a letter from you. My best love to all yours.

Ever   Henry Adams.

MS: MHi

1. In recalling Petrarch's sonnet "De l'empia Babilonia," HA slightly altered the phrase *Qui mi sto solo* (Here I am solitary).
2. "Verweile," not "Bleibe." "Still delay! Thou art so fair." Goethe, *Faust,* part I, scene 4.

To Charles Milnes Gaskell

St Thomas. 16 Feb. '95

My dear Carlo

This happens to be my birthday, and as I am bound to have a celebration somehow, I start out by beginning a letter to you. Perhaps you may re-member my age. No one else does, I am sure, and in America, as far as I know, no one can remember when I died; which must have been in your time, though it was a long way back, and I hardly remember it myself. You yourself are not now quite a chicken, and your own birthdays are running close on mine as we come to the finish. In whose Consulship was it that I was a good quarter ahead?

I have chosen an out-of-the-way spot for my festa; no other than the quarantine at St Thomas where I have been nearly a week, and must stay ten days more, to atone for the pleasure of having passed a night at San Juan de Puerto Rico where there are a few cases of small-pox. I left about as much small-pox in Washington three months ago, but here in the West Indies the islands are more particular, and your British colonies quarantine furiously, which obliges all the other islands to imitate them. So here I am! It is pleasant enough. No lovelier spot could be found without considerable inquiry. I have just had my bath in the surf at sunrise, and have made my coffee, and smoked my cigar; no mean enjoyments, for a sunrise bath in the tropical sea, and Porto Rican coffee, and Havana cigars are among the best things that this small globe contains. Presently I shall take an hour of Spanish, and then dabble with my water-colors, and at eleven go down to breakfast with my half-dozen fellow-prisoners. Then another cigar, and a siesta and so start fresh again. I have often been more bored, in places supposed to be gayer, and have passed more time in places far less beautiful.

Since December 1 I have been wandering in Spanish countries. Mexico took a month or more, and I think that I saw the Mexicans down to the roots. Not that I have any longer the ambition to acquire useful knowledge, but because the Mexicans came in my way and I had to sleep in their huts, and eat their tortillas and chile, and wear their leather riding-suits, and their silver spurs, and their serapes, and ride their mules over their blazing mountains. All to no purpose, for my young companion broke down with fatigue and sun, and scared my wits out of me with fear of sunstroke, so that I turned short, half way to Acapulco; came back by moonlight; and took steamer from Tampico to Havana; from there to Porto Rico, and so here. We have wandered seven or eight thousand miles, and, as soon as we are released, we hope to reach our object, which is Trinidad and the windward Antilles. Probably any other persons would have had adventures on such an excursion; but I never have anything out of the common. The world always presents, like the moon, its same side to me. Always mankind is absorbed with more or less success in the same solemn human duty of making money. The tiller of the soil is always being exploited by the trader and the money-lender; the trader and the money-lender are always exploiting the tiller of the soil. Religion, art, politics, manners are either vulgarised or dead or turned into money-making agencies. Every country is a variation on the same theme, as monotonous as Baker Street or the Rue de Rivoli. In all my wanderings I have never met a gentleman or a lady, nor do I know where to look for them. Perhaps you may come across them in

Europe, but I have not been so lucky. To me, railway-trains, hotels and steamers carry only one constant stream of money-makers, or their wives or children. Not even an artist or an archbishop crosses my dusty track. Robin Hood lived in much better society.

I have had no letters for a month or more, and can get none until we reach Barbadoes. Probably I am none the worse, but you must bear this in mind in case anything has happened that I ought to know. Here in the tropics they talk of nothing but sugar and coffee, low prices, ruin and discontent. I ought to except Mexico where all is prosperity and satisfaction, but Mexico is a fragment of the later Roman Empire miraculously preserved as it must have existed two thousand years ago in Spain and Africa; and what ruins us, profits it. Here in the Antilles our civilisation struggles on, in a losing battle with barbarism, much as Froude described it, only worse. The negro, the half-breed, and the broken planter are the results of Columbus and the four hundred years of triumphant civilisation which we celebrated at Chicago the other day. It is not flattering, nor even picturesque, but nothing can spoil its natural beauty, and its fruits and roots are still uncommon good. As yet, beets won't make coffee, pineapples, mangoes or bananas.

Adios, querido! hasta luego! I may have to come over this summer to hunt documents at Seville. If so, I shall see you, and give my own love to your wife.

Ever   H. Adams.

MS: MHi

To Charles Francis Adams, Jr.

1603 H Street. 16 April, 1895.

My dear Charles

On returning here after a winter's absence I find various communications from you, all bearing more or less directly on the necessity of enlightening a perverse generation in regard to the importance and merits of our family and friends. In the remote atmosphere which surrounds me, this debased and degraded race seems to care about us or our friends as little as they do for a Periplaneta Orientalis;[1] and, to judge from the supreme indifference of this generation, that insignificant coleopter will be far more important than we, to the generations which may follow the present. Nevertheless I suppose we are bound to behave as though the universe were really made to glorify our works, so I heartily approve your proceedings. Pray make any use of me that you like, just as though I were real.[2]

As for the governor, the world has little use for him, now that he is dead, and not much more, while he lived. Judging from the intolerable dulness of the various Lives already published: Seward, Chase, Sumner, Motley, Longfellow, &c—in fact, of all, except Lincoln and the Generals—I should say that the less we insisted on exhibiting our papa, the better. He stands on the merits of his course and speech in one session of Congress, and his diplomatic papers and conduct. For those two results, his character, mind and training were admirably fitted. His defects and limitations were as important, and as valuable, to him, as his qualities, within the range of those fields. Had there been a little more, or a little less of him, he would have been less perfect. As he stands, he stands alone. No other public man of his time begins to compare with him, within the range of his action. He is almost like a classical gem. From the moment he appeared anywhere— at Washington, London, Geneva—his place was never questioned, much less disputed. Russell, Palmerston, Disraeli, Bright, Cobden, Gladstone, Seward, and all the Americans, were bunglers in work compared with him, as his state-papers show. His instinctive sense of form, combined with keenness of mind, were French rather than English. His simplicity was like the purity of crystal, without flash or color. His figure, as a public man, is classic,—call it Greek, if you please.

Of course you cannot expressly say all this, but this is really all that the public wants to know, and your business is to make them feel it. Sons are not the proper persons to do such work, but I know of no one better suited, so we may as well try.

A light hand is necessary; total effacement of oneself; rigid abstention from paradox, smartness or pedagoguery; and a single purpose of painting the figure, and nothing else. Our business is to let the governor have his own say; to show him as simply as he showed himself. With his youth, or his local politics, the world cares mighty little to trouble itself. With his limitations, still less, except that his limitations, like the limitations of painting, were necessary for the relative perfection of the figure.[3] My own notion is to represent him as the contrast or complement of his father and grandfather, with an eye to the grouping rather than to the individual attitude.

The story you told of Sumner and John is quite fresh in my mind,—more so than I care to think, for newer things seem older.[4]

Love to your family   Ever   Henry.

MS: MHi

1. *Periplaneta Orientalis:* oriental cockroach.
2. CFA2 to HA, April 15: "Having at last fairly got to work on the C.F.A. biography, I

propose, as I go along, from time to time 'to try it on the dawg,'— you serving in this case as the canine objective" (Adams Papers, MHS).

3. HA was responding to CFA2's remarks on the limitations of CFA as revealed in his early diaries.

4. CFA2 had sent HA a copy of *Dinner Commemorative of Charles Sumner and Complimentary to Edward L. Pierce, Boston, December 29, 1894* (1895). In his after-dinner speech, published therein, CFA2 had recalled an incident of the early 1850s:

"It was at the old house at Quincy. Mr. Sumner, the guest there for some Sunday . . . got talking with us, as he was wont to do, earnest for our improvement. My younger brother, Henry Adams . . . was there, and Mr. Sumner was endeavoring in his rather direct way to instil into him a love of historical study . . . Mr. Sumner in his appeal used this expression, no less homely than strong, 'Why, Henry, I am sure you never would let a slice of pudding stand in your way to a slice of history!' Suddenly, my brother John spoke up very greatly to the point, 'You bet your life, Mr. Sumner, he would n't let it stand in the way *long*.' I can see still the puzzled look of the Senator over the great enjoyment of the future historian at the realistic turn thus given to the exhortation" (p. 40).

To Brooks Adams

Washington. 5 June, 1895

Dear Brooks

My movements are still uncertain. Expecting every day to hear the voice of some devil telling me what to do, I have put off all other devils, like yourself, who only want me to do something.[1]

Probably—no! *possibly* I shall go over with the Lodges, July 5, with the intent to return in October. By that time, or a little later, I hope to see all our immediate problems solved. By this, I mean that we should know, or be able to foresee whether the bankers can or will carry us over the presidential election. If they can and will, we may safely leave everything to them, financially, and to their agent, whom I suppose to be Mr Platt, for politics.[2] My common-sense tells me that this is what ought to happen,—what is the direct, proper and inevitable course of our history—and what will bring us quickest to the next stage. Historically I support Pierpont Morgan for President on a distinct gold monometallic platform.[3] This I hold to be political orthodoxy.

On the other hand I feel constant doubt whether the bankers can carry us so long. Their great spring boom is now over, if I understand my New York Times, and has been a severe effort, with results not such as to decide anything whatever. I do not feel sure that the bankers can even carry out their contract till October. The drift of exchange is stronger than ever against us, and the risk of a silver scare, both in Europe and America, is greater. If, when Congress meets, the finances are not already on a secure footing, and the elections have not been decisive for gold, I shall look for confusion. As a man of sense I am a gold-bug and support a gold-bug government and a gold-bug society. As a man of the world, I like confusion, anarchy and war. If the gold-bug government and society is to break down, I shall stay here to grin in its face. In case, by December next, the struggle should be still going on, with any chance of gold-bug defeat, I shall probably stay in Washington till the result is fixed. Platt alone can tell me what it will be, and even he cannot know much before next winter. The next Congress is probably free silver in any case. All that the bankers can hope for is a President sure to veto a free-silver bill. Against that, Mr Platt will find some pretty shrewd silver-men, not without money, ready to play fairly high stakes.

As free-silver, in my eyes, means fun, and especially implies a direct trial of strength with England, to whatever extent the new President may choose to force it,—*j'y suis!* After the insolence of Sir William Harcourt's last declarations—in no whit different from the declarations of George Canning about the Orders in Council—I see no dignified course for our government except that of a trial of strength.[4] Towards that, all my little social buzz has been directed since September, 1893. I think it time that the political existence of England should cease in North America. Whether we can allow it to develope in South America, particularly on the Orinoco, is a matter that will depend on England herself.[5] A free-silver administration will be thoroughly coached on these points. I think I can effect that much, even though there were not already an active ferment at work in the press and Congress. All depends on the *man,*—the next President. The *policy* can only fail by wanting vigor.

One's mind goes far, and dreams much over such a field of vision, but in the end it always loses itself in Asia. Russia is omnipotence. Without Russia, such a scheme might fail. I fear Russia much! Why can one never penetrate that polar mystery? What chance is there of repeating the diplomacy, the blunders and the disasters of 1812? What chance is there of achieving that success on which Madison had a right to reckon, and which nothing but the unripeness of the age prevented his achieving?[6] Our true point of interest is not India but Russia, yet Russia is impenetrable, and any intelligent man will deal with her better, the less closely he knows her. You ought to be,—like your grandfather,— minister to St Petersburg under another Madison.

These are the dreams over which I brood in the solitude of 98° Fahrenheit, with slight congestion of the brain.

With this clue, you can tolerably well reckon where I shall be, and what I shall be doing until the Presidential election.

Now, for your book!

Allow me, first, to strike out the dedication. Between *us,* it is not needed. For you, it is a mistake, because it would suggest to critics the idea of saying or hinting that the book was really mine; and critics are sure to think the first ill-natured idea that is suggested to them, a God-send. For me, the dedication is an embarrassment. The book is wholly, absolutely, and exclusively yours. Not a thought in it has any parentage of mine. Not only am I not in it, but it is strongly contrary to my rigid rules of conduct. I believe silence to be now the only sensible form of expression. I have deliberately and systematically effaced myself, even in my own history. I can conceive of nothing but harm, to our society, from the expression of its logical conclusions. I look on our society as a balloon, liable to momentary collapse, and I see nothing to be gained by sticking pins through the oil-canvas. I do not care to monkey with a dynamo. If you choose to do it, well and good! I never try to stop any man from doing anything— or woman either. They act as Brahma wills, and I not less so. By all means work out your full destiny; but work it out alone. My destiny—or at least my will, as an element of the social mass in movement—lies in silence, which I hold to be alone sense. Even my name, on a dedication, talks too much to please me.

Next, the Preface!

I would first go through it carefully, and strike out all the egoism you can reach. The ego may pass in a letter or a diary, but not in a serious book. You should be able to get all the literary advantage that the pronouns *I, me,* and *my* can give, by restricting yourself to a definite scale; say once on an average of five lines. Further, if my opinion has any value, you will find it only in my general rule of correction: to strike out remorselessly every superfluous word, syllable and letter. Every omission improves. I have suggested possible condensations by pencil-marks on the text. [*The rest of the letter is missing.*]

MS: MH

1. In late May, BA had sent the manuscript of *The Law of Civilization and Decay; an Essay on History* (1895) to the London publisher Swan Sonnenschein & Co. to be considered for publication. In June BA asked HA, if he were going to London, to talk the matter over with Sonnenschein and to arrange for an index. He also asked HA to comment on the draft preface and on a chapter of conclusions.
2. Thomas C. Platt (1833–1910), boss of the New York State Republican party.
3. John Pierpont Morgan (1837–1913).
4. Sir William Harcourt (1827–1904), M.P., leader of the Liberal party; George Canning (1770–1827), M.P., influential British statesman before the War of 1812. Harcourt reputedly had said that if a new international bimetallist conference were held, "the Government would not allow the gold standard for England even to be drawn into dispute" (*Nation* 60 [June 6, 1895], 435–436). HA regarded George Canning's note of Sept. 23, 1808, in which he refused to withdraw the Orders in Council, as a "sweeping assertion of British power" which left the United States "no alternative but war or submission" (*History*, IV, 336, 338).
5. In the Venezuela–British Guiana boundary dispute, British claims threatened Venezuelan control of the Orinoco River.
6. Russia's recognition of American maritime rights and its readiness to mediate between the

U.S. and Britain were, in HA's view, diplomatic triumphs of JQA that had been negated by the war hawks of Madison's administration (*History*, V, chap. 19; VII, chap. 2).

To Brooks Adams

Washington, 21 June, 1895

Dear Brooks

Thanks for your letter and letters. I am not likely to go far into the crowd in London. I am curious for gossip only.[1] As far as concerns me, I want the gold-bugs to win. I have never regarded silver as anything but a medium for prolonging and extending the present stage of society.

The immediate problem is, however, a curious one. For the first time in history, as far as I know, the capitalists have deliberately undertaken the stupendous job of controlling international exchanges. Now let us see the effect. Here are the figures so far, of the balances in exports and imports. The syndicate took control in February:

1895.	Merchandise	Silver	Gold	
Jan.	13,682,000	2,125,000	24,700,000	40,507,000
Feb.	−2,333,000	2,000,000	−4,067,000	−4,340,000
March	−4,137,000	2,000,000	−4,120,000	−6,257,000
April	−3,322,000	2,600,000	−2,029,000	−3,750,000
May	−1,762,000	4,000,000	−4,144,000	−1,906,000
	2,128,000	12,725,000	10,340,000	

In round numbers, $25,000,000 against a usual, normal average of $75,000,000 for the half year.

As far as the mere deficit goes, it amounts to little. Our average foreign payments for the last ten years have not exceeded $100,000,000 a year, although for the last four years they have averaged $189,000,000. We could make up the deficit without much trouble.

The trouble is that the syndicate, by giving an artificial stimulant to us, has at once checked exports, stimulated imports, and also foreign travel, until nothing can end it but another crash. Wages have been raised, prices put up, capital put out to support the bubble, and it all rests on a poor $30,000,000 of bonds (not stock) sold in Europe.

This is bad financiering; a good deal worse than the somewhat similar Sherman Act. It cannot, in my opinion, be stretched over the presidential election. I think we shall find that the syndicate will not dare to renew its contract in October. It has had no such success, even now, as I had anticipated; and the three hardest months are to come. Everything depends on our exports in August, September and October. If those are bad, the bulls must go down. No matter who is on top of the bull crowd, Morgan, Rothschild, or Baring, there are always bears enough and Jews enough to sell them out on a bad turn.[2]

What I want to learn in London is whether the bears understand the situation as I do, or can give me bull points that I cannot get here.

Of the political situation I know nothing. I rarely see the papers, and have had no talk with any of the politicians since you left. Indeed I do not know that any politicians are now here.

Socially also I am quite alone, or see only the few stray summer stay-overs. Washington is still very pretty and very pleasant.

I have been amusing my idleness by working up the history of our foreign exchanges since 1850. The figures are quite amusing, and sometimes rather surprising. If you come on any light which can clear my unaided intellect, treasure it for me. As far as I can work it out, our annual payment to Europe is not more than $110,000,000, or less than $100,000,000, leaving the capital account aside. Apparently we pay this sum under three heads: Interest or profits on foreign capital; expenses of travel, and freights. Estimates on these three heads are very wild. Some put freights as high as $30,000,000; a very moderate estimate for 80,000 tourists would make $30,000,000 more; but that would leave only $1,250,000,000 of foreign capital drawing four per cent, invested here. What say you?

Of one thing I do not doubt. We have certainly repaid more than $200,000,000 to Europe in solid capital, in the last five years. I am greatly curious to know whether they are still hard up and want more.

Love to your wife   Ever Yrs   Henry Adams.

MS: MH

1. In his letter of June 19 (MH), BA sent letters of introduction for HA to London financial authorities; HA did in fact consult them.
2. Nathan Meyer Rothschild (1840–1915), 1st Baron Rothschild, headed the leading international banking firm in England. He was a member of a prominent Jewish family of European financiers.

To Mabel Hooper

Paris. 1 Sept. '95.

Dear Infants[1]

Two days ago, on arriving here, I got Looly's and Fanny's letters, which gave me all the news in the world, or at least all I am likely to get, for no one else writes. By the time you get this, summer will be waning. My own passage is taken for October 12, and by the 20th I hope to be running the house at Washington. I want one of you—and of course that means Looly who is the only one of you worth a monkey—to write to Miss Baxter,—I suppose Aunt Daisy knows her address—and ask her to make us a visit at Washington. You will have to arrange the whole thing, if she accepts, as two of you will have to be there to matronise her, and you must find a date to suit you all, bearing in mind that I shall be best pleased with the earliest date after October 20. If Ellen and Mabel both feel like matrons, all three of you might perhaps pack into the house some way, but I shall need two anyhow, and I don't suppose Fanny and Mabel care for such advanced society. You had better fix a term, too, for Miss Baxter's visit. One always feels easier for knowing how long one is wanted. Say a fortnight, or a month, or anything you like, so it be understood.

Mrs Lodge and I are going out shopping, and we shall try to find the linen that Maggy wants. In London I bought a warehouse of furniture and glass for her. She devours tables and chairs by herds. I don't believe all five of you wear out as much furniture as I do. I found some rather nice things at Gregory's and was extravagant, so that I will bust your paw yet.

I forgot my travels. Where did I leave off? At Tillypronie, I think, near a month ago. I left poor Lady Clark very,–very broken.[2] When I rejoined the Lodge's in London the town was deserted and we had a week of it without society or gossip. I think I managed to do all I wanted, or at least all I had jotted in my memoranda, but I left to the last the decision whether you girls were to have solitaire pearl necklaces or ruby diadems. Of course you are too old for diamonds, and they are too common. Perhaps you had better decide for yourselves next year, on the spot.

We all left London on Sunday, the 18th, and, with lovely weather, crossed to Amiens where we passed Monday in the Cathedral. Of course I had been there often, but it is always newer and more wonderful every time, and it never seemed so fresh as now, or so marvellously perfect. Then we went on to Rouen and passed Wednesday there, also on old ground, but interesting, and we might well have staid longer. We kept on then to Caen, Thursday, which was new to me, and full of William the Conqueror and his buildings. On Friday we stopped some hours at Bayeux to see Matilda's tapestry and another early church; and we had time at St Lo to bag another curious early Cathedral, still reaching Coutances in time to see the sun-set from the top of the Cathedral there.

We thought Coutances the most charming of all these places, but perhaps it was only a surprise. The Norman Cathedral there was something quite new to me, and humbled my proud spirit a good bit. I had not thought myself so ignorant or so stupid as to have remained blind to such things, being more or less within sight of them now for nearly forty years. I thought

I knew Gothic. Caen, Bayeux and Coutances were a chapter I never opened before, and which pleased my jaded appetite. They are austere. They have, outside, little of the vanity of Religion. Inside, they are worked with a feeling and a devotion that turns even Amiens green with jealousy. I knew before pretty well all that my own life and time was worth, but I never before felt quite so utterly stood on, as I did in the Cathedral at Coutances. Amiens has mercy. Coutances is above mercy itself. The squirming devils under the feet of the stone Apostles looked uncommonly like me and my generation.

On Saturday we came on to Mont Saint Michel, among a mob of tourists. About Mont St Michel I can say little because it is too big. It is the Church Militant, but if Coutances expressed the last—or first—word of Religion, as an emotion of self-abasement, Mont Saint Michel lifted one up to a sort of Sir Galahad in its mixture of sword and cross. We passed two days there, in the most abominable herd of human hogs I ever saw at the trough of a table-d'hôte, but the castle was worth many hogs. When Rafael painted St Michael flourishing his big sword over Satan, he thought, no doubt that he had done a good bit of religious painting, but the Norman architecture makes even Rafael vulgar. The Saint Michael of the Mount is as big as Orion and his sword must be as high as Sirius, if Sirius in these days has any Faith, which may be doubted; and if stars anyway are of any use, which is more questionable still, both stars and swords being now better understood, or more antiquated, than in the eleventh century. So we bade good-bye to Sir Galahad St Michael, on Monday, with the proud thought that we could smash him with one cannon-ball, or the gold resources of a single Wall Street Bank, and we rode and we rode and we hunted and we hollowed till we came to Vitré to sleep, and there too we saw what is left of a very old town, and walls, above a green valley, and a great Castle of the Tremoilles, grands seigneurs s'il en fût; and the old Chateau of Mme de Sevigné, a few miles off, untouched, and for all the world exactly like our Scotch castles. From Vitré to Le Mans, with another Cathedral; and, last of all, two long hours at Chartres on a lovely summer afternoon, with the sun flaming behind Saint Anne, David, Solomon, Nebuchadnezzar and the rest, in the great windows of the north transept. No austerity there, inside or out, except in the old south tower and spire which still protests against mere humanity. I've a notion that you saw Chartres, and know all about it. If so, I can drop it. If not, I hope to take you there. Of course I studied the windows, if only for La Farge's sake, and tried to understand their makers. On the whole, as a combination of high merits, religious and spiritual; artistic, as architecture; technical as engineering; for color, form and thought; for elevation of idea and successful subordination of detail; I suppose Chartres is now the finest thing in the world. At least that would be my guess; but I've no confidence in it; and if you say you prefer St Paul's or St Peter's, so let it be. It does not matter much now-a-days. I believe a vast majority prefers the Houses of Parliament and the State Department at Washington. You can take your own line.

The same evening we came on to Paris, and here we are: Hotel des deux Mondes, Avenue de l'Opera. Mr and Mrs Lodge, the two boys, and I, occupying one apartment. We have not quarreled or differed, and our journey since leaving New York has been highly successful. I hope they have enjoyed it as much as I have. I find the Cunliffes here, which is another joy to me. The Luce's also, our other sister, are here, and two thousand million Americans sitting at every café, with penetrating voices proclaiming that they only wish they were in New York.[3] I wish they were, and I further still, for I love Paris only so very little that I would not quite utterly destroy it, as I would destroy London; but would leave the Louvre, and Notre Dame, and the Café Riche or Véfour's. The only real objection I have to France is that there is no good Champagne in it. Otherwise it is a tolerable place enough, except for the Jews and Americans.

Now I have written you a very long letter, and must finish my coffee and dress, or some one will come in. Give my love to paw, and to Martha and Hitty and Elsie and all the other brats.[4]

Ever affectionately   Henry Adams.

MS: MH

1. The five daughters of MHA's brother, Edward William Hooper: Ellen (b. 1872), later Mrs. John Briggs Potter; Louisa ("Looly") (1874–1975), later Mrs. Ward Thoron; Mabel (b. 1875), later Mrs. Bancel La Farge; Fanny ("Susan") (1877–1963), later Mrs. Greely S. Curtis; and Mary ("Molly") (1879–1972), later Mrs. Roger Warner. HA was trustee for them of MHA's estate.
2. Charlotte Coltman Clark (1823–1897), wife of Sir John F. Clark.
3. John Dandridge Luce (1855–1921), Boston banker; and Louisa Davis Luce.
4. Abigail ("Hitty") Adams (1879–1974), daughter of John Quincy Adams II (1833–1894); Elizabeth ("Elsie") Adams (1873–1945), daughter of CFA2.

To Elizabeth Cameron

Paris, 3 Sept. 1895.

Your letter from Newport arrived Saturday morning, and the following one, from Beverly, arrived Saturday evening. Such are the eccentricities of steamers. At least the second came quick.

Of our doings there is not a great deal to say. Paris is hot, even for me, though I like it. At about seven in the morning I get up and write a letter to you or somebody and take my coffee, as I am doing now. At about ten

I decide where to breakfast, and what part of the city or suburbs to honor with a visit. To say the truth I find it safer to be alone. I am apt to be cross and queer before noon, and dread to show it as much as though my hair were dyed and my teeth false. I feel the months turning to years and the years piling up to the sixties, and between the life I lead and the life I imagine is so vast a gulf, that the world irritates me. I cannot even retire into the past where I belong, for the present is everywhere, yet when I try to live in the present, it turns into sour small beer. Gluttony is my favorite resource, yet thus far I have been unable to get a good breakfast or dinner in Paris, or a single well-cooked dish. The restaurants which I once haunted, and where the cooking was always good, are now careless, and little better than tables-d'hote. They never give one the old choice of dishes. They all have their wretched plats du jour. They cook for Americans and English, and seldom, at this season, see a Frenchman, or at least a Parisian within their doors. It is no use trying to find a haunt where the American has not penetrated. He—and she—go everywhere, and by preference to the best places; and where the American, Englishman, or German, goes, there life has no longer an interest except for market-values.

Naturally it exasperates me, and I long for ruined countries, like the South Seas or the West Indies, where the Englishman has wreaked his worst, and has at least gone away and left the ruins alone. The desert is a happy home. Last year, in the black cañons of the Yellowstone, I was in a better place than this.

If the Americans seemed to enjoy it, I might be more contented, but even in that, I see a distinct change. Paris has become an American city, as much a matter of course as New York. The American has no longer a standard here but himself. Even the vulgarities of the second empire were standards to him once, but the republic holds up nothing either to admire or reject. He has no barrier, and sees no limit to his own Americanism. Far better to stay at home.

Add to this dreary, eternal sense of my own moral death, the anxiety I feel about you, and you can imagine that I am poor company for pleasurers. About you I have said all I can. It is no use. I know only too certainly that all the reason in the race has nothing whatever to do with a disordered cerebrum, or cerebellum,—which means that a sick brain must work wrong, or at least differently from a well one. I can only look on. For that matter, I am used to it—God knows!

At the same time, although quite aware that you are, and will be, incapable of seeing things straight—or at least as I see them—about yourself, you need not necessarily be wholly incapable of seeing them straight about others if your own eccentricity can for a moment be lost. You know that from the moment of my return last April, I told you two things. One was that you were threatened with nervous prostration. The other was that your husband was already suffering from it. I was then, and am still, more troubled about him than about you, not only because at his age the symptom is very alarming, but because of its retroactive effects on you. Of the fact, I have no doubt. You remember that in 1893, in Europe, he was in a state of cerebral excitement which astonished me. You remember how it lasted through all the silver debate, surprising even those who knew him best. This spring I saw that the reaction had set in, and was already strongly marked. I noticed it, as you did, in many ways, and it was immaterial to me whether he had suffered some shock or not, since the cerebral condition was in any case the same, accompanied also by the infallible symptom of pecuniary anxieties. The symptoms, as far as I have seen them in my own experience, are the precursors of decline, which may be slow and may be rapid. It may be a matter of ten years, of ten months, or of ten days. It may be that the brain is hardening or softening, or is suffering disease. The symptom of *embutissement*[1] would be, or might be, common to all. At least it is better than violence. You have a dreadfully difficult experience to face at a time when you are yourself hardly responsible. You hold him responsible, and perhaps he holds you responsible, when you should both be put under guardianship, and treated as *aliénés*.

This is pretty plain speaking, but it is not the first time I have said it to you. I am at my wits' end to devise some means of helping you. The only person who can help you is Jim, and I know you will rather die than call him in.[2] He should be ready to act as his father's guardian if his father should need it. In fact, I suppose that without him nothing could be done. Next to Jim is Wayne, but Wayne is in Italy, and anyway would rather not be drawn into so serious a matter, though he might be willing to advise.[3] All these questions I had to deal with in the case of my father: and, as you may remember, long after he was irresponsible, only the accident of his falling into the hands of sharpers forced us to make my brother John his guardian, and I know not how we could have acted with a divided family.[4] To the last, my mother never could realise her husband's loss of mind. She was impatient over it as though he were to blame.

Of course another result is possible. You may pass the crisis and react, for you are young and strong. He may be suffering only from temporary overexcitement, and, when the reaction is over, may recover his nerves as before. In that case you may go on, *tant bien que mal,* as of old, till the next strain; only, in the interval, just please hurry up and bury me, for I had long ago my fill of these cerebral troubles, which have already wrecked my life, and cost me much more than life is worth; and rather than go through any more I prefer to clear out, and start fresh,—say as a clam or a coral. Any kind of organised creature that has no nerves will suit me for my next incarnation. Meanwhile, if I could send you off somewhere, to vegetate like a cow in a pasture, with Martha for a rabbit to amuse you, I would do it. I would not mind being a turkey-buzzard myself.

MS: MHi

1. *Embutissement:* apparently HA's coinage from *embu*, flatness of color, deadness of dried paint.
2. James McCormick Cameron (1865–1949), Pennsylvania steel company executive, was Senator Cameron's son by his first wife.
3. Wayne MacVeagh was Senator Cameron's brother-in-law.
4. On March 28, 1882, CFA was swindled out of $18,000 by cardsharpers who took advantage of his senility. An earlier incident, in May 1880, had led to the guardianship.

To John Hay

Paris, 7 Sept. 1895.

My dear John

No word from you has arrived to soothe my perturbed spirit,[1] nor has my band of fellow-travellers supplied me with anything more than the faintest kind of an echo from your world. No doubt a letter will arrive soon, since I bethink me to write again. That occult association is too common to be despised. The Lord loves it.

For all this week, Paris has been a Roman bath. The oppressiveness of the heat would have seemed homelike in Washington. At this moment, as I write, at my open window, in the lightest of silk pyjamas, at nine o'clock in the morning, I am moist with perspiration, and drowsy with sleeplessness. Is it not curious how Paris imitates foreign vices. Trinidad is more comfortable.

Luckily we were cooler in Normandy, and our trip there was very successful. Not for several days or more have I enjoyed happier moments than among my respectable Norman ancestors, looking over the fields they ploughed and the stones they carved and piled up. Caen, Bayeux, St Lo, Coutances and Mont St Michel are clearly works that I helped to build, when I lived in a world I liked. With the Renaissance, the Valois and the Tudor display, I can have had nothing to do. It leaves me admiring, but cold. With true Norman work, the sensation is that of personal creation. No doubt Amiens and Chartres are greatly superior architecture, but I was not there. I was a vassal of the Church; I held farms—for I was many—in the Cotentin and around Caen, but the thing I did by a great majority of ancestors was to help in building the cathedral of Coutances, and my soul is still built into it. I can almost remember the faith that gave me energy, and the scared boldness that made my towers seem to me so daring, with the bits of gracefulness that I hasarded with some doubts whether the divine grace could properly be shown outside. Within I had no doubts. There the contrite sinner was welcomed with such tenderness as makes me still wish I were one. There is not a stone in the whole interior which I did not treat as though it were my own child. I was not clever, and I made some mistakes which the great men of Amiens corrected. I was simple-minded, somewhat stiff and cold, almost repellant to the warmer natures of the south, and I had lived always where one fought handily and needed to defend one's wives and children; but I was at my best. Nearly eight hundred years have passed since I made the fatal mistake of going to England, and since then I have never done anything in the world that can begin to compare in the perfection of its spirit and art with my cathedral of Coutances. I am as sure of it all as I am of death.

The other sights were a pleasure, but not the same. I enjoy them, but in an intellectual kind of way. Chartres especially was fascinating. I expected it, and was not disappointed. The thirteenth century had more money than the eleventh. The nineteenth has more money than either; but I was happiest just eight hundred years ago when my great Dukes lived, say from 1038 to 1100. We got life then down to a point.

The return to this momentary passing period does not amuse me. Obviously I am not in it. Of course I see more clearly than ever, after my visit to my Norman grandfathers, that this thing is rot, and is no concern of mine, and that I had better go to rest again for another eight hundred years; but for the moment I am here, and am obliged to see it; the first time I have seen Paris in summer for many years. The crowds have doubled in numbers, and to me look rather improved. Unlike England where the laboring class seemed to me much run down, the French have an air of health and cleanliness. Of course art has pretty near gone. Even cooking is practically lost, but this is because the moderately rich class, which maintained standards of taste, has been wiped out, and the tourist, who has no taste, has taken the place. The tourist is really startling. He comes in processions and armies, like the old pilgrims. When the head of such a column enters where you are, it is like an advancing flood. It rolls you over, and crushes you. The tourists themselves are what pilgrims always were, only without the slight glimmer of an idea which faith gave. I have watched their faces by hundreds, and compared them with the pilgrims of my own time.

Of acquaintances, considering that the Lodges presumably know people, they have seen fewer than I expected. For once, I am well off, for Robert Cunliffe is living here, and Gaskell has come over to be with us. Poor Gaskell, who cannot stand heat, is unable to leave his hotel till sunset, and almost suffocates even then, but thus far we have managed to keep dining.

Bay Lodge and I go about together a good deal; so do Cabot and I; but I prefer Bay who is a nice fellow, with only one failing, which is the kind of ambition and aspirations which you and I had forty years ago.[2] I have tried to teach him better, but I fear he really is not equal to being a money-lender. He is otherwise my favorite, and I find him sympathetic, intelligent, well-educated and unselfish. Of the three—father and two sons—I like him best. His mother has stood heroically all the dirt and weariness of the middle-ages, most of which is still preserved in the inns of Normandy, but the heat has rather floored her. Sally Loring has beguiled our sports, but has now gone across to Scotland.[3] Of others I know less than nothing—that is, very little. In short, on the whole we have got along remarkably well, and without disappointments. At times I feel again the old sinking of the stomach which indicates hopeless spavin in the motor muscles of the spirit, but I console myself with the reflection that it can't last long, which always did encourage the wicked.

Love to all yours.   Henry Adams.

MS: RPB

1. *Hamlet,* I, v, 183.
2. George Cabot ("Bay") Lodge (1873–1909), a son of Henry Cabot Lodge, poet, *Song of the Wave* (1898) and other volumes, served as gunnery officer in Spanish-American War.
3. Sally Pickman Loring (1859–1912), later Mrs. Theodore Dwight.

To Brooks Adams

27 Dec. '95.

Dear Brooks

Assuming that you are interested in our affairs, I write you a line this week to keep you posted.

There has been less reaction than I expected, after our grand drunk of last week.[1] Of course Lombard Street, Wall Street, State Street, and all the other Juden-gassen, did what they always have said they would. They sold everything, and made a first-class crisis not unlike '93. They are still keeping it up, I believe, but as I read the papers only once a week, I do not follow very close. It is not necessary. We knew what they would do. All I cared about was to know what effect they would have. The shock was as violent as they could make it. State Street has been frantic. You were very lucky to be absent. The telegrams and letters that have poured in on Olney, Reed, Lodge, and the rest, have been incredible.[2] Poor Henry Higginson and even your friend Howard Stockton have written in terms that no copperhead in 1861 surpassed.[3] They have raged and whined and threatened, until I have felt positive pity for them. I need not say that when the President's financial message appeared, in the midst of all this frenzy, I gave myself up for lost. We were all deeply depressed, and assumed that the President would surrender. That was a week ago. Since then, I hardly dare guess what has been doing; but as far as I can see, the country is all right. No one has yet given way or shown outward sign of alarm. I am told that Congress is unanimous in fact as in appearance. Little or nothing has been said there. Of the President, who is a kind of Veiled Prophet, we know nothing. When the dethroned monarch, J. S. Morgan came on, a few days ago, the President did not send for him or see him. Olney is very reticent, but very firm. The rest of the Cabinet, as far as I hear, talk well. You understand that I am now speaking not of the President's first message and the Monroe doctrine, for on that, we are all right, except that some people blame Olney's manners. Congress has acted on that message without a word, unanimously. The struggle is over the second, financial message, and the question is whether we shall borrow further of the Jews, or borrow of the Russian government, or go on to paper, or to silver. Of course I want free silver, but I am willing to take paper, or the Russian alliance, or anything except the Jews. Wall Street wants Rothschild, I suppose; since Wall Street *is* Rothschild. We all see here that political independence implies financial independence, which means either silver or paper. All my knowledge is bounded by the certainty—which is to me a vast relief—that the administration feels the point and that the quarrel with Wall Street is even more bitter at the White House than it is at mine across the way.

I assure you that any little outstanding account you may think still open between you and State Street, is for the moment almost if not wholly balanced. For a week we have had them under our feet. We have kicked and cuffed them as we did in '61. They have not dared make a popular appeal, as yet, and their attempt at a clerical peace-meeting in New York was a failure. How long we can hold them down I do not venture to guess, but in my youth I was taught a little Latin, and of that little, almost the only fragment I retain is a line of Horace about "ille potens sui laetusque deget, cui licet in diem dixisse: Vixi!"[4] If only for a week, we have rolled them in the mud once more. Doubtless we may, and probably shall, have to return to our bondage, but like Spartacus we have given a mighty unpleasant little entertainment to our masters. I rather hope to see Lombard Street howl like State Street, before we get through with it; but *cras*, as Horace continues, I leave as an open question.

The administration seems to be still wabbling between the Jews and the Gentiles, and the only advantage we have gained as yet is the irritation of the President. Olney is even more frank than the others of the Cabinet, and his battle with State Street is more of a settled thing. Naturally I feel more sure of his ultimate point. The Attorney General, Harmon, seems square. I think Lamont is right, but very cautious.[5]

In the midst of this strife I have rather neglected the foreign one, which is really secondary just now. Olney is apparently engaged in extending his diplomatic connection over the rest of America. The next step will be another session of the Pan American Congress, if the diplomatic outlook favors. Russia as yet seems too far to reach. We have not come to that point. Probably we shall never get there. Thus far we have been carried ahead by the impetus of the first leap. England has let us go. Whenever she begins to act, we shall know better the length of our chain, and I am much too old and wearied a prisoner to imagine it very long. We have had a gay dance for a week, but the cage and the whip are still there. Luckily, in one's sixtieth year, life is short, and its terrors more easily born.

The humors are gay and grim. State Street, including your brother Charles, is furious, pathetic and desperate, about Olney's manners! That is the main burden of complaint. I think Charles a grand spectacle on the deportment issue, but State Street on Manners will be sublime. As for me, I quite decline to defend Olney's manners, or Cleveland's or State Street's, or my own, or yours, or those of your grandfather, who wrote the Monroe doctrine, or of your great-grandfather who helped to write the Declaration of Independence, or of your great-uncle Sam, who must have been really rude to Governor Hutchinson and others.[6] Boston manners are beastly bad. I've been saying so for forty years, and am glad State Street agrees with me. True sympathy between State Street and me is so rare!

To sum up, Cleveland and Olney, as the Evening Post rightly charges, have become the leaders of the anarchists. That is fixed! They are not likely to abandon this position. Both of them are exasperated with the money-lenders, and indifferent to their doings. The cabinet is with them. Both parties are following them. They have the country on the run, and will force foreign affairs forward as the issue in the general election. I suppose Olney will be the democratic candidate. By the time you get back, in May, I expect to see some very remarkable points settled in history, both abroad and at home. At the rate of movement since November, 1890, we ought, within another year, to see universal anarchy.

Other news I have none. Hitty Adams and Molly Hooper are now with me. Also Edward Hooper! I am dumb! Why talk, since for once we are on top.

Love to your wife.   Ever Yr   H.

MS: MH

1. In the boundary dispute between British Guiana and Venezuela, England refused to arbitrate. President Cleveland sent a blunt warning through Secretary of State Richard Olney

(1835–1917) to England warning of "grave consequences" if England did not accede and cited the Monroe Doctrine for his authority. At Cleveland's request Congress appropriated money to set up a boundary commission. Olney's aggressive language touched off a "war scare."
2. Thomas B. Reed (1839–1902), Speaker of the House.
3. Howard Stockton (1842–1932), Union officer 1861–1871.
4. "That man is master of himself and happy, who chooses daily to say, 'I have lived'"; Horace, *Odes,* III, xxix.
5. Judson Harmon (1846–1927), attorney general 1895–1897; Daniel Scott Lamont (1851–1905), former private secretary to Cleveland, secretary of war 1893–1897.
6. The Boston Tea Party illustrated Samuel Adams' (1722–1803) rudeness to Thomas Hutchinson (1711–1780), colonial governor of Massachusetts, 1771–1774.

To William Hallett Phillips

Paris, 26 July, '96.

Dear Flops

Your letter of the 16th has just arrived.

From the evident desperation of the Spanish government and its measures, obviously directed to our address rather than to Cuba, I have supposed likely that it had received official warning that our government must act before Congress meets.[1] The poor Spaniards are terribly distressed, and are flinging themselves at the feet of France and Russia in utter despair. Both France and Russia, through their official press, have replied that help is out of the question. Canovas must give way, or the dynasty must fall, and I fear both may happen.[2] My heart bleeds for the Spaniards whom I like more than any other people in Europe; but poor Don Quixote! He is very dangerous in a world of shop-keepers, and can neither run a hotel nor meet his notes. His only chance is that the whole concern will go to pieces with him.

In fact, he is only one of the gangrened toes of Europe. Another is Turkey, and much worse. I am grimly entertained by the frantic howls and yells of the New York bankers and eastern money-lenders about Bryan and silver.[3] Bryan is American conservatism itself, as every movement must be that rests on the small land-owners. The issues here are of a kind that make ours a joke. When I read the French newspapers and books which talk of little else but the difficulties of the political and social situation, I turn sick and green with terror and despair. Between war worse than 1870, and rot worse than 1893, there is nothing to choose, not even a path. The worst is that no one can guess when another spasm will come. We had a violent one in 1890. Another more violent in 1893. The convulsions of 1895 were too horrible even to think about, and all Europe shuts its eyes with shame when it remembers Armenia.[4] Now, before 1896 is fairly half over, all

Europe is wondering what the devil is to be done to prevent a general
convulsion which every government is doing its best to avoid, and which,
even if avoided, is not escaped. The financiers are predicting collapse of
inflated values and bubble joint-stock companies. The politicians are scared
about Crete, Macedonia and Egypt. The manufacturers are scared about
everything—competition, war, socialism, strikes, ruined markets, legislation
and want of legislation. As far as I can see, everybody—without exception,
everybody—now expects a grand collapse of some sort; and sits down
before it in despair, almost indifferent to what may happen, and half glad
to give up the struggle. The mass of capital accumulates unused. The
hoarding of gold seems to have extended to private people. The stock-
exchanges can find nothing to do, except to force up the apparent values
of the few securities that still seem solid, or to force down those of doubtful
credit, but the creation of a great new industry—like the railway or steam-
shipping industry, is no longer hoped. Bicycles are the best they can create
now. The unrest and anxiety are universal, and no remedy is even suggested;
and the worst sign is that the rich and the poor alike accept the situation,
and agree to carry it on till it stops of itself.

You know how blue I was in 1893, and how I foresaw bloody destruction
at every turn. Since then every month has made the situation more strained.
Every month, something has crumbled, and never once has anything been
built. Even since I left Washington, barely two months, the silver agitation
has broken out; the stock-market has gone to panic values; the old syndicate, which failed to hold up the exchanges last year, has been forced to
try it again, to prevent losses which were likely to bankrupt the street;
while on this side, Crete has rebelled; Macedonia is disturbed; Syria is in
disorder; Russia has declared her intention of driving England out of Egypt;
the Matabeles are in revolt; and not one of the sores already open, has
been healed.

God only knows whether the disintegration will go on at the same rate
as for the last two or three years; but, if it does, even a banker must now
see that the equilibrium, such as it is, cannot last another year—or even
another six months. At that rate, by next January, Bryan would be President,—or we should have no President, which would be worse; the United
States would be at war with Spain; our stock-market would have cut its
own throat; the Turkish empire would be at an end; Russia would be at
war with England; and South Africa would be a chaos. The sequence must
be broken somehow between now and next January, or the game is up.

My whole interest here is to watch for the moment when Europe tries
seriously to meet its difficulties. According to my calculations Russia must
be now straining all its influence to bring about some modus vivendi that
will carry the machine along, at least politically, for a few years. I think it

must succeed. The interests on that side are life and death to civilisation itself. Yet its success in the international field will only stimulate the social, financial and economical evils. War or rot! Rot or war! Europe turns from one to the other, and despair settles down all over it.

As for our election, the result must be the same anyway. Bryan would no doubt be a great shock to credit and even to society, but McKinley would lead to the same end, by a slower process, perhaps, but as surely. The stock-market is a good guide in such matters, and for three years the stock-market has persistently foretold ruin.

I do not know why you should object to valuing your work for me this last year at five hundred dollars. Still, you can do as you like, and if you prefer to consider it as a debt, call it one. Also take what you want for your vacation.

As for me, I am here quite alone. The Hays and their cohort went to London on the 22d and sail on the 29th. I remain here another week, and then expect to go to Homburg to waste a time with the Wayne McVeaghs. It should be a good place to catch onto diplomatic gossip. In Paris I know not a human being. The theatres are so hot that I avoid them. The music-halls are so idiotic that I shun them. My occupation is to read till noon; to get into the country and stroll till sunset; and to dine in the open air. The weather is warm; the drought severe; and solitude is now a habit. Go you and do otherwise.[5]

Ever Yrs   H.A.

MS: MH

1. Secretary of State Olney had sent a secret note to the Spanish government on April 4 offering the good offices of President Cleveland in the Cuban civil war. The offer was rejected.
2. Antonio Canovas del Castillo (1828–1897), prime minister of Spain, assassinated Aug. 8, 1897.
3. William Jennings Bryan (1860–1925) advocated the free coinage of silver. At the Democratic national convention he had won the nomination for the presidency with his dramatic "Cross of Gold" speech.
4. In the face of the recent massacres of Armenians, officially sanctioned by the sultan's government, the Western powers declined to act.
5. Luke 10:37.

To Elizabeth Cameron

Sunday, Aug. 9, '96.

The weather has turned cold and wet, which makes Paris dull, but the McVeaghs are still wandering in Russia, and I don't care to go to Homburg alone to be colder and duller than here. So I am hanging on from day to day, doing nothing, and having nothing to write. Stimulated into activity by discomfort, I went to the office of the American Line yesterday and took a stateroom on the St Louis for October 3. I believe Rachel and her party go by that ship.[1] They are the only Americans I know in Europe. I might as well have some one to identify me at the bankers' in case of shipwreck on a desolate island. Apparently, then, I shall be in Washington on October 10. I rather dread it. Whatever way the election turns, it will do no good as long as this hive of money-lenders in London and Paris stand ready to buy up the result. Until London and Paris are wrecked and ruined, there can be no independent life for us. No doubt, free-silver would be a momentary blow to them; but a Jew thinks nothing of a blow. In five years we should be absolutely in his hands. So I play Sister Anne on the house-top, and look in every direction for the dust of the coming avenger; and, as for avengers, I see plenty of them.[2] They don't take the trouble to hide, or even to hurry. As yet, in all my reading in the press, in current literature and in religious discussions, I have come across no single voice that questions the approaching overthrow of the present system of society. Absolutely no one believes that it can resist its own tendency to disintegration much longer. But how much? Will it last five years? or ten? or fifty? or a hundred? Rome lasted five hundred after it was apparently sicker than we. Free silver is no use to me unless it is another decided element in a disintegration that I can expect to see. If it is to end in mortgaging us beyond hope, like India and Mexico, in order to support this rotten European fabric a few years longer, I would rather keep the country on its cross of gold. Then, at least, we shall have the Passion, the Agony, the Bloody Sweat, and the Resurrection.

But I doubt and doubt and keep on doubting whether Europe can go on another five years without a collapse—not perhaps permanent, but enough to suit our end. You ask for new books! There are no new books except such as deal with this subject. Everything else is dull and flat. Zola, in his Lourdes and Rome, deals with nothing else, and his critics follow him.[3] As for newspapers, as you go along the streets you notice that four men out of five read Rochefort's Intransigeant or Drumont's Libre Parole, if they read anything; and Rochefort, the atheist, agrees with Drumont, the Catholic mysticist—or, at all events, miraculist—in loathing the Jew régime, and in outspoken sympathy for the commune of '71, and the anarchists of today.[4] Get Rochefort's "Aventures de ma Vie," four volumes; not reading for girls or Pennsylvanians; but uncommonly amusing! Get Gyp's "Gens Chics," and "Ohé! les Dirigeants!" with their ludicrous illustrations by "Bob."[5] I would send all these books to you, except that it would be scandalous. The curious thing is that Paul de Cassagnac in his "Autorité," frantic imperialist, teaches the same doctrine;[6] and even up to Pope Leo XIII, the influence is destructive and anarchistic. Books swarm on the Church question, and our friend Bishop Keane figures largely in the disintegration of Catholic conservatism.[7] As for Italy, disintegration has gone perhaps even further than in France. If you care for German scandals, you can read the worthless but rather curious little book which the man Friedmann—a Jew lawyer, I imagine—has just published on the Kotze scandal and Kaiser William.[8] The Kaiser has had the book seized and prosecuted,— I cannot see why, except that it affirms the one secret of his policy and passion of his life to be hatred and mortal hostility to the socialist and anarchist spirit which is inevitably to overcome him. The substance of all the literature and political movement of the time is that governments now exist only to protect capital lent out at interest—Jew money—and that a big bankruptcy is inevitable. In France, the contempt for the republic of Jews and protestant usurers and bourgeois is an accepted popular fact. Indeed the word "bourgeois" is now universally adopted, instead of "aristo" as the expression of everything unpopular and arbitrary. France, too, is not financially strong. The South African collapse, last November, hit her hard. Taxation is awful; practically it is confiscation. Agriculture suffers terribly in spite of protection. Another year like '93 and '94, or a serious shock to financial confidence, would go far to break the wretched camel's last hump. The government, with one of its four legs deep in mire in Algeria, and another still deeper in Tonkin, has plunged a third up to the haunches in Madagascar, and the Lord only knows where it can find solid ground for its last. The next election here is a very grave matter. In Italy the Crown dares not try an election. In Germany the Kaiser will probably have to make a *coup d'état*. In Austria, the whole panjandrum depends on the Emperor's life. You know what the situation is in Turkey and Spain. And finally, the Pope's death can hardly fail to complicate matters extremely.

So I sit on the housetop and watch the lightning in the sky, and while I thank the stars that the storm will hardly come quick enough to destroy anything that I care for, I curl up with a delightful shiver of dread and excitement when I think of the next great convulsion, compared with which the convulsions of '70 and '71 will be—so everyone says—just a *lever de rideau*.

To come home, merely to watch blind forces at work, without even the pretence, on any side, of intelligent direction, or relation to a system, or a consciousness of an ultimate end, is the more trying because I see that the mess would be worse if the forces were intelligent! What I really want is to have Martha here for a companion. It is cold as November, and mostly rains, but I see that you are again stewing in the nineties. Martha and I would ride on the tops of all the omnibuses and trams, and go to all the shows, and all the restaurants and confectioners, and ramble in all the woods within fifty miles, and buy a ruined castle to play in. We would sometimes invite you to play with us. I have received the big photograph, but—Lord! Lord!! as Mr Pepys says—how it makes her look like a matron advanced in matrimony![9] I have also received your letter of July 27. You ask if I have read Hardy?[10] No! I have met him. Few men will stand reading after one knows them. No one has written anything in France. I should have sent you "Lysistrata" for Réjane's sake, except that it was really too—too!—Greek! I hear nothing of Sala's arrival.[11] Literally I have not exchanged a word with anyone but a servant for these ten days past, nor seen a face I recognised; but Americans absolutely fill this part of Paris, and the boulevard before the Grand Hotel is worse than the side-walk before the Fifth Avenue.

Tuesday. August 11. At last comes a telegram from McVeagh. He seems to have succeeded in getting to Homburg, but as he is to come to Paris, and return, I think I will wait, and go back with him Friday night. It will give me time to get my letters and change my address at the bankers'. I suppose I shall stay a fortnight at Homburg, and then return here, and cross the channel about September 1. My English friends will take me a month, and by that time I expect to be ready to do nothing in Washington for a month or two. Do you know—earnest Cuban as I am, and much as I want to go there for my winters—the present chaos and ruin seems to be better than our exploiting it; at any rate, a more orderly proceeding; and as it is certain to ruin Spain, and help considerably to ruin France, I am curious to see it work out its problem. Of course I shall take up the fight again as soon as Congress meets, but I am almost pleased to think that, as long as our monumental prize hog remains in the White House, all our efforts can effect nothing, and probably the present situation must last at least another year. If Cleveland were a Machievelli or a Caesar Borgia, he could not have invented a more diabolical method of spreading ruin throughout the world, without risk to himself. Curious how the utmost intelligence is identical with the utmost stupidity. Crete and Cuba are drifting along, peaceably, in spite of all mankind's interest or neglect.

H.

MS: MHi
  1. Rachel Cameron (b. 1871), later Mrs. Chandler Hale, stepdaughter of Elizabeth Cameron.
  2. In Perrault's tale Blue Beard's wife discovers that he has killed his former wives. She escapes a similar fate when her "Sister Anne" sees her brothers arriving. They kill Blue Beard.
  3. *Lourdes* (1894) and *Rome* (1896), novels by Emile Zola.

4. Henri Rochefort (1831–1913); Edouard-Adolphe Drumont (1844–1917), author of *La France juive* and editor of *Libre Parole*, the chief organ of the anti-Semitic movement.
5. "Gyp," the pen name of the comtesse de Martel de Janville (1850–1932).
6. Paul Granier de Cassagnac (1843–1904), Bonapartist and political journalist.
7. Bishop John Keane, a church liberal, was forced to resign as rector of Catholic University of America in Sept. 1896.
8. Fritz Friedmann, *L'Empereur Guillaume II et la révolution par en haute. L'affaire Kotze* (1896). The book told of sexual misconduct in court circles while Leberecht von Kotze (1850–1920) was master of ceremonies for the German emperor Wilhelm II (1859–1941).
9. Samuel Pepys (1633–1703), *Diary.*
10. Thomas Hardy (1840–1928), English novelist, an edition of whose works was published in 1896.
11. Count Maurice Sala, French consul general at Havana 1891–1897.

To John Franklin Jameson

1603 H Street. 17 Nov. 1896.

Dear Mr Jameson[1]

Your obliging letter of the 14th has had the luck to find me here; an accident which rarely happens. Long absences are one cause which has broken my relations with the world. The other and more serious cause is that, in the chaotic and unintelligible condition in which I found—and left—the field of knowledge which is called History, I became overpoweringly conscious that any further pretence on my part of acting as instructor would be something worse than humbug, unless I could clear my mind in regard to what I wanted to teach. As History stands, it is a sort of Chinese Play, without end and without lesson. With these impressions I wrote the last line of my History, asking for a round century before going further. Five or six or even more years have passed since then, and I am still a student and a scholar—and a mighty modest one too,—without consciousness of a mission as teacher. In short, I am like most other men who have studied much, and know that they know nothing. I have nothing to say. I would much rather wipe out all I have ever said, than go on with more. I am glad to hear other men, if they think they have something worth saying; but it is as a scholar, and not as a teacher that I have taken my seat.

Pray accept this as my answer to your request.

Very truly Yours   Henry Adams.

MS: DLC, Jameson

1. John Franklin Jameson (1859–1937), professor of history at Brown University, had apparently invited HA to lecture there.

To George Cabot Lodge

1603 H Street. 17 Jan. '97.

Dear Bay

Your duties are probably absorbing, if they require the study of Latin and German, or either of those languages which are incapable of being learned, and, when learned, are incapable of any really artistic purpose.[1] Yet an intelligent man may be—as intelligent men have been—obliged to use those tongues, which obliges us to pursue them. Therefore I write to pray you, (if in case of your contact with the German world, you meet up with any German mind,) that you will incontinently pack it up, and send it to me. More than that, I want to follow the fight over the Agrarian laws, and the Bourses; and, as Springy undoubtedly must know all about it, I want you to get from him what lists of pamphlets, &c, you can, and send them to me.[2]

Who knows the future? Perhaps these writings may be useful. Do I not sit here, peering far into the darkness, and laughing to my harmless senility at all the futile ways of man and god; and shall I not be better and wiser if you teach me more? And may I not impart your wisdom to other futilities? They need it. Betray me not, for, by the horns of Moses,[3] my life pays now the penalty of indiscretion, and the Gold-bug reigns forever; but all the same, there are those who are not happy, and among them are your honored father, and my beloved neighbor next door. They have suffered much, and they are in one great and glorious helplessness. The wheels of the chariot have passed over them. The Ohio standard of statesmanship cuts so low that it leaves not a noxious weed behind. The new cabinet has turned to dust and ashes, which beats any previous emetic so composed. Your honored father is a companion to dragons and John Hay is a brother to owls.[4] Each in his way has found that the Lord does not appreciate his servant Job, and that friends are a vexation to the soul of the upright. I will not describe to you the interior of their garnitures, for it would be a difficult task. All is said when I observe that of all the gold-bugs known in this country, the species peculiar to Cleveland is the coarsest, the biggest and the cheapest, and that Mark Hanna is a museum specimen.[5] I still hope that my neighbor will pull off his mission, for I want to stay with him in England, but no man can see anything for your father to pull off except sackcloth and ashes.

Let this teach you, my son,—to hold your tongue, and send me all the literature which is likely to be of use at the next election. If you have a grain of common-sense, you will work hard and write a play, with comic songs and dances, and a Cleveland comic character, as for instance, Hanna, to beat Francis Wilson.[6] Cultivate a sense of humor, and be versatile. If you could see your elders here laugh and jest, you would learn how. I have the material for an American novel that would make your literary fortune and oblige you to live in Europe forever. Compared with ten years ago, life is as dramatic and amusing as in the days of Nero. But beware how, in your letters or conversation, even to Springy, you betray the slightest knowledge of what I say. I write to you solely—solely, solely—to ask for agrarian literature and for whatever throws German light on the plans and policy of Russia. I'm an old man, and a poor old man, and a damned ugly old man, and I've gone and voted for M Kinley. So does history repeat John Phenix.[7] Consequently I am treading on egg-shells, and keep uncommonly still. You had better do likewise or you will tread on me.

Give my love to Springy. Society here is raging as usual, but your mamma probably tells you all you want to know about that. I saw her last night at the Opera, looking bright and as fascinating as ever.

Auf Wiedersehen.

MS: MHi

1. Lodge had gone to Berlin in early January to study German philosophy.
2. Spring Rice was second secretary at the British embassy in Berlin 1895–1898.
3. Moses is referred to in Deuteronomy 33:17 as wearing horns and was traditionally so represented, as in the Michelangelo sculpture for the tomb of Pope Julius II.
4. "A brother to dragons, and a companion to owls"; Job 30:29. Hay was about to be named ambassador to England.
5. Marcus Alonzo Hanna (1837–1904), Cleveland capitalist and political boss, U.S. senator 1897–1904.
6. Francis Wilson (1854–1935), American musical-comedy star.
7. John Phoenix, pseudonym of George Horatio Derby (1823–1861), Massachusetts-born Western humorist whose *Phœnixiana* (1856) included the vignette of an elderly citizen who was "overcome by excitement and spirituous potations" on election day: "'I'm an old man, gentle-*men*,' sobbed he, 'and a poor old man, and a d——d ugly old man, and I've gone and voted for Bigler!'" (1889 ed., pp. 108–109).

To Worthington Chauncey Ford

St Germain en Laye   1 August, 1897.

My dear Ford[1]

Your letter of July 21 with its valuable inclosure arrived last evening here where I should say that the nineteenth century was already forgotten, and the sixteenth alone remembered. By dint of effort, I too had almost lost consciousness of affairs, and shut my eyes tight to passing events. During a month passed in London, I became satisfied that no serious change in the situation was likely to take place, and that the best thing that a student could do was to go to sleep for a year. So I came over to Paris in May, and have slept since. My five blonde nieces like many modes of amusement, but as yet they have not tried exports and imports. They do not even heartily enjoy French subjunctives, but they open their hearts to Valois kings and other dress-makers, and they ride and drive in the forests with extravagant disregard of the balance of trade. They nurse my senility and decrepitude with ideal care, and take from me every excuse for waking up to calculate figures.

Nevertheless I have tried to measure the bearings of your complete statement for the year. It differs little from what we calculated on April 1. The importations have been much greater, but the exports have been better, than I expected. We have a balance of $274,000,000 in our favor, which seems to exceed all precedent.

Yet we have not turned the exchanges, and gold continues to flow out. We have now the six full years since '92, and the correct balance paid by us, over and above the apparent trade-balance, is just $200,000,000 a year. I conceive that to be at present our normal situation as far as regards relative years. What the actual situation is, unshown on the returns, I do not know, nor is it essential to know.

There are in fact two accounts which should be kept separate in our minds. One is the legitimate industrial trade account; the other is the money-dealer's, or bankers' account; and these have now very little to do with each other. Money is a commodity, and the most important single commodity now manufactured or exchanged, but as it grows in importance, it needs a separate account.

My present interest is not the money-account, but the industrial. From what we have seen of late years, I think it indubitable that while industry, in twenty-five years, may have doubled its product, capital has decupled its mass. Ten million dollars in 1870 could hardly be carried so easily as a hundred millions today. I see no reason to suppose that this creation of capital will be checked until civilisation itself is checked, and, with the present organisation of capital, that sort of civilisation is not likely to be checked.

What interests me is the effect of a capitalistic domination on an industrial society. England and France are the real field of struggle, now as ever. Europe, under its present capitalistic regime has proscribed war and violence because they endanger debts; but it has stimulated and extended industrial war and economical competition to an extent which is already almost as exciting and destructive as war.

French industry has suffered very severely, but I am more curious about the English. The curious movements of gold this last year, and the total failure of the Bank to draw gold from abroad, leads me to think that even now the true industrial balance is so vastly against England that even the vast bankers' balance in her favor cannot overcome the drain. A banking-community like London must be hard up when it cannot or will not send gold to pay her debts to us, but creates long-exchange, as it did last winter; and then exacts instantly every dollar of gold it can get when the industrial balance turns in its favor. Naturally I have waited with great curiosity to know what would happen when our tariff should be settled, imports stopped, and the autumn crops begin to flow out. This time, can England refuse to pay cash? Can her bankers again make fictitious book-entries on a scale that will stop the flow of gold? If not, how much gold can they spare? The Bank certainly can spare none.

For these reasons I shall wait with curiosity to see the British trade-returns for the next five months; for in the struggle now going on, it is life or death to us all; and unless we can economise and squeeze industrial Europe, capitalistic Europe will bleed us to death.

As for the currency question I can see no reason why all parties, except dealers in foreign exchange, should not unite in withdrawing our green-backs. Naturally we must substitute silver, at least for the time, and we must not contract, if only for political reasons; but if the banking class is honest,—which, by-the-bye, is a supposition that I should never dream of making of any exclusive interest,—there ought to be no serious difficulty in freeing the Treasury wholly from the domination of Europe in that respect.

With a favorable industrial trade-balance, and with our Treasury strengthened to protect itself against foreign pillage, the industrial and economical war is likely to become rapidly more and more intense. I do not care to live to see it, for it is not an elevated spectacle, and no one is the nobler for dying in order that others may get cheaper and worse clothes and food; but if I live five years more, and the machine works steadily, as of late, I ought to see quite enough of it to satisfy any slight appetite I still have; and the European trade-returns will be my delight. If you can, I should be extremely curious to see you make out for England, France, Germany, Holland, Belgium and Switzerland—and Austria, if Austria is also a creditor country—a series of tables like that for us; and in the end make a general table for all the creditor countries, since 1889. The debtor countries matter less. We are debtor enough for all. The industrial movement of the creditor countries is the essential; for, if the capitalistic system works to injure the industrial system under its immediate influence, the end must come in the form of industrial decline and decay. Capital may survive indefinitely, as in Byzantium, by propagating cheaper forms of labor, like coolies and negroes, but with that form of society I feel no particular concern, once our chapter is closed.

Anyway, accept my warm thanks for the table which is a foundation for all future study.

Ever Yrs   Henry Adams.

MS: NN

1. Worthington Chauncey Ford (1858–1941), chief of Bureau of Statistics at the Treasury 1893–1898, supplied many statistical tables on international trade in reply to HA's inquiries.

To Cecil Arthur Spring Rice

16 Rue Christophe Colomb
Paris, 11 Nov. 1897.

My dear Nephew

Before your extremely interesting letter gets lost in my drawer under a heap of bills, and before the varying changes of the year cause me to forget all that is a week old, I hasten to acknowledge and to appreciate your attention, and to give you what news I can of the small world I know. Your inquiry about Mrs Cameron covers us all, in fact, for the two nieces are more or less immediately with her. She has her apartment at 61 Avenue Marceau, we have ours nearly opposite. She has taken passage on the 27th. My girls have taken passage on the same steamer. She has bronchitis bad, and is likely to kill herself by going home, even if she is able to go. My girls, I hope, will get off, even if she breaks down. Enfin! Was wollen Sie? Many years ago, before I lost my mind, and when people were still partially human, I gave up the struggle of life. Kismet! All America and most of England is—or are—in Paris. The autumn has been lovely. The Touraine was charming. The sun shines as bright on the Champs Elysées as it did under the Empire, and all my schoolmates who were here with me then, are here with me now,—except the dead ones,—with white hair and senile eyes and apparently as little sense as forty years ago. How do I know which is best, sixty years or twenty—the Republic or the Empire? Both are Progress! Or are they not?

Make your own answer to Life as it asks its questions, and hang on to one fact: that that particular question is only another form of the kinetic theory of gases, of which your German problem is an illustration. Do you know the kinetic theory of gases? Of course you do, since Clerke Maxwell was an Oxford man, I suppose. Anyway, Germany is and always has been a remarkably apt illustration of Maxwell's conception of "sorting demons."[1] By bumping against all its neighbors, and being bumped in turn, it gets and gives at last a common motion, which is, and of necessity must be, a vortex or cycle. It can't get anywhere except round a circle and return on itself. It has done so since the time of Varus and his legions. The struggle between the industrial and the military impulses was at the bottom of the Reformation. It has been at the bottom of every political change since Merwig.[2] We can now pretty well measure the possible x which is the ultimate quantity we want to eliminate. Another generation will have the figures, and the limit of ultimate concentration will then be calculable,— barring war, which may of course delay, or wholly defeat, further vortical movement. The point to study is, however, not primarily the social move- ment, but the industrial, and I am always wondering at my own ignorance, and at the European conspiracy of silence on that point. What is the rate of progress of the creditor nations in exports and in capital. What is the rate at which credit increases with reference to its base, if it has one, in exchange? What is the rate of production compared with the possible markets? I can get absolutely no serious information as to the amount of credit now existing, or its equivalents in previous decades. With these two elements: the industrial and the capitalistic, I think I could fix approx- imately the elements of the human orbit, which is necessarily limited by the same conditions of mass, &c, which limit the orbit of the planet itself.

But this is something approaching thought, and our intelligent classes now permit no one except Jews to think. Beware how you betray such a vicious tendency. All governments particularly regard it with jealousy, and Universities and Society are very shy of all who indulge in the habit. Only Socialists and Anarchists can afford to think.

Ever Yrs   Henry Adams.

MS: MHi

1. See HA to Samuel P. Langley, May 3, 1893, note 2.
2. Merovig (c. 411–c. 458), chief of the Salian Franks, from whom the first royal dynasty of France took its name.

To Elizabeth Cameron

Paris, 13 Jan. '98.

This has been rather a curious week of rumors, stories, imaginations and events, private and public. Most of them are of the sort for which Paris is so famous,—apparently insane and purposeless inventions, calculated to make a self-respecting mosquito hold his tongue. None of them are likely to do good by spreading, and none of them directly concern me; but one of them seems to concern you, or at least Mr Cameron, if it is true. It comes from London and runs literally thus: "A man who has just come from Rome (January 9) says that Chandler has given it up there, and gone to Paris."[1] This is all! If it is true, probably Chandler will avoid his friends, as before, and I shall not see him. Probably they will know about it in Washington before we know anything here. Of course, if true, it is very serious. I had hoped he would last at least till the warm weather. You will not mention the story, least of all as coming through me. I want no contact with the Hales. But such rumors have got to be reckoned with. And no doubt Rachel will take refuge with her sister in Paris, if she needs help, and if her sister comes. In any case, I shall not be likely to see or hear anything of them, as I leave Paris on the 21st with the Hays for Egypt, and mean not to return before June, if I can manage to get to Russia, after the Nile. You know my old instinct of running away and hiding in a hole, which has always puzzled my family and friends? I have it strong just now. I don't want to go back to Washington; still less to Boston; until the world and all society has finished its somersaults so that I can settle down to a new situation. The smash of last spring was only partial, and settled nothing, not even a boom in real-estate; and this autumn has left everything dragging,—even Cuba. I've not even married a niece, and the Lord knows it's high time to work off some of my stock. Brooks needs help, for he is a singularly impatient and unsteady workman. Enfin, the situation over here is much more interesting than the situation at home. I can watch it better by hanging about Europe.

So I expect to pass next summer on this side, and perhaps next winter too, if the old rubbish still sticks; but please don't whisper it, for I hate to have sticks poked down my hole. Meanwhile, the rubbish goes on rotting, and does it fast. You saw how emphatically the Army, through the Court-martial, set its foot on the Jews and smashed the Dreyfus intrigue into a pancake.[2] Aristarchi who dined with me last night, and with whom I discussed the whole European situation, insists that, whether Dreyfus is guilty or not, (and he has little doubt of the fact that he was, but this is no longer important except to him), the campaign which the Jews have made for him, the very large amounts of money they have spent on the press and on the effort to pass by the government and control public opinion against it, has resulted in enormously stimulating the anti-semite feeling in France, which has now reached the point where violence has become only a matter of time. I believe Aristarchi to be right.[3] The current of opinion is running tremendously strong, now that the whole extent of the Jew scandal is realised. For no one doubts now that the whole campaign has been one of money and intrigue; and the French are very furious. Of course all the English and the Americans are with the Jews, which makes it worse.

If the financial situation should turn bad, there would be many sudden changes all over Europe; and no one knows what the financial situation is. I am very curious about Russia which just now holds everything up. Russia shows some signs of being pressed for money; and Austria is decidedly in a bad way. England can't much help them, for India is pressing her on one side, and we are shovelling imports into her, without asking pay, on the other. Of course, Europe has lots of bonds and stock still to sell, but she can sell nowhere except in New York, and she has already sold most of her loose paper there, and borrowed more. If New York took alarm now, and withdrew her money from London, I think the Bank of England would have to shut up. Of course, the Jews will never permit that to happen, and they have the power to maintain credit by banding together; but meanwhile the outside world pays the whole bill, and just now the unlucky victim is India.

So you see why it amuses me to look on. Unluckily for me, my eyes and ears have always been women. Without acquaintance with women of high position and social faculty, I am blind and deaf. Here I know none, and know of none. I'm half inclined to move over to London for a season, and try to catch on there. Whom do you recommend for an ally? Apparently I should have to educate her, and the chance of finding what I want, is small. Time is short. I am already too old to make love, and too dreary to be amusing. What is worse, society is older and drearier than I, and the women have lost the art of society. They are frankly bêtes.

And this condition of rotten instability may last ten years, or fifty, or a hundred, and I can't wait. If I had common-sense, I'd crawl back and die; but I want to see the fun, if it's coming; and the last six years I've seen a good deal, and there's a good deal going now.

Friday, 14th.   Parbleu! it was quicker than I thought! When I strolled down the Boulevard after dark last evening, there was an ominous hum in the air that made me look about me; for, if anybody was going to visit Alphonse Rothschild, I've a sort of notion that I'd like to go too. It appears that Zola kicked the boiler over.[4] The situation is now worse than ever. For the first time in twenty years, the Army has put down its foot with a stamp that has scared Cabinet, Senate, Bourse and Boulevards. The Cabinet and the Senate crouched down under the table. Scheurer Kestner was shuffled out of the way quicker than that venerable fool ever guessed it. Colonel Picquart found himself shut up in Mt Valérien before he could breakfast.[5] But Zola howled; and the Bourse actually fought—Jews and Gentiles—till the police came in. A good day's work! and rioting too in Havana! and a new outbreak in India! Tiens! ça marche!

One can't expect larks like this every day, to be sure; and after a little explosion, the kettle will doubtless simmer down, as it did in '94, provided the finances are right. That is the point of my curiosity:—the Berlin Bourse, the Russian Treasury, and the Bank of England! If one goes, all goes.

Ralph Palmer is coming over tonight to pass a few days. He goes on Tuesday. On that day the Hays arrive, and on Thursday, the 20th, I break up here, and move back to the Brighton. The leaving Paris just now is rather a doubtful advantage to my friends, though for myself I don't mind. Brooks and his household need me more than I supposed. On the other hand, I am not sure whether the Hays need me or not, though I rather guess that John does, since he has no other companion than Spencer Eddy.[6] Anyway, no one is the worse for vanishing, especially when he has vicious political and social tendencies like mine. If I stayed here a year, I should drop into the circle of Reclus and Krapotkin, and should be sent home by Porter in chains.[7]

Ever

MS: MHi

1. Chandler Hale (1873–1951), HA's companion in Mexico and the Caribbean, had married Rachel Cameron, a union which had disappointed her family. Hale had been secretary of the U.S. embassy in Rome and had resigned because of ill health.
2. As a result of Colonel Georges Picquart's discovery that an incriminating document had been forged, the supporters of Alfred Dreyfus pressed to have the case reopened, claiming that Major Marie Charles Ferdinand Walsin Esterhazy was the forger. The army refused, and its court-martial acquitted Esterhazy.
3. Grégoire Aristarchi Bey (b. 1843), longtime Washington friend of HA, had been Turkish minister to the U.S. 1873–1883. He was now a journalist in Paris.
4. Baron Mayer Alphonse de Rothschild (1827–1905), head of the Paris branch of the family bank. Emile Zola's open letter, which filled the front page of *L'Aurore* on Jan. 13, denounced the war office and charged criminal injustice in the Dreyfus case.
5. Auguste Scheurer-Kestner (1833–1899), vice-president of the senate, had interceded on behalf of Dreyfus, and the Paris *Herald* reported that his replacement was "almost a foregone conclusion." Georges Picquart was arrested after Esterhazy's acquittal and imprisoned.
6. Spencer Fayette Eddy (1874–1939), private secretary to John Hay.
7. Elisée Reclus (1830–1905), French geographer and revolutionary; Prince Peter Kropotkin (1842–1921), leading anarchist thinker; Horace Porter (1837–1921), U.S. ambassador to France 1897–1905.

To Elizabeth Cameron

26 Feb. '98.

Tomorrow we reach Cairo, and all sorts of ends and beginnings and questions and answers, with perhaps some letters and possibly an incident or two that may not be older than Cleopatra. Two days ago a flying mail-steamer stopped to give us a mail, including your short despatch just before going to Boston and blizzards. There was also a letter from H. Blaine and one from Mabel. With that exception, nothing has occurred to divert my mind from hieroglyphs and Pharaohs. All runs on like the life on an ocean voyage. On the whole, there is little virtue in travelling with such companions. I am the only one who aggravates and irritates. The others are provokingly patient and tolerant, and even headache fails to spoil their tempers. They do not even stick pins into one, which is an occupation that I have been accustomed to suppose all women and most men adepts in practising, by the sole light of nature. I find myself sticking the pins just to keep up the tradition. Peace reigns within our ship, and beyond is nothing. Since leaving Luxor we have seen nobody, and, except for one or two donkey-trips, have seen nothing. You do not want to hear about tombs and mummies, and if I brought you as a present the complete parure of Hatasu or Arsinoe, you would neither care for it yourself nor find anyone in New York to admire it; for the Egyptians did not know the diamond, and the New Yorker knows nothing else—unless it is the ruby or the emerald, which come to the same. It is no use my trying to interest you in Egypt. The best I could do would be to interest you in Lord Cromer, and him we have missed.[1] The next best would be to interest you in Lord Cowper's valet, who was murdered a week ago a few miles from here, but the newspapers will already have told you more than I know about it myself, and the British Lord, even in his incarnation as valet, does not spell-bind me. I am almost more interested to hear that Zola is sent to prison.[2] If he did not deserve it for the special offense, he did for his novels; and on the whole I think he had better have joined his friend Dreifus on the Devil's Island some time ago, with as much more French rot as the island would hold, including most of the press and the greater part of the theatre, with all the stock-brokers and a Rothschild or two for example. But the horror of my British-American world is positively heart-rending. Since Louis Seize was sent to the scaffold, France has done nothing that made the hair rise on end like the sending of Zola to jail. The incredible and indelible infamy and disgrace of the French people rouses deeper indignation and disgust than the crucifixion, or the massacres of Nero or of his majesty the present Sultan, ever did in the breasts of the British nobility and gentry, not to speak of the middle class, and their New York clients. The gold-bug is outraged beyond expression. How hard I try to sympathise! But, by the soul of Pharaoh and the Rock of Moses,[3] one is not a scarabeus of that kind without inward agony and self-mortification. If you could see me act the beetle, you would know at last what a silent ocean of heroism lies beneath the smile of the Sphynx. I am going to have a coat embroidered with a scarabeus pattern in green, and the hieroglyphic for:—Men Cheaper Ra on the back.

All the same, Egypt is better than opium. It soothes and smooths one's creases out with the patient weight of a German philosopher trying to be intelligible. Hay and I ponder painfully over the strange state of mind which results from learning to regard Homer as a modern poet and Herodotus as a trivial Cook tourist. Go where we will in this singular land, one has to look down on all human knowledge or experience as modern and insufficient, but we are used in a degree to that, and we have known since childhood that, from the top of the pyramids one looks down on Alexander the Great, Julius Caesar, Napoleon and Lord Cromer foreshortened to the same plane, of the same apparent scale and proportions. From the sarcophagus of Cheops all look alike; only their methods may seem slightly personal or peculiar to their barbarian variety of origin. This we knew. It is a commonplace of Murray and Baedeker and of the Howadji[4] when we were young. Five-and-twenty years ago, I learned to regard the Third Dynasty as that of my contemporaries. What passes far beyond this, and reduces us to powder, so pulverised is the imagination at sixty, comes from too great familiarity with Cheops and Chefren.[5] Every day we are forced to realise that they were themselves modern, and that relatively they must run with Evelyn Baring and Cambyses as of the same general age.[6] We see dimly already a hundred thousand years behind the pyramids, almost as clearly as we see our Indians behind the Pilgrims. I have got to reconstruct my youth on the scale of at least fifty thousand instead of five thousand years. As far as I can see, society in Egypt when I was young and really active ran to seed fully ten thousand years ago, and was as rotten then as it is now. Since then the only change has been that the rot has spread outwards.

After all, I have felt sure for years that I had made a mistake somewhere, and perhaps a mere trifle of fifty thousand years in my age is one of the least of my errors.

A mail-steamer has just come by, and whistled, and stopped, and put on board a mail with your letter from Boston, telling of snow and ice and weddings and people older than Ramses. Also a letter from Mme Chose in St Germain offering me the Chateau d'Hennemont. Queer jumble! In sight of the Pyramids with 80° degrees of heat!

Cairo. Monday. 28. Here we are again, and the change is curious! Yesterday morning we all rode across to Saqquara to see our friend Ti in his lovely tomb,—us young people on donkeys, and Mrs Hay like Cleopatra, on a throne borne by strong Nubians, and visible from miles across the plain, like Memnon.[7] At four o'clock in the afternoon we were installed at Shepheards, and I took Helen and Alice for a long tramp up the Mouski to see the streets of Cairo. At eight we found ourselves at dinner; the Ham Fishs at the next table, the Angells beyond them, and so on.[8] After dinner, talk in the thronged hall and cold plunges into the hottest of water. Then I heard what I have tried to put off so long, a little of the story of the "Maine,"—as much as can be learned here—and, from step to step, was dragged back to the life I fled.[9] I fled once more, and as soon as my cigar was out, I escaped unmarked in the crowd, and hid myself in bed. Hardly had I turned off the stupid light, when a bang on my door started me up again. It was Hay's valet Creber, bringing your letter of the 13th, and I retired to bed to read how you were already worked up to the old excitement by the mere escapade of Dupuy.[10] Three long hours of midnight was the price I paid for my return to life from the tombs! As I am drawn back into the fascinating and horrible whirlpool of politics and finance, I thank the ill-luck that drove me away. Last winter was too much of a nervous strain, and this winter in Washington, without your help, would have broken me all up. As for you, another Washington winter like the last would have been the end. Let them run their machine as they like, now; the wisdom of all Egypt could see no way out of the situation. Spain is clearly in convulsions, and what she may drag down in her ruin, no one can guess. France, and even England, may sink; but we, I think, not yet.

Love to Martha. I will write to her next week.

Ever

MS: MHi

1. Evelyn Baring (1841–1917), 1st Baron Cromer, plenipotentiary of the British occupation of Egypt 1883–1907.
2. On Feb. 23 Zola was found guilty of criminal libel. After a retrial, he fled to England to escape imprisonment.
3. Exodus 17:6.
4. *Howadji*: Muslims who have made the pilgrimage to Mecca.
5. Cheops (fl. c. 2680 B.C.), Chephren (fl. 2565 B.C.), builders of the Great Pyramid and the Second Pyramid at Giza.
6. Cambyses II (d. 521 B.C.), Persian conqueror of Egypt.
7. The tomb of royal architect Ti, noted for its remarkable reliefs; the colossi of Memnon, two seated statues of Amenhotep III.
8. James B. Angell (1829–1916), president of the University of Michigan, minister to Turkey 1897–1898.
9. The battleship *Maine* had been blown up and sunk in Havana harbor on Feb. 15.
10. Enrique Dupuy de Lôme, Spanish minister to the U.S., was obliged to resign because his indiscreet private comment on President McKinley was published in the press.

To Elizabeth Cameron

Athens. 10 April, 1898.

I had half a hope of getting a letter from you today, and put off writing in consequence, but nothing arrives since your telegram which I answered to Paris. It would be gay to be with you at Venice. I am torn greatly in mind. On one side, the pleasure of being with you and Martha would be far greater than any other possible enjoyment. On the other, I promised Rockhill to go with him to Servia and Bulgaria to present his credentials, and Rockhill is quite pathetic in his isolation out here, and clings to his friends stoutly. To see the Balkan States and Constantinople with him would be a vast spread of wings, and a serious spread of knowledge. I must do it, for it is not one of those chances that are refusable. But, behind all the rest is my invincible repugnance to returning to the west till politics get decided somehow. I make desperate efforts to hear and think as little as possible about the situation, but, do what I will, I hear and think too much, and as I sit on the platform of the Pnyx, or wander over the hills at Phaleron or Eleusis, my mind wanders terribly fast between Salamis, where Xerxes is before my eyes, and Key West where our ships are waiting orders.[1] The moment is perhaps a turning-point in history; in any case it can hardly fail to fix the lines of a new concentration, and to throw open an immense new field of difficulties. The world is abjectly helpless. It is running a race to nowhere, only to beggar its neighbors. It must either abolish its nationalities, concentrate its governments and confiscate its monopolies for social economies, or it must steadily bump from rock to rock, and founder at last, economically; while it will founder socially if it does concentrate and economise. Even so weak and wild a political member as Spain or Turkey has the power to pull down the whole fabric of the world, and the whole of Europe quivers with terror if she threatens to use it. Germany, Russia and England can agree in nothing but a division of thefts, and a tacit understanding that no part of the world shall be exempt from the exercise of their power. Behind it all, there lies an economical war which is vastly more fatal in its effects than any ordinary war of armies.

Slowly and painfully our people are waking up to the new world they are to live in, and I am, as you know, for these five years past, so absorbed in it that it gives me nervous dyspepsia, insomnia and incipient paralysis if I have to face a crisis. Now, one can stand dyspepsia and paralysis, but one would rather not, unless one is needed or rewarded for it. As I have certainly never been rewarded, and have never received the smallest hint from anyone that I am needed, being sixty years old and therefore not fitted to carry cannon or march with extreme probability of arriving, being, moreover, a tax-payer and a steady supporter of every administration (except Cleveland's), it seems to me that I show considerable intelligence and amiability by keeping my nose out of this mess, and remaining as far away as possible. Three years ago, when the danger was ahead, I joined in howling warnings. Probably I might have saved my wasted energies. The result must be the same, whatever foresight we have. Just now, if I howl, I should only get my head punched.

So I dread coming west, and dread still more the thought that I may be obliged to come west. I am too glad to remain here, and to haunt the poor, old, ridiculous, academic, pedagogic, preposterous associations of Attica. What a droll little amusing fraud of imagination it was, and how it has imposed its own valuation of itself on all respectable society down to this day! Fifty years of fortunate bloom at a lucky moment,—a sudden flood of wealth from a rich silver-mine, the Rand of that day,[2]—was all that really dazzles us; a sort of unnatural, forced flower, never strong, never restful, and always half-conscious of its own superficiality. So ridiculous a city, without excuse for existence, and without land to cultivate, water to drink, or trade to handle, no historian ever saw elsewhere. Aristophanes and Lucian are the only people who really understood it. Still, it had a certain success that I could wish had been commoner. Without being a superstitious worshipper of Athenian art, I shouldn't mind if a little of it could have survived. My brother Brooks says: No! it cannot be! man is made to be cheap, and Athens was costly.—After all, other and greater arts have gone;—Chartres and Amiens are as dead as Athens, and Michael Angelo deader than Phidias. It is a comfort to find one city that never kept shop, and where art never smelt of per-centages. I prefer it to Venice,—or should, if you were not to be there.

Rockhill and I roam all over the place, for Mrs Rockhill and Dolly[3] have gone to Olympia for three days, and left us here. One afternoon we passed at Eleusis, really an exquisite spot. All day today we have rambled along the sea-shore of Phalerum and the Piraeus. We haunt low quarters where I bargain for coins with dirty pawn-brokers and greasy Greek peddlers. As they sell me for a dollar or two the same coins which the shops and collectors at Athens will not sell for less than ten or twenty or a hundred dollars, naturally I prefer their friendship. My coin-collection is becoming weighty. I must have bought more than a hundred since Assouan, and they afford me not only much amusement but lots of instruction. A new king turns up every day or two, of whose existence I never heard, but whose head is a medallion that all the Caesars since Julius have never been able to approach—unless it be Napoleon, who did pretty well on medals as on some other rivalries with classic triumphs. But of course the only real charm of Athens, as of all these other dry countries, is the color and the water, the mountains and the sea. I wish you were here. You would hate it.

April 13.   Another mail last night, with London papers to the 9th. But no letter from you or from England except from Gaskell on the 6th; yet you had been in London a year or two then,—I can't remember the odd months,—and Hay might at least have sent me a line to tell me so. I shall get nervous if another mail brings nothing. And I'm keeping this because I don't know your Venice address. This contretemps quite overshadowed the political tempest. Poor dear old McKinley stands like Olympian Zeus with his thunder-bolt ready, and Sir Julian Neptune with the lesser Gods offering him burnt-incense.[4] I only hope he will keep it up. The real issue is now European, and, to me, a veritable turning-point of the hinges of Hades. If we only get round that corner safely—and that corner means the Kaiser Willy to me! Then they can pick up the pieces of various shattered empires at our leisure. To think that the gold-bugs, instead of squeezing us into obedience, have squeezed Paris and London till they howl, and have forced the Bank of England to put up its rate to 4 per cent in order to borrow more of our money when she can't pay what they already owe! As the exchanges now look, I think the Bank will have to stop payment this year. If that does not first squeeze the life out of us, we take at once the hegemony of the world—the head of the column,—the pride of the biggest purse—and all the Jews will emigrate to New York. But the struggle to survive will shake society in Europe and America to tatters.

Ah! I've been thinking so long of this crisis, and have cast up so many columns of figures, not to speak of our prodigious Cameron Reports of the Senate Committee, on which, as far as I can see, the President and Congress have taken their stand. After all, it was you and I who did all the real fighting against the odds when that hangman dog of an Olney went back on himself and us. It was a mauvais quart d'heure, the Christmas holidays of '96, and poor Willy Phillips never lived to see the fight recovered. If only this week holds out right!

Meanwhile I have become an Athenian, and have half forgot that countries exist without dust and Greece. I live mostly at Rockhill's, and do little of anything. Our plans are now settled. We are all to start Saturday (16th) for a week's trip to Mycenae, Corinth, Delphi, &c; and on our return, as soon as possible, we go to Constantinople; from there to Bucharest, ending up at Belgrade, probably about May 20. I shall then strike for Vienna, and Rockhill will return here to his family, for the ladies do not go with us to the north. By the end of May, therefore, I shall be searching Europe for you, if I do not hear more than I've heard yet. But all this may still depend a little on politics and today's, or tomorrow's, doings in Madrid and Washington.

April 14. All today we have passed in an expedition to Sunium. Rockhill, his wife, Dolly, and I. I would not neglect it, for Byron's sake;[5] and, for once, it was almost exactly what I imagined. I am glad to have got it right. How I wish you and Martha had been with me to see the Aegean at its best! The wind was strong from the south, and the blue was streaked with white along the coast, as the blue of the sky was marked by the strong white of the ruined temple. I won't bore you with scenery, especially as I am very homesick when I think of you at Venice, and how I would like to take you, on a soft, spring, afternoon, in a gondola to Torcello, to worship my mosaic Madonna over the old bishop's chair. And Ravenna, too, and San Vitale and San Apollinaris. I would not trouble you with criticisms of Venetian Gothic more than I could help, but at Torcello and Murano I would be really sympathetic. There is nothing so full of feeling in Greece.

And now I have waited till the last moment for the mail, but nothing comes, and I must send off this letter, for the mail goes early in the morning. Where ought I to address it? I don't want to send it all the way to Paris. It would lose a week, if you are at Venice. Apparently I must send it to Morgan's correspondent in Venice, and trust to the telegraph to let you know it is there, in case I hear from you. I have received from Beirut a letter from Martha with some charming little photographs. I will write to her later. There is nothing more to say. I am quite alone here, except for the Rockhills, and they are as solitary as I. The tourists are many, but unknown to us. I shall hurry all I can, to join you.

Ever Yrs.

MS: MHi

1. The U.S. North Atlantic Squadron was assembling for action against the Spanish. In 480 B.C. the Greek fleet drawn up at Salamis had awaited the battle that was to end the Persian dominion.
2. Beginning in 483 B.C., the silver mines of Mount Laurium in Attica became a new source of wealth for Athens. Beginning in 1886, the gold mines of the Rand (Witwatersrand) in Transvaal became a major new source of wealth for England.
3. Dorothy Woodville Rockhill (b. 1878), the Rockhills' daughter.
4. McKinley, his war message ready, delayed sending it to Congress in order to allow time for the evacuation of Americans from Cuba. Meanwhile, European ministers to the U.S. prepared jointly to urge a peaceful solution. Sir Julian Pauncefote joined their effort on condition that, as dean of the Washington diplomatic corps, he compose the note. After consultation with Acting Secretary of State William R. Day, he adopted American wording about "re-establishment of order in Cuba" (April 7).
5. "Place me on Sunium's marbled steep"; Byron, *Don Juan* (1819–1824), III, LXXXVI, strophe 16.

To John Hay

Belgrade, 5 May, '98.

Dear Infant

Here I am, and have been for a week, travelling about to inspect the President's representatives in the Balkans, and to keep Rockhill in order, but have got to the end of both; for King Milan has shut up Rockhill here for an indefinite time,—apparently during his good pleasure,—and I can't go on alone to Bucarest.[1] So I have got to turn westward at last, and, if you keep an eye out to windward, you will probably see me running into port somewhere about June 1st.

Naturally I use nautical terms, seeing that we are all nautical just now, and have our eyes fixed seaward. Queer that in our day, good Bostonians should be still trembling, like their ancestors in the 16th century, for fear of a Spanish armada! I hardly know myself whether I am reading the Critic or Amyas Leigh.[2] In a day or two more, I suppose we shall see that Spanish fleet which is not yet to be seen because it is not in sight, or for some other reason. I am dying of sheer curiosity to learn what Dewey has done at Cavite, for the Spanish account obviously omits all his serious work. Still more anxious am I for Schley's turn-up on the Atlantic.[3]

Of course, in theory, not a single Spanish ship or land-soldier ought to escape capture or destruction. They have taken risks far greater than those of the old Armada. If they succeed in winning any successes, things will be drawn out; but I expect in any case that diplomacy must now become pretty active, and as this is likely to be the last considerable settlement I shall witness, and as London is likely to be the spot where one can see most, I intend to bestow on that commercial and rotten metropolis a portion of the coming summer. You may as well, therefore, resign yourself to that infliction.

Europe has stood the financial strain of Spanish collapse without a total break-down, and is evidently delighted. Apparently our strength saved her, for the Bank pulled through only because we wanted no more gold. They seem to admit that we had the means of insisting on it, if we had needed it. Our financial supremacy is, for the time, established. But the worst and most nauseous dose Europe has yet had to suffer is the sight of our flag over Manila. Will not England—or Russia—want us to stay there? You have a new game to play, and I hardly see my clue. My own little game of two years ago is played out and won in far less time than I expected.[4] I had not prepared myself for the new deal, and don't quite feel as though I knew the value of the cards or of the players. Whose hand is the heroic

President playing, anyway? Is it New York and Cleveland? Is he on the make? Who is behind him? Is it a syndicate, financial, political, or what?

At Belgrade, one sees the Danube, or a piece of it, but not far across it, and the Cardinal Major President is more of a problem to me than all the Balkan peninsula. At this distance I see none of his tricks—real or assumed,—I see only the steady development of a fixed intent, never swerving or hesitating even before the utterly staggering responsibility of war. It is no use to tell me that McKinley has wavered or weakened or has had to be forced on. He has done it; and, though I call myself rather a reckless political theorist, he has gone far beyond me, and scared me not a little. No wonder if he has scared himself. In his place I should have gone to bed and stayed there. What does he want next? What should I want, in his place? To clear out the West Indies! That is as good as done!—Hawaii! He can take it with a word! But what of China? What of the East? What of Europe? By the horns of the moon, I know not where the ambition of the man may stop, for he holds the sceptre of the world—if Schley puts in his work.

Naturally I have stayed here in order to escape the bother of noise and idiocy that always begins a war, and I have tried to think of everything rather than it. If we get a licking, I don't want to be there; and if we win, I expect to turn up to watch the next hand. So I have wandered in the ruins of Baalbeck, and Ephesus, Eleusis and Mycenæ and Tiryns and Delphi, and have explored ancient Byzantium and modern Athens, and tracked the failures of civilisation over thousands of miles of country where every village is historical and every stream has run with blood, and all is now more desert and more barbarous than it was in the time of Homer. This is cheering—it is even a beautiful dream. But it has really taught me only one lesson, and that at an expense of three or four pounds bestowed on the noble oriental. You remember the Greek coins which so much puzzled me at Cairo. I could not comprehend how the finest Greek coins, worth anywhere from five pounds to fifty, should be held in the bazaars, by adjoining shop-keepers, at prices differing between four shillings and forty. Accordingly I bought specimens—naturally at the lowest price—wherever I met them—at Cairo, Damascus, Smyrna and Athens,—with increasing wonder, for the specimens became rarer and finer and cheaper as I went on. At last I had eight or ten of these coins, with the peculiarity of washing clean and bright, unlike genuine coins which usually wash down to the stain of time, and show a more or less rich oxydation. I had no means of weighing them, which is one of the surest tests. At last, at Constantinople, I ran the thing down. A scamp of a jeweller at Alexandria, by collusion with the guardian of the coins at the Museum there, made a series of about a hundred and fifty forgeries, which would deceive the righteous, and with these he has deluged the Levant. The forgeries are large and small, and I suppose include gold coins, and especially the rarest. I have seen only about thirty. The Syracuse is one; the Alexander another; and so on. I am curious to see whether the scamp has managed to keep the weights. I am also curious to get a complete set of them, for protection and comparison.

Rockhill sends his professional and personal regards. Convey the assurances, &c, to your amiable family.

Ever Yrs   Henry Adams.

MS: MHi

1. The former King Milan Obrenović IV (1854–1901), who had abdicated in 1889, had been appointed commander in chief of the army in 1894 by his son and successor, Alexander.
2. Richard Brinsley Sheridan's comedy *The Critic, or a Tragedy Rehearsed* (1779) includes a bombastic mock play, "The Spanish Armada." Amyas Leigh, the hero of Charles Kingsley's patriotic historical novel *Westward Ho!* (1855), takes part in the defeat of the Spanish Armada.
3. On May 1 Commodore George Dewey (1837–1917), commanding the U.S. Asiatic fleet, destroyed the Spanish fleet at Cavite; Commodore Winfield Scott Schley (1839–1911).
4. Having been enlisted by Clarence King in the cause of Cuban independence in the fall of 1895, HA made his house a kind of headquarters for the Washington agents of the revolutionaries and drafted for Senator Cameron the report of the Senate Foreign Relations Committee supporting the right of the U.S. to intervene.

To Mabel Hooper

Paris, 28 May, '98.

My dear Mabel

I've not thought it worth your while to hear from me of late, while you were settling your own affairs to your own liking.[1] If I have a horror in the world, it is that of meddling in other people's concerns, and if I had a commission from the Infinite to concentrate all practical wisdom in the most condensed form of dying advice to my fellow-beings, I should without a moment's hesitation say to Infinite Wisdom: "Hold your tongue and mind your own business!" Above all, I have nothing to say or to do with young people's love affairs; although I would much rather meddle with them than with older people's concerns. So I have carefully refused to answer your questions or to give you any advice except on the one point, that you had better marry. Even that is going further than most of my friends would approve. My father, who was the wisest man I ever knew, contented himself with giving that advice to his children, and never gave any more, nor did his children ever ask for more. You will get along very well in life with that, and nothing else.

Yet I have often told you more than this, and have opened to you the unfathomable depths of the feminine character, such as probably I ought to have kept secret. Women go shipwreck, in ninetynine cases out of a hundred, from two causes: one is that they cannot hold their tongues; the other is that they cannot run in harness with each other. The woman is made to go with the man, and will not go together. The better they are, the purer in character and the higher in tone, the more domestic in tastes, and the more irreproachable in life, the more impossible they are with each other. Aphrodite was easy to manage, compared to Pallas; she could get along with the other Goddesses if they would only have left her alone; but Pallas would have been on cold terms with every other Goddess in the Pantheon just because she felt herself superior. The mugwump attitude is murderous to women, but at bottom it is not the attitude—it is the feminine instinct which lies at the bottom of the tangle, and a woman, before thirty, has so little experience of her own instincts that she may be regarded as a child. When she loves, when she hates, when she is jealous, she does not know it until someone tells her,—and then she is furiously angry at being told, and wont believe it. Of course in that respect we are all fools, more or less. The woman's difficulty is that she is fooled by her instincts and her sentiments which are at the same time her only advantages over the man. And the worst of it is that no life can be so quiet or so simple as to escape the play of these instincts. Two sisters in East Bridgewater can annoy each other as much as though they were Marie Antoinettes or Messalinas. Mother and daughter can be as jealous as two girls of eighteen.

Why do I tell you this now? Because I shall never have a chance to say it again. You are already in a new life where your woman's instincts will come immediately in contact with the objects that rough it; and from that moment you can no longer generalise; you have got to take each difficulty separately as it comes. Then I can't teach any longer. Education is finished. You have got to apply it.

With that I quit. You must do your own educating henceforward. I'm not much worried about it. You are tolerably certain to be happy, as happiness goes among the good, and Bancel is tolerably certain to help you, and be a very sympathetic companion. The only thing worth having in life is the first five or ten years of happy marriage. During that time, one asks nothing of the world except to be let alone, and one's life is so full that one needs the outside world only as a background more or less complementary to the colors of one's personality. When one emerges from that comfortable content, into the region of middle life, one has unconsciously learned to stand and walk alone; but whether one has learned it or not, one has to do it, for, by that time all the papas and mammas and uncles are dead or imbecile. That time will take care of itself. You need not worry your poor little imagination about it.

So I leave you to your own world, which will very soon teach you how thin and poor all else is, and how gloriously and sublimely selfish real happiness must necessarily be. Don't try to struggle against it! Unselfishness is essentially unhappiness—or perhaps I should say, want of active happiness; and a really happy person can be unselfish only through the exuberance of her own selfish enjoyment. To her, unselfishness must be a sacrifice; and it is a singular trick of our natures that makes us all resent a kindness that comes in that form. What we accept with gratitude from a brother pauper, we take with a grudge from a Rothschild. Among paupers, all is common; but the rich stand apart, and cannot be unselfish.

To these hunks of wisdom, I would gladly add any practical advice if I had any to suggest, and if I did not know that you were surrounded by people more competent and better informed than I, in those matters. If you want anything, you will let us know. But I am pretty sure that all you will want is to have the feeling that we all sympathize with your state of mind, and that we neither criticize nor see anything unusual in it. As a matter of fact, the world is in a conspiracy with lovers, and they are quite safe even if they shut all their eyes. It is the only stage of life after infancy when we can be fairly sure that no one will intentionally do us a wrong.

As for myself, I have had my teeth put in order, and go over to England at once. The time has come when we must start in to make peace with Spain, and as I had a finger in the quarrel, I want to have a finger in the pie now that it is cooked. Our good people have behaved very well, but have wildly exaggerated their enemy's power, and now I fear much more difficulty in quieting down their ebullition and suddenly discovered ambitions than I do in bringing Spain to terms. Don Quijote is always *doublé* with Sancho Panza, but I never quite know what lining to expect on Yankee Doodle's half-sewed clothes.

Give my love to Bancel—who now comes first, I presume,—and to all the chicks and shrimps. It seems droll to be here without you. I avoid St Germain.

Ever affly   Henry Adams.

MS: MH

1. Mabel Hooper was engaged to Bancel La Farge (1865–1938), son of John La Farge.

To Elizabeth Cameron

Monday 21 Nov. '98

A whole week slipped away, with only the dull sensation of having no longer the use of still another sense. I was blinded before; now I have lost you, I am deaf. The days slip away, for the most part, in the mild amusement of destroying all the papers, books and other rubbish that I can lay hands on, or in weighing and cataloguing Greek coins, until noon, when some one generally comes to breakfast: Rebecca, or Ward Thoron, or once Jeff Coolidge and Nora (is it Nora) Sears, or Elizabeth.[1] At four o'clock, Hay generally comes for a walk, and we tramp to the end of 16th Street discussing the day's work at home and abroad.[2] Then at five we get back to Mrs Hay's tea where some one, agreeable or otherwise, generally drops in. About six I return to my den, and close my day. So ends the first lesson. Edward Hooper arrives tomorrow with Ellen. So begins the second.

The impression I get is rather sympathetic and pleasant. Washington at this season is almost as villageous as ever, and people are as informal and simple as in the First Dynasty and the age of Cheops. Mostly they are rather soothing, as I felt by contrast one evening when Wayne dropped in, trying furiously to be genial. Hay is especially loyal. I am sure he makes an effort to show that office is a pure fungoid, and not a part of his nature. Yet, as far as I can see, his office has been so thoroughly looted, or is so pawned in advance, both in patronage and in policy, that he might as well look on from outside as stand within. He was not even allowed to appoint an Assistant Secretary. If he has anything to say about the British Embassy, he affects a secrecy which contradicts all his apparent behavior. He tells me that such and such candidates are out of it; that Hitt and Walcott and McMillan are for different reasons impossible; that Choate is most favorably considered; that Platt and Quigg are playing with Depew and Whitelaw Reid, and nothing they say can be trusted.[3] But at the same time he says that, while he could create an efficient diplomatic service, he is not allowed to use even the instruments he has at hand—meaning Rockhill and me—and has not a single diplomatic agent who can be utilised to advantage. I believe all this to be true. You will appreciate how glad I am of it. To refuse him my help would be most disagreeable to me; but to accept office would be misery. What I like—for I am, as you have often truly said—a mass of affectation and vanity, is to have people make me pretty speeches, which they do, and to grin behind their backs, as they do behind mine.

As for policy, the helplessness matters less, because no question of policy is involved. All was fixed in advance, and has no credit for Hay except the cheap success—or failure—in trading with the Senate to carry it out, and even that will be done by McKinley who is easily first in genius for manipulation. McKinley is more than all I thought. He is just the President for us in our present condition. Clearly we are bound to go, soul and body, into the hands of the gold-bug—wealth individualised,—until a violent convulsion sweeps away the Cimex, and substitutes the socialistic hemiptera commonly called lice. As Dr Johnson once remarked: "Sir, there is no settling the point of precedency between a louse and a flea."[4] Between

McKinley, with his Hannas, and the coming trades-union administration with its cheaper and feebler Bryans, I will give no precedence except in time, but surely McKinley is better than we had any right to expect.

There is a new Russian,—Cassini,—with a pretty niece. Speck is *très répandu,* quite the leader of mankind. Rebecca is enthusiastic about Mrs Griggs Attorney-Générale, a Cleveland charmer like all charmers. O'Beirne has gone.[5] The Lodges have not come.

The Ames's have come back to Cambridge. Awful dinners rage for the Kanucks.[6]

Tuesday. [22 Nov.]   Last night Mrs Hay made me go to the theatre with Hay and Eddy to occupy some box at some one's request. The play was impossibly Oshkosh, a weary thing of dance and song; but the Pauncefotes were in the next box, and I had a chat with Maude, of course chiefly about you. Also Lord Herschel came over to complain of the slowness of his Kanuck commission, while Jeff Coolidge complains tearfully of Herschel's long speeches.[7] I met Mrs Townsend yesterday at Fischer's, and she also wanted to know all about you. Alas, we all want to know about you. The void you have left is not filled or approached.

Nothing else worth noting. Joe Choate is now far away at the head of the field for England. Platt does it to spite Whitelaw and break him down. It will be a very brilliant and excellent appointment, but a terrible pecuniary sacrifice and expense to Choate. The expense of that Embassy has become a serious difficulty in filling it, and practically shuts it up in New York.

This morning I have Martha's letter of the 9th.

Also a long letter from Tati with much love to you both. He talks of coming officially to the exposition.

MS: MHi

1. T. Jefferson Coolidge (1831–1920), a member of the Joint High Commission on various Canadian-U.S. questions; Eleanora Randolph Coolidge (Mrs. Frederick R.) Sears (1856–1912), his daughter; Elizabeth Warder (1875–1952), later Mrs. Ralph Ellis, daughter of Ellen Ormsbee Warder (1844–1928) and Benjamin H. Warder (1824–1894).
2. Hay became secretary of state Aug. 16.
3. Robert A. Hitt, Republican representative from Illinois 1881–1903; James McMillan (1838–1902), senator from Michigan; Joseph H. Choate (1832–1917), eminent lawyer, appointed U.S. ambassador to Britain 1899–1905; Lemuel Ely Quigg (1863–1919), Republican representative from New York 1894–1899; Chauncey Depew (1834–1928), Republican senator from New York 1899–1911.
4. Quoted in James Boswell's *Life of Samuel Johnson* (1791).
5. Count Artur P. Cassini (1835–1919), Russian ambassador to the U.S. 1898–1905. Because his marriage was a misalliance, he presented himself as unmarried and his daughter as his niece. Baron Hermann Speck von Sternburg (1852–1908), German chargé d'affaires 1896–1900, ambassador to the U.S. 1903–1908; Laura Elizabeth Price Griggs, wife of John William Griggs, U.S. attorney general 1898–1901; Hugh J. ("Paddy") O'Beirne (1866–1916), 2nd secretary at the British embassy 1895–1898.

6. Kanucks: Canadians.
7. Farrer Herschell (1837–1899), head of Anglo-American commission.
8. Mary S. (Mrs. Richard H.) Townsend (d. 1931); Victor G. Fischer, a prominent Jewish Washington art dealer.

To Elizabeth Cameron

Tuesday, 29 Nov. '98

Winter has come down on us this time like a howling herd of office-seekers, so that my autumn has run away before its time, and spring seems near again, when I can see you and Martha, and play with the lambs, and chase the sheep; but just now we are certainly not yet there. Much to the contrary! If you were only here, I should enjoy it much, for we are really almost alive at last, or think we are; and the scene is a singular contrast to that of the last winter I was here, and the moment, two years ago, when I was writing that famous Cameron Report which is now the law of America,—or would have been, if everyone had not then been afraid of it. Without you I can no longer lay down the law; but truly I have no need. Those who trembled and ran away two years ago, are now lightly taking risks and asserting rights that turn me pea-green. Only yesterday, Hay swallowed, without a tremor, two or three continents, and told two or three Kaisers to go hang.[1] Tomorrow the country would scream with delight at a war with Europe; and it is not one but a dozen questions that threaten to gratify the public in that respect.

I hardly know where to begin my running commentary on the times, unless I casually acknowledge your letter. Between ourselves, our diplomatic servants abroad have by no means made a success at our own palace, and the new experiment of sending Joe Choate out to raise the average, though certainly the best choice by far that could be made to please and conciliate the mugwump and anti-imperialist classes, is yet an experiment, and will make the deadliest enemy of Whitelaw. Choate ought to make a very brilliant ambassador; but these are going to be times when wise diplomates hold their tongues, and, above all, avoid being funny. He will need two seasons to learn his business, and he will wander blindly among pitfalls. Still, I am heartily pleased to see anybody there, so long as it is not me; and am annoyed only because an idea seems to have got about, founded I suppose on a false notion of Hay's influence, that I might have had the post, had I wanted it, whereas the absence of wish and of power were equal,—that is, absolute.

While on the subject of diplomates, I will stuff in here, quite out of place, the visit of poor Quesada who sat an hour with me yesterday pouring out his story. I say *poor*, but in reality Quesada single-handed won the biggest diplomatic match of our recent times, and is now only busy in scooping in the stakes. He is to bring Calixto Garcia and the other commissioners to dine with me this week, and there is no Dupuy de Lome now to denounce us.[2] Quesada has made clean sweep of his enemies. To be sure, he is still regarded askew by the Departments, but, as I told him—Paciencia y barajar[3]—that too shall pass away.

The story Quesada told me was to me intensely interesting, not because it was dramatic, but because it was the burial-service of my—or rather my grandfather's, doctrine of foreign relations, and of the scheme which lay behind our Cuban Report and the Senate Resolutions, and our dinner two year's ago for Mendonça and Romero.[4] Quesada, as you know, did his best to work through the brambles by that path. He went again to Mexico; he importuned Diaz and Romero.[5] All the South American States were implored to interpose in order to bring Spain to terms in the interest of their common blood, and to save Cuba to the Spanish race. Instead of coming round to that course, all the Spanish Republics backed round the other way. They grew more and more afraid of the United States in proportion as they threw more work on us, and they ended by throwing their whole passive weight on the side of Spain. How like dead weights we poor mortals are! For eighty years our ablest men—Jefferson, J. Q. Adams, Clay, and nearly all the rest, down to Blaine, have toiled to build up an alliance with the Spanish American Republics to support the Monroe Doctrine and protect us from England and Spain; suddenly, at the first strain, the Spanish Americans desert their own kith and kin; fly back to Spain; throw us into the arms of England, and force us into the position of a domineering tyrant.

Anyway, they have done the job thoroughly. With the usual Spanish bull-headiness, they have thrown everything into our hands, and they are all left out in the cold, and hate us now without disguise or limit, because their fear is at last founded on their own treachery and cowardice. Except Brazil, which is not Spanish, and is strong enough to stand alone, all Spanish America is now for sale to Europe, with us forbidding the transaction. You can imagine the fire-brands that are lying round loose, and underneath is the Nicaragua Canal, all cut and dried, to fan the fears of every republic from Mexico to Chili, into a frenzy.[6]

This is the reason why the Cubans resigned themselves so willingly to our exclusive assumption of power over them. They were cast off by their own blood, and angry with everything Spanish. They were at their last gasp, and when we struck in, they cared little what else we struck provided they got their revenge.

Of course, all this is secret, probably known to very few people, and not talked about even by them. Quesada hinted at parts of it, rather than told it as I tell it. The sum of it is that we cannot help ourselves. The law of nature is stronger than a mere doctrine. We are in for a sort of Athenian hegemony over the hemi-sphere and we may yet have our Syracuse to besiege, and our Nikias-Shafter to ruin us.[7]

With the kerosene-can so handy, the fire is always on tap. All Central and South America is the fuel. Germany is the kerosene-can. All Europe is already arrayed with Spanish America against the British-American combination. And a jolly row it already promises to be. And I think not even the anti-imperialists fully realise the situation, although it has driven Andy Carnegie as mad as a Bedlam Christ.[8] The anti-imperialists are perfectly right in what they see and fear, but one can't grow young again by merely refusing to walk. I fear that the American calf itself is now too old to get much more nourishment from sucking the dry teats of the British cow.

So much for politics! As for society, this is my busy season. Edward Hooper has already been here with Ellen and returned yesterday to New York. The Lodges arrived Sunday, and Cabot came to lunch at once, and found Jeff Coolidge, Austin Wadsworth and George Eustis.[9] Hatty Blaine has been much here. The boy is huge, and rattles away to me in unintelligible boy-language which I pretend to understand.[10] Elizabeth Warder is a daughter of my house. Rebecca Rae is constant, but is not easy about Charley's health. Also Mrs Blaine and Mrs Lippitt are both visibly losing faculties.[11] With the Hays, I make practically a common household, shifting forward and back as state-exigencies require; but the noble Baron Speck is the most portentous speck-tacle. Not only did he write to the steamer to welcome me, but Hans Breitman gave a barty[12]—a Sunday tea—for Lord Herschell and asked me by special note. I was rather amused at his imperence,[13] and went. For tip-top hig-lif I never yet rose to that water-mark before. Imprimis: The Misses Pauncefote, accompanied by Lord Herschell; his Secretary; Frank Dugdale, and Paget; Secondo: Mrs Leiter and Daisy; Tertium quid: Mr Henry Adams—and nobody else![14] Apparently, but—I never said it, thought it, or had any feeling but the deepest contempt for anyone who ever repeated it,—Speck is—well! may be willing, with imperial permission to become—or might some day like to visit India en famille— or—enfin! Speck is something more than nothing in the Leiter household. As for me, why was I asked, and without Hay whose shadow I am? I thought milord Herschell looked as though I were asked to ask him to dinner, but in some forty years that I have haunted London, I never yet heard that Lord Herschell had ever asked me or anyone else to dinner, and I like reciprocity. Lord Herschell may go dine with a better man.

Everyone asks for you, and I admit the soft impeachment,[15] and describe in glowing terms the charms of your Paris aery. What would I give for just an afternoon there! From this letter, one would say I was rushed by the world of society and politics! In truth I am solitary as a moulting owl, and only pass my time in cursing the weather that prevents a daily walk to the Rock Creek haunt. One's life does not run quite like a chainless bicycle.

———

MS: MHi

1. By the agreement reached on Nov. 28 with the Spanish commissioners in Paris, the United States acquired a protectorate over Cuba and possession of the Philippines, Puerto Rico, and Guam.
2. Gonzalo de Quesada (1868–1915), chargé d'affaires of the so-called Cuban legation at the Hotel Raleigh in Washington; Gen. Calixto García (c. 1839–1898) headed the commission sent by the Cuban national assembly to learn the U.S. government's policy on Cuba and to obtain funds to pay off the Cuban army so that it could be disbanded.
3. *Paciencia y barajar:* patience and shuffle the cards.
4. Salvador de Mendonça (1845–1913), Brazilian minister to the U.S. 1891–1898; Matías Romero (1837–1898), Mexican minister to the U.S. 1882–1898.
5. Porfirio Díaz (1830–1915), president of Mexico 1877–1880, 1884–1911.
6. After the French failure to complete a canal, there was increasing pressure in the U.S. to undertake the task, one group urging Panama for the site and the other group, currently more influential, urging Nicaragua.
7. Nicias, commander of the disastrous Athenian expedition against Syracuse, where he was killed in 413 B.C.; William Rufus Shafter (1835–1906), commander of the expeditionary force in Cuba.
8. Andrew Carnegie was a vice-president and leading benefactor of the Anti-Imperialist League, recently founded in Boston with headquarters in Washington.
9. William Austin Wadsworth (1847–1918); George P. Eustis (1864–1936).
10. Walker Blaine Beale (1896–1918), son of Truxton and Harriet Blaine Beale.
11. Eliza Gilman Dodge Lippitt (1827–1903), mother of Rebecca Rae.
12. Hans Breitmann, the beer-swilling German-American of *The Breitmann Ballads* (various editions, 1857–1914), humorous dialect verse by Charles Godfrey Leland.
13. "Imperence": impudence, in British substandard usage.
14. Frank Dugdale (1857–1925); Capt. Alfred Wyndham Paget (1852–1918), naval attaché at Washington; Mary Carver Leiter, wife of Levi Z. Leiter (1834–1914), retired Chicago merchant.
15. Richard Brinsley Sheridan, *The Rivals* (1775), V, iii.

To Worthington Chauncey Ford

1603 H Street. 19 Dec. 1898.

My dear Ford

Your remarks on the budget-situation start my curiosity. The economical theory of history requires the extinction of the wasteful, and the substitution of the cheaper forms of life, until the forms become too cheap to survive; but we have reached the point where further cheapness can only be reached by a social system growing rapidly more and more socialistic. Plutocracies are wasteful, and yet we are building up the greatest plutocracies that ever existed. If you are right, government has now got to feed on accumulated capital, which will speedily bring about the Russian millennium of a centralised, despotic socialism. Europe is some fifty years ahead of us, in that line of motion, but the speed, on both sides, is sufficient for comfort. You might almost figure out for us an arithmetical ratio which would fix the date of our arrival at the terrestrial Paradise. Please try and let me out.

You remember the Table you made for me of Trade-balances for England, France, Germany and the United States from 1870 to 1896. It is my ocean-chart in the currents of politics, but I much want to add the years '97 and '98 to it, and I've not the means of doing so. Can you give me the figures? If you wish, I will return you the Table, for insertion.

I see that Mr Lloyd, in the last Statist (December 10) fairly commits himself to the statement that the adverse trade-balance of England is a delusion, and that "never before have we been so rich."[1] No one will accept this view more gladly than I, if it means that England will continue to pay us five or six hundred millions a year, without dropping prices on us. On his own showing, I doubt it very seriously, but as long as England and her industries will consent to prolong the situation, we have every interest in not disturbing it. On the other hand, I see increasing uneasiness in nearly all the industrial circles of Europe, and the Bank statements of Russia and Germany, Austria and France, show that a general and somewhat painful effort has been made for contraction, which must press their industries hard. I am at a loss to see how, under such conditions, at present prices, their industries can compete with ours. The whole of western Europe is already tributary to us. The British trade-return for November is again deplorable, and that for the eleven months is awful. France, this year, is apparently running behind. Russia can no longer borrow in Europe, and wants to borrow of us, with the pledge to spend all the loan here. In short, I have terrible qualms about the bottom of that European money-bar'l as our next general election approaches. The next turn of the screw may hurt our thumbs.

My brother Brooks has gone back with many conundrums for you. I trust he is in a contrite spirit. In spite of talk-for-effect in the newspapers, I think we are pretty serious-minded here, and disposed to view the future with no purple illusions. The problem is certainly calculated to set the whole menagerie to chewing its tails in religious silence.

Ever Yrs   Henry Adams.

MS: NN

1. T. Lloyd, "Are We Living on Our Capital?" *The Statist* 42 (Dec. 10, 1898), 865–866. Lloyd argued that import statistics included remittances of capital.

To Anne Palmer Fell

24 Dec. '98.

Dear Lady[1]

I am glad it is no worse, though sorry to see that you, too, who held out longer than anyone against the tyranny of money, should find the struggle beginning to become severe. Curious how the whole world groans under it, and sacrifices existence to it. And yet we shudder at Moloch and his furnaces.[2] And yet our terrestrial paradise and economical heaven is over-flowing and bursting with wealth and prosperity. And yet—and yet—and so on, till the whole cargo of commonplaces is exhausted, and at the last, Dreifuss reigns. Never mind! We rolled 'em in the mud last winter. We kicked and cuffed 'em all round the ring. We pulled their hooked noses and their somewhat defective teeth. We made our dear President, who has not a ghost of an idea except theirs, carry out every sort of measure most obnoxious to them. We fought for the Cubans, and we annexed Hawaii, and we slapped Europe in the face, and we did everything that the gold-bugs had said we shouldn't do, and we had a raring tearing good time. To be sure, the Dreifussards will get all the loot, and will be as despotic, four years hence, as they were four years ago; but I shall be out of it soon, and, after all, the solemn experience of the ages tells me that gold-bugs are made to be stuck against walls on pins. Others shall see the fun, even if I am done.

Such is our present state of Washington. We are disgustingly fat, oily, greasy and contented—Esquimaux after a blubber-feast. As I take no interest in the realisation of an economic paradise, I rather regret my artistic inferno at Paris, where the world is far from prosperous, and has fits. The fits are great fun. Some day perhaps some one will get hurt, and I never take my afternoon walk up the boulevards without looking up the Rue Laffite to see whether there is a chance to observe how a Rothschild would ornament a lamp-post.[3]

Writing to you in the distant desolate island of Florida, I can say frankly how our American philistinism bores me to frenzy, but here one smiles and grins and holds one's tongue. I cannot think you would enjoy it. Books? there are no books. Except Helen Hay's little volume of poems, which I send you, I know of nothing but the dregs of magazines, and even in them I like Zangwill better than Kipling, because he is an honest Jew, and Kipling isn't.[4] I will send Marian anything she wants, but I can no longer undertake to choose.[5] If you will tell me what to order, I will order it; but I've no one any longer to help me get books or clothes or anything for her, and am as helpless as a turkle on his back. In fact, I scare myself with my solitude, and would give a dollar for a white mouse to play with.

To amuse you I have been telling everybody that I had a friend in Florida who kept a pension in a watery pine-forest, and I would get them admission to this saurian paradise if they need rest and air. Unluckily all the girls now have malaria, and their doctors find herds of small alligators in their blood. It is quite the rule for every well-bred girl to be swallowing arsenic by ounces, and having headaches by the month. They are all sent to the north pole to freeze up. None is allowed to be warm. How much benefit they will get from the new treatment I do not know, but the alligator-business works both ways; for if you won't have alligators inside of you, you can't play with alligators at Narcoossee. Still, I hope the doctors will catch some new fad soon, and let the alligators alone.

Give them my love; also the children.

Ever Yrs   H.A.

MS: MHi

1. Anne Palmer Fell (1857–1937), onetime friend of MHA, had married a British mining engineer and settled in Narcoossee, Fla.
2. Leviticus 18:21; 2 Kings 23:10.
3. The Rothschild bank was in the rue Laffitte, comparable to Wall Street.
4. Helen Hay (1875–1944), daughter of John and Clara Hay; *Some Verses* (1898). Israel Zangwill (1864–1926), foremost Jewish author and Zionist in Britain, known for his realistic depiction of Jewish life.
5. Anne Palmer Fell's daughter Marian (1886–1935) had been named after MHA.

To Elizabeth Cameron

Christmas, 1898.

I am uncommonly homesick for you and Martha, and more perversely discontented than usual when I've nothing to complain of; but Christmas always was a dreary day to me, and it is, at least, gayer now than when I was a boy, and felt depression more acutely. Gay or not, however, nothing shows much on the surface, for the house is full of young people, and I have nothing to do but to look on, and play the benevolent grandfather. Somehow, I like better to think of your quatrième in Paris, but then I turn anxious, and wonder whether you will have trouble before I can get there. My economical demonstration is complete that Europe cannot get through the winter without trouble. All its discontent is caused by the pressure of our competition, and as long as I thought that this pressure might let up, and the last two years might prove to be exceptional, I thought that European affairs might run along quietly; but now that money is 8 per cent in Berlin and 2 per cent in New York, while our exports and imports show a trade-balance in our favor 25 per cent greater than the utterly unheard-of balance of last winter, the game is up. Under such conditions, further competition is ridiculous. We shall just rake in the stakes as long as the poor Germans and English can put up the money. Last year we, and India, pocketed the whole gold-product, more than two hundred million dollars, and left not a blossoming ounce in their vaults, but we loaned them at least as much more. This year they are 25 per cent worse off, and their credit is getting shakey. England and Germany are reckless gamblers and will go on borrowing till they break, but France hates the Jews and debt, and therefore I expect the first collapse to appear there. My reasoning is perfect, but its results depend on the correctness of my estimates of stocks and credit. Of course I cannot know the unknowable, but this month has settled lots of things. Europe has tried, rather timidly, to drop the prices on us, and for about a week she sold everything short. She had to give it up. In the attempt to economise, she had let down her stocks of wheat, iron, copper and even cotton to so low a point that she had to buy. If she stops buying for a week, she must stop eating and stop working. I want you to understand this, for a timely understanding may save your lives, not to speak of fortunes. Europe must go on, buying our goods at our prices, on loans of our money. Sooner or later we shall call those loans; Europe must then stop buying; and the result is, in theory, that her people must die, on a great scale, of starvation. The single unknown quantity is the date when we shall call those loans. The longer we defer it, the worse will be the crisis; and, as I have said, I regard the crisis as already certain to be accompanied by the most sweeping revolution that has ever been known, which can only end, if it has an end, in the concentration of life in two last centres, one probably in Russia, and logically on the Black Sea; the other in the Mississippi Valley.

To you, and indeed to me, this reads like lunacy; but within the last five years we have seen so much lunacy realised that we cannot afford to disbelieve in the moon. Indeed the whole situation is the outcome of the silver struggle five years ago. Gold is doing its work faster than I expected.

I don't believe you can read all this with patience, but, if you can, I wish you would, because it affects you much more than me. You hate McKinley with all that vindictive hatred which, I think, women alone feel. Your only chance of revenge on McKinley is in the trouble which financial confusion will cause. To me McKinley is totally indifferent, but I like amusement, and it will amuse me to help run our affairs without having to take responsibility. The more closely I see McKinley's administration, the more clearly I see his incompetence, but also his suppleness and keenness of instinct. I think you will have your revenge, but you will have to take it in a very nasty form of the vilest and most degrading personal intrigue, in the ratio of John McLean to Mark Hanna.[1] Even then your revenge depends on the world's total ruin. I've no objection, as far as it affects me, and indeed should be highly amused, but I want you to understand better than Cleopatra did, how a world is to be well, or ill, lost.[2]

Meanwhile the Commissioners have arrived. I found Whitelaw Reid at Hay's when I went there for my cup of tea last evening. Poor Hay had to bear the brunt of Whitelaw's insane voracity for plunder, at a moment when he was barely able to walk, after a sharp attack of illness, and when the promotion of Hitchcock to the Cabinet had depressed him once more with the consciousness of his—and the President's—total inability to cope with the greed of the Senate.[3] In the great crisis of concentration which our country must pass through, it is already quite clear that the Senate is the chief obstacle, and will have to succumb. I have always been impressed by the parting speech of that otherwise overrated scoundrel Aaron Burr, on going out of office as Vice President: "If the Constitution is to perish, its dying agonies will be seen on this floor."[4] Burr cribbed the idea from the commonplace of Roman history; but we have now arrived near the time of Tiberius Gracchus, and either Julius Caesar must come, or must fail to come, which means our failure to reach the next stage of life. The Senate is already an impervious obstacle to concentration and economy of government, and I see its resemblance to the Roman Senate in every twist and turn of our tortuous Executive. For instance, Hay would give his head to put life into the Department at home and the service abroad. I've no doubt he would like to tear the whole machine to pieces. It is not the President that prevents him; it is the Senate; it is Cabot Lodge, Mark Hanna; Stephen Elkins; old Morgan; Eugene Hale, Platt and Vest.[5] There can be no executive efficiency while the Senate remains what it is; and there can be no room for Whitelaw—or, if you prefer it, for me, or for Rockhill,— so long as all patronage must go to the Senate.

So I left Hay struggling like the angel, with Jacob Whitelaw Reid,[6] and returned peacefully to my own fire-side to think of you and Martha, and to chatter with Looly and Elsie and Arty, as Helen Brice calls him, and to thank God that I was not like other men, and wanted nothing but the kingdom of heaven.[7] For that may the Lord make us duly thankful!

Your thoughtful telegram arrived this morning promptly. The day has passed without incident, Elsie and Arthur going to a Christmas junket at the Wolcotts, while Looly and I dined in quiet.[8] I passed the better part of the afternoon with Hay at the Lodge's, talking, as one does talk, about things. Rebecca came in at noon to say that she had a letter from Charley saying that he had not felt so like himself for years as on this voyage. In the evening, to my horror, Miles came in.[9] Oh, Lord! I had not called there! Did you want me to? I never did before, and I call nowhere, not even on my own grandmother, but I will do it now. Miles was quiet and inoffensive, and we kept off dangerous ground. He seemed chiefly curious to know whether your husband meant to go back into politics.[10] Or did he?—or was it my ear that is now supernaturally sharpened for distant whispers? I do not—do not—do not know. But it would be funny and as good as Anna Held to see your husband and Wayne and John McLean and Carl Schurz and Godkin and Grover Cleveland and Bryan and Edward Atkinson and Eugene Hale and Frisbie Hoar and Bailey of Texas and my brother Charles *and* my brother Brooks—and me, join to elect Miles President on an anti-imperialist platform!!!![11]

Tuesday. [27 Dec.]   Your letter came yesterday, and Martha's Christmas card, and Paddy complaining that you did not write;[12] and I called on Mrs Miles who was not at home, and on Mrs McVeagh who was, and I learned that Wayne had been in bed for a week with the usual cold and cough. Of Rachel and Chandler I hear not a word. H. Blaine is the same as ever to me, but we do not mention them. Of Mr Cameron, too, I hear only that he went to Donegal. That is all my family news. Today Margaretta and her guest Catherine Dexter come to breakfast, and this evening Rebecca Rae has made me ask the Santo Thyrsos to dinner. Madame is said to be charming. Monsieur is a round little minister from Portugal.[13] I asked Maude Pauncefote, but she too is in bed, as most of the population are, including all the servants. Next door, Mrs Hay returned all right from her three-day trip to Cleveland, where she found her mother evidently failing, and her sister at a rest-cure. Hay is all right, and we have resumed our evening walks, discussing the day's news and the morrow's prospects. The British Embassy still drags. Choate's appointment has been practically decided for weeks past, and I don't know why the President delays it; but the more I hear of Choate, the more I regret Whitelaw. I fear that Choate has neither taste, tact, diplomatic sense, nor money. He is only a little mugwump God, like Bayard and Edmunds and Phelps and so many other lawyers. At St Petersburg we must have another western man. Of course no western man is fit, but I know of no eastern man more so. It is now the most important of our foreign posts, and we have absolutely no one in the least degree trained for it. We need a grand seigneur there, with languages and money.

Happy New Year.   ——

Thanks for check.

MS: MHi
1. John R. McLean (1848–1916), editor of the *Cincinnati Enquirer*.
2. John Dryden, *All for Love, or The World Well Lost* (1678). The play is about Antony and Cleopatra.
3. Members of the American delegation to the Paris peace conference ending the Spanish-

American War. Reid was one of the commissioners. Ethan A. Hitchcock (1835–1909), designated secretary of the interior Dec. 21.

4. "If the Constitution be destined ever to perish by the sacrilegious hands of the demagogue or the usurper, which God avert, its expiring agonies will be witnessed on this floor"; Matthew Davis, *Memoirs of Aaron Burr* (1858), II, 362.

5. Stephen B. Elkins (1841–1911), senator from West Virginia; Sen. John T. Morgan of Alabama; Eugene Hale (1836–1918), senator from Maine; Sen. George G. Vest (1830–1904) of Missouri.

6. Genesis 32:24. Reid pestered Hay for the ambassadorship to Britain.

7. Arthur ("Arty") Adams, young son of CFA2; Helen Brice (d. 1950), daughter of a former senator.

8. Edward Wolcott (1848–1905), senator from Colorado; and his wife, Frances Bass Wolcott (c. 1852–1933).

9. Maj. Gen. Nelson A. Miles (1839–1925), a brother-in-law of Elizabeth Cameron, testified before the War Investigation Commission on the incompetence of the War Department.

10. Senator Cameron's term had expired in 1897. He did not seek reelection.

11. Anna Held (1865?–1918), music-hall comedienne; Sen. George Frisbie Hoar (1826–1904) of Massachusetts; Joseph Bailey (1863–1929), representative from Texas. Spain relinquished its colonies to the U.S. There was some opposition to annexation as being imperialist.

12. "Paddy," or "Mademoiselle," nurse or housekeeper for the Camerons.

13. Carlos C. Machado (1865–1919), viscount de Santo-Thyrso, Portuguese minister to the U.S.; Katharine Dexter (1875–1967), later Mrs. Stanley McCormick.

To Elizabeth Cameron

8 Jan. '99.

Your letter arrived Friday, rather to my relief, for I was beginning to worry. We are here all dead, or dying, or getting well. Just for a day or two, the getting well has been fashionable. Wayne and John McLean and Mrs Lippitt and my cook and chambermaid and various senators have been reported better. Hay has been in bed again with head-ache and throat, just as before. He begins to think it is bores, and that his strength has given out. I should not wonder. The boredom is monstrous, and, after office, think of ten cabinet dinners within six weeks!

Such dinners! The President has a table for seventy, laid in the long corridor. Always the whole cabinet, comprising eighteen persons including Vice Presidents and such; and of course precedence fixed and invariable. Not a man or woman in the lot whom one would ever cross a room to speak to, except for their offices; all bores, and all liking it.

While they are amusing themselves in your house[1] and in Hay's, I dine pleasantly en tête-à-tête with M. le Duc de St Simon who is amazingly good company.[2] The other evening over my modest pint of Champagne I listened to his account of the death of Mme de Montespan in 1707,—so good,— so good—that I cried to think that such writing cant now be written and wouldn't be read, even if the society of our time gave the material. Look at the passage beginning: "Toute le France y allait." And "un langage particulier, mais qui était délicieux." Mme de Montespan would never have had me as a scullery-boy, but she was as good to look at, and as picturesque, as Mrs Lyman J. Gage, I guess, or as Mrs Russell A. Alger.[3] Two centuries hence, no doubt, even Mrs Alger will be picturesque, but, for that, one needs much perspective.

Just now my sister Anne gives me all the perspective I want, and you know that, if sister Anne happened to care to play Mme de Montespan or any other part, it is not the rôle that would dash her, but only the want of a competent audience. So, last Thursday or Friday evening, when the Vice President gave a cabinet dinner, he invited sister Anne, with some other of the court ladies, to come in later, and sister Anne went there, and was ushered up into your great Louis Quatorze Pompadour Régence Marie Antoinette gilded drawing-room, where she found all the court-ladies seated about, in solid splendor, and, in the middle, Mrs Faulkner, her senatorial colleague from W. Virginia, in a dark street walking-dress, with a hat and veil, not in the least embarrassed by the singularity of her costume.[4] Mrs McKinley was lecturing Mrs Hay on her favorite topic, that of husbands. Hay was at home, having gone to bed with a head-ache. "I don't understand these wives," quavered poor Mrs McKinley, "who put their husbands to bed, and then go out to dinners. When I put Mr McKinley to bed, I go to bed with him." Sister Anne told this to me at the opera yesterday afternoon, in the intervals of Melba, and I fear that our ribald laughter was indecent, as, indeed, were some of the poet Bay's comments. Certainly Mrs McKinley's suggestion that Mrs Hay was going to bed somewhere else, was poetic and even lyric, and could be used as a "Song of the Wave," much more effectively than some of its actual motives.[5] The fact is that Mrs McKinley is impayable, and the stories about her now quite take the place of those about poor Mrs Leiter.[6] Sister Anne also greatly delights in the Vice President, who addresses her as "Bir-r-rdy" and presses affection in the shape of wine and such New Jersey seductions.

The Court is a bore, but it is of a respectability that the angels in heaven have never attained, and never could, if their associates are those described in the Holy Writ, which savors of much that we do not now mention; even Mrs Cush Davis has not yet égayéd it;[7] but while Mrs McKinley was protesting against the morals of Clara Hay, Mrs Warder was giving a ball, and—oh, my stars all the respectability of the Cabinet vanished, and the Treaty was forgotten, and even Frisby Hoar must, I think, have stopped for a moment talking about imperialism, when he heard of that ball. I had heard much of it from far away back. I was engaged to lead the cotillon with Elizabeth. Hay and I had been summoned in, while passing, to see the castle which Speck and Maude Pauncefote were painting for the last figure.[8] Speck and Maude ran hand-in-hand round here to breakfast while at work, that Mrs Warder might not be care-worn. Maude was quite exhausted. So was Mrs Warder. By this time you will have heard the awful tragedy, and the world will have rung with it. I do not understand why the society-journals have not yet told it; but as I can find nothing to clip, and as you may not have got letters, I will condense and abstract the tale thus far, to say: that Alice Warder chose Mr Andrews, known as Pinkie, to lead with her; that Pinkie, at risk of sudden death, rose from his grippe-bed, dined with his friend Lord Abinger, and brought him to the ball, where he sat smiling on everybody in a state of jag so advanced that Pinkie was requested to remove him, and when his persuasion failed to convince milord, the services of the British Embassy had to be invoked.[9] Young Owen, the Attaché, summarily dragged Abinger out and ejected him from the house. I judge that some physical effort was found necessary. Between grippe, dinner, Lord Abinger and Mrs Warder who insisted on an improper arrangement of the chairs, Pinkie lost such mental balance as he ever has, and became more and more obnoxious in his behavior and remarks, until, after all was over and he was taking his leave, he said to Mrs Warder that she had ruined her party, and that he would never enter her house again. Upon that, Ward Thoron, who was looking and lounging about, mildly took him by the arm, and walked him too down stairs and out doors, and bade him good night with a civil request that it should be the last.

All this was promptly brought to me next day by H. Blaine Beale or Beale Blaine, who has reason to be willing that other men than hers should be drunk and disorderly; and was confirmed by Mrs Hay and added to by sister Anne. Pinkie the next day crawled. Apologies fell like snow-flakes. Pinkie fled to New York. I know not what has become of Abinger, but he was notorious for a cad at best. Poor Mrs Warder will never give another party, this being a judgment upon her because her husband died only five years ago.

Est-ce canaille, hein? but rather funny, too, I think, as an illustration of a Richardson house and a Byzantine simplicity.[10] It is not régence, but it is about as good as an English and German civilisation could be asked to give. I don't myself mind people being brutes; what I dislike is their being ignorant, stupid and boorish in their instincts. On the whole I prefer Pinkie to Abinger, and Russell A. Alger to Lyman J. Gage. I rather like a fool; that is why I like Frenchmen—at a distance. We are not wicked. We have not the senses for that. We drink, as all boors always do, and we prefer whiskey to wine. We laugh at Francis Wilson. Sister Anne and Mrs Hay dragged me to see him last Monday, and I wept while the others shouted with laughter. What is rather worse, we pretend to like Wagner, and laugh at the humor of the Meister-Sänger and the Siegfried and the Rheingold, as heavy and beery as a Blut-wurst. This week sister Anne and I had a box at your theatre, and I went to Tannhaüser and poor old Rossini's Barbiere. Much as I delight in Tannhaüser, which is not Wagner at all, or but embryonically, I must reaffirm that Rossini runs better, and shows the voices better. Melba made me feel fifty years younger, as I did when I first went to the opera and heard Grisi in Norma. I thought of Vernon Lee's musical ghost at Venice, but there was no Mario for Melba.[11] From the opera I walked up to sister Anne's to see Constance who has run on here for a change. The senator came in, with his usual story of Bill Chandler whose chaff of Hoar and Hale delights our own statesman from Nahant.[12] Chandler is an impudent dog, but he does not cant, and Hoar is equally impudent and does cant. As for Hale, he has been saved solely by Frye, and we believe Frye's reason to be that, mean a dog as Hale is, he is not so bad as Tom Reed would be, as a colleague.[13] Chandler gravely complimented Hale on the cheers which his speech in caucus had called out for Frye. As for Tom Reed, he is quite anathema, and the wit that delighted society five years ago is so eclipsed that I rarely hear it mentioned. He and all the anti-imperialists are bitter, like most beaten men, but they are also violently excitable, and Carnegie quite mad. I sympathise in their anti-imperialism, for all my antecedents lead that way, but they bore me with their arguments which are weak as wash, and with their temper which is childish.

Cabot anticipates no extra session, and meditates an early start for Europe. In fact he has authorised and instructed me to engage March passages to Naples by the southern route, via New York, Gibraltar, Marseilles, &c. I write today to inquire. How will this suit you? Can you be in Italy in April? If so, we can meet in Rome or Naples; but do not mention our plan until you hear it from sister Anne, or outside, for as yet it is much in the air.

Tuesday. [10 Jan.] This is a busted society. Everybody comes in here collapsed and desperate. Luckily Wayne is still in bed, not yet able to sit up. Whether John McLean has mastered his hiccoughs I do not yet know. Rebecca was here yesterday with one of her worst throats, and her mother still in bed, weeping cheerfully in expectation of approaching death, her temperature and pulse being normal. Hay, who has not been ill, has twice taken to his bed, and now drags himself about with a weary effort. Quesada is totally broken down, without having been ill, and is a mere bundle of bones with some hair and eyes, weak and desperate. As for the statesmen at the Capitol, I leave them to the newspapers, but Dingley is having the closest kind of a call.[14] As a society, I do not call it gay, but the weather is excellent. Last night another great dinner at the White House. Cabot and sister Anne went there, and Constance came here with Bay and John to dine with me. Constance looks more pale, thin and nervous than ever, but seems as full of the devil. Her mother appears rather particularly fit. Your letter of Christmas has just arrived. I wrote you that Mr Cameron was known to have gone directly to Donegal. Since then I have heard nothing, and have not seen Gensler.[15] Yesterday in the street I met Rachel walking with Chandler and Jim. I did not stop to speak, as they seem now to have broken definitely with all my circle. But I imagine it is about time for your husband to reappear. I am told that your sister Mrs Miles somehow damaged her face, and could not appear at Court the other evening. Helen and Alice Hay have been at Philadelphia to adorn Pansy Griscom's stage-entry,[16] and only today return. I am quite alone, and, as the world goes, about the most easy of martyrs. Poor dear McKinley rouses my stupor at his gay way of conducting government, but it is not I that seek reelection. I'm pleased you had Ralph.

———

MS: MHi

1. Vice-President Garret A. Hobart was renting the Cameron house on Lafayette Square.
2. Louis de Rouvroy (1675–1755), duc de Saint-Simon, gave an intimate picture of life at the Court of Versailles in the last years of Louis XIV and the Regency period; *Mémoires* (1872, rev. ed. 1882).
3. Cornelia Washburne Gage (d. 1901), wife of Secretary of the Treasury Lyman J. Gage; Annette Henry Alger (c. 1840–1919), wife of Secretary of War Russell A. Alger.
4. "Sister Anne": Senator Lodge's wife; Virginia Whiting Faulkner, wife of Sen. Charles J. Faulkner.
5. "Song of the Wave," title poem of George Cabot Lodge's 1898 volume.
6. Ida Saxton McKinley (1847–1907) was a nervous invalid given to fainting spells. Mrs. Leiter was known for her many malapropisms.
7. Anna Malcolm Agnew Davis, wife of Sen. Cushman K. Davis of Minnesota.
8. At the Warder cotillion a representation of the siege of Morro Castle.
9. Frank W. Andrews, Jr.; James Yorke Scarlett (1871–1903), 4th Baron Abinger.
10. The Warder house on K Street had been designed by H. H. Richardson.
11. Vernon Lee, the pseudonym of Violet Paget (1856–1935). The narrator of her tale "A Wicked Voice" (1890) is haunted by the ghost of an opera singer.
12. William E. Chandler (1835–1917), senator from New Hampshire.
13. William P. Frye (1830–1911), senator from Maine, apparently stopped the Republican caucus from disciplining his fellow senator, Eugene Hale, an antiexpansionist.
14. Nelson Dingley, Jr. (1832–1899), Republican representative from Maine.
15. Henry J. Gensler, debate reporter of the U.S. Senate, former private secretary to Senator Cameron.
16. Frances ("Pansy") Griscom (1879–1973), daughter of Mr. and Mrs. Clement Acton Griscom.

To Martha Cameron

2 February, 1899.

My dear own only daaarling Mother, do you know what a dreadful shock I had when your little photograph came, in uniform, on the parapet? I threw it into water to soak it, before pasting it to the mount, and this is what I found when I went for it! Just dirty white paper! Please send me another! I wont soak it next time, though I must say that a photograph which wont wash is rather too French for my own mother Dulliver.[1] I am just as homesick for you as ever. I have all the little children paraded here for inspection but they can't any of them take the place of Dr Dobbitt's little girl. Corker Blaine is a terror. His mother can't manage him now, and in a year or two he will be awful; but he is a splendid great big fellow. Benjamin Thoron is just the opposite; elderly, and like his father; precocious and not handsome. None of our old friends seem to be here. I believe Marie Brown is in the country. Matilde Townsend is a young lady, and her photographs are in the New York World among the leaders of society. I wonder whether I should like your new girls. I never knew French girls. Are they like us?

You know that I am coming back to you in about six weeks. I suppose you've got all through Miss Strickland, and will have all your ideas in French.[2] Can you correct mother when she talks bad grammar? That would be rather fun! Is French or English easier to talk? Do the girls at school learn English? Are they Dreifussardes? I've no one to play with, now, except the Secretary of State, and he's such a little boy that it's no fun; and I thought of going down to the island to play with Daddy, but I'm going to sail so soon that it's hardly worth while to leave here. We've a little touch of winter now, with snow on the ground, but the days are getting longer and Lent is almost here. The girls say it has been a very dull season, and no dances. You will have the Leiter girls in Paris in a fortnight. And their mother too.

Ever yr affte   Dordy.[3]

MS: MHi

1. HA's playful variant of Martha's childhood nickname "Mrs Gulliver." "Dr Dobbitt" was a name HA assigned to himself. Martha, now 13, was attending a convent school in Paris.
2. Agnes Strickland, coauthor of *Lives of the Queens of England* (1840–1848).
3. Another of Martha's nicknames for HA. He was George ("Dordy") Washington, and she was Martha Washington.

To Elizabeth Cameron

Girgenti. Tuesday. [25 April 1899]

Is it April 23 or 24 or 25? I have kept no run of the month, but it is certainly Tuesday, and so life gets done. Another stitch picked up, and my last Greek cities running off like the time-machine![1] Here I am at last, looking down over the temples and the Mediterranean, where for nearly forty years I have meant annually to come, and now it is done, and another small object in life wiped out. Of course it's not worth while. One Greek temple is just like another, when it is ruined. Girgenti as a landscape is Athens with improvements. Two thousand, or twentyfive hundred years ago, it must have been immensely charming, like Japan in its prime, but now it is a landscape with hardly ten lines of history, and no art. So we will turn it down and catalogue it. Please consider Cabot and Bay and John and Winty Chanler as having reached Palermo punctually Sunday morning, and taken me to see the mosaics which I came for, and which make another old bird-of-travel flushed and killed.[2] When I came to Palermo in June, 1860, I came to see Garibaldi and a fight. There was a barricade at every fifty yards on the main street, and I chatted with the red-shirted hero in the Municipal town-house as he supped with his staff. I could see no sights but that. All the brigands in Sicily seemed to be in the streets, and the fleas were thick as dust. If Garibaldi were Hannibal, he could not seem further away now, and if I were Empedocles and Matt Arnold to boot, I could not be older;[3] but at last I saw Monreale and the mosaics, and, for a wonder, these were worth while. They make even Ravenna modest. Also some Greek metopes from Segeste or some other old ruin, which we struck in the Museum, seemed to me of the very first class. To bag two first-class art-works in one place, when I know so few in the world, was a triumph. I was glad I came. And after all, Girgenti is typical; altogether the most beautiful Greek ruin I know; far more charming than Athens or Corinth or even Delphi or Smyrna, and of course out of all comparison with places like Ephesus or Alexandria. I've done fairly well, therefore, and game has been good.

Of course our party has been amusing and pleasant, rather young for me, but almost as much so for Cabot, and old enough to make allowances for each other and the universe. Winty Chanler makes most of the fun and the go, and keeps us properly mad. We have seen no one worthy of being called even pretty, though the boys are of an age to find beauty in a harpy, and naturally we have seen no one that is good, or at least good enough to notice. The weather is cool—almost cold. A fire in the evening would never be out of place. I am rather shivering now, before an open window, at seven o'clock in the evening, in my heaviest winter clothes. I think I had better get ready for dinner, and at the same time get warm. Tomorrow night we expect to reach Syracuse.

Messina. Saturday morning. [29 April]   Prompt we are! Cabot rattles us through, on time, tourists such as Cook should love; but I don't much mind now. Nothing matters much, except money, I judge; even in the best days of the Greek Gods, money seems to have paid for all. We are now very learned about our Greeks; we have done our Syracuse and we understand our politics and economics as well as though we lived in 415 B.C. and had a hand in the Peloponnesian War. Even Bay admits that our Greeks were somewhat wanting as economists and politicians, but on the other hand we are quite overwhelmed by their superiority as landscape-gardeners. Girgenti and Syracuse were interesting studies in that profession, but yesterday came the climax at Taormina. Nothing in Japan compares with the vigor and genius which the Greeks put into this poor little colonial mountain-side, to make every inch of beauty count for its utmost value. For the hundredth time I flung up the sponge and stopped chattering before my Greek. It's no use to talk. The fellow's genius passes beyond discussion. Taormina in itself is one of the most beautiful spots in the world. I've seen most of the great landscapes, including the slopes of Fuji Yama and Kilauea and Orizaba and Popocatapetl and Turquino. They are all divine, but the Greek is the only man who ever lived that could get the whole value out of his landscape, and add to it a big value of his own. His share counts for almost as much as the share of nature. The wretch was so complete an artist that big or little was equally easy for him to handle, and he took hold of Etna just as easily as he did of the smallest lump of gold or silver to make a perfect coin. Some day I hope you will come here—it is an easy trip—and pass a week at Taormina, just to quiet your trouble about educating Martha. Education is a fraud. It's of no use at all. No one, for two thousand years has ever been more than barbarously educated. No one ever will be educated again. There is nothing to be educated for. We may as well be contented in our vulgarity, and be satisfied with dry champagne and the electric light, for at least the Greeks did not have these.

This evening we cross to Reggio and bid good-bye to Sicily, which is a poor place enough as far as it is modern. I am glad to have seen it at last, though I shall never use my new knowledge. It would make a grand chapter for Brooks, but I am past literary ambition. We shall see Paestum tomorrow and reach Naples. Chanler leaves us at Salerno to go on to Rome whither we follow on Wednesday. Sister Anne should arrive there tonight.

My chief regret through all the journey is that you are not with me, but the travelling is rather hard, and if you should come, I should rather leave southern Sicily out, and bring you directly to Palermo, and here to Taormina. Girgenti and Syracuse are interesting historically, but hardly worth your labor. If you ever come here without me, think of me occasionally, when you are tired of mosaics and Greek theatres.

Love to Martha. I almost dread getting back to Rome for fear of hearing that you have decided to sail.

Ever ——

MS: MHi

1. An allusion to H. G. Wells's *The Time Machine* (1895), which, however, propels its traveler into the future.
2. Winthrop Astor Chanler (1864–1926).
3. Matthew Arnold's poem "Empedocles on Etna" (1852).

To Louisa Hooper

Florence, 20 May, '99.

My dear F.N.[1]

Here we are, having finished our trip, at least as far as I am concerned, for I have seen all I came to see, and linger on only to be with my crowd. Although a good deal of the old light and simple crime has gone out of Italy, and I see no longer what I felt once, and feel no longer what the middle-ages felt, I find St Francis, or at least his church, and Michael Angelo, or at least his Chapel,[2] quite of my own time. After getting done with my Greeks and Normans in Sicily, who interested me very much, I found that the only kind of brandy that could get me up an emotion was Michael. He was chief of my school of Conservative Christian Anarchists. I am altogether consoled, quited and at times entertained by the vigor of vehemence of the old man's loathing. Not that he was much of a Christian, or a Conservative! All the Christianity in the Sistine Chapel consists in sending everything to the devil with a gesture of unpardoning severity. He swept all the world away at once,— Giottos and Angelicos, Christian saints and Papal chamberlains—all huddled together, saved and damned, and I'd nothing to do but to go with the crowd; so I came to Florence solely to look once more at the Medici figures. I sat a long time yesterday before them, trying to worry their thought out of them, and I came away quite ecstatic and depressed and self-contented and desperate. I cannot quite fix their relative order. First comes Giuliano, no doubt, the young man, rather sad but hopeful and handsome, ready for life.[3] Then I want to place the so-called Dusk, the soul of man laying out his work, looking it square in the face, practical, ready to back his judgment with money or sword or speech. Then the so-called Dawn, the waking-up to what one has undertaken, the painful discovery that life is going to be hard; the farewell to Early Christianism, Giottos, Angelicos, Virgin mothers and Greek Gods; the knowledge that the Christ-child, if he comes at all, comes to be crucified. Then the broad glare of Day, fierce, terrific; a mere formless effort, impossible to complete, useless to define, furious to think about; a mere, blind, brute endurance, without aim or hope or understanding; a primal energy, not even bound or aspiring, as in the Slave at Paris. At the end, not the exquisite exhaustion and beatitude of the Slaves, but only Sleep and not easy sleep at that, for the attitude is that of momentary rest, and the mask is always below. Then, above all, resuming it all, comes Lorenzo,[4] pondering over it, but not seeing either Hope or Consolation or Faith; only his finger on his lip, saying to me as clearly as though he spoke:—You know it all! You and Michael and I, and poor, sad, Giuliano, poor devil, are all in it! But we don't talk about it. What's the use!

The contrast in handling the same subject between these figures and the Slaves is highly amusing. Of course the Slaves are more beautiful.[5] The struggle and the apparently happy extinction, are more to our fancy. But what a mad old maniac Michael was, and how did he dare practice on human stupidity to such an extent as to put up these symbols of brutality and despair over princes' tombs in a Christian church? They say Giuliano was weary of life. If he was aware of Michael's intentions about his tomb, I am sure life would have amused him enormously.

It amuses even me, with a four-hundred-year dilution, and here I write you a long letter on nothing else. In fact there is nothing else to say. Our journey is nearly done. The Fred Shattucks are here.[6] So are about twenty Bostonians whom I've not seen for forty years. I've no news. I don't know how I'm to pass the summer. I have nothing to send but love to you all. Thanks for your letters.

Ever affecly   H.A.

MS: MH

1. F.N.: Favorite Niece.
2. The Medici Chapel (1521–1534), church of San Lorenzo, Florence.
3. The statue of Giuliano de' Medici (1479–1516).
4. The statue of Lorenzo de' Medici (1492–1519).
5. Statues by Michelangelo in the Louvre.
6. Dr. Frederick C. Shattuck (1847–1929), professor of medicine at Harvard; and his wife, Elizabeth Lee Shattuck (d. 1931).

V

Conservative
Christian Anarchist
1899–1905

FOR HENRY ADAMS the dynamos silently turning at vertiginous speed at the Paris Exposition of 1900 seemed to symbolize the drastic change of scale that separated the nineteenth century from the twentieth. All his tables of international trade and his coal and iron statistics pointed to the unimaginable power nexus of the future. He therefore advised his brother Brooks to drop "Money" from his global calculus and substitute "Power." Thanks to his friendship with Samuel P. Langley, the secretary of the Smithsonian Institution, he kept abreast of the new science with its revelation of radioactivity and the possible unleashing of the power of the atom.

The unsettling implications of these discoveries seemed to parallel the political disintegration which ushered in the new century. In Africa the Boer War challenged the stability of the British Empire. On the European continent a resurgent Germany entered the naval race on a menacing scale. In France the aftermath of the Dreyfus Affair opened political and social abysses: the Church lost control of public education, and socialism seemed on the march as the lockstep of the future. Far off in China the Boxer rebels besieged the legations and threatened to upset the spheres of influence of the great powers. The expulsion of Spain from the Americas and from the Philippines marked a fresh dislocation of international relations.

In a world that seemed topsy-turvy and headed, as he prophesied, for an "ultimate, colossal, cosmic collapse," Adams took frequent refuge in the Christian art, architecture, and philosophy of the Middle Ages. The contemporary world seemed abandoned to amoral international bankers and predatory capitalism. In the medieval Age of Faith the churches dedicated to the Virgin Mary had fostered, he believed, the moral values now lost to his own era. To express his contempt for his depraved age Adams began to refer to himself as a Conservative Christian Anarchist, though paradoxically relishing the luxuries of the world that "gold-bug" capitalism had made. The counterpointing between the Virgin and the dynamo would hereafter color his thinking and would run as a leitmotif through his letters.

The period from 1899 to 1905 was dominated by research for and the writing of two masterpieces—*Mont Saint Michel and Chartres* and *The Education of Henry Adams*. Adams' deepening interest in church architecture took him back to France for several months each year and regularly interrupted his close relations with Secretary of State Hay. But even when away from Washington, he kept up his role as devil's advocate in global diplomacy, his letters challenging as always with extravagant metaphor and sardonic wit. Those to Mrs. Cameron continued his weekly diary as they pursued her on her incessant travels. "Gossip," as he confessed to her, "drips through me," and he kept her richly supplied. He frequently introduced for her benefit, amidst the ceaseless flood of personalities, his picturesque and cynical commentary on world affairs. As the wife of one senator and the daughter of another, politics had been her daily bread, and now that her husband was out of office Adams' intimacy with Hay and Lodge provided fresh sustenance. That she caught all the literary and learned allusions which embellished his reports may be doubted; for him they were clearly an important dimension. His letters were, in fact, like his talk, as he sometimes acknowledged, a form of self-communion. When he traveled he reserved for Mrs. Cameron's eye his most evocative descriptions as he had when writing to her from the South Seas.

The death of John Hay in the summer of 1905 marked a turning point in Adams' life. The long meditative walks together and the intimate visits between their adjoining houses came to an abrupt end. Adams confessed to one of his English friends, "I've no longer any concern in politics." Removed from his privileged position close to the levers of power, he lost whatever influence he had had on American foreign policy. He retained sufficient ties to officialdom and the diplomatic corps, however, to be able to regale Elizabeth Cameron with Washington political gossip, embroidered as always with irony and exaggeration. On his "high stool" above the crowd he especially relished his continued surveillance of the self-assured Rough Rider in the White House.

To John Hay

Paris, 20 August, '99.

My revered Secretary

I should not have stood on the order of letters, or waited to receive one from you, had I had anything to say or to ask; but my life has been such as suits my years and my decrepitude. I have had neither news nor views to give, nor gossip to repeat, nor imagination to invent. I have met no one, read nothing, and stolen no ideas. Paris delights me, but not for its supposed delights. It is the calm of its seclusion that charms; the religious rest that it diffuses, and the cloister-like peace that it brings to the closing years of life. I reflect on the goodness of all things, and enjoy the peace of God.

In this there is very little to write about. And I've not even seen your representative, though he lives just across the way. Spencer Eddy seems to feel the same influences, for I never see him—even at his office; which leads me to suppose that, at this season, embassies are little busier than I. Once in a while, St Gaudens drops in to dinner, or I am asked to a lunch.[1] Ralph Palmer has just passed the week with me, and we have excoursed to the environs. In a few weeks, people will be returning to get their winter clothes. You know the routine.

Public affairs have offered nothing to interest me. To be sure the Dreifus business has proved to be even more grave than I feared, and has struck a blow at the republic and at France and at society itself, that seems to me fatal. I can see now nothing ahead but sooner or later the socialist experiment. Sedan was merely a military defeat like many; but the Dreifus affair is a moral collapse that involves soldiers and civilians alike, and the capacity of the French to maintain a character of any sort in a world like Europe. The socialists alone profit by it, and what a socialist France would be, is a grave question for America. France could then be only an appendage to what Dewey so happily and indiscreetly called central Europe, and with central Europe, as he justly said, we must by the nature of things be at war.[2] France is our oldest ally, and if her weight is to be thrown decidedly into the opposite scale, your successor some day will need help.

There has always been, for me, the real kernel of the Dreifus, and there it is for Jaures as well as for Drumont, for Déroulede as well as for Casimir Perier.[3] They all see it, feel it and say it, and there I leave it, for the thing is done, and, I think, must stay done. The army, the navy and the civil government have all admitted and proclaimed their incapacity to maintain France as one of the great powers. In that case, a new world must come.

Meanwhile, as long as the gold product doubles up, and business flourishes, and the laboring class is employed, nothing is likely to happen, and ministries are tolerably safe. You can tell better than I whether this prosperity will last over the next election, but I see no reason to doubt it. I should even allow a whole generation of prosperity, barring momentary reactions. Of course, things go faster than I can ever get used to, but we can now see further ahead. As that seems the case, and as you will not probably be called upon for heroic statesmanship, why should you be bothered by the easy job of drifting along a placid current of expedients? Your business is to devise a set of arrangements by which you can run the machine along without settling anything. You want to invent a new modus vivendi for every dispute, which shall not need the approval of the Senate, and shall not leave any more record than is necessary. The process is more troublesome, but, with tact and good-nature, it does not seem necessarily less effective, than that of negotiating permanent treaties, usually unsatisfactory in the end. Your predecessor Clayton was an awful warning.[4]

In any case, why give it up? You will find life dull, in the reaction, and I cannot see that you will gain anything. You have stood it a year, and the first year is usually the hardest. You gain, all the time, in ease and habit. Length of service has much to do with future reputation, and if you did not take office for reputation, what the deuce did you take it for? I imagine that the Cabinet is greatly improved by its changes, and that things will run the better, both for you and for the public. Last winter was probably the worst. Anyway, every day brings you nearer a necessary end.

I never like resignations. They always need excuse and defence. They imply doubtful reasoning. In ordinary conditions they proclaim a defect of some kind in the resigner. In extraordinary conditions they imply opposition or discontent. How can you explain that you're bored? or that you want to curse the Senate? we all want often to curse the Senate—and do it freely; and we sometimes throw in the House and the Judiciary and the Executive—and Edward Atkinson on top;[5] but we can't resign. At least, we can only resign ourselves; which is the proper course for you.

Then probably you will soon become imbecile, like me and some others; and then you'll be sorry to have lost position.

In short, you know it wont do! You've got to stay, and whether you wanted that dyeplomatic position or not, you have no dignified choice.

I've written so much on this point that I've come to the end of any moral letter. My brother Brooks wants to drop his wife, and drag me to Russia, but I prefer Paris or even Washington to that. My own Mary does not write, and leaves me to infer that I am not expected at Simla.[6] Mrs Cameron wants to eject me here. My only hope is in Don. The Lodges are at Zermatt rolling in glaciers. Bigelow has gone home. Paris is absolutely filled with American girls guided by the genial Cook. I took Palmer into the Luxemburg gallery yesterday, and saw nothing but swarms of girls from Minneapolis or the suburbs. Joe Stickney, who was very faithful, has fled to the Tyrol.[7] St Gaudens to Boulogne. None of them have anything to say, or the vestige of an idea in their heads, but it doesn't in the least matter. I've learned to study French prepositions and to understand that the French conditional is the sum of human depravity.

Paris itself is a wreck. The Exposition has ravaged it with unheard-of violence. All the great streets are impassable, and the river is chaos. Let us hope it may get into order, when you come over next year on your leave.

Please don't let the girls tell Eddy that I chaffed his office-hours.[8] He is too sensitive on that side, and takes himself seriously as you know. As he has nothing, I imagine, to do, and Vignaud does that, I suppose he can't well pretend to be working a diplomatic dynamo.[9]

My best love to Mrs Hay and the lambs. At the Walter Gays, last Sunday, I found the George Howlands.[10] They are babes in the woods,— very much—but seem—all the rest. Apparently they have enough to live on, at present, but death from starvation always comes in the end.

Ever truly   ——

MS: MHi

1. Augustus Saint-Gaudens (1848–1907), lifelong associate of John La Farge, muralist and sculptor, commissioned by HA to execute the figure placed on the grave of MHA in Rock Creek Cemetery in 1892.
2. In a Trieste interview Admiral Dewey declared, "Our next war will be with Germany."
3. Jean Jaurès (1859–1914), French socialist leader; Paul Déroulède (1846–1914), nationalistic political leader; Jean Casimir-Périer (1847–1907), president of France at the time of Dreyfus' first trial.
4. John M. Clayton (1796–1856), secretary of state 1849–1850, was harshly criticized for negotiating the ambiguous Clayton-Bulwer Treaty concerning a future isthmian canal.
5. Edward Atkinson, a founder of the Anti-Imperialist League, was conducting a pamphlet campaign against U.S. military intervention in the Philippines.
6. Lady Mary Victoria Leiter Curzon, wife of Lord Curzon, viceroy of India.
7. Joseph T. Stickney (1847–1904), poet and doctoral student in classics at the Sorbonne, close friend of George Cabot Lodge.
8. Spencer Eddy was now second secretary at the U.S. embassy in Paris.
9. Henry Vignaud (1830–1922), first secretary at the U.S. embassy in Paris.
10. Walter Gay (1856–1937), expatriate American art collector; George S. Howland (1865–1928), Clarence King's half-brother.

To Brooks Adams

Paris, 10 Sept. '99

My dear Brooks

I have written to Rockhill to ask him to send letters of introduction for you, to Athens, care of the Legation, where you will call for them.

I know no one at Athens. Except Rockhill's house and the American school, I never have entered a private residence.

If you propose to pass a month there, you will find plenty to occupy you, provided you can find anything to occupy your wife. Athens is a hole, and always must have been one. Greece is a fraud—I mean that it has no qualities which justify its existence except its geographical position—and I never wondered at the colonising instincts of the inhabitants. They were better off everywhere else.

At Athens you are in a good position to begin the study of Greek civilisation by the Mykene collections in the Museum. For the collation of authorities, the best and most recent work is *Busolt. Griechische Ge-schichte; First Vol. 1893.* Three volumes are now out, and as far as they go, are a complete Encyclopaedia for all recent Greek study.

Of course the most solid basis of study, from your formula, is the coinage. At the Library of the American school and in the Museum, you will find the material for working it up. With that clue, you can keep Athens in its proper place as an influence in the development of the west, or the resistance to the east.

Sicily was of course the point where the stress centered, and the drama has its real *mise en scène.* The coinage of Sicily tells the story. You will have to go to Sicily, if you want to feel Greek.

By way of variation, I would provide myself with an Aristophanes. The contrast between the shop-keeping bourgeoisie of Athens, with their so-called wit, and their damnable scepticism and their idiotic Socratic method, on the one side; and the dignity, grace, decorative elegance, and almost complete want of religious depth or intensity, of Eleusis, Delphi, and their symbol the Parthenon, on the other, is what I felt most strongly on the Acropolis. Aristophanes and Euripides are perfectly intelligible there, and alive still. Under those influences I should certainly have voted to hang Socrates.

With my growing antipathy to Professors and Universities, I feel a re-prehensible instinct of hostility to Athens as the Professor's paradise. If history is to be written on your formula, Athens cannot be taken seriously except for the short time her mines lasted. Her siege of Syracuse tells her story.

There is rather a handy little book:—Origines de la Monnaie. Ernest Babelon. Paris, 1897.—which I will send you to Athens if I can remember it. *The* book on Greek Coinage is Barclay Head's Historia Numorum.

You are not more out of the world than I; only I live in the twelfth century, which amuses me much. The economic and political situation is still hanging doubtful, but the interests involved in getting along without violence or political disturbance are so much greater than ever before, that I cannot believe in serious difficulty. The French army is the only organisation that seems still to have the courage of its profession. The Kaiser Willy has surrendered to the Jews and Gentiles, and Chamberlain, I suspect, is only driving a bargain.[1]

                              Love to your wife.   Ever   ——

MS: MH

1. HA apparently alludes to the dismissal on Sept. 4 of the Prussian ministers of education and of the interior, who had offended both radicals and conservatives, and to Chamberlain's belligerent stance in the Transvaal negotiations.

To Elizabeth Cameron

Paris, 23 Oct. '99.

Your letter of the 12th arrived this morning. Since it was written, things have moved fast. Everything always gets going at this season, and the months of November and December generally cut out the work of the year.

What you tell me of the Dewey movement troubles me a little. Setting aside the question of party, about which I am not violent, there remains the personal question which is rather serious to me at Washington. How the deuce I am to get on, with Hay and all my friends on one side, and you and Brooks and that dear John McLean and Emily, on the other, I don't know.[1] In fact, I can't do it. Inevitably I must lose something. Generally I have been able to keep clear of these passions, but this time all of you are too deep in the mud. Hay and Cabot, and such-like as Teddy, have too much to lose. Your temper, like mine, is becoming too bitter with age. It is likely to be a scrimmage wanting in the commonest decency of manners. I dread going home to it all the more because there is not a vestige of principle involved, and I can only sit on the very uncomfortable fence, indulging in the luxury, which is long ago a faded joy, of entertaining the deepest contempt for you all. Balanced by the loss of relations, the gain on my part is small. As a convinced, conservative, Christian anarchist, the turning out a set of cheap politicians in order to put in a cheaper, seems to me scavenger's work, necessary but low, at least as compared with the bomb, which has some humor in it, and explodes all round, making an effectual protest against the whole thing. Altogether I am not comfortable about it. As for mixing with the Gorman-McLean-Whitney-Croker crowd, they wouldn't let me in if I asked.[2] I don't mind Bryan, who is just an ass, but these eastern democrats are intelligent and exclusive. They know an anarchist when they see him. They are not as bad as Cleveland was, but practically, for me, they would make Washington equally impossible.

It brings me blue. Apparently I must abandon Washington altogether, and on the whole, while I am about it, the simpler and pleasanter solution seems to be to clear out of the planet once for all, as it is a question of brief importance anyway. Washington was the last tie. It is now a very weak one. Little will break it, but less will break me, who only keep going by a sort of constant tours-de-force, and prestidigitation. You are all drifting from me; I feel it and see it daily; and I know that the currents ahead are going to be violent for two winters to come. I can't choose a current, for that would at once throw me out. I can't drift with the current, for that is only possible in quiet waters. I can't even run away without cutting myself off from communion. So I linger in Paris, and bask in the warmth of the twelfth century, and write letters about nothing, as much as possible. You know my badge; not that of Valentine: "Rien ne m'est plus; plus ne m'est rien,"[3] but "Nothing matters much." How would it be in Valentine's French: "Beaucoup ne vaut Rien."

The twelfth century has been active this week. I went to Chartres last Tuesday and passed a long day studying it out so as to square it with the books. I passed Wednesday in running out to Chantilly and driving about three or four miles across to St Leu d'Esserent, a very beautiful church, high on a terrace over the Oise, with a stone flèche of the most delightful originality and grace, and the ruins of the Abbey Farm about the church, most pleasing. That evening the George Howlands dined with me, and I got the Curtis's to come up, as they had got me to go down to meet Mrs Cooper Hewitt.[4] From that lady I received a douche of New York and Newport, of Mr Eugene Higgins and Mrs Sammy Howland, which made the twelfth century singularly charming;[5] but from the Howlands I got only the clack of George's tongue on my nerves. Some day, when I have guests, they will be surprised by my suddenly sitting down in the middle of the floor and blubbering like a boy with a stomach-ache. The sound of certain voices becomes at times unendurable—my own the worst.

One gain I got. The sixth of my party was St Gaudens. By-the-bye, I hope to manage for him—and her—a medallion head, which Curtis seems to want. St Gaudens was going down to Amiens on Friday with two Frenchmen, and offered to take me. Naturally I went. The two Frenchmen were like all the Frenchmen I see, bourgeois of the timid type—one an architect, one a lawyer—afraid of everything, conventional as death, serious as a French *noces*, but very nice, courteous in the bourgeois style, and friendly. Of course I had for once to rattle French, which was hard on them; but we were met at Amiens by another bourgeois, the Archiviste, who acted as guide, and we did the town under his direction. Of course Amiens is far from new; it is almost as old as I am. If I did not know the Cathedral intimately, I had at least a bowing-acquaintance with it, these many, many years. If it is as old as I am, it has the advantage of not showing its years. Nothing was ever younger or fresher, and I went all over it again, officially as it were, with more interest than ever. Curiously enough, it was new to St Gaudens. As for the French lawyer, he had never even seen Saint Denis. I found it impossible to be *ingénu*;—not to patronize them. Is one odious! How can one help it? These *boutiquiers*—I except the architect and the *archiviste*—belong to a wierd world of childish information about like Marco Polo. Anyway I learned much, and enjoyed it greatly. As for Saint Gaudens, it was a new life. It overpowered him.

My photographs too are an occupation, and by the way a fairly expensive one. The mere *clochers* and *flèches* number hundreds in the Monuments Historiques series alone. Your rooms are becoming a school of romanesque architecture. Volumes lie about the floor. Last evening Joe Stickney and St Gaudens dined here, and floundered in architecture on all the chairs.

Mademoiselle writes to me for news of you. She is bored in her village, and wants to come up. If I have to quit, how would it do for me to send her 500 francs and tell her to come up, and clean and close up here? She would like it, and I should feel easier. Also, hadn't I better leave an order with Hottinguer to pay the rent as it comes due? There will be another quarter in January. By April, either you or I will be back.

Was it true that Frohman threw Miss DeWolfe over? The story troubles me, for I'm afraid she had run in debt for her costumes for the Gentleman of France.[6] She certainly thought she had an engagement in form.

The Transvaal War also makes me uneasy. It has already squeezed down cotton, wheat and copper, and I fear that silver is going to nothing, owing to George Curzon and his council.[7] Meanwhile I can make little out of the fighting, and for all I can see, the English may be in great trouble. The loss of officers is stupidly English.[8]

Your remarks on my housekeeping are just; but remark that nearly all that you paid on Joseph's book goes now on the cook's. Victorine has only the lamps, &c. I calculate the waste and peculation at about five francs a day; ten is an excessive allowance. It increases rapidly, and I dare say nothing for I know that both the women want to go, and I can keep them through November only by this means. Practically it will be like doubling their wages. If they will only stay quiet! but I fear next week.

———

MS: MHi

1. The "Dewey boom" for president was increasing, and J. Donald Cameron, a Dewey supporter, declared he would return to Washington to live if Dewey were elected.
2. William Collins Whitney (1841–1904), New York political leader, financier, and owner of a famous racing stable. A Democrat, he refused to support Bryan's candidacy.
3. "Nothing matters any more to me; anything more means nothing to me"; heraldic motto adopted by Valentina Visconti, duchesse d'Orléans, after the murder of her husband.
4. Ralph W. Curtis (1854–1922), expatriate American artist; his wife, Lise Colt Curtis; and their daughter, Sylvia, lived in the apartment directly below Elizabeth Cameron's, which HA was occupying. Lucy Work (Mrs. Peter Cooper) Hewitt (1842–1934).
5. Eugene Higgins (1874–1958), American artist; Samuel S. Howland (1849–1925) and his wife, Frederica.
6. Charles Frohman (1860–1915), American theatrical producer; Elsie de Wolfe (1865–1950) was expected to appear in *A Gentleman of France*, but appeared instead in another play.
7. Lord George Nathaniel Curzon (1859–1925), governor-general and viceroy of India, and his council put India on the gold standard on Sept. 15.
8. The Boers captured a train and took several British officers as prisoners.

To Cecil Arthur Spring Rice

Washington. 1 Feb. 1900.

My gentle Diplomate

Your letter of Nov. 30 reached me last night. Your's of the same date to Mrs Hay arrived January 13. Apparently it takes three weeks to register a letter in the wilds of Ahriman.[1] Evidently my friend Alexander the Great is needed again, and, from what one sees and guesses, I rather judge that he has come since you wrote. I would I could have an hour's talk with you today, "a flask of wine, a book of verse, and Thou"; for, in truth, my son, I am weary and oppressed by the stupidity of your class, and am desperate at finding in this waste of imbeciles not one poor wretch who can tell me why I consent to talk with him. The entire diplomatic class has, in my forty years of acquaintance with them, supplied me with just two interesting specimens; and you are one. I pay you that compliment free of charge. Don't grow fat on it! For it is wrung from me in bitterness of soul.

I have thought much of you and your position of late, and I doubt whether you have yourself been so anxious as I, about your welfare. Truly I have had much night-mare, these three months past, as you, who know my previous incarnations, can easily imagine. Many times in my life I have seen the earth shake under me, and the empires fall and rise like bubbles, but I thought all that was over for me, and that I could do my Hafiz, or champagne-fiz, our modern equivalent, in peace, with a happy Heaven secure. Suddenly, out of the clear sky, comes the devil on a broomstick in the shape of a mob of howling Jews who upset my world, send all my friends to Heaven before me, and bedevil man and beast beyond recognition. And the worst of it is that my poor world can't help itself. Stupid it is, and was, and will be,— stupidity is dear to the Gods and their best gift to man,—and if the diplomate were not stupid, how could he serve? Nature did not make you stupid, and consequently my sympathies are acute for you, until habit shall have accomplished what nature denied.

Mrs Hay and Mrs Cameron will have told you the gossip, such as there is; and I have little to add except that, on my return here a fortnight ago, I found the Washington world thinking about new people and new things, more or less, and, in comparison with Europe, also thinking very well of themselves. After nearly a year of Paris, the contrast seemed a trifle sharp. Europe seemed anything but satisfied with itself. New York was just humming with self-content. I left Mrs Cameron and Martha in their perch over the Bois de Boulogne, surrounded by the Paris colony, just as my uncles and aunts used to live forty years ago, and I tumbled back into an America which my uncles and aunts would not recognise, full of occupations and ideas that hardly existed here yesterday. To you, in Persia, Russia looms over the whole horizon. To us, in America, ourselves are the centre of the Milky Way. My time is wholly taken up in running as hard as I can to catch the procession before it gets out of sight round the next corner. Paris makes on me the impression of Chartres, as something pertaining to the twelfth century. Yet the Boulevards were never so crowded, the streets are dangerous with furious automobiles and fiery trams, and the Exposition is a huge architectural Inferno of unfinished domes, minarets, Greek temples, and iron frames. All the same, France cannot do the pace. She is really out of the running.

My breakfast-table resumed its habits without an effort on my part. Nieces run in and out like pigeons in a dovecote. As fast as I marry one off, two more come on. Statesmen are less plenty. Having made my great success on Cuba, I have dismissed my Cuban conspirators to their various functions in fortune-making, and content myself, like the Pope, with giving everybody my blessing. John Hay negotiates a treaty a day, or thereabouts, and sends it to the Senate to sleep forever. By some incomprehensible oversight, the Senate has accidentally approved one of his Treaties, which happens to be the most important, and naturally in my view the most likely to be opposed. The arrangement about Samoa has got through.[2] I hardly dare express my astonishment for fear some Senator should see the point. The elections are coming on; the opposition is at its wits' end for a grievance; the administration is in terror for fear of giving them one; the Philipinos are groaning under our cruel despotism; Bryan is orating; McKinley is smiling; and Moreton Frewen has arrived,—for once not quite hilarious.

At your embassy there is a wedding on hand. At the Lodge's, there is not. Probably some of your gossips have told you the love-secrets of Polichinel Lodge, which are no secrets at all.[3] If you could only be trusted not to repeat, I would repeat too, but Persia is a whispering-gallery, that would return my confidences to confound me after both the Lodge boys had married other women and forgotten their many early heart-breaks, and were swearing at the love-scrapes of their own sons. My sister Anne is absolutely rose-colored. My brother Brooks and his wife are in St Petersburg, and you can imagine whether that philosopher is interested or not. Knowing him slightly, I incline to suspect that he has, by this time, acquired views which may extend even as far as Teheran. I wish he could go there. You might have so comfortable a fight among the primitive roses, and you could knock down his concentric theories with all sorts of Persian history!

As for myself, after passing the summer in the twelfth century, thinking only of Norman *clochers* and *flêches* and of apses and choirs and glass; after scouring the country round Paris for twelfth-century churches, and after attending service at Chartres most of the Sundays, I was rudely disturbed by the return of winter and of Mrs Cameron who ejected me from my summer-quarters and drove me across the winter-ocean. I am now trying to compel Hay to go down to South Carolina with me, and pass a week with the lord of Coffin's Point. Mr Cameron is anxious to have us come down, but Hay pleads his beautiful treaties.

Of treaties and wars I will say as little as possible, partly because a letter is indiscreet, and partly because Moreton Frewen tires me. I am not an exaggerated hog. I do not want to require too much from human nature, for I never knew much good of it, and, as the new century advances, (on that point I follow humbly the Kaiser), the little good I ever knew of my own century quite disappears and is lost to my eyes in the dazzle of having, since the first year of my era—according to Christians, 1838,—won all my stakes, triumphed in all my interests, betrayed all my principles, lost all my self-respect, and been mistaken in every opinion I ever held. The consequence is that I am respected, sought, and, if I live to be wholly, instead of partially, imbecile, shall be admired. Under these favorable circumstances I try not to be impatient of—other people's—cant or hypocrisy or lies. Yet temper, to men past eighty, is not an easy servant, and at times,—not infrequent,—I swear.

Chiefly I swear at blunders which are worse than crimes, and at stupidity which is infinitely more wicked than the murder which I am impelled to commit in order to satisfy my artistic instincts which require revenge on the stupid. Twelfth-centurian that I am, I detest a university under all circumstances, and loathe science more than knowledge. Let us abolish Congress!

Ever your attaché ——

MS: MHi

1. Spring Rice wrote from Persia. Ahriman is the evil deity in Zoroastrianism who rules over the kingdom of darkness.
2. The Samoan treaty signed by Germany, the United States, and Great Britain on Dec. 2, 1899, was ratified by the Senate on Jan. 16.
3. George Cabot Lodge was engaged to Matilda Elizabeth ("Bessie") Davis. As in the Polichinelle puppet shows, everybody knew the fact but honored the secret. The marriage took place Aug. 18.

To Brooks Adams

Washington, 7 Feb. 1900

My dear Brooks

A month ago, today, I sailed from Cherbourg, and have neither written to you, nor heard from you since. Of course I know you want news, and of course I am happy to gratify you; but I want first a little news for my own account.

It is not easy, after a year of lying in bed, to get up, and jump onto a railway train going at full speed. The sensation of arriving in this country becomes stronger after every absence I make. A year of France and Italy had somehow dulled my sense. From the moment of landing in New York, I was conscious of a change of scale. Our people seemed to sling at least twice the weight, twice as rapidly, and with only half the display of effort. There is now almost no sense of effort, for instance, about our great railways; but the sense of energy is overpowering.

I was instantly struck, too, by the equivalent of this changed scale, when I came to Washington. Only three years ago, I was quite alone here, except for Rockhill, in the atmosphere of foreign affairs. The Cleveland régime suffocated us. Today the whole menagerie knows, or thinks it knows, all about foreign affairs, and Hay negotiates a treaty a day to keep the Senate's appetite supplied. The octopus is stretching its tentacles everywhere, quite blindly, like octopuses or octopodes elsewhere, but with an accurate sense of touch. As for traditions, constitution, principles, past professions, and all that, the devil has put them back into his pocket for another thousand years. By common agreement, we all admit that the old slate must be washed off clean. We all admit that we cant help it if the world does tip over. We are only glad we are on top.

This sense of being on top is what strikes me most sharply after the sense of being left behind which I felt so much in western Europe. I find myself actually slow. I, who was alone here three years ago in trying to get the country to assert itself and its strength, am now alone in trying to persuade stray passengers that, after all, America needn't load up with what wont sell. Every day I am discouraging some new scheme. Wall Street has fairly cut loose from Europe, or thinks it has, and no longer attends to European sales. The financial articles say that Europe has sold all she has, and that the balance is in our favor now. They dont care a damn whether England is ruined or not. France and Germany are more scared about it than we are. Our people seem willing to shoulder the whole British empire.

Of course I don't share this gaiety altogether, nor does Hay, nor the President, nor cautious men in general, but there it is, and I see no reason why it should not stay. All depends on the solidity of England's wealth. As you know, I have had, and still feel, grave doubts on that point. As I watched her adverse trade-balance jump from 2.47 per capita in 1889 to 4.41 in '98, (I haven't calculated it for last year), and simultaneously saw her sell our securities—the only asset she could sell—at a rate which has certainly exceeded a hundred million dollars a year, naturally I inferred that if she went on long enough at that rate, she would end in insolvency. If Wall Street is right in thinking that she has come to the end of her American securities, the insolvency is near; but, in my calculation, Europe still holds more than a thousand million dollars of American investments on which she could realise in these flush times; and the exchanges are not so bad for her as they were. If she is pushed, she can still draw heavily on us, unless she is much further gone than I can figure out.

The proofs of our strength are plenty. The coal and iron tell our story. But the proof of our position in exchanges is our gold. We are now all agog about our new gold-fields at Cape Nome. There, at the narrowest part of Behring's Straits, north of the Yukon, and just opposite the East Cape of Siberia sixty miles away, is a sand beach forty miles long, and two to four miles wide under the tundra, in which every shovel-full contains a dollar, more or less, of gold. At the first start, last summer, a few hundred people took out two-and-a-half millions. In April, as soon as navigation opens, the whole Pacific coast will pour in there, and Heaven only knows what they will do. The mere gold is only the direct immediate result, and the geologists are as curious as the miner's, for they say that the geology is uniform for an unknown distance, and across into Siberia, and the possibilities altogether indefinite. Meanwhile our other gold-fields are more productive than ever, and our gold reserve in the banks and treasury is piling up into figures quite unexampled. We have let England take a little,—at a price,—but practically we cannot get rid of it except by loaning it abroad. No one knows what our foreign balance is, even now, but if we begin lending money, we shall soon own all Europe.

This is our situation, as it appears to me on landing. Can Europe check it? Evidently England leans on us. We may have to carry her, but she will never again dare to hurt us. Evidently, too, the Transvaal war has taken the military nations quite by surprise. The value of offensive armaments has fallen one half. No one will fight in future, if he can crawl under a bed. If England can get out of this war, she will never in our time get into another. Already those mines have cost a five-hundred-million-dollar war, and the most humiliating licking that any civilised nation ever got. It is quite on the cards that within five years the mines themselves may be abandoned as worthless, like the silver-mines. Even if England were to march into Pretoria tomorrow, with that astonishing fool Sir Redvers Buller, leading the legions, the lesson of the war would be the same.[1]

Beyond this point I am lost. You must teach me the rest. When I try to think further, I dream nightmares. The stupidity of the English grows like the giant of Solomon in the Arabian Nights. It comes in a great cloud out of a beer-bottle, and calls me names.[2] They can't in nature be so stupid as I see them. My vision is distorted. No man can be such a fool as Buller. No one can be as blundering as Hicks Beach.[3] No one has a right to be as fatuous as Arthur Balfour.[4] Nobody is virtuous enough to appreciate the morality of Joe Chamberlain. All that,—nightmare! let it fade! but let me know what Russia has taken for small change; what Germany means to take, and what France will say to the change, small or large. The Persian Gulf, I judge, between Germany and Russia! Herat, as well! Which means that England must seize Lorenzo Marquès! What becomes of the Transvaal is already a minor point. The greater concentration is already sure.

Your democratic friends seem to me to be quite desperate. They want to get rid of Bryan, but would do no better with anyone else. They flounder pitiably. Nothing but the unexpected can help them. Practically they are all for sale—and a fair share are bought. I have ceased even to be shocked at the corruption of money. It will at any rate carry over my time, and it has the exceptional trait of apparently including everybody down to day-laborers. When the rot comes, all will be in it.

The family news is brief. Charles and his household are here. I see them frequently. Charles has, I believe, ceased to lecture in public. I think he has taken a hint, and learned the wisdom of silence. At least he does not talk to me except of his patricide.[5] The Lodges seem unusually well and cheerful. From Boston I hear nothing worth writing. Of myself, there is nothing to say. No one insults me, which proves that I am in no one's way.

Love to your wife.   Ever Yrs   ——

MS: MH

1. Gen. Sir Redvers H. Buller (1839–1908) had been defeated by the Boers in two recent battles.
2. Allusion to "The Tale of the Fisherman and the Jinni" in *The Arabian Nights*.
3. Sir Michael E. Hicks Beach (1837–1916), chancellor of the exchequer, accused of obstructing the War Office and Admiralty defense activity.
4. Arthur Balfour (1848–1930), leader in Parliament, criticized for his role in the Transvaal negotiations.
5. *Charles Francis Adams*, CFA2's biography of his father, was published Feb. 17.

To John Hay

Paris, 26 June, 1900.

You are getting on my nerves. I thought that here, buried in the twelfth century, I should escape the jimjams of your politics. Last winter we saw enough. We diagnosed the whole menagerie. We killed and buried, in advance, half the world and the neighboring solar systems. You laid down for me the profound political fact that the Boer war was the greatest blunder England ever made, and I humbly bowed. What am I that I should question?

Apparently you are the sacrificial Isaac; not I. You ought to know best what hurts you. Three months ago you said that, and today I am squirming under it worse than ever. While England has broken her teeth on a perfectly inessential European difficulty in South Africa, instead of concentrating herself on the one great difficulty in Asia, the Chinese have imitated the Boers; they have taken the offensive, and have knocked you silly, first of all. How the deuce are you to get out?[1]

For a fortnight I have been utterly aghast about it. First, the unequalled horror of those wretched people shut up in Pekin to be skinned and burned, half of them our personal acquaintances (lucky Bax Ironside to be so offensive as to be sent away before skinning);[2] then, the question what you are going to do about it.

I note, day by day, your frantic cry in the newspapers that you are going to do nothing about it. Of course! One never does anything! The other feller does it. When the sky falls, one stands on one leg in the water and makes another. Nobody cares! It's nobody's business. Make an arrangement with Yu or Me or Him to let our citizens loose, and we'll promise never to go there again.[3] We won't ask damages even for the lost skins.

I hope you may do it, but we all know you can't. What *can* you do, then? That's where I begin to turn green. You've got literally the world on your shoulders.

It is all very well for us—we, us, America, England, perhaps France too, and even Germany—to be afraid of Russia; but just now I am beginning to shiver *for* Russia. If Russia breaks down now, I'm not dead certain but that the whole flowery menagerie might break loose. Apparently Russia herself has nightmares too. What killed Mouravieff?[4]

Russia, or Japan, or both, have got to go to Pekin, and I hope they may get there soon. What then? Has the military genius of your great conquering administration told you yet what military value Pekin has? Who is to do the rest? Two hundred thousand Europeans were not enough to hold Cuba or the Transvaal. England's war-bill for her fun in South Africa cannot much fall short of a thousand million dollars. How many men are needed to garrison the valley of the Yellow River?

My preliminary chill is the fear that the Chinese rising may react on Persia and Central Asia, and start off a general Mahometan outbreak; but this is only a side-show in my World's Chaos. What may happen is infinite, but what must happen is finite and very intim*i*te, seeing that you have got to do it. Granting that Russia and England are able to stand the strain, even then I don't see how to get in or out.

Your open door is already off it's hinges, not six months old. What kind of a door can you rig up?

Oh, but I don't want to go into it! Not I! The twelfth century is good enough for me. But, after all, politics is a matter of the conflict of forces. Forces are chiefly mathematics. What's the mathematical formula for the world now?

Leaving out unknown quantities, like the Asiatic peoples, what is the mathematical value of Japan, and is it plus or minus Russia?

Assuming Japan to be plus, or in other words, assuming that Japan and Russia will unite to take care of northern China, what forces remain to take care of the Yangtse and Hoang-ho?

England is already there, and has got to stay. How many men must she put there to keep order? She is already quite aware that she has not the strength. She must ask for help. She must ask you.

There you are! Joint occupation of Southern China, with England, and, if possible, with France; for you need to drag France in, rather than keep her out. Germany will have enough to do in the centre.

You're a nice hand for such a job! Shade of George Washington! And Congress! And that giddy old Constitution! And the Senate! And the Supreme Court!

Suppose you refuse! England must then go over to Germany and capitulate. She sinks anyway, but, that way, she disappears, and we too. Then it becomes a world of all Europe and Asia, with America a fake-show in the Midway Plaisance.

The fun of it is that it should be just you who have got to decide the thing, supposing that it comes to a decision anyhow, and we are not all wrecked first. As one who belongs wholly to the past, and whose traditional sympathies are with all the forces that resist concentration, and love what used to be called liberty but has now become anarchy, or resistance to civilisation, I who am a worm—and trodden upon, at that—am quite Chinese, Asiatic, Boer, and anarchist; but, if I ran the present machine, and saw that anyway I had got to run into the gutter, would I shut down, or put on steam?

I am a coward and should shut down, but the next man would put on all the more, and the result would depend on the forces, as before; so we come back to study the forces, and there we stick. Yu don't know, and I don't know more than Yu or than Li,[5] for that matter; perhaps not so much.

It's droll, but no one seems to mind. Since we turned grey last winter, foreshadowing the consequences of the Boer war, all those consequences have been realised, and no one seems to know it, or to care. No one seems to care for our friends who are suffering the terrors and torments of the damned in Pekin and Tien-tsin. We go to the Exposition and look at the Danse du Ventre and the fantoches. I suppose it is the best we can do, and the worst would be to get scared. All the same, it doesn't seem to help you much, and it's not original in Paris or in the twentieth century. And the stock-market does not seem satisfied.

God bless you, my son! I will go back to my cloister and pray to the Virgin for you. That is rather more intelligible than to go and represent you at the Danse du Ventre; but it may not solve your problem. You need pure mathematics for that, and, above all, you need to know the values of at least two fixed elements. I wish you may find 'em.

All Americans are in Paris. I pass my life in hiding from them. Yet the women are pretty, intelligent, and young. The men are chiefly at races. I see Mrs Cameron and Martha, but no one else; and read only St Thomas Aquinas.[6] Thus far, the summer has suited my complaints.

I take note of what you say about office.[7] In that, as in other respects, you have got to accept the law of the sum of forces. Perhaps you will be able to get out. Perhaps, like Teddy, you will not. If the present shower passes over, so! if not, so! and again! and you may not find the door open! though you set it so! Best pray to the Virgin, after all, for you'll probably lose your breath anyway. Don't kick and don't swear and dont say: Fountain, I will drink of thy waters on a given date per schedule of the P. & O. Steamers. On the whole, you had better stay where you are. It amuses *me*.

––––

Yours of the 15th has arrived.

MS: MHi

1. The previous September Hay had asked the powers having concessions in China to accept an "Open Door" policy in China, granting all nations free and equal trading opportunities.
2. Henry Bax-Ironside, secretary of the British legation at Peking. The anti-foreign Boxer uprising had spread to Peking, and foreigners took refuge in the legations in the inner city, which were besieged.
3. Yü Lu, viceroy of Chihli province, in which Peking was situated.
4. Mikhail N. Muraviev (1845–1900), Russian minister of foreign affairs, died of a cerebral hemorrhage June 21.
5. Li Hung-chang, viceroy of Canton.
6. St. Thomas Aquinas (1225–1274) was to be the subject of the final chapter of *Mont Saint Michel and Chartres.*
7. Hay had written to HA on June 15 that nothing would induce him to stay on in office.

To William W. Rockhill

Paris, 12 Juillet, 1900.

My dear Rockhill

Pardon the affectation of *juillet!* It's a bore to start over again on a miserable date.

I write to acknowledge your William of Rubruk from Quaritch's.[1] The amount of work you have put into it was known to me before, but is obvious at every page.

To me, the book is more interesting, perhaps, for what it does not contain than for what it tells. The French literature of the 12th and 13th centuries is my hobby, but hitherto I have read chiefly the poetry and the metaphysics. Except St Thomas Aquinas and his scholastic predecessors back to Abelard, there is little 13th century prose. Joinville comes first in that character.[2] I am much interested in this contemporary and rival of Joinville, and probably his friend.

Friar William is naïf, but not so much so as I should expect; not nearly so much so as Joinville. For a Friar he is singularly wanting in imagination. The marvelous hardly shows; even the good daily miracle of his safe journey—a miracle if ever there was—seems simple matter-of-fact in his narration. The Friar is not modern. He never seems to be vain or self-conscious; he never displays his learning, but what is more curious to me, he does not show care for his Order, or for any particular Saint, or for the Trinity or the Virgin. I imagine him finding Joinville a pretty credulous and ignorant soldier. I suppose he had a knowledge of metaphysics; certainly he had the usual monkish theology; like everyone else in that century, he was always yearning to explain how easy the Trinity was, and how simply the miracle of God's unity in the wafer could be explained if you would only see it as he did; but that was all shop to him, and in the day's work. On the whole, I should call him a wonderfully good example of the men trained by all the great Orders to the practical work of the age. I can imagine him conscientiously and laboriously superintending the masons who were building the cathedral at Amiens. He makes me understand how those great churches got built; and how Albertus Magnus and Thomas Aquinas, and Duns Scotus managed to pile up the enormous structure of their philosophy.[3] The world never saw more patience or labor or sustained energy than these men showed. They did immense things, and I don't know but what Friar William's journey is as astonishing as anything that was done. The chances against him must have been fifty to one.

I have felt the want of you this last month. The Chinese business has hung heavy on my soul; not merely the Chinese part of it, although I would have given much for an intelligent guide to the mysteries of the Pekin situation; but what troubled me more was what seemed to me the collapse and cowardice of Europe. They don't want to face the situation at home. Russia and England are both timid. Both have learned to fear themselves. So has France. All of them cling to any straw that will float them another hour in security. They know that if the situation in China is the best they can conceive, they must still choose between a joint occupation and a partition. No native government is likely to stand on its own legs. But between joint military occupation, and joint military partition, the choice would puzzle the devil. I should prefer partition as the easier, safer and cheaper. Apparently England is afraid to divvy, or is still hankering for the whole trade. Certainly if a fatal blunder can be made, England will make it, and I can see not the least difficulty in making a dozen blunders any one of which might swamp Europe. But November will no doubt, as usual, see the problem settled.

I had a kind letter from your wife, which was itself an answer unanswerable. Of her I hear nothing but the most enthusiastic accounts, and I shall have nothing to do but to applaud them. This will be easy. I will begin with the winter. You will tell her that I am a cooing dove, a regular tumbler.

With sample regards Ever Ys Henry Adams.

MS: MH

1. *The Journey of William of Rubruck to the Eastern Parts of the World, 1253–55, as Narrated by Himself,* William Woodville Rockhill (1900). Quaritch's, London bookdealer, included early travels as one of its specialties.
2. Jean, sire de Joinville (c. 1224–1317), *Histoire de Saint Louis.* Joinville accompanied Louis IX (Saint Louis) on the Seventh Crusade (1248–1254) and was with the royal court in the Holy Land when Louis sent the Franciscan friar William of Rubruck (c. 1215–c. 1295) on a mission to the Mongol empire.
3. All three philosophers appear in *Mont Saint Michel and Chartres.*

To Charles Milnes Gaskell

50 Ave. du Bois de Boulogne
27 July, 1900.

My dear Carlo

Thanks for your letter of the 24th. I had not written because there seemed to be so little that was pleasant to say. I had nothing to send; no books; no plays; and no bric-à-brac that seemed up to your standard. The Exhibition has many good things and much that interests me, but it has no one new excitement and is a failure as a show. The attendance is not half what was calculated. Of course the heat counts against it, but anyway the world seems to have lost interest in Exhibitions. The heat is certainly exceptional, but the drought is much worse, and is rapidly becoming disastrous. Add to that the Chinese complications, and general nervous fear of political trouble after the Exposition;—you see, there is a dearth of youthful confidence and eternal joy.

I leave your English affairs quite outside. You understand them better than I do, and know my feelings, which I suppose to be not much different from yours.

Anyway, if things do not clear up soon, I look forward with anxiety to the autumn. November and December are trying months. They always scare me, and this year more than ever.

I have moved back to my last summer's quarters. My brother-in-law Edward Hooper is visiting me, and I expect your old myth Ralph Palmer today or tomorrow. You had better for the present avoid us. I am a tropical bird, who nest in the forests and caves till dusk, and then enjoy the cool of the evening like poor dear old Monckton Milnes. Lord of Life, how old we are! You would have to see things, and the Exposition is a perfect bakehouse for heat. I never enter it now, and you could not do it safely.

All day long I read metaphysics, and study Saint Thomas Aquinas. It is as amusing as Punch, and about as sensible. St Thomas is frankly droll, but I think I like his ideas better than those of Descartes or Leibnitz or Kant or the Scotchmen, just as I like better a child of ten that tells lies, to a young man of twenty who not only lies but cheats knowingly. St Thomas was afraid of being whipped. Descartes and the rest lied for pay. You remember Pascal's famous avowal of it, in the simile of the wager.[1]

What is more curious, not to say startling, is that all these gentlemen seem to me to be talking of something serious. This is a new and eccentric idea. I thought we were all agreed that metaphysics were a mediaeval absurdity.

All this is a side-play to my interest in twelfth-century spires and Chartres Cathedral.

It also serves to distract my mind from the barometer, thermometer, and China. Especially the latter, which touches me closely in many ways, as it does you, and which seems to me a mere labyrinth of necessary blunders. I can see no means of taking a correct course; the best is hopelessly blundering. My own government and poor Hay are already floundering in imbecile helplessness; and that deliberately, seeing nothing but worse ahead of any direct course.

> My love to all yours.   Ever truly   Henry Adams.

MS: MHi

1. Blaise Pascal, in a famous passage in his *Pensées* (1670), appeals to the unbeliever's self-interest: in betting that God exists, you stand to win eternal happiness; if you lose, you lose nothing.

To John Hay

Paris, 7 Nov. 1900.

My only infant

Now that the circus is over and the beasts put to bed, I take for granted that congratulations are in order. Accept mine! I have no more to give. My little all is at your service. You have had an excessively complicated job, and have, I imagine, very much contributed to the happiness of the excellent Major.[1] You have shown infinite patience, uncommonly correct judgment, and an amount of ability which no one about you knows enough to understand, and no one here is intelligent enough to appreciate. You have made no mistakes that I know of. And you have held your tongue.

To a twelfth-century monk in a nineteenth century attic, in Paris, the whole menagerie seems a queer struggle for reality, and impossible to judge or censure; so my congratulations have only the value of a Latin epitaph on a marble slab at the base of your bronze equestrian statue in Roman armor and a laurel wreath. Let it pass for that: Hic jacet J.H.; vir nobilis, &c, &c, insignis &c, &c, praecipue felix, &c, &c, amicus Adamus, &c, &c, &c, d. d. d.

Even to discuss it all must be a bore; yet I find it occupies more of my thoughts than anything else except the color-theory of the Chartres glass and Ming vases. You don't expect to be taken as seriously as a Ming jar, of course, so I won't flatter you. Still the Ming dynasty is in it, much more than the Manchus. From the first, I have been absorbed by the conviction that the worst possible solution in China was that of a joint military occupation, which is the solution now inevitable. Joint military partition was to me much safer and more advantageous, and in my belief easier, as it required for the moment only a division of seaports. England would have got a bigger slice this year than she is likely ever to get again, and we could stand outside supporting her.

The whole question is in that last proposition about England. I own up that England has got on my nerves. Every week I see a big drop in her scale, till I get to think she will drop on my head tomorrow. Hicks Beach seems to me to grow in colossal dimensions of incompetence, and when I see that old rat Goschen scuttling out of the ship, and all the intelligent ones, even up to Salisbury, trying to escape, and a young lot coming in, about of the style of George Curzon, leaving Joe Chamberlain and Hicks Beach, and every sort of difficulty close ahead, I turn greener than ever with terror.[2]

The management of the Treasury and the Bank has been such that at last public confidence is affected. The continent shows distinct tendencies not to trust England with its balances. The exchanges are set dead against her, on all sides. If Gage can let her have a hundred millions of gold now, he can carry her and Russia over, till the gold mines are reopened. Otherwise I see no chance that England can maintain her credit, and for at least five years she has kept her head above water only by credit. She has been insolvent since 1895. Almost invariably I have found the public catch an idea in five years; first, a few theorists; then the most far-sighted Jews; and at last the crowd of speculators for the settlement. The shock of last November very nearly upset England. This November her situation is very much worse, and the hatred of her is intensified to a degree at which an explosion becomes almost inevitable. Financially and politically the current seems to run even stronger against her than it does economically; and I don't wonder; for to me, who look on her as our only ally and our outpost in our future struggle with Europe, her stupidity, brutality, ignorance and senility, have been unendurable since the bimetallic contest in '93 when she so nearly cut our throats.

So I regard the Anglo-German agreement as in effect a capitulation to draw Germany away from Russia; a scheme I have believed to be hopeless.[3] To me, the only correct card is France; but I am only a theorist, without the smallest knowledge of the hands. If we could draw France into a combination which should secure the Philippines and all southern Asia up to the Hoang-ho, it would be all we could hope. Failing that, we lose the game when England falls.

You too want to scuttle. Everybody wants to scuttle, apparently, who sees the mess before him; except perhaps the Major who has a genius for just such situations. Never impatient and never discouraged, he is sure to win because he has the cards. There is to be a new deal after December, and no one can tell how the next hands will fall, but he seems safe for two years. Anyway, to the diseased mind of a Dominican monk like me, seven hundred years old, the lead is no longer his. In this game, Germany leads trumps.

I would give a sixpence, or a string of pice, to know what trumps Germany holds. I can't believe in Germany. She is not big enough to swing the club. If she could unite herself either to eastern or western Europe, she could do it. As it is, I see nothing but a repetition of my own thirteenth century.

This by way of compliment to your success. Of personal matters I have very little to say. The Exposition is closing. To me it has been an education which I have failed to acquire for want of tutors, but it has been an immense amusement and only needed you to be a constant joy. It has brought me so near the end that I hardly care to wait for the last scenes. There are things in it which run close to the day of judgment. It is a new century, and what we used to call electricity is its God. I can already see that the scientific theories and laws of our generation will, to the next, appear as antiquated as the Ptolemaic system, and that the fellow who gets to 1950 will wish he hadn't. The curious mustiness of decay is already over our youth, and all the period from 1840 to 1870. The period from 1870 to 1900 is closed. I see that much in the machine-gallery of the Champ de Mars. The period from 1900 to 1930 is in full swing, and, gee-whacky! how it is going! It will break its damned neck long before it gets through, if it tries to keep up the speed. You are free to deride my sentimentality if you like, but I assure you that I,—a monk of St Dominic, absorbed in the Beatitudes of the Virgin Mother—go down to the Champ de Mars and sit by the hour over the great dynamos, watching them run as noiselessly and as smoothly as the planets, and asking them—with infinite courtesy—where in Hell they are going. They are marvelous. The Gods are not in it. Chiefly the Germans! Steam no longer appears, although still behind the scenes; but one feels no certainty that another ten years may not abolish steam too. The charm of the show, to me, is that no one pretends to understand even in a remote degree, what these wierd things are that they call electricity, Roentgen rays, and what not.[4] The exhibitors are dead dumped into infinity on a fork.

So my solitude prepares itself for heaven, with a constant eye to the London exchanges. With an humble and contrite heart[5] I prostrate myself before the Major and the dynamos, and wait for the day of judgment much as I did in the reign of St Louis. St Thomas Aquinas and you are my only friends. Sturgis Bigelow is here, and Alice Mason, and the Warders. Mrs Cameron has got back, and has a winter of black before her. Martha is sixteen feet high and gawky. Zorn's portrait, as I wrote you, is fun.[6] Joe Stickney comes down to moralise and dine. I buy only Ming porcelain. I read only romance French, and you.

Give my love to Mrs Hay and the babe-hays.

Ever Yrs ——

MS: MHi
1. McKinley was reelected. He had been brevetted major in 1865.
2. George Joachim Goschen (1831–1907), first lord of the admiralty. With the dissolution of Parliament, Goschen announced that he would not stand for reelection, and, as expected, he was elevated to the peerage Dec. 18. In the reorganization of the cabinet after the October general election, Lord Salisbury remained prime minister but gave up his other post of foreign secretary.
3. The Anglo-German agreement was at first taken to mean that Britain and Germany would take concerted action against Russian territorial expansion in China. Germany soon denied that the agreement was directed against Russia or that it would oppose Russian occupation of Manchuria.

4. Compare *Education,* chap. 25, "The Dynamo and the Virgin."
5. An echo of Rudyard Kipling's "Recessional" (1897).
6. Anders Zorn (1860–1920), Swedish artist, painted a portrait of Elizabeth Cameron.

To John Hay

Private most privately private.

Paris, 4 Dec. 1900.

My dear Statesman

You are not very encouraging to a poor banished citizen who wants to come home and can't find a steamer. You threaten him with Teddies and terrors enough to scare a boer. And my brother Charles is said to be thinking of a second parricide this winter in Washington.[1] And my brother Brooks is there now. And Mme Albertini starts next week with costumes enough to redeem you all from the wild Mohocks.[2] And the Perry Belmonts are to be there.[3] And Cabot is the worst terror of all. How does one live!

Here I have only Boston to struggle with,—almost all of it, I admit, but not yapping like mongrels for bones. They get here neither offices nor duchesses. So they and I are wheeled about in our bath chairs, and drivel.

I have Sturgis Bigelow; my sister-in-law Mrs John and Hitty; Mrs Brimmer at the Brighton; Jeff Coolidge just gone from the Vendome; the Tom Newbolds; the Alan Johnsons just gone; Paddy O'Beirne; all the Warders; Mrs Cameron and Martha; Becky Grant; the Michael Herberts; next week Louisette returns.[4] It is too much for me. I stay just as I did a dozen years ago, with Martha in a corner behind the sofa, while Rodin or Helleu or Zorn or some other swell is talking of himself to Martha's mother in the next room.[5] By day I wallow in the twelfth century. By night I go to bed at ten o'clock. I've been once to the theatre and am still recovering. Paris is very Brumy and the sun, like me, mostly abed. You know it all. Only we change with years. The Arc d'Etoile and the Princess Matilde are above decades.[6]

You excite my wildest admiration! Whenever I think of you, I glow. How do you carry that load? Look you! friend! I am but a waif on the waters of eternity, and I care not one French sour grape how soon or how late this damned humanity breaks its neck, for I know mighty little good of it, yet I assure you I lie awake of nights and kick off the bed-clothes merely at thinking of the risks we are now running, and the rate of our speed. You say you are a bore about the Senate. You know I am two double-barreled bores about England. I can do nothing but think and talk about it. The Senate is a good, brutal, conspicuous ball to kick. England is one of the wierd mysteries of God's afterthought. Spain in the sixteenth century was nothing to it. China today is a trifling problem beside it. And both Spain and China were simple old mediaeval military problems, while England is the last word of divine wisdom. I tell you, divine wisdom has said some pretty rotten words!

Soul of my body! I can make nothing of it! That England has stood through the last year upsets all my facts and figures. I have been wholly wrong. I have got to figure out a balance-sheet totally new, and to me totally incredible. I look on now in superlative bewilderment. I cannot conceive what holds England up. With broken prestige, admitted failure, and no money, how do Hicks Beach and the Bank go on! With the entire world, every solitary human being between the Ural Mountains and the Bay of San Francisco longing to hit her and plunder her, how does she keep her purse in her pocket? And now Mr nephew Kaiser William has taken charge of her precious welfare! A lunatic, just barely outside of a mad-house, protects his venerable grand-mamma from other wicked robbers. The twelfth century never saw anything more grotesque!

Believe me, my angel son and sovereign, I am not fretting much for the sake of England. If her venerated interests alone were at stake, it is not I who would lie awake for anxiety about them. My alarm is strictly and grossly selfish. What I fear is that, if English credit really gets that shock which is now common expectation in half the newspapers of the world, you would see the fair fabric of your popularity vanish in a single telegram. If England can no longer borrow or buy, she can no longer pay. Your markets may disappear over night. Your produce might be thrown back on you by the wholesale. Values would vanish in the call of a stock-board, and all of you at Washington would be sprawling on your backs in an instant, and the worst of it would be that though I get no profit out of your success, I should get just about as much of the kicks in your reverse. I can't win, but I stand to lose about as much as you. At bottom it's only the income that counts; the honor is now cheap. You see why I am a double-quick-firing-machine-gun of a bore about England.

For, to anyone who has all his life studied history, it is obvious that the fall of England would be paralleled by only two great convulsions in human record; the fall of the Roman empire in the fourth century, and the fall of the Roman Church in the sixteenth. Big as the catastrophe was when Spain went down, and France, neither was anything like England; they were small in comparison. Spain has taken at least two hundred years and a score of wars to founder completely. France has convulsed our century in doing it. For God's mercy, what will England do!

As necessary residuary legatees, you and Russia have got to administer the estate, with the Kaiser claiming the whole. He has always wanted to be

king of England. By the sword of the Archangel Michael, I almost think
he'll succeed! England seems to me to have no longer the strength to stand
alone. The feeling there, I am told, is now one of universal depression and
self-distrust. Furious with Salisbury for his last batch of family jobs, no one
seems now to see future salvation in Joe Chamberlain. The opposition is
scared to death at the thought of being offered power, and would support
Salisbury against his own party to prevent it. There might be stranger solutions than grandson William. A bigger bid for it than yesterday's refusal
to see Kruger, would be hard to make.[7] In international law I take it, his
yesterday's telegram to Kruger is an abandonment of neutrality. I
suppose England would regard a similar telegram to Queen Victoria as a
declaration of war.

In short, my venerable friend, I respect and admire you beyond measure,
and in another month I expect to be hurrying back to swing incense and
flattery under your precious nose. I hold on tight to you as my last tie to
the nineteenth century. You keep my brain, on one side, a little less wobbly
than usual. Otherwise I have to read the letters of Symmachus to steady
me.[8] Do you know the letters of Symmachus? If not, ask my brother Brooks
for Gaston Boissier's charming volume on him.[9] Symmachus is Salisbury,
or you, or Kaiser Willy, or somebody, after whom the deluge.[10] Symmachus
is mighty good reading. So is Saint Simon!

Réjane has got a new part; I've not seen it, but they say she has little
acting to do. Also a new play at the Gymnase; another at the Variétés; what
know I? Lots more! Paris is waking up. No new books, I think. For me, I
buy a Greek coin every week; or, as I said in my last, a Ming jar, by alternation,
or a big book on twelfth century glass; but what I yearn to buy is illuminated
manuscripts, and I would, too, but no one now knows enough to enjoy
them, and all alone I can't worship indefinitely without rheumatism in my
joints. A dynamo is what I need.

Hasta luego, amigo! I am pleased to see how kindly the Message speaks
of Spain and France.[11]

———

MS: MHi

1. CFA2 projected "a magnum opus" on his father centered on the diplomatic history of the
   Civil War.
2. Mrs. Leander Albertini (1855–1933), an in-law of Reynolds Hitt.
3. Perry Belmont (1851–1947), capitalist and politician, had been a student of HA at Harvard.
   Recently involved as a corespondent in a divorce action, he married the delinquent wife,
   Jessie Robbins (Mrs. Henry T.) Sloane.
4. Mary Ann Brimmer, widow of Martin Brimmer (1829–1896), prominent Bostonian,
   founding president of the Museum of Fine Arts, Boston; Rebecca (Mrs. David Beach)
   Grant (d. 1917); Louise Bonaparte Moltke-Huitfeldt (1873–1923).
5. Auguste Rodin (1840–1917), leading French sculptor; Paul-César Helleu (1859–1927),
   fashionable French painter.

6. Princess Mathilde Bonaparte (1820–1904) had presided over a leading literary salon for more than fifty years.
7. Stephanus J. P. Kruger (1825–1904), Boer statesman, president of the Transvaal Republic.
8. The letters of Quintus Aurelius Symmachus (c. 340–c. 402) barely allude to the disasters overtaking the Roman Empire.
9. Gaston Boissier in *La Fin du paganisme* (1891) devotes a chapter to Symmachus.
10. "After us the deluge"; remark of Jeanne Antoinette Poisson (1721–1764), marquise de Pompadour, to Louis XV, quoted by Mme. du Hausset, *Mémoires* (1824), p. 19.
11. McKinley's State of the Union message to Congress proposed friendly relations with Spain. It also noted that U.S. interest in the Paris Exposition marked a year of goodwill between the U.S. and France.

To Anne Palmer Fell

1603 H Street. 25 March, 1901.

Dear Lady

I have just returned from a brief trip to New York to see Ternina in the Götterdämmerung, which was a world-shaking experience.[1] That I, in my dotage, should fall a victim to the Wagnerian religion is one of the wildest experiences in this wierd world. Evidently I near my end.

Not that so small a matter as that is calculated to disturb my philosophy. I am only bewildered to find that fifty years ago a great artist should have said all I have since learned, without my knowing he had said it; and that now another great artist should sing it out loud, and everybody should listen in frantic silence and absorption, when I feel sure they can't know what it means. If they knew, something would happen.

Indeed I would like to come down to talk religion with you. Nothing would suit me so well. The truth is that this American world, or rather this twentieth century, strains my nerves to a point which needs rest. You perhaps are in a quiet eddy of it. Here I feel as if it were a Niagara whirlpool. Other people take it gaily. I live too much abroad to feel the happy confidence of the hog-market. My precious donkey-ears are glued to a telephone which says all sorts of startling things. I almost think I shall live to see wilder menageries than any I have yet danced in, though I've danced in some gay ones. It would take too long to explain my columns of figures and my measures of speed, so I won't try. You can take it for granted and play Wagner. The circus will not disturb your alligators and rattle-snakes. But I am to go abroad in a month, and am tied here till I go. I cannot paddle with the babes this time, though paddling is the only realisation of true religion.

On the whole, though I am glad to be through with it, and to have no more responsibility for the universe, I find it still very amusing to look at, from a front box. The spectacle does not lose its interest. Far from it! What a fascinating melodrama it is, when one has time to think; and what do the Kaiser and the Czar and Edward VII and Pierpont Morgan think of it? I presume that Marian can tell you, since she was born to it. As I was born in the year 1138, I don't catch on.

I passed all last summer in Paris living in my own time. I was crusading with various gentlemen; studying scholasticism with various others; praying to the Virgin with a third batch. We lived an active life in my day too; more active than now; and played lots of pranks with the universe; but the sudden change to New York, and the jump of seven hundred years, took away my balance, and it was hard to recover. You can have no conception of the contrast between Europe and America, or of the vertigo that it gives one. Paris is a capital of a mediaeval province. France is deliberately turning her back on the future, and reverting to antiquity. England is Matt. Arnold's "weary Titan" fifty years older, and more than fifty years stupider.[2] As for the other countries, they are waiting for burial, except Germany, and she is waiting to bury them. One and all, they dread and detest us. We are sapping their vitals, and they have got to make some stupendous effort to save themselves.

They can't save themselves even then. They have not the coal or the iron or the copper or the cotton or the grain or the energy, to do it; but they can make a big fight before they go under; and unless it is political, it must be social. They can sweep away a heap of costly rubbish like churches and armies and classes; they can pull the Jews' teeth, and abolish us. They know it, and are utterly staggered by the job. We don't know it, and are as innocent of ill-doing as the virtuous Boxer. They are being squeezed together by our pressure, and if we don't squeeze out a volcano, we shall gobble the mouse.

The "Götterdämmerung" is right ahead. I want to see the Ternina that will sing it.

Poor dear Agatha was half pathetic, or three quarters, for she was always half.[3] What a life! but she doesn't know it. At least she is still German more than Jew. If the Jew had got the upperhand, she would have been a tragedy.

No one knows, except Ternina and us, and we shall not tell. It's not of the slightest consequence.

Ever Yrs   Henry Adams.

MS: MHi

1. Milka Ternina (1863–1941), Croation opera singer, unusually successful in Wagnerian roles.
2. "Heine's Grave" (1867). Arnold echoes Heine's "sharp upbraidings."
3. Agathe Schurz (b. 1853), eldest child of Carl and Margarethe Schurz. Agathe's mother, born in Germany, came from a Jewish family of Hamburg named Meyer.

To Brooks Adams

1603 H Street. 22 April, 1901.

Dear Brooks

Welcome home! Your letter, as usual, needs six or eight folio volumes to answer, and offers no equivalent in news; but my reply will, as usual, match your letter, I imagine, in both respects.[1]

As far as concerns the Stone Age, you have as much field for theory as anyone else. Practically all we know of the Stone Age is the American Indian. Such as he was when the Puritans settled on Beacon Street, such you have a right to assume him in the pre-glacial period. Of course he had practically all that we have; he had crossed every sea, settled every continent; invented every society, and developed every idea. On which subject I myself, modest as I am, said five-and-twenty years ago, all there is to say in my lecture on the Primitive Rights of Women.

Who the original man was, God only knows. Probably he is sunk beneath the Indian Ocean. You have not to deal with him or with anything as near him as five million years. He sprang from a low-class monkey, far back in Eocene or Cretaceous time. Drop him!

Your starting-point is with man after he has colonised every continent in the world, and most islands. Whether he is Miocene, Pliocene or Pleistocene matters nothing to you. At all events, whenever he was, he preceded world-commerce, and he still knew metals. Copper and tin go back of anything you can find out.

You start with the Deluge in the Euphrates Valley. My only explanation of the original cradle of art is that the Euphrates Valley was formerly much more extensive and the river flowed at least as far as the deep water outside the Persian Gulf. In the great subsidence of the Afro-Indian continent, the latest event was the submergence of the Persian Gulf, and with it, the cradle of civilisation. (Read Suess, Face de la Terre.[2] Chapter I on the Deluge. His idea is different, but he illustrates the records, and his authority is scientifically dictatorial.)

If this was not the cause of the apparent break of continuity suggested by the Assyrian art and its complete development from the apparent start, you will have to look for it behind geological changes in the upper waters of the Euphrates Valley which have cut the ancient water communication with central Asia.

In either case you have not to deal with a stone-age. When we first strike commerce, metals were known. The North American Indian himself worked copper and gold, and he is older by some million years than anything you can touch in civilisation. At least, if he's not, they can't prove the negative, and you've a perfect right to assume the affirmative.

The only difficult point that worries me, after the initial Assyrian assumption is the Phenician extension. I cannot resist the suspicion that the Phenicians reached Brazil, as early as the Mycenae period. The pottery is even Greek, which makes the case worse. If the Brazil Indian came in contact with Phenician commerce a thousand years B.C; and the Malay civilisation came in on the west coast a thousand years A.D., the development of the *North* American Indian becomes less certainly isolated. At the same time, the working of the Lake Superior Copper seems to be beyond likely interference from either source. All one can say is that it is post-glacial. Even that is very doubtful about the California gold. The Calaveras skull, whatever age it may be, is a very serious fact, as you can see for yourself if you will look at it at Cambridge and get its chemical analysis. Don't allow yourself to be controlled on that subject by the authorities on either side.[3] The number of American languages—a hundred and fifty or more—is as sure evidence of the age of man in America as it is in Africa or Asia. You had better consult Putnam on all these points.[4] At bottom, my chief reason for accepting the pre-glacial age of the American Indian is the rupture of continuity between him and all the old-world types.

The Phenician extension is another matter, and requires very careful study indeed. On one side it possibly touches Brazil, on another it involves England, on a third it raises all sorts of questions about the Etruscans, Greece, the Black Sea and the Homeric poems. Who were the Mycenaeans, and who were the Dorians? How far back does Cypriote commerce go? Who were the Hittites? Who were the Trojans of the lowest town? You have struck all this in Greece, and know already, I suppose, what you think.

You can have all my coins if you want them. They are mostly boxed in a Safety-vault, but I have some of my own purchases too. Let me know!

As for Europe, I consider the game as thrown up. Hicks Beach's speech might have been made by you or me.[5] I am waiting from week to week for the economical readjustment, and I apprehend its reaction on us to be due this year. The rupture between America and Europe as economical systems is now a fact too conspicuous for discussion. How they are to be brought again to a common level is beyond my powers of foresight. I can only look on, and shiver.

As for personal recognition you are better off than you would have been in any previous time. You would have been burned or imprisoned formerly. One is not a prophet of evil cheap.

As for me, I shall make no plans for the present. Edward Hooper's illness has disturbed my calculations, and until I can get his affairs somehow arranged, I dare not move.

Love to your wife! I heard of you both from the Lodges.

Ever Yrs   Henry Adams.

MS: MH

1. BA had asked where he could find authoritative works on the Stone Age and on other topics suggested by his travels in Greece.
2. Edward Suess (1831–1914).
3. In 1866 the geologist Josiah D. Whitney reported that a fossil skull had been found in a mining shaft in Calaveras County, Calif. The authenticity of the skull was much debated among paleontologists.
4. Frederic Ward Putnam (1839–1915), curator of the Peabody Museum at Harvard 1875–1909.
5. Hicks Beach, introducing the budget on April 18, estimated a deficit of £55 million.

To John Hay

Paris, 9 June, 1901.

Gorged as you are with the sugar-plums of power and the comforts of a home, you will not want to know the trivialities of a frivolous people like me, but I got a pencilled line from you, just as I was sailing, which I answered only by telegraph, and that was four fertile weeks ago. Of your funereal return to Washington I have heard nothing, and only infer that if it had been your funeral, I should have known it.[1] Quantula sapientia![2] Upon my sacred vows to the Virgin, I turn green with horror o'nights in thinking that we trust ourselves and the world to a set of fellows like you who haven't even got sense enough to stay at home when you're imbecile.

You make me tired and bring me blue because you are so idiotically like me when I go automobilising which is my last proof of senile decay. Last Thursday I took Martha and her cousin Edith to Chantilly by automobile,[3] and the chauffeur rattled us back over a fearful paved-road, that can never have been touched since the Consulate, thirtyfive kilometres in an hour and a half; about three kilometres, or three fifths of a mile, in a minute; and I, all the way hanging on to my hair and ears, and asking myself what form of suicide I had better take if anything happened to those girls. That time we escaped. Yesterday I did it again, with my niece Elsie Adams, taking her to breakfast at St Germain, and steeple-chasing back through the forest of Marly and the Bois and the Fête des Fleurs expecting translation to Hades at every kilometre. This is all the consequence of quitting my own quiet, slow, early-Jacksonian country, where I was sleepy and sprinkled with cornmeal, in order to come over here, where the women insist on a uniform speed of twenty miles an hour across the Place de l'Opera. My tears avail nothing.

Tu es ille vir![4] You are that chauffeur! Only you break down and come home by freight. What history has told me, that I know. The chauffeurs that have for three thousand years run the world into every ditch in the whole fortieth parallel from China to San Francisco, are well burned in on my mind; but you and your associates scare me more than my little Frenchman or Napoleon the Third. What the devil are you all at! One long week I stopped in England. It was Whitsuntide,— and in my belief it always is Whitsuntide in England—and one huge debauch of beer and bicycles. They were trying to be French and to enjoy the light-hearted gaiety of their Anglo-Saxon ancestors. It was heart-rending. Harry White saved my life by carrying me down to Wilton for three nights, but he drove me, at my request, to Clieveden, and when I saw that dream of Italian beauty, and felt that Willy Astor might come in at any moment, and catch me there, I dragged White away in a panic. I did want to see Mary Curzon, and wrote to her. She answered from Windsor Castle, and I fled England. And now Bill Whitney has won the Derby and Foxhall Keene the Oaks.[5] As for Pierpont Morgan, he owns the empire, and last of all—what would drive to frenzy anybody except a beery boozy Whitsuntide Englishman, Andy Carnegie patronises and lectures the whole menagerie. And the beasts booze, and the beer bubbles!

Disgusting is not my word for it. Anarchist though I am, I know no anarchy that I can invent half equal to it. As far as I could see or hear, the whole English people are turned fatalistic pessimists, with no idea or hope except in their endless credit. They admit that they are living on borrowed money; that France and America have fought and are fighting the wretched Boers, not they, who can't even fight, or feed, or pay without our active help. They publish every day new fall in consols, decline in railways, falling off in exports; and at last even a serious falling off in imports. They are deadly sick of us, and look at us with absolutely French disgust as we swagger up and down Bond Street, and buy their worn-out clothes, and corner them on the stock-exchange. All Europe is sick of us, and detests us. Not that we do any harm, for we are all that carries them; but we are bigger, and in some ways, cleverer, and we are vulgar, and we are a kind of Jew somewhat altered by emigration. My own belief grows every year stronger that the alliance of Europe against us is an inevitable necessity for them, and that within a definite term, say twenty years, it will take shape. The approximation of France and Germany is this year an admitted fact. A very few years more, at this rate, will make them allies. Austria is already in advance of Germany, and the moment France comes in, all western

Europe follows. I am satisfied the thing is feasible, and that Germany means to take the hegemony of the world. In my belief, Russia must obey that combination, and England alone will drop out, from want of energy to keep in. What we are to do, I don't know, but I guess we are going to rot. Cabot Lodge and Teddy Roosevelt know. Bluster, in that case! Europe has still got the means to put up a big game, and, as usual, necessity makes the impossible easy.

What exasperates me most is that at this season, Paris is uncommonly amusing. Even one who refuses conscientiously to be amused, like me, cannot help grinning horribly at the fun. The Holy Virgin knows there is plenty of tragedy in it too, but not more than elsewhere; and indeed I know nothing so Promethean in tragedy as Arthur Balfour and John Morley and Joe Chamberlain.[6] At the Salon there are half a dozen interesting things; especially two amusing Besnards. At the Royal Academy I saw nothing except Sargent's Wertheimer Girls, which are du Sargent pur, and far from undefiled. America is here as usual. Mrs Cameron sails for New York on the 29th. Get her a house near you at Sunapee, for she knows not where to go. My Marbury-DeWolfe outfit at Versailles has broken at last with miladi of Anglesey, and set up a new salon.[7] Bay and Bessie had me to dinner in their palace of the Rue du Bac. Joe Stickney plods gloomily on his thesis. My printer does not a stroke on mine. I've not entered a theatre or heard of a play. I've not looked into a book. Martha is 5.8½ feet high. Mrs Cameron is good-natured enough not to show that I am more of a bore, though I think sincerely somewhat less of a jackass than I was when she still stood in her teens and we first met. It is a great comfort to me to see my friends too grow old and lose their memories and their teeth and their hair, like me and you and her, &c. To me it has never mattered, but to her and you it should be serious. Others travel on without changing more than the obelisk. Even our own O'Beirne chirps gaily on his perch; but Spring Rice chirped at Penrith, and I failed to see him.

This very day I have been to call on the Duchesse Stevens to see her apartment next door to the Trocadero, and I have been out to Malmaison dining with Tuck to see his electric outfit.[8] Verily I hardly know myself, though in London I dined with Joe Choate too. The weather has done it. One can't stay at home in a dry June. And now I am going to buy photographs of monuments to help Mary help George to build a Victorian Memorial.[9] Bon à tout faire, am I.

Ever ——

MS: MHi

1. A chaffing allusion to President McKinley's sudden return to Washington with his critically ill wife.

2. *Nescis, mi fili, quantula sapientia gubernatur mundus*: You do not know, my son, with how little wisdom the world is governed; Count Axel Oxenstierna (1583–1654).
3. Edith Hoyt, a cousin of Elizabeth Cameron, lived in France and was about Martha Cameron's age.
4. "Thou art the man": 2 Samuel 12:7.
5. Foxhall P. Keene (1865–1941), banker famed as a horse breeder and sportsman.
6. British statesmen confronted with the disasters of the Boer War.
7. Elisabeth Marbury (1856–1933), very stout and masculine theatrical agent intimately associated with the actress Elsie de Wolfe, had set up a salon.
8. Adele Stevens (1841–1912), a divorcée, had married Charles, marquis de Talleyrand-Périgord, whose father ceded to him the title of Duc de Dino. Edward Tuck (1842–1938), expatriate U.S. banker.
9. Lord George Curzon proposed the building of a monument to the late queen in Calcutta. When constructed it was built on a grander scale than that of the Taj Mahal.

To Elizabeth Cameron

Nuremberg, 3 Aug. '01.

So Bayreuth passes! We have finished our cure, and are on our way again. All went well and merrily. All was easy and archaic. Except that I am rather ashamed never to have done it before, I feel that virtue is rewarded. Not that I have got particular pleasure out of it, or that I am more Wagnerian than of old. I got more pleasure, by far, from the regular theatrical performances. I felt my Wagner much better in bits. Too much of him, or of any other artist, gives dyspepsia. His faults get on the nerves. As for Wagner, his German bad taste becomes the only thing I see, at last, and in Parsifal it culminates in a mass of flabby German sentimentality which passes patience, and makes me indifferent to what John Lodge assures me is the highest point he ever reached in music.[1] Of course I have learned a lot about motifs, and all sorts of things, but on the whole, except to have seen it all, without cuts or abbreviations, I do not think I am better off. My conviction that such a monstrosity of form is simply proof of our loss of artistic sense, is stronger than ever.

Germany deepens it. Forty years have added another layer of bad taste to all that went before. It sickens me to think that this is the result, and all the result, of my life-time. I saw the same thing in Italy, but there the effort has not been so gigantic. Here in Nuremberg I feel it the more because this was one of my first delights in art, way back in '59. It makes me happy to think that I shall never see it again. Altogether, Germany gives me the sense of hopeless failure. In fact, I have had more than enough of Europe altogether, and I'm afraid my appetite for America is not voracious either. The world has lived too long. So have I. One of us two has got to go. For the public good, it had better be the world that goes, for at least I am harmless.

Bay and Bessie and John seem better satisfied with it than I am, which may partly be accounted for by their more advanced education. To them it all seems to seem of course. Our party has run nicely together. I've seen no cloud on Bessie's face, and Bay's sunny humor seems unbroken. Cabot and I groan with indigestion, and sister Anne at times gets tired, but the youthful brooks flow on forever. There is less dispute than there used to be. All parties have come a step nearer, and perhaps are several steps older. Bayreuth was more or less full of acquaintances, and there were even one or two people whom I myself had seen or heard of before; but we got not much help from them.

Linz. Monday morning. [5 Aug.]   We came by rail yesterday to Passau, and by steamer here. Great success! the river is very beautiful, and quite untouched by commerce or industry. Except that the people looked rather better cared for, and were dressed in ready-made clothes from Vienna, I should not have noted the forty years that have passed since I saw it last. Some day, bring Martha down here, to show her how pretty Europe once was!

Salzburg. Tuesday. [6 Aug.]   Yesterday we came here to do Mozart, and here we willingly rest till Friday. The pretty little old dark town, along its mountain, under its castle, has turned into a fashionable summer haunt, and our big hotel is like Saratoga, filled with Americans and Jews. Everything is good and clean, but it is liker to America than to Europe, and still more like Lucerne, which also you know. I've nothing to say against it except that it tells me nothing, and I might as well be with you and Martha at Beverly, for anything I see of the people or hear of the language. In the hotel and in the streets I hear English everywhere, and generally American. Everybody looks like everybody else. One never seems curious to know anybody, or even to know who anybody is. Queer effect of civilisation and progress! Fifty years ago, and a hundred years ago much more still, one talked with people, and met everywhere travellers who interested or amused one. Lately I have travelled all over Europe with all sorts of young people, boys and girls, Hays and Lodges and Warders and Bessie Davis, and I don't know how many; but I have never seen them make an acquaintance or show the faintest interest in anyone we have met. The worst is that I can find no fault with them. I've not seen either anyone to suggest an inquiry. As for a lady or a gentleman, the thing has disappeared with the buffalo.

I see no earthly good in travel any longer. It helps to nothing at all. One learns geography, but railways do not pay much attention to geography. One sees towns and landscapes out of all relation with what is actual or ever was. As art, it is all misleading. As politics it has no meaning at all.

Even as hotel-keeping I do not see that many ideas are suggested. One ceases to care to complain. The only effect on me is to make me think of Paris as a quiet old forgotten village, where one can rust and die.

This is the first day of the Musik-Fest. At eleven o'clock we had a concert in the Academy Hall; two hours of Mozart music. The hall was as usual abominably hot; packed; with a durchlauchstigster; kaiser-könig-lichster; weiss-nicht-wasigster;[2] a certain Prince Eugene, who looked exactly like Egerton Winthrop;[3] and an audience, singularly ordinary and to me undistinguishable from any other musical audience in the world. We listened two hours to a selection from Mozart, very pretty, and easy, and familiar, and gentlemanly. Next to me sat a wild little nervous pianist who gave me his card,—Roderich Bass—and informed us, in the intervals, that he was to perform in the concert tomorrow. He amused sister Anne much. I was less amused by stumbling over Mrs Bob Chanler at our hotel, whose present haunt is, it seems, a short distance away, and who has also come up for the Fest.[4] Somewhere I suppose I shall strike also Mrs Bigelow Lawrence and Fanny Chapman, who were also at Bayreuth.[5] Americans swarm like bees. We have struck more rain too, and the rivers are in flood.

Cabot now proposes to go on to Vienna, and perhaps from there to Moscow and St Petersburg if sister Anne is not fatigued; and to get back to Paris about the middle of September. To me it is all the same. I am in no hurry to get back, and not violent to get forward. Only I shall be glad to get off my old tracks, and to see something that lies outside experience.

Your letter of the 17th from Donegal makes me hope that you are now quiet at Beverly, probably bored, but I hope comfortable. I've postponed sending off this letter, in order to report our happy arrival here.

———

MS: MHi

1. John Ellerton Lodge (1876–1942), son of Henry Cabot Lodge.
2. "Most august, most imperial-royal, most know-not-what-else-to-call-him."
3. Egerton Winthrop (1839–1916), New York lawyer, banker, art collector.
4. Julia Chamberlain Chanler (c. 1873–1936), wife of Robert Astor Chanler (1872–1930).
5. Elizabeth Chapman Lawrence (1829–1905), widow of Timothy Bigelow Lawrence of Boston, prominent socialite, seasonal resident in Washington; Fanny Chapman, her younger half-sister.

To Elizabeth Cameron

Moscow, August 21, 1901.

Done! Wipe out Moscow! We have seen the Kremlin at last, after I have said, since the year 1858, regularly every day or two, that really I must go there. What a comfort to meet my end with my task accomplished and wrapped in the appropriate napkin! It is true that, for pleasure, one ought to come here early in life, and especially before visiting Constantinople and Ravenna; one ought to start from Petersburg and pass down through here to Kiev and Roumania, and so to Byzantium and the rest and best; but anyway I've got it done, and it leaves a queer taste like caviar and vodki, semi-barbarous and yet *manqué.* Even barbarism is sometimes weak. The Kremlin is more than half barbarous, but it is not strong; it is Byzantium barbarised. The bulbous domes are weak. The turnip with its root in the air is not so dignified as the turnip with its root in the earth. The architecture is simply ignorance. The builders built in 1600 as they built in 1200 because they knew no more. They had no building-stone. Gold was their only idea of splendor. Crude blue and green was all their decoration when they had to stop on red. They had no fund of taste in themselves; no invention or sense of form or line or color. Where on earth did our tenth-century French get all these? Charlemagne was about on a line with Ivan the Terrible who reigned here somewhere about seven hundred years afterwards, and I can see no ghost of a reason why art should have had seven hundred years of wonderful wealth after Charlemagne, and should have stayed dead after Ivan. It is a fact, I can't see much anyway. You knew it already. This is only for the benefit of Martha's education. Decidedly I incline to advise her not to marry a Muscovite. The conclusion is rather broad compared with what led to it; but the more I see of Russia, the more terrific the business of Russianising becomes. Moscow is, à la fin de la fin, une ville manquée.

The Sunday high mass at the huge new church, or cathedral, gave me almost a sensation. As I watched it from the gallery, above the dense crowd, I thought that a crusader of the twelfth century who had drifted into Sta Sofia at Constantinople would have seen so nearly the same thing that he could have stood by my side and told me all about it without a sign of surprise; and I was almost ready to try and remember a little of Villehardouin to start a conversation.[1] The Russian mass is a marvellous composite of the Jewish tabernacle and the first Crusade. The robes are those of St Louis, Godfrey of Bouillon, Solomon, Justinian,—I don't know who not— and the ceremonies those of Solomon's temple. I never saw anything more fascinating. Except the Athanasian Creed I know nothing more Greek.

What lends power to the illusion is the wonderful tenth-century people, whose formal devoutness goes beyond what I imagine ever existed in western Europe, and whose process of crossing themselves is a very curious mathematical combination of gestures lasting a considerable time, so that, as they cross themselves before every street-shrine, they keep at it pretty steadily. The men show more persistence than the women, and make the bulk of the audience at mass. When the whole congregation happens to cross themselves simultaneously, the effect is curious. In some ways, I feel sure, the Russian of today is more primitive than the Frenchman or German ever was, if you call this passive attitude of subjection primitive. I never met with it in any primitive race I have struck before, and even a monkey shows occasional scepticism. I find my chief interest in watching the people in the churches and shrines. What I can't make out is whether the attitude is as completely passive as it seems, or whether there is an occasional gleam of fanatical fire. Thus far I've seen not a sign of individuality. All are run in the same tallow, more or less.

All these observations count on the general question which interests us all, whether we are going to be whacked, or not, by Europe, in the long run. Now, in the long run, the passive character exhausts the active one. Economy of energy is a kind of power. Russia and Asia may clean us all out, especially if Germany helps to run her. What will happen in five hundred years I can't even guess; but I'm clear that we've at least a hundred years' start, and that Martha, if she insists on marrying a Russian, had better keep him at home, and not come here on speculation.

At the same time I judge that the average Russian would make a very docile husband, obstinate only in small matters, and quite a baby always. He will need to be told what to do. Perhaps that may not suit Martha; at least not so well as it would suit some women I have read about.

Petersburg. Friday morning. [23 Aug.]   We came up here yesterday, a comfortable twelve-hour journey through endless forests, arriving at nine o'clock, and met by the Embassy at the station. Luckily the Towers are in Switzerland.[2] Berty Peirce, being our cousin, does not matter.[3] Here at the hotel I found your letter of August 6, with a batch of other letters, including one from Mrs Hay which reassures me in regard to her at least. I doubt whether the entire Trinity sitting on Judgment Day will upset her. Never did I meet such a pyramid of strength. Your letter, as usual, gives me more than all the others, and I have one from Mabel which does not altogether sound like Mrs Hay. I wish it did. Of Constance, nothing whatever has been said to me. From Mary Curzon I have a note from Braemar Castle where she seems to be staying with her mamma, but what the deuce is Braemar Castle? I have quite forgotten castles at Braemar.[4] Also a note from Henry Holt offering to dramatise Democracy![5] I thought my old— five-and-twenty-year old—sins were long dead and buried, but they rise like Mrs Bigelow Lawrence who will die convinced that she was meant as the heroine of that scandalous work. I saw it in her eye at Bayreuth. It would be fun for her to see herself on the stage.

Saturday. [24 Aug.]   Caviar and cold sturgeon! We made a night of it. After two hours at the Hermitage Gallery yesterday skimming the collections, and a long drive in the afternoon, the Embassy took us to a Summer Garden Opera five miles off, where we listened till half past twelve to a Russian opera by a certain Boradin, just like a Chinese play that has no beginning or end, but a ballet scattered about the middle.[6] Then we had to get supper, and it was hard on three before we got to bed. It was funny, mamma!

Cabot has got to have interviews with swells, and to be in Paris by the 14th. I want to run over Sweden. Plans are therefore a little vague, but if I can escape Berlin, I shall do it, even at cost of a swashing about the Baltic.

The Hermitage pictures are next to the Madrid for condition. I am not disappointed. Today I go there with sister Anne for a serious inspection, but yesterday was enough to tell me what I came for.

Sunday. [25 Aug.]   I will close up this despatch now, for I have little or nothing more to say. Petersburg is dark, raw and rainy. Already I am tired of it, but the gallery is still good for days. When I think that my poor grandmamma had to suffer this place for five years, and lost her only daughter here, I feel inclined to pity my grandfather.[7] But he was twenty years younger than I am, and had been in the United States Senate, which ought to have reconciled him to most atmospheres. Hay writes very bad news of King. I foresaw it last winter. What next!

———

Tuesday, 27.   I reopen my despatch to your and Martha's letters of the 13th. Kiki gives me a pang.[8] I saw that it was coming, as you did, but it is cruel. I am still in doubt of my next move, but expect to arrange so as to get to Paris on Sept. 16, when Emile finishes his 28 jours. I've done my Rembrandts and will get through the Greek things today. Tomorrow probably to Peterhof. My companions start Saturday for Berlin. I shall write to Martha soon, but there is little for me to tell her from here, and we have met no one.

———

This goes by the embassy bag.

MS: MHi

1. Geoffroi de Villehardouin, *History of the Capture of Constantinople by the French and Venetians,* covering the years 1198–1207. No contemporary MS survives. The first printed copy is dated 1585.
2. Charlemagne Tower (1848–1923), U.S. minister to Austria-Hungary 1897–1899, ambas-

sador to Russia 1899–1902, ambassador to Germany 1902–1908; and his wife, Helen Smith Tower (1858–1931).
3. Herbert Peirce (1849–1916) was a cousin of Mrs. Henry Cabot Lodge, in whose company HA was traveling.
4. A famous Scottish castle on the river Dee.
5. Henry Holt (1840–1926) had published HA's anonymous novel *Democracy* in 1880.
6. Alexander Borodin (1833–1887), *Prince Igor* (left unfinished and completed by Rimsky-Korsakov and Glazunov in 1889).
7. Louisa Catherine Adams lost her infant daughter, Louisa, when her husband was U.S. envoy to Russia.
8. Martha's dog was mistakenly thought to be dying.

To John Hay

St Petersburg. 26 August, 1901.

My dear Hay

Your account of King hangs like a nightmare over me, the more because, with my usual pessimism, I had fully realised the danger, when I bade him good-bye, and both of us knew that it was a chance if we met again.[1] Of late I have found my pessimism rather a serious load. One can afford to be pessimistic only in youth when the world sometimes gets a chance to be gay. Nowadays it is a bore to be always trying to see the world half as black as it is. Luckily my share in it is now very small, and if King goes today, it matters only a little the less to me that I go tomorrow. We can wipe the slate clean, and let the other fellows fill it again. They can hardly write as much on it as we did.

Coming up here does not tend to gaiety either. We have dragged ourselves across some thousands of dreary miles, mostly forest, and have seen many dreary peasants, and several dreary cities; but the result in accumulated happiness is to me not considerable. As far as companionship goes I have nothing to complain of. I hope my companions may say as much. As for pleasure of travel, this country is worse than our own. Nature has done nothing for it, and art almost as little. Moscow was amusing for twelve hours. Warsaw gave me a new astonishment,—the Polish Jew. Petersburg is distinctly *vieux jeu*; it reminds me of my grandmother; it says next to nothing of my own world. I am still asking where the deuce Russia is. Thus far I have seen only log-cabins in dense forests; or cities, without industry, separated by five hundred miles of barrens. Of Russia I know nothing.

Of course, my numerous questions about it must remain in my own usual dump of ignorance. No Russian can answer them. Cabot has duly had interviews with Witte and Lamsdorf,[2] but neither of them said much, although Witte said much more than I expected. Indeed, for him, Witte was quite garrulous. He talked freely of his difficulties in a general way, and made no concealment of his antipathies. But he did not say or hint that he wanted us to do anything about it. What he wants most is gold; after that, more gold; and finally, all the gold he can get. This must be the whole story, for he has to carry the entire load of Russian development and industry, credit and defence, court and people. He is quite ignorant. Of the world outside Russia, and especially of America, he knows little. He fears Germany, detests England, and clings to France. He is a force; a rather brute energy; a Peter-the-Great sort of earnestness; but he is not a literary philosopher with patented ideas and statistics complete, to answer my conundrums.

So I must answer myself. After all, it is simpler than I thought. Russia is, in these parts, not relatively advancing so fast as the rest of Europe. Her scale is greater, but her energy less. She is still a century behind; in certain respects her people are, I think, in a mental condition that western Europe has never known at all. It is the passive condition of a worn-out oriental society that we cannot estimate because we never had to work through it. Granting that this passivity will, at some future time, become an economy of force which will outwear western energy, still the centuries must pass pretty far before that time is reached. Anyway I think that for three generations we can look ahead with very little anxiety to rivalry on the part of Russia. She will need us more than we need her. As yet she has made no progress that I can see, towards becoming economical. She is still metaphysical, religious, military, Byzantine; a sort of Mongol tribe, almost absolutely unable to think in western lines.

All the same, the politics of eastern Europe are a big affair, awfully complicated, and liable to more convulsion than I see likely elsewhere. Germany, from this point of view, becomes a powder-magazine. All her neighbors are in terror for fear she will explode, and, sooner or later, explode she must. Ever since history existed, we have little else than records of the explosion of northern Europe; and if law is law, the next time it must blow out eastward. Austria and Russia are almost in a panic. As for us, we shall drain the whole economically, but if it comes to universal piracy again we must all suffer. At present pretty much all eastern Europe is collapsed. I see no reason for it, but the want of gold. The scale of development here needs great supplies, and the Boers have starved them. All these countries are trying to protect themselves, and as usual Germany threatens to strike first and hardest. She strikes at Russia and Hungary. The question now is whether Russia and Hungary will turn to us. It is a very complicated situation, and I hoped that Witte or Lamsdorf would have said something to clear it, but as yet there is nothing to be said. Apparently they are all waiting. Witte says his railway will be finished in three months, except of course the Baikal strip, and that he can already use it for troops. This surprises me a little; but probably it is more or less true, although he frankly announces that the railway must be rebuilt, and supplied with rolling-stock before it can pay.

Of course Russia is what we know! There is no sense in supposing that it is modern or American or economical. But it may still come out very much ahead on a hundred years' stretch. Its scale is so enormous that it is bound to dwarf its neighbors, and with such mass and momentum, speed is a subordinate element.

Anyway it is a question of mathematics and of forces and strains; and wisdom or knowledge is useless. Fate rules in these parts. One is fatalist by necessity.

I am hesitating where to go next. The Lodges start for Berlin on Saturday. I shudder at Berlin, and want to cut across through Sweden. In either case it is Paris about the 15th. Then, oh Lord! begins a new decision, and I am weak-minded, unfit to decide a straw.

———

MS: MHi

1. Hay wrote on Aug. 9 that King was dying. HA quotes from the letter in the *Education*, chap. 28.
2. Sergei Y. Witte (1849–1915), minister of finance; Count Vladimir Nikolaevich Lamsdorf-Duevnik (1845–1907), minister of foreign affairs 1900–1906.

To Elizabeth Cameron

Sunday, 12 Jan. 1902.

Slowly the legs that had gone to sleep have begun to tingle and get the blood moving again, but it's not a particularly exhilerating process, and it aches. The only real satisfaction is to count up the number of statesmen I've buried, and the graves of notorieties I have outlived. I want now to outlive the present crowd, and am counting my symptoms to figure out four or five years more for myself, so that I can bury the heroes of the Spanish war with those of the Mexican war who were my first admirations here fifty years ago. Even Theodore has not the face to pasture his charger in front of the White House as Zachary Taylor did in 1850, when my father took me to the White House first.

When was my last dinner at the White House? Before you were born! In 1878! Under the reign of Mrs Hayes. Though it was the happiest time of my whole life, associated with everything—and the only things—I ever cared for, that dinner between Mrs Carlisle and Mrs Conger is still a nightmare;[1] but it is curious that the Hays were also there, and that last Friday evening, Mrs Hay and John stopped in their carriage to pick me up and take me across to the slaughter-house. Mrs Hay was not—to say the least—more sprightly than I, though we were none of us bubbling, but we all played square, and shirked none of the cards.

That the house is to me ghastly with bloody and dreary associations way back to my great-grandmother a hundred years ago,[2] seems no particular reason why it should always depress me, or why it should seem to entomb a little family party of very old friends, in the private dining-room, and upstairs afterwards to smoke in the cheery octagon; but it did. We were only eight; Cabot and Nanny Lodge and a Mrs Selmes of Minnesota, whom I must have known in the Hayes epoch, and who came on me like a ghost.[3] We waited twenty minutes in the hideous red drawing-room before Theodore and Edith came down; and we went in to dinner immediately with as much chaff and informality as though Theodore were still a Civil Service Commissioner. We chattered round talk; Cabot was bright; Hay was just a little older and a thought more formal than once we were; Edith was very bright and gay; but as usual Theodore absorbed the conversation, and if he tired me ten years ago, he crushes me now. To say that I enjoyed it would be, to you, a gratuitous piece of deceit. The dinner was indifferent, very badly served, and, for some reason, nothing to drink but a glass of sherry, and some Apollinaris. Theodore's talk was not exactly forced or unnatural, but had less of his old freshness and quite as much of his old dogmatism. None of us had improved. When I think of what has passed, I see no reason why I should expect improvement. Even cognac will not improve much after sixty years of ripening.

One condition is clear! Hay and I are shoved up to a distinct seniority; we are sages. I felt it not only in Hay's manner, but in Roosevelt's too, and it is my creed now that my generation had better scuttle gracefully, and leave Theodore to surround himself with his own rough-riders. He will do it anyway before long, and would do it immediately if he had the men; but his two appointments thus far have betrayed weakness in material, for one is a third-rate lobbyist rejected by McKinley as below proof, while the other is an unknown quantity, very problematic to Wall Street.[4] Theodore is eager to change everything everywhere, but his suggestions are all more or less inadequate. The only effect would be to substitute his man for McKinley's man. We outsiders rather lose than gain.

Really Theodore is exasperating even to me, and always was. His want of tact hurts Congressmen and Senators more than it does me, but what annoys me is his childlike and infantile superficiality with his boyish dogmatism of assertion. He lectures me on history as though he were a high-school pedagogue. Of course I fall back instantly on my favorite protective pose of ignorance, which aggravates his assertions, and so we drift steadily apart.

But the most dangerous rock on Theodore's coast is Cabot. We all look for inevitable shipwreck there.

My lighthouse is little Quentin, the youngest boy, who comes in, and massacres the doll-house.[5] Little Constance set it in order again, and was miraculously docile.[6] Big Constance goes to Aiken Wednesday. Bay and Bessie walked in to dinner one night, Bay rather more docile than Bessie. As luck would have it, Willy Chanler came in later, very thick of utterance, and very fast running down hill. All the Chanlers now seem to be in a bad way, and even Winty finds gaiety laborious.

13th.   I cannot say that I find many bright spots here, but at least Helen and Alice seem contented and even happy.[7] Mrs Rockhill appears to be a qualified success socially; she dines here this evening. Mrs Townsend has given a ball, at which Toody[8] danced, though not yet out in society. Probably it was bigger than Martha's New Year's ball, but I guess it was no pleasanter. By the bye, this morning I have Martha's letter of the 3d, and yours. Edith's came last week. Your dear little old-fashioned quaint thirteenth-century cloister life of Paris seems here a sort of dream like Mark Twain's diary of Adam.

Of drearinesses and horrors I have my usual share, but this time not quite so close to me as last year. Young Cruger is the nearest to a family victim; but my sister-in-law Minny has imitated the fashion and broken her foot while staying on a visit of condolence with her sister.[9] Charley Stoddard has been forced out of the Catholic University and his house, into his usual hospital, and we have got to send him checks—put him on the check-rein—I suppose, for the future.[10] Probably Mrs Howland—Clarence King's mother—has come on the same list. We are trying to untangle King's affairs.[11]

Do you see Mr Dooly? He was distinctly funny yesterday about Miles and Theodore, and hit them both pretty fairly. The round-robin was neat. We all chuckled. I am curious to know how Theodore took it. Poor Miles never had the faculty of taking a joke, and the best of us do not enjoy jokes about ourselves, especially when we have been kicked first.[12]

Tuesday. [14 Jan.]   Sister Anne says that Theodore roared with delight over Dooley. Sister Anne came to bid goodbye to Brooks and his wife, who started off yesterday afternoon to visit your hospitable husband, and go on to Havana and Mexico. Brooks has helped me to catch on to the machine a little, but Brooks himself is as far from catching on as ever, I think, though he is slowly acquiring a certain reputation. He is like Clarence King, Richardson, La Farge and all my crowd, whom cleverer and richer men exploit and rob. It is the law of God! It is also the law of common-sense. Every now and then the victim comes back on the victor, and squashes him, which is why the bourgeois is afraid. Brooks is too brutal, too blatant, too emphatic, and too intensely set on one line alone, at a time, to please any large number of people.

The Rockhills and Helen Hay dined with me last night. Mrs Hay and Helen go to New York today for wedding garments, and Hay comes to me for dinner. Looly and Mabel and Bancel and Oliver La Farge,[13] or most of them, are expected here towards Thursday. My campaign, you see, has begun, and the winter is fairly set in, dry, sharp and clear. But people seem to me, somehow, to be more ill-natured than usual, and to gossip more superlatively, like me.

———

MS: MHi

1. The dinner actually took place on Feb. 17, 1881. As described by MHA, HA took in to dinner "a simple-hearted old lady from Michigan, wife of Senator Conger" (Omar Dwight Conger). On HA's left sat the wife of John Griffin Carlisle, then a Kentucky congressman. The conversation turning to the etiquette of dinner invitations, the two women revealed that they had not answered theirs for that occasion, "not thinking it a thing to do"; *The Letters of Mrs. Henry Adams, 1865–1883*, ed. Ward Thoron (1936), p. 268.
2. John Adams (1735–1826), the first president to live in the White House, moved in alone from Philadelphia, the previous seat of government, because Abigail Adams was ill in Massachusetts. She arrived from Quincy in Dec. 1800 with the news that their son Charles, aged 30, was dying of cirrhosis.
3. Martha Flandrau Selmes, widow of Tilden Selmes, lawyer and rancher in Dakota Territory. They became friends of Roosevelt when he was ranching in the 1880s.
4. On Jan. 8 Roosevelt appointed as postmaster general Henry Clay Payne (1843–1904), Wisconsin businessman active in Republican politics, and as secretary of the Treasury Leslie Mortier Shaw (1848–1932), Iowa banker, governor 1898–1902.
5. Quentin Roosevelt (1897–1918), the youngest of Theodore and Edith Roosevelt's five children.
6. Daughter of Constance Lodge Gardner ("Big Constance") and Augustus Peabody Gardner (1865–1918).
7. Helen and Alice Hay (1880–1960), daughters of John and Clara Hay.
8. Nickname of Martha's friend Mathilde Townsend.
9. Ogden Cryder (1884–1902), son of Duncan Cryder and Elizabeth Ogden Cryder (Mary ["Minnie"] Ogden Adams' sister), died Jan. 2.
10. Charles Warren Stoddard (1843–1909), California author, *South-Sea Idylls* (1873), professor of English at Catholic University of America.
11. Besides his mother, Clarence King left a wife, Ada, and five children. The marriage had been kept secret because Ada King was black, though John Hay evidently knew about it. Twenty-eight years after Hay's death, Ada King stated that King's friend James Terry Gardiner had administered an $80,000 trust set up by King for her and the children and that, when Gardiner stopped sending money, Hay had continued to send her support

payments (New York *Daily Mirror,* Nov. 21 and 22, 1933). Whether HA knew of the marriage has not been established.

12. Mr. Dooley, pseudonym of Chicago newspaper humorist Finley Peter Dunne (1867–1936). Miles went to the White House on Dec. 21 to urge the president to suppress the reprimand sent him by Secretary of War Elihu Root, but Roosevelt refused, lecturing Miles loudly in front of others. In a parody of the interview, "Mr. Dooley" scored Roosevelt for preaching what he himself had not practiced when he criticized military operations in Cuba in the round-robin letter of Aug. 3, 1898. He quoted Roosevelt as saying to Miles, "ye shud know that an officer who criticises his fellow-officers, save in th' reg'lar way, that is to say in a round robin, is guilty iv I dinnaw what" (*Washington Post,* Jan. 12).

13. Oliver Hazard Perry La Farge (1869–1936), third son of John and Margaret La Farge, had studied architecture and civil engineering at Columbia University and was a banker in Seattle; Bancel La Farge, another son, was a designer of jewelry and mosaics.

To Elizabeth Cameron

9 March, 1902

I am short of gossip. The world is dull, and not even as ridiculous as usual. Those astonishing foreigners are abating. We have got rid of Prince Henry, but I trust you may some day see the bronze bust of his brother which he has unloaded on the White House.[1] Perhaps I am as big a fool as I think, and the future man will be a bigger fool than I, but it is absolutely impossible for anyone to be as big a fool as the Kaiser without being shut up. This bust is the kind of German-brass art which makes one bitterly regret the stone-age. Poor St Gaudens or Rodin would do what Ruskin once did when some one suddenly called his attention to a similar product of art.

To Prince Henry succeeded Lord Grey, and why Lord Grey is here, except to boom Mrs Westinghouse's social success,[2] I know not, though I do know the caustic comments that his British queerness starts up like quail in South Carolina whenever he appears. Still less can we conceive what brought Mrs Moreton Frewen here.[3] Sister Anne thinks it was unexpected to Moreton himself. They imposed themselves on the poor Pauncefotes to the agony of Maude, and Moreton ran about town, getting dinners for them all wherever he could beg one, because the cook at the embassy was bad or ill or drunk or dead or in South Africa. The British do not change, and I understand my Britisher well enough for a perfectly stupid brute; but my American woman is a curious sort of parasite on that blundering whale, and I have in vain implored sister Anne to find out what Mrs Moreton wants, and why she has suddenly broken out in a gush of affection for us which certainly portends trouble. Sister Anne is even more surprised than I, although I have been much staggered by the love I have apparently excited in the childlike bosom of Mrs Moreton. Still, certainly I am an agreeable young man, quite good-looking, very rich, and with fine shooting, but Sister Anne has none of these attractions, and yet Mrs M.F. gushes all over her.

They asked themselves to dinner, and with great trouble I got the Ward Thorons to dine with them, and tried not to insult them much.[4] Yet I lie awake o'nights, and curl up like a sick monkey when I think how grossly insulting I am to all these frauds and jack-a-napes's who pervade political haunts. Some day perhaps you will understand why Wayne is bitter. The varnish and gloss and gilding is all worn off, and he sees only the lead and brass beneath his own veneer and that of his neighbors. The constant skin-irritation exasperates his nerves. Last night Edith Roosevelt sent for me to dine and go to see cousin Maude in "Quality Street."[5] Cabot was at dinner, and Root, and no one else, but Theodore and the wives.[6] You will think me morbidly diseased, but I am not much worse than other men of eighty, and it is positive that, entirely for fear of insulting somebody, I never exchanged one word with any of the three men. Honestly, I dare not. Theodore is living in a political fool's-paradise where not a breath of healthy air ever penetrates. Cabot and Root are obliged to stoke his furnace whether they like or not. Any remark of mine would be like a poison, and my silence is a sort of gloom. With all the vivacity of a happy nature I talked with Sister Anne and little Edith, who is an ugly little girl, but at least is a child. Roosevelt, Cabot and Root talked across the table to each other about Congressmen and Senators. At the theatre it was the same thing, only I hid myself in a corner and talked with Mrs Root who is a fool, but, fool as they all call her, she is like many female fools, much more intelligent than the men. My cousin Maude acted with great effort a dri-velling play, and a crowded audience stared at our box.

Do you feel the full jest of that? Actually! I am a courtier! an *intime* at the White House! a neighbor of Respectability Row! Like a true courtier, I hold my tongue. Or rather I think Wayne and I are skeletons, not in the cup-board, and not even able to teach them their mortality. The dance goes merrily on. Every week Theodore makes a new fight. If Root remonstrates, Theodore slaps his face too. Hay is already outside. Cabot himself is dragged by the heels. Congress is as sulky as Wall Street. Theodore is inflated with his own popularity; he wants to be candidate for the demo-crats too; and tries to slap the face of everybody who elected him. Luckily for a Christian Conservative Anarchist, he is not my President. Not that I have a candidate of my own, or care even to offer a wiser man in his place. Times are too problematic. Sooner or later, England and Turkey and Aus-tria and Poland and Finland and Russia and Japan, and the rest of the boiling, may boil. South Africa still boils. The other evening Hay was here to dinner, and just as we were sitting down, the front-door opened, and Montague White rushed up the stairs.[7] Of course neither Hay nor I objected particularly to Montague White except that he is a slimy snob of the worst British middle-class city-Jew type; but what I do object to is that he is not a Boer, and would like to sell them out if he could. He never knows anything, and can never tell me anything; but all the same the expenses of war go on, and the Irish and Japanese and all true anarchists, like me, rejoice. Mrs Hay is about again. Alice is to walk a few steps today. Looly and Hitty are still here. When are Rodin's things to come? Will mine come too? Or will you keep it?

Tuesday. [11 March]   I knew it! Last week I wrote it! You are seriously ill, and I'm scared. Poor Alice Hay too is in bed again and this time with something rheumatic! This is a howling wilderness. Summer has come, or is coming. The Cass Canfields sail this week.[8] You must go south quick. Helen Payne arrives today and stays till April. She sails about the middle. Miss Marbury sails early too; Miss DeWolfe on May 7. Little Horstman runs along too; and all go to Italy with you. When am I to go? What am I to do when I go? Boo-hoo! I'm little boy Dordy, two years old, and I can cry, though little Quentin says its nonsense; I'm nine.

The Lodges senior came to dinner Sunday; and I fixed Cabot so tight that he never once had a chance to speak of politics. Sister was very bright and humorous in her old way. If only you had been here, it would have been fifteen years ago. Not that I care to go back, but that you looked so pretty, and Martha so fascinating at a year old! No one will be like you. Yet the gutters are flooded with pretty girls, and bright ones too, who flit in and out of my doors, and rattle in the next room while I lean over sheets of twelfth-century in my study. Hitty goes home tomorrow. Looly is still my type-writer and slave.

And now comes the news of Methuen's rout and capture! What a ridiculous optimist I have always been! Ashamed as I am of my drivelling stupidity, I appeal to you or to Moreton Frewen against harsh judgment. For years I have wept and howled that the English are too stupid to live! I've written ten volumes about it, which nobody but old Edward Everett Hale ever read![9] I've suffocated with suppressed fury, and exploded with denunciations. Latterly I've said to everyone, in despair, that nothing remained but to remove the English race bodily from England, and repopulate it from central African negroes who would show traces of intelligence, courage and humanity. All this is so feeble compared with the facts!

And now! my first thought is for ourselves! as yet of course I do not know whether Pierpont Morgan can once more hold up the market, and save a panic; but I'm not so nervous about South Africa as about Manchuria. If a Russo-Jap. war-scare starts on the back of Methuen's disaster, the game is up. Why it has not started, I don't know; for Russia is making no secret of her expectations, which involve a war in India. I've written you all that. I am pretty well satisfied that all the parties are hiding the cards, collecting gold, and postponing the war-scare till their preparations are made. My informant here continues to scream the alarm in our eyes:— "You do not appreciate the gravity of the situation." For once, he is, I guess, convinced of his own truth; but that means little. Actual war is not necessary to bust England; the scare would be enough.

Well! Well! Well! I've croaked like a Pennsylvania bull-frog for five years, about England; but I never said anything as mean about her as Lord Roberts did yesterday in open Parliament, and never have I talked disaster as terrible as those Irish cheers.[10] But what can we do here? Suppose I were President, what could I do? I suspect I could only seize Canada, west of the Lakes, and today I think the chances about even that my deputy will do it before he gets through. The wreck of the European empires tumbles on us, whether we will or no. That infernal job of the Philippines hampers our action horribly.

Do not imagine that we here are blind or sold to anybody; but really we do not know how to get clear of the wreck. What is the use of our talking? Honestly, seriously, solemnly, the conduct of England is that of a sort of Moreton Frewen; it is not common-sense; it is not intelligible; no one explains it, not even Lansdowne to Pauncefote.[11] The conduct of Germany is not so boorishly beerily brutally dull-witted, but is equally extravagant and more absurd. France is the only serious government and people in Europe.

If ever a world blew up, I guess it was much in the situation of ours; but I guess also that the Dobbitt's of that world were as little able to find a window to escape out of, as Martha's Dobbitt.

———

MS: MHi

1. Prince Henry (1862–1929), German fleet commander, brother of Kaiser Wilhelm II.
2. Albert H. G. Grey (1851–1917), 4th Earl Grey, British official; Marguerite Westinghouse (1842–1914), wife of George Westinghouse, leading inventor and industrialist. Grey was staying at the Westinghouse residence after visiting the earl of Minto, governor-general of Canada.
3. Clara Jerome (Mrs. Moreton) Frewen (1850–1935), sister-in-law of Lord Randolph Churchill.
4. Ward Thoron had married Ellen Warder (1871–1959) in 1893. She was the eldest daughter of Benjamin H. and Ellen Ormsbee Warder.
5. Maude Adams (1872–1953), no relation to HA, was appearing in *Quality Street*. She had been a shipboard acquaintance.
6. Elihu Root (1845–1937), secretary of war.
7. Montagu White (1857–1916), consul general of South African Republic.
8. Augustus Cass Canfield (1852–1904), yachtsman and marine architect; and Josephine Houghteling Canfield (1864–1937), New York City social leader.

9. Edward Everett Hale (1822–1909), Unitarian minister, prolific writer, *The Man without a Country* (1865).

10. Frederick Sleigh Roberts (1832–1914), Lord Roberts. His report to the House of Commons on a British disaster in the Boer War was cheered by Irish members.

11. Henry C. K. Petty-Fitzmaurice (1845–1927), 5th marquess of Lansdowne.

To John Hay

Inverlochy Castle, Fort William, N.B.[1]
26 July, 1902.

My dear Hay

As an atom I consider myself a success. Whisked one way or another by any petticoat that passes, I have hardly left Touraine than I am whirled up to Scotland and dropped on a moor. What I am doing here may seem intricate to some, but not to me. I am doing nothing. The world, if there is a world, belongs only to possibilities. You may be in it; so may Prester John or the great auk; but not Lord Salisbury or Roosevelt or I. We are a part of the infinite eternal silence.

How I came here is a mystery like the Procession of the Holy Ghost.[2] Don Cameron willed it, and I was. Why Don willed it is another problem. His head seemed suddenly to turn. He took a fancy for his supposed ancestors. Bang went a sax-pence![3] He took the Abinger castle at an hour's notice, and gave me a day to catch on.

Apart from companionship, I certainly prefer Paris; probably most men of eighty-odd, like us, would do the same; but Don prefers his moors, on which nothing would induce him to set a foot; or thinks he does. To be sincere, I fully expect that he will be so tired of his moors in a week that he will fly to Arizona or elsewhere; but then I shall get back to Paris.

We are very jolly, quite alone, and Dordy takes care of the little girls when their mothers is busy. The house is not as big as Surrenden, but newer. Ben Nevis rises from the front door, and Loch Eil looks in at the back windows. When it doesn't rain, it is very pretty; and it doesn't rain nearly all the time. We've no neighbors. Thus far, no guests but little Edith Hoyt who is just *brêvetée*.

Your letter of July 11 dropped suddenly into this salmon-pool. It reminded me that somewhere there are people doing things. Since all the nations of the earth suddenly turned round this spring and sang in chorus: 'God bless my soul, let's all do what Hay wants!', I've lost interest in the matter. While all the mules were kicking, it was fun. Now that it has come to the mere drudgery of work, I don't care a copper-share of Amalgamated. Even Joe Chamberlain has come back to orthodoxy, and when I can no longer swear at Joe, what's the use of a devil?

Paddy O'Beirne says that if you are in a way of regularly appointing British ambassadors, couldn't you make him one.[4] I told him that little things like that were hardly suited to our interference as a rule, but, if he wished it, I would attend to it. Spring Rice must have gone back to his post without a sound. No one has had a word from him. In London I caught only a glimpse of the Embassy, and had but half an hour's chat with Carter and White.[5]

On the whole I have seldom known a quieter Europe. Apparently the lid is at last screwed down. Practically there is no longer any bucking against the American régime. Everything is sold ahead. I am only a little curious to know what will become of the Church, which is now getting kicked all round.

I wonder how you would like to be back with us here, as we were in '98 at Surrenden. It gives Don rheumatism, and I am myself as stiff as a Senator; but it might help young kids like you, and I'm sure Mrs Hay would like it. As for Treaties, you might negotiate one with the barometer, which needs it bad.[6]

I hope Helen got back well, and Mrs Hay has you all under her wing. Give them my love.

Ever Yrs   Henry Adams.

MS: MHi

1. The castle had been rented by Donald Cameron.
2. A much-mooted element of the Nicene Creed concerning the sequence of the elements of the Trinity.
3. A reference to a *Punch* cartoon in which a Scotsman exclaims at the speed with which money goes.
4. An allusion to the recent appointment of Michael Herbert, a personal friend of President Roosevelt, as British ambassador to the U.S.
5. John Ridgely Carter (1864–1944), U.S. embassy officer in London.
6. Hay had written that he had drafted a new treaty with Colombia for an isthmian canal in Panama.

To Brooks Adams

Inverlochy Castle, Fort William, N.B.
10 August, 1902.

My dear Brooks

Thanks for your letter. I am glad to hear that the business-arrangement has run to your satisfaction.[1] I can see no reason why everybody's business should not now run satisfactorily, for the entire world ought to be starting in for a prodigious development, with no longer any resistance that I can see, except their human limitations. Of course, the problem that bothered us so much between '93 and '98 is now settled. The returns of our iron-production are alone decisive about that, and our country is established for at least a century as the centre of human energy. As for western Europe and England, I do not think they are likely to give more trouble for a long time to come. They are very rich in accumulated wealth, and very poor in natural resources, but England has had her bumptiousness well knocked out of her, and has settled down to work. She will last our time, no doubt, in her new attitude, and we need not expect any further great change for the present. If my calculations were near the mark, they never proved that England was running behind-hand more than one, or at most two, hundred million dollars a year, and at that rate she can run on for fifty years without perceiving it. On the Boer war alone, she wasted twice as much.

I do not know what is the matter with the Share Market in Mines, for the dulness is not confined to the Rand or to London. It is becoming probable that the gold will cost more than before, but that can hardly be the cause which killed the expected boom. Nor can it be the want of money, for the banks on the continent are now gorged with gold. I imagine it to be only the after-effect of heavy losses and long waiting under heavy loads. Just now, we are helping to tide them over, especially by taking their dead stock of surplus iron. Barring the unforeseen, I should say that another six months ought to put Europe on her legs again. Anyway, she has stood the strain vastly better than I feared, or than would have been possible fifty years ago. I suppose it is her accumulated capital that enables her to hang on.

In any case, the chapter seems to be over, and I imagine it to be the last in my lifetime. Like a cautious and somewhat cowardly Scotchman or Jew, I have got through, I hope, without loss and without much profit. Our contemporaries have made their piles, or lost them, and in either case are not much better off than we. I see no one, except the "captains of industry," who seems to have the smallest importance. The most brilliant men of my time have died, like Bret Harte, without rousing a ripple.[2] Lord Salisbury dropped out the other day without exciting a remark.[3] There is not now a politician in the world whose name is likely to be remembered a dozen years, unless it is Chamberlain,— et encore!

I apprehend for the next hundred years an ultimate, colossal, cosmic collapse; but not on any of our old lines. My belief is that science is to wreck us, and that we are like monkeys monkeying with a loaded shell; we don't in the least know or care where our practically infinite energies come from or will bring us to. For myself, it is true; I know nor care at all. But the faintest disturbance of equilibrium is felt throughout the solar system, and I feel sure that our power over energy has now reached a point where it must sensibly affect the old adjustment. It is mathematically certain to me that another thirty years of energy-development at the rate of the last century, must reach an *impasse*.

This is, however, a line of ideas wholly new, and very repugnant to our contemporaries. You will regard it with mild contempt. I owe it only to my having always had a weakness for science mixed with metaphysics. I am a dilution of a mixture of Lord Kelvin and St Thomas Aquinas.

You probably know that I came up here as a guest of Don Cameron, and that I sprained my ankle a fortnight ago, and he got thrown into a ditch last week. He is still in bed. I am shuffling about the house. The weather is the most infernal ever known, as is always the case in this dog-tail country. To me it matters nothing, for I can read and write here as well as in Paris, but it is idiotic to call the season summer.

This is all my personal news. Probably I shall get back to Paris in about a month. If I were just a trifle richer, I should set up an automobile stable, which is now the only amusement worth cultivating, but it would cost me a little too much for my comfort, more in bother than in money, but an excess of both.

Bored I am, no doubt! but Odysseus cannot now start off into unknown seas, since his predecessors—les Ennuyés—have explored them all.[4] He can only strike into paradox.

My love to your wife. Mary Charlton is to come up here next week;[5] and Ralph Palmer; and I know not who else. The world seems quieter than I ever knew it before, but it is putting in big work, and making oceans of wealth.

Ever Yrs   Henry Adams.

MS: MH

1. BA had reported that the family property had been divided, that their brother Charles was practically eliminated from the family trust, and that they would henceforth be freer to make investments.
2. Bret Harte (1836–1902), popular author of Western tales, had died in May.
3. Prime Minister Salisbury (Robert Cecil) had retired from office.
4. HA's fanciful word play on Erinyes, the mythological Furies. He identified them with a plague of bores.
5. Mary Campbell Charlton, widow of William Charlton (1850–1894), a secretary of the British legation in the 1880s. After MHA's death she became, along with Mary Endicott Chamberlain and Mary Leiter Curzon, one of the "three Marys" who frequented HA's breakfast table.

To Brooks Adams

Paris, 10 Nov. 1902

Dear Brooks

Thanks for yours of October 16.

The date of my return depends entirely on the chance of my finding a party to make the voyage with. I hate solitary seas. I may come any day that gives me companions.

As usual in November, all the symptoms of political and financial strain seem to have come together, and the bears run loose. I can't believe it serious. After Christmas we shall all get under way again, and bump on for another year. Even a great smash could hardly affect us long. Any considerable relaxation in activity would create an almost instantaneous accumulation of capital, gold, and commodities, which would find way at once to new expansion. The gold product alone guarantees us a rapid recovery from prostration. The weak point, as I see it, is still Germany; and her weak point is Russia. Although we have lifted half her load—the iron,—and France has lifted the other half—the coal,—she is still very sick. As for Russia, she is always sick when she does not borrow; and she is not likely to recover much for the present. We have got to carry those two invalids for a while; but, barring suicide or accident, we can do it easily. America, England and France can carry the solar system if they take the contract. They contain, according to my figures, six-sevenths of the energy of the world; and the other seventh is much divided and scattered. These three countries now make an Atlantic system, which will swing any possible Asiatic system for at least two generations more. Add the Rhine countries and northern Germany and Scandinavia, which must always belong to the Atlantic system, and it is clear that we embrace practically the whole motive power of the actual world. I cannot conceive how this machine can help running at accelerated speed.

What we grossly fail in is intelligent attention to science. Our dependence on coal, which encourages the coal owners and miners to blackmail society with such clock-work regularity, is not necessary. Science, properly equipped, can solve this problem without much trouble. Indeed it has already partially solved it, and the water-powers are actually and regularly storing their surplus energy in the form of Calcium Carbide or Acetylene. The Calcium Carbide is in all respects a better storage medium than coal or coal oil, and science can easily improve and perfect and enlarge its usefulness. Our people ought also to be obliged by law to keep a year's supply of coal on hand. A steady and intelligent application of our scientific and capitalistic resources could make us independent of coal-owners or coal-miners in a very short time. This is absolutely necessary, for the modern form of war is economic, and an economic civil war on a big scale would probably lead to anarchy and starvation like old-fashioned wars.

This is the chord on which I have pounded for five-and-twenty years, and very slowly the capitalist has waked up to it. I suppose every great industrial corporation now runs on its employed scientific advice. The isolated capitalist concerns have only to organise a somewhat larger system in order to master the whole situation. There is no reason, except the primary outlay, why the world, within ten years, might not be able to defy the coal people.

The iron problem is a more difficult one, I imagine, but even that is not insoluble. Metals are numerous; some of them are more common than iron. Many have very valuable properties now quite unutilised. We ought at once, without a moment's delay, to spend, if necessary, a hundred millions a year to achieve such an increase of our resources. Until we learn this lesson, we are still stupid and infantile insects. The whole universe to us, now, lies there. Curiously enough, Philosophy, Metaphysics, Mathematics, Dynamics, Chemistry,—all branches of human study since study began—have at last pretty well come on to this common ground. All are concentrated on this field of Energy.

This alone is worth study and preaching today, whether in the pulpit or in politics or in workshops. Economics is a wholly subordinate branch. Your economical law of History is, or ought to be, an Energetic Law of History. Concentration is Energy, whether political or industrial. If I were ten years old, I would educate myself to write that book, and teach that lesson, but I care too little now for God or man to teach anything.

My love to your wife. I hope to see you in Washington.

Ever Yrs   Henry Adams.

MS: MH

To Elizabeth Cameron

Sunday, 11 Jan. 1903

A fine dreary snowy day that lends itself to letters. After a week ashore, one welcomes snow; it is more sympathetic than streets.

My letter from New York gave you what there was to give; a general notion of hurry, confusion and squeeze. Of your sister I could learn no more than I saw with my eyes; of your brother-in-law I knew enough without his telling me of the great Ohio dinner he has got up for the 18th, for John Hay, and to which he has asked all the ambassadors to meet him—Hay—for the glory of Colgate.[1] Hay and the ambassadors are equally disgusted, but your brother-in-law has such winning ways, as you know, that he has corraled them all, and is coming down in a private car on the 17th to pen them.

My day in New York on the 6th,—the day I wrote—was worse than the day to Karlsruhe which I imagined you making. After scratching off my note to you, I drove down to Mabel's and passed half an hour with the babies; then went with her to the glass-shop to see Whitney's second window,—Autumn,—which is absolutely the most marvelous color I ever conceived possible. Nothing has ever equalled it, or will, for splendor; and it tires me to think of the animal and his females living with it, and treating it as an ape would treat an ivory Madonna, or worse.[2] Then La Farge took me to the Art Rooms to see Mrs S. D. Warren's pictures, for sale, and his own Marquand window, five-and-twenty years old, and made of better glass than he can now get, also to be sold; a jewel too exquisite for New York hogs to see, unless the dealers show it.[3] How I would like to have it for my dining-room! but already I am aghast to find that income has dropped off, and expenses increased so as to make a difference of five thousand dollars between this year and last, which is already twice my margin for bric-a-brac. My fifty millions are going, not coming, and the scale of expense has doubled. To buy anything is now fantastic, but I can try to make others buy. So after lunching with Lucy Frelinghuysen, and a long talk with her, I took La Farge up to Oliver Payne's house, and the Colonel showed us his things.[4] Of course his things are such as kings mayn't now have; they are what I want; especially his Rubens; but he has also one 15th century tapestry, which equals our Spanish tapistries of the Exhibition, and in fact is one of the same lot. Stanford White has framed it exceedingly well. The Colonel's personal passion is for his Turner, the Piazza by all sorts of lights; but I have known that picture for forty years,[5] and was more interested in a Velasquez head of the Infanta. It is pitiable to see how the Colonel is pleased to build Helen's house, and how Helen and Payne try to like what he does, and to fit their bourgeois or bohemian tastes to his. The Colonel has gone the road that you and I and all the grown ones have gone; and cares for nothing but the best; but young people don't want the best, and ought not to be allowed to have it. You and I and our friends ought to have it all. The Colonel is far more interested in the house than the children are; and I bluntly told him to buy the Marquand window for it, if he wished to give it a cachet once for all. I wonder whether Stanford White would let him do it. Anyway, it is not my business and with that I left it.

At the Club I was assommé by your friend Hitchcock—Centre, is it not,—and then went back to the Knickerbocker at eleven, to find Henry Higginson supping, and to talk with him till one.

Henry had much to say about many things, but the most serious was himself. He says the doctors have given him his first call. He broke something in his brain this autumn, and had to stop. He suspects that Pierpont Morgan is stopping too, and that the enormous sales on the stock-exchange are his closing of accounts. The Jews, he says, are all alert to jump on his leavings and divide them. No one can now stop without a catastrophe. The mass and velocity of these great interests are appalling. You saw that the Pennsylvania Road quietly doubles its stock and bonds? No one is surprised. Most of us doubt whether even that will do much good. The country has outgrown all possible machinery. Five years ago, when this thing began, I saw people show surprise and incredulity; then, every year when I came back, I saw the feeling change to astonishment, exultation and growing effort to realise it; but this is the first year I have seen consternation, as though the flood had risen above danger-mark.

When I went to bed on Tuesday night, I had talked twelve hours without stopping, and I was fairly sick of the universe. And to think that Theodore Roosevelt does this thing every day, and does not yet go mad—quite!

I also saw Bob Chanler at the Club, and he harped still on his wife and child. The loon wants them here! and I think he counts on the new Delano money to bring them. Estimates vary between $500,000 and $1,000,000 apiece for the heirs, and all divide equally.

Wednesday was a day of rest and depression. I got here to dine solemnly alone, and go to bed with about as much gaiety as though bed were Hades.

Then began the effort to catch on to the train again. The job of paying bills double one's old scale; of hearing the reports of one's accounts and household; of asking questions and guessing riddles. Sister Anne came like an angel. John Hay trotted me off to inspect Larz Anderson's and Walsh's houses.[6] On Friday, Mrs Roosevelt sent over for me to come to dinner with the Owen Wisters, and Cabot Lodge came to explain that I was to take the Wisters off their hands for Saturday evening because of their Cabinet dinner.[7] Which part is best, in this play: the President's, the Senator's, the Wister's, or mine? Of course I executed myself with all the apparent cordiality of my nature, and dined as badly as usual with the Lodges and Wisters in the beautiful new state dining-room at the White House, where we seven innocents looked quite lost in the vastness. Theodore was less excited than a year ago, and occasionally let some one say a word or two. We were shown over the house which is now quite a gentleman's place, mostly done in white, and where the safe white is abandoned for red and green velvet, less successful. The state dining-room in oak is charming. Theodore innocently delights in its space which dwarfs him.[8] Mrs Roosevelt, who has in her mild way, rolled Bammy quite out of the house,[9] and very properly; and who is, I am sorry to say, obliged almost daily, to snub some of our other friends who ought not to need snubbing,—we have, this winter, *five* American women as ambassadresses or ministresses,—Mrs Roosevelt, I say, accepts the state-rooms with even more pleasure than Theodore does, and looks less lost in them, although she too needs a crown.

Actually I staid with Sister Anne to the musicale, and saw all the reception, from the Michael Herberts and Sunie Draper down or up to Charley

Macauley in his beautiful gold lace and *spurs*.[10] For once I indulged in the sense of feeling more at home in the White House than in my own. Sister Anne and I sat on a distant sofa and looked on. The birds were all there, and some of the beasts, but the tragedy of Holleben hung over the beasts. No one understands it, but certainly it is another case of Eisendecker, and we are all shuddering for poor little Speck who is going to be crushed between these two stupid tumbling masses, without a chance of salvation.[11]

Of course I did what I had to do, and asked the Owen Wisters to dinner, and went to get Bessy and Bay to amuse them. The Owen Wisters do not amuse me; he has the qualities of his race, and I of mine, and Bay of his, and acids rarely mix well; but a dinner is no great matter, and I was fully repaid by the baby who is a beauty. I passed an hour with it. Indeed I am now an admitted baby-expert. Mrs Johnny is to sit on one side of the cradle; Sister Anne on the other; Mrs Bancroft Davis in the centre with the baby on her lap; and I, a little St John, at her knee.

Sister Anne brought Hetty Sargent to breakfast. Wendel Holmes has come in, with that vague look of wondering bewilderment which you see always on the face of the Bostonian who for the first time has discovered America.[12] Cabot has talked an hour about all things big and little. Hay has opened his soul. You see I am *lancé,*—and deadly low!

Tuesday. [13 Jan.]   At sister Anne's on Sunday afternoon I met Wendell Holmes again, and upon us descended Theodore with Wood and Wister, from tramping in the slush.[13] Theodore rattled away as usual about all sorts of matters, big and little, but always announcing his own views, and never stopping to invite or consider those of other people. There is a hitch in the Philippines. Taft now wants to stay. This will throw out Rockhill, who had already lost Japan by taking the Philippines. What other changes are at hand seem known to nobody. Root's intentions are in doubt. Theodore has upset the whole diplomatic service in order to make the Bellamy Storers an embassy, because the Kaiser, in deadly fear of Mrs Bellamy, took refuge with Mrs Charlemagne. So everyone had to dance across the board, and the unfortunate Mrs David Jayne Hill, heart-broken, sought peace at Berne.[14] As far as I can see, the women take mostly what they want, and I stand more than ever in fear of them. The heart-burnings are many. In fact, I dimly perceive that they are likely to become more. Poor Langley came in to dinner, much depressed by heart-burnings and enmities which are rampant against him too, but he seemed to dislike explaining their cause.[15] He made me feel quite cheery, he was so low.

Helen's baby is a week behind time, and thereby considerably deranging things. H. Blaine came to breakfast yesterday, and we discussed her situation and Truxton's. She says that Truxton's new girl is respectable, and pretty;

a kind of summer-girl; a little like some of my old friends forty years ago,—say Fanny Ronalds. There was some newspaper attack for which I believe that Truxton shot the editor and promised to marry the girl after his trial; but of this I am vague, for H. was more concerned with discussing her own situation in it. To her it is an enormous relief everyway, and she hopes that all will now work out well. If the new marriage succeeds,—and Truxton can't afford two divorces,—and if there are children, H. hopes that she and her Walker will have peace, but it is a close thing. Last year she was seriously afraid that she should be driven back to Truxton by his incessant pursuit of the boy. But if the new wife comes here to live, H. will go away. Her mother is failing steadily, and is now living in the past. The mind is gone.

Mabel La Farge arrived at eight o'clock, two hours late, to dinner. Bancel did not come. Bancel too has disappointments, and indeed the artists seem all to be complaining of want of work. Mabel seeks points about Paris. Her friends frighten her with stories of expense. Mrs Stickney walked in to call on Mrs Nott the other day, and then and there bought her house without looking at it, and has gone off, leaving Lucy here at the Randolph with strict orders to do nothing.[16] The Winty Chanlers have arrived, or arrive shortly, at Sister Anne's. *Enfin!* you see my work is cut out. I've written to your husband. I've done all the duties I know of, except calling on the Michael Herberts and the Berty Peirces and Rebecca Dodge and Chauncy Depew.

———

MS: MHi

1. Colgate Hoyt (1849–1922), New York banker, president of the Ohio Society. The dinner was got up by Wayne MacVeagh.
2. The La Farge windows were designed for William C. Whitney's Long Island house.
3. Susan C. Warren (d. 1901), widow of Samuel D. Warren and, like her husband, a collector of paintings; La Farge's early windows for Henry G. Marquand (1819–1902) were up for auction and were purchased by a daughter of La Farge.
4. Lucy Frelinghuysen, daughter of the late Frederick Frelinghuysen, secretary of state under President Arthur; Col. Oliver H. Payne (1842–1917), industrialist and financier.
5. *St. Mark's Place, Venice,* bought by Payne in 1901, now called *Juliet and Her Nurse.*
6. The Anderson house is now the national headquarters and museum of the Society of the Cincinnati; the Thomas Walsh house is now the chancery of the Republic of Indonesia.
7. Owen Wister (1860–1938), author of *The Virginian* (1902), friend of Theodore Roosevelt.
8. A major renovation of the White House had just been completed.
9. Anna ("Bamie") Roosevelt (Mrs. William S.) Cowles (1855–1931), Roosevelt's eldest sister.
10. Susan Preston Draper, wife of William Draper, former envoy to Italy; Charles L. McCawley (1865–1935), brevetted major of marines for bravery, June 1, 1898.
11. Theodor von Holleben (1838–1913), the German ambassador, had been abruptly recalled Jan. 7 without explanation. In 1884 the German minister Karl von Eisendecker had been similarly recalled.
12. Oliver Wendell Holmes, Jr. (1841–1935), recently appointed a justice of the U.S. Supreme Court.
13. Gen. Leonard Wood (1860–1927), military governor of Cuba.

14. Storer was appointed to Austria-Hungary, Charlemagne Tower to Germany; Julia Packer
    Hill was the wife of David Jayne Hill (1850–1932), appointed to a post in Switzerland.
15. Samuel P. Langley was then working on a power-driven aircraft.
16. Lucy Stickney (1866–1918), sister of poet Trumbull Stickney.

To Edwin A. Alderman

1603 H Street. Washington.
10 Feb. 1903

Dear Sir[1]

Your obliging letter of the 4th inst. has just arrived, and I hasten to acknowledge it. If I could give you any assistance in pursuing your object, I would do so with great pleasure.[2] Unfortunately the same difficulty has pursued us all, in the field you have chosen. The southern society has left very little trace in literature of its own. Almost no intimate letters, memoirs or records of any kind, exist to fill a biographical outline. Politically, the southern statesman, like all statesmen, was a self-conscious actor on a stage, and sometimes he acted well, sometimes ill, but his acting, though it became a second nature, was never worth a biography. Nothing succeeds less than biographies of statesmen, compiled out of their speeches. Few volumes are duller than those made up of pomposities; and we, who have to struggle with them, are forced to see that Webster and Calhoun and Clay and all their school, took themselves too seriously for our amusement. Your business is to be an artist,—to make a picture,—to paint a character,—not to preach, or lecture, or flatter. You want to be read. With all its faults, Parton's Andrew Jackson remains the best biography we have.[3] Much could be done with Calhoun, if it were done with a sense of relation and background; and so also with Jefferson Davis. As a rule, the man who makes the most mistakes, makes the best biography.

I am very truly Yrs   Henry Adams.

MS: ViU

1. Edwin Anderson Alderman (1861–1931), president of Tulane University 1900–1904.
2. For a study of Southern contributions to American character, Alderman had written to more than twenty prominent persons asking what, in their opinion, these contributions were and requesting the names of those they considered most significant in this respect.
3. James Parton, *Life of Andrew Jackson,* 3 vols. (1860).

To Alexander Agassiz

1603 H Street. 12 April, 1903.

My dear Alex

Your splendid volumes have occupied my time since they arrived, interesting me much, as you knew they must. I wish I had something better to offer in return than the modest family sketch I sent you.[1]

Naturally I did not need to be convinced of Darwin's eccentricities. Never was there a scientific theory which rested on a slenderer basis of evidence,—unless it may be the parallel roads theory, or the evolution theory itself. We, who lived before creation, knew how little we had to stand on. We guessed. Some of our guesses were wild. We heaved up continents at will, and sunk them on wire cables or dropped them overboard. We are doing penance for it now, and not only in the Pacific. A month or two of most superficial study satisfied me that I could squeeze out two or three theories as satisfactory as Darwin's; and now your voyage comes to raise a new class of questions that make my blood run cold. I have already a haul of doubts as profound as the Nero Deep.[2] You have introduced some new forces into geology which seem to me to be very general and highly destructive. Nothing less than the total abandonment of all the old sciences, and their reconstruction, from top to bottom, seems to be possible, if any new or considerable generalisation is to be reached in any direction, either in geology or anything else. You have upset time itself. I do not know on what evidence the geologists have held that Tahiti and the other volcanic masses thereabouts were of tertiary origin. If there is the slightest proof of a date, I know nothing about it. Also I may deferentially add that I don't believe a word of it. If denudation has taken place on the scale that appears on the surface, it may very well have begun as far back as the denudation of the Laurentian or African continents. If the volcanoes are, in some cases, seven miles in height, from the presumed source of activity beneath the sea-bottom, they are cosmic forces, and must go into the category of elements. All the low continents, Australia, Africa, &c, must come under the same head of early planes of denudation, and the mineral-beds will be proof of age.

I am always a little worried by the absence of metals in these volcanic series; but still more by the question, which, since Suess's book, has become to me the most important of all questions, whether the sea or the land changes level. At Tahiti, I ended by admitting that it was the sea-level that had risen and fallen. Your photographs show to me a vast amount of future dispute on the subject.

With many thanks.   Ever Yrs   Henry Adams.

MS: MH-Z

1. *The Coral Reefs of the Maldives* (1903) and *The Coral Reefs of the Tropical Pacific* (1903), reports on the expedition of the *Albatross* from August 1899 to March 1900. HA apparently sent Agassiz his *Memoirs of Arii Taimai*, privately printed in Paris in 1901.
2. A trough over 9,000 meters deep in the Pacific, southwest of Guam.

To George Cabot Lodge

22 April, 1903.

My dear Bay

I return the manuscript.[1] The mere fact that it is far better than anything I could do, and that it has some of that freshness which is worth all the finish that time is sometimes supposed to give, would not prevent my trying to offer suggestions, if I saw any that were likely to be of use. Practically I know but two, and have practised these with so much success that at last I have ceased to practise at all. For that reason I do not recommend them to others, but I will state them, merely to excuse myself.

The ordinary criticisms I leave aside, knowing that you are much better posted in them than I am. As a matter of course you go over your work, as you would go over anybody's work, with a comb, combing out all the inevitable knots, and straightening the crooked angles, and filling the defective lines. The point is, not so much to do, as to see; once seen, a defect is easily handled.

The defects of technique are the alphabet of art, and half the time we care too little about them to correct them till the last moment. You go on correcting these as long as you live, and never get to satisfy your ear. You can take up any volume of any master of style, and go over him with a pencil in your hand; you will always find something to invite correction. This part of criticism is mere technical work. I leave it wholly aside.

What troubles me most in my own work is where its defects are the faults of its qualities. One cannot exact from one's mind that it shall be its own opposite, and reflect what lies beyond its field of reflection; but one can find fault with it for being flat where it is really reflecting a hill, or sharp when it reflects shadow, or insensitive to a high light when the light is obviously the essential thing in the picture. The fact, which all the psychologists insist on, that the mind really reflects only itself, is to me the most exasperating thing in the world. Until I read over my own work, I

never see the holes and bare spots in my own mind; and only then I feel
how hard it is to scratch about, and put on false hair and rouge and a grin.
As writers grow old, they all do it, some well, some ill; and call it art. The
young ones don't know enough to do it. They are like girls who can trust
to their freshness to cover their faults of feature. A pair of blue eyes carry
young verses over a heap of troubles, as well as they carry the summer-girl
over a flirtation.

Anyone who means to be an artist has got to study his defects, and the
only way of studying one's own defects is to lay one's work aside until it
is forgotten, and then to go over it again with no other thought than to
see where it is wrong. As a rule one finds that it is mostly wrong. A man
is generally artistic in proportion as he sees what is wrong, and most work
is good in proportion not so much to what one leaves in it as to what one
strikes out. Hardly anyone who has any faculty of perception can write a
volume without saying something worth keeping, but generally he swamps
it in a mass of stuff that prevents the reader from noticing it. As matter of
solemn truth, we read mostly things that challenge no notice, and are a
little irritated and annoyed when an artist tells us that we have overlooked
what he meant. We prefer the mush. I do so myself. I shrink from a tragedy
or an effort. I loathe the strenuous life. I've had more than enough of
analysis and synthesis. You must forgive the weakening fibre of senility. It
is true that even in extreme youth I never loved strenuosity either mental
or physical, because it always ended in giving me a licking, and consequently I have always associated it with bullying me, unless it was I who
bullied the littler fellow; and it is still the same thing. When I feel strenuous,
I know I am going to be rude to somebody whom I think I can bully.

The application of all this twaddle is perhaps too obvious. You can see
it all, at a glance; and of course, as usual, by that tiresome faculty of seeing
oneself, you will see it as you feel it. Never—never—never—can you see it
as I feel it, for in that case you would be somebody else. Yet, by that stupid
mental process on which men foolishly pride themselves—called reason—
you can construct a doll-figure of my literary form, and see how it fits, or
does not fit, yours. To me, a story-teller must be a trivial sort of animal
who amuses me. His first quality should be superficiality; for this quality,
as a fundamental, I take Miss Austin and generally the women-women, not
the men-women like George Eliot, as examples; and Dickens, if you like,
as a warning of what happens when one tries to be serious in order to fill
up the holes in one's mind. Balzac tires me from the instant he becomes
moralist. You know all this. I don't insist. Art comes in at the corner of F
and 20th,[2] when you want to get a moral into me without my knowing it.
You've got to do it, because that's what you are for; you won't grin through
a horse-collar just to make the clowns laugh. Yet, when I get to the corner,

I tell you to go to the devil; I won't take pills! How are you going to grab me by the throat, after the strenuous presidential manner, and jam your pill down? That is the whole subject of dispute. That is art. One man tries to do it one way; another man fetches you a hit in the stomach; and a woman tickles you behind the left ear; but an old, hardened, vicious, reptile, like me, just runs off—to Paris, if possible. You have got the hardest kind of a job to find a new trick for me. To make Saint Thomas smile, though the object of all our ambitions, is not easy, but, once discovered, the old trick will always fetch him unless he has a stomach-ache; whereas the old trick does not fetch me any longer. The New Yorker bores me in real life; how can he amuse me in fiction? Doubtless it can be done; but I am singularly on my guard against his tricks. You have got to study me,—not him. If I know myself, the only possible way of interesting me in a New Yorker would be to make him funny and sympathetic because I never should recognise him in that light; but, as New Yorker—no! in my opinion, you can't make me swallow that pill,—art or no art;—no, not even the diabolical cunning which your mother attributes to Sargent's portrait of the President can make me swallow it. Brute, fraud, mountebank, millionaire, cheat or philanthropist, all is one to me. I wont swallow him.

In face of this stupid and mulish obstinacy, what are you to do? I am a pig; I'm sorry for it; but I am a public too; and I want to be amused. Make for me a comic Mrs Hull, braining her son-in-law with a rocking-chair, and probably you would amuse me to the end;[3] but I don't care a straw whether one New Yorker brains another, or how he does it; and the more accurate the types, the less I care. You can't make me care. No art could ever make me swallow that pill. This is my solemn conviction. Of jelly I am nervously suspicious. As a cocktail, it has ceased to deceive. Pure brandy I loathe. Even with a crowbar it wont go. Your only chance is to make me laugh, and slip it into my mouth while it's open. For this reason I say, as I began, that I want you to reflect on what you are trying to do. Remember that, after all, I am, or have been, human, and that nothing human has any longer the slightest interest to me, if it resembles myself.[4] That particular form of boredom, in all its varieties, can only be saved by putting into it what never was there—a sense of the ridiculous.

Please lock up the volume for a year. Then read it over—carefully—and tell me your conclusion.

Ever Yrs   Henry Adams.

MS: MHi

1. The manuscript was George Cabot Lodge's New York society novel, *The Genius of the Commonplace*, first published in 1976 (ed. John W. Crowley).
2. Bay and Bessie Lodge were living at 1925 F Street, at F and 20th streets.

3. In the Burdick case, recently in the news, Marie A. Hull was the victim's mother-in-law, but was not implicated in his murder.
4. HA's revision of Terence: "Homo sum; humani nihil a me alienum puto" (I am human; I think nothing human is alien to me).

To Charles Milnes Gaskell

23 Avenue du Bois de Boulogne
14 June, 1903.

My dear Carlo

From your letter I infer that you are in town. Apparently it is the best place to be in. As yet I've not been tempted to leave it, and, except for the length of day-light, I have to guess the season. It suits me very well.

What suits me less well is the apparent dead-high-tide about us. For my immortal soul, dyspepsia from over-feeding has become chronic. Your letter instances several cases:—e.g. Lord Kelvin with his radium and atheism, and his frank confession that neither he nor his antagonists know what they mean. Forty years ago, our friends always explained things and had the cosmos down to a point, *teste* Darwin and Charles Lyell. Now they say that they don't believe there is any explanation, or that you can choose between half-a-dozen, all correct. The Germans are all balled up. Every generalisation that we settled forty years ago, is abandoned. The one most completely thrown over is our gentle Darwin's Survival which has no longer a leg to stand on. I interpret even Kelvin as throwing it over.

Our friend Joe Chamberlain is a political example of the same thing. He has thrown over all our old laws of politics, and really is right, at least in the sense that Kelvin is right. No one knows.[1]

The automobile business is a practical illustration. It has exploded all our nineteenth century commodities. Our roads are little more than the old mule-tracks of the Romans. Every great city is now constructing a three-tier system:—underground; ground-level; and high-level, electric railways; and already this is insufficient. New York will have twenty million people in another fifty years, and all will have to be carried up and down, every day.

We have got to spend something fabulous on our roads alone. In America we must create them.

To you respectable old country-gentlemen of the sixteenth-century, all this muddle comes easy; but to Americans it does not come easy at all. We are looking ahead to a kind of strangulation. Three hundred million people running an automobile of a hundred million horsepower, at full speed, without roads to run on, and without the smallest idea where we are going or want to go, is a new problem in planetary history. I've been watching it all winter in Washington, with the whole apparatus of government to enlighten me; and now I'm studying it here as history and science. The only result is to figure out, by both processes, an *impasse* within thirty years. The mechanical problem is easily figured out, for one arrives at the limits of the possible very soon; the difficulty begins with the impossible. We know so very little, and all wrong.

Poor old nineteenth century! It is already as far off as Descartes and Newton.

You have not answered my question about our breakfast at Sir Henry's and William Everett's dinner, if it was a dinner, at Cambridge.[2] What year was it, '62 or '63; and what year did you come up to read law? I want to make some calculations of figures on it. What will be the next term of an equation or series like this:—

$$1823 : 1863 :: 1903 : x.$$

Figure it out in coal-production; horse-power; thermo-dynamics; or, if you like, just simply in fields—space, energy, time, thought, or mere multiplicity and complexity. My whole interest is to get at a value for that x before I break up, which is an x more easily calculated.

The gentle mathematicians and physicists still cling to their laws of thermo-dynamics, and are almost epileptic in their convulsive assurances that they have reached there a generalisation which will hold good. Perhaps it will. Who cares? Already it is like all the rest of our old structure. It explains nothing. Science has given up the whole fabric of cause and effect. Even time-sequence is beginning to be threatened. I should not at all wonder if some one should upset time. As for space, it is upset already. We did that sixty years ago, with electricity. I imagine that in another sixty years, if my x sequence works out regularly, we must be communicating throughout space, by x rays, with systems infinitely distant from us, but finitely distant from each other; a mathematical problem to be solved by non-Euclidean methods.

Anyway we are to reach the impasse within another Kelvin life-time, as far as I can understand the figures. Whether we stop there, or break our necks, is singularly unimportant to us.

I've nothing new to send you from here. Books swarm like maggots, but I no longer read pornography and no one now writes history, criticism, travels or poetry. Rostand's Academy speech was pretty.[3] Would you like it?

Love to yours.   Ever truly   Henry Adams.

MS: MHi

1. On May 15 in a speech in Birmingham, Chamberlain challenged the free trade system in effect since the repeal of the Corn Laws in 1846.

2. Sir Henry Holland (1788–1873), the queen's physician, writer, friend of American ministers at the U.S. legation.
3. Edmond Rostand, *Discours de réception à l'Académie française, le 4 juin 1903*, a eulogy on the dramatist Henri de Bornier, Rostand's predecessor in the French Academy.

To Charles Milnes Gaskell

23 Avenue du Bois de Boulogne
30 Oct. 1903.

My dear Carlo

I am sorry you did not get the Lodges down to Wenlock, although I knew she hardly had the strength to go. From what is said of the weather, I'm afraid the country at best has not been dry. Apparently you have done it, this time.

Tell Evelyn[1] clearly that if he wants to see us, he must get to Washington not later than April. If he does not care to see us, but only the country, he can travel comfortably till July. After July 1, he had better stay in Canada or not go at all. A few sea-side places alone are habitable.

I am reading Morley's Gladstone with interest, especially the first volume.[2] Having written a good deal of biography myself, its difficulties present themselves to my eyes with some bluntness. The ice is always thin in spots. Gladstone's mind at best was feebly polarised. A weak magnet deflected it. I have read nothing about the wonderful experience I lived through in England, in 1863, that has astounded me quite so much as Morley's Vol. ii, pp. 75–86. Gladstone's own biographical note, p. 81, raised my few remaining white hairs stiff with horror. Can it be credible that he could dream that such a confession,—however acceptable to a priest in the confessional, acting for a respectable deity who can't be hurt,—could be admitted by a serious critic whose life was very nearly the sacrifice of his deliberate attack?[3] You can tell Morley, if you ever talk with him about it, that one of his readers, who thought he could understand and even accept Manning, finds himself totally unable to understand Gladstone.[4] Of course I mean understanding in any sense of logical consistency. In the jesuitical sense, it is only too easy.

As for Chamberlain, he is just such another, as I see him, only his is a Birmingham jesuitry. As my brother Brooks and I were among the first to study and open this problem in 1893-7, and as we emptied it to our own satisfaction, I have read Chamberlain's statements and followed his policy with interest. My own conclusions were different. It seemed to me that a country enjoying England's unapproached advantages, and running probably half the artificial power of the world with one third the output of coal, was already protected enough. If she failed to compete with a poor and heavily handicapped people like the Germans, or an isolated, distant and high-priced people like the Americans, it must be for want of energy or of intelligence or of will. If this is the case, you may as well shut yourselves up as not. Nothing will do any good. The only chance was to let starvation and ruin stimulate energy again; but if the energy is exhausted, protection may ease decline. It is an opiate in such a rheumatic state of the system; and at the age of England and me, opiates are sometimes life.

So I stand neutral. Build up the wall, and lie down inside on your colonies! France did it ten years ago successfully, though, to be sure, France lives on our vices—the richest kind of revenue!

I'll ask about French books. I see none.

Love to all yours   H.A.

MS: MHi

1. Gaskell's son.
2. John Morley, *The Life of William Ewart Gladstone*, 3 vols. (1903).
3. Gladstone wrote in 1896 that he had made a "singular and palpable" error when he declared that Jefferson Davis had made a nation. He admitted his mistake was of "incredible grossness." See HA's account of the incident in the *Education*, chap. 10.
4. Cardinal Henry Manning, a convert to Roman Catholicism, retracted his Anglican "errors" in *The Temporal Mission of the Holy Ghost* (1865).

To Henry James

23 Avenue du Bois de Boulogne
18 Nov. 1903.

My dear James

Although you, like most men of toil, hate to be bored, I can hardly pass over your last work without boring you to the extent of a letter. We have reached a time of solar antiquity when nothing matters, but still we feel what used to be called the law of gravitation, mass, or attraction, and obey it.

More than ever, after devouring your William Story,[1] I feel how difficult a job was imposed on you. It is a *tour de force*, of course, but that you knew from the first. Whether you have succeeded or not, I cannot say, because it all spreads itself out as though I had written it, and I feel where you are walking on firm ground, and where you are on thin ice, as though I were in your place. Verily I believe I wrote it. Except your specialty of style, it is me.

The painful truth is that all of my New England generation, counting the half-century, 1820–1870, were in actual fact only one mind and nature; the individual was a facet of Boston. We knew each other to the last nervous centre, and feared each other's knowledge. We looked through each other like microscopes. There was absolutely nothing in us that we did not understand merely by looking in the eye. There was hardly a difference even in depth, for Harvard College and Unitarianism kept us all shallow. We knew nothing— no! but really nothing! of the world. One cannot exaggerate the profundity of ignorance of Story in becoming a sculptor, or Sumner in becoming a statesman, or Emerson in becoming a philosopher. Story and Sumner, Emerson and Alcott, Lowell and Longfellow, Hillard, Winthrop, Motley, Prescott, and all the rest, were the same mind,—and so, poor worm!—was I!²

Type bourgeois-bostonien! A type quite as good as another, but more uniform. What you say of Story is at bottom exactly what you would say of Lowell, Motley, and Sumner, barring degrees of egotism. You cannot help smiling at them, but you smile at us all equally. God knows that we knew our want of knowledge! the self-distrust became introspection—nervous self-consciousness—irritable dislike of America, and antipathy to Boston. *Auch ich* war in Arcadien geboren!³

So you have written not Story's life, but your own and mine,—pure autobiography,—the more keen for what is beneath, implied, intelligible only to me, and half a dozen other people still living: like Frank Boott; who knew our Boston, London and Rome in the fifties and sixties.⁴ You make me curl up, like a trodden-on worm. Improvised Europeans, we were, and— Lord God!—how thin! No, but it is too cruel! Long ago,—at least thirty years ago,—I discovered it, and have painfully held my tongue about it. You strip us, gently and kindly, like a surgeon, and I feel your knife in my ribs.

No one else will ever know it. You have been extremely tactful. The essential superficiality of Story and all the rest, you have made painfully clear to us, but not, I think, to the family or the public. After all, the greatest men are weak. Morley's Gladstone is hardly thicker than your Story. Let us pray!

Ever Yrs   Henry Adams.

MS: MH

1. Henry James, *William Wetmore Story and His Friends* (1903).
2. George Stillman Hillard (1808–1879), Boston lawyer, editor, associate of Charles Sumner, legislator, and writer; William Hickling Prescott (1796–1859), historian of Spain in the Americas.
3. *Auch ich . . . geboren:* I, too, was born in Arcadia. HA quotes from Schiller's poem "Resignation, Eine Phantasie" (1786). James had explicitly noted Boston's "Arcadian" aspects.
4. James describes Francis Boott, Boston expatriate in Italy, as the "earliest of all precursors."

To Elizabeth Cameron

Sunday 14 Feb. '04

I hurried off my last letter on Monday for fear of more bad news. News there was in plenty the next day, bad or good or middling, that made us all jump. The 8th of February will be a pretty serious and solemn anniversary I reckon, a good while after I have done my yawp.[1] You can figure my delight in chirping pessimistic dirges to every body in the fifteen skies. Never was I happier. I told 'em all that the bottom had dropped out; that my reign had come; that anarchy was in sight, and that my Louis XV chateau in the Ave. du Bois was already in flames like Baltimore. Bay and Bessie came to dine and we chorkled. Of course next door we were very busy. Poor Kassini whined and Jusserand fumed, and Durand was stupid, and no one had a ghost of a notion what had hit them.[2] No one yet has it. I've done my best to spread the joyful tidings and convince them all that universal anarchy, ruin and ravage will cover the world within a year, but they've no sense.

Russia *habet!* she has got it. Never never no never or hardly ever shall she stand up again. I am giving odds that the Tsar won't live through the year, and that the Russian Treasury will be bankrupt before next December. Also that the French republic will fall; the Bank of England suspend, and I be hung to a lamp-post on the Place de Grève. My dear family portraits! my beautiful *potiches!* my sweet bed! my lovely commodes! I sob to bid them good-bye, but you shall have them. Please raise a monument to the memory of one who anarched for martyrdom.

To dance on volcanoes is fun, but I've got a little bit tired this week. I had time to write you that the Baltimore fire had burnt up Chartres.[3] I am still trying to find out whether anything is left of it. I am painfully calculating when Hottinguer who is up to his ears in Russians, will walk off with my money.[4] What is much worse I hear bad news of your sister Mary, and have tried in vain to catch your sister Lida who was here again this week.[5] She will have told you. On top of this, and Hanna's collapse which is nothing to me, comes a break-down of Charley Rae, to Rebecca's despair. My nephew Charley has iritis again, which embarrasses our affairs. Brooks is at Hot Springs with eczima, and his wife at Sister Anne's with mighty powerful weakness. Oh, but it's gay, and I was never in so cheery a temper!

Meanwhile Washington is full and running over. People actually sometimes drop in. Joe Stickney, after a phenomenal social success, has returned with hearts to Cambridge. Edwin Morgan dined here last night before starting for Manchuria.[6] Zorn is here, and is coming to breakfast or dine;

and the Barensons too.[7] My niece Fanny has gone home to pick up her young man and start fresh. Elsie is with me, and Looly.

Yesterday the gossip from Wall Street affirmed that Bill Whitney left practically no property. I have been very curious to know whether he could have made a fortune, with habits so madly extravagant. One says also that George Vanderbilt has been hard hit. Schwab has run away. Le Roy Dresser is uncommonly near the penitentiary.[8] Another such year as the last will squash all our summer pumpkins into pie.

Tuesday. 16. My birthday! Sixtysix years old! It is time to quit, and I shall be glad to take leave. Yesterday was my worst day for a long while. It began with a letter from Milnes Gaskell which warned me that he is little likely ever to see me again.[9] Then your letter followed from Sta Margarita which threw me into the blackest despair. That you should kill yourself, though an annoyance, matters little to me, since a few months pass quickly at sixtysix, but my feelings were keen for Martha, and I tried to calculate how much reckless carelessness and extravagant exposure had done for all you three sister's children. After all, your sister Mary has had the sense and foresight to live to a fair age, but poor Martha! I imagined her worry and distress. All alone, too, in Rome! What *can* she do! I want to start at once to be with her when the worst comes, but there are limits to unavowed insanity. In a universe where I alone am sane, I have to act as though other people were also responsible. This was bad enough, but it was relatively nothing. With my mind in this condition of dark purple gloom, there came in on me to breakfast a slew of people: Dolly Rockhill and her chum Miss I-do-know-who; Lucy Stickney and an écolier Normale named Aubert; at last—Barenson and his wife! Well, you know, you see, you know, I *can't* bear it. There is, in the Jew deprecation, something that no weary sinner ought to stand. I rarely murder. By nature I am humane. Life, to such people, is perhaps dear, or at least worth living, and I hate to take it. Yet I did murder Barenson. I cut his throat first, and chopped him into small bits afterwards, and rolled the fragments into the fire. In my own house I ought not to have done so. I tried to do it gently, without apparent temper or violence of manner. Alas! murder will out! I fear Lucy Stickney will betray me, and bring me to ultimate conviction.

The ill-luck that brought such a victim into my lair on precisely the worst day I've had for years, pursued me throughout. I tried to hide. People persisted in coming in. My only quieting thought was that Mark Hanna next door was drawing his last breath. Not that I wanted Hanna to die, but that the thought of somebody else worse than I was, calmed my nerves. I felt pleased to know that Myron Herrick was already in town, announcing his candidacy for Mark's shoes before the wearer was dead.[10] The sense of universal, overwhelming, final and sufficient ruin does soothe. I forgot the Barensons. I thought only of you, and I wept.

Today I am calmer. Although bad news goes on accumulating, and the débâcle is visibly upon us, I am for the moment superficially calm. If I can only get a few hours when a dearest friend wont die, or when no one will write to beg for money to save an old acquaintance from the alms-house and her children from starvation, I can perhaps live over a day or two more. Yet, after one's nervous system is wholly broken up, poppies turn neurotic.

George Vanderbilt has not rented his house for fifteen years; only his forest and the shooting. I am not sure that the Steel Trust will have to foreclose. Sam Mather doubts it.[11] Pierpont Morgan's collapse is greatly to be regretted,—says Oliver Payne—because he is the last Christian banker in exchanges. The small interior banks are failing daily by twos and threes. The total collapse will doubtless wait till Europe busts. I apprehend that Russia is now an entire chaos without administration, and must go bankrupt financially, politically and socially as well as in a military sense, within a brief time. France must follow. England cannot stand up. We are already tottering. I guess I've got home.

Since July, 1861, I've not been so gay about public affairs. Brooks comes up today to *égayer* me more. Oh Lord! oh Lord! that cough of your's! poor Martha!

———

MS: MHi

1. In a surprise attack on Feb. 8 the Japanese overwhelmed the Russian ships at Port Arthur. The czar proclaimed war Feb. 10; the mikado did so the next day.

2. Count Artur P. Cassini, Russian ambassador to the U.S.; Jean J. Jusserand (1855–1932), French ambassador to the U.S.; Sir Henry Mortimer Durand (1850–1924), British ambassador to the U.S.

3. In the great fire that destroyed 75 city blocks of the business district of Baltimore, part of the printer's copy of HA's *Mont Saint Michel and Chartres* disappeared.

4. Henri Hottinguer of the Paris banking family.

5. Mary (Mrs. Nelson A.) Miles; Lida Sherman (Mrs. Colgate) Hoyt (1853–1908).

6. Edwin V. Morgan (1865–1934), former professor of history at Western Reserve University, on duty at the State Department.

7. The art historian and connoisseur Bernhard (Bernard) Berenson (1865–1959) and his wife and collaborator, Mary Smith Costelloe Berenson (1864–1945), were on a 6-month visit to the U.S. from Italy, where they lived. They came to Washington with a letter of introduction from John La Farge to HA.

8. George W. Vanderbilt (1862–1914), capitalist, owner of Biltmore, a magnificent estate at Asheville, N.C.; Charles M. Schwab (1862–1939), president of U.S. Steel Corp., organizer of the bankrupt U.S. Shipbuilding Co. He settled with the bondholders on Feb. 4 and left for Europe on Feb. 12 amid reports of a criminal investigation by the New York legislature. Daniel L. Dresser (1866–1915), bank president involved in the bankruptcy of the shipbuilding company.

9. Gaskell had been seriously ill.
10. Hanna died Feb. 15; Myron T. Herrick (1854–1929), Cleveland financier, governor of Ohio.
11. Samuel Mather (1851–1931), industrialist, brother-in-law of John Hay.

To Charles Milnes Gaskell

23 Avenue du Bois de Boulogne
22 July, 1904

My dear Carlo

Lady Catherine says that you would not be bored if I write to you.[1] I've very little to write, but lots of time, almost as much as you have. I am not in bed, I admit, but except for meals twice a day, I hardly leave my desk. The weather is superb, but I am lazy.

To compel myself to do something I bought an automobile, a very pretty Mercedes, 18 h.p., and hoped to live in it, but, to my great relief and satisfaction, the inspector delays for weeks to give me a number, and the chauffeur always has a reason for sending the machine to the shops. Between them I am quite happy, and never have to go out-doors.

Paris is deserted by all my acquaintance, and occupied by a million and a half Americans whom I don't know, but see every evening when I walk out to the Bois to dine in the open air.

One would think that the whole world everywhere was in *fête*, amusing itself and dancing. No one is willing to face the danger. The French are carefully shutting their eyes to the situation of their friend Russia. You know how scared I have been about this war. The situation grows more intense every day, and its interest keeps me awake nights. I am terribly curious to see the end; it is all I care to see in politics now. Russia is very rapidly foundering. At least the old Russia has got its death-blow. Either she must go to pieces, or found a new system. Every day brings a new shock to the old one. It is the greatest event that has taken place in our time, as a catastrophe,—even greater than the war of 1870 and the catastrophe of France. Really I am glad to have lived to see this old chapter closed, and want only to know whether it will end in a big tragedy like Louis XVI, or in a tragi-comedy. Never has so great an empire sunk without dragging the world down with it. The confusion will be vast. It already is serious as everyone knows, though no one likes to talk of it. I am glad not to be in Lansdowne's place, and am quite willing not to be in Hay's. The whole world may be in a turmoil before they know it.

With this melodrama to watch, I've not cared for other theatres, and hardly go into Paris at all. Would you like me to send you the albums? Of course you don't read—and neither do I—but you may look at caricatures. You can take them in five minute doses, if you like; which is about as much as I can stand of them myself. As serious occupation I usually play solitaire, but many people think this too much effort, and in fact I generally try to find a lady to do it for me. Just now all my ladies have gone. Mrs Cameron is at Nauheim curing her heart, and all the others are at Aix or Carlsbad or S. Moritz. I recommend you to try this altruistic method as you get more minutes to spare. You only look on and criticise.

Ever Yrs   Henry Adams.

MS: MHi
1. Gaskell was still ill.

To Elizabeth Cameron

23 Avenue du Bois de Boulogne
Friday, 5 Aug. [1904]

Your postal from Imst arrived last night.

What you are to do in September may be a question, but you must devote August to finishing your cure and giving Martha some mountain air. You can do nothing at home until cold weather. As far as your sister could see or tell me, there was nothing even she could do. She leaves here today.

You are by this time, I hope, in mountain air, and will be tonight above roasting. Here, yesterday was alive. Elsie de Wolfe pitched precisely on yesterday to ask me to take them down to Fontainebleau to a sale which she thought would be good. I got out to them at about half past nine, and we started off with a blazing day. At Longjumeau we creved a pneu with a nail, and stopped half an hour sizzling. Going on, we took a zigzag route, by the Routière, and did not reach Fontainebleau till one o'clock. The thermometer above our table on the cool side marked 32° (90° Fahr.) and for two hours after breakfast we tramped to sales and antiquaires till I expected Miss Marbury to have a stroke. As for me!—After all, it is funny, and so am I! At 4.20 we started back, to do time, the sky without a cloud, and the air in blasts of heat. We ran as hard as we could, by way of Melun to Choisy-le-Roi. I hate going at sixty kilometers. It spoils me pleasure, ruins my clothes, and scares me out of my senses. Just at Villeneuve, the meanest place about Paris, our new pneu gave way, my third in two days. Probably the heat of the road, and sixty kilometers an hour, did it; but we had another half hour on the pavement. When we crossed the bridge at Choisy-le-Roi,

I saw some light clouds on the horizon, and congratulated the party on a hope of some shadow. We ran ahead by Sceaux, and by that time, in effect, the sun was a little overcast. In another fifteen minutes, we saw light showers to the south. We were then within ten or twelve kilometres of Versailles, and took little notice of weather. It was about 6.30, and in twenty minutes we should be at home. In ten minutes we ran into a howling deluge. We had just time to get our water-proofs on; but nothing protects against such wind and water. We simply went through it, and it through us. I was glad the machine had no hood, for it would have been an extra danger. We were in a warm bath, but all right, and I got them into their house at 6.50. I waited twenty minutes hoping for a let-up, but then started out again and struck up to the Vaucresson road. In about five minutes, or less, a deluge of rain fell, and I found that, after all, an umbrella was the best protection. We could not go fast. The rain and wind blinded. We ran on beautifully, for the rain had cooled the road, and I was just thanking my machine for its good behavior and my own arrival at No. 23, when we ran down the last hill before St Cloud into a sheet of water covering the road for 200 yards or more. The rain had stopped, but the water was pouring into the road in a river, and could not drain off. We ran into it, and in the middle, up to our wheel-tops, came to a stop. There I was, sitting solitary in a waste of waters, wondering what more could happen. My man went overboard and struggled in vain to get his machine to work under water, but after fifteen minutes of failure, he let me call a wet bicyclist to help him push us ashore; an easy job, but one that chauffeurs hate.

Once across the awful chasm, and our engines going again, my spirits rose; and just then a big Panhard rolled down the hill from St Cloud. A lot of people were by that time looking on, and out of the house-windows; and as the Panhard chauffeur seemed half inclined to slow up, they all laughed and shouted: "Allez!" *Aller* he did with a splash, and I drove off, crying bravo and clapping my hands with the rest, just as the four inmates of the Panhard rose to their feet and looked about them with consternation over the raging waters just as I had done.

My troubles began again at the race-course at Longchamp where the road all round was a long lake of water. I turned back twice before getting across at Bagatelle. A glad man I was when I reached No. 23, just at eight, with the last daylight.

These are the triumphs of civilisation. All I can say is that, in spite of heat, delays, floods and tempests, at least I was not bored. Whether the two ladies were pleased, I cannot surely say. The sale was hopeless rubbish, but the spree was theirs, not mine; and anyway they got home to dinner.

I also got home to dinner at Henry's, but an hour late. I was moist.

This morning I get a note from Suzanne asking me to breakfast at 12.30 to meet the Gherardesca.[1] Suzanne must be very short of men, so I will go, to oblige her, which is more than I did for the Versaillaises at dinner on Wednesday.[2]

Nothing yet has been so bad as my wanderings with Bay and Bessie, but I shall catch up.

I found my thermometer on the balcony registering 40° (104° Fah.) with its back to a lead plate. Today is no slouch either.

Tell Martha to read the adventures of Odysseus!

———

MS: MHi

1. Suzanne Bancroft Carroll (Mrs. Charles Carroll); Count Giuseppe della Gherardesca, honorary attaché of the Italian embassy in Washington 1903, and his wife (d. 1934), the former Harriet Taylor of New York.
2. Elsie de Wolfe and Elisabeth Marbury at their villa in Versailles.

To John Hay

23 Avenue du Bois de Boulogne
8 Sept. 1904.

My dear Hay

As far as a poor Porcupine sees, which is but the length of his tail, you are in pretty deep water, and my humble prayers rise every day to the Virgin to help you through.[1] No such squeeze as this has occurred in my time. The balance of the world is upset, and the whole rotten fabric will certainly fall. The war is over. If it lasts ten years more, it is over all the same. Russia has had her *coup de Jarnac*.[2]

Peace must now be made, and we can trust Germany and France to make it. Their interests require it. My trouble is that having been so strongly Russian hitherto, I am now as strongly German.

Just look at it! What is Germany to do? The practical extinction of Russia for years to come leaves Germany, in the east, face to face with the combination of England, America and Japan. If you were the Kaiser what would you do about it?

I have been strutting round, twisting up my moustache, playing Kaiser in imagination for the past week, trying to think of a way to protect myself. The more I study it, the tighter my quarters become. Of course I can make peace pure and simple, and deliver myself, tied up in a roll, to Japan and England, who, at a flash, could clear out every German interest or possession east of Suez. I can do this only as the result of defeat and helplessness. First I must try to keep my head above water.

You ask, of course, what will satisfy me. Hang me if I can see that anything will satisfy me short of readjusting the world. All China would not satisfy me, since I should hold it only as long as Japan gave leave.

I am not unreasonable. My situation is exceedingly difficult. My true compensation ought to come in Russia, but if I take the Baltic provinces I must give back Alsace. Anyway the Baltic provinces are hardly worth it. Poland would answer, but I've too many Poles already. What I need is the Volga, but it is too far away.

I must therefore insist on protection in China. What can you give me? I asked Takahira this question last spring, and scared him greener than ever.[3] Would I like Shanghai? Perhaps! I don't know! Offer it, and I'll see! but bestir yourselves, and hit on something, or I shall have to act!

Do you mean to refuse me all consideration? If England and you are going to back up Japan in such crying injustice as this, I must throw all my strength for Russia, and bring France into the combination. It will be a fight for life.

You had better pay my price. The aggrandisement of England by this war has been immense. To America, it is all profit. Japan has become the first power in the east. Germany alone is very cold.

You reply that I get my consideration in Europe where I am now dictator, and that the ruin of the Russo-French alliance ought to satisfy me amply. For the first time, my elbows are free. The facts, as I see them, argue just the other way. The stronger I am in Europe, the stronger I must be in Asia.

I am very shy of suggesting an extension of my concession at Kiau-chau. It is a trap, of which the Japs hold the spring. It is much more dangerous than Port Arthur.

No! if Russia has to give up Port Arthur, England then is bound to give up Wei-hai-Wei, which leaves the Japanese in full control of all those seas down to Hongkong. Kiau-chau is in constant danger, and is indefensible by Germany. I had better give it up, too.

I am the walking soul of justice and unselfishness, but I implore you to reflect on my difficult position. The collapse of Russia leaves me in the air. I must fall on something. England and America between them must find a soft place.

One thing more! If I dislike one trait of your diplomacy more than another, it is your tendency to intrigue. I bar further intrigue between England and France. I propose to do all that myself.

———

This is what I did when I played I was Kaiser. I have caught the habit, and can now imagine myself nothing else; not even Cardinal. I am dying to hear that you've squared me, but I cannot conceive how! As I see it, I must save Russia.

———

MS: MHi

1. Augustus Saint-Gaudens had made a bronze medallion caricature of HA on which the inscription read, in part, "Porcupinus Angelicus." HA's head is attached to a porcupine's body with angel wings.
2. *Coup de Jarnac:* an unexpected and decisive blow, proverbial phrase from Guy Chabot, sieur de Jarnac, who in a famous duel in 1547 treacherously attacked his opponent and then, when he was helpless, killed him.
3. Kogoro Takahira (1854–1926), Japanese minister to the U.S. 1900–1906.

To Charles Milnes Gaskell

1603 H Street. 20 Dec. 1904

My dear Carlo

Your letter of the 4th arrived just in time for me to show it to Brooks, who sails next Saturday for Antwerp *en route* for Berlin where he thinks he has something to study. He and his wife are profuse in thanks, and regret only that their path is the straight and narrow road that leads to Germany which is a hole.

I returned here early in November rather than stay alone and dreary in Paris. Washington is now rather more amusing to me than other places, because I can laugh at all my friends who are running what they call a government. They are droll, like most men who run governments. We have arrived now at that age when we are allowed to laugh, because no one cares what we do as long as we don't ask for money. Your audacity in begging for a University takes away my breath.[1] I am at a loss to learn what function a University now performs in the world. They are ornamental but expensive; and, as you say, not one graduate in ten retains a shadow of liberal education. Of course we see it here more clearly than you. For this I could make my mourning with philosophy, seeing that it has always been so in my time, but the flamboyant self-esteem and moral platitude of the odd tenth man reconciles me to the premature demise of Thomas Aquinas and the late Duns Scotus.

Talking of Thomas Aquinas, I have just finished printing my *Miracles de la Vierge*. The book will run up to a pretty bulky size, but I print only a hundred copies, one of which will be for you. It is my declaration of principles as head of the Conservative Christian Anarchists; a party numbering one member. The Virgin and St Thomas are my vehicles of anarchism. Nobody knows enough to see what they mean, so the Judges will probably not be able to burn me according to law. If there has ever been in the world a greater blockhead than the schoolmaster, it has been the judge. On the whole, I think the bishop has had an advantage over both, in so far as he had a sort of general idea what he represented.

This country is terribly interesting. It has no character but prodigious force,—at least twenty million horse-power constant; about as much as all the rest of the world together, by coal-output. We are running very fast indeed into the impossible, which you can measure on our coal and ore output. I cannot conceive what will happen. Logically we must strangulate and suffocate in just fifteen years,—at the point of 50-million tons annual steel output. Luckily I am out of it, and perhaps it has all been only a dream. I'm not sure. If so, Russia has been an ugly one, and turns me green with horror.

All the same, our great managers of industry are dead scared.

The rest is rubbish. I've no news.

Love to all yours   Ever truly   Henry Adams.

MS: MHi

1. Gaskell was trying to raise money for the University of Leeds.

To Henry Osborn Taylor

1603 H Street. 17 Jan. 1905

My dear Taylor[1]

Many thanks for your letter and its literary references. I imagine you are almost the only man in America who are competent to supply them to me, and I shall use them with proper care.

My own interest in the subject is scientific to such an extent that my play with it is awkward, like a kitten in walnuts. I am trying to work out the formula of anarchism; the law of expansion from unity, simplicity, morality, to multiplicity, contradiction, police. I have done it scientifically, by formulating the ratio of development in energy, as in explosives, or chemical energies. I can see it in the development of steam-power, and in the various economies of conveyance. Radium thus far is the term for these mechanical ratios. The ratio for thought is not so easy to fix. I can get a time-ratio only in philosophy. The assumption of unity which was the mark of human thought in the middle-ages has yielded very slowly to the proofs of complexity. The stupor of science before radium is a proof of it. Yet it is quite sure, according to my score of ratios and curves, that, at the accelerated rate of progression shown since 1600, it will not need another century or half century to tip thought upside down. Law, in that case, would disappear as theory or *à priori* principle, and give place to force. Morality would become police. Explosives would reach cosmic violence. Disintegration would overcome integration.

This was the point that leads me back to the twelfth century as the fixed element of the equation. From the relative unity of twelfth-century conceptions of the Prime Motor, I can work down pretty safely to Karl Pearson's Grammar of Science or Wallace's Man's Place in Nature, or to Mach and Ostwald and the other Germans of today.[2] By intercalating Descartes, Newton, Dalton and a few others, I can even make almost a time-ratio.[3] This is where my middle-ages will work out.

I tell you this in order that you may explain to Prof. Robinson why the volume is not offered to the public.[4] It is what it professes to be, and I do not propose to invite attention to it by offering it to any one except personal friends. You can lend him your copy, and if, on looking it over, he seriously wants the volume, I will with the greatest pleasure send him one, but I do not want him to treat it as anything but what it is,—a sketch-study intended for my own and my nieces' amusement.

Your work is of a totally different kind. I have no object but a superficial one, as far as history is concerned. To me, accuracy is relative. I care very little whether my details are exact, if only my *ensemble* is in scale. You need to be thorough in your study and accurate in your statements. Your middle-ages exist for their own sake, not for ours. To me, who stand in gaping wonder before this preposterous spectacle of thought, and who can see nothing in all nature so iconoclastic, miraculous and anarchistic as Shakespeare, the middle-ages present a picture that has somehow to be brought into relation with ourselves. To you, there is no difficulty in transporting ourselves into the middle-ages. You require serious and complete study, and careful attention to details. Our two paths run in a manner parallel in reverse directions, but I can run and jump along mine, while you must employ a powerful engine to drag your load. I am glad to know that your engine is powerful enough.

Time is very short, but at any rate our middle-ages are long, and the rest matters little to us now. What I most want is an intelligent man of science, a thing I never shall find.

Ever Yrs   Henry Adams.

MS: MH

1. Henry Osborn Taylor (1856–1941), historian and former student of HA, had responded to *Mont Saint Michel and Chartres* with glowing praise and detailed suggestions of complementary readings.
2. Karl Pearson, *The Grammar of Science* (1892); Alfred Russel Wallace, *Man's Place in the Universe* (1903); Ernst Mach (1838–1916), Austrian physicist and a founder of modern positivism; Wilhelm Ostwald (1853–1932), German physical chemist.
3. John Dalton (1766–1844), English chemist who devised the first atomic table.
4. James Harvey Robinson (1863–1936), professor of history at Columbia University, described by Taylor as his "chief companion in the Middle Ages."

To Cecil Arthur Spring Rice

1603 H Street. 25 Feb. 1905

Dear Niece[1]

I waited for a letter before returning the enclosed, imagining that you would possibly give an address. Vain image! I should have known you better. So I return to your wife's address the despatch that she wasted on you.

I am grateful to you for reading my out-cryings of the atrophied. Indeed I know of no one but you and Mrs Winty and Martha who could have read them, and poor Martha could not help herself. Our world passionately interests me for the traits our women have discarded. Men of cold blood, as I figure them, never had these traits, and have driven them out of women. What sex will the American woman develop?

I get a singular pleasure in everything most strange to myself, and this is one reason for delighting in your oriental and Persian poetry[2] but I am most curious to know where it all began, because I am inclined to suspect that the earliest pre-Vedic poets must have been the best. The delight in complexicating thought (good word, that!) is an excessive refinement of complex society. To one who, in his heart, fears deep water and likes to boat on shallow streams, the greatest charm of art is just before the water becomes brackish. Oriental thought seems to me always elaborated. Our western thought seems to me always childlike. An Englishman, German or Norman (not intermarried with Jews) can no more think orientally than he can fly ornithologically. I know it because I can never do it myself after forty years of effort. We want to do it, but can't. I infer that thought never existed in northern races. It was the product of India or the Euphrates, and only trickled westward in drops to the Greeks.

Was ever anything so childlike as western Christianity? Put it in the present tense, if you like! Is any oriental capable of understanding how the western mind thinks in the Church of England? I take it that the Persian could understand the Virgin or the Trinity, as a decadence from his own principles, but could he follow the decadence down to its total disintegration?

I have been so long trying to catch this flying Thought by the tail, that I feel I must bag it before I cut out. I am clear that our western thought rapidly grows more complex, and in my own time has made a big stride. I incline to think that sixty years more at the same rate of movement will bring us close to the oriental mind. Radium was a violent shock which may not show its full effects for a generation. Marconi rays knocked us silly. My object in studying the 12th century was childish, for I wanted only to get the first term for the curve or acceleration of western thought, so that I could carry it down and project it into the future. The Unity—that is, the birth—of western thought, calculated by centuries, terminates in the complexity of orientalism just about a hundred years hence—three generations.

This is a historical view of Persianity, and I drop it. Since you left, we seem to be steadily drifting—drivelling—drowning. The exhibition is painful all round. We are all out of temper, mortified, furious with ourselves, and disgusted with each other. Russia is a simple nursery-tale compared with us, but as yet we are not murdering each other. The collapse of Russia in face of her energies would naturally precede our collapse, but at our acceleration we can not run our machine another thirty years without some similar convulsion. Complexity will trip us up. We are not made for it, and the Forces increase by the square of the velocity, while the Mind lags along barely as the legs walk.

I had momentary catalepsis last week when I suddenly saw Sir Mortimer walk into my den.[3] If these horrors can happen in a civilised state, what am I to expect in Satan's? Nevertheless I said it was probably your doing, and hid my horror. He was still harping on my daughter—I mean my niece—I mean you. I was a little impatient and asked him why he didn't have you ordered here if he wanted you so much. I gathered from his answers, that he was something like the late President Abraham Lincoln who said he had very little influence with this administration.

I ended by telling him that anyway he need not lie awake nights, for the government would wholly disappear after March 4, when the new people would have to learn their trade, and he would have no one to speak to till next December.[4] Sleep, pretty baby, sleep!

Need I say that I have no news and that I have more nieces than ever. The north is invading us in hordes of nieces for March 4. I have unloaded the freight on the White House in block. Bessy Lodge's baby Abélard had a close call last week with a throat, but pulled through, and they dine here tonight. Sister Ann's cough is worse—confound it! I want her to run away with me, but Micawber cannot be deserted.⁵ Hay is stalwart and runs me off my legs. I think no one knows anything about politics.

My homage to your wife.   Ever Yrs   Thos Aquinas

MS: Churchill College, Cambridge

1. Alluding to his gift of *Mont Saint Michel and Chartres,* HA kept up his fiction of an audience restricted to nieces.
2. *The Story of Valeh and Hadijeh,* translated from the Persian by Mirza Mahomed and Cecil Spring Rice (1903).
3. Sir Henry Mortimer Durand.
4. After the inauguration and a brief special session of the Senate to confirm presidential appointments, official Washington would remain relatively quiet until the Fifty-ninth Congress convened on Dec. 4.
5. "I never will desert Mr. Micawber"; Charles Dickens, *David Copperfield* (1849–1850), chap. 12.

To John Hay

23 Avenue du Bois de Boulogne
3 May, 1905

An attic in the wilderness is as good a place as any other celestial constellation for reading the diabolic squeals of our pigs in Pigsburg. I return the howl in another envelope.¹

Our dear scholar is bent on fear. Nothing shall calm him. Truly I am myself the biggest coward on earth, and I have lectured for a year on the mathematical certainty of general disturbance when a great vacuum is suddenly made in space. Also I hold that a further centralisation is logically due, and must of necessity tend towards the centre. What strikes me most is that I seem to be wrong.

This happens so rarely that you may perhaps never have noticed a case before, and even I am perplexed to account for it. Hitherto in my life I have been always right; it is other people who are wrong. I suspect this to be now the correct explanation. All that is eccentric, unexpected and irregular, is individual, accidental and negligeable. In this case, all such perturbations are due to the individual weaknesses of the two men who stand on top of the heap.² You may look over the whole world outside, and you will find no other sign of eccentric energies or inexplicable action—no! not even in Colorado among the bears.³ All is orderly,—even the cowboys.

Spring jumps to the conclusion that there can be no revolution among people who can't revolve.⁴ How much revolution makes a revolution for Springy, I don't know; but for my simple wants, as compared with eighteen months ago, eastern Europe has done about the most active bit of revolving as Europe has ever seen. One may be sure that it will go on, as long as the conditions, and especially the man, are constant.

The other case is more personal still. For ten years I have sat here and watched the intrigues to detach France from Russia and England and us. Suddenly and violently comes an explosion which flings France beyond all recovery into England's arms. Spring says it is the result of the eastern war.[5] The bank, which is run by the German Jews as the N.A. Review says (p. 562), suddenly sacrifices all its ten years' profits on the table, and plays a wild *coup* not in the least Judaic. Granting that it means war and a new centralisation,—Holland, Austria, Salonika, and what you like,—it is a wild *coup* still; a false move; a blunder, which betrays the whole vacillating direction of policy. It is mere idiosyncrasy. Had the Germans meant it seriously, they would not have made the scandal. If they made the scandal, they have nothing to gain by following it up with open warnings to all their neighbors to prepare for war. I infer that they have other things in mind. Germany's difficulties are always great. My preference is to disregard her manners,—which are, after all, not so bad as those of her neighbors have often been,— and help her all one can. Let her have her way! Why not! She has asked nothing very serious; she has only talked abruptly, and even this is apparent. She has been talking openly enough in private, all along.

I rather agree with Jaurez.[6] What he and I want is to make politics follow mass. We want our Atlantic system,—which extends from the Rocky Mountains, on the west, to the Elbe on the east, and developes nine tenths of the energy of the world,—to control France and Germany as far as it goes. Germany tries, and has always tried, to be independent, and she faces east, south, and west, jumps over our heads, and intrigues with every bankrupt beach-comber, to maintain a continental system like Napoleon's, independent of our's. The law of mass is against her, thus far, and, except in Silesia, she has no real balance to her western strain. All western Germany is American, Atlantic and anti-military. We need only to work with it, and help it to what it thinks it wants; and above all, to remove, as far as we can, the inevitable friction with France and England. This is the hardest job. Fear will not listen, and we can't tell which of all the powers is now the most scared. At any moment we may have a blind panic. Nothing saves us now but the Jew banking-interest.

I hope France and England will try to let Germany have her way. As yet she has asked for nothing very serious. The time must come when she will ask for Holland or Austria or the Baltic Provinces, or a strip of Poland. Her manners are almost as bad as those of England or France were, a hundred years ago; and this doubles the danger. One cannot discuss the matter beforehand. One hardly sees a means of preparing any solution at all. Yet war would be fatal to everyone, except perhaps to us; and victory would almost necessarily be fatal to Germany as well as to France and Europe. The difficulties of Germany are not such as war can relieve. Victory would only raise greater dangers and more enemies. What she needs is to emigrate into Russia.

Meanwhile my skies are still cold and my attic is solitude, and that brute of a chauffeur comes daily for orders.

———

MS: MHi

1. Spring Rice, in a letter to Hay from St. Petersburg on April 26 (MHi), had given his views on the rampant disorders there and on the crisis precipitated by the kaiser's speech of April 2, calling for equal rights with the French in Morocco.
2. Czar Nicholas II and Kaiser Wilhelm II.
3. Roosevelt was bear hunting in Colorado.
4. Spring Rice had written that he believed "in all sorts of horrors to come—murders & tumults & robberies—but not in an organized revolution."
5. "As soon as the Battle of Mukden is fought Germany declares publicly that she *has* interests in Morocco, that France has neglected them and that she intends to look after them" (Spring Rice to Hay, April 26, MHi).
6. Jean Jaurès, a socialist and internationalist, discounted German military policy.

To Margaret Chanler

23 Avenue du Bois de Boulogne
2 June, 1905

Dearly Beloved[1]
—if I may venture on so early Christian an expression with a proper respect for you and Winty,—your very kind letter of May 11 was followed at a long interval by the volume of Mr Henry Thode, though I may not understand why he does not go the whole hog Heinrich.[2] I have accordingly perused his Germanity on the subject that concerns us; but as I verge closer and closer to my seven-hundredth anniversary, the instinct to contradict a German becomes obsession. Truly I love all Germans, but they all have Mme de Stael's single fault.[3] Accuracy is their disease and professorship their antidote. I know not why I love St Francis better as an Umbrian, but I think it because I do not know what an Umbrian is.[4] At all events I feel almost sure it wasn't a German. Henry has spared us that.

You are wonderful! How can you do such things! If I were really of the Church, the only thing I would insist on would be that all the Germans should get out of it. Honestly I think you don't mind. The Church should have been so deeply grateful to Luther and Calvin and Knox and the rest, for ridding her of Germans and Swiss and Scotch and Dutch and all the most disagreeable people on earth! They all insist on our swallowing what they call Truth, which is always themselves *au lard*.

Do you ever read Kant? In the whole history of human thought, nothing so German ever was known. Kant was short of a God, and deliberately made one out of himself in his official character of German professor. His categorical imperative is the Dean of Königsberg. If any German,—not Jew,—had ever been endowed with a sense of humor, Kant would have been the noblest jest of Deity. He is the drollest of all serious solemnities. I don't get over him at all. Old as human conceit is, and weary as I am of it, Kant's simple-minded German-professorial conceit knocks me silly, not on account of Kant but on account of the German Kantists, who still keep it up, as solemnly as in the fifteenth century when the Professor reigned unchecked.

So let's leave our Francis an Assisian, and repudiate the Piche grandpapa. I've nothing against Piche, but I prefer Pica. After all, the southern French in those days were more Italian or Spanish than they were French. In any case he wasn't a Norman! Is it not curious that St Thomas, just his opposite, should have been both Norman and German?

All this is parenthesis, for I've no one to play with here, and none of my beautiful ladies ever heard of the twelfth century. I am swept down the torrent of hats. Whether Mrs Cooper Hewitt or Charlotte Sorchan, Mrs Tams, Mrs Henry Clews or the Brices know what hats are precisely right day by day, I gravely doubt, and I try to help them.[5] I've just run the Hays up to the Gare du Nord in my auto, and have seen them and Lady Herbert off for England. I ran the Brices down the Seine as far as the Andelys yesterday and showed them sixteenth century glass and we dined at Ritz afterwards. They disputed my views on hats. Certainly women *are* vain!

I have asked every woman here to elope with me daily, and have great hopes for some of them, no husbands being expected, but of course this is but idle play with their affections due only to you're being false. If you had come over, we could have had the chateau. As it is, even the Warders go to England. I dine in vain.[6]

The Lodges are in Florence, due here towards July. I am glad they put it off, for the confusion and noise here is now too buzzy for anyone but an imbecile with senile complications. It suits me, but my weakness of head becomes more marked every week, and I can't last long at the pace. You would laugh like a saint to see the queer things I do, and the way I get tied up. Laura will have to untie me.[7] Yet I've dozens of nieces here, all devoted to my best interests and earnest to nurse me en auto.

Come soon to save!

Ever Yrs   Henry Adams.

MS: MH

1. Margaret Terry (Mrs. Winthrop Astor) Chanler (1862–1947), musician and writer, intellectual friend of Edith Wharton.
2. Henry Thode, German art historian, *Franz von Assisi und die Anfänge der Kunst der Renaissance in Italien* (1885; rev. ed., 1904).
3. Mme. de Staël, *De l'Allemagne* (1810).
4. Thode argued that Pica, the mother of St. Francis, was Provençal.
5. Charlotte Hunnewell Sorchan (1872–1961), wife of Victor Sorchan and daughter of HA's college mate Hollis Hunnewell; Blanche Cruger Tams (c. 1860–1944), wife of James F. Tams (c. 1847–1928), architect and yachtsman; Lucy Worthington Clews (1852–1945), wife of Henry Clews, New York banker.
6. Ellen Ormsbee Warder and her daughters Elizabeth and Alice (1877–1952).
7. Laura Astor Chanler (1887–1984), daughter of Margaret and Winthrop Astor Chanler.

To Brooks Adams

23 Avenue du Bois de Boulogne
5 June, 1905.

My dear Brooks

I have kept your exceedingly kind letter on my table for a week or two, as I rather like to do with all letters that have a personal value, before answering them; because if I replied at once I might perhaps say the right thing, and in that case I should certainly be wrong. The right thing for you would be the wrong thing for me.[1]

This will be clear to you if you reflect a moment on the fact that you are, as far as we know, the only man in America whose opinion on this subject has any value; that is, whose opinion is decisive because it's all the opinion there is. No one else, to our knowledge, has been over the ground, or has tried to approach it from the same side. Setting aside a few women who have touched the emotional side, and a few architects or decorators who have never got far enough to touch anything, you are alone.

This is a singularly suggestive fact. You are alone, because it was you who shoved us into it. You started me ten years ago into this amusement. You mapped out the lines and indicated the emotions. In fact I should find it difficult to pick out of the volume what was yours from what was mine. The family mind approaches unity more nearly than is given to most of the works of God. You and I think so nearly on the same lines that, even when not directly interacting, the two minds run parallel, and you can hardly tell whether they are one or several.

For this reason I take your approval more or less as though it were my own, and I were praising my own work. As between you and me, your judgment is final, since there is no one competent to dispute it; but excepting this, it leaves both of us exactly where we were. You are a sufficient audience for me, since I know of no one else whose opinion I should seriously consider. As a matter of friendship I keep a few copies to give away as personal compliments, but not because the donees are competent to contest your judgment. I want, from time to time, some such means of showing a civility. It is cheaper than keeping an automobile to drive them, or a cook to feed them; yet I do both, and this comes in handy beside. But if you asked me to find out five hundred persons in the world to whom you would like to give the volume, I could say only that, as far as you and I know, five hundred do not exist,—nor half that number—nor a quarter of it.

"As far as you or I know," and I suspect we know of everybody worth knowing. Thousands of people exist who think they want to read. Barring a few Jews, they are incapable of reading fifty consecutive pages, or of following the thought if they did. I never yet heard of ten men who had ever read my history and never one who had read Hay's Lincoln.

Therefore I am inclined to think that I have got to be satisfied anyway with you for an audience, and it is more appreciative in me to say at once that you are audience enough. The reading-world will say what you do better without trying to read than with it. There are already some fifty copies afloat, and I'll bet ten to one that half of them have not been once read. Yet they've been given only to the most appreciative and cultivated personal friends.

Of course there are several hundred thousand persons in Boston and out of it, who are lecture-goers and frequent libraries; and there are one or two million young women who read poetry in Browning Clubs, and mostly come to Paris to study art when they can. I imagine that neither you nor I care much to be admired by these, but in any case they will admire us the more at second hand. We need not lift a finger to reach that class, who are quite passive, and mere mud-ponds of receptivity.

This sounds contemptuous to my fellow men, and perhaps it is so; but I am quite sure that whatever my fellow-men may say about it, or think they ought to say about it, both they and my fellow-women in their hearts agree with it, and will like me better for not being on sale.

Meanwhile, much else presses on the hungry generations and treads them down. I see dim new complexities rising on the horizon as we go, and I am pretty nearly out of my saddle, myself, barely clutching at empty air.

Probably you know how to run the caravan. I cannot say that I do. I can see very clearly a dozen ways for it to break its neck in the dark, but not one clear path. Not that I greatly care, for my own neck is pretty well broken already.

Love to Evelyn.   Ever   H.

MS: MH

1. "I have this moment finished your book . . . I perhaps alone of living men can appreciate fully all that you have done, for I have lived with the crusaders and the schoolmen—but this book of yours will stand, believe me, even in this dying age—for Henry, we are dying.

"I have now but one request to make. I think I have a right to insist, that you should put this work of yours, this crowning effort of our race, into a form where it can be read and preserved. I want you to publish an edition and let it be sold, or at least distributed to the libraries. You have no right to let the best thing we have ever done die" (BA to HA, May 12; MH).

To Clara Stone Hay

23 Avenue du Bois de Boulogne
4 July, 1905.

My dear Mrs Hay

I had not the heart to telegraph. All the world will have done that, and will have overwhelmed you with messages of condolence. I can say nothing. You will understand it. You made a superb effort, and I feel sure that it delayed the result for two or three months, but the doctors led us all wrong, and John was alone right. I am still aghast at their ignorance.

You still have duties and interests—growing ones—and a life of usefulness before you. My warmest good-wishes go with you. You are more essential than ever, because you are the sole remaining head and centre of the family. You cannot lay aside your active interests. As for me, it is time to bid good-bye. I am tired. My last hold on the world is lost with him. I am too old to make new efforts or care for new interests. I can no longer look a month ahead, or be sure of my hand or mind. I have clung on to his activities till now, because they were his, but except as his they have no concern for me, and I have no more strength for them. He and I began life together. We will stop together.

I have tried to catch Helen by letter, but take for granted that she must return to you at once.

Affectionately Yrs   Henry Adams.

MS: DLC, Hay

To Brooks Adams

23 Avenue du Bois de Boulogne
11 July, 1905

Dear Brooks

I return the deed, signed and witnessed, by this mail. I merely write to notify you.[1]

Yours from Woodstock dated the 2d arrives with Palfrey's.[2] I do not mean to answer it now, because it involves the universe, but I want to try to ask you to make an attempt to consider—before you commit yourself irretrievably to recommending any new panacea for society—that you had better hold your tongue. This is pure egotism on my part, equivalent to suggesting myself for imitation. Still, as a reasoned policy, I hold it to be scientific certainty. Your social *impasse* merely reflects the position of human thought altogether. No matter where you follow it, you reach the same diffusion. Chemistry would tell you the same; Physics the same; your own mind, the same. You will make matters worse by meddling with the United States Constitution or any other relic of ancient order. Within thirty years, man himself must make a big jump or break his neck. He must develop new mental power or perish. He has set in motion energies which he cannot control. It is he, you must develope, not the law or the machine.

Once more, thanks for what you say about the volume. I took the precaution to copyright it, in order to prevent its being copyrighted against me. As for piracy, I love to be pirated. It is the greatest compliment an author can have. The wholesale piracy of Democracy was the single real triumph of my life. Anyone may steal what he likes from me, and no one can do much better than has been done heretofore; but I don't want to be made *particeps criminis*. I don't want to steal my own property. I prefer to help him away with the swag.

Further, I regard it as immaterial about the volume because it is a question of a very short time. I've always told you I should not last beyond seventy. I doubt reaching that age—at least with normal faculties. Hay's death settles it. I am out of the game. In a year or two, the volume is yours—or my executors'—to sell or burn.

Love to your wife   H.A.

MS: MH

1. The deed established the Adams Manuscript Trust to run for fifty years. Although CFA2 proposed making the family papers accessible for educational purposes, BA prevailed in having them closed for the period of the trust. The papers were placed in the custody of

the Massachusetts Historical Society under control of the family trustees. At the end of the fifty-year period, the trustees made a gift of the papers to the Society.

2. John Gorham Palfrey had drawn up the "declaration of trust" under BA's direction and sent it separately.

To Theodore Roosevelt

Private and *Personal*.   23 Avenue du Bois de Boulogne
                                                       6 Nov. 1905

My dear Roosevelt

You have established a record as the best herder of Emperors since Napoleon. I should long ago have written you my gratitude had not men— and women—taught me to hold my tongue before my betters. On public affairs I am still a scholar, not a professor; and when I think I know enough to help you, I will do it; but for the present I am bothered most by private matters. You have taught us how to herd Emperors, but also you have shown that, of all cattle, Emperors are most easily herded. I need your views about the relative docility of Kings, Presidents of South American Republics, Railway Presidents and Senators, but mostly and immediately about Mr McNutt.[1]

Of Mr McNutt, I know, of my own knowledge, only that he has held official station under the United States Government and under His Holiness the Pope. I had hoped to know no more of him. At the cost of a shock verging on apoplexy I have been obliged to hear that he is about to sail for New York on the 18th in the "Amerika," and that, after transacting some private business, he hopes to visit Washington.

If you think it necessary to let Mr McNutt enter your fold, and frolic with your lambs in the Senate and House, I shall still have to ask you what your neighbors on La Fayette Square are to say about him, if asked; for this is a case where we must carefully conform to the Law and particularly to the Prophets of the White House.

I am not concerned about my own social relations. You know that I have none. My fear is that the sudden appearance of Mr McNutt in La Fayette Square might give public annoyance to persons whom we would rather protect than expose,—among others, to his harmless wife.[2] The press is pitiless. You know how audaciously violent our newspapers are, when they are seized by virtue; a sublime spectacle; but loftier than convenient for those who are underneath, and receive the filth.

Possibly a word from you, conveyed in private, through a proper agent,— by preference in the church hierarchy,—might prevent the visit to Washington. You know all about it. I know next to nothing.

I hope to reach Washington as usual in time to help you open Congress and exhort the impenitent. I have now no one else to help.

Ever Yrs   Henry Adams.

MS: DLC, Roosevelt.

1. Francis A. MacNutt (1863–1927), an American resident in Rome and a papal chamberlain. Found guilty of unspecified "disorderly conduct," he was dismissed from his post. The rumors about the scandalous nature of his misconduct appear to have shocked HA.
2. Margaret Van Cortlandt MacNutt (1851–1936).

VI

The Benevolent Sage
1906–1918

THE PRIVATELY PRINTED *Mont Saint Michel and Chartres* that Adams sent to his circle of friends and relatives in 1905 elicited an admiring chorus of appreciation which was followed by discreet entreaties by outsiders for copies. He was already well advanced in the writing of the autobiographical sequel that would introduce his "Dynamic Theory of History." Whereas he had made occasional allusions in his letters to his progress on the Chartres manuscript, he was completely secretive about *The Education of Henry Adams* except for a few cryptic hints. It was a prudent precaution, for persons familiar with his satiric chaff might well have worried among themselves at the figure they would cut.

When the privately printed *Education* went out to his confidants early in 1907, he insisted that it was merely a draft lent for their criticism, correction, and censorship. Scarcely a handful of the fortunate recipients took him seriously and returned their copies. He professed to fear only the judgment of Charles W. Eliot, perhaps remembering his refusal to accept Eliot's offer of an honorary degree. Eliot returned the book without comment. Long afterward he was heard to say, "An overrated man and a much overrated book." Many of those first readers, baffled by the philosophical drift of the *Education,* succeeded in extracting from him a variety of figurative explanations calculated to send them back bemused to his text.

As Adams approached seventy he felt increasingly that time was running out for him. In his mind there loomed menacingly the recollection that his father had showed signs of the onset of senility at seventy-three. This sense of impending danger accompanied his curious feeling that his had been a posthumous existence since his wife's death in 1885. He had worn his bereavement as a protective shield against the disturbing world and often expressed the wish that he could escape and join his wife beneath the Saint-Gaudens monument. These mortuary reflections were reinforced for him now by the signs of a disintegratinig society on almost every continent.

Time was indeed growing shorter, and there was all the more need to pierce the veil of the future even if as an impotent Cassandra. His scientific theorizing about the future of mankind needed more precise calculation. He therefore plunged into the study of higher mathematics and the latest theories in the physical sciences, psychology, and sociology. The result was an essay, "The Rule of Phase Applied to History," in which he bowed rather distantly to Josiah Willard Gibbs's recondite theory, but he soon laid it aside unprinted for the more devastating metaphor suggested by the Second Law of Thermodynamics and the principle of entropy. Discarding the abstruse mathematical formulations which lay beyond his range, he seized upon the general idea of entropy, the irreversible movement of heat from a hotter body to a colder one, to symbolize the inexorable degradation of all energy in the world, both physical and mental. He kept a sharp lookout for every sign in scientific literature and the daily press of social and psychological deterioration and poured them all into a small book demonstrating that the steady degradation of civilization was like that of "a clockwork that is running down." He titled the book *A Letter to American Teachers of History* and distributed it broadcast to academia in 1910 as a cautionary guide for historians to help society to face its desperate future. To his disgust, academia proved impervious to his advice.

During this period Adams also helped to produce an edition of the letters of John Hay that his widow emasculated by identifying persons in largely impenetrable initials. Another task, which he accepted from the Lodge family, was the preparation of a biography of the poet George Cabot Lodge, whom he had cultivated among his Paris circle as a promising disciple. Bay Lodge had died in 1909 at the age of thirty-five of a heart attack. Published in 1911, the biography was a graceful if rather wintry memorial to the dead poet.

All this cerebral activity accompanied his social responsibilities to his nieces, real and imaginery, at home and abroad. He kept them and his other correspondents diverted with irreverent and whimsical chaff. In Paris he squired his various "wives," as Edith Wharton termed them, to the fashionable tables at the Ritz and to other elegant restaurants in the Bois. With his archaeologist friend Henri Hubert of the ethnological museum at Saint-Germain-en-Laye he discussed the progress of the search for Cro-Magnon man in the caves at Les Eyzies, a project which Adams helped finance. He also became addicted to the motorcar in his sojourns in France and as their erudite guide carried off his guests to the Gothic churches of Normandy.

Global politics no longer preoccupied him, for the deepening tensions among the powers and the recurring wars in Europe, Africa, and Asia simply confirmed his long-standing diagnosis of impending disaster. He turned with relief to the partial revision of the *Chartres* and reprinted it in a private edition in 1912. In the spring of that year he suffered a stroke that after a few months left him with a trace of paralysis. Strength returned and zest for a new hobby, the recovery of Old French *chansons* which his talented young companion Aileen Tone played and sang for him and his visitors.

Driven back to Washington from France by the outbreak of World War I, he resumed his role as benevolent sage, and, though advancing age and infirmities gradually restricted activity, his "breakfasts" continued to attract political leaders and foreign dignitaries. He welcomed America's entrance into the war as a step in forming the "Atlantic Alliance" of which he had dreamed. His running commentary on the life about him lost none of its bite even when, no longer able to hold a pen, he was obliged to dictate his letters. In the last letter he dictated, two weeks before his death on March 27, 1918, he stoically declared, "I am one of the lucky ones who have got through with the game and care nothing, any more, for my stakes in it."

Henry Adams lies beside his wife in Rock Creek Cemetery. The only identification of the gravesite is Saint-Gaudens' enigmatic figure in its hooded cloak.

To Isabella Stewart Gardner

Knickerbocker Club   9 Feb. 1906

My dear Mrs Gardner[1]

You have given me a great pleasure and greater astonishment. You will not feel it strange that I should write to thank you for it.[2] Not that I know what to say that could be new to you, but that you can have no objection to hearing the same things said and re-said.

As long as such a work can be done, I will not despair of our age, though I do not think anyone else could have done it. You stand quite alone. Only I must admit that no one has ever done it before you, though many have tried. If I were obliged to treat it like the scientific gentlemen of our world who preach of Evolution, I should have to say that your work must be classed as a *tour-de-force*,—no Evolution at all,—but pure Special Creation in an adverse environment. You are a creator, and stand alone.

Creators are so rare as to have no atmosphere to live in, but must create it all. You would have been almost equally alone two thousand years ago. America is a terribly pathetic picture to anyone who wants something else, but it is hardly worse off than Germany or Sweden or Russia or England have nearly always been; only the reasons are different. We are not quite so stupid and impenetrable as some. We can, in a certain proportion,—say one or two in a hundred,—feel what you do and have done.

All the same, this living with one or two in a hundred—or a thousand— is living in a rarified air. The effect of an hour with you is that of the Absolute,—vertigo,—loss of relation,—absence in space, time and thought. It is peace, repose or dream, rather like opium; but the return to air and dust is painful. It hurts me. I feel as though you must need something,— not exactly help or flattery or even admiration,—but subjects.

I bring you the only offering I can, which is thanks.

Ever truly Yrs   Henry Adams.

MS: Isabella Stewart Gardner Museum

1. Isabella Stewart Gardner (1840–1924), wife of John Lowell Gardner of Boston (1837– 1898), daughter of New York merchant prince David Stewart. She was a Boston social figure noted for her imperious ways. Her great art collection contained many masterpieces of Italian Renaissance painting.
2. HA, in Boston for the wedding of his niece Dorothy Quincy, had just seen for the first time Fenway Court, the Italianate palace built (1899–1903) by Isabella Gardner to house her art collection.

To Charles Franklin Thwing

1603 H Street. 19 Feb. 1906.

My dear Master

I found your card and was sorry to miss you. I wanted to chaff you unmercifully about your Hay memorial, but I reflected and was mute.[1] Only too well I knew that if I were in your place I should do the same thing. What is the use of talking about it? Does not our dear press and our pure legislature resound with virtue, and denounce graft? they got the money, and can afford now to kill the men they blackmailed? Colleges and churches are at least clean of hands. They get precious little money, and kill nobody but themselves.

I thought of Hay's wrath at being used that way, and smiled, because at my age friends never die, and I never admit that anyone is dead, if they were mine. We are a big majority on the other side, and can afford to laugh. I laugh most at the idea of my giving money to anyone but a street-beggar. The self-conceit of money-giving is a marvel. Mr Rockefeller may properly give. So may anyone else whose means are double his demands; but we modest wretches who never have enough to make our nieces a square meal and who write history too, would show culpable vanity by giving. Come along soon, and I will lecture some more.

Ever Yrs   Henry Adams.

MS: OCIW

1. Thwing had written HA proposing to establish as a memorial to Hay a fund to purchase books for the Western Reserve University library.

To Brooks Adams

1603 H Street 12 April, 1906.

My dear Brooks

You are obviously right in feeling discouragement. I suspect that God Almighty felt some discouraged, after all his trouble, when Eve played him that apple-trick. His remarks indicate it. Touching, in historic sequence, on every considerable person who has tried to run the Cosmos since, including God the Son and God the Holy Ghost, I note a general tone of discouragement until you get down to Mr Albert J. Beveridge and other great statesmen who are paid to be optimists.[1] At moments I have felt brief intervals of doubt myself, though never lasting. I notice a kind of tired look even on the face of our President. If I offered advice, which I never do, I should advise yielding to it. God tried drowning out the world once, but it did no kind of good, and there are said to be four-hundred-and-fifty thousand Jews now doing Kosher in New York alone. God himself owned failure.

Under these circumstances I see no shame in owning failure too. Nobody seems to care whether I do or not, and I cannot, for the life of me, see why I am called upon to instruct them. If any damneder fools ever lived on earth than my generation of Americans, my laborious studies have not discovered them, and the proof is that they were self-satisfied beyond record. Nothing could teach them better. Why try?

But please give up that profoundly unscientific jabber of the newspapers about MONEY in capital letters.[2] What I see is POWER in capitals also. You may abolish money and all its machinery, the Power will still be there, and you will have to trapeze after it in the future just as the world has always done in the past. On the whole, our generation has suffered least of any. The next can run its own machine.

Before I quit these shores on May 5, I will send Chartres to the Athenaeum, the City Library and Harvard College. Everyone has read it now who is interested in the subject, and it may as well be forgotten in Libraries. I will put a couple of copies for you with the Bérard, and you can do what you like with them, but I will myself take care of the Athenaeum.

Faith is my only everlasting staff, and I rarely find it fail. My faith in Man is absolute, and if greater in one respect than another, it is greatest in 23 Court Street.[3] Whether I have any concern in it still, I do not know, but clearly it has none in me. It is like my publishers. Never a sign of an account do I get.

Love to your wife   Ever Yrs   H.

MS: MH

1. Albert Jeremiah Beveridge (1862–1927) of Indiana, Republican senator 1899–1911, was an enthusiastic advocate of U.S. imperialism.
2. "There is no coherence in anything except money, and I can see nothing before us now but a complete reorganization on the money basis . . . The President has been unable to organize any coherent opposition to money and the result will be to turn the courts into the exponent of money" (BA to HA, April 10, MH).
3. The Adams Building, where BA maintained the Adams family offices, was at 23 Court Street, Boston.

To Charles Milnes Gaskell

1603 H Street   23 April, 1906.

My dear Carlo

Your letter of the 17th arrives just as I am closing up to depart. I sail next Saturday, and should be established at No. 23 Ave. du Bois this day fortnight. I rather hanker to get over to you, but perhaps I had better wait till summer. If I dared, I would come *en auto* and harry you out of Wenlock, but I am quite senile. Any new exploit scares me.

Your old friends are of the heroic age. Sir John is Shakespearian. Here I am alone. Everyone is dead. Yesterday I was struck by seeing my own name in the columns of the New York Times, mentioned as *the late* H.A. *Tant mieux!* At least it is over, and *nil nisi.*[1] Please read Horace Walpole again and note his ridiculous affectations of age—and everything else, for that matter. I pardon nobody for bad Gothic and Venetian taste. Yet I once read Ruskin and admired! we even read Carlisle and followed! Lord, but we date!

My winter has been more mundane and yet more solitary than ever. Politically I am extinct. Domestic reform drivels. Reformers are always bores, as we knew in our youth, except when we meet our Gladstone's who are worse. Theodore Roosevelt is amusing at least, and I find him exceedingly conservative, but he scares the timid wayfarer into fits. He talks of measures that ought to have been taken of course fifty years ago, and that all Europe adopted in our youth; and all our shop-keepers shudder. Talk of bourgeois, shop-keepers, middle-class and philistines! Come here and study them! Nobody ever knew them till now!

To me, it is all one. I listen and assent to everybody. Why should I care? San Francisco burned down, last week, and I have been searching the reports to learn whether the whole city contained one object that cannot be replaced better in six months.[2] As yet I've heard of nothing. Only the Stanford University at Palo Alto was a very charming group of buildings, and I'm sorry it is hurt. Yet San Francisco on the whole was the most interesting city west of the Mississippi. I was fond of it, and my generation made it. It produced many of my best friends and had more style than any town in the east.

What is the end of doubling up our steam- and electric power every five years to infinity if we don't increase thought-power? As I see it, the society of today shows no more thought-power than in our youth, though it showed precious little then. To me, the whole lesson lies in this experiment. Can our society double up its mind-capacity? It must do it or die; and I see no reason why it may not widen its consciousness of complex conditions far enough to escape wreck; but it must hurry. Our power is always running ahead of our mind, especially here.

It's rather fun to see our successors tackle it. But, Lord, how silly we are.

Ever Yrs   Henry Adams.

MS: MHi

1. *De mortuis nil nisi bonum:* about the dead speak nothing but good.
2. The San Francisco earthquake and fire occurred on April 18.

To Lord Curzon

23 Avenue du Bois de Boulogne

30 July 1906

Dear Lord Curzon

I had not the heart to write to you while the whole world was overwhelming you with condolence, and even now I write rather to quiet my own memories than with any idea of quieting your pain.[1] Twenty years ago when I went through the same suffering, I found relief only in the sudden revelation that I was not alone; that others were nursing the same acute memory of intolerable loss, like a secret society that silently opened its arms to let me in. I have lived in it ever since, and in twenty years search have found no other life worth an effort; but this is my weakness, and I sincerely trust will not be yours.

I cannot talk of her. What you would say, I should only repeat. Some visions are too radiant for words. When they fade, they leave life colorless. I do not understand how we bear such suffering as we do when we lose them; but we have to be silent, for no expression approaches the pain. You know it all now. If you can put it in words you will speak not only for yourself, but for all of us who suffer.

I owe myself these few lines. Forgive their weakness.

Ever truly Yrs   Henry Adams

MS: Lady Alexandra Metcalfe
1. Lady Curzon had died July 18.

To Charles Milnes Gaskell

23 Avenue du Bois de Boulogne
1 Nov. 1906.

My dear Carlo

Thanks for your farewell note.[1] The compliment which the Minister paid you is your due, and yet not the less gratifying, since dues are not always paid. It pleases me, as much as it does you, to see my judgment in men affirmed by the world, and I am not disturbed by the Privy Council affair which seems to me natural and reasonable. I think the P.M. is right. If he took into the Privy Council anyone outside of the servants of the Crown, he would upset the institution.[2]

I am much more in doubt as to your refusal of a peerage. I should have refused, certainly, for the same reasons, but I have no family to decide for. Your children are poor judges of their own interests, and you must in effect always decide for them.[3] Lord Houghton's case was our chief lesson in this line of life.[4] What is the market value of a peerage today? What will it be, fifty years hence? The market has its values for this, as for all other assets, and till one knows what this value is, one cannot know what one is refusing.

In our youth, the old or new levelling doctrines led us to the self-denying practices of Stoicism and Jesuitism. In age, I incline to think that science— the science of a mechanical theory of the universe—regards the Stoics as merely a form of self-conscious misconception both of oneself and of mankind. The true ideal of the future is the average, as the socialist sees it; and if the average includes social values, the future inclines us to accept them.

I admit that they have no values for you. At our age, all responsibilities merely wear out our nervous systems. I have seen it with all my friends. One by one the heavily weighted have broken down. Yet a peerage cannot be a very severe weight; though, if I remember right, the West Riding has hardly its share of them; but I think of it forty years ago.

Personally I am rather glad not to have to learn a new name for you. I am always forgetting my friends titles.

I shall be again on my way before you receive this letter, and look forward to another winter of vanishing interests. I have won all the political stakes my youth played for, and have seen every object more than attained. The next game belongs to its own players, who seem to see it fairly well. What no one can see is the effect of indefinitely cheapening mechanical power. Costless energy will be a condition new to nature. I worship it in the form of a bomb. Others call it the auto-bus.

Give my regards to all yours. Honestly I mean to come over to see them next summer.

Ever Yrs   Henry Adams.

MS: MHi

1. Gaskell and his wife had returned to England after seeing HA in Paris in late October.
2. Prime Minister Sir Henry Campbell-Bannerman (1836–1908) had offered Gaskell a peerage. Whether he had also offered him the honor of becoming a privy councillor is unclear.
3. Campbell-Bannerman wrote Lord Ripon, leader of the Liberal party, that Gaskell may have been influenced in his decision not to accept the barony because "It wd. involve a step down for his wife & also for his dau.-in-law," both of whom were daughters of earls (Oct. 27, 1906; quoted in John Wilson, *CB: A Life of Sir Henry Campbell-Bannerman* [1973], p. 580).
4. Robert Pemberton Milnes had refused the peerage offered him in 1856. In 1863 his son Richard Monckton Milnes, presented with the same offer, accepted the honor.

To Margaret Chanler

1603 H Street   23 Nov. 1906.

The happy saints alone know,—oh Lady of Light,—how much I have missed and needed you, or how dark my world is without you, but Winty need not be jealous, or do the Thaw business.[1] At my age, the regret is because of the future which disappears so fast. I pass my time calculating the chances that remain of ever renewing one's quatre-vingt *ans*. I am glued to my table here; the machine has begun to revolve, and I spin. On reaching New York last week I telephoned all round—to Miss Marbury, Mrs Jones, and so on,—but they were all silent and absent.[2] Not one of you was in reach. I fled to Washington for resource. Now I am engaged with guests straight ahead, and if you were only one of the guests, life would be gay. You had better come to me.

My dreary hours of ennui last summer were drifted far back of our twelfth century. I read nothing but third and fourth,—fascinating and lurid,—full of St Augustine, St Jerome, St John Chrysostome and the Alexandrians. It is highly amusing, but for edification, not to be recommended. On the whole, one would not be an early Christian. Indeed, if the saints' language about each other may be trusted, one would rather not be a saint. Even dogma, in the atmosphere of Constantinople and Ephesus, lacks charity. I mention this only to excuse my disappearance from our twelfth century, which, by comparison, seems so modern. The eastern patriarchs were more amusing than our mild western beatitudes, and the way they murdered each other helps out Chicago manners.[3]

You are going to Paris,—nicht wahr?—you and Mrs Wharton, and will find the Church persecuted anew, but the humorous side very much in evidence.[4] My Church friends were dumb. You can imagine Suzanne Carroll, Mrs Bellamy Storer, Mrs Walter Gay and Bessie Marbury, in face of the *non possumus*.[5] My business in life is now that of a retired father, with charity to all, but the worst of retirement is that *ennui* has no resource but humor. The American *possum* is not *non*, and can always climb a tree when he must, but he makes one laugh at his expression of features.

Nothing matters much! if I could find the proper classical expression for this maxim I would have it engraved on the door of the White House and embroidered on the President's pajamas. But we are learning.

Come on! I can offer you no gaiety, but a sense of duty should be enough. You are bound to sacrifice yourself to save souls.

Ever Yrs   Henry Adams.

MS: MH

1. On June 23, 1906, Harry Kendall Thaw (1871–1947) had shot and killed Stanford White in a jealous rage over a woman.
2. Mary Cadwalader Rawle (Mrs. Frederic R.) Jones (1850–1935), close friend of Henry James, the Roosevelts, and Edith Wharton (her sister-in-law), was noted for her informal salon in New York City.
3. The so-called Robber Council, convened at Ephesus in 449, was marked by violence. When Flavian, patriarch of Consantinople, denied the authority of the council, he was beaten by soldiers and died soon after. The just-reported murder and suicide of a Chicago businessman and his actress wife reflected Chicago manners.
4. Edith Wharton (Edith Newbold Jones) (1863–1937), novelist, author of the recently published *House of Mirth*, a central figure in the upper-class Anglo-American colony in Paris, tended toward agnosticism. Margaret Chanler was a devout Catholic. The disestablishment of the Catholic church in France under the 1905 Law of Separation encountered varying degrees of resistance.
5. Maria L. (Mrs. Bellamy) Storer (1849–1932), a Catholic convert, had been active in Vatican politics; Matilda Travers Gay (1856–1943), wife of Walter Gay (1856–1937), American art collector and painter. *Non possumus* (not possible) refers to Pope Pius X's refusal to allow French bishops to form religious associations to take title to church property as required by the Law of Separation.

To Mary Cadwalader Jones

1603 H Street   10 Jan. 1907.

Dear Lady

I feared things might be proceeding to slow music, so, like the abject coward that I am, I pulled the bed-clothes over my head and shivered. Never again will I stand up in the ranks. I've been shot at, all I want, and now I've lain down to die like a gentleman, and will never pretend to be alive again. The truth is, I've made mighty little pretence at it, these twenty years, but this time it's going to strike seventy and I won't. I've but one thought, and that is to clear out with a courtesy, like a well-bred young woman.

This accounts for all my lapses and laches, and I wish you would explain it to Mrs Schuyler.[1] To me the dead are the only live companions; I live with them almost wholly, and when two or three more have gone, I shall live with them entirely. I have no longer any sense of parting or distress or despair, and nothing more to say. The world goes its way, and I am left behind with every body I ever cared for, as outside of life as they. I wish I could help Mrs Schuyler to reach this Nirvana without passing through the acute stage of suffering; but if she could do that, she would not need the Nirvana, and, at best, words count only for instants. When I was in the same need, twenty years ago, the only glimpse of real relief I found was the discovery that everyone else seemed suddenly to turn round and tell me that they were all in it; that each of them had been through some loss that never left their minds. Since then, life has had to me an outside and inside for everyone, and one does not need to talk about it to know that we all feel.

Mostly just now the young seem most to need help, and all of them are breaking down like one's own automobiles. It is going on to a year since Mabel La Farge caved in.[2] She is still, like me, telling her family, the universe in general, that she must not be agitated. Beatrix was much in the swim.[3] I get pathetic tales from Mrs Tams about her anxieties for Violet.[4] Health is rare, and happiness does not seem to rage like pneumonia or murder, but I could get on, even in abject solitude, if I had a clear conscience. My form of nervous collapse is in thinking of my sins, chiefly social and mostly of omission. What joy must Mrs Bellamy have in the certainty of right![5]

Poor La Farge![6] I've been afraid to write to him, only to invite him to renew his nightly tale. It must be horrid enough without writing.

Ever Yrs   Henry Adams

MS: MHi

1. Harriet Lowndes Schuyler (1843–1915). Her husband, Gen. Philip Schuyler (1836–1906), had been killed in a train wreck Nov. 29, 1906.
2. Allusion to her nervous breakdown.
3. Beatrix ("Trix") Cadwalader Jones (1872–1959), daughter of Mary Cadwalader Jones and Frederic Rhinelander Jones (a brother of Edith Wharton) and later wife of Max Farrand, was a landscape gardener.
4. Violet D. Cruger (d. 1944), daughter of Blanche Spedden Cruger Tams and her first husband, Eugene Cruger.
5. Maria Storer's involvement in Vatican politics had embarrassed President Roosevelt. On her refusal to desist, he recalled her husband from his diplomatic post in Rome. To defend himself and his wife, Storer published a pamphlet quoting from Roosevelt's letters to the two of them.
6. John La Farge had had a nervous breakdown and was confined in a Providence asylum.

To *Whitelaw Reid*

1603 H Street   12 Feb. 1907.

My dear Mr Reid[1]

In Mrs Hay's absence, I venture to acknowledge yours of the 1st.[2]

You have to settle the same difficulties that fret me. I feel no great hesitation in ignoring the order to "burn when read," because I believe it meant only as a safe-guard during his life-time, and if I wrote it on letters of my own, I should regard it as equivalent to "personal" or "private"; but I feel more hesitation about allusions to persons, dead or living, public or private. There I think Mrs Hay would probably prefer that you should edit the letters yourself, and send only what you pass.

As editor I have always strained liberality of assent. No editor ever spared any one of my family that I know of, and, in return, we have commonly printed all that concerned other people. Whether this state of war ever injured anyone I do not know; but it lasts to this day, and makes me rather indifferent to conventional restraints. On the other hand we have never willingly hurt anyone's feelings, and yet have sometimes been compelled to do it.

Therefore it will certainly be better for you to do your own editing. Anyway, I act for the present, only as a sort of reservoir for collection, and have merely to receive what you choose to offer. I fear rather want of civil-war and reconstruction material.

Ever Yrs   Henry Adams.

11:30 A.M.

P.S. On beginning to read over the package of letters,—to me most deeply interesting,—of the Tribune period, in the seventies, I am arrested—short—by your correspondence about declining the Berlin mission in 1879. Hay's letter to you of March 30, 1879, is wholly dependent on your exceedingly interesting letter to him of March 20. May I take extracts from that? I admit that the tripartite correspondence between Evarts, Hay and you delights me all round, and that I much wish to print it all; but at least I would like a copy of it. What do you think? Might the whole be used?

H.A.

MS: DLC, Reid.

1. Reid had become U.S. ambassador to Great Britain.
2. HA had agreed to help John Hay's widow prepare an edition of his letters.

To Theodore Roosevelt

1603 H Street   March. 11. 1907

My dear Roosevelt

Trained to abject submission under the iron heel of despotism, I shall submit to your tyranny willingly if you only pull the boy through and yourselves.[1] You have given us a 60-horse-power Daimler-Mercédes fright, and have shaken our nerves like a railway collision. Please consider our future under Fairbanks![2] I don't want—any more than Charles II did—to begin my travels again.[3]

Having passed your censorship, and Cabot's, and Speck's, I have a greater than you all to face,—Charles Eliot's! I am still trembling before him as though I were always an undergraduate, while the thunders and lightnings of my own family are as gentle cooing of doves. If they scold or sneer, I can happily suppress the whole thing, as is my wont; but Charles Eliot's sentence will be damnation forever.

Love to Mrs Roosevelt and the boys

Ever truly   Henry Adams.

MS: DLC, Roosevelt

1. HA had professed, with how much tongue in cheek can only be guessed, that he expected the recipients of the *Education* to return the volume with their corrections and emendations. Roosevelt had replied that he would neither return nor correct the volume. Roosevelt's son Archibald had been dangerously ill, and the Roosevelts had suffered great anxiety.
2. Charles W. Fairbanks (1852–1918), U.S. vice-president.
3. England's Charles II (1630–1685) was twice driven into exile.

To Elizabeth Cameron

1603 H Street   13 March, 1907.

You are kind as ever, and I am as obliged as always, but you have hit on the only moment of the year when my knots are tied up beyond loosing. Everything centres on the last week in March. I am fixed.

For a wreck, I am much tossed about. You see in the papers all the news that concerns the public, but nothing about our noses, eyes, ears, &c, which concerns the private interests of our friends. Sister Ann came in yesterday to breakfast and we compared noses, as I do with Mme Jusserand. Sister Ann's eyes, or optic nerves, have gone back on her, so she is going to Boston to help nurse Mrs Luce, but wants to sail for Europe if she can, and try to pick up. The Specks are going for a severe arsenic cure.[1] I am dodging Bryce dinners all over the place.[2] Elsie comes today. Ellen Hooper on Monday. The Opera on the 28th. Looly has departed, and Brooks is due on the 25th for his argument.[3] The weather has been very bad, and the snow still clings to us.

Mr Cameron writes me a note granting the *imprimatur,* and the President and Cabot have also passed the permission; but I am far from willing to publish, and am driven to it only as defence against the pressure to write a memoir of Hay, which I will not do, not on my account but on his. All memoirs lower the man in estimation. Such a side-light is alone artistic. Yet I would gladly wipe out all that is said about his friends and contemporaries if it were possible to keep an atmosphere without it. If any of them, from the President and Cabot and your husband downwards would hint a wish to be left out, I would do it gladly; and still more gladly would omit myself. To gibbet myself for a friend's sake is no agreeable thing, and must be disguised by all sorts of ornaments and flourishes, landscape backgrounds, and weeping Magdalens.

Thus far, no one has objected, not even my brother Charles as yet, or Brooks, though I expect protests from them, not so much on their account as on mine. They will certainly point out to me what I am pointing out to you,—that my art fails of its effect. In that case I can still suppress the whole thing, and stand ready to do so at a moment's notice. Cabot is the worst treated, but is lamblike, and John weeps that I have spoiled it all, and hopelessly ruined its good discipline for him, by concluding that he "interests."[4]

Bessy has just sent down the baby, and I have admitted her to Dr Dobbitt's school, to her vast excitement.

MS: MHi

1. HA refers to Levico, Austria, a spa with arsenical springs.
2. James Bryce (1838–1922) was the new British ambassador to the U.S.
3. BA was going to argue the *Endeavor* case before the Court of Claims; it was, however, postponed.
4. John Lodge, a son highly critical of his father.

To Henry White

1603 H Street   March 26, 1907

My dear White

Your letter of the 16th arrived yesterday, and the package has just come. I have barely had time to read over the letters.

Naturally as a sub-editor I am greatly tempted to print everything, but am worse bound to advise Mrs Hay against it. Although I imagine that Cabot knows what kind of treatment to expect, a good many others, like Whitelaw Reid, would be unpleasantly surprised. Even governments like England and Russia might find certain epithets keen.

And yet—! What do you really think? I fear I can hardly resist the letter of May 22, 1903 about Cassini, Lamsdorf and the secret treaty.[1] Russia has so gone by the board since then that no one but Cassini would be affected. I would pay handsomely to hear Cassini tell his own story about the Manchurian business; for I feel confident it would be more severe than Hay's. More and more I suspect that Cassini was deliberately sacrificed by his Manchurian gang, but I doubt if he will ever tell the story.

As for the Senate as a whole, Hay's comments were so general and so free that an editor had better not try to conceal them. A dozen letters are on end in the heap, each more bitter than the other. Everyone knows how Hay felt and talked. The best way is to show him justified.

Mrs Hay is still in California, and I shall turn over to her the whole material I have sifted out from the mass, since she went off, for her to take opinions about it during the summer. As soon as this is done, I expect to sail for Paris, say about May 1st, or earlier if any of my habitual lady-protectors carry me away under their kindly wings. I am old and imbecile, and need coddling. This work over one's friends' dead bones is not cheery. Not that anything matters much now, but the constant load of depression is wearisome. To beguile my mind with cheerful and juvenile gaiety I can only cast up quips and jests with my last surviving contemporary, my neighbor Sam Ward—now ninety-odd.[2]

So you may expect me in Paris about May 1, curious to know how you will have solved your house-problem. I hope Mrs Cameron may bring me.

Anyway I hope to find you and Mrs White contented with what the Lord grants—such as it is.[3]

The general impression of this town is that we all feel tired. Three or four persons close to the President have assured me that, for the first time, even he complains of fatigue, and shows it. Wall Street shows it a little too much for good manners. As I pass my life trying to avoid knowing things, and am now quite without means of hearing anything, I can give you no notion what is passing over my head, but I suspect it to be chiefly fatigue and a free saturation of ignorance. The President is trying to find out what effect a dose of hard times and unemployed labor will have on the republican vote. For the first time, he is transparently hesitating.

The Lodges are in Boston. James Bryce has begun his spell-binding career. Speck and Jusserand soon start oceanwards. We are at peace. I hope it also for you and Mrs White.

Ever Yrs   H.A.

MS: NNC, Nevins

1. In April 1903 Russia had made evacuation of Manchuria conditional on a seven-point convention that it was secretly forcing on China. Hay revealed in his letter to White that the United States had a verbatim copy of the convention, the existence of which Cassini officially denied.
2. Samuel Gray Ward (1817–1907), onetime American representative of the Baring Brothers bank.
3. Margaret Stuyvesant Rutherford White (d. 1916), wife of Henry White.

To Mary Cadwalader Jones

1603 H Street
Thursday, 11. [April 1907]

Dear Lady

Your letter of yesterday, just received, is a great relief to me, for I began to imagine a thousand terrors, of which the least was a summons to everybody's funeral, beginning with you, Trix and Harry Thaw. Now I feel better, and hope to save you all.

The more because I have been in abject terror about that new volume, and on the point of throwing it into the fire once for all. I imagined even La Farge outraged in feelings, and St Gaudens furious for my blood. I've not yet sent it to St Gaudens for his permission because I did not know where to find him. Everybody else, except Milnes Gaskell, has assented either expressly or in silence, but I've not yet felt at liberty to take into my confidence any but those with whose names I've taken a liberty. I will send you a copy, but don't betray me! You shall count as *belle-soeur!*

Please bear in mind that I don't mean any harm. The motive of the first part is to acquit my conscience about my father. That of the second part is to acquit my conscience about Hay. *Ego* exists only for the last three chapters, which tie on to the last three chapters of Chartres, as my little say in life. Properly you should read these six essays as one, and the rest as prelude, background, detail or side-light.

With that—and St Gauden's figure—adoo! I'll dine on the 26th if you still approve.

Ever Yrs   Henry Adams.

MS: MHi

To Charles Milnes Gaskell

23 Avenue du Bois de Boulogne
10 May, 1907

My dear Carlo

Once more I find myself pitchforked across the ocean into this inconceivable kettle of absurd humanity, and the only change is that I feel each time more bewildered than before by the fact of my own continued existence, which seems now to connect back with nothing. This world has no relation whatever with my world, and I go on living in dream, whether in the company of Presidents and Senators at home, or of the spring models and automobile fiends here. Before sailing, I mailed to you the volume I had already announced, as my last Will and Testament, which is intended for you to strike out whatever you find objectionable, and return to me. As I have to ask the same favor of everyone else mentioned by name in the volume, the process is slow; but as the volume is wholly due to piety on account of my father and John Hay (the rest being thrown in to make mass), I am wholly indifferent about what shall be struck out, and almost equally so what shall be left in. You may lop liberally at your will. Indeed I am only waiting for the smallest objection from anyone of my family— or of Hay's,—to suppress it all. Thus far they have not dared squeak. Even the President and Cabot Lodge bow the neck in submission. As my experience leads me to think that no one any longer cares or even knows what is said or printed, and that one's audience in history and literature has shrunk to a mere band of survivors, not exceeding a thousand people in the entire world, I am in hopes a kind of esoteric literary art may survive, the freer and happier for the sense of privacy and *abandon*. Therefore I stop at no apparent *naïveté*.

Presently I am coming over to see you, and incidentally to see one or two other distinguished citizens like yourself, but just now I am quite cold enough here, and too wet. As all America is here, and I have rather more entertaining to do than at home, I do not see that it much matters whether I am here or there, but they are a simple-minded crowd, as they always were, and the intellect does not count. I hear of little done in my absence. One or two books. No music. No pictures. A drama or so; but no *clou* or surprise. My doctrine that the human mind is steadily weakening as in a saturated solution of a salt, holds here.

I left things in America much as I find them here,—much noise and no progress. All the great and impending social or political issues are more impending than ever, but Roosevelt has merely embroiled them, without plan or solution; and I do not see that your government, or the French, German or Russian has done more. Probably there is no solution—only expedients.

Love to yours   Ever Yrs   Henry Adams.

MS: MHi

To Oliver Wendell Holmes, Jr.

1603 H Street   31 Dec. 1907.

My dear Wendell

Your letter is a noble New Year's gift. I should think that an ant, having risen on his hind legs in a gigantic effort to look over a grain of sand, must be immensely pleased if a honey-bee, flying by, stops to tell him that he sees right. I know I am the ant, and the sense crushes me.

At seventy, it is hard not to take one's helplessness seriously. Just now I am desperately struggling to understand the new electro-æther which has been injected into chemistry and physics as the ultimate substance or deity of the new dispensation. You will find it in Whetham's "Recent Development of Physical Science," and in Gustave Le Bon's "Evolution des Forces."[1] With the effort to recover a few logarithms, I am driven to the conclusion that the law of mind in motion follows the same formula as the law of electric mass. The curve is given on p. 177 of Gustave Le Bons "Evolution de la Matière."[2] The idea seems reasonable. But in that case, the curve of Progress would be, starting with the—

20th century	1,000,000
19th "	1,000

18th	"	32
17th	"	5.5
16th	"	2.7

and so on, in a practically straight line like the comet of 1843. This law is well enough for past history, but brings us into infinite speed, and contradiction in terms, within no time at all. We must be there now.

Perhaps we are! I am! Never have I studied harder than in the last three months, and my mind succombs. It is well! Elinor Glynn and her sister will be here next week.[3] Are you ready?

Ever Yrs   Henry Adams.

MS: MH

1. William Cecil Dampier Whetham, *The Recent Development of Physical Science* (1904); Gustave Le Bon, *L'Evolution des forces* (1907).
2. Gustave Le Bon, *L'Evolution de la matière* (1905).
3. Elinor (Mrs. Clayton) Glyn (1864–1943), author of the sensational boudoir novel *Three Weeks* (1907); Lady Lucy S. W. Duff Gordon (1863–1935).

To Homer Saint-Gaudens

1603 H Street, 24 Jan. 1908

My dear Mr Saint-Gaudens[1]

I will send you all I can find of your father's letters. They shall go to you by mail today.

I have only one favor to ask of you in return. Do not allow the world to tag my figure with a name! Every magazine writer wants to label it as some American patent medicine for popular consumption—*Grief, Despair, Pear's Soap,* or *Macy's Mens' Suits Made to Measure.* Your father meant it to ask a question, not to give an answer; and the man who answers will be damned to eternity like the men who answered the Sphinx.

Undoubtedly a beneficent Deity, whether he exists or not, will some day commit our entire American—and European—society to eternal Hell fire for *not* trying to answer your father's question; but this is no reason why we should undertake to act the part of Savior,—much the contrary.

Source: Harold Dean Cater, *Henry Adams and His Friends* (1947)

1. Homer Schiff Saint-Gaudens (1880–1958), editor, requested the letters for his father's memoirs, which he subsequently edited and amplified with biographical material: *The Reminiscences of Augustus Saint-Gaudens,* 2 vols. (1913).

To James Ford Rhodes

1603 H Street   10 Feb. 1908

My dear Sir[1]

I owe you many thanks for your kind letter of the 8th, and for your very gratifying comments on my attempt to realise the Unity of Thought in the Thirteenth Century. You call on me for a much more risky experiment when you ask for my attempt to realise the Multiplicity of Thought in the Twentieth. Every artist is fascinated by the temptation to try to do the undoable, and I am not exempt from this weakness. After many years of weary effort, I have managed to get my scheme into such a shape that I can begin to see it. If you can imagine a centipede running along in twenty little sections (each with a little mathematical formula carefully concealed in its stomach) to the bottom of a hill; and then laboriously climbing in fifteen sections more, (each with a new mathematical problem carefully concealed in its stomach), till it can get up on a hill an inch or two high, so as to see ahead a half an inch, or so,—you will understand in advance all that the Education has to say. You will understand also why I believe the literary problem insoluble, and keep the experiment private.

I hate to bother you with all this introduction, but it is only meant to explain that the Education is a volume sent out exclusively for revision, correction and suggestion,—that its shape is provisional,—and its proportions intended to be shrunk at least one fourth. As a personal favor I have to ask that you will note on the margin all the corrections, omissions and suggestions that occur to you, and that you will, when done with the volume, return it to me so that I may adopt them in the text.

In fact, the two works are designed as one, but no one will ever find it out except the author.

With many thanks, ever truly Yrs   Henry Adams.

MS: MH

1. James Ford Rhodes (1848–1927), author of *History of the United States from the Compromise of 1850* (1893–1906), had commented appreciatively on *Mont Saint Michel and Chartres.*

To William James

1603 H Street   11 Feb. 1908

My dear James

You are as kind as possible, to write me a long letter.[1] I am grateful, for I can find no man to play with. The American is a singularly unsocial animal. For social purposes,—as far as I have read the records of society,—he is the most complete failure ever known; and I am the champion failer of all.

As for the volume, it interests me chiefly as a literary experiment, hitherto, as far as I know, never tried or never successful. Your brother Harry tries such experiments in literary art daily, and would know instantly what I mean; but I doubt whether a dozen people in America—except architects or decorators—would know or care.

I care little myself, and have put too many such *tours-de-force* into the fire, to bother about explanation. This will probably follow the others, for I have got it so far into shape that I can see the impossibility of success. It is the old story of an American drama. You can't get your contrasts and backgrounds.

So fully do I agree with you in having no use for time, that I expect soon to dispense with it altogether, and try the experiment of timeless space; but I am curious to know what our psychic friends think of it. Are they bored in space as much as I am in time? Lodge is less clear on that point than I could wish.[2]

Ever gratefully Yrs   Henry Adams.

MS: MH

1. James had written that the "boyhood part" of the *Education* was "really superlative" but that "'education' was stirred in too much for my appreciation" (William James to HA, Feb. 9, 1908, in *The Selected Letters of William James*, ed. Elizabeth Hardwick [1961]).
2. Sir Oliver Lodge (1851–1940), physicist and a leading researcher in psychic phenomena; *Signalling Across Space Without Wires,* 4th ed. (1908).

To William James

1603 H Street   17 Feb. 1908

My dear James

As a wit and humorist I have always said that you were far and away the superior to your brother Henry, and that you could have cut him quite out, if you had turned your fun that way. Your letter is proof of it. Did you ever read the Confessions of St Augustine, or of Cardinal de Retz, or of Rousseau, or of Benvenuto Cellini, or even of my dear Gibbon. Of them all, I think St Augustine alone has an idea of literary form,—a notion of writing a story with an end and object, not for the sake of the object, but for the form, like a romance. I have worked ten years to satisfy myself that the thing cannot be done today. The world does not furnish the contrasts or the emotion. If you will read my Chartres,—the last chapter is the only thing I ever wrote that I almost think good—you will see why I know my Education to be rotten.

You do not reflect that I am seventy years old—yesterday,—and quite senile. It is time to be gone. I want to burn the Education first, but it does not press. Nobody cares. You do not even care to come on here to see real greatness, like the President.

Ever Yrs   H. Adams.

MS: MH

To Owen Wister

1603 H Street   20 March, 1908

My dear Mr Wister

Before I go off for the summer, I have to thank you for several hours of enjoyment over your George Washington.[1] The subject is a never-failing interest, and you have added a new charm to it. I hope to see future editions and additions indefinitely, for you cannot want material, and the book will be better for doubling its size. Of the life on the plantation alone, I would like to have a whole volume, since it accounts for his character better than any other part of his education does. I cannot but think that it was partly the reaction of the master against the slave that gave the Virginian occasionally much of that elevation which we admire.

I find but two characters in our eighteenth century which greatly interest me. Others are strong and even lofty, but only two command my constant attention,—Washington and Franklin. They are a perpetual conundrum,—a wonder,—and their psychology passes my comprehension. Luckily Franklin has to a certain extent explained himself in that bit of autobiography which stands alone at the head of American literature; but Washington's interior development will always remain to me more or less mysterious. I know American nature well enough to know my ignorance of it. Washington's breadth defies me, and his balance passes comparison.

With many thanks I am very truly Yrs   Henry Adams.

MS: DLC, Wister
1. Owen Wister, *The Seven Ages of Washington: A Biography* (1907).

To J. Laurence Laughlin

1603 H Street   6 April, 1908.

My dear Laughlin[1]

I am happy to hear from you again. The world grows dim and crawls far away, so that I seem to see now only vague outlines and motions. Any real figure or voice is doubly welcome.

Of course you can have the volume, but it is sent out only for revision, correction and suggestion, and is to be returned when annotated. For publication, it will need to be shortened one fourth.

Sugar-coated an inch thick, the pill is intended to show the necessity of purging education. As an old man, I have excuse for insistance, and I dare risk what young men dare not. I risk the consequences of saying in this volume that the time has come when our whole system of education is to be reconstructed from the bottom, on some broad generalisation that will make it intelligible to the future student; and I suggest that the department of history is the agent for doing it. Please read it with the understanding that I am trying to state and prove a mathematical theorem, not a personal view. To me, the problem has not the value of a *carte de visite*. I shall be dead before the Universities begin to discuss what they must do to meet a necessity foreseen for generations.

Therefore please regard it as merely a repetition of all my old views, by way of testamentary bequest.

Yrs truly   Henry Adams.

MS: MH

1. Laughlin, who had been one of HA's doctoral students at Harvard, was a professor of political economy at the University of Chicago.

To Henry James

23 Avenue du Bois de Boulogne
6 May, 1908

Mon Cher Jacques

Mea culpa! Peccavi! Parce, frater![1] It is but a form and a phrase, yet this volume is supposed to be lent out only for correction, suggestion and amendment, so that you are invited to return it, with your marginal comments whenever you have done with it. I need hardly tell *you* that my own marginal comment is broader than that of any reader, and precludes publication altogether. The volume is a mere shield of protection in the grave. I advise you to take your own life in the same way, in order to prevent biographers from taking it in theirs.

Also—you being a literary artist, and therefore worth the trouble of forewarning—I note for your exclusive use the intent of the literary artist—c'est moi!—to make this volume a completion and mathematical conclusion from the previous volume about the Thirteenth Century,—the three concluding chapters of this being only a working out to Q.E.D. of the three concluding chapters of that. This is only for my own horizon; not for your confusion.

Ever Yrs   Henry Adams.

MS: MH

1. I am guilty! I have sinned! Spare me, brother!

To Elizabeth Cameron

23 Avenue du Bois de Boulogne
Thursday, 7 May 1908

You are a woman, therefore superior to me, and you can keep your head in crowds. Mine wobbles. What I've seen or heard since I left Washington a fortnight ago seems curdled and—to say the least—unodorous; certainly unprofitable to me, or you. Yet, such as it is, you shall have it.

The voyage was a bad one. Two days of it were as sea-sicky as I have known for many years, and I was left alone at table. Luckily the party was gay and large, and I was the only man, much to be petted by nieces. Your Shontzes were on board in deep mourning, and confiding their terrible loss to all who came near.[1] Of the loss, something will be told later; but for myself I rather preferred not to enter into relations with the ducal family, for the Shontzes are visibly of a naïveté impossible. They pass the bounds. Edith Deacon, very pretty, very headless, and also very *naïve*, hardly inspired me with such heartrending pity.[2] Laura Chanler, seeking her parents in the vast, seemed a monument of prosaic worldly wisdom beside these others, and the Brices and Bessy Marbury became monuments of cold and crude worldliness. Never can mankind have seen such foolishness. The ship was otherwise empty as in midwinter; only sixty cabin-passengers.

Into this group, Marconi slung a telegram announcing Jean Reid's engagement.[3] I was to have passed the week conducting the Brices through Normandy, but at Cherbourg a telegram from Miss Reid called Kate Brice to Paris, and I came up by train with Miss Marbury, arriving Sunday afternoon, and dumped myself into my room with a deadly homesickness and hollowness, which was not helped by dining alone at Paillard's next to an odious old American whom his ladies addressed as Mr Widener.[4] Monday evening at the same place, I was literally walked on by an elderly man, whose face bore a nose that years only defy, and that does not successfully meet the defiance. Mr Morgan did not see me, or anyone else. He seems to avoid eyes, and I don't wonder; but, for once, I felt perfectly at ease carrying my white hair and wrinkles at Paillard's between Mr Widener and Pierpont Morgan.

On Monday the effort began, to catch up with the tail of the procession. To shorten the tail, I will say only that since then I have sunk in self-degradation to a point beneath my wont. I have lunched with the Whites, and have sat with Edith Wharton and Harry James who is with her; and have breakfasted at Paillard's with Miss Marbury who brought wierd tales of Ellen Mason and her Polish tyrant just leaving the Villa Trianon after some months of stay. I skip that for other wierdnesses. Just hear what I did last night! I dined with Mrs Whitelaw Reid at the Hotel Vendome, *en famille*, to meet the young man and Jean. You can't be so bewildered as I at this new family tie. Yes! I was literally one of the wedding party, only a pair of Harrimans helping. Jean was pretty, bright, engaging—and engaged. Of the young man,—what can I say? that he is *type de* King's Equerry? Why do the girls choose that type? Why not? He seems pleasant; he is good-looking; he is not dull; he is livelier than Alan Johnson on one side, and has not half the charm of my dear Lindsay on the other.[5] Who, by the way, came up to see me in the afternoon, as sympathetic and inscrutable as ever. By inscrutable, you know what I mean,—youth, unlike what I ever knew for young.

I don't know how to describe Equerries! They seem to me double; one on view; the other, not. Lindsay seems to me straight. The Equerry may be straight or crooked, but in the eye, he is evasive. Harry White has a droll story about the marriage having been made by the King,—a second attempt, the first having been shattered by papa Mills.[6] But I must hurry!

Muriel White had a dance last night, and Harry took the trouble to write me to come. I was much more weary than Jean who was too tired to go; but I went. Yes, I did; though you won't believe me. And I fell into the arms of the Gays and Jaffreys and Mrs John Drexel, and what do I know who? It was pretty and the ladies were very swell and all that; but Mrs Jaffrey supplied me with buckets of gossip. Of course she, like all the others, wailed about you and Martha, when I told them that they must find you a tenant;[7] but everybody does that, and Nancy in particular is in despair. Nancy has been in Italy, and in going *en auto,* was pitched out, on her head, near Nismes. Only her thick hair seems to have saved her. Her mother had a scare such as I have when nothing happens,—blue-green. You can imagine! But it is now five weeks, and the girl seems right. She looked to me rather more delicate than usual but quite herself.

Then Mrs Jaffrey told me the Chaulnes story as current in the beau monde. Chaulnes disappeared for four days in a cocaïne or opium den; lay there all that time without taking off his clothes; collapsed; was brought to the Langham; given a bath; put to bed, and died, then and there. All this mixed up with much worse things, about women.

Between intervals, tales about everybody having lost money, some by the *crac* and some,—including the Equerry,—on the King's Colt, just beaten by Augy Belmont.[8]

And at midnight I walked up the Rue François I in the rain, meditating bombs.

Yet the girls are so pretty and well-dressed and *do* they know better? What can *they* do?—even a Shontz? much more a Gladys or Jean?[9]

I am glad to be done with it, and to quit the world tomorrow by lunching with James and Howells at White's.[10]

Meanwhile your apartment weighs on my mind,—and you! and Martha! and much else. Every day, my nerves weaken.

———

MS: MHi

  1. Theodore Perry Shonts (1856–1919), midwestern railroad magnate and head of the New York subway system; and Harriet Amelia ("Milla") Drake Shonts. In February their daughter Theodora had married the duc de Chaulnes, who died in April.
  2. Edith Deacon (1887–1963), one of four sisters. Gladys (1881–1977), the famous beauty, became the duchess of Marlborough in 1921.
  3. Jean Reid (1883–1962), daughter of Whitelaw Reid, married Sir John H. Ward (1870–1938), equerry to Edward VII.
  4. Peter Arrell Brown Widener (1834–1915), Philadelphia street-railway magnate and art collector.
  5. Ronald Charles Lindsay (1877–1945), second secretary at the British embassy, had recently become a suitor of Martha Cameron.
  6. Ogden Mills (1856–1929), brother of Mrs. Whitelaw Reid.
  7. Helen Smythe Jaffray (1850–1932), widow of William P. Jaffray; Helen Frances ("Nancy") Jaffray (b. 1885), daughter of Helen and William Jaffray.
  8. After the arrest of Henri Rochette, head of the Crédit Minier et Industriel, a series of bank failures had taken place in April. On May 6 the king's colt Perrier, the favorite, lost to August Belmont's Norman III, an outsider.
  9. Gladys Vanderbilt had married Count László Széchényi Jan. 27, 1908.
  10. The luncheon, given by Ambassador Henry White, included Henry James, the American novelist William Dean Howells (1837–1920), and Howells' daughter Mildred.

To Elizabeth Cameron

23 Avenue du Bois de Boulogne
14 May, 1908.

Your letters telling me of your sister's accident do not encourage too much my naturally extravagant bent towards a frenzied gaiety;[1] but we have been over all that ground too often already. I was relieved to learn that your apartment is off your hands till August. This is so far good. We shall perhaps be able to look ahead a little further in October. At present I am in my usual scared state, and trying to adapt my future to the theory of a Bryan administration and prolonged industrial trouble. At least I get down to hard pan by that process, and can hardly be surprised. I had a long talk with Mrs Whitelaw Reid when I dined with her, which scared me blue. Where *is* Truth? Can one believe a politician?

Meanwhile I am in the usual singular state of Paris, altogether morbid, unhealthy, *ennuyeux,* and fit only for a boy of twenty, or a race-course. The boy and the race-course are equally remote from me; but I am driven back to my rooms every afternoon by the infallible shower, and shut up till I have to go out to seek dinner at Paillard's or the Elysée Restaurant. I have been playing a little with Edith Wharton. Yesterday I lunched at Voisin's with the Brices and Minot. In the background sat Eliot Gregory. Minot took us up to Mme Langweil's afterwards to seek wedding-presents.[2] He is himself going over to paint Jean Reid. Bessy Marbury has already gone over. Naturally the two Brices are hatting.

I dined last night at the Harry Whites' on a sudden call, I hardly know why, for I was not needed. I sat between Edith Wharton and Mme de Ganay, of Courances, where I had fortunately been taken last year by Mrs Gay.[3] *Très Juive,* and of course intelligent! and of course the rest! Helen Valençay was there, looking so old that at first I took her for Mrs Vanderbilt.[4] I must call, for her mother is also here. Reginald Lister listered after his fashion.[5] Also other men—Frenchmen—amusing. I felt—just so,—I need not say,—but tonight I have Lindsay to dine *à deux* at Paillard's, and he is always restful and cheery. Tomorrow I dine with the Gay's. I hope it is because they want me, for it is certainly not because I am ornamental. I have had a cold, and it is cold anyway,—so cold that last night Mrs White and the ladies were driven out of their salon into our smoking-room for warmth.

I tried an hour or two of Jeanne Granier at the Vaudeville the other evening, but found it enough, without the Third Act.[6] Edith Wharton and Henry James had the same experience with La Vallière at the *Variétés;* but

Mrs Wharton saw Mary Garden appear at the Grand Opera as Thaïs, and says it was a full and uncontested success.[7] It seemed never to have occurred to her or anyone there to question the power of Mary Garden's voice. Droll! we were told so habitually that she had not voice enough. And now she has simply taken possession of the Grand Opera without a doubt of it.

Mme de Boigne's fourth volume has made success.[8] It is to me very interesting, for it comes down to 1848, and gives me my first idea of Louis Philippe and the Orleans family. Among the vast number of elderly people who regret the good old times, I hardly remember to have ever met anyone who enthusiasmed over Louis Philippe, and I see why, from Mme de Boigne who did.

Harry James has been painted by Blanche.[9] Who is Blanche? He was at the Embassy dining last night, but I know his work no better. The Salons are as usual growing worse and worse every year, according to Mme de Ganay. I told her that I began with that understanding just fifty years ago, and that as far as I could see, the worseness varied only in its quantity; the quality averaged much the same even this year when neither Besnard nor Flameng exhibit, and the Jean Bérauds and Boldinis are ordinary.[10] Sargent too is absent. Minot says that Sargent insists he cannot any longer paint; he has lost his faculty. Sargent must, I fancy, be about fifty to fiftyfive; it is a pity to reach that stage so early; at sixty it is natural.

Friday, 15. I am horrified to see the death of Charley Rae telegraphed this morning.[11] For him, perhaps, it is an escape, but for Rebecca it must be a sentence. And I must write! oh, Lord.

I sat an hour yesterday with Mrs Wharton and the Bourgets, &c.[12] Mrs Wharton really does make a social effort, and I approve it, as I always do with my numerous female adoptions, though rarely do I find it pay in small change. The individuals bring little reward. The Bourgets are Bourgeoises,—very! But in the mass, probably the woman gets something and by reflection I gain. I like, too, to watch you do your work, when you do it well, though the contrasts are picturesque. Poor Mrs Harry White sits like a *fauteuil Louis Quatorze*, quite helpless before a group of two.

Lindsay and I dined at Paillard's as I said. He is agog about coming changes in his *corps,* and expects to go to the Foreign Office in the autumn. Thence to Petersburg if he can. He thinks that Regi. Lister will have to vanish into a legation somewhere, and is curious about Brice. Gerald Lowther is eager for Berlin or something; and all the young men are squirming, but not a whisper can be got from the F.O.[13] Diplomacy is dull just now. There are no questions, unless in the Balkans. Even Kaiser Wilhelm has taken to vamping up old castles, and worrying his own favorites.[14]

How am I to crawl through the next six months? And you? Luckily the

President is as optimistic as I am pessimist. I pin my hopes to his coat-tails and to Taft's good nature. As long as Washington keeps open to me, I can take refuge there at least so far as to be useful to my aunts and *belles-soeurs* with Elsie de Wolfe's approving help.

———

MS: MHi

1. Lida Sherman (Mrs. Colgate) Hoyt had suffered a broken hip from a minor accident and was not expected to walk again.
2. Joseph Otis Minott (born Minot; 1864–1909), American painter residing in Paris; Eliot Gregory (1854–1915), American artist and writer; Mme. Berthe Langweil, a dealer in objets d'art whose shop was frequented by Mrs. Cameron and HA.
3. The marquise de Ganay (d. 1921), the former Emily R. Ridgway of Philadelphia.
4. Helen Valençay (1876–1952), daughter of Levi P. Morton and Anna Street Morton (1846–1918).
5. Reginald Lister (1865–1912), minister-counselor at the British legation in Paris 1905–1908.
6. Jeanne Granier opened May 8 in *Mariage d'Etoile*, a comedy by Alexandre Bisson and Georges Thurner.
7. Eve Lavallière, stage name of Eugénie Fenoglio (1866–1929), opened April 24 in *Le Roi*, a comedy by Gaston-Arman de Caillavet, Robert de Flers, and Emmanuel Arène. Mary Garden (1877–1967) made her Paris debut on May 11 in the title role of Jules Massenet's *Thaïs* (1894). She had made her first appearance in 1900.
8. Comtesse de Boigne (1781–1866), *Récits d'une tante. Mémoires* (1907–1908).
9. Jacques-Emile Blanche (1861–1942), portrait painter, writer, and noted conversationalist.
10. Paul Besnard (1849–1934); François Flameng (1856–1923); Jean Béraud (1849–1936); Giovanni Boldini (1845–1931).
11. Adm. Charles W. Rae died May 14, aged 60.
12. Paul Bourget (1852–1935), novelist; and his wife, Minnie David Bourget (d. 1932).
13. Lindsay became assistant secretary of state for foreign affairs 1908–1911; Lister became minister to Morocco 1908–1912; Sir Gerard Lowther (1858–1916; knighted 1907) became ambassador to Turkey 1908–1913.
14. On May 13 the kaiser took possession of his newly restored castle, Hohkönigsburg, in Alsace. On the same day his old favorite, Prince Philipp zu Eulenburg, held in prison for perjury, was refused bail.

To Elizabeth Cameron

23 Avenue du Bois de Boulogne
Sunday, 24. [May] 1908

Nothing from you this week, since you were just starting for Richmond, and I grow worried about it. But I worry anyway, and if it were not you, it would be the universe or the fleas. I am too ridiculous to live loose. I ought to be shut up.

You would not know it if you saw me here, dancing about among my *fantoches*[1] like an aged Pierrot. Nieces by scores flatter and pet me till I blush and shrink. Luckily Pussy Wharton—as a few irreverent contemporaries still call her—sailed yesterday, after spoiling me by planting me in her *salon*. I told her what fate waited her, and how she was floating into the fauteuil of Mme Récamier before the fire, with Chateaubriand on one side and Barante on the other, both drivelling; only Chateaubriand would be Henry James and Barante would be Henry Adams.[2] She has her little suite, but they are not passionate. The Bourgets and so on; Blanche, the young painter, who has perpetrated a rather brutal, Sargenty portrait of Henry James; Fullerton, the young Times correspondent;[3] in short, a whole train of us small literary harlequins who are not even funny. And she goes to plays and things, and reads.

Well, she is afloat today, and I am playing with Mrs Winty, and the Brices, and—Mrs Marie van Vorst, into whose salon I tumbled the other day, escorting Mrs Wharton, and found old Rodin making old eyes at the fair Marie, as at others whom we remember.[4] Old Rodin is rather disgusting. The cohort of ladies are going out to Meudon this afternoon, under the charge of Mrs van Vorst, and they very kindly offered to take me with them, but I pleaded engagements which did not exist. I will go down and call on Matilda Gay. Yet I am wrong. If I were not so much older than Rodin, I would put my dignity in my pocket, and go to Meudon, and say *qu'il baisse,*[5]—which is true.

To amuse Laura, I took her and Harriet Wadsworth to lunch at Laurent's in full summer heat, and then took her with her mother for chaperon to dine at the Pavillon de l'Elysée, with Lindsay. You and Martha may go hang; but Lindsay is the only satisfactory and sympathetic young man I know, and I only wish I were a girl and could marry him myself. I will try to marry him to Laura if you go back on him. He is pathetic too, and pretty solitary.

I took Mrs Chanler and Laura and Nancy to Bagatelle yesterday afternoon to see portraits of Louis Philippe to illustrate Mme de Boigne. Nancy quite exquisite and taller than ever, squealing shrill cries for Martha. I dropped in to dine at La Rue's and fell on Constance and Gussie and the wierd little girl, and when they went at nine o'clock, I moved my seat to the opposite table where Dolly Rockhill and little Tebaldi were dining. You can judge that America is in force. If I wander down to see Mrs Harry White, I find Ann Vanderbilt, and Lady Anglesea, and their sequel.[6] If I follow the Brices or some other niece up to Minot's rooms, I find—who else—Wideners! Bessy Marbury from London sends me a long Scenario from Sardou to translate, and I have to refuse, because they won't give me time. Mrs Ralph Curtis, to whom I try to make desperate love after the manner of old George Bancroft, has me to dine tomorrow with—I imagine—Mrs Cooper Hewitt, just arrived; and we go to see Brasseur and La

Vallière in Le Roi at the *Variétés*. And in the intervals of these fatuous follies, I sit long hours alone, glaring at a pile of new books, and trying to play I am alive. I have just waded through another fat volume on Trucquage by Eudel who wrote the previous one;[7] and I wanted to make it an Appendix to illustrate the last chapters of my Education. One's mind dissolves before this dissolution of art.

Meanwhile I get a series of shocks from home. Constance had a list of new ones. Her aunt suddenly called to be operated on—Cabot's sister, Mrs George James,—at a moment when Nanny was in bed with shingles! H. Blaine operated on, for appendicitis. I am still waiting for the details of Charley Rae's death. I am worrying all the time about your sister and you and Martha. I am shaping all my arrangements to suit the assumption that Bryan will be our next President, and that we shall have to endure a new social revolution at Washington,—this time, my last. My one solid comfort is to have got rid of my automobile.

———

Monday, 25. Still no letter from you, but one from Sister Ann countermanding our July arrangement and adding that you had come to see her the day before, the 14th as I read it. Your last to me was the 3d, so I am posted ten days forward. Bad enough all round! It turns me green—*verdâtre!*

Having funked the Meudon excursion, I was summoned last night to a Dutch feast at La Rue's where Minot had collected his victims, Helen Brice, Mrs Winty and Laura, and Mrs Cooper Hewitt, who has just arrived from Italy. We were seven, and very gay as you may fancy, but I gleaned no great light. Mrs Fred Jones writes from London that she and Trix come over on Thursday. Constance writes that she wants me to take them— herself and the child I imagine—to Versailles on Thursday. The Brices say they are coming on Thursday to take me to Mont St Michel. Apparently *femme dispose* and *propose* as well, but what will *l'homme* do?

———

Tuesday, 26. At last comes your letter of the 17th,—just about as bad as I expected. As poor Lindsay pathetically sighs:—"Very well!" When one is beaten, one goes somewhere else; but I hardly recommend Paris. It is exasperatingly gay and horrid. I dined last night with Mrs Ralph Curtis. There was Mrs Cooper Hewitt, Mrs Lor. Ronalds, and two McGees. Did you know "Bertha" Ronalds?[8] I never saw her before, but one knows the type,—the rattling little *nez-retroussé* type of latent ambition and self-conscious self-distrust under self-assertion. We went on to the *Variétés* to see *Le Roi,* which was to me a sort of mouldy Offenbach without the music. It bored me horribly, and always does,—this attempt to satirize the republic as in old days we satirized the empire. Poor old Leopold is worn threadbare, and the *sous-préfet* is worse. But everybody is crying out that it glows with wit and sustained style. In fact, it is rot such as even I have never seen, and made bores of even Brasseur and La Vallière.[9]

We go to Normandy till Tuesday. Chanlers too!

MS: MHi

1. *Fantoches*: marionettes.
2. Prosper Brugière (1782–1866), baron de Barante, statesman, historian; *Souvenirs* (1890–1901).
3. William Morton Fullerton (1865–1952), American journalist, correspondent for the London *Times* 1891–1911.
4. Josephine Treat Van Vorst, widow of Hooper C. Van Vorst. "Mrs. Marie": mock deference to her famous daughter Marie Van Vorst (1867–1936), social reformer and novelist.
5. *Qu'il baisse*: how feeble he is becoming.
6. Anne Harriman Rutherford Vanderbilt (d. 1940), wife of William K. Vanderbilt (1849–1920); Lady Anglesey (d. 1931), the former Mary Livingstone King of Sandhills, Ga., widow of Henry Cyril Paget, 4th marquess of Anglesey.
7. Paul Eudel, *Le Truquage: altérations, fraudes et contrefaçons dévoilées* (1903); *Trucs et truqueurs* (1907).
8. Bertha Perry (Mrs. P. Lorillard) Ronalds.
9. The plot of *Le Roi* turns on two seductions. King Leopold of Belgium was notorious for his sexual exploits. Albert Brasseur (1862–1932) played the part of the king.

To Elizabeth Cameron

23 Avenue du Bois de Boulogne
Tuesday, 9 June 1908.

Your letter of May 31 arrives this morning. It makes me shiver,—but to you the shivery state in me seems my nature. I have shivered myself and you for many years till it has become habit.

Curiously enough, of late I have been too much occupied to shiver. You should have seen me last Friday lunching at Laurent's between Mrs Gambril and Mrs Cooper Hewitt, with Mrs Lanier opposite, and Mrs Ralph Curtis at the foot. The men were Egerton, Ralph Curtis and Moncure Robinson. Do you see me at home in the crowd? After all, Egerton, Curtis and I are not far from the same age, and we are the only young men in Paris. On Saturday I lunched at Harry Jones's en famille, and took Mrs Fred to see the pastels.[1] She is in a tub of trouble and distress, of which I will perhaps tell you some day, but which hardly bears setting on record. Poor woman! she is always in trouble, chiefly owing to what she calls her "gaffs," which means her nervous restlessness and craving to do good to everybody,—or to tell everybody how much she would like to do them good if she could. She is not the only one! and her "gaffs" are innocent. But on Sunday, after I had lunched at the Curtis's to help them with Okakura,[2] and the men went off, I stopped to see the children, and Mrs Curtis drew me into a corner to ask me, under her breath and a catch in her voice, and fire in her eye, whether I had read Edith Wharton's last story in the June Scribner.[3] Luckily I had not. "It's all about me," she said, "and Ralph, and our house, where Teddy made us a visit, and his wife has put down his whole account of it even to the furniture of the bed-rooms, and describes me as a rich widow without any mind, who has let my artist husband give up his career which he found himself to have failed in." You can imagine my incredulity, but the good-natured Mrs Ralph was on the war-path, and kept it up. She had read it to Mrs Hewitt who thought it outrageous. "I am furious" she said, and ended by giving the thing to me to say what I thought of it. What I really thought of it, I took care not to say, and I wrote her a note trying to laugh it off, because what I think of it is no great matter, but what all you ladies will think of it is not likely to be affected by me. You will say what you please, but, by all the commandments, don't tell on me. I repeat gossip only to amuse you and give you an occasional variety. I am too old to be drawn into a battle of ladies, and am an intimate friend of all parties. But—!

Lindsay and I dined at La Rue's. He is going to the naval review to Norway.

Yesterday (Monday) Miss Marbury joined me at Paillard's to lunch, and also had much to say, but her grief was over her favorite chauffeur who had shot himself to death on the French steamer coming over, and had apparently been calmly ignored by the Compagnie which had handed over the whole affair to the Marine, and had notified nobody. Miss Marbury was as furious as Mrs Curtis; but, to me, the shiver was due to the idea that the man was certainly suffering from acute mania, and might just as well have had his attack *en automobile en route.*

Tomorrow night I take Nancy and Mrs Jaffray to dine at the Café Anglais and hear Maggie Teyte come out as Melisande at the Opera Comique. Larry Butler will be interested in this tremendously ambitious effort of the young girl whom I first heard at his rooms sing "Du premier jour" with a mastery that astonished me.[4]

Harry White sat an hour with me yesterday afternoon, also rich in gossip diplomatic which I dare not repeat.

Friday, 12. My record of young *marcheur* goes on apace. I took Trix and her mother to Paillard's on Tuesday to educate Trix up to the wildest Paris dissipation, and, if it had not been for the violinist, we should have gone to sleep. Trix had never been at a fashionable restaurant here. She was profoundly impressed by its modern excitements—twenty Americans and six Germans. No one else!

Wednesday I breakfasted at the Café Voisin with the Wintys and the Roman matron commonly called Jane San Faustino.[5] I had met that Sempronia in Rome of yore, but did not recall the relation. The Princess is as mad as Bob Chanler, but more amusing. I would like to give you a phonograph of her conversation, but it would not end. She most interested me by her description of the Ogden Mills's at Ritz, in their room filled only with Braganzas and other royalties.[6] Apparently Bob Chanler was not in attendance; Winty says he is at Versailles with his late wife and children.[7]

In the evening I took Nancy and her mother and young Johnson, a portrait-painter doing Nancy, to dine at the Café Anglais and see Maggie Teyte come out in Pelleas. We got fairly into the theatre before it was announced that Pelleas was put off and Manon, with Vix, would take its place.[8] It had already been once postponed. My wrath was deep, but it was my party, and I had to tie myself up. We sat through four Acts of Manon, which were not very well done; and I brought them home.

Yesterday I was busy. At 12.30 I picked up Mrs Cooper Hewitt at Ritz's and took her out to the Pré Catalan to breakfast. She had never been there; it was very pretty; not too full; and of course dotted with hats. I think it amused her. Then I had an hour with my dentist to make an average. I put in a half hour at the Embassy where Mrs White was enthroned with old Steurs, Mrs Chanler and Laura. Then I dressed and went to dine with the Blair Fairchilds, to meet the two Brices, old Mrs Baldwin and young Aldrich.[9] I had a long talk, of the most intimate, with Mrs Baldwin (whom I never saw before) about Edith Deacon. Upon my life, I am becoming a Cardinal-Jesuit-confessor in a way that requires the robes!

The Brices brought me home, and so closed my week's social running. If it were not that, on my seventieth birthday, I had declared myself dead and irresponsible,—a mere ghost, without further business in a world that is obviously a dream without connection or intelligence,—I should be ashamed of myself. As it stands, it is no more ridiculous than it was forty years ago, and these phantoms are no more absurd than their grandmothers. Who, by the way are still in it;—at least I breakfasted with a little mad Mrs Ronalds only the other day, and dared not ask about Fanny Carter, her mother-in-law.

Well! the Grand Prix is here, and the butterflies will soon scatter. Ward Thoron and Looly Hooper arrive tomorrow. My brother Brooks is hovering somewhere. The Lodges will probably be here within a month. The swarm shifts rapidly, and I shall be again bored to death with solitude. It would amuse me more to be running the Taft campaign at home; but, thus far,

Roosevelt's points on that race have been perfectly accurate, and have left me with nothing to add of my own. In three or four months the panic about Bryan will begin, I suppose, and I shall be more concerned.

I write you all my gossip only because I hope it may serve a little to vary the atmosphere. I wish I could do anything to help. Your sister is going through what I may have to go through, any day, and must probably go through very soon. We are all in the same boat, and all are about equally near the falls.

———

MS: MHi

1. Henry Edward Jones (1850–1922), brother of Frederic Jones and Edith Wharton.
2. Kakuzo Okakura (1862–1913), adviser to the Museum of Fine Arts, Boston, and, beginning in 1910, curator of its department of Chinese and Japanese art.
3. Edith Wharton, "The Verdict," *Scribner's* 43 (June 1908), 689–693.
4. Maggie Teyte (1888–1976), English soprano, was chosen by Debussy himself to succeed Mary Garden in *Pelléas et Mélisande* (1902) in June 1908. "Le Premier Jour de mai" (1855) by Charles Gounod. Lawrence Butler (c. 1876–1954), later a notable member of Long Island society.
5. Jane Bourbon del Monte (c. 1863–1938), Princess San Faustino, was the former Jane Campbell of New York.
6. Ogden Mills and his wife, Ruth Livingston Mills (d. 1920).
7. "Late wife" refers to Julia Chanler, who had divorced Robert Chanler in 1907.
8. Geneviève Vix (1879–1939), French soprano, in Jules Massenet's *Manon* (1884).
9. Blair Fairchild (1877–1933), American composer residing in Paris; Mrs. Florence Baldwin, assumed name of Mrs. Deacon, mother of the four Deacon sisters. Her husband had killed her lover in 1892. Chester H. Aldrich (1871–1940), New York architect.

To Charles Milnes Gaskell

23 Avenue du Bois de Boulogne
18 June. 1908

Dear Carlo

I wonder whether you would care to read the *éreintement* of a historian? I think I will send you Aulard's little book on Taine.[1] It is a piece of evisceration, but it makes me cold to think of what would be the result of the same process applied to me. No man's mind and memory are comprehensive enough to carry the relations of a long story. I cannot even rewrite a chapter without greatly changing it, and I think I never have written a chapter less than five times over, unless it were from sheer collapse. If I went on forever, I should always do it differently, and of course each version is a correction. Such a scorching as Aulard gives would skin anyone. He admits it, and tries to deprecate attacks on mere blunders.

If I were forty years younger, I should come over to Jean Reid's wedding as an excuse to see you all. Instead, I am going to charter an automobile and go south for a few weeks. I have been doing a regular season here, and going about as I've not done these five-and-twenty years. One can't do this with impunity at my age, so I made a diversion to Normandy *en auto* with various ladies and twelfth-century expansions. I managed to pick up two or three bits I had missed. Normandy was lovely in apple-blossoms and the weather too. Mont Saint Michel is not wholly spoiled. At least some sand is left.

I am now thinking of doing Provence and the south,—perhaps even a bit of Pyrenees. It will serve to break up the long summer.

Our world rides fast, as the ballad says. Your government has upset the whole tub of socialism on us, and mine is plunging into an unknown ocean. I suppose my friend Taft is being nominated now while I write. He is a charming fellow, altogether the best man I have ever had a chance to support; but I have grave doubts of his election. Apparently my doubts are shared by other people, for I cannot see a sign of improvement in confidence. The cutting down of expenditure goes on, and insolvencies are beginning on a great scale. No one will spend money. The Parisians complain bitterly. They run a mile to ask you to enter their shops, and they knock off twenty per cent at the suggestion of an offer. The place is full of Americans, but they don't spend. Their money must be accumulating, but it is quite likely that, if the election seems close, people will economise still more. And meanwhile the laboring class is squeezed flat. Many hundred thousands have no bread.

No one knows what may be the political effect of such a situation, but it makes everyone cautious. For my own part I wonder only that society is so calm. Fifty years ago, we should have had riots and fury.

My little world at home is not in very good form. One's friends and connections are breaking down or dying in a rather promiscuous way, and I dread every fresh letter. There is more and more comfort in feeling oneself the oldest man alive, and ready at a moment's notice, to quit. Paris always fosters one's most anarchistic tendencies, and one sees so little in society worth saving that one does not feel much regret at not saving it, but the poor things can't help themselves and don't seem much to want to. Men and women, French or American, seem to me almost equally dulled and helpless. They give no reaction.

Books are numerous but nothing very good, nor plays, nor pictures, but Paris is pretty and awfully crowded.

Ever Yrs   Henry Adams.

MS: MHi

1. François-Alphonse Aulard, *Taine, historien de la révolution française* (1907).

To Margaret Chanler

23 Avenue du Bois de Boulogne
4 Sept. 1908

Dear Saint

Your letter filled me with the usual contradictory emotions,—first, of pleasure that you should be coming here, and, second, of despair that you should not be coming to Washington or New York. I am facing another awful catastrophe in my social existence in Washington. La Fayette Square is to be as archaic as the Roman Forum. Andrew Jackson and I sit there alone, wondering why we too are not removed as cumberers of the soil. Nothing beside remains. Round the decay of that preposterous wreck, the bare and level streets stretch far away.[1] Not a friend have I left.

Even the Roosevelts will be gone six months from today. Poor dear Taft can bring nothing to take the place of what has gone, because he can find nothing to bring. The despair that drowns me is due to the failure of all your generation to fetch on a new one to amuse me. I beg you all, one after another, to bring me a new man. You bring me charming women in plenty, but when I ask them for men, they look blank,—they don't even blush,—they don't know what a man is. Then I ask the Lodges, father and sons; the Roosevelts; Henry James or his brother William; John La Farge or his sons; or the whole covey of Chanlers,—when I ask them to tell me who is their agreeable and amusing companion, they say they have none; that I know everybody that exists.

It can't be! The men we want are surely there. They will turn up just to spite me when I am dead. I wring my few remaining hairs with fury that they do it on purpose. I abuse with outrage all my young acquaintance; and the only result is that my brother Brooks comes here and drives me wild by telling it all over again to me as a discovery he has just made.

I hate to poison your mind, but I feel a blue fear that Rome will not be Rome to you any longer. It seems to me that even from here, I feel a change—not only in myself. Still, I shall be glad to hear that your spirit of unfading youth supplies the lost freshness, and that you are rich enough to make good the losses that we poor ancients suffer. We are bankrupt. One is not ten million years old for nothing.

As for science, it has become lovely and metaphysical and idiotic and delightfully human. It is much more passionate than our friend Saint

Thomas. Did I tell you how deeply I was touched—in my own sense—by Lord Kelvin's dying confession,—that he had totally failed to understand anything? I, who refuse to face that admission, am delighted to have somebody do it for me by proxy. There is rather a suggestive volume by Emile Boutroux on Science and Religion in Gustave Le Bon's Scientific Series.[2] It came out last March, and tries to state the situation in my own terms. The French are making great efforts to deal with the question of Unity, and as they have a sense of it—which the English and Germans never had,—their study is interesting. Sometimes I seem almost on the point of seeing where it must come out; but, as in Scholasticism, and in Philosophy in general, the last Unit is so big that it crushes man, and we don't like to be crushed. We object to being left to build spiderwebs on a dynamo.

And now this morning arrives your volume, or Hanna Thomson's volume from you, which we will discuss hereafter.[3] That is to say, if I have any longer the power of talking, for it leaves me at times, so that my mind refuses to do more than muddle, and lie on its back like a baby, mumbling at intervals. I think our American and English writers do no more. Muddle and mumble is all I can gather from them. We are back in the babies.

I am glad to hear that yours flourish. My nerve has been so completely broken by the disasters of most of my friends that I cling to the few who still swim. I see, however, that the Adriatic swam into New York yesterday with its cargo of our friends, so that they have managed to survive the storms which have nearly wrecked my physical system here. For sheer depression, the last fortnight has been a record-breaker. Paris in constant rain and wind is gory.

I can tell you nothing of gossip. The Harry Whites have been in England for ten days. Of Mrs Fred Jones I hear no word. From America come mostly wails of wretched horror. I've had to try to write to poor Baroness Speck.[4] Mrs Cameron is in oceans of difficulty between her sister and Don and Martha. Mrs Hay is in another ocean with her sister Mrs Mather.[5] Positively I dread opening every letter, but the wicked flourish. I never repeat scandal unless as a joke, but I roared with laughter the other day at Ritz's when Joe Minot announced to me that Willie Vanderbilt had gone off with—no! I won't repeat such stuff.

Love to all. Ever Yrs Henry Adams

MS: MHi

1. Echo of Shelley, "Ozymandias."
2. Emile Boutroux, . . . *Science et religion dans la philosophie contemporaine* (1908). It appeared in the series Bibliothèque de philosophie scientifique, edited by Gustave Le Bon.
3. William Hanna Thomson, *Brain and Personality* (1907).
4. Baron Hermann Speck von Sternburg had died at Heidelberg Aug. 23.
5. Flora Stone (Mrs. Samuel) Mather (1852–1909) was fatally ill.

To Elizabeth Cameron

23 Avenue du Bois de Boulogne
Sept. 15, 1908.

Yours of the 5th arrives with much more punctuality than the hands of my clocks. Your account of the situation is as bad as possible. We have foreseen it precisely as it comes. I should not console her much by telling her that she is not alone. As our time comes, we all face more or less the same certainties. The absolute inevitability of it, which young people cannot understand,—or old ones either—is to me the most fascinating part of it. I have already told you that I had got my first warning. With me, as with many other fools and some geniuses, the weak spot is what is known as Brocas convolution of the brain, which contains the shelves of memory.[1] Suddenly or slowly the shelves close and can't be opened. Mine have been closing normally and slowly, but one day in July I happened to go into Audrain's place to ask a question, and, to my consternation, my French tumbled out all in a heap.[2] The words came without connection. The man looked at me queerly; I mumbled something, and got out into the street; by the time I got back to my rooms, the paralysis had passed; but I knew quite well what it meant; and was not surprised when I told Austin about it, to find that I knew more than he did.[3] The thing may be a mere momentary upset, and never recur. The more likely chance is that my Brocas convolution is slowly hardening, as I have seen it in so many cases. In my experience, as in my father's case, or R. W. Emerson, or your uncle John, or old George Bancroft, the average time is about ten years, the last five or six being more or less helpless. If I can get two years more, without a breakdown, I shall do well enough, but I doubt it. The margin is wide. M. Broca might shut up in seven days or seven years, but he is sure to do it in the end, and meanwhile keeps me much on the watch. Luckily for me, the process is generally placid and painless. Poor Speck would have been glad to exchange, and perhaps even Charley Rae would have preferred it. What surprised me most was to find, a few days ago, in the Life of Faraday, that he, the most active-minded Englishman of the century, and the greatest genius, suffered for five-and-twenty years under the steady loss of memory until he died quite senile at seventytwo.[4] Let us be grateful we are not geniuses.

Meanwhile I get out of life all the quiet and beauty I can. After the great storm, some days of great beauty have come, and I slip off, into the country, to enjoy them. Sunday I went to Versailles where were various callers amusing themselves as they might. Bessie Marbury has at last come to my view of chauffeurs, after a chaotic year of trial that only a woman's nerves could stand. Yesterday I suddenly took the train to Chartres and once more studied my windows to see whether I could correct anything in my account of them. The sun was intense and tried the glass severely. For days together I see no one to speak with, but the Fred Keep's came to tea, one afternoon, and Lindsay took me one evening to dinner at Ritz's where we saw great Jews and others, including the noble Harry Lehr amusing the Duchess of Westminster.[5]

Another active exchange of letters with Whitelaw Reid has been started. He wrote to ask for my Education, which I sent him, and he added a pressing invitation to Wrest, which I declined. He finds his palaces a little solitary now that his children have flown. I don't wonder; but his is a happy temperament and simply satisfied with the great merits of the world he owns.

———

MS: MHi

1. The convolution of Broca, discovered by the French physiologist Paul Broca (1824–1880), is the third convolution of the left frontal lobe; it is the center that controls articulate speech.
2. Audrain was a dealer in antiques.
3. A. K. Austin, an American physician practicing in Paris.
4. Michael Faraday (1791–1867), known for major discoveries in electromagnetism, died at 76. Henry Bence Jones, *The Life and Letters of Faraday* (1870).
5. Frederic A. Keep (c. 1858–1911), wealthy western lumberman who moved to Washington in 1900; Florence Sheffield Boardman Keep (c. 1864–1954); Henry S. Lehr (1869–1929), a dandy known as "King Lehr."

To Charles Milnes Gaskell

23 Avenue du Bois de Boulogne
27 Sept. 1908

My dear Carlo

I hasten to acknowledge your letter from Tillypronie. Though almost as stalwart as Sir John at eightyeight, I still feel that this infernal racket is playing the deuce with me. Especially my memory and mind are as slippery as monkeys. I am so scared at their tricks that I daren't leave home. I've seen this process so often that I know quite well what it means. If I take care of myself and avoid strains, mental and physical, especially women, wine and anxieties, with good luck I may be able to go about alone for some two years more; but I may have to protect myself from myself at the shortest possible notice.

Most of my elderly friends, and some of my younger ones, have gone
that way. If you feel curious about it, you can easily read it up in the
medical books under the heading Brocas Convolution. It is really a very
curious study. To my delight, I happened to discover that Faraday suffered
for five-and-twenty years from this affection before he died of it, absolutely
senile, at seventy-two. This is Sir John's complaint; but only Scotchmen
can do without memory. I notice, too, that while everybody in Great Britain
lives indefinitely, I have now buried everyone past eighty in America. Man
or woman, I know no one, now, older than my own generation. Last winter
swept all the old people away.

The subject may seem a little lugubrious, but it interests me on account
of my theory, that, on the physico-chemical law of development and dynamics, our society has reached what is called the critical point where it is
near a new phase or equilibrium. In America, we do not stand the pressure.
Neither the individual nor the society is any longer stable. We have got to
go up or go under. Probably in England, enough of the old society exists
to mask the process more or less; but in America it is flagrant; especially
in a general election, where you see all the forces of society, moving at a
tremendous pace, and without the faintest conception of what they are
doing. The spectacle resembles that of swarms of insects changing from
worms to wings. They must get the wings or die. For our salvation, Mr
Wilbur Wright is providing wings.[1] He will also have to provide a new
insect to use them.

I would have much liked to talk with Lord Kelvin about it, but he too
said with his last words that he had failed to make a magneto-electric-
etherial theory that would stand up; and this is the same problem as mine.
The solution of mind is certainly in the magnet.

It is useless to talk, of course, and especially because hundreds of people
are working, experimentally and mathematically, on the same subject. I am
waiting for their results, and am rather annoyed to have only two years to
spare, when I probably need at least ten, at the rate they go.

Then their infernal mathematics handicap me to a degree that practically
throws me out of the race. The French physicists alone are making really
a considerable effort to state the problem in a literary form, and if it
weren't for them, I could not even see it. For I find Sir Oliver Lodge,
curiously enough, quite unintelligible.[2] The only man who seems to me
quite honest about it, both with himself and with his public, is Gustave Le
Bon; but even he has not ventured into the social *mélange*. He can't tell
me whether our society is now a solid, a fluid or a gas.

On these books, I have been laboring some six hours a day, all summer,
and now, with nothing accomplished, I am preparing to emigrate again. I
have taken rooms on the Kaiser Wilhelm II for October 28. This will bring

me to New York the day after election. Either we shall be then out of the woods, or we shall be in convulsions. My own circle is still in great tribulation of all sorts, and I go back early on their account.

I fear I shall not pass through London. With much hesitation I have declined two invitations to Wrest, from the Whitelaw Reids, and feel now as though I must not fall in their way. They are superb in their hospitality, but I dread going about in more or less new circles, when I feel not quite at home.

By the way, if you see Augusta Harvey, can you tell her that, after a correspondence with the magazines, I failed to place her article, even with the help of photographs, and that I still think she had better adopt my scheme of historical illustration and comment. It would not be difficult; at any rate, with your help to make a first architectural restoration of the plan and appearance of the Abbey. You remember how I tried to begin one, years ago.

Americans swarm. I dined at Ritz's a few nights ago, and found myself literally circled by Americans whom I wanted to avoid. They are a set of bores, and I always want to carry a bomb with me to Ritz's. I cannot conceive that society would lose perceptibly now by drowning all its good society. Socialism may come when it pleases; it cannot be a greater bore than what it will sweep away. Nor can it be sillier, though it may be shabbier.

My love to all yours.   Ever   Henry Adams.

MS: MHi

1. Wilbur Wright (1867–1912), airplane inventor, had that year made test flights at Le Mans which attracted worldwide attention.
2. Sir Oliver Lodge, *Modern Views of Electricity* (1889).

To Theodore Roosevelt

1603 H Street   16 Dec. 1908

My dear Roosevelt

If you were talking last night as President, I have nothing to say. Whatever the President says goes! The authorities used to say that Parliament had the power to do everything except make a man of a woman. Some day we will put that into the Constitution as an Executive Power—not requiring confirmation by the Senate. In regard to most of us elderly people, I admit that there is little or no difference between an old woman and an old man, even when Senator. Not for a moment would I challenge the fate of Pulitzer by affirming that there is,—for I am with you on that as on other points.[1]

But!!! After March 4, should you allude to my bronze figure, will you try to do St Gaudens the justice to remark that his expression was a little higher than sex can give. As he meant it, he wanted to exclude sex and sink it in the idea of humanity. The figure is sexless.[2]

Such is life! When you are 1,235,452,000,000 like me, you will repent too.

> Ever Yrs   Henry Adams.

MS: DLC, Roosevelt

1. An allusion to the president's reprimand of Joseph Pulitzer (1847–1911), who had accused Roosevelt's brother-in-law of profiting from the government's purchase of the New Panama Canal Co. In a special message to Congress Roosevelt threatened the publisher with prosecution for criminal libel.
2. Roosevelt replied to HA that he had simply taken it for granted that the figure was a woman and attached no importance to its portrayal as such.

To Whitelaw Reid

1603 H Street   15 Feb. 1909

My dear Mr Reid

I have to thank you for your letter of the 5th. When Mrs Reid was here I took occasion to tell her that I was in no way responsible for the omissions or insertions in the Hay volumes, beyond the material which I placed in Mrs Hay's hands. With that material she has done what she pleased. I have never been informed except by you, of her decision to omit certain letters, especially yours. Of course I gave her what I thought appropriate for publication; beyond that, I had nothing to do, and was in Europe when the volumes were printed.

I am forced to say thus much to you, in order to explain that I was not even aware of having wasted your time at Wrest on preparing material that was not used. To no one else am I bound to make explanations, and with Mrs Hay I have had no talk whatever, except to suggest that it would be easy to print a Key containing the suppressed names.

As you know, I am not myself delicate as to the use of names. My view is that we, who set up to be educated society, should stand up in our harness, and should play our parts without awkward stage-fright of amateurs. We may not always like our parts, but we ought to respect ourselves enough to respect them. God knows, I have no love of notoriety, but I never have shrunk from it, if it seemed to be a proper and becoming part of social work. You have always acted on the same rule, and on a vast theatre. To us, therefore, the attempt at anonymity means only amateur weakness.

For my own pleasure I have rescued all the names that came within my reach. You can insert in your copy, on p. 246 of Vol. I, the names:—Dyer, Wise, McBlair, Pyne, Ivers, Forbes, Ives, Tom Welles, Foster, Reid of the Gazette; and, of course, D. D. Porter and Captain Steadman. Grant's remark about Sherman, p. 248 was made to Mr Forbes; you will remember what Forbes; I took the person to be old John Forbes of Boston.[1]

I had the notion that, as our American literature was barren of what used to be called Table Talk, a few volumes of the Table Talk of one of our best talkers would fill a yawning gap in our somewhat meagre library. Therefore I tried to select everything that resembled conversation;—everything that he said to you and me, without literary purpose. The result is desperately muddled; but let us hope that enough of the scheme remains to answer a part of the intent.

Yes! Theodore is whacking his last critics. He is, beneath it all, a little saddened, I think, although he bears it all bravely. In a few days more, Washington will groan with dulness without him; and then will come your own Ohio to the rescue.

Frankly, our friend Taft has begun with a series of what the French call *bêtises,* stupidities which have thrown me into consternation. He has done, undone, and left undone, a quantity of things that bewilder me. The selection of Knox knocked us all silly, and seemed to me a calamity, not so much because of Knox, as because of the measure it gave of Taft. The avowal of intention to surround himself with lawyers reduces me to silence, for I despise the political lawyer, because I am his client and can not be his equal. Knox did not know enough law to know that he was ineligible,[2] and did not know enough diplomacy to organise his Department which he has thrown into confusion. He is not in the remotest degree fit for the post. In regard to the Treasury Taft has made a still worse muddle; he has hawked it over the country; Burton, Herrick and I know not how many more, have refused it.[3] As for the Department of Justice, he has put his brother's representative into it,—Wickersham—a perfectly respectable appointment, but one that invites criticism from every enemy he has to make.[4] Meanwhile, in the midst of the muddle, Taft went off to Panama to decide an engineering matter for which he was incompetent, leaving all the old and new incumbents here, in a temper which you can imagine.

This unexpected revelation of character comes on me with a shock. I may be mistaken, of course, but, if so, I am mistaken in company with everyone else. I am only an echo of underground society. My impressions are impersonal. I have no candidates to offer, and no scheme to suggest; but if the new President is so bent on making a clean sweep of Roosevelt's men, why did we elect him expressly to carry on the Roosevelt régime?

But I forget my rôle of benevolent sage! Ben Franklin is my idol and model. Let us all smile, like our President, and go on to "cultiver notre jardin."

Ever Yrs   Henry Adams.

MS: DLC, Reid

1. HA continued for years to fill in names in Hay's letters. His handwritten list of these names and his annotated volumes of the letters are at the Massachusetts Historical Society.
2. Philander C. Knox (1853–1921), Republican senator from Pennsylvania, secretary of state 1909–1913. While Knox was a senator, a law was passed which raised the salary of the secretary of state and prohibited appointment of any member of Congress to a federal office of which the salary had been increased during his term in Congress. A bill repealing the salary increase (and removing Knox's disability) was promptly introduced.
3. Theodore Elijah Burton (1851–1929) of Cleveland, Republican senator 1909–1915. Myron T. Herrick, governor of Ohio, had returned to his financial affairs in Cleveland; he served as ambassador to France 1912–1914.
4. George Woodward Wickersham (1858–1936), attorney general 1909–1913, was a New York lawyer and partner of Henry Waters Taft (1859–1945), the president's brother.

To Brooks Adams

1603 H Street   17 Feb. 1909

Dear Brooks

The decay of my faculties about which you allow yourself such painful levity has now proceeded so far that I derive from it much humor, constant amusement, and some instruction.[1] At the slightest strain or care or worry, I go to pieces and become a jelly. In that state I contemplate my fellow men with more pure joy than ever. They dance as though they were flies in the sun, and are a joy to watch, even though I am old, ugly and idiotic. Yet this mental paralysis has practical drawbacks. One of these is my nauseous indigestion of American history, which now makes me physically sick, so that only by self-compulsion can I read its dreary details. This accounts for my slowness with your great work. You have toiled through a gigantic labor from which I shrank; you have accomplished an immense task which no one but yourself could have done; and which crushes me under its responsibilities and consequences; but I go all to pieces whenever I attempt to handle it, and roll on the ground in agonies of weakness. Your picture of our wonderful grandpapa is a psychologic nightmare to his degenerate and decadent grandson.

I make progress in the reading, but I reverse it in the criticism. Every effort sets me further back. The psychological or pathological curiosity of the study takes possession of me. The unhealthy atmosphere of the whole age, and its rampant meanness even in violence; the one-sided flabbiness

of America; the want of self-respect, of education, of purpose; the intellectual feebleness, and the material greed,—I loathe it all.

If our dear grandpapa had been favored by God with a touch of humor
in his long career! if he had indulged in a vice! if he had occasionally
stopped preaching! but only when he goes for blood and slays some savage
rival, does he provoke my filial regard.

I hate to gibbet him, but since his Diary has already done it, I suppose
we can do no worse. The curse of a Diary is fatal. No man has ever taken
his own life in that way without damnation.

The warning to me comes direct from Hell. It tells me never—never—
never—to be didactic. Thank God, I have done little preaching in my life.
I have tried to tell stories, and sometimes to found them on a carefully
concealed foundation of idea; but I trust I have never tried expressly to
improve my fellow-insects. Senile as I am, I still hope I may cling to that
salvation. I would gladly amuse my world; but I refuse to improve or
reprove it. The only form of preaching that ever appeals to an old man is
the familiar advice to repent, for the kingdom of heaven is at hand. This
is for himself!

So, you may do what you like with the paper I sent you, which was, in
my point of view, only a sort of jig-saw puzzle, put together in order to
see whether the pieces could be made to fit. Too well I knew the inadequacy
of the public mind, to let me imagine that anyone could derive amusement
from such trifles. The fools would begin at once to discuss whether the
theory was true. I cannot, even here, after months of search, find a physicist
who can be trusted to tell me whether my technical terms are all wrong.
The technologists cannot go beyond their laboratory materials. The American mind refuses even to amuse itself. It is a convention as flat as the
surface of the ocean.

Perhaps my language seems excessive, but you must make allowances
for me. I am sorely beset. Yesterday I achieved my seventyfirst birthday.
At that age, mind and body and nervous energies enfeebled, I am obliged
to look directly into four years of Ohio fog. Four years of Bill Taft will
kill me—thank God for that!—but four years of Bill Taft with Philander
Knox on top of him, make a nightmare such as Sinbad never dreamed.

Forgive me for unloading on you these morbid visions. Just now they
are poisoning our peace a good deal. We are mostly vagrant dogs about to
be asphyxiated.

Ever Yrs   Henry Adams.

MS: MH

1. In an attempt to buttress the dynamic theory of history which he had postulated in the
Education, HA worked up the essay "The Rule of Phase Applied to History," which took

its point of departure from the famous "Rule of Phase" by Josiah Willard Gibbs (1839–1903). BA, impressed by the essay, responded, "After this I hope I shall hear no more for the present about the decay of your faculties" (BA to HA, Feb. 15, MH).

To Brooks Adams

Washington   February 18, 1909.

My dear Brooks

Just one hundred years ago, President Jefferson was bidding good-bye, and President Madison was offering to J. Q. Adams the mission to Russia. Much water has flowed down the Potomac since then, but the meanest refuse it has swept along is I,—Ego,—to wit, the grandson of J.Q.A.—who am a blind beetle employed by you to sprawl over the history of the grandparents, whom I pity with the keenest sympathy, and wish had never been born.[1]

You have shouldered the load, and my business is to help you in carrying it, if you wish; but I never felt less confident of my ability. The danger of doing harm,—of obstructing you,—discouraging you,—or leading you wrong,—is the most trifling part of my difficulty. Of course I shall do harm! I see the dangers acutely, and I do not see how to escape them. By no literary machinery known to me can J.Q.A. be made a literary or popular success. "Nitor in adversum"[2] is the motto for a man like him. I fear making him even less attractive and engaging than if I let him alone; but what scares me most is the reflection that I have never known a biography which raised the reputation of its subject, and I have known hundreds that did the subject fatal harm. You can recall McClellan and Chase as examples. Hay's and Nicolay's Lincoln was the only exception, and must stand as your only model. In truth, it is not a biography, and they very properly called it a History.

Your book is also bound to be a History, but you cannot make J.Q.A. the center of it. He was always fighting on the outskirts,—a kind of free lance, following the march of forces which he never commanded. You are infallibly forced to violate your literary law; you must make two movements, one of history, the other of biography, and jerkily vibrate between them, inserting first a slice of history, then a slice of biography, and failing to maintain unity in the sum. The literary task becomes difficult just in proportion as you increase your centers of movement, and are forced aside from your personal point of view. Instinctively you will feel yourself drawn to sacrifice either biography or history, and if you do not, you will sacrifice both.

Diaries are vile things, and yet they have the great literary advantage of holding tight to one centre of motion. Histories are pretty vile things too, but chiefly because the writer is forced to multiply centres of motion. I think that this reason possibly explains why the French are so amusing in history; they coolly ignore every other interest than that of France. The Frenchman is an artist, and very properly refuses to sacrifice his art in order to run after what Germans call truth. The German is scientific and becomes dull and unreadable, because he is always making historical dictionaries,—trying to be true in every possible direction at once.

Therefore, at starting, I admit that you have undertaken a literary job which I shrink from facing. In my Gallatin I had to do the same thing, but I did it only as a study for the History to follow. I cared little whether I was read, for any literary object, since my *readers* would be obliged to read it all over again in a proper form and juster relations. Your object is, or ought to be, literary. You are, in reality, writing a romance, a political novel, and you need, above all else, Form.

There has been always my own gallows! All my life I have labored and sweated to get Form, and always I have failed, because the difficulties become enormously increased with every enlargement of detail. The details themselves require only patient labor, and I could sit patiently during long years writing paragraph after paragraph, over and over again,—chapter after chapter—volume after volume,—recasting, reconsidering, rearranging, without ever quite concluding, but I could never get to the point of seeing a big work as a whole. I doubt whether I have ever published a chapter in which every paragraph has not been re-written, with my own hand, fully three times, and reconsidered, pen in hand, fully thirty; yet even now I rarely read a chapter of my own without seeing that it ought to be re-written. You can imagine how I feel about a volume. My mind cannot carry it as a whole, but my eyes can see where the modelling, or drawing, or color, or conception, fails.

Failure matters little when it concerns only oneself. Henry James can fail as often as he likes in novels, but when he fails in biography, he leaves mighty little of William Story. In biography we are taking life. I would never have anything to do with the life of our father, for that reason. I felt sure that his position in history would be the lower for it. As he stood, the public imagination filled all gaps and voids. Had I botched it, he would have vanished. Even Seward has seemed to me lowered in popular esteem by it.[3] Magni nominis umbra[4] is an artistic secret, dead with Michael Angelo.

Magni nominis umbra would have been truer than it is, when applied to J. Q. Adams, without the Diary. Big as that historical monument is, and indispensable to history, I do not think it raised the reputation of its author. The impression it leaves is that of a man difficult to live with. One's imagination has no play. We cannot see the man of the world; we are held with our noses as tight to the grindstone as his own; we abjure our own faculty of fancy; we long to invent qualities that are missing, but are forbidden to do it.

There, then, is the enormous canvas which you have filled up, at least in the corner before 1810. You have done it so well that I am shy of making remarks on it. To satisfy you, I have gone over it, line by line, and made comments to the extent of forty or fifty pages, but these are mostly verbal.[5] Only now and then I have expressed my feelings; not to affect you, but to show you how a reader would probably be affected. You had evidently felt it too. The lowness of tone, which in you and me would be called dyspeptic, becomes monotonous. We lose patience, not so much with the despondency, as at the monotony. We yearn for a high light of wit or humor somewhere.

For my own part, I feel still more the old man's want of judgment. He had a nasty temper. Not that his temper was bad, but that it fooled him. He was always telling his guests that he didn't believe they had ever tasted Tokay. I can't forgive him his vote for the Embargo or his defence of Andrew Jackson. He was not punished half enough for either. His patriotism, too, has a savagely humorous side. His whole behavior shows that he loathed and hated America. He never quarreled in Russia; he was happy as a King in society there; he enjoyed it all, and was never so pleasantly situated; yet we know what Petersburg is, and what his circumstances were. Beyond dispute, he never thought of going home without nausea, but he, and his son, and his grandchildren, had to be trained to profess a passionate patriotism which very strongly resembled cant.

His limitations, too, were astounding. Though he was brought up in Paris, London and Berlin, he seems to have been indifferent to art. I do not remember that he ever mentions interest in architecture, sculpture or painting. His taste in literature was wholly didactic. I wonder what he thought of Walter Scott; the Lay of the last Minstrel came out in 1805, and Scott was precisely his contemporary within four years. I do not conceive that he could have cared for Wordsworth or Turner who were also of his generation; but I half-remember that among his books I could never find Goethe or Schiller. I do not think he ever enjoyed Voltaire, and I would give much to be assured that he ever bothered himself to look at the Rembrandts at the Hermitage.

These limitations cramp you horribly. You have no atmosphere. You can make a little play at St Petersburg with de Maistre, and I fear that you had better avoid Greek art or literature, while you coquette with the French stage; but on the whole, you must avoid art.[6] On looking into the index of the Diary, I see one mention of Walter Scott, as late as 1816, and it is really pitiable.

As we are now a great deal older and more mature than he ever was, these limitations shock us,—or at least they shock me,—and make the task more trying. They drive me back on the political side which is nauseating, and was as nauseating to him as it is to me. After he went home in 1817, I doubt whether he ever could have had a chance to talk with anyone except about politics. The generation of Americans that succeeded Jefferson was one of pure and simple provincial barbarism, much like the society of Australia or New Zealand now. He was the only man in it who had ever known the world, and he must have lived a life of pure void. For that matter, I do not find it scintillating in 1909.

Somehow you have got to put all this into some harmonious shape. You will have to skin your skunk. My first care would be to look over it as a matter of proportion, and trim down excrescences. You will have to allot space to the episodes:—so much to the Senate; so much to diplomacy; so much to the State Department; and trim unmercifully. I do not mean that you should prune movement, but that you should break up monotony, either of action or of thought. I would hunt for possible repetitions. For example, his battle to escape the bar and bench may be found to contain needless repetitions. His journeys and voyages, with their discomforts, may bear economies. The worst of it is that you will surely find omissions to make good. For instance, as far as I can see, you have made no allusion to his behavior about the Louisiana Purchase in November, 1803. Your own discursions into history may be susceptible of modelling, but will be more likely to expand than to contract. I think you might make a sentence about the drift of his legal arguments,—his way of approaching a subject. My recollection is that his work, though vigorous, was apt to be diffuse,— wanted form—and that he frankly said he was bored by the effort to correct.

Perhaps you will see better the technical method of the job, as I under-stand it, if I add that I find my work easiest when chopped up into chapters of not more than 24 pages (400 words a page.) That number of pages I can manage as a unit, and by stringing the units together, I can keep a sort of general oversight on them, and rip out a defective bit anywhere it shows. I can also see more clearly what can best be cut out, if the chapter tends to over-run its limit. The short chapter always tends to become a unit, for the space is hardly large enough to admit more than one subject, and if it admits two, it fixes their limits, as well as,—to a certain degree,—their treatment. The longer the chapter, the harder the task; in experience I have found the chapter of 10,000 words the largest I can readily handle. The most successful British biography I have read in twenty years is Purcell's Life of Cardinal Manning,[7] and I observe that its 1500 pages are divided into 58 chapters, or 25 pages a chapter, and its page averages rather less than 400 words. This,—I take it,—is the result of long experience in readers as well as writers. The average mind cannot comfortably carry more than 10,000 words in one group.

I have no scruple, in my own theories, about handling my material in view of a climax, and for artistic purposes, the climax must always tend to tragedy. No one with the intelligence of an average monkey will try to tell a story without leading up to its point. Your tragedy will be indicated, as it is in the lives of us all, by the chief failure, which is, in your case, the Presidency. To me, the old gentleman's Presidency appears always as lurid,—which is not the impression made on me by his father's defeat,—and I see the age of Andrew Jackson and the cotton-planters much as I see the age of the Valois or Honorius,—that is, profound horror. Americans are afraid of tragedy; they fly it, or shut their eyes to it; they are irritated if you insist on it; but they do not so much object to the suggestion of it, and are willing at times to admit that certain persons,—like Abraham Lincoln— may be treated in that tone. Once, in the course of my many literary experiments, I tried to put some depth of shadow into my picture,—John Randolph,—and although nobody liked it, not many people expressly complained. J. Q. Adams is, to my artistic fancy, a tragic picture, and his Presidency is the most tragic shadow of it. He is the prophet who ends in secret murder and open war, violence and fraud and hideous moral depravity. Americans dare not look at it as such a Shakespearean or Sophoclean plot, and would turn their backs on it; but in their miserable consciousness of meanness they know it, and they have still enough left of atrophied imagination to feel the suggestion of it.

Finally, after all is said, our good grandpapa must always be, in a historical point of view, the most important figure of the half-century, 1800–1850. The historian must roll half-a-dozen of the other figures into one, in order to balance his value in the picture. Even on the single side of Foreign Affairs, he is the only Foreign Minister we ever produced who was trained and competent to his task, until the time of John Hay. All the others were mere American politicians or lawyers of more or less ability; those two men were alone educated, from youth upwards, and knew the whole field on which they were to act. By a happy chance, you are the only person competent to deal with the subject. I am not quite sure whether this compliment to you is also a criticism on our time, but it is certainly true that the list of our Academy and Institute contains every name that has yet been discovered in our ranks, and I can see in it no name but yours which carries any weight for such work as this. Indeed, except McMaster, no one on the list carries any weight at all;[8] old Parton was a brilliant biographer compared with any of them.

In conclusion I revert to my first fact,—that I am the poorest shot of the lot! My only business in social life, just now, is to play the rôle of Sage,—to sit solemnly in my chair and listen to one person after another unfolding insoluble problems for my opinion. Today I have had three. Each takes an hour. In the intervals I take up a fourth,—your's! The problems are always insoluble, else they would not come to me. My answer is always the same,—let the other fellow talk till he has said all there is to say; and then, with proper gravity, advise him, or her, above all, to keep his temper.

This is the whole story!

Ever Yrs   H

MS: MH

1. BA had completed the manuscript draft of his biography of JQA and sent it to HA for criticism.
2. *Nitor in adversum*: I strive against opposition; Ovid, *Metamorphoses*, II, 72.
3. *An Autobiography from 1801 to 1834. With a Memoir of His Life, and Selections from His Letters,* by Frederick W. Seward, 3 vols. (1877–1891).
4. *Magni nominis umbra*: the shadow of a great name; Lucan, *Bellum Civile*, I, 135.
5. HA's detailed critique eventually ran to 81 long sheets.
6. Joseph de Maistre (1754?–1821), Sardinian ambassador to Russia when JQA was there, author of *Les Soirées de Saint-Petersbourg* (1821).
7. Edmund Sheridan Purcell, *Life of Cardinal Manning, Archbishop of Westminster* (1895–1896).
8. John Bach McMaster, *A History of the People of the United States, from the Revolution to the Civil War,* 8 vols. (1883–1913).

To Charles Milnes Gaskell

23 Avenue du Bois de Boulogne
2 May, 1909.

My dear Carlo

So you have got your medicine! I am too ignorant a capitalist to understand it, but I can console the British land-owner by the reflexion that if he will only grow old enough, he will not mind being taxed out of existence.[1] Nature has done it already. Merely my forced abandonment of vices, not to speak of virtues, has—I calculate—cheated my governments out of fully half what I paid at thirty.

The process of levelling down,—of growing laterally instead of vertically,—is one which has been going on since the starfish first crawled—if they do crawl,—and is near completion. We have now only to cut off the heads of a very few more poppies, and our dear friends the socialists will alone remain. I am glad to see every country hurrying the process, for I am curious to know what sort of society can be duller than this. As it shows itself to me, at home or here, it has not only lost its old features, which were ugly enough, to be sure,—but has taken on no new ones, and is a formless lump of globular lumps, like Pierpont Morgan's nose. This is, I believe, what the socialists say, and I think they are about right. I have been to the Salons and the restaurants and the weddings and the little private talk-talks; and have seen nothing but what the socialists see. I try to read, and to walk, and to hunt bric-à-brac, and to smile like my sweet President; and the whole impression is one of regret that I can't jump a hundred years, and see what worse rubbish can grow. You will have a bad attack of moral dyspepsia if you come over here. You will growl like a venerable Bengal tiger. As for me, I smile.

What does it matter? I've been studying science for ten years past, with keen interest, noting down my phases of mind each year; and every new scientific method I try, shortens my view of the future. The last—thermo-dynamics—fetches me out on sea-level within ten years. I'm sorry Lord Kelvin is dead. I would travel a few thousand-million miles to discuss with him the thermodynamics of socialistic society. His law is awful in its rigidity and intensity of result.

You talk about imbeciles being gloomy reading![2] An absolute imbecility of social mind is worse. I wish I could think it was all my own, but every newspaper and Mr Bernard Shaw and about a million socialistic orators yesterday howl it.[3]

The consequence is that I've no news. Everybody is more or less on edge—irritable in a feeble way. We have no interests except weddings. I have no amusement but hunting up wedding-presents. Half a dozen ladies whose daughters have left them, expect me to hold their hands. I growl meekly with ambassadors, and weep softly with their wives. We talk of oriental politics and taxes. Also of Germany and wars. Secretly I doubt whether enough of the primitive energy still exists to fight one real war. The society does not look it. But they may have energy enough to fire off missiles one or two hundred miles away.

The best book I could send you would be a bound volume of Le Rire for 1908.[4] Nothing of a serious sort has been shown me. Even Edith Wharton cannot help me, though she abides among the high-lights and talks only with *gens-d'esprit à la Louis Quatorze, chez Ritz.*

Ever Yrs   Henry Adams.

MS: MHi

1. The Lloyd George budget of 1909 included land taxes (20 percent of unearned increment in all land transfers and a small capital tax on undeveloped land) as well as increases in income, inheritance, and liquor taxes.
2. "The Commission on imbeciles has just printed its last volume & very gloomy reading it is!" (Gaskell to HA, April 11, 1909, James Milnes Gaskell Collection); a reference to

Report of the Royal Commissioners on the Care and Control of the Feeble-Minded, vol. 8 (1908).
3. George Bernard Shaw (1856–1950), Irish-born playwright, leading exponent of Fabian socialism. May Day, designated in 1889 by the Second Socialist International as a labor holiday, was observed with demonstrations, parades, and speeches.
4. *Le Rire*, a humor magazine.

To Henry James

23 Avenue du Bois de Boulogne
Sept. 3, 1909

My dear Friend

Your letters, few as they are, have always the charm of saying something that carries one over the gaps; and when you describe Bay Lodge as a great and abundant social luxury, you paint a portrait rather more lifelike than anything Sargent ever did.[1] You paint even a group, for I believe we are all now social luxuries, and, as for myself, I am much flattered if regarded as bric-à-brac of a style,—dixhuitième by preference, rather than early Victorian. Nothing matters much! Only our proper labels! Please stick mine on, in your wonderfully perfect way, and I will sit quiet on the shelf, contented, among the rest.

As for what the newspapers report as the realities of life, I grow everyday too detached to feel them, and as for the volume you mention—which I did, in fact, at one time, mean to recall in order to give it completion of form,—I do not care what is done with it, as long as I do nothing myself. Bay Lodge's experience last winter completed and finished my own. When his Heracles appeared absolutely unnoticed by the literary press, I regarded my thesis as demonstrated. Society no longer shows the intellectual life necessary to enable it to react against a stimulus. My brother Brooks insists on the figure of paralysis. I prefer the figure of diffusion, like that of a river falling into an ocean. Either way, it drowned Bay, and has left me still floating, with vast curiosity to see what vaster absence of curiosity can bring about in my Sargasso sea.

Mrs Wharton, in spite of her feminine energy and interest, is harder hit, I think, than I by the loss of Bay Lodge, but she has, besides, a heavy anxiety to face in the uncertainties of her husband's condition. We are altogether a dilapidated social show, bric-à-brac or old-clo' shop, and I find smiling a rather mandarin amusement. Mrs Wharton has told you about it, no doubt, but she will not have cared to dwell on it. My most immediate anxiety is Sturgis Bigelow, whose condition is very alarming to my shattered nervous system; but there are a dozen more such, in my close neighborhood, and Bay's catastrophe makes the solidest stars reel.

I speculate occasionally on your doings and interests, and those of your fellow Englishmen, if you have fellows still; and I have even gone so far as to ask such insects as return, from time to time, after penetrating the hive,— Mrs Wharton, the Ralph Curtis's, Berenson, and such,—what they have found in the way of wax or honey to store or consume, leaving small particles for me; but the sad heart of Ruth was nothing worth mentioning, compared with the small crop of gleanings that I have effected among that alien corn.[2] As usual, I got more active information from Berenson than from all the rest, and yet Berenson,—well! Berenson belongs to the primitives.

God be with you, all the same! though I associate only with aviators, and talk of the north pole with proper scepticism.[3]

Ever Yrs   Henry Adams.

MS: MH

1. George Cabot ("Bay") Lodge had died suddenly Aug. 21 from a heart attack at the age of 35.
2. "Alien corn": echo of Keats, "Ode to a Nightingale."
3. On Sept. 1, 1909, Dr. Frederick A. Cook announced that he had reached the North Pole on April 21, 1908. Experts received the announcement with skepticism, convinced that Admiral Robert E. Peary was the one who had actually reached the pole as he announced on Sept. 6, 1909.

To Margaret Chanler

23 Avenue du Bois de Boulogne
Sept. 9, 1909.

My dear Friend

Thanks for your letter of August 25. Among the props of life which have fallen, or are falling, you are a column of support without match. My summer has been mostly an effort to keep pace with the ruin,—if one can keep pace with ruins, like other wrecks,—and I have no one left but you to serve me for a fixed star to measure my altitude. Bay is a crushing loss, but I am almost worse demoralised by the fear that his death will sweep Nanny and Bessy and Cabot and the whole family beyond my range of touch and feeling. No one can foresee what swath time's scythe will cut, when it starts in with a swing like that.

Well! being a poor bit of materialised *Energetik,* I have no resource but the old one, taught by one's brothers in childhood—to grin and bear it; nor is this refuge much ennobled by calling it stoicism. The defect in this old remedy is that it helps others not at all, and oneself only by a sort of moral suicide.

I try to busy myself with our favorite philosophy but I rather agree with you and your friend Bergson that St Thomas said all there was to say.[1] On the whole I think I like to keep my milk and my flies separate. Bergson does not much amuse me. I like my Schopenhauer, and I like my Kelvin,— I like metaphysics and I like physics,—but I don't much care to reconcile them, though I enjoy making them fight. What I like most in the schoolmen is their rule of cutting infinite sequences short. They insist on stopping at the prime motor at once. Bergson and all the speculators who follow Kant, start with Space, and then merge that Space in Thought, and are bound to merge that Thought-space in Hyperthought-space and so on to infinity like our friend Keyser; but become scared and stop, without explaining the reason for stopping. They give me no sort of help. Time and Space are conditions of Thought, and so far good; but I can reckon an infinite hierarchy of them in mathematics, one just as good as the other,—concepts of concepts,—and why, in space, should I stop?

I have not seen Keyser's last paper;[2] it will be an amusement for winter; but I have been amusing myself with a fable for instructors of history. I've a notion of printing a Letter to Professors. Pure malice! but History will die if not irritated. The only service I can do to my profession is to serve as a flea.

I like best Bergson's frank surrender to the superiority of Instinct over Intellect. You know how I have preached that principle, and how I have studied the facts of it. In fact I wrote once a whole volume—called my Education—which no one ever saw, and which you must some day look into,—borrow William James's copy, in hopes that he may have marginally noted his contempt for me,—in order to recall how Education may be shown to consist in following the intuitions of instinct. Loeb calls it _Tropism_, I believe; which means that a mother likes to nurse her own child.[3]

No! on the whole, I wont make you go back to my destroyed volume; but will some day get you to read Fabre's dozen volumes of Souvenirs Entomologiques; the most fascinating and bewildering of anti-Darwinian philosophies.[4]

I am glad that you mean to resume your duties in New York society. Except for women, society is now an infinite solution; a mere ocean of separate particles; and you can help it to one little centre. I own that the centre will do nothing; but it may play itself to be real.

Love to all yours.   Ever   Henry Adams.

MS: MH

1. Henri Bergson, _L'Evolution créatrice_ (1907).
2. Cassius J. Keyser, "The Message of Modern Mathematics to Theology," _Hibbert Journal_ 7 (Jan., April 1909), 370–390, 623–638.

3. Jacques Loeb (1859–1924), professor of physiology at the University of California, mechanistic philosopher.
4. Jean-Henri Fabre (1823–1915) remained opposed to evolution, believing in the fixity of species.

To Henry Osborn Taylor

23 Avenue du Bois de Boulogne
22 Nov. 1909.

My dear Taylor

Your kind letter of the 2d finds me still in Paris, comforting the rich, and vituperating the wretched, as befits a child of wrath. From day to day I put off my steamer as though it were a monthly bill for taxes. Sometime, I shall find myself at sea; I feel confident that the day of sea-sickness will come, and that the sun of New York will dawn again; but I still linger here, as one lost.

Thanks for your flattery. Of course I love nothing so much as flattery, and am furious with no villain so much as at a critic. Murderers are meritorious compared with men who tell you the truth; not because truth-tellers always murder, but because one always thinks one could do it better. Murder is so easy, and art so long!

I have written you before—have I not?—that I aspire to be bound up with St Augustine. Or rather, I would have aspired to it, if it were artistically possible to build another fourth-century church. It cannot be. The Leitmotif is flat. One can get one's artistic effects only by flattening everything to a level. Perhaps that is why I so love flattery.

As for the readers whom you suggest, I would gladly encourage them to read, if I had the impudence to think anything worth reading. As for Sherman Evarts, he has a right to the volume anyway, and has only to send for it;[1] since it was put in print only to enable the persons named in it, to object or reject or correct whatever concerned them. Any person whose name is mentioned in it, has a right to it. Thus far, no one has objected, or has made any objection that has come to my ears, but I still hold myself ready to strike out whatever is objected to, by anyone authorised to object.

Really nothing matters. No one cares. In another generation, the proportion of *us* to all, will be as unity to infinity. I am satisfied that it is immaterial whether one man or a thousand or a hundred thousand read one's books. The author is as safe as the 17th century clergyman who printed his Sermon on Righteousness,—his pet sermon, that his congregation so much admired!

Thus far I have never given a copy of the "Education" to anyone.

Occasionally some bandit, like Theodore Roosevelt, has told me that I need never expect to see his copy again, but this is piracy, and *force majeure*. Theoretically all the copies are to be recalled, for the corrections, &c. As time goes on, I doubt more and more whether the volume is even worth correcting. It served its only purpose by educating *me*. If Mr Potter should ever hear of the book, and want it, I should be delighted to send him a copy; but I cannot think it. Even my regard for his father cannot inspire me with such a flight.[2]

As for your wife—it's another matter! When a woman says anything, it's so![3] I've said it in print, and stick to it. *They* may not be right,—who is! but the man is wrong.[4]

Ever Yrs　　Henry Adams.

MS: MH

1. Sherman Evarts (1859–1922), son of William Maxwell Evarts.
2. Arthur Bayley Potter (1853–1935), whose father was Thomas Bayley Potter (1817–1898), Manchester Liberal, associate of Cobden and Bright, and supporter of the Union cause. Arthur Potter on a visit to New York had seen the book at Taylor's apartment. In response to a direct request, HA later sent him a copy.
3. Taylor's wife, Julia Isham Taylor (1865–1939), had read it aloud to him and would not let him make marginal notes.
4. "No woman had ever driven him wrong; no man had ever driven him right" (*Education*, Chap. 6).

To Brooks Adams

1603 H Street　　30 Jan. 1910

My dear Brooks

In reply to your letter I know only that I supposed myself to be returning all the heirlooms, of every description, in pursuance of a deed I executed transferring to you all my share and interest in the Quincy house for a family memorial. I supposed that this deed covered the whole transaction, and that nothing remained but for the lawyers to create such a trust as would best serve the purpose. Of that, they are better judges than I. The whole thing being once accumulated in your hands, subject to your disposal, I have no further advice or instructions to give. At most I could only name a counsel to represent me and assist you.

I know nothing whatever about the porcelain,—not even the name of the fabric. Long ago I made over the whole family-business to you and Charles.

As I have often told you, I have but one idea left, and that is to get out of the world as soon and as silently as I can. Your forebodings do not affect me at all. To me the curtain has already dropped. I can't honestly say that I admire the play very much, but it has had good scenes and moments. I'm not going to abuse it. Still less am I going to make myself unhappy about the next one, which is none of my business anyway.

I have known you for sixty-odd years, and since you were a baby I've never known you when you weren't making yourself miserable over the failings of the universe. It has been your amusement, and a very good one. I always say that no one can afford to pose for an optimist, short of an income of a hundred thousand a year. Up to fifty thousand, the pose of pessimism is the only dignified one, just as it is after sixty years old. Both are about equally good rôles. Voltaire settled all that in Candide.

Your sorrow for the British would affect me more if I saw anything left in them worth saving. On that subject Mr Wells has said in his Tono Bungay all I have seen or thought.[1]

As I see the entire world today, it has already reached its lower level, and is likely to stay there. It cannot get much flatter. You may cut off the heads of every rich man now living,—of every statesman,—every literary, and every scientific authority, without in the least changing the social situation. Artists, of course, disappeared long ago as social forces. So did the church. Corporations are not elevators, but levellers, as I see them. I cannot see, for example, how France, which is the best type of future society, would be changed by changing anything any more. It is resolved into individuals without tie.

My generation has worked this out and it is done—finished—complete. I'm going home, to bed. As for my little book, it is a mere bit of amusement to make me forget being bored, for a few hours.[2] It is a jibe at my dear historical association,—a joke, which nobody will know enough to understand. It can't help you in the least. Jokes never do.

Meanwhile give my benediction to everybody.

Ever Yrs   Henry Adams.

MS: MH

1. H. G. Wells's (1866–1946) novel *Tono-Bungay* (1909) depicts the end of the old rural order in England and the advent of modern capitalist society.
2. *A Letter to American Teachers of History,* privately printed in 1910.

To Bernhard Berenson

1603 H Street   6 Feb. 1910

My dear Mr Berenson

On arriving here last month I found a copy of Songs and Sonnets with your card, and your Sienese Painter with the author's compliments.[1] Naturally I read both, and re-read them, with the conscientious interest and attention which their *provenance* roused. Little by little my mind has given way under the effort to carry on, at once, two lines of thought as far apart as Assisi and Washington. Siena helps me little. Every day, I find the straddle more agonising. The old exclamation,—IT CAN'T BE!—in all sorts of accents and keys, comes to my lips every hour of every day, and, so far from becoming quieter, grows more hysterical. So, you must not expect me to have anything to say about Sassetta or Giotto.[2]

The things do not belong to the same universe with La Fayette Square. This is the last word of life to me, and nothing irritates me so much as to see that people won't understand me. You remember how I tried to prove it, by their own methods, in the paper you so kindly read for me, last year. The whole meaning of life, for me, is concentrated into this single conviction that the phases of human consciousness have no more likeness to each other than ice, water and steam; and that American consciousness is the limit. We have reached the end, as water reaches the end when it falls to sea-level. Sassetta yells this at me. I see no going further. Every year this town drives the lesson further into me, until I begin to fear that I shall have to be shut up. It becomes an *idée fixe*.

This year I am trying to exorcise the evil spirit by setting him free, in the shape of the small volume which will contain about two hundred pages such as you read. For fear of betraying my insanity, I have tried to disguise it, but, for further security, I shall send it privately to the people interested, of whom you are one. As a work seeking publicity, it would seem quite foolish. As a scientific demonstration of the relation of our century to the twelfth, it may serve to calm some of our irritations. For one, I feel much less annoyance with life, from the moment I understand that nobody is to blame. The poor wretches know no better, and I should derive no more real peace of mind even by murdering a senator. Not that I would willingly forego the joy of murdering a Senator; but I feel that it would not be lasting. I should want to murder more senators to renew the pleasure.

Therefore, if you receive such a volume within a few weeks, you will know where it comes from.

My state of mind is the worse because of the great social change here. The few people who ran in machines of their own,—the few who were not syndicated,—are gone. Cincinnati looms like a flood in the Ohio. I am directly in its path, and rather glad to be drowned. At least it saves the trouble of more struggling. I hand the job over to the V. G. Fischer Art Co.

Ever Yrs   Henry Adams.

MS: I Tatti

1. *Songs and Sonnets,* commonly known as *Tottel's Miscellany* (1557), the first great collection of Elizabethan lyrics; and Berenson's *A Sienese Painter of the Franciscan Legend* (1909), a reprint of his 1903 articles in *Burlington Magazine.*
2. A comparison between Sassetta (c. 1392–1450), the subject of Berenson's book, and Giotto was central to the argument.

To Elizabeth Cameron

1603 H Street   Sunday, 6 March 1910

you scare me blue!

you always do!

Oh, Lord! what awful thing is going to happen now that worries you so much? Not for five-and-twenty years have my nerves been in such a condition as now. I see black mystery all round me, and whether people seek me or avoid me, I get the same sense of anxiety and dread. Enteritis is nothing to it. Politics is bad enough. Our poor dear Taft seems to me to be smiling on a vast ocean of treachery and desertion. Universal disgust is the social fashion, and comes to me from all sides. No one has uttered a cheerful word this winter except Harry White who has most reason to be bitter and furious.[1] You can imagine the state of my brother Brooks. Ward Thoron tells me that New York is blacker than soot. My own circle is black enough, God knows, but I could stand the blackness if it were not for the mystery. What has become of Edie Hoyt? She has not been near me this winter, and I know no one to ask about her. Sherman Miles has been as mysterious as Edie. William says he stopped here once, but when he knew I should be out, and he doesn't answer notes or invitations. I try to put it down to absorption in hymeneal happiness, but one becomes so nervous about hymeneal happiness that it needs constant reassurance.[2] Yesterday your McCallum cousin got her divorce. Why under the sun do Ellen Thoron and Elizabeth Ellis and Alice Warder all herd together at Woodstock without their husbands? Ward seems blue about it, or I imagine he does, but he gives no reason. As for sister Ann, I only wish she had some of the same disease. Her mania is that of sticking to her husband when she is so weak that she can't walk to the next corner. The only giant of strength is Mrs Hay, who has carried loads that might break down Saint Michael and the Dragon.

Of course every time you talk of worries, I think of Martha and shiver, for that is my last vulnerable point. Black night veils my eyes like Dido's.[3] Yesterday I went out to Rock Creek hoping for a minute's content and repose, but the ocean of sordidness and restless suburbanity has risen over the very steps of the grave, and for the first time, I suddenly asked myself whether I could endure lying there listening to that dreary vulgarity for ever, and whether I could forgive myself for condemning my poor wife to it. The grave itself has become a terror.

I think the newspapers depress me most. They seem to convey a scent and taste and touch of rot and disintegration all over the world, perhaps worst in England, but most avowed in France. This morning I have gone over five of these great bundles of so-called news, and I feel as though I had rolled in slime.

Finally I just get this note from Rebecca Rae.[4]

I get a certain relief in spraying you with my melancholia, for I've an idea that you are so bad that it can't make you much worse; yet I am not sure even of that. You have never felt fear, while my worst horror is that I am made sick by terror; and if I infect you with that disease, you might as well go to bed in a hospital and stay there.

I've asked about the Baltic, and can have my deck suite for $400; but I've not seen Florence Keep.

———

MS: MHi
1. Henry White had been replaced as ambassador to France.
2. Sherman Miles had married Yulee Noble in 1909.
3. Vergil, *Aeneid*, IV, 461. At the shrine of her husband, Dido seems to hear his voice crying out, "when dark night concealed the earth." Martha had had a nervous collapse in 1907.
4. Mrs. Rae reported that her operation was a success and her condition excellent.

To Barrett Wendell

23 Avenue du Bois de Boulogne
18 May, 1910.

My dear Wendell[1]
Your letter of May 1 has just caught up with me, like the comet, and carries me sailing diffusively into space.[2] I am glad to sail into something—besides snuffles, rheumatism and cough. These infinities have, at least, large breath.

No! my Letter to Teachers is just simply a Letter to Teachers, and no more! to teach teachers how to teach. Or perhaps, how not to teach! and how close they have come to their long-prophecied ultimate. As an application of practical method, it is meant to nail down their wriggling tails to the fact that they are there! It is a scientific demonstration that Socialism, Collectivism, Humanitarianism, Universalism, Philanthropism, and every other ism, has come, and is the End, and there is nothing possible beyond, and they can all go play, and, on the whole, base-ball is best. Eduard von Hartman's introductory paragraph, I conceive to be the last word of life (p. 20).[3] Schopenhauer prophecied it nearly a hundred years ago, and I have only collected and grouped the statements of the allied sciences. To my mind, they are final.

And what is the harm? The Declaration of Independence, Jeffersonian Democracy, the Principles of 1789, the Trades Unions, the Old Age Pensions, Death Duties, Andrew Carnegie and John D. Rockefeller, all preach it, and why not I?

All I have added is only the simple announcement that we have arrived. Nothing remains but to simmer out and stop the appearance of boiling,— of motion. There *is* no more motion, and can be none, except to recognise the fact.

Here in France, the fact is so self-evident that no one would regard it as anything but a commonplace. Is it otherwise in Germany? My only decisive authority is Jean Cristophe.[4] In England? I trust to Tono Bungay. The Europe of my youth is as old as I am. There are youths in it, but no more youth. I will give it a dozen more years to accept and act on the fact.

Of course nothing is to be gained by preaching this lesson as a form of energy. It would act as a dissipator of energy. Therefore I have taught it, or tried teaching it, only to the few men who could profit by it to economise their scholars' energies,—to save them from wasting it on past processes. Economy is all I can see now, as a true scientific object for education to pursue. Certain branches of education may soon be lopped off, to advantage. Economy is an end in itself, as the prolongation of life. Naturally all healthy pleasures, the arts, the theatre, the ball-field, are in that sense, economies. So, I judge, is morphine, when one is in pain,—or death!

But I did not care to work out the details. The trouble is that economy will also be the measure of lost energy. You can grade the steps of decline by the values of the economies.

Anyway my only fear is of rot,—sudden decomposition at a very high temperature, or motion. Things are fearfully rotten in Europe. Any interference may hasten, or may check it. Which? Ostwald talks of the possible new catalytic action of some new mind.[5] As I see it, the new mind can only break the machine's back. I don't want to help or hurry that.

Voilà! it is as simple as that.

Ever Yrs   Henry Adams.

MS: MH

1. Barrett Wendell (1855–1921), professor of English literature at Harvard and a former student of HA's.

2. Halley's comet passed the sun May 18, 1910.
3. Eduard von Hartmann, *Ausgewählte Werke*, VIII (1904), 572–573.
4. The first four volumes of Romain Rolland's *Jean-Christophe* (1904–1912), a ten-volume novel about a musical genius and his times, are set in Germany, the rest in France.
5. Wilhelm Ostwald, *L'Energie* (1910).

To Charles Milnes Gaskell

88 Avenue du Bois de Boulogne
31 Dec. 1910

My dear Carlo

I use a few of the last moments of this departing year to acknowledge your letter of the 29th and express my regret that I shall not be here to see you, and especially Lady Catherine whom I've not seen for years, as you pass through on the 16th. On that day I should be arriving in Washington.

I know not why I go, but I know equally little why I should stay. In a sort of paroxysm of despair I ask everyone I meet to tell me whom they have for people to talk with, and they all tell me the same thing,—that they don't talk. I have repeated this to you so often that I am deadly tired of it myself, but what else can I say? I have nothing to tell. I met only this morning an old French friend, who is a Deputy, and asked him the same question. He replied that he would arrange for me to meet Jaures. Except that Jaures represents to me, as a sound anarchist, a feeble type of political commonplace *bourgeoisie,* I've no objection to listening to his talk. Clemenceau is much stronger, and the most agreeable type of public man is Lépine, the Prefect; but I don't seem to see myself at home with politicians at all.[1] They have nothing to say that I care about. The literary lights are worse. Society does not exist for them, or for University people, or generally, too, for artists. They all live solitary lives. Society is a totally disintegrated crowd. Here, as at Washington, I have no life.

This does not prevent my seeing a good many people, and writing a good many letters, or even in being interested in a certain number of things and doings, or having influenza and rheumatism, or being depressed by gloom, and almost cheered by sunshine. My new apartment is but a few steps from Mrs Cameron who lives at No. 80, and who now has her daughter and her son-in-law here for Christmas. The Bacons, our actual ambassador, are very good in asking me to meet anyone of interest who passes.[2] The Harry Whites, after Mrs White has been through two severe operations for apendicitis, go home with me on the Adriatic next Wednesday. Mrs Wharton plays family, and we all live in one constant circle. I've nothing to complain of. Nobody seems to care to read by my light, but by whose light does anybody read? Even Rudyard Kipling's has already died out. Henry James is forgotten. I doubt whether all the Magazines can now rake up a writer who would be sure of sale. I am still surer they could hardly rake up one who would deserve it.

This is my epitaph on the departing year which has swept away many people and things, without producing, for my purposes, either a thing or a person. I have not made a new acquaintance. I have had to turn off my *bonne,* or housekeeper, after six years service, and to pay her racing-debts, amounting to a miserable forty or fifty pounds which has convulsed the whole shopkeeping quarter. How much she robbed me of, I shall never know. I have lost three or four of my most valued friends. I have seen three or four more, in politics, shockingly whacked by the public. The whole result to me is only what it was with Thackeray, that I still sit here, alone and dismal at seventythree year, dipping my nose in the Champagne brut, and cursing dyspepsia.

There will be no more Champagne in my time. All good things go. What does it matter to us? But I am sorry for the babe unborn.

Ever Yrs   Henry Adams.

MS: MHi

1. Georges Clemenceau (1841–1929), prominent deputy who had been premier until July 20, 1909, when he was succeeded by Aristide Briand; Louis Lépine (1846–1933), prefect of police in Paris. HA had met both men the year before at a dinner at Ambassador Henry White's.
2. Robert Bacon (1860–1919) served as ambassador to France 1910–1912.

To Charles Milnes Gaskell

1603 H Street   7 March, 1911.

My dear Carlo

Your letter of Feb. 21 from Torquay suggests a number of reflections. The first is that just fifty years ago I set out on that career of failure which took its start in the first great collapse of society I ever witnessed, and which has passed through half a dozen more, in various societies, till it has arrived in a general collapse in them all. Here in Washington, all has broken down except the mere machinery. We have not a notion how we are to pick ourselves up. Our experiment of a great paternal, protective system has fallen into political chaos, and we doubt whether we can lift it out. My friends are all prostrate, and only wild and cheap politicians are in control of the legislature. As a result of fifty years' career as a reformer, I reckon it rather brilliant. In France I've done better still, if I understand

M. Monis and his new Cabinet.[1] England I leave to you. My only literary authorities are Mr H. G. Wells, and Mr Bernard Shaw, with Mr Chesterton to make the Trinity.[2] Last evening I had a young Russian Secretary dining with me,[3] and I gathered from his genial prattle that Russia expected next year an election rather worse than any of ours. Society has disintegrated till it can't stand up.

Amid all this droll mud-puddle, you and I are giant wrecks. Somehow we find ourselves afloat, though dismantled, and to my astonishment, the only part of my career which seems distinctly not an entire failure, is that I've always managed to have all the money I wanted. As society grows bankrupt, I grow rich, at least in the sense of not growing poor. To be sure my standard of wealth is very low, for I regard even the miserable millionaire, with £10,000 a year, as sufficiently comfortable, if he does not go to coronations; but that standard was a high one fifty years ago.

Tired of all this, I go back to my twelfth century, and find peace. Having given away all my copies of the volume on Chartres, I am now reprinting it, for it has become a favorite book with the Professors of Middle-age art and literature, so that they worry me for copies. I will see them roasted before I will let it be published, for I've published books enough, and there is hardly anyone now living who is worth writing for, unless for money; so I spend my vast wealth lavishly on printing as a form of senile vice. It comes high, so I don't keep an auto.

The enfeeblement of the social mind has reached a point where paralysis has begun, and I am amused and happy, as in an asylum for idiots. The daily press is all. I know, because I read it. As Dr Forbes Winslow says:— These are facts![4]

Fifty years! Think of me, reaching Liverpool fifty years ago, to begin this mad career! We've beaten the record.

Ever Ys   Henry Adams.

MS: MHi

1. After Briand was forced to resign, Feb. 27, Ernest Monis (1846–1929) formed an anticlerical and leftist coalition cabinet and won his first vote of confidence on March 6.
2. G. K. Chesterton (1874–1936), a conservative essayist, often engaged in controversy with Wells and Shaw.
3. Constantine Nabokov (1866–1922), first secretary of the Russian embassy.
4. Dr. L. Forbes Winslow, *Recollections of Forty Years, Being an Account, at First Hand, of Some Famous Lunacy Cases* (1910).

To Charles Milnes Gaskell

88 Avenue du Bois de Boulogne
29 July, 1911.

My dear Carlo

Thanks for your notification of the Stepney marriage![1] Generally such eccentricities are hard on the mother. I hope our old friend will not find it so. Give her my warm regards, should you see her.

Wenlock should be a charming watering-place now. Here we are short of water, and the greenth is browned. You should have had showers enough to keep you alive. You should have, too, a few degrees less heat than we. My thermometer every day hangs about 90° Fah. Of course I lock myself up, and go out only at sunset, and dine under the trees in the Bois towards nine o'clock; but I like it, being of a tropical nature and habit, given to indolence and sloth.

This habit of body and mind requires much literature to keep it going, and I devour books by the ton, but they are all of a kind that involve conundrums or puzzles that I can chew and very slowly digest. In the last six weeks I have worried half a dozen such questions which have no answers, but which crop up at intervals all through life. E.G: St Augustine's views on Grace; St Thomas Aquinas' view of Free Will; Darwin's ideas on Sexual Selection; Mâle's view of the Charlemagne window at Chartres and the Pseudo-Turpin of Rheims;[2] the relative merit of a score of MSS. of the Pseudo-Turpin in the Bibliotheque National and the Arsenal; the extinction of the Tertiary Vertebrates and the action of the Glaciers; the meaning of the paintings in the Cro Magnon caverns, and of the carvings on ivory and stone of the same period. Each of these matters has given me at least a week of reading, and the last has had a certain direct importance to me as history; for the Cro Magnon race covered all the country from the Loire to central Spain and Italy, and had an art so high that, after it disappeared, some twenty thousand years followed before the Egyptians again raised the standard to approach it. That is to say, we professors of history have found a totally new field which pretty nearly upsets all our old notions. We are busy trying to find a peg to hang it on. The puzzle amuses me more than the extinction of the Lords does.[3]

Yet the extinction of the Lords amuses me too, almost as much as that of the great Tertiary vertebrates. Nowadays the Extinction of Species has become a matter of perplexity quite as irritating as the Origin of Species, and the whole theory of the Cosmos turns on it. The Lords serve exceedingly well to illustrate the process. If you care to read the geological history of the hog, you will have it all. After endless forms and experiments, the hog family died out, leaving only our domestic pig, which I take to correspond to our common Cook's tourist.

As everyone contradicts everyone else, nothing matters much, except that I should have fresh supplies of these jig-saw puzzles. For that, I scour land and sea.

Ever Yrs   Henry Adams.

MS: MHi

1. Catharine Cowell-Stepney (1876–1952), daughter of Margaret Warren Cowell-Stepney and Sir Arthur Cowell-Stepney, was engaged to marry Sir Edward Stafford Howard, a widower 25 years her senior.
2. Emile Mâle, *L'Art religieux du XIII siècle en France* (1898).
3. The Parliament bill to limit the power of the House of Lords to oppose acts passed by the Commons was under continuing discussion and was expected to pass.

To Elizabeth Cameron

1603 H Street   April 16, 1912.

Saturday evening will be a date in history. In half an hour, just in a summer sea, were wrecked the Titanic; President Taft; the Republican party, Boyce Penrose, and I.[1] We all foundered and disappeared. Old and sinful as I am, I turn green and sick when I think of it.

I do not know whether Taft or the Titanic is likely to be the furthest-reaching disaster. The foundering of the Titanic is serious, and strikes at confidence in our mechanical success; but the foundering of the Republican party destroys confidence in our political system. We've nothing to fall back upon.

In a work which you never heard of, called the Education of Henry Adams, I figured on the values of society, and brought out my date of stoppage,—did I not,—at 1917, with a possible error of time to 1927. I feel today as though I were shaving it close. The confusion and consternation here are startling. If it were a question only of a democratic administration, they were resigned to that, but no one now knows whether the people want representative government at all. They seem to want an Athenian democracy without representation. Last night the Lodges came to dinner; Jack White and a young Biddle came; Bessy brought Langdon Mitchell later.[2] I listened to the talk. Mrs Keep had already repeated to me the talk of Crane.[3] Much was quoted from the talk elsewhere, among all parties. Through the chaos I seemed to be watching the Titanic foundering in a shoreless ocean.

By my blessed Virgin, it is awful! This Titanic blow shatters one's nerves.

We can't grapple it. Taft, Titanic! Titanic—Taft! and Boyce Penrose! and I! Where does this thing end![4]

And my apartment! I shall not get to Paris before May 10, which gives me six weeks to move. Can I do it! If not, what? Poor Mabel La Farge is struggling with the same conundrum with four boys on top.

I've shifted my passage to the Olympic on May 4. Of course, the Olympic has a bad record; but nerves are now so shaken that no ship seems safe, and if I am wrecked, I might as well go under.

Edith Eustis has just been in, naturally upset, but telling me of a dinner she had last night, where the admirals derided the possibility of such a disaster, and said it would upset the navy if true.

And Mexico down in the cellar!

Can't you imagine how happy I am! and your heart would glow over the gloom of my brother Brooks. We have all got a delightful shudder on us. We all sqwauk like guinea hens! Isn't it gaudy! Telegraph at my expense if you see light.

———

MS: MHi

1. On the night of April 14 the *Titanic,* the largest and fastest liner afloat, struck an iceberg on her maiden voyage. Of the 2,200 passengers, including many notables, over 1,500 lost their lives. Roosevelt's victory in the Republican primary split the party and paved the way for the election of Democrat Woodrow Wilson (1856–1924). Senator Boies Penrose (1860–1921), the party boss in Pennsylvania, was unable to block Roosevelt's nomination at the Republican convention.
2. Langdon Mitchell (1862–1935), a prominent playwright; John Campbell ("Jack") White (1884–1967), son of Margaret and Henry White.
3. Charles R. Crane (1858–1939), Chicago industrialist, treasurer of the National Progressive Republican League.
4. Echo of "Chaos, Cosmos! Cosmos, Chaos! who can tell how all will end?"; Tennyson, "Locksley Hall Sixty Years After" (1886).

To Ward Thoron

South Lincoln, Mass., July 27, 1912.

My dear Ward:[1]

I should have written to you more than once since I was condemned to the solitude of this wilderness if it had not been that I thought from day to day I should get some clearer idea of what my future was to be. When you are knocked down, so to speak, by a tramcar,—let us say one of your own—and pick yourself up, you are somewhat dazed and disconcerted, and want somebody else to tell you what to do next. I have not yet the faintest shred of an idea what I shall be allowed to do or shall be able to do. I do not even know whether I am really gaining strength or not. They all say that my recovery is wonderful. Leave it at that. Perhaps they may next winter send me off to escape the winter here, and I may, after all, drift back to Europe as an invalid, to prolong the somewhat stupid process of growing old.

In that case, I may again recover the thread of my thirty-thousand-year-old babies.[2] I may possibly, if things should be uncommonly fortunate, get down to Dordogne with you, or even resume that work upon Turpin which was so suddenly broken off last spring, when I was still in the middle of the "Chanson de Willame."[3] Thus far, I have been obliged to throw them all aside, with the understanding that it was finished forever. At the same time I have a yearning desire to see our new Turpin in print; and if you really feel as though it were an amusement that tempts you, I should like to see you go on with it. You could consult Picard as to the cost, and I could at once deposit with him the necessary amount with which to proceed to the work. I do not suppose that it would be very ruinous, but at all events there is no harm in asking. You can do all the preliminaries, and, unless I die entirely in the meanwhile, we can go on with it just as though nothing had happened to me.

To this moment I don't know what has happened to me.[4] I should suppose it was a stroke, except that the doctors say it is not, and I should suppose that I was idiotic and paralytic, except that I read more than I have done for many years. To be sure, I do not understand it; but then, I have strong reason to believe that there is nothing in it all to understand. The books strike me as singularly empty. I have not read a book,—naturally excepting my own—for a year or more that struck me as worth reading. But my table is covered with them, and I do nothing but pretend to study. My memory is as bad as you know it was, but not very much worse, which is rather surprising to me, for I thought that my illness would have abolished my memory for all things recent. Nevertheless, here I am,—a good deal feebler, but, so far as I can see, not otherwise very different from what I was when I bade Paris good-bye last autumn.

I need hardly tell you that everything here in this country that I see is quite as feeble-minded, not to say idiotic, as I am myself. Our friend, Theodore Roosevelt, is, I think, hovering on the edge of a collapse somewhat like mine. Our friend, Taft, as far as I can see, arrived there some time ago. And of Mr. Woodrow Wilson I know nothing except that everybody seems to think the chances very small of his remaining on friendly terms with any of his party. There is very little doubt in my mind that he will be our next president, provided nothing happens in the interval to do him injury with the public. But he is so very doubtful a person, so little known to the public, and so skeptically known to his acquaintance, that I think nothing is impossible, and anything that happens is sure to be for the benefit of Theodore. So you may, after all, see your friend, Theodore, in the White House again, which will not hurt my feelings as much as it will hurt yours. As you are aware, I care very little for the man in the White House, and very much for the woman; and if Mrs. Roosevelt is there it will atone for much, in my eyes, in her husband.

By the way, Mrs. Cameron, who has just arrived here to inspect me, has made a visit at Oyster Bay, and seen Theodore as well as Edith, and says that Edith looks exceedingly well, young, and fresh, and in excellent spirits, but complains curiously of very much the same thing that I have complained of for ten years past,—that is, of having totally lost her sense of smell and taste.[5] This is worse than my case, because I partially lost my sense of smell, but I kept my sense of taste. I thought that everybody under any circumstances kept their taste for sweets, acids, salt and such things; but apparently Mrs. Roosevelt has totally lost her sense of taste, which is very disastrous, and I should like to sympathize with her if I were not afraid that she would think I was joking.

I hear of you from Mabel, and I am glad that you have found a spot to rest your wearied feet in. I think for a time that the Lake of Geneva may serve to charm you, if not to amuse. I wish I could offer you the smallest diversion.

I hope this afternoon to see your sister, who is coming over to lunch with my sister-in-law, Mrs. Charles Adams, and I shall probably get more news of you. As it will no doubt be more or less what I know already, I don't think it worth while to keep my letter open to hear. Still, if she has anything very exciting to say I may add a postscript.

Ever yours,   Henry Adams.

MS: Faith Thoron Knapp; dictated, typed, signed

1. Ward Thoron was doing research in France for HA.
2. HA was financing Henri Hubert's archaeological work in the Dordogne caves.
3. Turpin (d. 800?), archbishop of Rheims, erroneously considered the author of *Historia de Vita Caroli Magni et Rolandi*, 12th-century compilation of legends.
4. HA had suffered a cerebral thrombosis on April 23. In mid-June, though still partially paralyzed, he was moved to a cottage on his brother Charles's estate in South Lincoln, Massachusetts.
5. Mrs. Roosevelt had lost her sense of smell and taste as a result of a riding accident in Sept. 1911.

To Bernhard Berenson

Birnam Wood, South Lincoln, Mass.
4 Sept. 1912

My dear Prophet,

Your letter descends on this remote province like an aerolith (or is it an aerolite) with an evident intent to wipe us out. We are a primitive people. I know no community so naturally depressed as ours always was until the mild rays of Unitarianism struck it; but then we suddenly turned our backs on the darkness, and with almost one accord agreed to be cheerful. We walked about, slapping each other in the stomach, saying:—'Let's be gay!' New England trying to be gay beats the German jumping over chairs to be sprightly, but we did it, and are doing it still. We think it bad form to be anything else. Therefore we don't read and never think. Our newspapers are a constant wonder to me. They never allude to any thought, past, present or future, and are under a ban in regard to the world outside of Boston. Europe is never mentioned. We agree to ignore all but ourselves, and above all to be gay. The world is gay,—ought to be gay,—must be gay, shall be gay,—damn it, sir, *you* must be gay! Only, our gaiety is a peculiar species, as you know!

And now comes our Theodore! He preaches that the other people are all wicked,—everybody is wicked,—damn you, sir, *you* are wicked!—but he will save you, though he is not so damn good either, and you must have faith in the Peepul who are all right, and anyone who says anything at all is a liar and a *European,* and a pessimist son of Taft; but if he too is gay and believes in Theodore, all will be well.

The gospel, in sum, is that you must all be gay and teach the young to be happy and go to the foot-ball games. Like you, they cheer with comfort to see *their* world go to the devil, because it is so much more popular to be gay over the new world to come. In private they all talk like crows, but in the world, optimism is sweet and the Peepul with money like it.

Yah! what do I care? I dropped out of it on April 23, last. The world I left was as done—finished,—flat,—as I was. Not an idea or a thought or a novelty left in it, or possible even to grow from it. The thing was played out. The situation was plain. The damn thing might spin on as long as you please, but the only new idea about it was its spinning out. I would not go back to it for a prize pig. The proof of it was that all the people, whether they thought so or not, agreed that it was bad form to say so. Tragedy was *vieux jeu.* No one now goes to Hell. Dante and others were good for a stage-scene, but to believe in Tragedy is the mark of a humbug, a liar, and a busted delusion, when you have Lloyd George, Keir Hardy and various Jews to believe in, and a glorious hope in Woman's Rights.[1] Nobody believes in Woman's Rights, but it is Progress,—or Progressive.[2]

For three months I have been contemplating this happy scene, and rejoice in perfect content at having quit it. I've no more to say, and no one to abuse. I cannot conceive that anyone will ever take any interest in me, or in anything that interests me. I went to Boston the other day, and stood in Beacon Street, and wept over its shrunken ruins. One or two squares of houses are all that remain; the world about is mere adipose tissue hanging on the old skeleton. I thought of Rome and the Capitol. Honestly it was not unlike, but Boston was the more ruin of the two.

What else have I to write about? What could you write about if you were here? Mrs Cameron writes that Tuxedo is worse; they abuse Theodore even more persistently than here. At Newport Mrs Vanderbilt gave a party, and that party is already departed, leaving no echo. At New York they have had a police scandal worthy of Rome in the 16th century, and beating Russia and Turkey; but it is not dramatic as it should be. I admire it, but it does not appeal to me, like Mme Steinheil.[3] You know! I can tell you nothing! There is a charming odor of rottenness about our Theodore and Becker and the rest, but, damn you, you shall be hopeful and play ball.[4]

All right! Good bye!

MS: I Tatti

1. David Lloyd George advocated the National Insurance bill and reform of the British land system; James Keir Hardie (1856–1915), M.P., Scottish mining-union leader.
2. The Progressive party platform called for women's suffrage. On Sept. 3 Ohio voters rejected a women's suffrage amendment to the state constitution.
3. Marguerite Steinheil (1869–1954) had been the mistress of President Félix Faure and had been acquitted in 1909 of the murder of her husband and her mother; *Mes Mémoires* (1912).
4. Charles Becker, a New York City police lieutenant, had been accused in the press of having instigated the gangland murder in July of Herman Rosenthal, a well-known gambling house owner. The investigation of the crime and its connection to the system of payoffs to the police for criminal protection had become a press sensation. Becker was found guilty and was executed in 1915.

To Bernhard Berenson

1603 H Street   28 Jan. 1913.

My dear Mr Berenson

I think I might partially recover my mind if I could perceive in the rest of the world any symptom of sanity. Not that I see much sign of what we used to call insanity,—mania,—but only of drivelling feeble-minded-ness.

It tires me, and I want to die. I cannot bear the thought of ten thousand years more, like this.

Luckily I shan't have it. My own feeble-mind warns me that I can't possibly get worse. I should say that about four-and-twenty hours was my limit. After reading the morning papers I cut it down to twelve.

Naturally I have nothing to write about. As far as I know, this town is without knowledge on any subject whatever, and the result of sixteen years republican rule is one long wail of disappointment and disgust. No one expresses any confidence in the new rule or the new men, and the only new idea is that of pulling down all that has been built up. Worst of all, no one has energy enough to feel really disappointed. The Church goes on talking, the Parliaments go on talking, the Courts go on talking, the communists go on talking, the suffragists go on talking, Theodore Roosevelt goes on talking (not so much), and only the scientific people scratch their heads and ask themselves where they are at. Between 1850 and 1910 they have twisted their own tails into a hard knot.

As for me I am gone to the bottom—that is, to the 12th century,—deeper than ever. Thanks to Miss Aileen Tone, my best new niece, I've got into the music of 1200,—Church, Court, Bourgeoisie, Pastourelles, dances, and all the rest,—which she decyphers, plays and sings to me after dinner, and we discuss half the night.[1] French, Germans, English and Italians, all help to confuse the subject, and we grow more joyful every day because everyone tells everybody else he's a liar, but more particularly a fool. I suspect all are right, and this adds much to our amusement. I hope to come over about April 1 to Paris, and continue the study. Perhaps I shall extend it to the songs of my 30,000-year-old baby in his palatial residence at Eyzies among the hippos.

It is quite a happy life,—I mean not the hippos, but that of the senile imbecile in 1913 at Washington. There are a half dozen of us here, and while I am the most imbecile, I am also the happiest. Busy every hour, I do nothing and see nobody. I never write, never read, and never eat. I'm a sweet, gentle creature who loves his fellows. I know a Lemur at the Zoo. He is quite the most ideal creature ever made—except some beetles. We love each other and he turns all sorts of tricks for me. I want to go where lemurs are, and have some society. It is Madagascar. Think of it! Our ancestors survive in Madagascar, lovely as Cain in Eden.

Farewell till later! May all go well!

Yrs ever   Henry Adams.

MS: I Tatti

1. Aileen Tone (c. 1878–1969) of New York, a trained musician and friend of Louisa Hooper and Mabel Hooper La Farge, had been engaged as a companion for HA.

To Henry Cabot Lodge

6, Square du Bois de Boulogne
18 Oct. 1913

Dear Cabot

It is rather absurd for me to condole with you about illness. After my own smash-up, last year, I make a precious poor example. Yet my collapse was final, and left me on my back once for all, while I am glad to hear that you will come out smiling, or perhaps are already practising your beguilements on your world. Let it be so! the sooner the better for us all. I hear good accounts also of Winty. At this rate I shall save my autumn harvest in good order. I would like to be as positive about myself but dare only say doubtfully that I think I am no worse.

Of course this is statistically untrue. I am one year worse, and am reminded of it by receiving a copy of your Early Memories.[1] Forty-odd years are as serious facts as several illnesses. Of course I am deeply affected by your allusions to me, not only for that they are friendly but that they are humane. If I had been you, I should have commented on the subject in a much less forbearing spirit, for I have always felt inclined to severity towards myself. Not that I really debased myself below other people, or was afraid to face either man or beast, but because, looking on the whole affair from outside,—absolutely, as a wilderness without road,—I could rarely see which way to go, and was fantastically conscious that others knew less than I, and were doing heaps of harm. I did not want to do harm. To this moment I am at a loss to know how I could have done good. I cannot even say that in the actual situation I see any clear path to it, and only the other day I wrote to my brother Brooks that I had doubts whether the path he pointed out was either wise or historically correct, though I was quite willing to see him try it.

This attitude of mine I hold to be imbecile, and in effect I said so in my Education. It deserves reprobation and scorn, and I am ready to say that too,—But! I still see no more clearly what to do about it. Should I follow you? I am willing enough, but just where do you stand? Shall I follow Mr W. J. Bryan?[2] Good! but tell me, my pastor, where to seek him!

Anyway, here I am, at the end of the passage, and unlike Ruddy Kipling's nightmare, I've seen nothing, and must leave you to tell about it, only not by anything in my eyes.[3]

I expect to be in Washington in a month, and wish I might find you there, or even that I might take you to warmer lands for a few months, but I fear I need, more than you, some one to take me. To get across that ocean and into America is a big feat for a paralytic old fool.

Your grandchildren are enough to atone for all my failures. They are worth doing! Come and see!

Love to Nanny and all.   Ever Yrs   Henry Adams.

MS: MHi

1. Henry Cabot Lodge, *Early Memories* (1913).
2. William Jennings Bryan had been largely instrumental in nominating Woodrow Wilson for the presidency in the 1912 convention. As Wilson's secretary of state he was negotiating treaties that required the signatories to accept one year's arbitration before resorting to war.
3. In Rudyard Kipling's "At the End of the Passage" (1890), an Englishman is found dead with a look of horror in his eyes.

To Charles Milnes Gaskell

1603 H Street   19 Feb. 1914

My dear Carlo

The winter is nearly over, I am seventysix years old, and nearly over too. As I go, my thoughts turn towards you and I want to know how you are. Of myself, I have almost nothing to tell. It is quite astonishing how the circle narrows. I think that in reality as many people pass by, and I hear as much talk as I ever did, but it is no longer a part of me. I am inclined to think it not wholly my fault. The atmosphere really has become a Jew atmosphere. It is curious and evidently good for some people, but it isolates me. I do not know the language, and my friends are as ignorant as I. We are still in power, after a fashion. Our sway over what we call society is undisputed. We keep Jews far away, and the anti-Jew feeling is quite rabid. We are anti-everything and we are wild up-lifters; yet we somehow seem to be more Jewish every day.

This is not my own diagnosis. I make none. I care not a straw what happens provided the fabric lasts a few months more; but will it do so? I am uneasy about you. I judge you to be worse than we. At least you are making almost as much howl about it.

I have no complaint to make. Everyone is civil enough to me. I do not think anyone knows my name, or ever heard of it, but they know an old man when they see one, and are decent. I don't show myself in public. My brother Brooks goes much beyond me, and so does my brother Charles, but I am timid.

Really I have nothing to tell. Since my shock of two years ago, I read very little and write not at all, but we sing our twelfth-century songs, and get more and more manuscripts copied, and have much amusement over them. It is innocent! no one cares. Sometimes one person or another condescends even to listen, but usually we are protected by a big wall of German or Russian stuff, which keeps out all other taste. As for literature you probably know about what there is, but none of it gets to me. History is dead. Philosophy never reaches me. I am sure that young people have it, but they won't give it to such as me. Much as ever if I can catch echoes of it from Spring-Rice.

My notion is that our great effervescence of the last century has now come to an end, and that society is simmering down to a cold solution; but I need ten years more to decide this, and I shall not have it. Of course, society does not take that view. Society cannot, as a whole, feel its own pulse. Moreover, society cares, and I don't.

By the way, the Society of Architects has stolen my volume about Mont Saint Michel, and I would have sent you a copy if I thought you wanted it.[1] As you have my edition, I did not think you wanted another. Still, it is droll! Here am I, telling everyone that I am quite dotty and bed-ridden, and the papers reviewing me as a youthful beginner.

Send me a line about yourself.

Ever Ys   Henry Adams

MS: MHi

1. HA's facetious reference to his gift of the copyright to the American Institute of Architects.

To Henry Osborn Taylor

15 Feb. 1915

My dear Scholar and Master

As you know, I am a poor and ignorant, besides being a senile, reptile, and in one respect also am morally bad, for I never loved or taught facts, if I could help it, having that antipathy to facts which only idiots and philosophers attain; but with these drawbacks perhaps you will allow me to thank you for your last volume.[1] I have read it with grateful attention.

I cannot criticise. The field is not mine. I am concerned in it only as a spectator, and now a very blind one. I cannot correct or suggest, but I can do what may be equally useful,—I can tell you what effect your treatment has on me, and as I am probably an extreme case, you may infer its effect on opposite natures.

Perhaps I ought to say first, that once, at the most trying crisis of my life, and of his,—our old teacher in wisdom, Gurney, said to me that of all moral supports in trial only one was nearly sufficient. That was the Stoic. I cannot say that I have found it so, except in theory, but I am talking theory. Putting myself in that position, I read your book.

You see at once what must follow,—what did in fact follow. Of course, all that goes before is futile except as failure; all that follows after is escape—flying the ring,—by assuming an unprovable other world. Logically, the religious solution is inadmissible,—pure hypothesis. It discards reason. I do not object to it on that account; as a working energy I prefer instinct to reason; but as you put it, the Augustinian adjustment seems to be only the Stoic, with a supernatural or hypothetical supplement nailed to it by violence. The religionists preached it, and called it Faith.

Therefore to me the effect is of ending there. The moral adjustment, as a story, ended with Marcus Aurelius. There you lead us with kind and sympathetic hands; but there, over the door to the religious labyrinth, you, like Lord Kelvin, write the word Failure. Faith, not Reason, goes beyond.

What you intend, either as reason or faith, is another matter. I am giving only the effect on one mind. At the present moment, perhaps, the moral is somewhat pointed,—to me decidedly peaked. If you are writing Failure over one door and Lord Kelvin over another, and the Germans over the third and last—that of energy without direction,—I think I had better quit. I said so ten years ago, but I put it down to my personal equation then, and I cannot believe that you mean it now. Are we, then, to go back to Faith? If so, is it to be early Christian or Stoic?

The early Christian I take to have been abandoned long ago by the failure of Christ to reappear and judge the world. Whatever faith is to save us, it cannot be that. Is it, then, the Stoic?

I do not ask these questions for answers,—only to show you what questions are roused by your book, in order that, if you like, you may in any case, insert some provision against misapprehension. Of course, had I been the author, I should perhaps have been drawn into giving different values to the solutions, and should very likely have labored damnably over the Buddhists and the Stoics. Marcus Aurelius would have been my type of highest human attainment. Even as it is, I would give a new cent to have a really good book on the Stoics. If there is one, lend it me. I need badly to find one man in history to admire. I am in near peril of turning Christian, and rolling in the mud in an agony of human mortification. All these other fellows did it,—why not I?

Ever Yrs   Henry Adams.

MS: MH

1. Henry Osborn Taylor, *Deliverance, the Freeing of the Spirit in the Ancient World* (1915).

To Lawrence Mason

Washington   1 April, 1915.

Dear Sir[1]

Your singularly kind letter of March 28 deserves a better answer than I can give it.[2] Even in calm times, age often brings us to helplessness, even more of mind than of body, when we look about in despair at the things we have done, and in wonder at the impudence of doing them; but in these days, silence seems imposed. Barely five years have passed since I ceased to write, and already I see about me a totally new world, before which I feel like Saint Augustine at Hippo, fifteen hundred years ago. If God won't help me, I might as well quit, for I can see no escape elsewhere. A world whose social, political, scientific and moral systems rests on a religion of high explosives has no use for me.

Therefore, with you, I welcome mysticism in any of its forms. On the high-explosive revelations,—or revelation—I have hopelessly failed. So did Kelvin, as he took pains to affirm. He fell back on the absolute necessity of a creation. I am inclined to think that my logic drives me further, to the unreality of all phenomena. Unfortunately this conclusion abolishes mysticism too, as well as the Ego and the Non-ego, and ends in the Unknown. Q.E.D.

So I am obliged humbly to beg pardon of everybody and to take back all I've ever said. Not that it matters! No one knows or cares, and all has been often said before; but one hates to feel silly. To take refuge in the unknown is to avow imbecility,—or at least, senility which is a curious form of wisdom analogous to the ultimate. To us old people, the universe resolves itself into an effort of the Ego to maintain an illusion of continuity, which is to be solved very soon by disease, senility or death. This means, alive or dead, merely lack of the illusion of continuity. Of all the solutions offered for the universe, this is the only one which seems to be demonstrated by universal and daily experience, but only we old people may use it. You younger ones are obliged to deal with the illusions of continuity alone, though Science is getting precious close to chaos.

Mysticism as much as you please—or as much as you can,—but on your life, do not let it lead you to lose sight of continuity. Cling to that as your compass. No matter what other illusions distract you, or how scientific you want to be, don't hurt the world's illusions of unity. I speak strongly because I lost my own illusion of unity and continuity thirty years ago, and I know how fatal the rupture is to one's scheme of life. Once hit by Zeno's arrow, one is a mere mad rabbit.[3]

I printed all this ten years ago in my Education and merely drivel in repeating it. You need not read it. At least, not till you are seventy.

With many thanks   Ever Yrs   Henry Adams.

MS: CtY-B

1. Lawrence Mason (1882–1939), instructor in English at Yale University.
2. Mason wrote that HA's *Letter to American Teachers of History* had profoundly unsettled him but that he had found hope in mysticism.
3. Zeno of Elea (c. 490–c. 430 B.C.), Greek philosopher, formulated the paradox of the arrow in flight, conceived to be at rest in every consecutive instant and thus demonstrating the impossibility of continuous motion.

To Elizabeth Cameron

1603 H Street   March 1st [1918]

Are you not surprised to see what looks like me?[1] You well may be! Really it is not exactly I, and you need not suppose I am writing news. As you know, the game came to its end for me some four years ago, and I have not moved a finger since, nor do I mean to begin again. Your letters still entertain and delight me, but I have nothing to say in reply. As for the war, I said all I had to say ten years ago, in the last Chapter of my Education. Whatever is to follow, it will be none of mine. It is already a century away.

I write now *d'outre tombe* for another matter. You know that for ten years past I have tried to drape myself and my friends neatly for their final tableau before the audience that is to take stall-seats in the movie-show when we go. Slowly it is getting itself done. The fresh Life of John Hay by W. R. Thayer is the last step in the path.[2] It does not matter whether you like it or not, so long as it helps to build up the legend of our Square, and to open the road to more and better. Unfortunately I could do nothing with Nanny, and the only chance now rests on you. As far as I know, you are the only letter-writer and letter-receiver living, and if you have kept your letters, you must have tons which you can select to print together with your own. I have all your letters for thirty years in a box. You can easily choose volumes of them to be copied, and unite them by a mere thread of editing. You need not publish or print, unless you like. Just lock them up, and name a literary executor.

I suggest this—supposing you to have preserved the letters,—as much because it would occupy and amuse you for years, as to immortalise you or us. I do want you and Nanny to stand by the side of John Hay and Clover and me forever—at Rock Creek, if you like,—but only to round out the picture.

Of course, if you can't, say no more. Sometimes I succeed, sometimes I fail, and my failures are far the most common. Only—I would like to feel you there, with Clover and me, and Nanny, and Hay, till the St Gaudens figure is forgotten or runs away. It is all that I have left.

The scene here is too phantasmic for serious treatment, and becomes more so every day. To me it seems like a bad dream,—so bad that I dare not wake up. Some of the old friends are still here but you know how they would swear with the background! The Harry Whites prattle! Wayne gibbers! I mope and drivvle. I can't say that Springy seems to me much more real or hilarious. No one can guess what is to happen to us, and still less what to you! Of course I threw up the sponge ten years ago, and stopped even croaking, but you can go on with it in my place.

Elsie goes to Boston tomorrow to hear Cabot talk about my brother Charles.[3] Ward is now here, but Looly in bed at Danvers.[4] Aileen is in New York trying to get clothes and getting pneumonia. Winty Chanler left me yesterday after a good report from Johns Hopkins. The usual crop of divorces is ripe. The usual aimless talk about elections is spinning itself about the usual meaningless people. Yet you had better come back if you can. We had all best keep out of sight, and out of mischief. No one can foresee an hour ahead. Luckily you never believed me or minded my croaks, and had better not do so now, for I am certainly an idiot, whereas you may have happened, once or twice, in thirtyfive years, to have had traces of sense. Not that I remember any, but then my memory is gone.

This letter is a week's hard work, so don't read it.

Ever   Henry Adams.

MS: MHi

1. The crayon sketch of HA by John Briggs Potter (1864–1948) was reproduced in the November issue of the *North American Review.*
2. William Roscoe Thayer (1859–1923), historian, editor of *Harvard Graduates' Magazine* 1892–1915, had borrowed HA's corrected copy of the *Education* for use in his *Life of John Hay* (1915).
3. Lodge was preparing a memorial address on CFA2.
4. Ward Thoron and Louisa Hooper married in King's Chapel, Boston, Oct. 2, 1915.

To Henry Cabot Lodge

1603 H Street   1 March, 1916

My dear Cabot

I send you herewith a sealed packet containing a copy of my Education corrected and prepared for publication. Should the question arise at any future time, I wish that you, on behalf of the Hist. Society, would take charge of the matter, and see that the volume is printed as I leave it.

With this view, I have written a so-called Editor's Preface, which you have read, and which I have taken the liberty, subject to your assent, to stamp with your initials.

Also, may I beg that you will bar the introduction of all illustrations of any sort. You know that I do not consider illustrations as my work, or having part in any correct rendering of my ideas. Least of all do I wish portraits. I have always tried to follow the rule of making the reader think only of the text, and I do not want to abandon it here.

Pray bear in mind that the publication itself as well as the manner of it is left at your discretion. The volume has now been ten years in existence, and I have never thought its publication likely to benefit anyone at any special moment, but I will not undertake to control your judgment, after my own disappearance.

I might add that, if the Society should ever care to resume, on my behalf, the publication of the Chartres, it might follow the same rule, besides correcting some of the rather annoying misprints.

                                        I am very truly   Henry Adams.

MS: MHi

To Charles Milnes Gaskell

                                        Beverly Farms   Mass.   June 8, 1917.

I was awfully pleased yesterday to get your letter of May 19th and am ashamed to think that I have not written to you for so long a time that I can hardly remember when it was. The truth is that I have been more and more impressed this last year with the singular wisdom of holding my tongue.

To my very great surprise everybody seems more and more to have come round to my way of thinking and for once in my life I have found myself wondering how on earth it happened that I was with the majority and had better not criticize or find fault. If the public and the politicians have not always done things as I would like to have had them done, they have come out thus far infinitely better than I expected and I have no wish to say a word about my own superior wisdom; as you know our role in life has always been to be wiser than anyone else and the consciousness of that is the only reward we are likely to get from it.

Meanwhile, here we are, for the first time in our lives fighting side by side and to my bewilderment I find the great object of my life thus accomplished in the building up of the great Community of Atlantic Powers which I hope will at least make a precedent that can never be forgotten. We have done it once and perhaps we can keep it up. Strange it is that we should have done it by means of inducing those blockheads of Germans to kick us into it. I think that I can now contemplate the total ruin of our old world with more philosophy than I ever thought possible. You and I have seen so much and helped to do so many foolish things that it is really a joy to feel that we have established one great idea even though we have pulled all the stars out of their courses in order to do it. And, after all, it is a curious reflection that we never intended it.

I have carefully kept myself out of sight while the foreign commissions have made their triumphant march through America and have hardly so much as seen a single member of them. Spring Rice did, it is true, bring Arthur Balfour to breakfast one day, but it was a purely domestic affair and we talked only about Lord Robert Cecil in Mansfield Street about fifty years ago. You should have been there to join in the conversation, for Arthur Balfour had not then come up to London and was improving his mind at Oxford in the first stages of childhood. He has grown old since that time, and his whole career has passed, as you know, without my ever having seen him. He complains, too, of growing deaf. And I complain of growing blind, but I am ten years older than he and have a right to my decrepitude. I saw no other of the Englishmen except a young fellow named Amos who came to me from Egypt, nor did I see the great Joffre, nor his collègue the "grand jaloux."[1] The young women made such desperate love to them all that old men had not a chance to get near them. I did see my old friend Pierre de Chambrun for ten minutes, but that was all.[2] Perhaps I was lucky in my modesty, for they managed to kill my old friend Jo Choate because he adored speechifying, which I always abominated.[3] Otherwise I have been more interested in the humors of the situation and the singular cleverness and success of His Excellency the President of the United States especially in upsetting his rivals and making the whole cohort of Republicans and Rooseveltians follow after him and obey him with as much docility as if they were not all the time cursing him with a vocabulary worthy of my extreme youth. As far as I know we have obeyed like lambs and have done everything we were told to do. Never could I have conceived that in a short three months we could have gone into a great war and adopted a conscription not unworthy of Germany itself, at the bidding of a president who was elected only a few months ago on the express ground that he had kept us at peace. We are now proceeding in the same path to starve ourselves for the benefit of Europe and, before long, I shall be writing to you that, like my ancestors the primitive American Indian, I am living on "yams" and Indian corn. It will not be very different from my actual regime.

And now, I have returned here to the house which I built in 1876 and left in 1885, thinking that nothing on earth would ever bring me back. It is much as though your last abbot of Wenlock should return in spirit to visit you in the ruins of the abbey, and to tell you of the wickedness of Henry the Eighth. I am sure he would amuse you more than the return to fifty years ago amuses me. But with both of us, the moral is the same; it is all over now, and neither Henry the Eighth nor Ulysses S. Grant have longer any importance. I live here with my nieces as you might live at Wenlock with your daughter; and my only effort is to smile, to look benevolent, and to hold my tongue. The people strike me as being less amusing with much less sense of humor than fifty years ago, but they are almost pathetically conservative and in a *world* of Socialists they are more early Victorian than ever. I scarcely dare speak for fear of saying something disrespectful of Prince Albert. There are just three of my contemporaries living on this Shore, but we have all lost our minds or our senses and no one thinks it worthwhile to tell us so. No books come out. I am not aware that there are any writers left, certainly none in my branch which was extinct five and twenty years ago or more. No one even remembers the name of Lord Macaulay. I once wrote some books myself, but no one has even mentioned the fact to me for nearly a generation; I have a vague recollection that once some young person *did* mention an anecdote to me that came from one of my books and that he attributed to someone else. Harry James's niece also wrote to me, asking for his letters, which I gave her, and which is the last I shall ever hear of them.[4]

From Paris I get gloomy letters from Mrs. Cameron while the child Martha who was born, it seems to me, only last year in this very house, is now a kind of queen in Egypt after the manner of Cleopatra.[5] I shall yet hear of you too, riding on a white dromedary to Bagdad. I'm sure you will enjoy it.

Give my love to all yours and thank Mary for her letters. The sooner she writes again, the better.

Ever yours   Henry Adams   *per Aileen Tone*

MS: MHi; dictated

1. Marshal Joseph Joffre (1852–1931), commander in chief of the French Army, and René Viviani (1863–1925), a former prime minister and recently resigned minister of justice, were heads of the French mission. Viviani was being referred to as the "grand jaloux" (the great envious one) because he resented the fact that people wanted to see Joffre rather than him.
2. Pierre de Chambrun (1865–1954), marquis de Chambrun, deputy and diplomat.
3. Joseph Choate, chairman of the committee to receive the French and British commissions, had died May 14, the day after the final ceremonies.
4. Margaret Mary James (1887–1952), daughter of William and Alice James.
5. Martha's husband, Ronald Lindsay, was serving as British adviser to the Egyptian government.

To Elizabeth Cameron

Beverly Farms Aug. 3rd [1917]

Here comes your letter of the 12th telling me that you were going to cross the Channel on the 15th and at the same time comes a telegram from Elizabeth saying that she was going to stay with you in the Square du Bois on the same date[1] and everybody else is at sea, chasing torpedoes or writing letters at headquarters while I sit all alone wondering when I lived. I distinctly remember, some sixty years ago, being tumbled head over heels in the same way and everybody going to war and getting killed, or staying at home and getting abused for it, and whether that was now, or *now* was *then,* I haven't got clear in my mind. On the whole, I rather think I was more upside down *then* than now, but perhaps that was only because I was younger and more literally in the swim.

Of course I am not going to talk about the situation, which is altogether too complicated for any human being to get hold of. I don't believe anybody connects his thoughts or acts for two consecutive moments, and I am quite sure as I have always told you that the relation between this year and the year when I last saw you is entirely lost. No one remembers his own identity as long ago as that. This is no harm, I suppose, and is no worse than it has been before in the course of one's life, but it interferes with writing a letter. Here, on the North Shore, I find myself set back about forty years and everybody playing pretend that nothing has happened. Last Sunday an escort of nieces, all charming including Florence Keep—and Lulu Norman—took me in their arms, over to the Myopia Club and gave me a sort of reception in the middle of a crowd of young people—in flannels and white tennis shoes headed by Eleo Sears, all pretending that I was their age while, at thc same time, weird phantoms came up to me calling themselves Coll Warren and Bobby Grant, my contemporaries or scholars, who were no more like the men *I* knew under that name—than *I* was like *myself;* and in the middle of them, bounded in like a bomb, Mrs. De Koven, who might have come from outside the solar system for all she had to do there.[2]

Two days ago my niece Aileen who has the courage of several lions induced Annie Lothrop, now eighty-three years old, to ask Ruth Draper to give a monologue at her house on Smiths Point, and there she had all the oldest people there are—who never come out of their houses—to come and hear Ruth give all her most frivolous monologues, as *I* should select them.[3] Never did you see such a queer old crowd as we were. The first person whose arms I fell into was Alice Howe, who began by challenging me to tell her who she was.[4] I peered into her ancient visage which had not a feature I had ever seen before—and shouted "Alice Greenwood," a *marvelous* shot, hitting it perfectly right at the first jump. Then there was old Mrs. Putnam who is also above eighty, and of course the Henry Higginsons, while we by some accident left out Mrs. Jere Abbot, on whom I called last week, and who remarked to me, in a casual manner, that her first visit to Paris was under the presidency of General Changarnier, in the year '48.[5] All these old people would be easy enough to get along with if they weren't mixed up in a most exasperating way with the young ones. Here is Edie Hoyt who has been with us for a week, almost dead from trying to travel with the thermometer at 100. And Ruth Draper flying like a torpedo up and down the coast, giving monologues for the Red Cross, and poor little Hester Chanler staying with the Pickmans, like a widow with two babies, afraid even to mention the name of her husband for fear something will happen to him before she can finish what she has to say,[6] and all one's nephews at sea—or in camp—at the same time that four new and unknown nephews and nieces come over from the "Glades," chattering all the time like magpies about their little games exactly as their uncles and aunts and mothers and fathers did forty years ago.[7] As for you and Martha, you are comparatively a modern memory here, and fit in reasonably well, but so many other people have stayed in this house since you were here and so many have been born here that no one could keep the account even if it were worthwhile. Over at Wenham Lake there's a whole city of Phillipses, headed by William and Caroline, while a short distance off, Peter Higginson and Hetty are creating a new English country house, to be stocked with charming children now about two years old whom we visit now in their ancient quarters at Coolidge Point, dancing over the hayricks at eight o'clock in the morning of superhuman hot days. At Danvers also, flourishes Ward Thoron's "yearling," also a nephew of mine, and a little way further off near Coffin's Beach two pairs of Warners have planted nurseries of nephews and nieces in which there is one red-haired girl, quite fascinating. I will not try to explain to you what the relation between all these old and young people is for you would never make it fit, but the curious part is that other people are more buzzy than I am, and only last evening I was quite knocked silly when Edie, who was reading to me from Gosse's life of Swinburne, calmly read out a quotation from myself which was attributed to some apparently well-known "Mr. Adams," who turns out to be, in all probability, my own father.[8] How you expect me to keep my head in such a confusion as all this amounts to, I don't know, but I really think I do it about as well as the other fellows do, which is not very much to my credit, for they do it very badly. My brother Brooks and his poor wife have actually taken refuge in Chestnut Street while he attends a so-called

Constitutional Convention and she sits by herself not knowing where to seek refuge. To complete my bouleversement, the other day Gladys Saltonstall telephoned that she was rushing down the coast with a live duke and should bring him in to see us—and sure enough, a very good-looking young Frenchman in khaki was whirled into our drawing room by Gladys, playing pretend that he was a duc de Guiche committed to our care by Bobby Bliss.[9] *Do* you wonder if I radote? And in the middle of all this, Emily Tuckerman and Alick Sedgwick write postal cards from Chartres, as though I owned it.[10]

It's no use trying to send this letter until we know where you are, so don't be surprised if it's a day or two late. How on earth can one aim at a bird which is trying to fly between Paris and Stepleton and doesn't herself know which she is after?

Ever yours   Henry Adams   *per A.T.*

August 6th. Your letter of the 18 from Stepleton has this moment arrived and delighted us.

MS: MHi; dictated

1. Elizabeth Hoyt (1885–1954), head of the Women's Bureau of the American Red Cross, was in France.
2. The Myopia Hunt Club (Hamilton, Mass.) was so called because all the founders were nearsighted. Louisa P. ("Looloo") (Mrs. Guy) Norman; Eleanora Randolph (Mrs. Frederick R.) Sears (1881–1968); John C. Warren (1842–1927), Harvard '63, Moseley professor of surgery at Harvard 1899–1907; Robert Grant (1852–1940), Harvard '73, novelist and judge.
3. Anne Hooper Lothrop, a first cousin of MHA. Ruth Draper (1884–1956), monologist, gave private performances impersonating a variety of characters. She made her professional debut in 1920.
4. Alice Greenwood (Mrs. George) Howe (d. 1924).
5. Nicholas Changarnier (1793–1877), commander of the national guard during the revolution of 1848.
6. Hester Chanler Pickman (b. 1893), a younger daughter of Margaret and Winthrop Chanler. Her husband was Edward Pickman (1886–1959), son of Dudley and Ellen Pickman of Boston. The pair were married in 1915 amid some tension, since the groom was Unitarian and the bride Catholic.
7. The Glades, on the South Shore of Massachusetts Bay, was a summer hotel acquired in the late 1860s by a number of Boston families who turned it into a private resort. Two of HA's brothers had bought into the club in the early 1880s.
8. Edmund Gosse, *The Life of Algernon Swinburne* (1917). The quotation ("A tropical bird, high-crested, long-beaked, quick-moving, with rapid utterance and screams of humour") was drawn from *The Education of Henry Adams* but attributed by Gosse to "Adams, C."
9. Gladys Rice Saltonstall (1886–1984), wife of John Lee Saltonstall, later wife of Van Wyck Brooks; Robert Woods Bliss (1875–1962), former secretary of the U.S. legation in Belgium.
10. Alexander Sedgwick (1867–1929) of Stockbridge, Mass., was in France in the Ambulance Corps; Emily Tuckerman (d. 1924), daughter of Elizabeth and Lucius Tuckerman, member of Roosevelt's inner circle.

To Elizabeth Cameron

1603 H Street   March 1st [1918]

Your letter of the 7 of February arrived two days ago and we shall telegraph today for news of Martha through Elizabeth who is still with us, and who takes charge of the telegraph. As we have heard nothing for the three weeks since you wrote, it is better for me to say nothing just now and wait with patience for all the news that these days bring, having the enlivening sense that whatever comes is always bad and that we are no better for hastening it.[1] You can imagine how my ancient pessimism revels at the sight of a world infinitely more pessimistic than I ever was and seeming on the whole rather to enjoy it. At least they have not much time to cry over their spilled milk. In fact they haven't much milk to spill, for everything we have is now promptly taken away from us and sent to imaginary heroes at the front—I say "imaginary" because nobody will tell us where they are or what they are going to do. Meanwhile all our friends male and female are in uniform and Sherman Miles is a colonel. To be sure I believe that Mabel Boardman is a general, and I don't know *what* Elizabeth may be, she hides it so carefully.[2]

Meanwhile we're dying as fast as is respectable. I consider myself to be doing very well in that way, and I have bets with all my doctors that they can't keep me running for three months, but I was certainly taken aback by the announcement of Springy's sudden departure when I supposed him to be relatively safe.[3] I wish very much that I were twenty years younger, and could collect and edit his letters to you, as well as the others that you have, for he was a charming letter writer, and almost the only man who would stand reading by the side of John Hay. I think probably that his wife will try to prepare a memoir of him, but I do not know who is fit to do it, and it would need a very delicate hand. Indeed I think it would need an editor as good as Springy himself to give the right light and shadow to all the changes of characters and scenery. It is hardly to be done now, when this wretched war has swept our literary class out of existence and threatens to carry our whole leisure class after it. I look forward with great curiosity to the year *1938* which is my centenary because I expect by that time to be buried under the Great Pyramid in company with Cheops—all equally forgotten!! It is *ridiculous*. I can find no words to express my sense of the situation which has not been seen in the world since the days of the Stoics and Marcus Aurelius. Even our poor old town of Washington is changing fast and my once quiet study is pervaded by rampant automobiles and puff-puffs.[4] *Sleep* has become impossible. I envy you at Stepleton and wonder whether in the wreck of worlds I may not drift back to seek a quiet grave by the side of Elizabeth's friend who was "born a fool and died one."

All the same, my quiet house is actually invaded by people who wear all sorts of uniforms and are here on all sorts of errands and might, you would suppose, do very well to take the place of the senators and secretaries you used to know, but who pretend to regard me with a feigned deference which reduces *me* to dust! I think that here and there one of them may be aware that my generation did something, or said something, which no one remembers, but the entire stream of existence to them is limited to the administration of Mr. Woodrow Wilson and the literature of the war.

Crowds of charming young women, all of them working or trying to work for their country, flutter about our houses which are now mostly near Sheridan Circle, but they *do* occasionally get back as far as Lafayette Square and I think may sometimes look in at the windows of your house which is now a part of the Cosmos Club. There are few people left on the Square and are likely soon to be fewer, so that you would hardly feel happy here and would find very few old friends. I hear that Sallie Davis has been ill but that before falling a victim to her complaint, whatever it was, she became an ardent attendant on the religious exhortations of Billy Sunday.[5] In fact I am told that that tabernacle has been the most fashionable spot in Washington. This information comes from Florence Keep, who has struggled desperately to keep abreast of the time. As a rule I hear of the men only at second hand; even Harry White has become a stranger. Pretty much all the old English secretaries are gone or are going and their places are being slowly filled by second-rate English middle class, who are supposed to do "business." I have not had the advantage of meeting Mr. and Mrs. Isaacs who, I am told, are charming—but to whom I can be of no use.[6]

Cabot Lodge came in to dine last night with Bessy, in very good form, as I thought, and not so atrabilious as he has been of late. We actually avoided abusing anybody for the most part, perhaps because he was delighted to tell me that our famous secretary of war had actually been sent "to the front" and had sailed.[7] If I might guess from his appearance, he was more cheerful about the situation here, although I don't know enough to know why. Bessy was as handsome as usual, and Mabel La Farge, who is paying us a visit, listened to the conversation with respect due to her rural estate which she has now bought, not far from New Haven. She is weighed down by the effort of carrying four six-foot boys who have got to be prepared to kill somebody shortly. Of my own family I have little or nothing to tell you except that they seem to me as blue as I could wish. Pretty nearly all of them have husbands or brothers or sons at sea or in the trenches, and really I think they behave exceedingly well, and hardly suggest a complaint. The New Yorkers are also heroic, and make an appearance which really for the first time in their history gives them all, both men and women, a certain little air of being something in the world, which *I* regard as clear gain. The only situation which has suffered and which I fear may suffer seriously is our universities, for whom the outlook is dark.

We are waiting with *extreme anxiety* for your next news, and all this letter is mere chatter to fill up the time. I suppose that really the entire world is now hanging on to itself for the next month, waiting to drop into some *new* bit of darkness that it can't escape, but meanwhile we try to be cheerful and whistle our twelfth-century melodies.

Ever yours ——— per Aileen Tone

MS: MHi; dictated

1. Martha Cameron Lindsay was still dangerously ill at Stepleton in England. She died, aged 31, April 28, 1918.
2. Mabel Thorp Boardman (1860–1946), Red Cross leader and fundraiser for war relief.
3. Ambassador Spring Rice had been recalled without previous notice, ostensibly to consolidate British war agencies in the U.S.
4. "Puff-puffs": locomotives.
5. Sarah ("Sallie") Frelinghuysen (Mrs. John) Davis, mother of Matilda Elizabeth ("Bessie") Davis Lodge, widow of George Cabot Lodge; the Rev. William ("Billy") Sunday (1863–1935), spellbinding evangelist who attracted immense crowds with his acrobatic feats.
6. Rufus Daniel Isaacs (1860–1935), 1st earl of Reading, high commissioner and special envoy to the U.S.; and Alice Cohen Isaacs (1865–1930), countess of Reading.
7. Secretary of War Newton D. Baker (1871–1937) had left for France on a tour of inspection.

To William Roscoe Thayer

1603 H Street   Washington
March 15 [1918]

Dear Thayer,

Your letter of the 14th reminds me vaguely that perhaps I *was* really once alive and did write books so that I have begged Miss Tone to seek in all her forgotten closets for some copies of the volume you mention and now that she has found some, I do remember me that many years ago I was driven by hounds from Hell to utter a dying protest against everything as it is, and especially the historical school of Harvard College which I had done so much to injure and vilify but which I now confess I had better have left alone.[1] I had better have left all colleges alone, and everyone else, but at least I can flatter myself with the confident certainty that no one ever read me, or cared what I said, and that I might use all the bad language that came into my wicked brain, without ever raising so much as a smile on the blessed countenance of Charles Eliot. As far as I can remember I have not seen the countenance of his successor since he left my own lecture room some forty years ago, so that I hope I may consider the harm I did him to be now mostly wiped away and forgotten.[2] In the despair of final explosion, some six or eight years ago, I flung this little book into these presidents' faces, with my last profane act of farewell, but no one ever read it or has ever spoken to me about it, so that I think I may venture to offer it for your amusement, without danger of perverting your morals. Of Worthington Ford's morals, I have no opinion whatever, and he has already done all the harm he can, in perverting you. So let him pass!

In those far distant days, before the war, I had a mad idea that someone endowed with energy could effect some sort of open alliance or still opener antagonism between our historical school, or part of it, and the biologists of the Jacques Loeb type who were also feeble enough to teach in universities, but such an alliance or hostility would have needed fifty years of youth and vast reservoirs of energy—to say nothing of a considerable amount of education and intelligence. I had none of these things, and my start was bound to stop short. Within a year or two I was knocked as flat as a flatiron, and within another year or two the world was knocked as flat as I, and never lifted its head so far as to draw free breath again. Personally you can imagine how, after dragging myself through the mud, I climbed up onto the stile, in a disheveled condition, where I have continued to smile, ever since. I am one of the lucky ones who have got through with the game and care nothing, any more, for my stakes in it. As far as I can see, I am involved to the extent of looking on while you fellows do the shouting. Whenever you get through doing the shouting, you will turn to something else, which will not be connected with anything that ever interested *me*. You are therefore that wonderful object in creation, my last reader, and I give you herewith my final blessing, with the prayer that when you reach the same point long hence, you may also have a last reader as sympathetic as yourself, and a Harvard College which you shall not have treated with disrespect, but which will furnish you a kind and sympathetic audience to the end.

Universities are our American equivalent for a church; they will give you peace. My error in life was in deserting their blessed peace. I do not think I would ever have done it if it had not been for their *smile*—which made me think that I should get to resemble Charles Eliot, if I stayed there long enough.

You say nothing of your eyes, but Mrs. Thayer's handwriting reminds me, through the medium of Aileen Tone, of my own, and I very sincerely hope that yours are not as bad as mine. I trust that the peace of Berkeley

Street furnishes balm for that and all your other discomforts, but I am afraid that this winter has not helped the desired effect by any joys of climate or of sunshine.

Of course the loss of Spring Rice is another great shipwreck, and I am now fairly crushed under all these losses which seem to me now and then rather unfairly numerous and altogether disastrous. Luckily there are lots of young people who are much better company than I ever was, and who make a very good show among themselves as well as a pleasant one for me to look at. The function of continuing to sit on the stile and of practicing that genial smile is, after all, a branch and even a meritorious branch of high art. I recommend it now to all who approach me and I judge from their expression that it bores them, as much as it always bored me.

Ever yours   Henry Adams[3]   per Aileen Tone

MS: MH; dictated

1. Thayer had asked for a copy of HA's *Letter to American Teachers of History*.
2. A. Lawrence Lowell (1856–1943), president of Harvard 1909–1933.
3. This is the last extant letter of Henry Adams. He died in his sleep early in the morning of March 27 of a stroke. His last words were to Aileen Tone when she was leaving his room after winding his clock as usual, "Goodnight, my dear."

    A simple funeral service, held at Adams' house on March 30, was read by the Rev. Roland Cotton Smith, rector of St. John's Episcopal Church, Lafayette Square. Burial was in Rock Creek Cemetery, at the foot of the Saint-Gaudens statue.

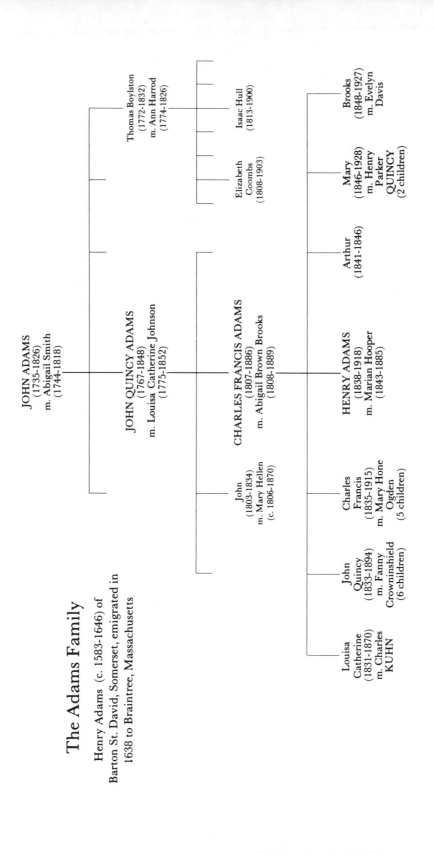

The Adams Family

Henry Adams (c. 1583-1646) of
Barton St. David, Somerset, emigrated in
1638 to Braintree, Massachusetts

JOHN ADAMS
(1735-1826)
m. Abigail Smith
(1744-1818)

Thomas Boylston
(1772-1832)
m. Ann Harrod
(1774-1826)

JOHN QUINCY ADAMS
(1767-1848)
m. Louisa Catherine Johnson
(1775-1852)

Elizabeth
Coombs
(1808-1903)

Isaac Hull
(1813-1900)

CHARLES FRANCIS ADAMS
(1807-1886)
m. Abigail Brown Brooks
(1808-1889)

John
(1803-1834)
m. Mary Hellen
(c. 1806-1870)

Arthur
(1841-1846)

Mary
(1846-1928)
m. Henry
Parker
QUINCY
(2 children)

Brooks
(1848-1927)
m. Evelyn
Davis

HENRY ADAMS
(1838-1918)
m. Marian Hooper
(1843-1885)

Charles
Francis
(1835-1915)
m. Mary Hone
Ogden
(5 children)

John
Quincy
(1833-1894)
m. Fanny
Crowninshield
(6 children)

Louisa
Catherine
(1831-1870)
m. Charles KUHN

Chronology

1838   Born in Boston, Massachusetts, on February 16, third son of Charles Francis Adams and Abigail Brooks Adams, grandson of President John Quincy Adams, and great-grandson of President John Adams.

1854–1858   Enters Harvard College. Contributes to the *Harvard Magazine*. Graduates as Class Orator.

1858   Sails September 28 with several fellow graduates for the traditional Grand Tour of Europe. Plans to attend the university in Berlin as a student of civil law. Enrolls in a German secondary school and writes an article on his winter's experience there (published in *American Historical Review*, October 1947).

1859   Resumes private study of civil law in Dresden. Travels in Austria and Germany with classmates and in Italy with his sister Louisa Kuhn.

1860–1861   Travels in Italy and Sicily until June. Publishes his Italian travel letters in the *Boston Daily Courier*. Interviews Garibaldi in Palermo after the surrender of the Bourbon troops. Returns to U.S. in October. In December joins his father, who has been reelected to Congress, as his private secretary. Serves as Washington correspondent of the *Boston Daily Advertiser*.

1861–1867   Sails for England May 1. Serves as private secretary to his father, who has been appointed minister to England. Acts as secret London correspondent of the *New York Times* until January 1862. Travels to Scotland and on the Continent.

1867   Publishes "Captain John Smith," "British Finance in 1816," and "The Bank of England Restriction" in the *North American Review*.

1868   Publishes review of Sir Charles Lyell's *Principles of Geology* in the *North American Review*. Returns to U.S. in July and begins work in Washington as a freelance political journalist in the service of reform. Contributes occasional pieces to *The Nation*.

1869   Publishes "The Session" and "Civil Service Reform" in the *North American Review*. His article "American Finance, 1865–1869" appears in the *Edinburgh Review*.

1870   Publishes "The Legal Tender Act" (with assistance of Francis A. Walker) and a second "Session" critical of Congress. Summoned to his sister Louisa's bedside at Bagni di Lucca, where on July 11 she dies of tetanus. Appointed assistant professor of history by Charles W. Eliot, the new president of Harvard. Begins teaching courses in medieval English and European history and becomes editor of the *North American Review*. Places his sensational exposé "The New York Gold Conspiracy" in the *Westminster Review*.

1871   Publishes with his brother Charles Francis Adams, Jr., *Chapters of Erie,* a collection of their reformist articles.

1872–1873   On June 27 marries Marian ("Clover") Hooper, daughter of a prominent Boston physician. Wedding journey takes them to England, Egypt, and the Continent. Consults with leading European and British historians and renews friendships in England. Returns to Harvard in August 1873.

1876   Publishes *Essays in Anglo-Saxon Law,* which includes his own essay and three essays by his doctoral candidates. Publishes "The Independents in the Canvass" urging support for the Liberal Republican faction. The publisher finds it offensive, and Adams resigns as editor. In December gives Lowell Institute lecture, "Primitive Rights of Women."

1877   Resigns from Harvard after accepting invitation to edit the papers of Albert Gallatin, Jefferson's secretary of the Treasury, and prepare his biography. Moves to Washington to work in State Department archives. Publishes *Documents Relating to New England Federalism* in defense of the anti-Federalist policy of John Quincy Adams.

1879   Publishes *The Life of Albert Gallatin* and three volumes of *The Writings of Albert Gallatin*. Begins acquaintance with a long succession of politicians and diplomats.

1879–1880   Travels in Europe researching archives in London, Paris, and Madrid for his projected history of the administrations of Jefferson and Madison.

1880   Publishes anonymously, in the U.S. and England, *Democracy: An American Novel,* depicting political corruption in Washington. It becomes a sensational success.

1881   "Five of Hearts" comes into being. Includes Clara Hay (Mrs. John Hay), John Hay, Clarence King, Marian Adams, and Henry Adams.

1882   Publishes *John Randolph,* highly critical of the Southern statesman, in the American Statesmen series.

1884	Under the pseudonym Frances Snow Compton publishes *Esther: A Novel*. He and John Hay begin construction of adjoining houses designed by Henry Hobson Richardson. Circulates six privately printed draft copies of the first section of his *History* to a group of intimates for their criticism.
1885	Circulates six privately printed draft copies of the second section of the *History*. On December 6 Marian Adams commits suicide.
1886	From June to October tours Japan with artist John La Farge. Father dies at Quincy at age seventy-nine after several years of mental decline.
1888	Circulates six privately printed draft copies of the third section of the *History*. Makes first visit to Cuba. Makes a circle tour of the Far West with English friend Sir Robert Cunliffe.
1889	Charles Scribner's Sons begins publication of the *History of the United States of America During the Administrations of Jefferson and Madison*. The fourth and final section is printed from the manuscript. Publication is completed in 1891 and includes a tenth volume, *Historical Essays*. Mother dies at Quincy at age eighty-one. He becomes increasingly dependent on Elizabeth Cameron for companionship. Commissions sculptor Augustus Saint-Gaudens to execute a bronze figure for the grave of Marian Adams in Rock Creek Cemetery.
1890–1892	From August 1890 to September 1891 travels with John La Farge to Hawaii, Samoa, Tahiti, Fiji, Australia, Ceylon, and France. Writes poem "Buddha and Brahma" aboard ship en route from Ceylon (published in the *Yale Review*, October 1915). Has reunion in Paris and London with Elizabeth Cameron. Leaves England for America February 3, 1892.
1893	Commences intellectual collaboration with his younger brother Brooks, whose radical *Law of Civilization and Decay* will appear in 1895. Privately prints *Memoirs of Mau Taaroa, Last Queen of Tahiti*. Twice visits the World's Columbian Exposition in Chicago.
1894–1895	Tours Cuba with Clarence King, February to March; travels to Yellowstone Park with John Hay and alone to Vancouver, July to September; tours Mexico and the Caribbean islands with Chandler Hale, December 1894 to April 1895. In December sends his presidential address "The Tendency of History" to the annual meeting of the American Historical Association to be delivered in absentia. In company of the Lodges, makes first systematic study of Gothic architecture of Normandy cathedrals.
1896	Prepares resolution, "Recognition of Cuban Independence," for Senator James Donald Cameron. In April travels to Mexico with the Camerons. Tours Europe with the Hays, May to October.

1897–1898   Prolonged stay abroad in London, Paris, Egypt (with the Hays), Turkey, Greece, the Balkans, Vienna, and Paris. Visits Ambassador John Hay at Surrenden Dering in England and is there when word comes of Hay's appointment as U.S. secretary of state. Sails for New York November 5, 1898.

1899   Tours Italy and Sicily with the Lodges. Resides in Paris, June to January 1900. (Until 1911 lives in Paris for part of each year.)

1900   Visits the Paris Exposition. Composes the poem "Prayer to the Virgin of Chartres," which includes "Prayer to the Dynamo" (published in 1920; reprinted in *Henry Adams* [New York: Library of America, 1983]).

1901   Privately prints revised and enlarged Tahiti book as *Memoirs of Arii Taimai*. Travels with the Lodges during July and August to Bayreuth, Vienna, Warsaw, Moscow, and St. Petersburg, then alone during September to Sweden and Norway.

1904   Privately prints *Mont Saint Michel and Chartres*. Contributes chapter on Clarence King to *Clarence King Memoirs*. In spring accompanies Secretary of State John Hay to the opening of the St. Louis Exposition.

1907   In February issues the private edition of *The Education of Henry Adams*. Circulates the volume to friends and to persons commented on. Invites corrections.

1908   Prepares an edition of the letters of John Hay, published by Clara Hay.

1909   Writes "The Rule of Phase Applied to History" (published by Brooks Adams in 1919 in *The Degradation of the Democratic Dogma*).

1910   Privately prints and distributes to universities and professors of history *A Letter to American Teachers of History*.

1911   Publishes *The Life of George Cabot Lodge*.

1912   Issues a second private edition, slightly revised, of *Mont Saint Michel and Chartres*. Partially paralyzed by a stroke, April to late July.

1913   Authorizes the American Institute of Architects to publish a trade edition of *Mont Saint Michel and Chartres*.

1913–1914   Spends summers again in France. Engages Aileen Tone, a musician, as secretary-companion.

1914–1918   Presides again at his noontime breakfast table at 1603 H Street in Washington, entertaining nieces, "nieces in wish," and visiting dignitaries.

1918   Dies in Washington March 27 at the age of eighty. Buried beside his wife in Rock Creek Cemetery. First trade publication of the *Education*. Awarded Pulitzer Prize posthumously in 1919 for *The Education of Henry Adams*.

Acknowledgments

My obligations to the Massachusetts Historical Society and its directors go back more than forty years to the time of director Allyn Bailey Forbes when I interviewed the late Henry Adams II there. Subsequently, Thomas B. Adams, the president of the society, kindly gave me access to the Adams Family Papers.

I am especially indebted to Stephen T. Riley, who succeeded Stewart Mitchell as director, for help and encouragement through the years and for his aid in sponsoring the publication of *The Letters of Henry Adams*. I thank the Massachusetts Historical Society, which controls the rights to the Henry Adams letters, and the present director, Louis Leonard Tucker, for permission to publish the letters in this edition.

I wish also to express my obligations to the many institutions and persons recorded in the Acknowledgments of Volumes I and IV of *The Letters of Henry Adams* (Cambridge, Mass.: Harvard University Press, 1983–1988) for the use of the letters selected here.

I am particularly grateful to my former associates at the University of Virginia in the preparation of the multivolume edition of the letters. They are J. C. Levenson, Edgar Allan Poe Professor of English, who directed the project, and Charles Vandersee, Associate Professor of English, both of the University of Virginia; Viola Hopkins Winner; Eleanor Pearre Abbott; and Jayne N. Samuels. The comprehensive annotations prepared by them and their assistants have been adapted for this edition.

The Chronology at the end of this volume is adapted, with permission from the Library of America, from *Henry Adams* (New York: Library of America, 1983).

I wish to thank Maud Wilcox, the former editor-in-chief of Harvard University Press, who invited me to prepare this edition. She has been generous with her advice and friendship through my long association with the Press. My thanks go also to Jennifer Snodgrass, who took over direction of the project. It is a pleasure to thank my editor, Ann Hawthorne, for her vigilant and discriminating editing of the manuscript.

Of all my debts to friends and associates, my deepest obligation is to my wife, Jayne Newcomer Samuels, whose tact and learning helped shape every stage in the making of this volume.

Index

Adams, Henry Brooks (*cont.*)
300, 307; camping trip to Yellowstone, 300; travels to Mexico, 302; on CFA's reputation, 306; travels to France, 311; investigates international trade, 331, 356, 358; on Dreyfus affair, 335, 357; travels to Egypt, 337; travels to Greece, 340; activities for Cuban partisans, 345, 352; at Paris Exposition, 375, 391, 394; on Boer War, 385–386, 398; travels to Russia, 408; travels to Scotland, 422; on Russo-Japanese War, 442, 445, 448; death of John Hay, 461–462; edits Hay's letters, 476, 479, 507; finances archeological research in Dordogne, 531, 534; on sinking of *Titanic*, 532; death of CFA2, 545; on World War I, 547, 549, 552; death, 556
—writings:
Aaron Burr biography (MS), 170; *Boston Daily Advertiser* letters, 31; *Boston Daily Courier* letters, 25–26, 31, 44, 50, 52; "Captain John Smith," 43–44, 86; *Chapters of Erie* (with CFA2), 123–124, 176; "Civil Service Reform," 108–109; *Democracy*, 169–170, 174, 410, 412, 462; "Eagle Head," 214; *The Education of Henry Adams*, 396, 414, 440, 477, 484–486, 488, 495, 504, 510, 520–522, 532, 539, 544–546, 551; *Essays in Anglo-Saxon Law*, 160; *Esther*, 192–193; *Gallatin* and Gallatin's *Writings* (editor), 150–151, 156, 512; *History of the United States . . .*, 156, 158–159, 175–177, 202, 204–205, 208–209, 310; "Holden Chapel," 47, 89, 91; *John Randolph*, 169–170; "The Legal Tender Act" (with Francis A. Walker), 110, 112; *A Letter to American Teachers of History*, 523, 544, 556; "Lyell's *Principles of Geology*," 96, 100; *Memoirs of Arii Taimai*, 433–434; *Mont Saint Michel and Chartres*, 389, 391, 442, 444, 450–451, 453, 455, 459–461, 469, 481, 484, 486, 488, 495, 500, 504, 530, 541, 546; "The New York Gold Conspiracy," 110–111, 120–121; *New York Times* letters, 41–42; "Palgrave's Poems," 134; "The Rule of Phase Applied to History," 510–511; "The Session," 114–116, 119; "Tennyson's *Queen Mary*," 137, 139; "Visit to Manchester," 50, 52
Adams, Isaac Hull, 48–50

Adams, John, 45, 79, 144, 283–284, 306, 417, 515
Adams, John (HA's nephew), 136, 139
Adams, John (of Samoa), 233
Adams, John Quincy, 45, 133–134, 148, 306, 310, 353, 411–412, 510–516
Adams, John Quincy II (HA's brother), 9, 11–12, 18–19, 25, 34, 37, 49–51, 61, 85, 92, 125, 133, 165, 201, 299, 306–307, 314, 316
Adams, Louisa Catherine Johnson (Mrs. JQA), 59, 396, 411–412
Adams, Louisa Catherine (HA's sister). *See* Kuhn, Louisa Adams
Adams, Marian Hooper ("Clover") (HA's wife), 125–126, 130, 136, 146–148, 153–155, 157, 160, 166–167, 182–186, 193, 314, 358, 417, 425, 526, 544–454; letter to, 180
Adams, Mary (HA's sister). *See* Quincy, Mary Adams
Adams, Mary Hellen (Mrs. John), 114, 116
Adams, Mary Hone Ogden ("Minnie") (Mrs. CFA2), 77, 79–80, 82, 91, 535
Adams, Mary Ogden (HA's niece). *See* Abbott, Mary Adams
Adams, Maude, 419, 421
Adams, Samuel, 321–322
Agassiz, Alexander, 170; *The Coral Reefs . . .*, 434; letter to, 433
Agassiz, Louis, 96
Albert of Saxe-Coburg, Prince Consort, 255, 548
Albertini, Mary S. Reynolds (Mrs. Leander), 396, 398
Albertus Magnus, 390
Alcott, Bronson, 179, 441
Alderman, Edwin A., 432; letter to, 432
Aldrich, Chester H., 498–499
Alexander the Great, 339, 381
Alger, Annette Henry (Mrs. Russell A.), 363, 366
Alger, Russell A., 364, 366
Alley, John B., 32, 35
Allison, William B., 118
Ames, James Barr, 128
Anderson, Larz, 277–278, 429, 431
Anderson, Nicholas L., 7, 9, 63, 180–181, 278
Andrew, John A., 66
Andrews, Frank W., Jr., 364, 366
Angelico, Fra, 370–371

522, 533–538, 547, 551; letters to, 463, 477, 506
Root, Clara Frances Wales (Mrs. Elihu), 419
Root, Elihu, 418–419, 421, 430
Rosecrans, William S., 62, 64
Rossetti, Dante Gabriel, 270
Rossini, Gioacchino, *The Barber of Seville,* 365
Rostand, Edmond, *Discours de réception à l'Académie française,* 438–439
Rothschild, Mayer Alphonse de, Baron, 336–338, 357–358
Rothschild, Nathan Meyer, Baron, 311, 320
Rousseau, Jean-Jacques, *Confessions,* 486
Rousseau, Théodore, 137, 139
Rubens, Peter Paul, 428
Ruskin, John, 138, 181–182, 195, 298, 301, 418, 470
Russell, Lady Frances Ann Maria, 39
Russell, Lord John, 39, 42, 255–256, 306
Russell, William H., 46, 48, 59–60, 70
Rutherfurd, Anne. *See* Vanderbilt, Ann Harriman Sands Rutherfurd
Rutson, Albert O., 154–155

Sackville-West, Sir Lionel, 172–173
Sackville-West, Victoria, 172–173
Sainte-Beuve, Charles, 121
Saint-Gaudens, Augustus, 289, 374–375, 379–380, 418, 480–481; Adams monument, 376, 483, 506–507, 545, 556; "Diana," 282, 284; medallion caricature of HA, 448, 450
Saint-Gaudens, Homer S., 483; letter to, 483
Saint-Simon, Louis de Rouvroy, Duc de, 362, 366, 398
Sala, Count Maurice, 327–328
Salisbury, Georgina Caroline Anderson, Lady, 108, 149
Salisbury, Lord (Robert Cecil), 108–109, 149, 154, 393, 395, 398, 422, 424–425, 547
Salmon, Lois ("Pree"), 244–245, 250
Salmon, Moetia. *See* Atwater, Moetia
Salmon, Mrs. Alexandre. *See* Ariitaimai, Princess
Salmon, Tati, 234, 240–244, 351
Saltonstall, Gladys Rice (Mrs. John L.), 551
San Faustino, Princess. *See* Del Monte, Jane Bourbon

Santo-Thyrso, Carlos Machado, Viscount, 361–362
Sarcey, Francisque, 274–275
Sardou, Victorien, 494
Sargent, Hetty A. *See* Higginson, Hetty Sargent
Sargent, John Singer, 292, 294, 492, 494, 518; "The Misses Wertheimer," 405; "Theodore Roosevelt," 436
Sassetta, 524–525
Saul, John, 282, 284
Scheurer-Kestner, Auguste, 336–337
Schiller, Friedrich von, 11, 24, 513; "Der Handschuh," 198, 201; "Resignation, Eine Phantasie," 441
Schley, Winfield S., 345–347
Schlözer, Kurt von, 147–148
Schmid, Reinhold, *Die Gesetz der Angelsachsen,* 128
Schofield, John M., 100
Schopenhauer, Arthur, 520
Schuyler, Harriet Lowndes Langdon (Mrs. Philip), 475–476
Schurz, Agathe, 400
Schurz, Carl, 118, 130–131, 133, 157, 161, 164, 293–295, 361, 400; letters to, 131, 139
Schwab, Charles M., 443–444
Scott, Sir Walter, 135, 255, 257, 513
Scribner, Charles, 205; letters to, 204, 208
Sears, Eleanora Coolidge (Mrs. Frederick R.), 350–351, 549, 551
Sebright, Olivia FitzPatrick, Lady, 108
Sedgwick, Alexander, 551
Sedgwick, Arthur G., 131–132
Sedgwick, Charles B., 32, 35
Seherr-Thoss, Muriel White, Countess von, 489
Selmes, Martha Flandrau (Mrs. Tilden), 415, 417
Sempronia, 498
Seumano, 224, 227, 233
Severance, Mrs. Henry W., 218, 222
Sévigné, Marie de, 313
Sewall, Henry M., 224, 230
Seward, Frederick W., 512, 516
Seward, William, 12, 18, 22, 24, 32–34, 36–37, 39, 41–42, 45, 58, 62, 71, 80, 82, 95, 99, 105–106, 306
Shafter, William R., 354–355
Shakespeare, William, 11, 55, 178, 470, 515; *Hamlet,* 136–137, 139, 271, 317,